YOU

AND

OTHERS

046046

DEMCO

YOU
AND
OTHERS

Readings in

Introductory

Anthropology

Edited by

A. Kimball Romney
University of California, Irvine

and

Paul L. DeVore
University of Massachusetts, Boston

WINTHROP PUBLISHERS, INC., CAMBRIDGE, MASSACHUSETTS

Library of Congress Cataloging in Publication Data

Romney, Antone Kimball, comp.
  You and others.

  1. Ethnology—Addresses, essays, lectures.
I. DeVore, Paul L., joint comp.   II. Title.
GN325.R65   301.2'08   72-14183
ISBN 0-87626-983-8

Cover by Donya Melanson

Copyright © 1973 by Winthrop Publishers, Inc.
   17 Dunster Street, Cambridge, Massachusetts 02138

Special Acknowledgments

The primary motivation for this collection has come from our association with various students and colleagues at the University of California at Irvine and the University of Massachusetts, Boston. Their questions and suggestions have stimulated the attempt to present Anthropology in a relevant and interesting manner. To the extent that either aim has been achieved, they are responsible. They are too numerous to include in total, but we are grateful to all.

We would like to thank Mary Bruce who spent long hours reading not only all of the current selections, but dozens of others that did not appear. Her perceptive insight in commenting on the articles in addition to her evaluations have been invaluable. We would like to thank also Margaret Kieffer who led us to explore several areas and items that we would not have otherwise come in contact with.

Thanks also to Jo White for spending hundreds of hours in the library, and for being the major bibliographic researcher for the volume. She also spent enormous amounts of time in the discussion of the content and implications of all of the items. Alice Macy has not only done all of the final typing but was of immense aid in giving editorial comments as well as in making useful substantive suggestions. Thanks are also due to Jim Murray and Muriel Harman of Winthrop Publishers for their encouragement and editorial suggestions.

046046

Contents

Preface

This reader is divided into eleven sections. Each section has been designed to be read as a whole unit along with its introduction. Any impact a given section may have frequently depends in part on the order and juxtaposition of various points of view. A conscious attempt has been made to present more than one viewpoint on any given topic.

Since, in reality, culture is an interrelated whole, not all of the selections fit neatly into a single categorical mold. In many cases the relevance of each of the selections to the other categories or sections to which it relates has been cross-referenced.

The first chapter reviews human evolution and prehistory as seen from the findings of the sub-fields of Physical Anthropology and Archaeology. The order of the following chapters proceeds in a very general way from the simple and concrete to the complex and abstract. Chapters Two through Seven emphasize the relations between the individual and his/her own cultural group. Chapter Two begins with the Patterns of Every Day Events and the succeeding chapters are Culture and the Concept of Normality, Roles and Statuses, Families and Sex, Rites of Passage, and Witchcraft, Mysticism and the Supernatural. Chapter Eight discusses the ways in which an individual's conformity to his/her own cultural patterns is virtually insured by his/her society. Chapter Nine describes Culture Contact and the outcomes of various kinds of encounters between cultures as a whole. Chapter Ten discusses and gives illustrations of Anthropologists at Work, and the last chapter examines Patterns of Communication, or Linguistics and illuminates the importance of communication and language in human interaction and cultural processes.

A. Kimball Romney
Paul L. DeVore

Acknowledgments

"A Survey of Physical Anthropology and Prehistory," by Victor Barnouw. Reprinted with permission from Barnouw, *An Introduction to Anthropology, Vol. II* (Homewood, Ill.: The Dorsey Press, 1971), pp. 2–22.

"Baboon Ecology and Human Evolution," by Irven DeVore and S. L. Washburn. Reprinted from F. Clark Howell and Francois Bourliere, editors, *African Ecology and Human Evolution* (Chicago: Aldine Publishing Company, 1963); copyright © 1963 by The Wenner-Gren Foundation for Anthropological Research, Inc. Reprinted by permission of the authors and Aldine Publishing Company.

"The Evolution of Hunting," by S. L. Washburn and C. S. Lancaster. Reprinted from Richard B. Lee and Irven DeVore, editors, *Man The Hunter* (Chicago: Aldine Publishing Company, 1968); copyright © 1968 by the Wenner-Gren Foundation for Anthropological Research, Inc. Reprinted by permission of the authors and Aldine-Atherton, Inc.

"The Origins of Agriculture," by Robert M. Adams. Reprinted from Sol Tax, editor, *Horizons of Anthropology* (Chicago: Aldine Publishing Company, 1964); copyright © 1964 by Aldine Publishing Company. Reprinted by permission of the author and Aldine Publishing Company.

"Daily Life Among the Yanomamö," by Napoleon A. Chagnon. From *Yanomamö: The Fierce People* by Napoleon A. Chagnon. Copyright © 1968 by Holt, Rinehart & Winston, Inc. Reprinted by permission of Holt, Rinehart & Winston, Inc.

"Daily Routine," by A. Kimball Romney and Romaine Romney. From *The Mixtecans of Juxtlahuaca, Mexico* by A. K. Romney and R. Romney. Copyright © 1966 by John Wiley & Sons, Inc.

"The Voices of Time," by Edward T. Hall. From *The Silent Language* by Edward T. Hall. Copyright © 1959 by Fawcett World Library. Reprinted by permission.

"Body Ritual Among the Nacirema," by Horace Miner. Reproduced by permission of the American Anthropological Association from *American Anthropologist*, Vol. 58, No. 3, 1956, and the author.

"Anthropology and the Abnormal," by Ruth Benedict. From *The Journal of General Psychology*, Vol. 10, 1934, pp. 59–82. Reprinted by permission of The Journal Press.

"The Sorcerer and His Magic," by Claude Lévi-Strauss. Excerpted from Chapter 9, "The Sorcerer and His Magic" translated by Brooke Grundfest Schoepf in *Structural Anthropology* by Claude Lévi-Strauss, © 1963 by Basic Books, Inc., Publishers, New York.

"The Wiitiko Psychosis in the Context of Ojibwa Personality and Culture," by Seymour Parker. Reproduced by permission of the American Anthropological Association from *American Anthropologist*, Vol. 62, No. 4, 1960, and the author.

"Disease and Curing," by A. Kimball Romney and Romaine Romney. From *The Mixtecans of Tuxtlahuaca, Mexico* by A. K. Romney and R. Romney. Copyright © 1966 by John Wiley & Sons, Inc.

"Psychiatric Illness in a Small Ladino Community," by Horacio Fabrega, Jr. and Duane Metzger. From *Psychiatry*, Vol. 31, 1968. Reprinted by permission of *Psychiatry* and the authors.

"On the Possibility of Friendship," by Craig MacAndrew and Robert Edgerton. From the *American Journal of Mental Deficiency*, Vol. 70, No. 4, 1966. Reprinted with permission of the American Association on Mental Deficiency and the authors.

"The Role of Women in a Changing Navaho Society," by Laila Shukry Hamamsy. Reproduced by permission of the American Anthropological Association from *American Anthropologist*, Vol. 59, No. 1, 1957, and the author.

"Sex Differences in the Incidence of Susto in Two Zapotec Pueblos: An Analysis of the Relationships Between Sex Role Expectations and a Folk Illness," by Carl W. O'Neill and Henry A. Selby. From *Ethnology*, 1968, pp. 95–105. Reprinted by permission of *Ethnology* and the authors.

"Begging in a Southeastern Mexican City," by Horacio Fabrega, Jr. Reproduced by the permission of the Society for Applied Anthropology from Vol. 30, No. 3, 1971, *Human Organization*.

"Children and Conduct in a Ladino Community of Chiapas, Mexico," by John C. Hotchkiss. Reproduced by permission of the American Anthropological Association from *American Anthropologist*, Vol. 69, No. 6, 1967, and the author.

"Is the Family Universal?" by Melford E. Spiro. Reproduced by permission of the American Anthropological Association from *American Anthropologist*, Vol. 56, No. 5, Pt. 1, 1954, and the author.

"Sex Roles and Economic Change in Africa," by Robert A. LeVine. From *Ethnology*, Vol. 5, No. 2, April, 1966, pp. 186–193. Reprinted with permission of *Ethnology* and the author.

"Marital Relations in the Jos Plateau of Nigeria: Women's Weapons: The Politics of Domesticity Among the Kofyar" by Robert M. Netting. Reproduced by permission of the American Anthropological Association from *American Anthropologist*, Vol. 71, No. 6, 1969, and the author.

"Some Aspects of Tagalog Family Structure," by Bartlett H. Stoodley. Reproduced by permission of the American Anthropological Association from *American Anthropologist*, Vol. 59, No. 2, 1957, and the author.

"Conceptions of Death Among the [Navaho]," by Clyde Kluckhohn. Reprinted with permission of The Macmillan Company from *Culture and Behavior* by Clyde Kluckholn. © 1962 by The Free Press of Glencoe, A Division of The Macmillan Company.

"Female Initiation Among the Maroni River Caribs," by Peter Kloos. Reproduced by permission of the American Anthropological Association from *American Anthropologist*, Vol. 71, No. 5, 1969, and the author.

"Endocannibalism Among the Amahuaca Indians," by Gertrude Dole. From Transactions of the New York Academy of Sciences, Spring II, 24:5, pp. 567–573. Reprinted with permission of the New York Academy of Sciences and the author.

"Rebirth in the Airbone," by Melford S. Weiss. From *Conformity and Conflict*, James P. Spradley, David W. McCurdy, eds. Copyright © 1971 by Trans-Action, Inc.

"Witchcraft Explains Unfortunate Events," by E. E. Evans-Pritchard. From Chapter IV, *Witchcraft, Oracles and Magic among the Azande* by E. E. Evans-Pritchard, 1937. By permission of The Clarendon Press, Oxford.

"The Frightened Witch," by Laura Bohannan. From *In the Company of Man*, edited by Joseph B. Casagrande. Copyright © 1960 by Joseph B. Casagrande. Reprinted by permission of Harper & Row Publishers, Inc.

"Sorcery and Structure in Fore Society," by Shirley Lindenbaum. From *Oceania*, June 1971, 41:4, pp. 277–287. Reprinted with permission of Professor A. P. Elkin, editor of *Oceania*, and the author.

"Gosiute Peyotism," by Carling Malouf. Reproduced by permission of the American Anthropological Association from *American Anthropologist*, Vol. 44, No. 1, 1942, and the author.

"The Dangerous Ingkantos: Illness and Social Control in a Philippine Community," by Richard W. Lieban. Reproduced by permission of the American Anthropological Association from *American Anthropologist*, Vol. 64, No. 2, 1962, and the author.

"Spirit Possession and Its Socio-Psychological Implications Among the Sidamo of Southwest Ethiopia," by John and Irene Hamer. From *Ethnology*, 5:4, 1966, pp. 392–408. Reprinted with permission of *Ethnology* and the authors.

"Informal Judicial Activity in Bunyoro," by J. H. M. Beattie. From *Ethnology*, 5:2, 1966, pp. 202–217. Reprinted with permission of *Ethnology* and the author.

"Dispute Settlement Among the Tolai," by A. L. Epstein. From *Oceania*, XLI:3, 1971, pp. 157–170. Reprinted by permission of *Oceania* and the author.

"The Taboo of Suicide," by Russell Noyes, Jr. From *Psychiatry*, Vol. 31, 1968, pp. 173–183. Reprinted by permission of *Psychiatry* and the author.

"Stereotyping," by Vine Deloria, Jr. Reprinted with permission of The Macmillan Company from *We Talk, You Listen*, by Vine Deloria, Jr. Copyright © 1970, by Vine Deloria, Jr.

"Wounded Knee," by Dee Brown. From *Bury My Heart at Wounded Knee* by Dee Brown. "Copyright © 1970 by Dee Brown. Reprinted by permission of Holt, Rinehart and Winston, Inc., and Harold Matson Company, Inc.

"Intergroup Hostility and Social Cohesion," by Robert F. Murphy. Reproduced by permission of the American Anthropological Association from *American Anthropologist*, Vol. 51, No. 6, 1957, pp. 1018–1035, and the author.

"Shakespeare in the Bush," by Laura Bohannan. From *Natural History*, Vol. LXXV, 1966, pp. 28–33. Reprinted by permission of the author.

"My 'Boy,' Muntu," by Ethel M. Albert. From *In the Company of Man*, edited by Joseph B. Casagrande. Copyright © 1960 by Joseph B. Casagrande. Reprinted by permission of Harper & Row Publishers, Inc.

"Anthropologists and Other Friends," by Vine Deloria, Jr. Reprinted with permission of The Macmillan Company from *Custer Died for Your Sins*, by Vine Deloria, Jr. Copyright © 1969 by Vine Deloria, Jr.

"Piltdown Man," by Kenneth B. Oakley and J. S. Weiner. From *American Scientist*, Vol. 43, 1955. Reprinted with permission of the American Scientist and the authors.

"Communication," by Edward Sapir. Reprinted with permission of the publisher from the *Encyclopaedia of the Social Sciences*, edited by Edwin Seligman and Alvin Johnson, Volume III, pp. 78–81. Copyright 1930 and renewed 1958 by The Macmillan Company.

"The Relation of Habitual Thought and Behavior to Language," by Benjamin L. Whorf. Reprinted from *Language, Thought and Reality: Selected Writings of Benjamin Whorf*, edited by John B. Carroll, 1970, by permission of The M. I. T. Press, Cambridge, Massachusetts.

"How to Learn Martian," by Charles F. Hockett. From *Analog-Science Fiction, Science Fact*, May 1955, pp. 97–106. Reprinted by permission of the author.

"Tabooed Words in Comic Strips: A Transparent Mask," by James R. Jaquith. From *Anthropological Linguistics*, 14:3, March 1972, pp. 71–77. Reprinted with permission of *Anthropological Linguistics* and the author.

General Introduction

In broadest terms, Anthropology may be thought of as the study of human cultural behavior, including its evolution, history and contemporary forms. Four major sub-fields of Anthropology are generally recognized within the field of Anthropology today. Each of these sub-fields deals with separate, but interrelated, aspects of cultural behavior. In the following paragraphs we will give a thumbnail sketch of each of these major sub-fields in the order in which they appear in this reader.

One sub-field of Anthropology, Physical Anthropology, deals with the evolution of human beings and the interaction between their present cultural position and the biological foundation on which it is based. It focuses a good deal of attention on the transition between early pre-human forms and the emergence of modern humans. It was during this time in the distant past that those distinctively human activities such as tool-making and the development of complex social organizations and language were developed. The biological and cultural revolution that occurred during this period resulted in the dramatic and distinctive differences that we currently observe between human beings and our closest relatives in the animal kingdom. An appreciation of the profound influences exerted by our biological heritage is both fascinating and useful in understanding contemporary culture in the variety of forms that it takes. The readings in the first section are meant to provide insight into the current knowledge concerning human ancestors and their influence on contemporary culture.

Archaeologists concern themselves with reconstructing human history before the time of written records. For this reason Archaeology is frequently called Prehistory. By detailed studies of the physical and cultural remains of human activities, Archaeologists provide a detailed understanding of many early human achievements. For example, the domestication of plants and animals took place prior to the invention of writing. The development of agriculture is perhaps one of the most revolutionary achievements in the early human development. It provided a base that resulted in the development of urban centers, occupational specialization, as well as a surplus that made occupations like writing, mathematics, music, etc. possible.

Social and Cultural Anthropology focus primarily on human cultural groups that exist in the contemporary world, or those for which we have considerable historical documentation. They deal with the vast variations in cultural patterns that govern the vast majority of human interactions over the world today. The majority of the readings in this book (Chapters Two through Ten) are focused in the area of Social and Cultural Anthropology. (We will speak at greater length about these sub-fields in the section introductions.)

Linguistics constitutes the fourth major sub-specialty within Anthropology. Language and patterns of communication constitute the fundamental bases upon which human culture has developed. Linguists are interested not only in the structure and function of individual languages, but also in the way in which languages develop and change through time. They also concern themselves with certain inherent characteristics that are universal in all human communication systems. The contributions of Linguistics are the subject of the last chapter in this book.

The central concept within Anthropology as a whole is that of culture. It is the concept of culture that provides a high degree of unity and common ground among the four subdisciplines referred to above. In the simplest sense, it refers to the sum total of the patterns of human interaction in group life. Each society provides its members with patterns of appropriate behavior in most of the situations in which they normally find themselves. The readings in Chapter Two illustrate how varied these patterns are in different cultural and ecological settings.

All human beings everywhere are constantly interacting with others; interactions which have profound influences on the people involved. Human interactions are always patterned by the cultural background of the people concerned. It is the aim of this book to explore the extent and nature of these cultural patterns as well as to give some feeling for their impact on the individuals involved. Hopefully, each of us may gain some understanding of ourselves by comparing our behavior, our concerns, and our feelings with those of others. These patterns are affected by thousands of years of human experience as well as by the biological base from which we have evolved.

The current view is that culture provides "patterns for living." Many patterns of culture may be viewed as answers to various problems met by the members of the given culture. These patterns dictate the language one learns, the way one reacts to illness, one's religious beliefs and practices, the number of wives or husbands one has, etc.

To view each culture as a set of patterns that could be understood from its own perspective was a concept that was slow to develop within Anthropology. The related insight that current cultural beliefs within any group had developed over very long periods of time in response to various universal problems was also slow to develop. Before expanding on these notions of culture as patterns of living and as providing individuals with solutions to certain problems, let us examine the historical context within Western civilization from which modern Anthropology has developed.

The effect upon European intellectuals of the discovery and conquest of the New World and of the exploration and partitioning of Africa and Australia was profound, for these intellectuals were brought face-to-face with peoples of radically different cultures and backgrounds in a way that had not previously been experienced. There was debate in the beginning as to whether these so-called "primitive" groups were really fully human or not. Some Europeans romanticized their way of life: the French philosopher, Rousseau, for example, concluded that the "savage" state represented a "noble" condition of humans to which Europeans might return by stripping away the frivolities of civilization and by getting back to the soil. The British philosopher, Hobbes, in contrast, concluded from the same data that these "savages" represented a "nasty and brutish" aspect of human development, and emphasized that civilization was a higher state. With few exceptions, these so-called armchair philosophers had not had first-hand contact with the people they speculated about, and it was not until this century that professional anthropologists emerged and began first-hand field work among non-Western cultures.

One of the earlier, but by no means the first, attempt to understand cultures in terms of their own perspective rather than our own was the work of the famed anthropologist, Bronislaw Malinowski. Malinowski defined one of the major goals of the anthropological field worker as follows: "To grasp the natives' point of view, to realize *his* vision of *his* world." Most modern anthropologists would pretty much agree with Malinowski. Some would like more concrete criteria for knowing when they understand the natives' vision of the world. For example, Ward Goodenough, a leading contemporary anthropologist, would say that the final test of the anthropologist's understanding would be his/her ability to perform appropriately in the native context. The test of an appropriate performance in this case would be the acceptance by the native of the anthropologist's performance. (Interesting attempts to do just this are reported by Laura Bohannan in Chapter Nine and by Ethel M. Albert in Chapter Ten.)

If one reflects for a few moments on what is really involved in order to behave and speak appropriately in a foreign tribe, for example among the Yąnomamö (see Chapter Two), it becomes apparent that the anthropologist is bound to undergo rather profound personal experiences in the process. He/she must learn to adopt perspectives that they previously could not even imagine or identify with because they were so radically different from their own.

For these reasons and others, anthropological field work has acquired great symbolic, as well as scientific, import in the discipline. Up until recently, most of the personal knowledge and experience were restricted by anthropologists to gossip or the tradition of visiting over cocktails at their annual meetings. In the last few years, anthropologists have begun to write and publish some of their experiences, many of which are shared in this volume.

Human beings everywhere share certain characteristics and attitudes while differing in others. There is a widely shared view among field workers that anthropologists may learn a good deal about themselves as well as about the people that they are studying. Kluckhohn in his book *Mirror For Man* (p. 11) holds that studying primitives makes it possible to see ourselves in better perspective. He points out that one would not expect fish to discover water because they have no experience with a contrasting medium, and he maintains that people who have not been exposed to horizons beyond their own culture would hardly be able to understand their own cultural behavior in a well-rounded perspective. As he phrases it: "Anthropology holds up a great mirror to man and lets him look at himself in his infinite variety."

Cultures, like individuals, have, on occasion, been spoken of in terms of single dominant characteristics, orientation, interests, or themes. Ruth Benedict's classic book *Patterns of Culture* is perhaps the most eloquent attempt to capture the distinctive flavor of cultural groups under a single rubric. She characterizes the Zuñi as Appolonian since she views them as a peaceful sedentary pueblo. The more competitive status strivers, the Kwakiutl, on the Northwest coast, who compete for prestige with their distinctive potlatch ceremonies, she calls Dionysian. Nowadays, anthropologists see culture as somewhat too complex to characterize with a single term, but it is still true that they each show a variety of characteristics of uniquely elaborated values, philosophies, and beliefs.

These attempts to see cultures from their own perspective have led current anthropologists to see culture patterns as providing a pattern of behavior for members of a given culture. The customs, beliefs and practices that make up these patterns of behavior and that constitute culture are frequently most apparent when viewed as solutions to given problems. The implications of this discovery were summed up in the so-called "theory of cultural relativity"—the notion that the *thousands* of different cultures in the world each represent a workable solution to the basic problems of human social life, and that there are no grounds other than ethnocentric prejudice for saying that one is essentially better than another.

It seems to be a universal characteristic of both cultures and individuals that their themes and interests which focus on particular problems of concern to the individual or culture are elaborated in terms of ritual and ceremonies. Some of these concerns are universal. For example, all cultures and individuals face disease or illness at one time or another, and they all find disease and illness uncomfortable and anxiety-provoking. Thus, in all societies, we find elaborate theories and practices concerning the cause and cure of illnesses. Culture here provides ready-made patterns of behavior for coping with illness.

Another universal concern has to do with questions such as, "Who am I?" or "Where do I fit into the universe?" In an attempt to answer such universal questions all societies have developed elaborate religious beliefs and rituals. We present a number of readings bearing on these questions, especially in Chapter Seven.

Other universal concerns arise out of the inherent biological facts of the human life cycle, and around each of these major universal events elaborate customs referred to as *rites of passage* arise. Those center on such events as birth, puberty, marriage, death (See Chapter Six). All societies also face the problem of enforcing at least minimum conformity to their major beliefs, practices, and customs. These are typically thought of as social control mechanisms. They are treated in the literature under a variety of headings such as conflict resolution, law, social control, or sometimes as psychological mechanisms such as guilt and shame. These mechanisms provide the focus of Chapter Eight.

In all societies it is also obvious that there are differences in individuals in terms of sex and age. These inherent differences provide an obvious focal point for the development of such things as division of labor, special initiation ceremonies, and beliefs concerning the relationship between male and female and the role of the sexes in the society. Sex and age differences may become an area of concern and become elaborated into social class and social stratification, or prestige hierarchies. We have brought together a number of readings relevant to these questions of roles and statuses in Chapters Four and Five.

Not all concerns, of course, need be linked to the universal factors mentioned above. It is a result of the universal factors that we are able to compare cultural groups on a worldwide basis and study their distinctive responses to the universal concerns and anxieties faced by all societies. It is important to note at this point that in the above discussion we have treated various concerns such as religion, illness, *rites of passage*, etc. as if they were conceptually separate items. In native theory it is far more usual for these areas to be conceptually interrelated into a coherent cosmology of some sort. For example, explanations of illness frequently are phrased in terms of good and evil and become inextricably merged with beliefs about religion, witches, sorcerers, diviners, etc. These beliefs also become merged with explanations of what goes on during *rites of passage*. Thus, for example, one cannot separate a funeral ceremony with its associated beliefs and practices from theories concerning religion and illness. Note, for example, that in our own society there is a strong religious component in our funeral ceremonies.

Special circumstances occasionally arise that affect cultures in an immediate fashion. Sometimes these circumstances are of long standing, and other times they may actually change the culture orientation in a relatively short time. For example, in the U.S., older people who lived and felt suffering during the great depression of the early 1930's have many more hangups and anxieties about materialism than do younger people who remember only the prosperous 50's and 60's. In any event, elaborate cultural or individual ceremonies or rituals (such as compulsive concern with "getting ahead") are indicators of areas of concern or anxiety. A special type of disturbance caused by contact between contrasting cultural groups forms the subject of Chapter Nine. Of course, these anxieties may vary in the extent to which an outside observer would judge them to be based on "realistic" factors. The society on the edge of starvation that has elaborate ceremonies and beliefs about food might be judged to have a fairly realistic anxiety. On the other hand, a prosperous society with elaborate rituals and beliefs about demon possession might be judged to be somewhat unrealistic. In the literature, social scientists tend to call these latter anxieties "psychological." We are not claiming that the pain caused by demon possession is not just as "real" as hunger pangs, only that the source is less obvious. Chapter Three provides a further discussion of the concept of normality.

A variety of methods have been used in Anthropology, none universally, and few well-standardized. In Cultural Anthropology, participant-observation in a community different from our own has been a frequent point of departure. The result of such a method of observation has been descriptive ethnography. Many of the descriptive ethnographies written between approximately 1915 and 1940 implicitly assumed that the various pieces or aspects of culture fit together into a coherent patterned whole. It was assumed that each item in culture contributed to the functioning of the whole. Thus, in writing an ethnography, the anthropologists made an attempt to show how each cultural item functioned in the overall pattern. This approach came to be known as the functional approach. It was the anthropologist's attempt to make coherent sense of the culture as a whole. Since that time there has been an increasing number of methods and approaches.

In the area of psychological and cognitive Anthropology a variety of psychological tests and standardized questionnaires has been used. Many of these use rather sophisticated statistical and mathematical models and techniques. Other anthropologists have become quite dissatisfied with attempts to quantify, and in order to convey more subtle and comprehensive viewpoints, have applied what might be characterized as humanistic approaches. The aim of such approaches is to convey a deeper insight into the essence of culture traditions through studies in depth. Literary techniques and theoretical interpretation may be utilized, either together or separately. Oscar Lewis, for example, in his well-known series of books on Mexico, conveys rather deep insight to the family life in selected parts of Mexico. By gathering his information

with a tape recorder, he lets the subjects speak for themselves, although it
reads like fiction in his sensitive writing style. Others have attempted, through
lengthy immersion into the life of a selected tribe coupled with wisdom
and theoretical analysis, to give insight into the workings of culture.

It seems to be an inherent fact of life that the more precise the method, the
more trivial the problem attacked. The converse follows: that is, the more
relevant and significant the problem, the less precise and replicable are the
methods that can be brought to bear on it. For the larger and more significant
problems it is still probably true that we have to rely on our wisdom. In
this particular volume we have chosen items that deal with broader and more
relevant questions rather than the more technical and narrow questions that lend
themselves to the more precise quantitative approaches. The results are diverse,
and viewpoints vary so widely that any simple characterization would be
grossly inadequate. In Chapter Ten we illustrate a sample of the range of
methods tried in recent times.

One primary aim of an introductory Anthropology reader is to aid one in
gaining some idea of the diversity of cultural practices and patterns—to provide
diverse materials for comparison with his/her ethnocentric ideas so that
he/she can, in fact, see his/her hopes and anxieties mirrored from many angles
in the variety of patterns that occur in other cultures.

YOU

AND

OTHERS

1 / Evolution and Revolution in Prehistory

Introduction

Archaeology and Physical Anthropology are two subfields of Anthropology that deal mainly with the past. Archaeology is primarily concerned with two major interrelated problems: first, to reconstruct the temporal sequences among prehistoric cultures; and, second, to reconstruct the evolution of their way of life from the material remains of these prehistoric cultures. Physical Anthropology deals with the evolution of human beings and the interaction between their present cultural position and the biological foundation upon which it is based.

Scholars in both fields attempt to trace the gradual development of modern biological and cultural capacities of the human being. Archaeology usually studies societies that existed before the time of written records and is, in fact, sometimes referred to as Prehistory. On occasion, archaeologists will investigate historic sites, which enables them to compare their inferences with those derived from written sources for a full reconstruction of the culture under consideration. Physical anthropologists study evolution and the transition between early prehuman forms and the emergence of modern man. They are also interested in such cultural activities as tool-making and social organization, in both human and prehuman forms.

Just as the work of Western historians enriches the interpretations of contemporary Western society by sociologists, economists and political scientists, so too the findings of archaeologists and physical anthropologists provide social and cultural anthropologists with fresh perspectives on contemporary cultures.

All the fields of Anthropology share a concern with understanding the behavior of humans as it is shaped by and adapted to different environments, both natural and social. The evolution of genetic factors which enable a species to adjust to different ecological niches, or *adaptation*, is a pivotal concept that archaeologists and physical anthropologists frequently use. An adaptational perspective is adopted by Barnouw in the first selection, entitled "A Survey of Physical Anthropology and Prehistory."

Biological evolution has been taking place on earth for hundreds of millions of years. Millions of animal species are represented in earth's history. Two trends in adaptation stand out as general patterns: first adaptation of various species to unique ecological niches has been achieved predominantly by biological and somatic means—"bodily" changes; e.g., fins for fish—with reliance on anatomical features and genetically-programmed behavior; and, second, the overall trend in each species of these somatic adaptations has been towards increasing specialization: finer tailoring of body, behavior, diet, etc. to a narrower and narrower ecological niche within a local environment.

Human evolution represents a dramatic exception to these two trends. Over the last ten million years the fossil populations directly in the genetic line leading to *Homo sapiens* initiated a unique strategy—*extra-somatic* adaptation—that rapidly began to counter previous evolutionary trends. Examples include tools, fire, language, and the harnessing of nonhuman energy. As a result of these evolutionary trends, *culture* gradually began to dominate and shape the course of hominid evolution. As the new hominid specialization of culture developed at an ever-increasing rate, it gradually brought somatic specialization to a virtual standstill and allowed hominids and, ultimately, humans to move in the direction of greater *generalization* of their adaptations. Our extra-somatic adaptations—e.g., the possibility of wearing a fur coat—enable man to live and adapt to almost any environment on earth, and even, as we have recently seen, in space. Culture, or the world as shaped by cultural activities, has expanded our ecological niche.

Evolutionists of the 1800's held that "purely biological" evolution of the hominid line must have been very nearly complete before cultural evolution began. They generally assumed that the hominid brain size *must* have reached the lower limits of the modern range before culture could have been "discovered." The accumulating evidence from archaeological sites now suggests a very different conclusion. The discovery that Australopithecines—with a cranial capacity (500cc) little more than one-third that of *Homo sapiens*—apparently used rudimentary stone tools showed that, at the very least, the two "levels" of evolution (somatic and extra-somatic) had proceeded in parallel for quite a while.

The current consensus among anthropologists is that cultural activities promoted the enlargement of the brain as much as the brain promoted the elaboration of culture. In other words, the increasingly-sophisticated skills, physical and conceptual, that characterize the course of cultural evolution were joined with other selective pressures in fostering our present highly-generalized neurological capacity for complex cultural activities such as language.

The second reading, by DeVore and Washburn, represents a new specialty within Anthropology that emerged into prominence in the 1960's and is designated as Primatology. The anatomy of nonhuman primates and the behavior of *captive* individuals and groups have been studied for decades in order to provide a base-line of comparison with the behavior observed in living humans or inferred for pre-*Homo sapiens* fossil populations. Present-day primatologists have the same comparative goal but are distinguished by their emphasis on the study of nonhuman primate groups living in their natural habitats. Recent studies reveal that many of the earlier generalizations based on captive animals were not representative of "natural" primate behavior.

DeVore and Washburn carefully *contrast* baboon social organization and behavior with that of human hunter-gatherers. They conclude that there are more continuities than had been assumed between generic primate behavior and that characteristic of humans.

There has been much attention in the recent past to the effects upon modern man of our biological heritage. Books such as Konrad Lorenz's *On Aggression* and Desmond Morris' *The Naked Ape* reflect such concern. They attribute much of man's aggressive and territorial possessiveness to our biological ancestry and evolution. However, when humans acquired language, culture, and technology, there followed an enormous qualitative cultural revolution that sets humans in a distinctively different niche from that of other animals. There are undoubtedly some parallels between behavior of other primates and certain behavior of humans, but there are still essential differences. DeVore and

Washburn's assessment of the parallels between human and nonhuman behaviors is both balanced and careful.

The final two articles in this chapter each treat profound turning points in the development of human behavior and culture. The first was the adaptation of human ancestors to a hunting culture. Washburn and Lancaster trace this evolution over a span of millions of years, carefully detailing the enormous cumulative effects on the biological and social characteristics of modern humans.

The second profound development, the agricultural revolution, is discussed by Adams, who provides a brief account of the period from the end of the Stone Age through the development of agriculture. This period is perhaps one of the most revolutionary periods in the entire human career thus far. In a few thousand years—a mere moment on an evolutionary time-scale—the basic features of classic, pre-industrial civilization took form. During this brief period, humans learned to produce food from domesticated plants and animals. Having freed themselves from the time-consuming acquisition of food, humans had more time to devote to cultural progress. As a result, urban centers, accompanied by occupational specialization and social stratification arose; writing and mathematics were invented; new problems arose also, including a population increasing by geometric progression. The peasant societies that are the subject of several readings in this book still retain most of the traditions, such as technology and religion, shaped during this period.

Finally, an article by Oakley and Weiner appears in Chapter Ten which is also relevant to Physical Anthropology.

A Survey of Physical Anthropology and Prehistory

Victor Barnouw

Anthropology is the study of man (from Greek *anthropos*, man, and *logia*, study). It is mainly concerned with a single species, *Homo sapiens*, rather than with many diverse organisms, as in the case of botany and zoology, although physical anthropologists also study the various primate species related to man. Our objective is to learn all we can about the single organism, man—how he has become what he is, what he has accomplished, and what his potentialities are. One obvious difficulty in this enterprise is that we are human beings ourselves and therefore find it hard to be objective and to obtain an adequate perspective on ourselves.

Of course, anthropology is not the only field which focuses on man. There are many others, including sociology, psychology, history, law, economics, and political science. We do not need to draw clear-cut boundary lines between these various disciplines. There are many areas of overlap among them, each field having its own distinctive characteristics and emphases.

Anthropology may be broadly divided into physical anthropology and cultural anthropology. Cultural anthropology may in turn be subdivided into three main branches: archaeology, linguistics, and ethnology.

One unique aspect of anthropology which distinguishes it from the other social sciences is that it contains a branch, physical anthropology, which is concerned with man as a physical organism and with man's evolution from simpler forms of life.

Whatever else he may be, man is an animal (not a mineral or a plant); he is a vertebrate, a mammal, and a Primate, the order of mammals which also includes, among others, the apes and monkeys. Man is more closely related to some organisms than to others. The animals with which he has most in common are the chimpanzee and the gorilla, but he also has much in common with the gibbon and orangutan and, more distantly, with the Old World monkeys and other primates. Physical anthropologists are concerned with tracing man's relationships to these related species and with reconstructing the evolutionary branching and differentiation of the primate order, particularly with respect to man and his closest relatives.

Physical anthropologists have pursued at least four kinds of research in this connection: (1) the analysis of primate fossils, with an attempt to place them in a geological, temporal sequence; (2) comparative anatomical study of living primates, including such features as blood chemistry, tooth cusp patterns, and many other features; (3) observation of living primates in the field; and (4) laboratory experimentation with apes and monkeys. One focus of physical anthropology, then, is primate and human evolution.

A second focus is human variation. All human beings on earth today belong to a single species, *Homo sapiens*. All human groups, in other words, are capable of breeding with others and of producing fertile offspring. Within this single species, however, there is a good deal of variation with respect to such features as skin color, hair form, and other attributes. . . .

THE CLASSIFICATION OF MAN

We pointed out that man is a vertebrate, a mammal, and a Primate. These categories represent progressive refinements of classification. Let us consider each category in turn, and in doing so trace man's evolution from simpler forms of life.

Vertebrates are bilaterally symmetrical animals which have segmented backbones. Running through the backbone is a spinal cord connecting with the brain, which is usually enclosed in a skull. Thus the brain and central nervous system are well protected. The backbone is flexible, since it is made up of a series of bony rings. These features provide for a more efficient, mobile system than the external skeletons which hold together some of the invertebrates. The advantages of the vertebrate system have made it possible for some vertebrates, such as whales and elephants, to attain huge size. Man, too, is a large creature compared to most animals.

Life seems to have originated in the waters of the earth, and the first vertebrates, which appeared about 480 million years ago, were probably jawless freshwater fish. First plants, and later animals, gradually invaded land areas.

The vertebrates are divided into classes of fishes, amphibians, reptiles, birds, and mammals. Amphibians were creatures which made a partial adjustment to a terrestrial environment, developing limbs which propelled them along the ground. Reptiles developed from an amphibian stage about 260 million years ago. Birds and mammals, both warm-blooded, evolved from reptilian forms and are the two most recent classes of vertebrates. Archaic mammals appeared on the scene about 160 million years ago. In the course of evolution, limbs replaced fins and became strong enough in some reptiles, and later mammals, to raise the animal's body from the ground.

Evolutionary changes also took place in modes of reproduction. Fertilization became an internal rather than external process. Reptiles, birds, and prototherian mammals (duckbill, echidna) laid eggs. With the mammals, however, particularly eutherian or placental mammals, the foetus could live for a long time within the mother's body and be born alive, without the covering of an eggshell.

Mammals are warm-blooded creatures which are able to maintain a constant high body temperature and have thus been able to live in various kinds of environments and climatic conditions. They have other adaptive features related to temperature regulation: an efficient circulatory system, a covering of hair, and a skin equipped with sweat glands. Since man has these features and others of the class, he is classified as a eutherian mammal.

Within the grouping of eutherian mammals, man belongs to the order of Primates, which also includes the lemurs, tarsiers, monkeys, and apes. An outstanding characteristic of the primates is their prehensile (grasping) five-digited hands and feet generally equipped with flat or slightly curved nails. Grasping hands and feet are well suited to life in the trees, where most primates spend their time, although some, such as the baboon, gorilla, and man, move about on the ground. Life in the trees demands good eyesight. Most of the primates, whose eyes are set close together on the frontal plane, have overlapping stereoscopic vision, and the higher primates also have color vision. Monkeys pick up objects with their hands and examine them, and they can feed themselves with their hands. Their forelimbs and hind limbs have become differentiated, with the forelimbs being used for exploration and the lower limbs for support, a differentiation most developed in man.

The Primate order is divided into two suborders: the Prosimii, or lower primates, including the lemurs and tarsiers, and the Anthropoidea, or higher primates, including the New World and Old World monkeys, the apes, and man.

The superfamily within the Anthropoidea to which we belong is that of the Hominoidea. Its other members are the apes, who differ from the monkeys in lacking external tails, cheek pouches, and some other features. The apes have long arms, rather short legs, a semierect posture, and a broader, more basin-shaped pelvis than those of monkeys. The gibbon and orangutan are Southeast Asiatic apes; the chimpanzee and gorilla are African ones.

Unlike many lower vertebrates, most of the primates are social animals which live the year round in groups consisting of males, females, and offspring. The young are relatively helpless at birth and depend upon maternal care more than most other mammals do. The period of dependency increases from the lower to the higher primates.

Terrestrial primates, such as baboons, move about in larger bands than arboreal ones and cover a wider range. They show more differentiation of dominant-submissive behavior than arboreal species and more sexual dimorphism, showing striking differences in size and strength between males and females.

Primates, represented by small prosimians, appear in the fossil record about 70 million years ago; they had become abundant by about 57 million years ago. In the Old World, fossil finds which consist mainly of teeth and jaw fragments and which perhaps represent ancestral types of Old World monkey and ape have been found in the Egyptian Fayum dating from around 30 million years ago.

Possible ancestors of ours are represented by the tooth and jaw fragments of Kenyapithecus and Ramapithecus, found in East Africa and northwestern India respectively and dating from about 14 million years ago. These teeth have been classified as hominid—more human than apelike—on the basis of such features as small incisor and canine teeth, V-shaped jaw, and relatively flat face. It has even been speculated that maybe, in keeping with these features, these creatures had upright posture and the use of tools.

This brings us to the characteristics of modern man and how he differs from other primates. These may be listed briefly:

1. Upright posture.
2. Very large brain and more complex nervous system in comparison with those of other primates.
3. Lumbar curve in the spine.
4. Broad, basin-shaped pelvis.
5. Well-developed *gluteus maximus* muscles of the buttocks.
6. Longer legs than arms.
7. Arches in the foot from front to back and from side to side.
8. Foot has a heel.
9. Big toe is in line with other toes and is not opposable.

10. No heavy brow ridges or crests on the skull like those of the adult male gorilla and chimpanzee.
11. Bony nose bridge and cartilaginous tip.
12. Presence of a *canine fossa*, a hollow in the cheekbones on either side of the nose.
13. Presence of a philtrum, a median groove in the upper lip.
14. Outrolled lips showing membranous red portion.
15. Presence of a chin.
16. No large, interlocking canine teeth.
17. Absence of a simian shelf, a bar of bone which binds together the right and left sides of the jaws of modern apes.
18. V-shaped or parabolic jaws in contrast to the long, U-shaped jaws of apes.
19. Central position of the *foramen magnum*, a hole in the base of the skull through which the spinal cord connects with the brain.
20. Relatively hairless body.
21. More developed breasts in the female.
22. Relatively large penis in the male and absence of a penis bone.
23. Slower rate of maturation.

Many of these features, such as the lumbar curve of the spine, the characteristics of the pelvis, the long legs, and the specialization of the feet, represent adaptations to upright posture and bipedalism. Some of the differences are matters of degree—larger brains, less body hair. Some of the features mentioned have been acquired rather recently by man and were not characteristic of our early hominid ancestors.

To conclude: we have seen that man is a vertebrate, a eutherian mammal, and a primate. In the order of Primates he belongs to the suborder Anthropoidea and the superfamily of Hominoidea. In the latter category, which also includes the Pongidae, or apes, man is classified in the family of Hominidae. *Homo sapiens*, or man of the present day, is the only living hominid, and all contemporary human beings are of the same species.

EARLY HOMINIDS

Between 1 million and 4 million years ago, there were apelike but upright bipedal hominids living in parts of Africa. The first fossil evidence of this was an immature juvenile skull found in South Africa in 1924 and named *Australopithecus africanus* (South African ape) by Raymond Dart. In the following decades, more such finds were made in South and East Africa, so that by now remains of over 100 individuals have been recovered. Despite the "ape" label originally given by Dart, it is now recognized that the australopithecines, as they have been called, were not apes but hominids, having more in common with ourselves than with the apes. They lacked chins and had brains which were not much larger than those of present-day apes, although their brains were relatively large in proportion to body size. The discovery of these remains has shown that man must have assumed upright posture before he developed a large brain.

There has been much debate about the archaeological evidence for tool use among the australopithecines, but it seems likely that at least some of them used tools of wood, bone, and horn as well as stone.

A later stage of hominid evolution was that of *Homo erectus*, represented by such finds as Java man and Peking man, living between a million and half a million years ago. These men were of about the same height as modern man. Their brains were much larger than those of the australopithecines but smaller than those of modern man, although the larger skulls fall within the modern human range. They had low skulls with heavy brow ridges and large chinless jaws with big teeth.

Homo erectus must have spread over much of the Old World, for his fossilized remains have been unearthed in Africa, Europe, China, and Indonesia. Since stone tools have often been found in the same geological levels, there is no doubt that *Homo erectus* had a culture, including the use of choppers or pebble tools and sometimes hand axes. Moreover, the use of fire was known at this time, as attested in cave sites in both Europe and China. Armed with tools and the knowledge of fire, some representatives of *Homo erectus* were able to move into cool northerly regions in Europe and China as well as occupying warmer zones in Africa, southern Asia, and Indonesia. By this time men must have acquired a language, and there must have been some division of labor, with men specializing as hunters and women as collectors and perhaps preparers of food. Home bases, to which members of a band returned, were a feature of this stage. There is also some evidence of communal hunting as in sites at Torralba and Ambrona in Spain where elephants mired in bogs were killed and butchered. Activities such as these are hard to imagine taking place without the use of language.

Neanderthal man is considered to represent a stage intermediate between *Homo erectus* and modern man. Although not formerly so classified, Neanderthal man is now regarded as having been a form of *Homo sapiens*. He lived in Europe and parts of Asia from around 100,000 to around 35,000 years ago. From the *Homo erectus* stage Neanderthal man inherited such traits as thick skull walls and brow ridges and low elevation of the skull, and large jaws, but he differed from *Homo erectus* in having a much larger brain, as large as modern man's. His skull was not high domed, however, but long and flattish, broadening out behind the ears.

Men of modern physical type, with chins and more high-domed skulls, lived in Europe during the Upper Palaeolithic period between around 30,000 and 11,000 years ago, and the earlier Neanderthal type then seems to have disappeared.

VARIATION IN MODERN MAN

Human populations today vary in skin color, eye color, hair form, and many other features. Physical anthropologists try to determine how variations in pigmentation, hair form, and other features have come about in different populations.

Physical anthropologists not only study the distribution of such observable traits as hair form and skin color, but they are also interested in the distribution of blood types, such as A, B, AB, O, M, and N, and other biochemical factors, and they study the incidence of ailments determined by heredity, such as sickle-cell anemia and hemophilia, and the relative susceptibility or immunity of different human populations to certain diseases.

Anthropologists used to be interested in classifying the "races of mankind";

some still are. There are various problems, however, about the concept of race. A race may be defined as a human population whose members have in common some hereditary physical characteristics which differentiate them from other human groups. Putting it in more genetical terms, a race is a breeding population which differs from others in the frequency of certain genes. Membership in a race is determined only by hereditary physical traits and has no necessary connection with language, nationality, or religion, although language, nationality, and religion often act as isolating mechanisms which may maintain to some extent the distinctiveness of a racial group. There is no such thing as an Aryan race, a French race, or a Muslim race.

Some anthropologists even argue that there is no such thing as race at all; "races" in their view are merely products of human imagination and reason which correspond to no actual reality in the world of nature. One reason why such men have rejected the race concept is that there is no agreement among physical anthropologists about how many races there are. Most anthropology textbooks list three major racial stocks: Caucasoid, Negroid, and Mongoloid. . . .

• • •

In addition to the three large categories of Caucasoids, Negroids, and Mongoloids, various other groups can be distinguished which have some distinctive characteristics, such as the Bushmen of South Africa, the Ainu of northern Japan, the Australian aborigines, and the Polynesians. In some racial classifications these groups are listed as separate races, apart from the three major ones, while other authorities lump some of them together as subdivisions of the larger ones. The Melanesians and Papuans used to be classified with the Negroes of Africa, since they have dark skin, dark eyes, and often kinky hair; but it has been shown that Melanesians and Africans are not genetically related, for they differ completely in the composition of their blood groups. Similarly, blood group studies show that there is no genetic relationship between the African Pygmies and the short-statured dark-skinned Papuan Negritos. Classifying people on the basis of common observable physical features may be misleading. Moreover, there has been much interbreeding among the human populations of the world.

There is a tendency in present-day physical anthropology to study the distribution of genetically determined single traits. When these are plotted, they often do not coincide very well with traditional racial groupings. There is, for example, a high incidence of blood group A in Western Europe and high concentrations of blood group B in northwestern India, West Pakistan, and northern China and Manchuria. These distributions do not accord very well with traditional racial classifications. The Caucasoids of northwestern India and Pakistan have blood types like those of the Chinese and unlike those of Western Europe, while the Mongoloids of eastern Asia have a different blood type from that of most American Indians. It is for reasons such as these that some anthropologists deny the validity and usefulness of the concept of race.

If we decide to follow the traditional custom of distinguishing particular races, we still cannot assume, as has often been done, that some races are more intelligent or more advanced than others. There has been a recent attempt by an American psychologist to show that American Negroes are inferior in native intelligence to American whites. He claims that efforts in compensatory education such as the Headstart program have failed to raise the level of scholastic performance among Negroes and that their inability must therefore be due to a genetic deficiency in intelligence. Some critics of this view have replied that most programs in compensatory education have not been effectively administered; their alleged failure need not imply any genetic inadequacy on the part of Negroes. It should be pointed out that some statistical calculations show that North American Negroes have about 28 percent white ancestry, while over 36 million whites are descended from persons of African origin. Neither Negroes nor whites are genetically homogeneous.

Writers with a racist orientation assert that when Negroes and whites of comparable status and educational level are tested, whites still come out ahead. But in what sense is status comparable? Negroes were slaves little more than a hundred years ago, and in the intervening years they have faced barriers of poverty and prejudice. . . .

The foregoing discussion involving relationships between physical and cultural factors leads us to consider what is meant by the term *culture*. The fields of archaeology, linguistics, and ethnology are all bracketed under the general heading of cultural anthropology, as distinguished from physical or biological anthropology. Culture refers to man's learned behavior, acquired by experience, as opposed to inborn genetically determined behavior. This usage of the term must be distinguished from older colloquial meanings expressed in phrases like "a man of culture." In the anthropological sense, all men have culture.

Although anthropologists sometimes use the word *culture* in a broad generic sense, they also speak about a culture, like Eskimo culture or Hopi culture. Here is a definition of culture in this sense: A culture is the way of life of a group of people, the configuration of all of the more or less stereotyped patterns of learned behavior which are handed down from one generation to the next through the means of language and imitation. The nub of this definition is the first clause: "the way of life of a group of people." This way of life has some integration and cohesion to it—hence the term *configuration*. It consists of patterns of learned behavior which are transmitted through language and imitation, not through instinct or any direct action of the genes, although the *capacity* for culture is determined by heredity. These patterns are only relatively fixed and are amenable to change; hence they are said to be "more or less" stereotyped. A person is destined to learn the patterns of behavior prevalent in the society in which he grows up. He does not necessarily learn them all, for there may be cultural differences appropriate to persons of different age, sex, status, and occupation, and there may also be genetically determined differences in learning ability. Moreover, the culture patterns of his society may change with the appearance of new inventions or through contact with other ways of life. We cannot understand human behavior very well without the concept of *culture*, . . .

Archaeology is the study of extinct cultures, while ethnology is the study of living ones. Archaeologists are usually, although not always, concerned with what are called prehistoric cultures, those which existed before the development of written records. Archaeologists willingly make use of written records if they are available, as in Mesopotamia, Egypt, and Guatemala, but often they have nothing to work with but the relics and remains of bygone peoples—potsherds, arrowheads, clay figurines, and tools of bone, stone, or other durable material. History begins with the appearance of written records; prehistory is the domain of the archaeologist. Both the historian and the archaeologist want to uncover the story of man's development through time. The historian is concerned with only a brief segment of man's existence on earth, for writing originated only about 5,000 years ago, while potassium-argon dates have shown that man's ancestors used stone tools about 2 million years ago. Prehistory therefore comprises an immense stretch of time. We depend upon the archaeologist, working with the paleontologist, geologist, physical anthropologist, and other specialists to reconstruct what happened during these hundreds of thousands of years. In many parts of the world—Australia, Melanesia, Polynesia, most of the New World, and Africa—writing was not known until its recent introduction by Europeans. Here again the archaeologist works to uncover the past.

Problems which face the archaeologist include selection of sites for excavation, excavation procedures, methods of dating finds, and interpretation of the evidence.

The presence of worthwhile sites is sometimes obvious, sometimes not. The appearance of local vegetation may indicate the presence of a former settlement. Air reconnaissance may discover telltale features not readily observable on the ground. The presence of buried walls, house foundations, and other features may be detected by the method of electrical resistivity, running an electric current through the earth between two electrodes and recording the amount of resistance. Proton magnetometers may be used like wartime mine detectors to discover the presence of underground iron objects, kilns, ovens, and solid structures.

There are different types of sites: living sites; butchering sites, where animals were cut up; workshop sites or "floors," where tools were made; quarry sites, where flint or minerals were extracted; ceremonial sites; and burial sites, such as graves and tombs.

After a site has been decided upon, the usual method is to survey it and stake it out on a grid plan, with the area divided into numbered squares. The location of all artifacts uncovered must be recorded, each within its numbered square and in depth. Photographs are taken in the course of excavation. The archaeologist preserves animal bones, charcoal, and remains of plants and pollen, both for dating purposes and for assessment of the ecological conditions formerly present at the site. Cautious inferences are made about former social and cultural conditions, settlement patterns, degree of cultural, technological advancement, and so forth, on the basis of the archaeological evidence.

Various techniques are used, preferably combining two or more methods, in dating archaeological sites. One is *dendrochronology*, dating by tree ring sequences, which has been used mainly in the American Southwest, and which provides a specific chronological date in years. The most widely used archaeological dating technique, however, is radiocarbon dating, in which the amount of carbon 14 in organic material is measured. This does not yield a specific date, but one plus or minus a certain number of years, giving a standard deviation. Other methods of dating include the analysis of pollen grains and of associated animal remains, particularly in the case of extinct animals, the date of whose disappearance is approximately known. Various other methods are also used. Excavation procedures and dating methods have become progressively more sophisticated in recent years. Archaeologists now depend upon a host of allied sciences for help in interpreting the data they uncover.

CULTURAL EVOLUTION IN THE OLD WORLD

In most of the period since man acquired speech and the use of tools he has been a hunter and gatherer. Settled village life and civilization are the achievements of only yesterday. Our knowledge of the long stretch of Palaeolithic (Old Stone Age) times down to about 8000 B.C. is based largely on imperishable stone tools, for most of the wood and other organic materials used by early man has decayed and vanished. Stone tools are divisible into core and flake tools, depending upon whether one uses the knocked-off flakes or the original core of stone from which the flakes are detached. Hand axes are core tools which were widely used in the Lower Palaeolithic in Africa, Western Europe, the Near East, and India. The Palaeolithic was marked by a gradual increase in the number and kinds of flake tools. These became more prominent in the Upper Palaeolithic, when hand axes ceased to be used.

It is in the Middle Palaeolithic period in Europe that we find the first implications of religious beliefs in the archaeological record: burials accompanied by grave goods and suggestions of a bear cult, implied by special treatment of bear skulls, which were sometimes set in niches in the walls of caves inhabited by Neanderthal man.

The Upper Palaeolithic in Europe has been dated by the radiocarbon method at around 32,300–11,000 B.C. It was characterized by a host of new inventions: spear-throwers, harpoons, and probably the bow and arrow. Improved stone tools were made, especially blades and burins. Various tools and decorated objects were fashioned from bone, horn, antler, and ivory, including spatulas, half-rounded rods, and pierced staffs. Bone needles were used, suggesting the use of clothing.

Well-executed artworks were produced in various media: clay sculpture, engraving in antler and ivory, and polychrome paintings on the walls of caves in Spain and southern France. The purpose of this cave art is not clearly known. It no longer seems sufficient to say that it was probably for the purpose of magically increasing and controlling the animals hunted by early man. The animals depicted evidently had some symbolic meaning for the hunters, since different species are depicted at different parts of caves, with horses, ibex, and stag being painted at entrances and backs of caves, while bison and "oxen" dominate the centers of the caves and are not found on the peripheries. Female human figures and "female" signs are found at the center, while "male" signs are found at the entrances and at the backs of caves, where male human figures also appear. While it is not clear what this all means, it is evident that Upper Palaeolithic cave art was more complicated and symbolic than was formerly imagined.

The Mesolithic period in Europe, dated at around 11,000–5,000 B.C., was a time of climatic change. The weather became warmer, and forests developed, replacing the open plains of Upper Palaeolithic times. Buffalo, wild horses and cattle, and other animals hunted by men of the Upper Palaeolithic disappeared from Europe, to be replaced by animals adapted to forest life. An increased attention was given to fishing, settlements spread along coast and streams, and various devices were developed for catching fish. Wood was employed for many kinds of tools; axes and adzes were used for chopping down trees, making dugout canoes, and perhaps house constructions. The impressive art of the Upper Palaeolithic disappears, with nothing comparable to replace it, as far as we can judge from what has remained of Mesolithic culture.

The Neolithic period, which began earlier in the Near East than in Europe, from around 8,000 to 3,500 B.C., was the most important transitional phase in man's history, bringing about sedentary village life based upon the domestication of plants and animals.

In the Old World the principal domesticated plants were wheat, barley, millet, and flax. The most important animals to be domesticated were sheep, goats, cattle, and pigs.

Settled village life brought many advantages, such as greater security for the aged, the very young, and the sick, and greater ability to preserve and store food. With permanent or semipermanent settlement, greater attention could be given to housing and furniture. Houses were made of varying materials, depending on the locality and the climate, employing mud bricks, reed and plaster, wood, and stone. Ground stone axes and adzes made advances in carpentry possible. Querns, rubbing stones, and mortars and pestles were used for preparing cereals. Weaving was facilitated by the invention of the loom. Woven textiles began to supplement or replace animal skins and furs for clothing. Pottery is absent from some of the lower levels of Near Eastern Neolithic sites but is usually found in late Neolithic settlements, sometimes beautifully painted.

Neolithic traits diffused westward into Europe and North Africa, both along the coast and through land routes. Megalithic cults involving passage graves, ancestor worship, and a mother goddess cult diffused by sea from the eastern Mediterranean to Spain and from Spain to France, the British Isles, and Scandinavia. These cults show that cooperation on a large scale was involved in the transportation and setting up of megaliths. Stonehenge further shows that some human beings in England in late Neolithic and Bronze Age times had acquired a considerable knowledge of the movements of the sun and moon and were able to predict the occurrence of solstices, equinoxes, and eclipses of the moon.

As Neolithic ways of life spread throughout the Old World, they had to be changed to adapt to many different kinds of environments. In Central Europe the early migrants encountered forests which had to be cleared for farming. They developed the pattern of "swidden" or "slash-and-burn" horticulture. This involves the clearing of a patch of land by burning, planting crops and tending them for one or several years, and then abandoning the plot to lie fallow for a while.

Neolithic ways of life spread eastward as well as toward the west. Northwestern India shared the basic features of the Near Eastern Neolithic complex. The same may be said of northern China, although millet was grown in preference to barley and wheat, and cows' milk was not consumed.

• • •

In the Bronze Age, between around 3500 and 1500 B.C., several centers of civilization quickly developed in the Near East and adjacent regions of the Old World. Mesopotamia seems to have been in advance of Egypt and the Indus Valley in this development, with centers in Crete and northern China emerging still later. In Mesopotamia, Egypt, and the Indus Valley, we find civilization developing along the banks of rivers which run through dry terrain. Irrigation was needed if farmers were to survive in such regions. This requirement may have encouraged centralized political control. Meanwhile, irrigation and new inventions such as the ox-drawn plow and metal sickle helped to provide an agricultural surplus, which made economic specialization possible. It was no longer necessary for everyone to work in the fields. Such specialists as the scribe, metallurgist, potter, weaver, carpenter, and barber now worked full time at specialized trades. A new class of peasantry appeared which depended upon city life and trade but which maintained its separate rural way of life. Within the city itself, class stratification appeared, not only distinguishing between the rich, the middle class, and the poor but also between freemen and slaves. Slavery, a recognized institution, was the focus of much legislation.

Bronze Age centers of civilization were characterized by the presence of monumental constructions—pyramids, mounds, ziggurats, palaces, tombs, and defensive constructions—showing that mass labor sources were available.

During this period, trade was not only local but far-ranging because of the needs of Egypt, Mesopotamia, and the Indus Valley to import metals and other basic commodities. Advances were accordingly made in communication. Larger, more seaworthy ships were built than formerly. Various animals were domesticated especially for their use in transportation: the donkey, camel, and horse. Merchant colonies became established in foreign centers of trade. Standardized mediums of exchange became recognized, first in grain and later in metal, especially silver.

The scale and range of warfare also increased in this period, involving larger numbers of persons than did the fighting of Neolithic times. At the same time, the Bronze Age saw great advances in knowledge, not only in the techniques of metallurgy and other technological advances of the period, but more importantly in the development of writing systems, mathematics, calendrical reckoning, and astronomy. This knowledge was largely limited to members of the priesthood and upper class, who attended schools and received formal instruction.

Patterns of culture spread from the centers of advanced civilization through various routes. Contacts between eastern and western Eurasia were facilitated by the opening up of the steppes to occupation by mounted nomads after the introduction of horseback riding soon after the 14th century B.C. and the invention of the covered wagon. Camel caravans across the deserts of North Africa brought luxury articles from the Mediterranean and Egypt to Ghana and Mali long before the period of European colonization in Africa. Evidence of high civilization in West Africa comes from the beautiful bronze portrait heads of Ife and Benin, made by the lost-wax process of casting between the 13th and 18th centuries A.D. in what is now southern Nigeria. At the same time, there was trade in communities along the coast of East Africa with ships from India and China. The islands of the Pacific were populated by migrants, probably from Southeast Asia, with a Neolithic horticultural and maritime culture, who must have settled first in the Philippines. According to radiocarbon dating, New Caledonia and Fiji were inhabited by around 800 B.C. or earlier. The Society Islands and the Marquesas were occupied around the second or third centuries B.C. The Society Islands in the heart of Polynesia may have been the point from which Hawaii, New Zealand, and other islands were settled. Hawaii became inhabited around the second century A.D., Easter Island in the fourth century, and New Zealand not until around A.D. 1000.

CULTURAL EVOLUTION IN THE NEW WORLD

Human beings of the *Homo sapiens* stage entered the New World by way of a land bridge in the Bering Straits region between 40,000 and 10,000 B.C. Very likely, there were several waves of migration. The early migrants brought with them a Palaeolithic culture. They probably knew how to make fire and may have made mats and baskets. The first clearly distinguishable culture in the New World archaeological record is the Big-Game Hunting tradition, organized around the hunting of herding animals, particularly in the Western Plains, and characterized by fluted projectile points. This tradition may date back to around 14,000 B.C.; it declined after 8000 B.C., when the large mammals (mammoths, mastodon, camel, horse, and extinct forms of bison) began to disappear. Other "traditions" coexisted with and outlasted that of the Big-Game Hunters in North America and Mesoamerica.

One of these, the Desert Tradition, slowly gave rise to the beginning of horticulture in Mesoamerica between 7000 and 2000 B.C. By the latter date, a complex of plants was being widely cultivated, including maize, beans, squashes, chili pepper, and the bottle gourd. These are native American plants, quite different from the domesticated species of the Old World.

This cultivation of plants was not accompanied by much domestication of animals, as in the Old World. Indigenous forms of wild horses and cows were not available for domestication in the Americas. In this respect, the American version of the Neolithic stage differed from that of Eurasia.

In other respects, however, we find parallels in housing, permanent settlement, and in the invention of weaving and pottery making. Some authorities have argued that Mesoamerican pottery was probably derived from Asia, as Woodland pottery diffused from Siberia, but this case has not been proven. It seems likely that most developments of culture at the "Neolithic" level were independent achievements on the part of the American Indians.

Some advanced civilizations developed in the New World, notably those of the Aztecs, Maya, and Incas. These three civilizations were quite different from one another in certain respects, just as were the civilizations of Sumer, Egypt, and Harappa. Nevertheless, like their Old World Bronze Age counterparts, the New World civilizations shared some common features.

Each of these centers saw the establishment of city life characterized by various features which were remarkably similar to those of the Old World: division of labor and class stratification, increased trade and communication, the appearance of a dominant priesthood-intelligentsia, emergence of a state, enlargement of the scale of warfare, and advances in certain spheres of knowledge, particularly systems for recording information, mathematics, and astronomical and calendrical calculations. Metallurgy developed around 700 B.C. in Peru, where gold and silver ornaments were made and the making of bronze was known.

The lost-wax process of casting, which was known in both Mesopotamia and Shang China, was practiced in Peru, Central America, and Mexico.

There seem to be many parallels between New World architecture and the architecture of the Old World Bronze Age centers of civilization. Pyramids appeared in Mesoamerica and Peru, temple mounds in the Mississippi Valley and the Southeast. The massive Inca fortifications at Sacsahuaman are reminiscent of Old World defense works.

The invention of zero and position numbering was an independent achievement of the Maya, paralleling the invention of the zero in India, but being dated even earlier in time.

There was some unevenness in the development of culture in these areas. Writing developed in Mesoamerica but not in Peru. Political organization, road building, and metallurgy were more advanced in Peru than in Mesoamerica. The Peruvians had llamas, alpacas, and vicuñas and were thus able to make woolen textiles, while other Indians were not. But there seems to have been more trade in Mesoamerica than in Peru. Special privileged classes of traders appeared among the Aztecs and the Maya. The Aztecs and Maya had slaves, but the institution of slavery does not appear among the Incas, although it might be argued that many of the commoners were virtually slaves. The many parallels in the development of Old World and New World civilizations give an impression of orderly sequences in cultural evolution, of certain cross-cultural regularities which have intrigued many theorists of cultural evolution from Edward B. Tylor to Julian H. Steward and his followers.

Baboon Ecology and Human Evolution

Irven DeVore and S. L. Washburn

The ecology of baboons is of particular interest to the student of human evolution. Aside from man, these monkeys are the most successful ground-living primates, and their way of life gives some insight into the problems which confronted early man. We have been concerned with an attempt to reconstruct the evolution of human behavior by comparing the social behavior and ecology of baboons with that of living hunter-gatherer groups, and applying these comparisons to the archaeological evidence (Washburn and DeVore 1961a). . . .

• • •

The men of the Middle Pleistocene, genus *Homo*, occupied the same range as the baboon-macaques but without speciation. Their way of life (based on tools, intelligence, walking, and hunting) was sufficiently more adaptable and effective so that a single species could occupy an area which ground monkeys could occupy only by evolving into at least a dozen species. This comparison gives some measure of the effectiveness of the human way of life, even at the level of Pekin and Ternifine man. Obviously, there is nothing to be gained by being dogmatic about the number of species of Middle Pleistocene men. Perhaps when many more specimens have been found it will be convenient to recognize two or three species, but the general form of this argument will still

hold. There is no suggestion that any of the known fossil men (genus *Homo*) differ in size or form as much as a chacma baboon and a drill, or a crab-eating macaque and a pig-tail macaque. Even in its most primitive form the human way of life radically alters the relation of the organisms to the environment. As early as Middle Pleistocene times man could migrate over three continents without major morphological adaptation.

Australopithecus may have occupied an adaptive position midway in effectiveness between the ground monkeys and early *Homo*. Small-brained, bipedal tool-makers probably occupied larger areas than baboons, and without speciation. It is most unlikely that the East African and South African forms of *Australopithecus* are more than racially distinct. . . . The presence of small and large Australopithecoids in South Africa at the same time suggests that their adaptation was much less effective than that of *Homo*. It may be possible to reconstruct more of this stage in human evolution with a more thorough study of the ecology of baboons, and by contrasting their mode of adaptation to that of man. With this hope in mind we will now consider the ecology of baboons in East Africa.

• • •

Troop Structure

A detailed description of the social relationships within baboon troops is given elsewhere (DeVore 1962). Here we have emphasized those aspects of troop life which are adaptations to life on the ground. Baboons are intensely social, and membership in a troop is a prerequisite for survival. Most of a baboon's life is spent within a few feet of other baboons. Baboon troops are closed social systems, individuals very rarely change to a new troop, and the troop regards any strange baboon with suspicion and hostility.

Within the troop, subgroups are based on age, sex, personal preferences, and dominance. When a troop is resting or feeding quietly, most of the adult members gather into small clusters, grooming each other or just sitting. Juveniles gather into groups of the same age and spend the day in these "play groups," eating, resting, and playing together. The most dominant adult males occupy the center of the troop, with the mothers and their young infants gathered around them, and the groups of young juveniles playing close by. These dominant males, and the small black infants near them, seem to be greatly attractive to the other troop members. During quiet periods the other troop members approach the adult males and the mothers, grooming them or sitting beside them. It is unnecessary for male baboons to herd the troop together; their presence alone insures that the other troop members will not be far away.

Around this nucleus of adult males, mothers, and young juveniles are the more peripheral members of the troop—the less dominant adult males, older juveniles, and pregnant or estrus females. Estrus females and their consorts usually stay at the periphery of the troop. Although the juvenile play groups will not wander far from the troop's center, peripheral adults may leave the troop for short periods. While the center of the troop moves slowly along, the adult and older juvenile (subadult) males and adult females sometimes move rapidly ahead to a new feeding spot. This may separate them from the rest of the troop by a quarter of a mile or more, and they may not rejoin the troop for thirty minutes or an hour. Although peripheral adult males may make such a side trip alone, or

in small groups, other troop members will not leave the troop unless accompanied by the males. Healthy "solitary males" observed during the early part of our study later proved to be troop members who had left the troop for a short while.

A baboon troop that is in or under trees seems to have no particular organization, but when the troop moves out onto the open plains a clear order of progression appears. Out in front of the troop move the boldest troop members—the less dominant adult males and the older juvenile males. Following them are other members of the troop's periphery, pregnant and estrus adult females and juveniles. Next, in the center, comes the nucleus of dominant adult males, females with infants, and young juveniles. The rear of the troop is a mirror image of its front, with adults and older juveniles following the nucleus and more adult males at the end. This order of progression is invariably followed when the troop is moving rapidly from one feeding area to another during the day, and to its sleeping trees at dusk. A troop which is coming toward trees from the open plains approaches with particular caution. The tall trees in which baboons sleep are found only where the water table is near the surface, usually along a river or beside a pond. Vegetation is usually dense at the base of these trees, and it is in this undergrowth that predators often spend the day. The arrangement of the troop members when they are moving insures maximum protection for the infants and juveniles in the center of the troop. An approaching predator would first encounter the adult males on the troop's periphery, and then the adult males in the center, before it could reach defenseless troop members in the center.

Because they are in front of the troop by twenty to forty yards, the peripheral adult males are usually the first troop members to encounter a predator and give alarm calls. If a predator is sighted, all the adult males actively defend the troop. On one occasion we saw two dogs run up behind a troop, barking. The females and juveniles hurried ahead, but the males continued walking slowly. After a moment an irregular group of some twenty adult males was between the dogs and the rest of the troop. When a male turned on the dogs, they ran off. On another day we saw three cheetahs approach a troop of baboons. A single adult male stepped toward the cheetahs, gave a loud, defiant bark, and displayed his canine teeth; the cheetahs trotted away. If baboons come upon predators while en route to their sleeping trees, the troop stops and waits while the males in the center move ahead and find an alternate route (the young juveniles and mothers with infants stay behind with the peripheral adult males). Eventually the dominant males return, the original order of progression is re-established, and the troop proceeds along the new route. These behavior patterns assure that the females and young are protected in the troop's center.

The ultimate safety of a baboon troop is in the trees. When the troop is away from trees, the adult males are very important in troop defense. We saw baboons near such predators as cheetahs, dogs, hyenas, and jackals, and usually the baboons seemed unconcerned—the other animals kept well away. Lions, however, will put a baboon troop to flight. From the safety of trees baboons bark and threaten lions but make no resistance to them on the ground. The behavior of baboons when near trees contrasts strikingly with their behavior on the open plains. If the troop is under trees, it will feed on the ground within thirty yards of predators, including lions.

Ecology and Sex Differences

The role of the adult male baboons as defenders of the troop has been described. This behavior is vital to the survival of the troop, and especially to the survival of the most helpless animals—females with new babies, small juveniles, and temporarily sick or injured individuals. Selection has favored the evolution of males which weigh more than twice as much as females, and the advantage to the troop of these large animals is clear, but it is not obvious why it is advantageous for the females to be small. The answer to the degree of sex differences appears to be that this is the optimum distribution of the biomass of the species. If the average adult male weighs approximately 75 pounds and the average adult female 30 pounds, each adult male requires more than twice the food of a female. If the food supply is a major factor in limiting the number of baboons, and if survival is more likely if there are many individuals, and if the roles of male and female are different—then selection will favor a sex difference in average body size which allows the largest number of animals compatible with the different social roles in the troop.

· · ·

The importance of sex difference in body size is reinforced by social behavior and the structure of the troop. As described earlier, some subadult and adult males are peripheral in the structure of the troop. They tend to be first, or last, when the troop moves. They are the most exposed to predators and are, biologically, the most expendable members of the troop. Interadult male antagonism results in a social order which both protects females and young and reduces feeding competition with females and young. Without altruism, the dominance behavior of a small number of males keeps a feeding space available to subordinate animals.

Juvenile play prepares the adults for their differential roles. Older juvenile females do not engage in the serious mock fighting which characterizes the play of older juvenile males. In this "play" the males learn to fight, and by the time the canine teeth have erupted and the temporal muscles grown to adult size they have had years of fighting practice. Play, social arrangement, and structural sexual dimorphism all supplement each other, producing a pattern in which the females and young are relatively more protected than the large males. Sexual differentiation must be seen as a part of this whole complex social pattern which leads to the survival of troops of baboons.

RANGE

On an average day a baboon troop leaves its sleeping trees at full daylight and moves rapidly to a spot where the animals feed intensively for two or three hours. In Nairobi Park this morning feeding period is often spent in a fig tree (if these are in fruit), along a watercourse, or out on the open plains. During the dry season in the Amboseli Reserve, feeding areas were usually at the edges of water holes. During the middle of the day baboons rest in the shade of bushes or trees, not far from the feeding place of the morning. The late afternoon is another period of relatively intensive feeding. It is often some distance away from the feeding area of the morning, and a different kind of food is usually eaten. If the morning was spent in a fig tree, the afternoon is usually spent eating grass on the plains; if the morning was spent on the plains, the afternoon meal often consists of the pods, buds, and blossoms of acacia trees. During such a day the troop completes an average circuit of about three miles in Nairobi Park, but this distance varies from a few yards on some days to six or seven miles on others. These figures refer to the distance between points on a map. As a troop meanders across a plain, however, the individuals actually walk twice as far as these figures indicate.

• • •

Daily routines tend to keep baboon troops apart. Although annual ranges overlap extensively, there is very little overlap of the core areas of adjacent troops. We saw no evidence that troops defend a part of their range as "territory" (Burt 1943), but in Nairobi Park one troop is seldom seen in the core area of another. The core area or areas of a troop contain sleeping trees, water, resting places, and food sources. A troop uses one core area and one grove of sleeping trees for many weeks at a time but may then shift suddenly to a new area. . . .

• • •

Ordinarily this pattern of range utilization segregates the troops into clusters which recognize and tolerate each other at short distances without any sign of nervousness or tension. If a small troop is at a water hole and a large troop which also uses that water hole arrives, the smaller troop feeds slowly away. When troop 171 came once to the water hole usually frequented by 185, however, both troops paid close attention to the other. Adult males clustered where the troops were closest. The gestures, noises, and indications of nervousness were very different from the apparent lack of attention which is characteristic of troops normally frequenting the same water hole. By comparison with the behavior of troops in Nairobi Park, troop 171 was probably at the edge of its range, and troop 185 was occupying its core area.

• • •

In summary, baboon range is based on the existence of refuge sites as well as sources of food and water. These ecological factors control population density, but the interrelations of troops are based on behavior. Troop size, number of adult males in the troop, and frequency of contact between troops determine the outcome of intertroop relations. Territorial defense is not seen, but core areas of different troops tend to space troops apart within ranges which may overlap extensively.

In the evolution of human behavior, hunting is the best clue to the size of the range and the area which is defended from strangers (Washburn and DeVore 1961a). The pattern of core areas around water, within a larger range, described here for baboons, is analogous to the pattern of land use by primitive hunter-gatherers in savanna country today. The major difference between baboon range and that of human hunters is the vastly larger area which humans, like the other large carnivores, must control. The aggressive protection of the hunting territory by humans also contrasts with the behavior which spaces baboon troops apart. African bushmen and Australian aborigines range over a hunting territory of from 100 to 1200 square miles. A range of this size is far more comparable to the ranges of wolves, wild dogs, and large felines than to the small ranges of the nonhuman primates. Within these large ranges, camp sites near water sources correspond to the core areas of baboon troops. Access to the resources within the core areas of these hunters is rigidly controlled by social custom, religious sanction, and the force of arms. Interband relations between human hunters distinguish between "friendly neighbors" and strangers, a distinction which has an ancient, prelinguistic basis in primate behavior. The most striking difference between the social organization of baboons and human hunter-gatherers is the closed social system of the former and the rules of local exogamy which are usually found in the latter. Although formal rules of exogamy depend upon the presence of language, the exogamous pattern itself may have arisen during the shift to a hunting economy by men of the early and middle Pleistocene (Washburn and DeVore 1961a).

· · ·

DIET

. . . [B]aboons may be described as very inefficient predators. Meat eating, to judge by the bewildered state of the female baboon who caught a vervet and of the young juvenile who caught a bird, would appear to be learned by each generation, and meat never becomes an important source of food for the whole troop. Only one baboon other than adult males (an adult female) participated in the eating of meat in any of the instances observed during the study. Accounts of meat-eating in captive baboons are contradictory. Kenya baboons kept near Nairobi Park ate meat readily, but Bolwig (1959) found that his captives refused it. In South Africa, where most reports of carnivorous baboons have originated, baboons are only now being systematically studied (Hall 1960, 1961), and we feel that the importance of meat in the baboon diet has been considerably overstressed. The usual reason given for the habit of meat-eating in South African baboons is that the hardship of drought creates the conditions under which it flourishes (e.g., Dart 1953), but when the two Thomson's gazelle were eaten in December the park was well into the rainy season, and the vegetable foods baboons ordinarily eat were more abundant than at any other time of year.

It would seem more reasonable to us, on the present evidence, to assume that meat has been a consistent but very minor part of the baboon diet throughout their evolutionary history. In localities where sources of animal protein can be obtained without danger, baboons apparently include these in their regular diet. At Murchison Falls, baboons are often seen digging out and eating crocodile eggs. Hall's description of the foods eaten by baboons along the coast of South Africa is very similar to the inventory of vegetable and insect foods discussed here, except that the South African baboons also eat marine foods such as mussels, crabs, and sand hoppers found along the beach. But baboons are ill-fitted anatomically to be carnivores, and too great a dependence on meat eating could have been detrimental to their wide exploitation of the vegetable foods they depend upon today. By their utilization of a wide variety of plant and tree products, baboons have been able to spread over the African continent, and, together with the macaques, to cover most of the tropical Old World.

In the evolution of the human species, meat-eating played a very different role. We have suggested that the earliest hominids may have been living on a diet very like that of the baboons, that is, vegetable foods supplemented by an occasional small animal (Washburn and DeVore 1961a). The freedom to carry a simple digging implement in the hands would greatly enhance this adaptation. During the dry season in Africa, human hunter-gatherers are also very dependent on the subsurface roots and tubers sought by baboons. A digging stick greatly improves the humans' chance for survival during this period of food shortage, and it may be that the presence of baboon skeletons at Olorgesaille indicates the result of competition between baboons and humans over a limited food supply. It would be an easy step from killing baboons to protect a source of vegetable foods, to killing them for meat.

Scavenging

Scavenging has been regarded as an important phase in the evolution of man's carnivorous habits. It seems reasonable that a primate liking eggs, nestling birds, insects, and an occasional small mammal might add to this diet and develop more carnivorous tastes and habits by gleaning meat from kills. This theory seemed reasonable, and we made a particular effort to examine kills and to observe the relations of the baboons to them. Although we saw over a dozen recent kills (including gnu, giraffe, zebra, waterbuck, impala, Grant's gazelle, warthog, Masai cattle, and goat) and have thorough records on some, we were primarily looking at baboons. The subject of scavenging is so important, especially in the interpretation of the deposits in which *Australopithecus* is found, that a much more comprehensive study is needed. However, here are our tentative conclusions.

The scavenging theory is not supported by the evidence, and primates with habits similar to those of baboons could get meat by hunting far more easily than by scavenging. There are several reasons for this. The first is that most kills are made at night and are rapidly and thoroughly eaten. When the hyenas leave at dawn, the vultures locate the remains and clean the last meat from the bones. Some kills are made by day. We saw the remains of a gnu which a pride of ten lions finished in an hour. A pride of four lions (two not fully grown) killed a gnu one afternoon and ate almost all of it in one night. The vultures finished the rest, and the bones were undisturbed for three days. Many bones disappeared on the fourth night. Similarly, we saw two lions eat a warthog, three lions eat a Grant's gazelle, and five cheetahs kill and eat an impala. Only the meat of very large animals is left for long, and Africa is well supplied with highly efficient scavengers which leave little meat to tempt a primate.

• • •

. . . A slight increase in predatory activity against young animals would yield a far greater reward than scavenging, would be much less dangerous, and would represent a smaller change in habit. The use of a stick or stone for digging would increase the baboons' food supply more than any other simple invention. Perhaps in *Australopithecus* we see a form which had such a tool to exploit vegetable foods and which also used this tool as a weapon. If tools were being used at all, their use in the deliberate killing of small animals would be only a small change from the behavior observed in baboons. Once man had become a skilled tool-user in these ways, he could extend tool use to the hunting of large animals, to defense, and to driving carnivores from their kills. Scavenging may have become a source of meat when man had become sufficiently skilled to take the meat away from carnivores, but the hunting of small animals and defenseless young is much more likely to lie at the root of the human hunting habit.

DISCUSSION

In this paper we have tried to stress those aspects of baboon ecology which are of the greatest help in understanding human evolution. Obviously, man is not descended from a baboon, and the behavior of our ancestors may have been very different from that of living baboons. But we think that in a general way the problems faced by the baboon troop may be very similar to those which confronted our ancestors. At the least, comparison of human behavior with that of baboons emphasizes the differences. At the most, such a comparison may give new insights. Many topics have been summarized above, and in this discussion we will call attention only to a few major points.

The size of baboon troops may exceed that of hunter-gatherers, and their population density far exceeds that of primitive man. The human group differs in being exogamous, so that many local groups form the breeding population. We believe that this radically different breeding structure has exerted a profound effect on the later phases of human evolution and has long been a factor in preventing speciation in man.

The social structure of the baboon troop is important to the survival of the species. Survival depends on the adult males being constantly close to the other troop members. Roles in the troop are divided between the sexes, but these are in the context of a compact troop. With man, the hunters leave the local group, sometimes for days, and then return to their home base. Such a pattern is radically different from anything known in monkeys or apes. Hunting with tools basically changed the social structure of the band, the interrelations of bands, the size and utilization of range, and the relation of man to other animals.

Diet has already been discussed and we will not repeat here, except to point out that our opinion of the importance of scavenging has changed through observation of the actual situation at the kills. It is not enough to speculate that scavenging might have been important. One must estimate how much meat is actually available to a vegetarian, and how dangerous it is to get meat by scavenging.

Finally, we would stress that survival is a complex process, and that all the factors which lead to reproductive success must ultimately be considered. Varied diet, social structure, and anatomy, all are important, but their meaning only becomes clear as they are seen making possible the behavior of a population. Sex differences, peripheral animals, and range—each of these has meaning only in terms of the survival of groups. With the coming of man, every major category is fundamentally altered and evolution begins to be dominated by new selection pressures. Some measure of how different the new directions are may be gained from the study of the ecology of baboons.

REFERENCES

BOLWIG, N., "A Study of the Behaviour of the Chacma Baboon, *Papio ursinus*," *Behaviour*, 14 (1–2):136–63, 1959.

BURT, W. H., "Territoriality and Home Range Concepts as Applied to Mammals," *J. Mammal.*, 24:346–52, 1943.

DART, R. A., "The Predatory Transition from Ape to Man," *International Anthropological and Linguistic Review*, 1:4, 1953.

DEVORE, I., "The Social Behavior and Organization of Baboon Troops." Unpublished Ph.D. dissertation, University of Chicago, 1962.

DEVORE, I., and S. L. WASHBURN, "Baboon Behavior." 16 mm. sound color film. (Berkeley: University Extension, University of California, 1960).

HALL, K. R. L., "Social Vigilance Behaviour of the Chacma Baboon, *Papio ursinus*," *Behaviour*, 16 (3–4): 261–84, 1960. "Feeding Habits of the Chacma Baboon," *Advancement Sci.*, 17 (70):559–67, 1961.

WASHBURN, S. L., and I. DEVORE, "Social Behavior of Baboons and Early Man." In *The Social Life of Early Man*, S. L. Washburn (ed.), (Viking Fund Publications in Anthropology), 31, pp. 91–105, 1961b. "The Social Life of Baboons," *Scient. American* (June 1961), 204 (6):62–71, 1961a.

The Evolution of Hunting
S. L. Washburn and C. S. Lancaster

. . . Human hunting is made possible by tools, but it is far more than a technique or even a variety of techniques. It is a way of life, and the success of this adaptation (in its total social, technical, and psychological dimensions) has dominated the course of human evolution for hundreds of thousands of years. In a very real sense our intellect, interests, emotions, and basic social life—all are evolutionary products of the success of the hunting adaptation. When anthropologists speak of the unity of mankind, they are stating that the selection pressures of the hunting and gathering way of life were so similar and the result so successful that populations of *Homo sapiens* are still fundamentally the same everywhere. . . . [W]e are concerned with the general characteristics of man that we believe can be attributed to the hunting way of life.

Perhaps the importance of the hunting way of life in producing man is best shown by the length of time hunting has dominated human history. The genus *Homo*[1] has existed for some 600,000 years, and agriculture has been important only during the last few thousand years. Even 6,000 years ago large parts of the world's population were nonagricultural, and the entire evolution of man from the earliest populations of *Homo erectus* to the existing races took place during the period in which man was a hunter. The common factors that dominated

[1]The term *Homo* includes Java, Pekin, Mauer, etc., and later forms.

human evolution and produced *Homo sapiens* were preagricultural. Agricultural ways of life have dominated less than 1 per cent of human history, and there is no evidence of major biological changes during that period of time. The kind of minor biological changes that occurred and which are used to characterize modern races were not common to *Homo sapiens*. The origin of all common characteristics must be sought in preagricultural times. Probably all experts would agree that hunting was a part of the social adaptation of all populations of the genus *Homo*, and many would regard *Australopithecus*[2] as a still earlier hominid who was already a hunter, although possibly much less efficient than the later forms. If this is true and if the Pleistocene period had a duration of three million years, then pre-*Homo erectus* human tool using and hunting lasted for at least four times as long as the duration of the genus *Homo* (Lancaster, MS.). No matter how the earlier times may ultimately be interpreted, the observation of more hunting among apes than was previously suspected (Goodall, 1965) and increasing evidence for hunting by *Australopithecus* strengthens the position that less than 1 per cent of human history has been dominated by agriculture. It is for this reason that the consideration of hunting is so important for the understanding of human evolution.

When hunting and the way of life of successive populations of the genus *Homo* are considered, it is important to remember that there must have been both technical and biological progress during this vast period of time. Although the locomotor system appears to have changed very little in the last 500,000 years, the brain did increase in size and the form of the face changed. But for present purposes it is particularly necessary to direct attention to the cultural changes that occurred in the last ten or fifteen thousand years before agriculture. There is no convenient term for this period of time, traditionally spoken of as the end of the Upper Paleolithic and the Mesolithic, but Binford and Binford (1966a) have rightly emphasized its importance.

During most of human history, water must have been a major physical and psychological barrier and the inability to cope with water is shown in the archaeological record by the absence of remains of fish, shellfish, or any object that required going deeply into water or using boats. There is no evidence that the resources of river and sea were utilized until this late preagricultural period, and since the consumption of shellfish in particular leaves huge middens, the negative evidence is impressive. It is likely that the basic problem in utilization of resources from sea or river was that man cannot swim naturally but to do so must learn a difficult skill. In monkeys the normal quadrupedal running motions serve to keep them afloat and moving quite rapidly. A macaque, for example, does not have to learn any new motor habit in order to swim. But the locomotor patterns of gibbons and apes will not keep them above the water surface, and even a narrow, shallow stream is a barrier for the gorilla (Schaller, 1963). For early man, water was a barrier and a danger, not a resource. (Obviously water was important for drinking, for richer vegetation along rivers and lakeshores, and for concentrating animal life. Here we are referring to water as a barrier prior to swimming and boats, and we stress that, judging from the behavior of contemporary apes, even a small stream may be a major barrier.)

[2] Using the term to include both the small *A. africanus* and large *A. robustus* forms. Simpson (1966) briefly and clearly discusses the taxonomy of these forms and of the fragments called *Homo habilis*.

In addition to the conquest of water, there seems to have been great technical progress in this late preagricultural period. Along with a much wider variety of stone tools of earlier kinds, the archaeological record shows bows and arrows, grinding stones, boats, houses of much more advanced types and even villages, sledges drawn by animals and used for transport, and the domestic dog. These facts have two special kinds of significance . . . First, the technology of *all* the living hunters belongs to this late Mesolithic era at the earliest, and many have elements borrowed from agricultural and metal-using peoples. Second, the occasional high densities of hunters mentioned as problems and exceptions . . . are based on this very late and modified extension of the hunting and gathering way of life. For example, the way of life of the tribes of the Northwest Coast, with polished stone axes for woodworking, boats, and extensive reliance on products of the river and sea, should be seen as a very late adaptation. Goldschmidt's distinction (1959, pp. 185–93) between nomadic and sedentary hunting and gathering societies makes this point in a slightly different way. He shows the social elaboration which comes with the settled groups with larger populations.

The presence of the dog (Zeuner, 1963) is a good index of the late preagricultural period, and domestic dogs were used by hunters in Africa, Australia, and the Americas. Among the Eskimo, dogs were used in hunting, for transportation, as food in time of famine, and as watchdogs. With dogs, sleds, boats, metal, and complex technology, Eskimos may be a better example of the extremes to which human adaptation can go than an example of primitive hunting ways. . . . [D]ogs were of great importance in hunting, for locating, tracking, bringing to bay, and even killing. Lee (1965, p. 131) reports that one Bushman with a trained pack of hunting dogs brought in 75 percent of the meat of a camp. Six other resident hunters lacked hunting packs and accounted for only 25 percent of the meat. Dogs may be important in hunting even very large animals; in the Amboseli Game Reserve in Kenya one of us saw two small dogs bring a rhinoceros to bay and dodge repeated charges.

With the acquisition of dogs, bows, and boats it is certain that hunting became much more complex in the last few thousand years before agriculture. The antiquity of traps, snares, and poisons is unknown, but it appears that for thousands of years man was able to kill large game close in with spear or axe. As Brues (1959) has shown, this limits the size of the hunters, and there are no very large or very small fossil men. Pygmoid hunters of large game are probably possible only if hunting is with bows, traps, and poison. It is remarkable that nearly all the estimated statures for fossil men fall between 5 feet 2 inches and 5 feet 10 inches. This suggests that strong selection pressures kept human stature within narrow limits for hundreds of thousands of years and that these pressures relaxed a few thousand years ago, allowing the evolution of a much wider range of statures.

Gathering and the preparation of food also seem to have become more complex during the last few thousand years before agriculture. Obviously gathering by nonhuman primates is limited to things that can be eaten immediately. In contrast, man gathers a wide range of items that he cannot digest without soaking, boiling, grinding, or other special preparation. Seeds may have been a particularly important addition to the human diet because they are abundant and can be stored easily. Since grinding stones appear before agriculture, grinding and boiling may have been the necessary preconditions to the discovery of agriculture. One can easily imagine that people who were grinding seeds would see repeated examples of seeds sprouting or being planted by accident. Grinding and boiling were certainly known to the preagricultural peoples, and this knowledge could spread along an Arctic route, setting the stage for a nearly simultaneous discovery of agriculture in both the New and Old Worlds. It was not necessary for agriculture itself to spread through the Arctic but only the seed-using technology, which could then lead to the discovery of seed planting. If this analysis is at all correct, then the hunting-gathering adaptation of the Indians of California, for example, should be seen as representing the possibilities of this late preagricultural gathering, making possible much higher population densities than would have been the case in pregrinding and preboiling economy.

Whatever the fate of these speculations, we think that the main conclusion, based on the archaeological record, ecological considerations, and the ethnology of the surviving hunter-gatherers, will be sustained. In the last few thousand years before agriculture, both hunting and gathering became much more complex. This final adaptation, including the use of products of river and sea and the grinding and cooking of otherwise inedible seeds and nuts, was worldwide, laid the basis for the discovery of agriculture, and was much more effective and diversified than the previously existing hunting and gathering adaptations.

Hunting by members of the genus *Homo* throughout the 600,000 years that the genus has persisted has included the killing of large numbers of big animals. This implies the efficient use of tools, as Birdsell stressed . . . The adaptive value of hunting large animals has been shown by Bourlière (1963), who demonstrated that 75 percent of the meat available to human hunters in the eastern Congo was in elephant, buffalo, and hippopotamus. It is some measure of the success of human hunting that when these large species are protected in game reserves (as in the Murchison Falls or Queen Elizabeth Parks in Uganda), they multiply rapidly and destroy the vegetation. Elephants alone can destroy trees more rapidly than they are replaced naturally, as they do in the Masai Amboseli Reserve in Kenya. Since the predators are also protected in reserves, it appears that human hunters have been killing enough large game to maintain the balance of nature for many thousands of years. It is tempting to think that man replaced the saber-toothed tiger as the major predator of large game, both controlling the numbers of the game and causing the extinction of Old World saber-tooths. We think that hunting and butchering large animals put a maximum premium on cooperation among males, a behavior that is at an absolute minimum among the nonhuman primates. It is difficult to imagine the killing of creatures such as cave bears, mastodons, mammoths—or *Dinotherium* at a much earlier time—without highly coordinated, cooperative action among males. It may be that the origin of male-male associations lies in the necessities of cooperation in hunting, butchering, and war. Certainly butchering sites, such as described by F. Clark Howell in Spain, imply that the organization of the community for hunting large animals goes back for many, many thousands of years. From the biological point of view, the development of such organizations would have been paralleled by selection for an ability to plan and cooperate (or reduction of rage). Because females and juveniles may be involved in hunting small creatures, the social organization of big-game hunting would also lead to an intensification of a sexual division of labor.

It is important to stress, as noted before, that human hunting is a set of ways of life. It involves divisions of labor between male and female, sharing according to custom, cooperation among males, planning, knowledge of many species and large areas, and technical skill. Goldschmidt (1966, p. 87 ff.) has stressed the uniqueness and importance of human sharing, both in the family and in the wider society, and Lee (personal communication) emphasizes orderly sharing as fundamental to human hunting society. The importance of seeing human hunting as a whole social pattern is well illustrated by the old idea, recently revived, that the way of life of our ancestors was similar to that of wolves rather than that of apes or monkeys. But this completely misses the special nature of the human adaptation. Human females do not go out and hunt and then regurgitate to their young when they return. Human young do not stay in dens but are carried by mothers. Male wolves do not kill with tools, butcher, and share with females who have been gathering. In an evolutionary sense the whole human pattern is new, and it is the success of this particularly human way that dominated human evolution and determined the relation of biology and culture for thousands of years. Judging from the archaeological record, it is probable that the major features of this human way, possibly even including the beginnings of language, had evolved by the time of *Homo erectus*.[3]

THE WORLD VIEW OF THE HUNTER

Lévi-Strauss urged that we study the world view of hunters, and, perhaps surprisingly, some of the major aspects of world view can be traced from the archaeological record. We have already mentioned that boats and the entire complex of fishing, hunting sea mammals, and using shellfish was late. With this new orientation, wide rivers and seas changed from barriers to pathways and sources of food, and the human attitude toward water must have changed completely. But many hundreds of thousands of years earlier, perhaps with *Australopithecus*, the relation of the hunters to the land must also have changed from an earlier relationship which may be inferred from studies of contemporary monkeys and apes. Social groups of nonhuman primates occupy exceedingly small areas, and the vast majority of animals probably spend their entire lives within less than

[3]In speculations of this kind, it is well to keep the purpose of the speculation and the limitation of the evidence in mind. Our aim is to understand human evolution. What shaped the course of human evolution was a succession of successful adaptations, both biological and cultural. These may be inferred in part from the direct evidence of the archaeological record. But the record is very incomplete. For example, Lee (personal communication) has described, for the Bushmen, how large game may be butchered where it falls and only meat brought back to camp. This kind of behavior means that analysis of bones around living sites is likely to underestimate both the amount and variety of game killed. If there is any evidence that large animals were killed, it is probable that far more were killed than the record shows. Just as the number of human bones gives no indication of the number of human beings, the number of animal bones, although it provides clues to the existence of hunting, gives no direct evidence of how many animals were killed. The Pleistocene way of life can only be known by inference and speculation. Obviously, speculations are based on much surer ground when the last few thousand years are under consideration. Ethnographic information is then directly relevant and the culture bearers are of our own species. As we go farther back in time, there is less evidence and the biological and cultural difference becomes progressively greater. Yet it was in those remote times that the human way took shape, and it is only through speculation that we may gain some insights into what the life of our ancestors may have been.

four or five square miles. Even though they have excellent vision and can see for many miles, especially from tops of trees, they make no effort to explore more than a tiny fraction of the area they see. Even for gorillas the range is only about fifteen square miles (Schaller, 1963), and it is of the same order of magnitude for savanna baboons (DeVore and Hall, 1965). When Hall tried to drive a troop of baboons beyond the end of their range, they refused to be driven and doubled back into familiar territory, although they were easy to drive within the range. The known area is a psychological reality, clear in the minds of the animals. Only a small part of even this limited range is used, and exploration is confined to the canopy, lower branches, and bushes, or ground, depending on the biology of the particular species. Napier (1962) has discussed this highly differential use of a single area by several species. In marked contrast, human hunters are familiar with very large areas. In the area studied by Lee (1965), eleven waterholes and 600 square miles supported 248 Bushmen, a figure less than the number of baboons supported by a single waterhole and a few square miles in the Amboseli Reserve in Kenya. The most minor hunting expedition covers an area larger than most nonhuman primates would cover in a lifetime. Interest in a large area is human. The small ranges of monkeys and apes restrict the opportunities for gathering, hunting, and meeting conspecifics, and limit the kind of predation and the number of diseases. In the wide area, hunters and gatherers can take advantage of seasonal foods, and only man among the primates can migrate long distances seasonally. In the small area, the population must be carried throughout the year on local resources, and natural selection favors biology and behavior that efficiently utilize these limited opportunities. But in the wide area, natural selection favors the knowledge that enables a group to utilize seasonal and occasional food sources. Gathering over a wide and diversified area implies a greater knowledge of flora and fauna, knowledge of the annual cycle, and a different attitude toward group movements. Clearly one of the great advantages of slow maturation is that learning covers a series of years, and the meaning of events in these years become a part of the individual's knowledge. With rapid maturation and no language, the chances that any member of the group will know the appropriate behavior for rare events is greatly reduced.

Moving over long distances creates problems of carrying food and water. Lee (1965, p. 124) has pointed out that the sharing of food even in one locality implies that food is carried, and there is no use in gathering quantities of fruit or nuts unless they can be moved. If women are to gather while men hunt, the results of the labors of both sexes must be carried back to some agreed upon location. Meat can be carried away easily, but the development of some sort of receptacles for carrying vegetable products may have been one of the most fundamental advances in human evolution. Without a means of carrying, the advantages of a large area are greatly reduced, and sharing implies that a person carries much more than one can use. However that may be, the whole human pattern of gathering and hunting to share—indeed, the whole complex of economic reciprocity that dominates so much of human life—is unique to man. In its small range, a monkey gathers only what it itself needs to eat at that moment. Wherever archaeological evidence can suggest the beginnings of movement over large ranges, cooperation, and sharing, it is dating the origin of some of the most fundamental aspects of human behavior—the human world view. We believe that hunting large animals may demand all these aspects of human behavior which separate man so sharply from the other primates. If this is so, then the human way appears to be as old as *Homo erectus.*

The price that man pays for his high mobility is well illustrated by the problems of living in the African savanna. Man is not adapted to this environment in the same sense that baboons or vervet monkeys are. Man needs much more water, and without preparation and cooking he can only eat a limited number of the foods on which the local primates thrive. Unless there have been major physiological changes, the diet of our ancestors must have been far more like that of chimpanzees than like that of a savanna-adapted species. Further, man cannot survive the diseases of the African savanna without lying down and being cared for. Even when sick, the locally adapted animals are usually able to keep moving with their troop; and the importance to their survival of a home base has been stressed elsewhere (DeVore and Washburn, 1963). Also man becomes liable to new diseases and parasites by eating meat, and it is of interest that the products of the sea, which we believe were the last class of foods added to human diet, are widely regarded as indigestible and carry diseases to which man is particularly susceptible. Although many humans die of disease and injury, those who do not, almost without exception, owe their lives to others who cared for them when they were unable to hunt or gather, and this uniquely human caring is one of the patterns that builds social bonds in the group and permits the species to occupy almost every environment in the world.

A large territory not only provides a much wider range of possible foods but also a greater variety of potentially useful materials. With tool use this variety takes on meaning, and even the earliest pebble tools show selection in size, form, and material. When wood ceases to be just something to climb on, hardness, texture, and form become important. Availability of materials is critical to the tool user, and early men must have had a very different interest in their environment from that of monkeys or apes. Thus, the presence of tools in the archaeological record is not only an indication of technical progress but also an index of interest in inanimate objects and in a much larger part of the environment than is the case with nonhuman primates.

The tools of the hunters include the earliest beautiful manmade objects, the symmetrical bifaces, especially those of the Acheulian tradition. Just how they were used is still a matter of debate, but, as contemporary attempts to copy them show, their manufacture is technically difficult, taking much time and practice and a high degree of skill. The symmetry of these tools may indicate that they were swung with great speed and force, presumably attached to some sort of handle. A tool that is moved slowly does not have to be symmetrical, but balance becomes important when an object is swung rapidly or thrown with speed. Irregularities will lead to deviations in the course of the blow or the trajectory of flight. An axe or spear to be used with speed and power is subject to very different technical limitations from those of scrapers or digging sticks, and it may well be that it was the attempt to produce efficient high-speed weapons that first produced beautiful, symmetrical objects.

When the selective advantage of a finely worked point over an irregular one is considered, it must be remembered that a small difference might give a very large advantage. A population in which hunters hit the game 5 percent more frequently, more accurately, or at greater distance would bring back much more meat. There must have been strong selection for greater skill in manufacture and use, and it is no accident that the bones of small-brained men (*Australopithecus*) are never found with beautiful, symmetrical tools. If the brains of contemporary apes and men are compared, the areas associated with manual skills (both in cerebellum and cortex) are at least three times as large in man. Clearly, the success of tools has exerted a great influence on the evolution of the brain, and has created the skills that make art possible. The evolution of the capacity to appreciate the product must evolve along with the skills of manufacture and use, and the biological capacities that the individual inherits must be developed in play and practiced in games. In this way, the beautiful, symmetrical tool becomes a symbol of a level of human intellectual achievement, representing far more than just the tool itself.

In a small group like the hunting band, which is devoted to one or two major cooperative activities, the necessity for long practice in developing skills to a very high level restricts the number of useful arts, and social organization is relatively simple. Where there is little division of labor, all men learn the same activities, such as skill in the hunt or in war. In sports (like the decathlon) we take it for granted that no one individual can achieve record levels of performance in more than a limited set of skills. This kind of limitation is partially biological but it is also a matter of culture. In warfare, for example, a wide variety of weapons is useful only if there are enough men to permit a division of labor so that different groups can practice different skills. Handedness, a feature that separates man from ape, is a part of this biology of skill. To be ambidextrous might seem to be ideal, but in fact the highest level of skill is attained by concentrating both biological ability and practice primarily on one hand. The evolution of handedness reflects the importance of skill, rather than mere use.

Hunting changed man's relations to other animals and his view of what is natural. The human notion that it is normal for animals to flee, the whole concept of animals being wild, is the result of man's habit of hunting. In game reserves many different kinds of animals soon learn not to fear man, and they no longer flee. James Woodburn took a Hadza into the Nairobi Park, and the Hadza was amazed and excited, because although he had hunted all his life, he had never seen such a quantity and variety of animals close at hand. His previous view of animals was the result of his having been their enemy, and they had reacted to him as the most destructive carnivore. In the park the Hadza hunter saw for the first time the peace of the herbivorous world. Prior to hunting, the relations of our ancestors to other animals must have been very much like those of the other noncarnivores. They could have moved close among the other species, fed beside them, and shared the same waterholes. But with the origin of human hunting, the peaceful relationship was destroyed, and for at least half a million years man has been the enemy of even the largest mammals. In this way the whole human view of what is normal and natural in the relation of man to animals is a product of hunting, and the world of flight and fear is the result of the efficiency of the hunters.

Behind this human view that the flight of animals from man is natural lie some aspects of human psychology. Men enjoy hunting and killing, and these activities are continued as sports even when they are no longer economically necessary. If a behavior is important to the survival of a species (as hunting was for man throughout most of human history), then it must be both easily learned and pleasurable (Hamburg, 1963). Part of the motivation for hunting is the immediate pleasure it gives the hunter, and the human killer can no more afford to be sorry for the game than a cat can for its intended victim. Evolution builds a relation between biology, psychology, and behavior, and, therefore, the evolutionary success of hunting exerted a profound effect on human psychology. Perhaps, this is most easily shown by the extent of the efforts devoted to maintain killing as a sport. In former times royalty and nobility maintained parks where they could enjoy the sport of killing, and today the United States government spends many millions of dollars to supply game for hunters. Many people dislike the notion that man is naturally aggressive and that he naturally enjoys the destruction of other creatures. Yet we all know people who use the lightest fishing tackle to prolong the fish's futile struggle, in order to maximize the personal sense of mastery and skill. And until recently war was viewed in much the same way as hunting. Other human beings were simply the most dangerous game. War has been far too important in human history for it to be other than pleasurable for the males involved. It is only recently, with the entire change in the nature and conditions of war, that this institution has been challenged, that the wisdom of war as a normal part of national policy or as an approved road to personal social glory has been questioned.

Human killing differs from killing by carnivorous mammals in that the victims are frequently of the same species as the killer. In carnivores there are submission gestures or sounds that normally stop a fatal attack (Lorenz, 1966). But in man there are no effective submission gestures. It was the Roman emperor who might raise his thumb; the victim could make no sound or gesture that might restrain the victor or move the crowd to pity. The lack of biological controls over killing conspecifics is a character of human killing that separates this behavior sharply from that of other carnivorous mammals. This difference may be interpreted in a variety of ways. It may be that human hunting is so recent from an evolutionary point of view that there was not enough time for controls to evolve. Or it may be that killing other humans was a part of the adaptation from the beginning, and our sharp separation of war from hunting is due to the recent development of these institutions. Or it may be simply that in most human behavior stimulus and response are not tightly bound. Whatever the origin of this behavior, it has had profound effects on human evolution, and almost every human society has regarded killing members of certain other human societies as desirable (D. Freeman, 1964). Certainly this has been a major factor in man's view of the world, and every folklore contains tales of culture heroes whose fame is based on the human enemies they destroyed.

The extent to which the biological bases for killing have been incorporated into human psychology may be measured by the ease with which boys can be interested in hunting, fishing, fighting, and games of war. It is not that these behaviors are inevitable, but they are easily learned, satisfying, and have been socially rewarded in most cultures. The skills for killing and the pleasures of killing are normally developed in play, and the patterns of play prepare the children for their adult roles. . . . Woodburn's excellent motion pictures showed Hadza boys killing small mammals, and Laughlin described how Aleuts train boys from early childhood so that they would be able to throw harpoons with accuracy and power while seated in kayaks. The whole youth of the hunter is dominated by practice and appreciation of the skills of the adult males, and the pleasure of the games motivates the practice that is necessary to develop the skills of weaponry. Even in monkeys, rougher play and play fighting are largely the activities of the males, and the young females explore less and show a greater interest in infants at an early age. These basic biological differences are reinforced in man by a division of labor which makes, adult sex roles differ far more in humans than they do in nonhuman primates. Again, hunting must be seen as a whole pattern of activities, a wide variety of ways of life, the psychobiological roots of which are reinforced by play and by a clear identification with adult roles. Hunting is more than a part of the economic system, and the animal bones in Choukoutien are evidence of the patterns of play and pleasure of our ancestors.

THE SOCIAL ORGANIZATION OF HUMAN HUNTING

The success of the human hunting and gathering way of life lay in its adaptability. It permitted a single species to occupy most of the earth with a minimum of biological adaptation to local conditions. The occupation of Australia and the New World was probably late, but even so there is no evidence that any other primate species occupied more than a fraction of the area of *Homo erectus*. Obviously, this adaptability makes any detailed reconstruction impossible, and we are not looking for stages in the traditional evolutionary sense. However, using both the knowledge of the contemporary primates and the archaeological record, certain important general conditions of our evolution may be reconstructed. For example, the extent of the distribution of the species noted above is remarkable and gives the strongest sort of indirect evidence for the adaptability of the way of life, even half a million years ago. Likewise all evidence suggests that the local group was small. Twenty to fifty individuals is suggested by Goldschmidt (1959, p. 187). Such a group size is common in nonhuman primates and so we can say with some assurance that the number did not increase greatly until after agriculture. This means that the number of adult males who might cooperate in hunting or war was very limited, and this sets limits to the kinds of social organizations that were possible. Probably one of the great adaptive advantages of language was that it permits the planning of cooperation between local groups, temporary division of groups, and the transmission of information over a much wider area than that occupied by any one group.

Within the group of the nonhuman primates, the mother and her young may form a subgroup that continues even after the young are fully grown (Sade, 1965, 1966; Yamada, 1963). This grouping affects dominance, grooming, and resting patterns, and, along with dominance, is one of the factors giving order to the social relations in the group. The group is not a horde in the nineteenth-century sense, but it is ordered by positive affectionate habits and by the strength of personal dominance. Both these principles continue into human society, and dominance based on personal achievement must have been particularly powerful in small groups living physically dangerous lives. The mother-young group certainly continued and the bonds must have been intensified by the prolongation of infancy. But in human society, economic reciprocity is added, and this created a wholly new set of interpersonal bonds.

When males hunt and females gather, the results are shared and given to the young, and the habitual sharing between a male, a female, and their offspring becomes the basis for the human family. According to this view, the human family is the result of the reciprocity of hunting, the addition of a male to the mother-plus-young social group of the monkeys and apes.

A clue to the adaptive advantage and evolutionary origin of our psychological taboo on incest is provided by this view of the family. Incest prohibitions are reported universally among humans and these always operate to limit sexual activity involving subadults within the nuclear family. Taking the nuclear family as the unit of account, incest prohibitions tend to keep the birth rate in line with economic productivity. If in creating what we call the family the addition of a male is important in economic terms, then the male who is added must be able to fulfill the role of a socially responsible provider. In the case of the hunter, this necessitates a degree of skill in hunting and a social maturity that is attained some years after puberty. As a young man grows up, this necessary delay in his assumption of the role of provider for a female and her young is paralleled by a taboo which prevents him from prematurely adding unsupported members to the family. Brother-sister mating could result in an infant while the brother was still years away from effective social maturity. Father-daughter incest could also produce a baby without adding a productive male to the family. This would be quite different from the taking of a second wife which, if permitted, occurs only when the male has shown he is already able to provide for and maintain more than one female.

To see how radically hunting changed the economic situation, it is necessary to remember that in monkeys and apes an individual simply eats what it needs. After an infant is weaned, it is on its own economically and is not dependent on adults. This means that adult males never have economic responsibility for any other animal, and adult females do only when they are nursing. In such a system, there is no economic gain in delaying any kind of social relationship. But when hunting makes females and young dependent on the success of male skills, there is a great gain to the family members in establishing behaviors which prevent the addition of infants, unless these can be supported.

These considerations in no way alter the importance of the incest taboo as a deterrent to role conflict in the family and as the necessary precondition to all other rules of exogamy. A set of behaviors is more likely to persist and be widespread, if it serves many uses, and the rule of parsimony is completely wrong when applied to the explanation of social situations. However, these considerations do alter the emphasis and the conditions of the discussion of incest. In the first place, a mother-son sexual avoidance may be present in some species of monkeys (Sade, 1966) and this extremely strong taboo among humans requires a different explanation than the one we have offered for brother-sister and father-daughter incest prohibitions. In this case, the role conflict argument may be paramount. Second, the central consideration is that incest produces pregnancies, and the most fundamental adaptive value of the taboo is the provision of situations in which infants are more likely to survive. In the reviews of the incest taboo by Aberle and others (1963) and Mair (1965), the biological advantages of the taboo in controlling the production of infants are not adequately considered, and we find the treatment by Service (1962) closest to our own. In a society in which the majority of males die young, but a few live on past forty, the probability of incest is increased. By stressing the average length of life rather than the age of the surviving few, Slater (1959) underestimated the probability of mating between close relatives. Vallois (1961, p. 222) has summarized the evidence on length of life in early man and shows that "few individuals passed forty years, and it is only quite exceptionally that any passed fifty."

That family organization may be attributed to the hunting way of life is supported by ethnography. Since the same economic and social problems as those under hunting continue under agriculture, the institution continued. The data on the behavior of contemporary monkeys and apes also show why this institution was not necessary in a society in which each individual gets its own food.[4] Obviously the origin of the custom cannot be dated, and we cannot prove *Homo erectus* had a family organized in the human way. But it can be shown that the conditions that make the family adaptive existed at the time of *Homo erectus*. The evidence of hunting is clear in the archaeological record. A further suggestion that the human kind of family is old comes from physiology; the loss of estrus is essential to the human family organization, and it is unlikely that this physiology, which is universal in contemporary mankind, evolved recently.

If the local group is looked upon as a source of male-female pairs (an experienced hunter-provider and a female who gathers and who cares for the young), then it is apparent that a small group cannot produce pairs regularly, since chance determines whether a particular child is a male or female. If the number maturing in a given year or two is small, then there may be too many males or females (either males with no mates or females with no providers). The problem of excess females may not seem serious today or in agricultural societies, but among hunters it was recognized and was regarded as so severe that female infanticide was often practiced. How grave the problem of imbalance can become is shown by the following hypothetical example. In a society of approximately forty individuals there might be nine couples. With infants born at the rate of about one in three years, this would give three infants per year, but only approximately one of these three would survive to become fully adult. The net production in the example would be one child per year in a population of forty. And because the sex of the child is randomly determined, the odds that all the children would be male for a three-year period are 1 in 8. Likewise the odds for all surviving children being female for a three-year period are 1 in 8. In this example the chances of all surviving children being of one sex are 1 in 4, and smaller departures from a 50/50 sex ratio would be very common.

In monkeys, because the economic unit is the individual (not a pair), a surplus of females causes no problem. Surplus males may increase fighting in the group or males may migrate to other groups.

For humans, the problem of imbalance in sex ratios may be met by exogamy, which permits mates to be obtained from a much wider social field. The orderly pairing of hunter males with females requires a much larger group than can be

---

[4]The advantage of considering both the social group and the facilitating biology is shown by considering the "family" in the gibbon. The social group consists of an adult male, an adult female, and their young. But this group is maintained by extreme territorial behavior in which no adult male tolerates another, by aggressive females with large canine teeth, and by very low sex drive in the males. The male-female group is the whole society (Carpenter 1941: Ellefson. 1966). The gibbon group is based on a different biology from that of the human family and has none of its reciprocal economic functions. Although the kind of social life seen in chimpanzees lacks a family organization, to change it into that of a man would require far less evolution than would be required in the case of the gibbon.

supported locally by hunting and gathering, and this problem is solved by reciprocal relations among several local groups. It takes something on the order of 100 pairs to produce enough children so that the sex ratio is near enough 50/50 for social life to proceed smoothly, and this requires a population of approximately 500 people. With smaller numbers there will be constant random fluctuations in the sex ratio large enough to cause social problems. This argument shows the importance of a sizable linguistic community, one large enough to cover an area in which many people may find suitable mates and make alliances of many kinds. It does not mean either that the large community or that exogamy does not have many other functions, as outlined by Mair (1965). As indicated earlier, the more factors that favor a custom, the more likely it is to be geographically widespread and long lasting. What the argument does stress is that the finding of mates and the production of babies under the particular conditions of human hunting and gathering favor both incest taboo and exogamy for basic demographic reasons.

Assumptions behind this argument are that social customs are adaptive, as Tax (1937) has argued, and that nothing is more crucial for evolutionary success than the orderly production of the number of infants that can be supported. This argument also presumes that, at least under extreme conditions, these necessities and reasons are obvious to the people involved, as infanticide attests. The impossibility of finding suitable mates must have been a common experience for hunters trying to exist in very small groups, and the initial advantages of exogamy, kinship, and alliance with other such groups may at first have amounted to no more than, as Whiting said . . . a mother suggesting to her son that he might find a suitable mate in the group where her brother was located.

If customs are adaptive and if humans are necessarily opportunistic, it might be expected that social rules would be particularly labile under the conditions of small hunting and gathering societies. . . . Murdock pointed out the high frequency of bilateral kinship systems among hunters, and the experts on Australia all seemed to believe that the Australian systems had been described in much too static terms. Under hunting conditions, systems that allow for exceptions and local adaptation make sense and surely political dominance and status must have been largely achieved.

CONCLUSION

While stressing the success of the hunting and gathering way of life with its great diversity of local forms and while emphasizing the way it influenced human evolution, we must also take into account its limitations. There is no indication that this way of life could support large communities of more than a few million people in the whole world. To call the hunters "affluent" (Sahlins, in Lee and De Vore, 1968) is to give a very special definition to the word. During much of the year, many monkeys can obtain enough food in only three or four hours of gathering each day, and under normal conditions baboons have plenty of time to build the Taj Mahal. The restriction on population, however, is the lean season or the atypical year, and, as Sahlins recognized, building by the hunters and the accumulation of gains was limited by motivation and technical knowledge, not by time. Where monkeys are fed, population rises, and Koford (1966) estimates the rate of increase on an island at 16 per cent per year.

After agriculture, human populations increased dramatically in spite of disease, war, and slowly changing customs. Even with fully human (*Homo sapiens*) biology, language, technical sophistication, cooperation, art, the support of kinship, the control of custom and political power, and the solace of religion—in spite of this whole web of culture and biology—the local group in the Mesolithic was no larger than that of baboons. Regardless of statements made . . . on the ease with which hunters obtain food some of the time, it is still true that food was the primary factor in limiting early human populations, as is shown by the events subsequent to agriculture.

The agricultural revolution, continuing into the industrial and scientific revolutions, is now freeing man from the conditions and restraints of 99 percent of his history, but the biology of our species was created in that long gathering and hunting period. To assert the biological unity of mankind is to affirm the importance of the hunting way of life. It is to claim that, however much conditions and customs may have varied locally, the main selection pressures that forged the species were the same. The biology, psychology, and customs that separate us from the apes—all these we owe to the hunters of time past. And, although the record is incomplete and speculation looms larger than fact, for those who would understand the origin and nature of human behavior there is no choice but to try to understand "Man the Hunter."

REFERENCES

ABERLE, DAVID F. et al., "The incest taboo and the mating patterns of animals." *American Anthropologist* 65:233–65, 1963.

BINFORD, LEWIS R. and SALLY R. BINFORD, "The predatory revolution: a consideration of the evidence for a new subsistence level." *American Anthropologist* 68(2), pt. 1:508–12, 1966.

BRUES, ALICE, "The spearman and the archer, an essay on selection in body build." *American Anthropologist* 61:457–69, 1959.

CARPENTER, CLARENCE R., *A field study in Siam of the behavior and social relations of the Gibbon (Hylobates lar)*. (Baltimore: Johns Hopkins Press, 1941).

DEVORE, IRVEN, and K. R. L. HALL, "Baboon ecology." In *Primate Behavior*, ed. I. DeVore. (New York: Holt, Rinehart, and Winston, 1965).

DEVORE, IRVEN, and SHERWOOD L. WASHBURN, "Baboon ecology and human evolution." In *African ecology and human evolution*, ed. F. C. Howell and F. Bourlière. (Chicago: Aldine Publishing Company, 1963).

ELLEFSON, J. O., *A natural history of gibbons in the Malay Peninsula*. Unpublished doctoral dissertation, University of California, Berkeley.

FREEMAN, DEREK, "Human aggression in anthropological perspective." In *The natural history of aggression*. (New York: Academic Press, 1964).

GOLDSCHMIDT, WALTER R., *Man's way: a preface to the understanding of human society*. (New York: Henry Holt, 1959).

GOLDSCHMIDT, WALTER R., *Comparative functionalism: an essay in anthropological theory*. (Berkeley and Los Angeles: University of California Press, 1966).

GOODALL, JANE, "Chimpanzees on the Gombe Stream reserve." In *Primate behavior*, ed. I. DeVore. (New York: Holt, Rinehart, and Winston, 1965).

HAMBURG, DAVID A., "Emotions in the perspective of human evolution." In *Expression* of the emotions in man, ed. P. H. Knapp. (New York: International Universities Press, 1963).

KOFORD, CARL B., "Population changes in rhesus monkeys: Cayo Santiago, 1960–1964." *Tulane Studies in Zoology* 13:1–7, 1966.

LEE, RICHARD B., *Subsistence ecology of Kung Bushmen.* Unpublished doctoral dissertation, University of California, Berkeley, 1965.

LEE, RICHARD B. and IRVEN DEVORE, eds., *Man the Hunter* (Chicago: Aldine, 1968).

LORENZ, KONRAD Z., *On aggression*, trans. by M. K. Wilson. (New York: Harcourt, Brace and World, 1966).

MAIR, LUCY, *An introduction to social anthropology.* (Oxford: Clarendon Press, 1965).

NAPIER, JOHN R., "Monkeys and their habitats." *New Scientist* 15:88–92, 1962.

SADE, DONALD S., "Some aspect of parent-offspring and sibling relations in a group of rhesus monkeys, with a discussion of grooming." *American Journal of Physical Anthropology* 23:1–17, 1965.

SADE, DONALD S., *Ontogeny of social relations in a group of free ranging Rhesus monkeys (Macaca mulatta* Zimmerman). Unpublished doctoral dissertation, (Berkeley: University of California, 1966).

SCHALLER, GEORGE B., *The mountain gorilla· ecology and behavior.* (Chicago: University of Chicago Press, 1963).

SERVICE, ELMAN R., *Primitive social organization.* (New York: Random House, 1962).

SIMPSON, GEORGE GAYLORD, "The biological nature of man." *Science* 152:472–78, 1966.

SLATER, MIRIAM K., "Ecological factors in the origin of incest." *American Anthropologist* 61:1042–59, 1959.

TAX, SOL, "Some problems of social organization." In *Social anthropology of North American tribes*, ed. by F. Eggan. (Chicago: University of Chicago Press, 1937).

VALLOIS, HENRI V., "The social life of early man: the evidence of skeletons." In *Social life of early man*, ed. by S. L. Washburn. (Chicago: Aldine Publishing Company, 1961).

YAMADA, MUNEMI, "A study of blood-relationship in the natural society of the Japanese macaque." *Primates* 4:43–66, 1963.

ZEUNER, F. E., *A history of domesticated animals.* (New York: Harper and Row, 1963).

The Origins of Agriculture

Robert M. Adams

The importance of agriculture for all that we know of a full and secure life hardly needs to be described. Great as are the cultural differences between peoples today who are dependent upon agriculture for subsistence, all of them have more in common than they share with the few surviving groups of independent hunters and collectors. Man's first acquisition of domesticated plants and animals not long after the end of the Pleistocene ice age, accordingly, has long been recognized as a great turning point or "revolution," perhaps comparable in importance only with the Industrial Revolution in which we are still engaged. Yet the direct, empirical study of this great transformation is still very young, hardly antedating the Second World War.

Not surprisingly, our understanding of the origins and early spread of agriculture is still very insecure and fragmentary. In fact, there is no area of the world for which the transition to food production can be traced step by step in adequate detail. But if general formulations about agricultural origins are thus somewhat hazardous, there is a corresponding advantage in discussing them here. The study of the rise of food production has been able to flourish only as a consequence of new conditions—the "explosion" of scientific manpower and research support which the postwar years have brought. Hence this problem perhaps can exemplify at least some of the anthropological work which these new conditions make possible, above all the crystallization of a group of major problems upon which the interests of many scholars, and even many disciplines, are focused intensively.

The problem of the early development of agriculture is rooted in the environmental and cultural conditions obtaining at the end of the Pleistocene, and we may begin by summarizing these very briefly. By this time, men whose skeletal remains were anatomically modern in type had made their appearance, and it can only be assumed that they were essentially modern in their capacities for cultural innovation as well. Although little survives other than material equipment devoted to the food quest, purposive human burials attended by a modicum of ritual hint at customs and preoccupations extending well beyond the realm of immediate subsistence requirements. Moreover, although most of the astonishing cave art of France and Spain during this period depicts animals to whom the hunt was devoted, both the technical quality of these paintings and the circumstances surrounding their execution clearly indicate that they were meant to symbolize and convey a world of conventionalized belief outside the practical requirements of the small bands who were responsible for them.

Relative at least to their predecessors in the Lower and Middle Pleistocene, these hunter-collectors during the last few millennia of the ice age were more specialized and better equipped, more numerous and widely distributed. In Western Europe, where the sequence is best known, groups not only successfully hunted great herds of reindeer, wild horse, and bison, but also harpooned salmon and caught rabbits and grouse with snares. Caves and rock-shelters in many cases seem to have been occupied fairly continuously over long periods. The finding of bone needles, together with suggestions of skin costumes in the Magdalenian art, implies that sewn clothing had been evolved which was well adapted to the cold climate. Hunters in Eastern Europe displayed comparable efficiency in the pursuit of the mammoth, and had developed earth houses as shelters in the absence of caves.

Increasingly able to adapt through cultural specialization to such challenges as the harsh subarctic environment around the fringes of the great European glaciers, man was able to increase the range of his occupation enormously. His first entrance into the New World, probably having occurred from twenty to thirty thousand years ago, was one apparent consequence since it must have involved exposure to comparable climatic conditions in the crossing of a now-submerged land bridge from eastern Siberia to Alaska. Australia, too, first may have been occupied during the terminal phases of the Pleistocene, possibly involving at least modest and accidental marine crossings by raft.

The end of the Pleistocene, marked by the gradual onset of modern climatic conditions, is usually agreed to have occurred about eleven thousand years ago. While the causes for the shrinkage and disappearance of the enormous ice sheets covering Europe and North America are still disputed, at least there is full agreement that the effects were dramatic. The concentric zones of treeless arctic tundra, boreal forest, and deciduous forest, successively more distant from the ice, marched north in the wake of the retreating glaciers, while the melting of the great weight of ice induced complementary changes in land and sea levels which substantially altered the continental margins. With the northward progression of climatic and floral zones came new fauna—generally smaller, less gregarious, less migratory animals—appropriate to the dense forests which now began to extend well into the northern latitudes. But even where open plains remained, as in western North America and large parts of Eurasia, many of the larger Pleistocene species failed to survive. Among those which disappeared altogether were the mammoth and mastodon, and the American camel, horse, and sloth—all within a relatively short time, and all under circumstances which leave little doubt that man's increasing proficiency as a hunter was a major contributing cause. This very proficiency may have served, in other words, to exterminate major resources of game and thus to help pave the way for radically changed patterns of subsistence.

As a general account of the end of the Pleistocene, what has just been said is incomplete or misleading in two respects. Firstly, most of the world open to human occupation lay at great distances from the main glaciated regions centering on the poles, and the climatic changes associated with the end of the Pleistocene in more equatorial latitudes involved decreases in precipitation more prominently than increases in temperature. Moreover, the whole problem of whether or not climatic changes in all latitudes took place closely in phase with one another is still not fully resolved. Secondly, it must be noted that the Pleistocene as a whole was not a time of continuous glaciation but rather of almost continuous climatic changes, changes whose sequence and correlations long have been a major theme of research. Shifting climatic, floral, and faunal boundaries at the end of the Pleistocene thus were not a new phenomenon but one which had gone on repeatedly through all of man's biological evolution as a separate species. What was new was neither the fact of an ameliorating environment nor the consequent enlargement of life-zones favorable for man's existence, but rather the increased exploitative efficiency and adaptability with which he took advantage of these conditions.

Compared with Europe and the United States, much less is known of the new subsistence patterns which emerged at the end of the Pleistocene in areas like the Near East and Middle America where the wild progenitors of our major domestic plants and animals flourished. To generalize from the more northerly areas, perhaps the dominant character of the post-Pleistocene response was its diversity. Faced with habitats whose differences were amplified as the ice receded, and with the extinction of many species of great herbivores upon which he formerly had relied heavily, man rapidly worked out a whole series of specialized adaptations based on a bewildering variety of new local resources. We find groups like the Tardenoisans, Azilians, and Maglemosians in Western Europe, for example, coexisting within short distances of one another and yet utilizing entirely different types of habitat. There is evidence that nuts, seeds, and wild fruits were relied on more heavily as sources of food than they had been in Pleistocene times, and that this increased emphasis on the gathering or collecting of vegetal products also was characteristic of roughly contemporary assemblages in Mexico and the western United States. Of course, this shift required the development of ground stone tools for pounding or milling in order to remove husks and render the tough kernels digestible—tools which later would be necessary for the processing of domesticated grains.

The increasingly intensive and localized, even semisedentary, character of these post-Pleistocene subsistence patterns is evident also in the faunal resources they sought to exploit. The bow and arrow came into use in northern Europe, and, perhaps as a consequence, much greater numbers and varieties of bird bones turn up in refuse deposits than previously. Especially rapid technological developments took place in fishing, with gorges, nets, fish-spears, weirs, and even boats and paddles, all employed already in preagricultural times. Among land animals, most of the common smaller species of the forest were hunted or snared, implying less reliance on collective drives and greater stress on the individual stalking of prey within a restricted territory. Here the dog played a crucial role, perhaps first becoming a scavenger around the hunting camps but before long being fully domesticated. Particularly along the rivers and sea coasts, where land marine resources supplemented one another, relatively permanent settlements made their appearance upon great heads of discarded shellfish. These characterizations apply first and most directly to Europe, but by 3- or 4,000 B.C. they also become applicable to subsistence trends in North America.

The potentialities of an agricultural mode of subsistence for transforming man's way of life do not remove the *origins* of agriculture from this early postglacial milieu that I have sketched, nor do they establish the appearance of agriculture as an inexplicable historical "accident." Instead we have here a series of broad cultural and environmental trends, alongside of which the introduction of agriculture in certain favored areas seems a consistent and harmonious development. The widespread diversification of food resources after the Pleistocene, the numerous corresponding elaborations in technology, the increasing sedentarism—these are circumstances which alone can explain the tide of still largely unknown innovations which led to the domestication of plants and animals.

At least on present evidence, the earliest agricultural hearth lay in the Near East. Recent studies there suggest the domestication of the sheep by perhaps as early as 9,000 B.C. While the age of domestication of the goat is somewhat more obscure, it is probably of comparable antiquity. Domestic pigs, on the other hand, do not appear in the archaeological record, as it is available at present, until around 2,500 years later, while the earliest domestic cattle yet known date from around 5,000 B.C. Meanwhile the domestic cereals, at first principally emmer wheat, einkorn and two-row barley, can be firmly traced to at least 7,000 B.C.; increases in cereal pollen suggest that they may have been in use considerably earlier.

While the material now available from which to generalize is admittedly fragmentary, we may infer from the long span suggested by these dates that the development of even a rudimentary subsistence agriculture probably did not take place as a single chain of events in a single small region. Instead it seems to have been a complex process which involved a prolonged period and consisted of many episodes not always closely dependent upon one another. The same conclusion emerges from a comparison of the substantially different life-zones in which our earliest known agricultural sequences occur.

One such zone is represented by the lowland Palestinian valley in which biblical Jericho later was situated, an oasis, where man and his potential domesticates gradually may have evolved a set of symbiotic relationships under hot, arid conditions. By not long after 8,000 B.C. the spring at Jericho and other neighboring Natufian sites had been occupied by small groups of hunter-collectors who also may have practiced some cultivation. At any rate, the presence of stone hoes and flint sickle-blades polished with use suggests that cereals were being reaped if not necessarily sown. Such are the accidents of archaeological discovery and preservation that this ambiguity as to the presence of purposeful agriculture at Jericho continues until much later. Before the end of the eighth millennium B.C. a substantial walled village apparently had grown up on the site, but even from these levels domestic plants and animals have not been surely identified.

By way of contrast with Jericho, the site of Sarab in a cool Persian mountain valley near Kermanshah possibly was only the summer encampment of herdsmen-cultivators who had adapted their own patterns of winter and summer movement to those of the flocks of wild sheep and goats which they must have domesticated by the early seventh millennium if not earlier. And between the environmental extremes of Jericho and Sarab at opposite ends of the Fertile Crescent, we find roughly contemporary sequences of incipient agriculturalists and settled villagers at sites like Karim Shahir, Jarmo, and others as distant as Çatal Hüyük in southwestern Turkey. In general, village life seems to have been fully established on an agricultural basis by the late eighth or early seventh millennium B.C., with settlements having sprung up on the Anatolian plateau and all along the foothills of the Zagros, Taurus, Lebanon and Anti-Lebanon Mountains wherever local circumstances were favorable. However, just as in the early post-glacial cultural adaptations of Northern and Western Europe, the most impressive features of these early agricultural manifestations are their apparent lack of contact with one another and the diversity of their responses to differing local resources and opportunities.

The picture which emerges from recent research in the New World is broadly similar. Taken in the aggregate, there is little doubt that the food crops upon which the Indians of the Americas relied prior to European colonization had been independently domesticated from wild forms native in the Western Hemisphere. Maize, by far the most widespread and most important crop, was derived from a wild progenitor which had flourished in Mexico and perhaps Central America. On present archaeological evidence its domestication probably occurred during the fifth millennium B.C., but preserved specimens from cave deposits as late as the mid-third millennium were still so small that they must have furnished only a very limited contribution to the diet. Even the earliest maize yet found, it may be noted, appears to have been derived from wild forms already divergently adapted to the pronounced regional differences in soils and climate which make Middle America what has been called "a geographical, cultural, and ecological mosaic." And this same observation applies to the even more numerous varieties of beans and melons or squashes (Cucurbita), the other members of a trinity of food plants which eventually provided the basis for a nutritionally adequate diet even without meat or dairy products from domesticated animals. Beans and the Cucurbita are also thought to have been of Middle American origin, first having been domesticated by 7,000 B.C. or even earlier. Yet a fully developed agricultural regime in which the cultivation of maize, beans, and squash provided a sufficiently assured level of subsistence to support the formation of settled villages apparently does not antedate 2,000 B.C. or so, anywhere in the New World.

The domestication of these crops reflects, in other words, the same kind of prolonged, independent experimentation in many diverse centers as that . . . for the Old World cereals. Moreover, the same process of many divergent, local derivations of food crops probably could be documented elsewhere in the New World. For example, the potato-oca-quinoa complex began in, and always was restricted to, the high plateaus of the Central Andean region of South America. We still await a concentration of archaeological attention on those areas and time-ranges of the prehistoric past in southern and eastern Asia (and sub-Saharan Africa) which will explain the rise of food production in those vast regions.

Thus the formation of settled village communities relying mainly on agriculture probably had taken place by 7,000 B.C. in the Near East and then, essentially independently, by 2,000 B.C. in Middle America. While the process of selecting suitable domesticates and developing the techniques for their cultivation and consumption had extended over several thousand years in both cases, the consequences of the new mode of subsistence were immediate and profound. To begin with, it permitted a substantial enlargement of the residence group which could be sustained by a given area of land. With the introduction of storage facilities for agricultural products (here the invention of pottery played a vital role), it also gave far greater assurance of secure, continuous occupation than was possible with the fluctuating returns from hunting and collecting. Further, agriculture created new opportunities for trade and for the growth of specialized craft skills, for it demanded the farmer's labor only during periods of sowing, weeding, and harvesting and left unprecedentedly long periods free for activities not directly concerned with subsistence. As V. Gordon Childe has argued, it must have stimulated population growth not only by expanding food resources but also by creating a new economic importance for children who became productively employed at an earlier age than was possible in hunting. Finally, the agricultural cycle itself, the yearly renewal of the plants and herds, furnished a stronger, more integrative focus of group belief than ever had existed previously. Perhaps for this reason small shrines or temples appear very early in the archaeological record of agricultural villages in all of the great nuclear areas of the Old and New Worlds. These temples, gradually evolving from small cults into great specialized hierarchies, in turn played a central organizing role in the subsequent growth of larger, progressively more complex and stratified societies that became the earliest urban civilizations. . . .

2 / The Patterns of Everyday Events

Introduction

Culture manifests itself in the patterns of everyday events of life. Our daily routine of activities such as eating, working, studying, sleeping, etc., is so highly patterned that we are frequently unaware of it as culture. Differences in these simple customs and patterns of living, however, are sometimes dramatically apparent when we visit other cultures in travels to foreign places.

Appreciation of the patterning of everyday events may be enhanced by recognizing the distinction between the concept of cultural belief and cultural practice. Cultural practice refers to actual behavior that can be observed or reported in terms of time and space by members of the culture. Belief refers to the thoughts and attitudes concerning an associated practice. Beliefs are frequently rationalizations to defend or explain a practice. In general, for each practice engaged in by a member of a culture, there is an associated belief. One practices brushing his teeth, and the associated belief is that it prevents decay, makes one feel clean or does away with bad breath. Religion, for example, may be viewed as a whole set of religious practices, together with a rather elaborate set of beliefs about God, Heaven and Hell, and other beliefs making up a theology.

Among beliefs a further distinction is sometimes made between overt and covert beliefs. For example, one may state overtly that he believes in non-violence while harboring covert feelings of aggression and hostility. It has sometimes been said, for example, that the reason Gandhi and certain sections of Indian culture put so much emphasis on beliefs of non-violence, is that, in fact, on some covert level, they harbored extreme hostility and aggression. The nature of certain Indian riots in which tens of thousands of people perished lends superficial credibility to such opinions.

The first reading in this chapter, by Napoleon A. Chagnon, is a characterization of daily life among the Yąnomamö, a primitive population (est. total: 10,000) living in small villages in southern Venezuela and northern Brazil. Some of their customs—e.g., the frequent use of hallucinogenic drugs—are quite distinctive, but some features of their life are typical of life in many primitive communities. For example, it is generally true of primitive societies that the division of labor and the distinctions among people hinge upon the same dichotomies as those recognized by the Yąnomamö—namely: male/female; child/adult; kinsman/in-law; and insider/outsider. Where so few distinctions underlie and regulate the entire social order, they are likely to be sharply-drawn and bound up with rules to a degree far greater than in the West, where a person's statuses are subdivided into many vaguely-defined, changing roles. Among the Yąnomamö, males and females live very different lives, from birth to death.

Similarly, the nature of the headman's authority is typical of most primitive communities where interaction is face-to-face. In such a setting the relations between leader and led is direct; a man is a leader as long as people find it useful to support him and follow his advice. There is little tolerance for an attitude of superiority, and little chance for abuse of authority. What Chagnon says of the village headman is true of most egalitarian, primitive communities: "Most of the time he leads only by example and the others follow if it pleases them to do so."

The second selection on daily routine by Romney and Romney describes in simple form a typical daily routine of people among a Mixtecan group in Mexico. The principal aim of this selection is to illustrate the extent to which daily events are patterned and scheduled in a rather homogeneous subsistence farming group. Over the four centuries since the Spanish Conquest, the Mixtecans have incorporated Catholicism, public offices, schools and even softball into their way of life. Yet in many vital regards their lifestyle is similar to that of the Yąnomamö or many other primitive groups.

Again, distinctions according to sex, age, and kinship status are fundamental to the division of labor and the distribution of authority. And as in primitive communities, the family plays a far more important role in the economy, in education and in providing for the aged and infirm than is the case in a Western, urban setting. And though they have their fiestas and other leisure activities, the near absence of animal and industrial power from the local economy means that every able-bodied member of the community is obliged to stay busy most of the time just to keep up a tolerable standard of living.

Culture provides each generation not only with most of the everyday answers to its daily routine but to its whole lifecycle as well. All rituals and customs are scheduled in time and space. We seldom stop to analyze our own attitudes towards time.

The third selection, by Hall, draws our attention to these attitudes, beliefs, and practices concerning time. He then compares our cultural concepts of time with a variety of other cultures including the Pueblo and Navaho Indians, the Tiv of Africa, the Truk of the Pacific, Tokyo city-dwellers, and others. In his comparisons of various cultural attitudes toward time, Hall also contributes to our understanding of patterns of Culture Contact, as discussed in Chapter Nine.

Hall turns the trained eye of an anthropologist to a feature of our worldview that pervades all of our behavior—namely, its temporal patterning. From the vantage point provided by his own cross-cultural experience, Hall is able to "look back" at the U.S. with a new sensitivity to the regularities and the limits of our shared concepts of time and its significance. As in any culture, he finds that what we express covertly ("unconsciously") by the timing of our activities sometimes belies what we say overtly, as in the case that he cites at the outset of his essay. This makes life complicated enough, but matters can get much worse when we are interacting with someone of a different culture. In this situation, the covert "messages" sent and received may seem so inappropriate and bizarre that they overwhelm all conscious efforts to establish a friendly, workable relationship. Almost certainly, much of the friction that often accompanies contacts between members of different ethnic or cultural groups (see Chapter Nine) stems from these unanalyzed sources. Whorf's article in Chapter Eleven provides a comparison of Western vs. Hopi conceptual categories, particularly spatial ones.

Miner's "Body Ritual Among the Nacirema" is a study of a lovable but bumptiously-ethnocentric people who arrogate to their union of 50 tribes a name which, properly speaking, belongs equally to all residents of North, Central and South Acirema. Miner's parody is two-edged: on the one hand, it stands as a reminder to anthropologists that their interpretations of non-Western societies and the exotic look of such societies "on paper" result partly from the nature of the quaint language in which they are described. On the other hand, his accurate description of our body rituals and the sense of arbitrariness that he evokes suggest that our behavior suggests the same regularity of patterns as that of more primitive groups.

Daily Life Among the Yąnomamö

Napoleon A. Chagnon

. . . [O]ne first has the impression that chaos rather than order reigns over the daily activities of the village members! Thus, while ideal rules about behavior definitely exist, individuals have a great deal of freedom to manipulate their behavior in such a way that they are not unduly encumbered by them. Most of the run-of-the-mill activities of daily life are not characterized by inflexible prescriptions regarding proper behavior.[1]

Male-female division

There are a number of distinctions based on status differences that are important in daily life. Perhaps the most conspicuous and most important is the distinction between males and females.

Yąnomamö society is decidedly masculine. . . . [T]here is a definite preference to have male children, resulting in a higher incidence of female infanticide as opposed to male infanticide. Female children assume duties and responsibilities in the household long before their brothers are obliged to participate in useful domestic tasks. For the most part, little girls are obliged to tend their younger brothers and sisters, although they are also expected to help their mothers in other chores such as cooking, hauling water, and collecting firewood. By the time girls have reached puberty they have already learned that their world is decidedly less attractive than that of their brothers.

As members of local descent groups, girls have almost no voice in the decisions reached by their agnates concerning their marriage. They are largely pawns to be disposed of by their kinsmen, and their wishes are given very little consideration. In many cases, the girl has been promised to a man long before she reaches puberty, and in some cases her husband actually raises her for part of her childhood. In short, they do not participate as equals in the political affairs of the corporate kinship group and seem to inherit most of the duties without enjoying many of the privileges.

Marriage does not enhance the status of the girl, for her duties as wife require her to assume difficult and laborious tasks too menial to be executed by the men. For the most part these include the incessant demands for firewood and drinking water, particularly the former. Women spend several hours each day scouring the neighborhood for suitable wood. There is usually an abundant supply in the garden within a year of the clearing of the land, but this disappears rapidly. Thereafter, the women must forage further afield to collect the daily supply of firewood, sometimes traveling several miles each day to obtain it. It

[1]Many fieldworkers do not begin to see the patterns of behavior until they have spent months of intensive contact with their subjects. I was convinced, after five or six months, that there were almost no guidelines for behavior. A part of the difficulty resulted from the language barrier. The patterns began to emerge only after about six months, and only then could I begin asking pertinent questions about many features of social organization.

is a lucky woman who owns an axe, for collecting wood is a tedious job without a steel tool. The women can always be seen at dusk, returning to the village in a procession, bearing enormous loads of wood in their pack-baskets . . . Good planners will spend a great deal of time collecting wood on some days so that they can take a vacation from this chore on others. If a woman locates a good supply of wood near the village, she will haul as much as she can and store it rather than let it be taken by her covillagers.

Women must respond quickly to the demands of their husbands. In fact, they must respond without waiting for a command. It is interesting to watch the behavior of women when their husbands return from a hunting trip or a visit. The men march slowly across the village and retire silently to their hammocks. The woman, no matter what she is doing, hurries home and quietly but rapidly prepares a meal for the husband. Should the wife be slow in doing this, the husband is within his rights to beat her. Most reprimands meted out by irate husbands take the form of blows with the hand or with a piece of firewood, but a good many husbands are even more brutal. Some of them chop their wives with the sharp edge of a machete or axe, or shoot them with a barbed arrow in some nonvital area, such as the buttocks or leg. Many men are given over to punishing their wives by holding the hot end of a glowing stick against them, resulting in serious burns. The punishment is usually, however, adjusted to the seriousness of the wife's shortcomings, more drastic measures being reserved for infidelity or suspicion of infidelity. Many men, however, show their ferocity by meting out serious punishment to their wives for even minor offenses. It is not uncommon for a man to injure his errant wife seriously; and some men have even killed wives.

Women expect this kind of treatment and many of them measure their husband's concern in terms of the frequency of minor beatings they sustain. I overheard two young women discussing each other's scalp scars. One of them commented that the other's husband must really care for her since he has beaten her on the head so frequently!

A woman usually depends for protection on her brothers, who will defend her against a cruel husband. If a man is too brutal to a wife, her brothers may take the woman away from him and give her to another man. It is largely for this reason that women abhor the possibility of being married off to men in distant villages; they know that their brothers cannot protect them under these circumstances. Women who have married a male cross-cousin have an easier life, for they are related to their husbands by cognatic ties of kinship as well as by marriage. Kaobawä, for example, is related to Bahimi as FaSiSo, and their marital relationship is very tranquil by Yąnomamö standards. He does beat Bahimi on occasion, but never cruelly. It is considered good to beat a wife every once in a while just to show your concern for her.

· · ·

It is not difficult to understand, then, why Yąnomamö women in general have such a vindictive and caustic attitude toward the external world. By the time a woman is thirty years old she has "lost her shape" and has developed a rather unpleasant disposition. Women tend to seek refuge and consolation in each other's company, sharing their misery with their peers.

A woman gains a measure of respect when she becomes old. By then she has adult children who care for her and treat her kindly. Old women also have a unique position in the world of intervillage warfare and politics. They are immune from the incursions of raiders and can go from one village to another with complete disregard for personal danger. In this connection they are employed as messengers and, on some occasions, as the recoverers of bodies. If a man is killed near the village of an enemy, an old woman from the slain man's village is permitted to recover his body.

Still, the women have one method by which they can exercise a measure of influence over village politics. All women fear being abducted by raiders and always leave the village with this anxiety at the back of their minds. Women always bring their children with them, particularly younger children, so that if they are abducted, the child will not starve to death because of the separation of the mother. They are therefore concerned with the political behavior of their men and occasionally goad them into taking action against some possible enemy by caustically accusing the men of cowardice. This has the effect of establishing the village's reputation for ferocity, reducing the possibility of raiders abducting the women while they are out collecting firewood or garden produce. The men cannot stand being chided by the women in this fashion, and are forced to take action if the women unite against them.

Child-Adult Division

Despite the fact that children of both sexes spend much of their time with their mothers, the boys alone are treated with considerable indulgence by their fathers from an early age. Thus, the distinction between male and female status develops early in the socialization process, and the boys are quick to learn their favored position with respect to girls. They are encouraged to be "fierce" and are rarely punished by their parents for inflicting blows on them or on the hapless girls in the village. Kạobawä, for example, lets Ariwari beat him on the face and head to express his anger and temper, laughing and commenting on his ferocity. Although Ariwari is only about four years old, he has already learned that the appropriate response to a flash of anger is to strike someone with his hand or with an object, and it is not uncommon for him to give his father a healthy smack in the face whenever something displeases him. He is frequently goaded into hitting his father by teasing, being rewarded by gleeful cheers of assent from his mother and from the other adults in the household.

When Kạobawä's group travels, Ariwari emulates his father by copying his activities on a child's scale. For example, he erects a temporary hut from small sticks and discarded leaves and plays happily in his own camp. His sisters, however, are pressed into more practical labor and help their mother do useful tasks. Still, the young girls are given some freedom to play at being adults and have their moments of fun with their mothers.

But a girl's childhood ends sooner than a boy's. The game of playing house fades imperceptibly into a constant responsibility to help mother. By the time a girl is ten years old or so, she has become an economic asset to the mother and spends a great deal of time working. Little boys, by contrast, spend hours playing among themselves and are able to prolong their childhood into their late teens if they so wish. By that time a girl has married, and may even have a child or two.

A girl's transition to womanhood is obvious because of its physiological manifestations. At first menses (yobömou) Yạnomamö girls are confined to their houses and hidden behind a screen of leaves. Their old cotton garments are discarded and replaced by new ones manufactured by their mothers or by older female friends. During this week of confinement, the girl is fed by her relatives; her food must be eaten by means of a stick, as she is not allowed to come into contact with it in any other fashion. She must also scratch herself with another set of sticks. The Yąnomamö word for menstruation translates literally as "squatting" (roo), and that fairly accurately describes what pubescent females (and adult women) do during menstruation. Yąnomamö women do not employ tampons; they simply remain inactive during menstruation, squatting on their haunches most of the time. After her puberty confinement, a girl is eligible to begin life as a wife and take up residence with her husband.

Males, on the other hand, do not have their transition into manhood marked by a ceremony. Nevertheless, one can usually tell when a boy is attempting to enter the world of men. The most conspicuous sign is his anger when others call him by his name. When the adults in the village cease using his personal name, the young man has achieved some sort of masculine adult status. Young men are always very touchy about their names and they, more than anyone else, take quick offense when hearing their names mentioned. The Yąnomamö constantly employ teknonymy when a kinship usage is ambiguous. Thus, someone may wish to refer to Kąobawä in a conversation, but the kinship term appropriate to the occasion might not distinguish him from his several brothers. Then, Kąobawä will be referred to as "father of Ariwari." However, when Ariwari gets older, he will attempt to put a stop to this in an effort to establish his status as an adult. A young man has been recognized as an adult when people no longer use his name in teknonymous references. Still, the transition is not abrupt, and it is not marked by a recognizable point in time.

• • •

Relatives by Blood and by Marriage

Many forms of interpersonal behavior stem largely from the social roles implied in the kinship system. To be sure, some kinship behavior reflects the two distinctions of age and sex discussed above, for the terminology of kinship itself employs discriminations of this kind. For example, there are terms to distinguish older siblings from younger siblings and terms used by members of one sex only in reference to those of the opposite sex.

The relationship between kinship terms and biological parentage is not the same in the Yąnomamö language as it is in our own. As was shown in the first section of this chapter, people may stand in a child relationship to a number of individuals; that is, it is possible to have multiple "mothers" and "fathers" in Yąnomamö society. The term for mother and father conveys as much of a social as a biological relationship between individuals, and in the daily activities of the Yąnomamö it is the social implications of kinship roles that are most important.

What is implied in the kinship roles can best be seen in the way the kinship terms themselves are formed. All primary kinship terms take the ending "-mou" when used to describe the relationship between individuals. Thus, osheya means "my younger sibling," but oshemou means that individual X behaves toward individual Y as a younger sibling. This ending, -mou, also occurs in nonkinship usage to express "a way of behaving," "to execute a particular activity in a specified manner," or "to perform the activity that is implied by the word to which -mou is affixed." For example, oko means fresh-water crab and okomou means "to go hunting for crabs"; *howashi* means "a mischievous white monkey" and *howashimou* means "to act mischievously, to monkey around"; *nowa naba* means "enemy," and *nowa nabamou means* "to become an enemy by behaving objectionably"; *waiteri* means "fierce" and *waiterimou* means "to behave ferociously."

Whenever I would ask the Yąnomamö a question such as, "What do you call Kąobawä?" the answers would always be in the form of a kinship term to which "-mou" was affixed, but rarely in the form "I say such-and-such to him." Calling an individual by a specific term is, however, implied in the "way of behaving" toward that individual. But despite the fact that the Yąnomamö can say, literally, "I call him father" (*kama kä iha, haya ya kuu*), they invariably say "*ya höömou*"—"I behave toward him as a child."[2] Thus, they express their relationships to others in terms of *ways of behavior*. Each kinship category implies a set of these behavioral norms, and one's social life in the community is established with respect to all other individuals by the kinship terminology employed in each particular case.

New individuals are incorporated into the community by an extension of kinship ties. Unless one is incorporated into the village in this fashion, there is no basis for social behavior vis-à-vis others, for the kinship system defines one's role in society. An orphaned teen-ager joined Kąobawä's group shortly before I began my fieldwork. He was from a distant Shamatari village and had no blood relatives in Kąobawä's group. He established his position in the community by calling Kąobawä "father." This defined his relationship to all of Kąobawä's kinsmen as well. As an exercise in kinship, I had the young man give me his relationship term for everyone in the village. He not only had specific terms for every member of the group, but he had also extended them to all the residents of Lower Bisaasi-teri and Monou-teri as well, since Kąobawä was related to these people. In short, the boy learned how Kąobawä was related to all the members of three different villages and logically extended his own assumed relationship to Kąobawä outward to the others; and he behaved toward them accordingly: He avoided women he called mother-in-law and refrained from sexual activities with women he called sister.

• • •

One of the most important characteristics of affinal ties is that they are capable of growing in strength over time because they can be solidified and reinforced by marriage exchanges between the groups. Ties between agnates, on the other hand, tend to weaken over time. For example, Kąobawä's local descent group could renew its friendship to similar affinally related groups in the village of Patanowä-teri by entering into marriage exchanges with them once again. There is no way, however, in which his own descent group could reinforce or strengthen the agnatic ties with the local descent groups of the *Sha* lineage in Patanowä-teri. By marrying into the affinally related Patanowä-teri descent groups, Kąobawä's group would enter into direct competition with agnatic counterparts in that village, further straining the relationships between the two communities.

There is another way of looking at this situation. Men who are related to each other as agnates (for example, brothers and parallel cousins) get along well with

2Although the word *höö* translates literally as "father," the expression *ya höömou* can best be understood with the translation given above.

each other when they are children and young men. As time passes and these men become old enough to seek wives, members of the groups to which they belong enter into competition with each other. The men themselves are under some pressure to display their personal autonomy, and they treat each other with considerable reserve as they get older. They cannot boss each other around or expect many favors from one another. Kąobawä, for example, cannot ask his adult brothers to perform menial tasks for him. This is because each man— particularly those men who compete for the same women—attempts to convince all others that he is capable of ferocity. The more remote the genealogical distance, the greater is the reserve with which mature agnates treat each other. That is, distant parallel cousins would behave toward each other with considerably more reserve than would actual brothers, although the men in question are all related to each other terminologically as brothers. If such men live in different villages, their mutual relationships are even more reserved when they meet.

The relationship between men who call each other brother-in-law, however, grows more intimate as the men get older. They can play and joke with each other, whereas agnates cannot, for they are not competitors and are not constrained to exhibit their fierceness to each other. They can cement their relationships to each other by merely promising to give their daughters to each other's sons. They can ask favors of each other, expecting them to be done without complaint.

· · ·

Daily activities begin early in a Yąnomamö village. One can hear people chatting lazily and children crying long before it is light enough to see. Most people are waked by the cold and build up the fire just before daybreak. They usually go back to sleep, but many of them visit and talk about their plans for the day.

The entrances are all covered with dry brush so that any movement of people through them is heard all over the village. There is always a procession of people leaving the village at dawn to relieve themselves in the nearby garden, and the noise they make going in and out of the village usually awakens the others.

The village is very smoky at this time of day, since the newly stoked campfires smoulder before they leap into flames. The air is usually very still and chilly, and the ground is damp from the dew. The smoke is pleasant and seems to drive away the coolness.

Clandestine sexual liaisons usually take place at this time of day, having been arranged on the previous evening. The lovers leave the village on the pretext of going to the bathroom and meet at some predetermined location. They return to the village by opposite routes.

This is also the time of day when raiders strike, so people must be cautious when they leave the village at dawn. If there is some reason to suspect raiders, they do not leave the confines of the upright log palisade that surrounds the village. They wait instead until full light and leave the village in armed groups.

By the time it is light enough to see, everybody has started preparing breakfast. This consists largely of roasted green plantains, easily prepared and steaming hot. If the family has any meat, it is taken down and shared, the children getting the best portions. Leftover meat is hung over the fire by a vine to keep the vermin off it and to preserve it.

If any of the men have made plans to hunt that day, they leave the village before it is light. Wild turkeys can be easily taken at this time of day because they roost in conspicuous places. During the dry season the *hashimo* (a kind of grouse) sing before dark and can be readily located. If any were heard the night before, the men leave at dawn to stalk them.

Tobacco chewing starts as soon as people begin stirring. Those who have fresh supplies soak the new leaves in water and add ashes from the hearth to the wad. Men, women, and children chew tobacco and all are addicted to it. Once there was a shortage of tobacco in Kąobawä's village and I was plagued for a week by early morning visitors who requested permission to collect my cigarette butts in order to make a wad of chewing tobacco. Normally, if anyone is short of tobacco, he can request a share of someone else's already chewed wad, or simply borrow the entire wad when its owner puts it down somewhere. Tobacco is so important to them that their word for "poverty" translates as "being without tobacco." I frequently justified my reluctance to give away possessions on the basis of my poverty. Many of them responded by spitting their tobacco into their hand and handing it to me.

Work begins as soon as breakfast is completed; the Yąnomamö like to take advantage of the morning coolness. Within an hour after it is light the men are in their gardens clearing brush, felling large trees, transplanting plantain cuttings, burning off dead timber, or planting new crops of cotton, maize, sweet potatoes, yuca, taro, or the like, depending on the season. They work until 10:30 A.M., retiring because it is too humid and hot by that time to continue with their strenuous work. Most of them bathe in the stream before returning to their hammocks for a rest and a meal.

The women usually accompany their husbands to the garden and occupy themselves by collecting firewood or helping with planting and weeding. In this way the men are sure that their families are safe and that the women are not having affairs with other men.

The children spend a great deal of time exploring the wonders of the plant and animal life around them and are accomplished biologists at an early age. Most twelve-year-old boys can, for example, name twenty species of bees and give the anatomical or behavioral reasons for their distinctions—and they know which ones produce the best honey. An eight-year-old girl brought me a tiny egg-like structure on one occasion and asked me to watch it with her. Presently it cracked open and numerous baby cockroaches poured out, while she described the intimate details of the reproductive process to me.

The younger children stay close to their mothers, but the older ones have considerable freedom to wander about the garden at play. Young boys hunt for lizards with miniature bows and featherless arrows. If they can capture one alive, they bring it back to the village and tie a string around it. The string is anchored to a stick in the village clearing and the little boys chase it gleefully, shooting scores of tiny arrows at it. Since lizards are very quick, and little boys are poor shots, the target practice can last for hours. Usually, however, the fun terminates when an older boy decides to make an end to the unhappy lizard and kills it with his adult-size arrows, showing off his archery skills to the disgruntled small fry.

Little girls learn very quickly that it is a man's world, for they soon must assume much of the responsibility for tending their younger siblings, hauling water and firewood, and in general helping their busy mothers.

Most of the people rest in their hammocks during the heat of midday, although they will collect fruits and other wild foods from the surrounding area, if any are in season. They avoid being in the direct rays of the midday sun.

If the men return to their gardening, they do so about 4:00 P.M., working until sundown. Otherwise, they gather in small groups around the village and take hallucinogenic drugs in the late afternoon shadows, chanting to the mountain demons as the drugs take effect. This usually lasts for an hour or so, after which the men bathe to wash the vomit or nasal mucus off their bodies. Kạobawä does not participate in the drugtaking, as he finds it unpleasant. Most of the men, however, do take drugs and enjoy doing it, despite the associated unpleasantries of vomiting and the pain that follows the blast of air as the powder is blown deeply into the nasal passages.

Whatever the men do for the afternoon, however, the women invariably search for firewood and haul immense, heavy loads of it to their houses just before dark.

The biggest meal of the day is prepared in the evening. The staple is plantains, but frequently other kinds of food are available after the day's activities. Meat is always the most desirable food and is always considered to be in short supply. It is a happy occasion when one of the hunters bags a tapir, for everyone gets a large share of it.

It is good to share meat with others. This attitude is expressed in the sentiment that a hunter should give away most of the game he kills. One of the obligations men take very seriously is providing adequate quantities of meat for their wives and children. They genuinely abhor hearing their children cry for meat; this calls into question their abilities as hunters and marksmen, both of which are associated with prestige. Rerebawä, for example, collected a large supply of game on one trip we took together. He gave it all to his wife and children and to his wife's parents. At the evening meal he refused to take a portion of the meat so that the others could have more. Later in the evening, he appeared at my hut begging for a can of sardines to satisfy his hunger for meat. He preferred to go hungry rather than risk the onus of being accused of poor marksmanship or stinginess.

Both sexes participate in the cooking, although the women do the greater share of it. Food preparation is not elaborate and rarely requires much labor, time, or paraphernalia. Spices are never used, although the salty ashes of a particular kind of tree are sometimes mixed with water to form a condiment of sorts. The food is dunked into the salty liquid and eaten.

Everyone eats in his hammock using his fingers for utensils. Some meals cannot be eaten from a reclining position, so the members of the family squat in a circle around the common dish. For example, large quantities of tiny fish are cooked by wrapping them in leaves and cooking them in the hot coals. When the fish are done, the package is spread open, and everyone shares its contents.

Animals are never skinned before cooking. They are merely put over the fire after their entrails have been removed, and roasted, head, fur, claws, and all. Most of the fur is singed off in the process of cooking. The animal is dismembered by hand. The head, particularly the head of a monkey, is highly prized because the brain is considered a delicacy. The most common meat is monkey, of which there are several varieties, so that this delicacy is enjoyed rather frequently by the Yạnomamö.

By the time supper is over it is nearly dark. The fires are prepared for the evening; if someone has allowed his own fire to go out during the day, he simply borrows two glowing sticks from a neighbor and rekindles his own hearth. The entrances to the village are sealed off with dry brush so that prowlers can not enter without raising an alarm. Before retiring to their hammocks, the Yąnomamö first sit on them and wipe the bottoms of their bare feet together. This rubs off most of the debris that has accumulated on them during the course of the day. Everyone sleeps naked and as close to the fire as possible. Despite the inevitable last-minute visiting, things are usually quiet in the village by the time it is dark.

Things are not always quiet after dark. If anyone in the village is sick, a shaman will chant to the malevolent spirits most of the night to exorcise them. Or, should anyone be mourning a dead kinsman, he or she will sob and wail long after the others have fallen asleep. Occasionally, a fight will break out between a husband and wife, and soon everybody in the village will be screaming, expressing opinions on the dispute. The shouting may continue sporadically for hours, dying down only to break out anew as someone gets a fresh insight into the problem. Once in a while someone gives a long, loud speech voicing his opinion on the world in general. Those who are interested may add their own comments, but the audience usually grumbles about the noise and falls asleep.

STATUS DIFFERENCES AND ACTIVITIES

Daily activities, except those concerning gardening and visiting, do not vary much from season to season. Much of the variation that does occur is a function of one's age or sex, as was shown above.

Other status differences do exist and account for some variation in the activities of particular individuals. Rerebawä, for example, is an outsider to Kąobawä's group and has no intention of joining the village as a permanent resident. Consequently, he does not participate in the gardening activities and has considerably more spare time than other married men. He spends this time hunting for his wife and her parents, one of his obligations as a son-in-law. He is quite dependent on them for the bulk of his diet because they provide him with all his plantains. This is perhaps why he takes his hunting obligations so seriously and gives his game away so unflinchingly. He is quick to make reference to his hunting skills and generosity, perhaps to draw attention away from the fact that he does not cultivate food for his wife and children. He has been able to avoid making a garden because of his status as an outsider; he plans to return to his own village as soon as his bride service is over. But his in-laws want him to stay permanently so that he will be able to provide them with meat and garden produce when they are old. They have no sons to do this for them and have even promised Rerebawä their second daughter on the condition that he remain permanently in the village. They prevent Rerebawä from taking his wife and children home by keeping at least one of the children with them when Rerebawä goes to visit his own family. They know that his wife could not bear to be separated permanently from her child, and Rerebawä invariably brings her back home so that she can be with the child.

By Yąnomamö standards he has done enough bride service and deserves to be given his wife. Also, by their standards he has lived in the village so long that he should be obliged to make his own garden. But he can legitimately refuse to do this because he has discharged his obligations well beyond what was expected of him.

Kạobawä, on the other hand, has the special status of being his group's headman. Apart from this, he is also some fifteen years senior to Rerebawä and has a higher sense of obligation and responsibility to his family. Rerebawä, in addition to refusing to make a garden, thinks nothing of taking a week-long trip to visit friends, leaving his wife and children with her parents. His attitude toward the children, compared to Kạobawä's, is rather indifferent. Kạobawä had planned to accompany me to Caracas to see how foreigners live until Ariwari began crying and appealed to his father's paternal sensitivities. Kạobawä stepped out of the canoe, took off the clothing I had loaned him, and picked up Ariwari; "I can't go with you," he explained, "Ariwari will miss me and be sad."

Kạobawä thinks for the others in the village, many of whom are not able to perceive some of the less obvious implications of situations. In political matters he is the most astute man in group, but he so diplomatically exercises his influence that the others are not offended. Should someone be planning to do something that is potentially dangerous, he simply points out the danger and adds parenthetically, "Go ahead and do it if you want to, but don't expect sympathy from me if you get hurt." Shararaiwä, his youngest brother, planned to take a trip to a distant village with me. I knew that the two villages were not on particularly good terms with each other, but they were not actively at war. Kạobawä arrived at my canoe just as we were about to depart and asked me not to take Shararaiwä along, explaining that the Iyawei-teri might possibly molest him and precipitate hostilities between the two groups. Shararaiwä was willing to take a chance that my presence would be sufficient to deter any potential trouble, but Kạobawä would not risk it.

• • •

Kạobawä keeps order in the village when people get out of hand. Paruriwä, for example, is particularly cruel to his four wives and beats them mercilessly for even slight provocations. None of his wives have brothers in the village, and few people are courageous enough to interfere with Paruriwä when he is angry. On one occasion Kạobawä was holding a feast for the members of an allied village. His preparations were being duplicated by an equal effort on the part of Paruriwä, an obvious attempt by the latter to show that he was also a leader. Some of the visitors arrived early and were visiting in Paruriwä's house. He commanded his wife to prepare food for them, but the woman moved a little too slowly to suit him. Paruriwä went into a rage, grabbed an axe, and swung it wildly at her. She ducked and ran screaming from the house. Paruriwä recovered his balance and threw the axe at her as she fled, but missed. By this time Kạobawä had seen the axe go whizzing over the woman's head; he raced across the village in time to take a machete from Paruriwä before he could inflict much damage with it. He did manage, however, to hit her twice before Kạobawä disarmed him, splitting her hand with one of the blows.

• • •

Kạobawä's personality differs considerably from Paruriwä's. Where the former is unobtrusive, calm, modest, and perceptive, the latter is belligerent, aggressive, ostentatious, and rash. Kạobawä has an established status in the village and numerous supporters, whose loyalties are in part determined by their kinship ties and in part because he is a wise leader. Paruriwä is attempting to share in the leadership and does not have a well-established position in this respect. It is obvious who the real leader is: When visitors come to Upper Bisaasi-teri, they seek out Kạobawä and deal with him, no matter how ambitiously Paruriwä attempts to emulate his position. Paruriwä does not have as many living brothers in his group as Kạobawä has, so his "natural following" is somewhat limited. In addition, two of his brothers are married to actual sisters of Kạobawä and have some loyalty to him. Paruriwä, therefore, has very little means with which to establish his position, so he is given over to using bluff, threat, chicanery, and treachery. This he does well, and many of the young men in the village admire him for it. He has gained the support of some of these men by promising them his wives' yet unborn daughters. Remarkably enough, some of them cling to these promises and do his bidding.

Finally, one of Kaobawä's most unpleasant tasks is to scout the village neighborhood when signs of raiders have been found. This he does alone, since it is a dangerous task and one that is avoided by the other men. Not even Paruriwä participates in this.

Kaobawä has definite responsibilities as the headman and is occasionally called upon by the nature of the situation to exercise his authority. He is usually distinguishable in the village as a man of some authority only for the duration of the incident that calls forth his leadership capacity. After the incident is over, he goes about his own business like the other men in the group. But even then, he sets an example for the others, particularly in his ambitions to produce large quantities of food for his family and for the guests he must entertain. Most of the time he leads only by example and the others follow if it pleases them to do so. They can ignore his example if they wish, but most of the people turn to him when a difficult situation arises.

Daily Routine

A. Kimball Romney and Romaine Romney

The day begins in the barrio household between 5:30 and 6:00 A.M. The woman gets up from the mat on which she has slept, smooths her clothes, perhaps shakes her rebozo and throws it around her shoulders. She does not stop at this hour to wash her face or arrange her hair, for she must start the fire, heat the coffee (if there is any) for breakfast, and begin the preparations for the rest of the day's meals. Firewood is kept stacked in the courtyard, and she goes outside to select some pieces for the day. She lights the fire with a match, tends it until it is going well, and then puts a little pot of water into the coals to boil for coffee. If she plans to have her corn ground at the mill, she must go at once. When she returns, she takes the *masa* (coarsely ground corn) to the metate for its second grinding. If she is doing all of the grinding herself, she will have ground it through once instead of taking it to the mill. While she is grinding, her husband awakens and gets up. She may stop her grinding to serve him some coffee and a cold tortilla or two which have been stored since the preceding day. When he has eaten, he goes to his field if it is nearby and does not return until breakfast time at about 9 o'clock. Meanwhile the children awaken. A mother does not stop grinding corn to attend to the children as they get up. There is little dressing to be done, for children as well as adults sleep in all their clothing and need only shake out their rebozos or serapes and put them on again. The children often sit outside in the sunshine to get warm and wake up. Then they too eat a cold tortilla before beginning to play or to help their mother.

The woman is occupied with the making of tortillas until breakfast time. The children play in the courtyard or in the cook shack while she works, and she seldom notices them unless some difficulty reaches her ears. The oldest of the little girls is in charge of the younger children and watches them play. An older boy may take this opportunity to lead the burro or other animal to pasture, or he may split firewood in the yard. The family gathers at about 9 o'clock to eat the morning meal. The time for this meal, as for all others, is not set and may vary widely from day to day, but the content—cold beans, fresh tortillas, and chile—is always the same. The man and boys are served first, all sitting on the floor, the woman waiting on them and sometimes making tortillas as they eat them. After eating, the man goes outside and sits in the sun while the children are fed, and then he returns to the fields. When the younger children have returned to their play, the woman and older girl (if she has been helping with the meal) sit down to eat. After the meal, the woman washes the bowls in clear water and sets them aside. She washes the empty bean pot also and leaves it ready for the beans she will soon set on the fire for the midday meal.

During the morning the woman of the household may go to the market (if it is Friday) either to sell some garden produce or to buy food. On other days she might make purchases in a store. However, many small items of food are obtained by barter within the barrio, among friends, and this sort of exchange is carried on later in the day. When a woman goes to market, she may take her children with her. It may be necessary for them to sit with her quietly for several hours at a time. There is never any noise or interference from these children. They are simply there. Nursing infants, who might create a problem, are usually left behind, often with a woman friend or relative who can nurse the baby if the mother is delayed. A mother of a young infant might send her daughters or her younger sons to the market or the store rather than go herself. Adults and children alike tend to go about their errands with dispatch. Women, especially, do not stand in the street to gossip with friends. They greet neighbors in a friendly way but do not stop to converse. Even if a woman should meet her husband in the street, she does not talk with him at any length until they have reached home. In contrast, in the market place itself there is a great deal of conversation between women who sit next to each other hour after hour.

At home there are many tasks to be accomplished before noon. Preparations for dinner begin soon after breakfast is over. Beans are winnowed by pouring them from one hand to the other, then rinsed and placed in a pot of water on the fire. Corn is removed from the ear and boiled in lime water, then drained and ground. Children—girls of all ages and younger boys—may help with the preparation of beans and may carry corn from the storeroom and help to shell it. Only older girls grind corn. Water must be brought in for use in cooking and for drinking during the day. The source of water is usually a well at some distance from the house, for not all households have wells; those with water share it with their neighbors. The woman will often leave her children in the care of their older sister and go to get water herself, for this is considered heavy work. However, children of all ages, both boys and girls, can and do carry water. Poultry and pigs must be fed by the woman or the younger children. The house must be straightened up and the house and courtyard swept. The woman rarely does this herself unless she has no children, for girls and younger boys do the work under her supervision.

An older daughter may go once a week to the river to wash, a task which requires spending the whole day. For this reason, a mother with a nursing infant is not usually called on to do the laundry, nor is a woman who has full responsibility for the preparation of meals. If there is a relatively unoccupied woman or girl in the compound, she goes to do the washing. Otherwise mother and children go to the river together, and the children play while the mother washes and spreads the wet clothes on the grass and on bushes to dry in the sun.

For much of the average morning the woman is either away from home on an errand or, more frequently, bent over the fire and the metate in the cook shack. Children who sit in the kitchen near their mother may be asked to hand her a utensil from time to time, to bring a piece of firewood from the yard, to chase the chickens away from the corn, or to drive the dog from the doorway. They may munch a cold tortilla, a piece of fruit, or a handful of pumpkin seeds as they watch her work.

Children of school age may spend the morning and the afternoon at school, coming home for dinner between 1:30 and 3 o'clock. However, only about half of the barrio's school-age children go to school at all, and even those who do attend do so irregularly. Thus, when their morning chores are finished, many barrio children are free to play. Some children play alone, particularly those who live in nuclear households and have only infant siblings or siblings much older than they. More often, children play in courtyard groups that include their siblings and their cousins. While children in the courtyard are young, play groups may include both sexes under the direction of an older girl in the family who is entrusted with the care of the younger boys and girls. As soon as they are old enough to do without a caretaker, boys tend to play with other boys and girls who have no caretaking responsibilities tend to play with other girls. When boys and girls beyond the toddler stage play together, they usually play on the boys' terms.

The man of the household may or may not come home for dinner. If his field is within easy walking distance from the house, he may be at home for both breakfast and dinner. If it is farther away, he may wait until breakfast is over before he leaves, and in this case breakfast is served well before the usual 9 o'clock. He also stays in the field until late in the day, and his dinner is brought to him there by his wife or often by an older boy who is not yet old enough to work in the fields for a full day. The boy stays with his father after dinner and returns home with him at the end of the day.

If dinner is not yet ready when the man arrives, he may take a few minutes to play with his children or sit among the children while he chats with the friends or kinsmen who have come home from work with him. When dinner is ready, the man and boys are again served first; when they have finished, they may smoke a cigarette outside. The man generally does not return to the field after dinner, but neither does he spend the late afternoon at home alone. He gets together with other men in his compound or in another to visit or to do business. The talk centers around the crops, prices, and coming fiestas. He may spend the time making something—leather goods, adobes, tile—which he will later sell. He may gather materials to build a new house at some future time. He may work with other men on the decorations for a fiesta. Older boys may spin tops or shoot marbles with friends in the street. Later they may cut hay for the animals and bring the animals home to be fed.

Meanwhile the woman and girls clear the kitchen after dinner, putting aside the leftovers—beans, tortillas, and chile—once again for the evening meal. (Second helpings, at least for children, are discouraged, and food left over after a meal is saved rather than distributed.) Then the woman may visit a neighbor, usually going with some sort of excuse, for example, an exchange of food or a question about plans for a coming fiesta. When this small business has been taken care of, the women sit and visit at length. The guest may be offered coffee, fruit, or squash cooked in brown sugar, for "little gifts make for good friends." The women may comb and delouse each other's hair and that of the children who have come along on the visit. Corn may be shelled by all of the women present. Some of them may sew or embroider. The children play in the courtyard largely unnoticed.

Instead of visiting in the afternoon, a woman may engage in some money-making project at home, such as butchering a pig and rendering the lard for sale, toasting pumpkin seeds, gathering greens and herbs, or picking fruit. Such activities are often shared by other women in the compound.

At dusk water is carried from the well for evening use. The fire is built up and the tortillas reheated or, less frequently, made fresh. Supper—leftover beans and tortillas with chile—is the end of the day for the family, and after the dishes are put away and the corn set to soaking for the morning, the adults sit and talk around the smouldering fire. Candles and ocote are used sparingly, so the room is usually dark, except for firelight, long before bedtime. The children lie down and sleep when they are ready, and even the adults are usually asleep by 9 o'clock.

Special events require a number of alternative routines. On Thursday afternoons some children of school age go to catechism class at the barrio church. On Sundays some women arise earlier than usual in order to attend mass, but not all women go, and attendance is rather irregular at best. Children may or may not go with their mothers to mass. Also, on Sunday, many people go to the river to bathe. The whole family may go at once, but more often the women of a compound and all the children go together. The bath takes place soon after noon, during the warmest part of the day, and the hair is washed and clothing changed. There is much visiting and chattering in such a group. On Sunday afternoons some barrio men play softball on a field at the edge of the barrio using equipment that they own cooperatively. A few younger, generally single, barrio men spend Sundays drinking with their friends, and there may be a drunk or two in the streets of the barrio on Sunday evening. These are the exception rather than the rule, except on fiesta occasions.

During the week the man of the household may, instead of going to the field, engage in some special semiskilled work. He may make or lay adobe or tile or do carpentry on contract, and while he is working, he may receive a midday meal from his employer. This is particularly true if he is working for another barrio person. On other days he may take part in a cooperative work group in the field of a friend, and on these days, he eats a festive meal with the group. During the dry season he may be called on to help on the same basis in the construction of a friend's house. The woman of the household that has requested cooperative help prepares the meal for the workers with the aid of her daughters and other women in her compound.

A man's labor may also be required by the regidor. The *tequio*, or communal work, includes planting and tending corn in the communal fields, street cleaning, repairs or improvements on the church, and so on. The church bell rings to announce the time, but the 30 men needed on any given day are notified in person beforehand. Records are kept by the regidor of each man's participation. The *tequio* is seldom accompanied by a communal meal.

Fiestas of all kinds alter the daily routine, even when the household is not directly involved in them, for the gift of food from someone else's fiesta makes it unnecessary for the woman to prepare a meal for the family. Besides providing good fare fiestas offer an opportunity for visiting and drinking. Barrio saints' fiestas also entail entertainment—dances, dramas, fireworks displays, and the movement of crowds. They include special masses which are attended by the majority of barrio residents. When the man of the household is a member of the society that is responsible for the fiesta, the routine is even more strikingly changed. For several weeks preceding the fiesta, especially if it is an important one, much of the man's time and energy goes into preparations for the event. He takes part in the purchase of food, liquor, cigarettes, and ritual necessities, such as candles. He participates in the gathering and arrangement of materials used in decoration of the church and adornment of the saint. He may help to build a structure on which fireworks are to be displayed. He spends much time in meetings with the other members of the society, planning and collecting money. On the days of the fiesta itself (which may last from two or three days to as long as two weeks), he rises early, attends mass, and then gathers with the other men of the society for a breakfast served by all of their wives. After breakfast they drink and smoke and make speeches until dinner. Between dinner and evening they drink again and watch the ceremonies that mark the particular fiesta. After dinner there are fireworks, a drama, or, often, a dance in which everyone participates until very late. Children sit and watch the dancing until they can stay awake no longer. Then they often go to sleep on the floor or in the arms of their mothers or sisters.

The woman whose husband is deeply involved in a fiesta is responsible for helping to prepare the food. Under the direction of the *mayordoma*, the wife of the head of the society, she works with other women (at grinding and tortilla making and the cooking of meat) from early morning until late, sometimes even sleeping in the fiesta cook house. The work is hard, but the interaction with other women is pleasant, and fiestas are anticipated with much excitement. Children may go with their mothers to the fiesta site, and here, as in the market, they sit and watch without interrupting. The youngest may be tied onto the mother's back while she works. Sometimes younger children are left at home with an older sibling; in this case, the woman leaves the fiesta at about 10 in the morning and again at 4 in the afternoon to take some of the fiesta food home to her children. Sometimes a woman arranges to do part of her work at home, for example, grinding and making a batch of tortillas. Then she sends her daughter with the finished tortillas to the fiesta place, and her share of the food is sent home to her. On fiesta days, meals are irregular, but children wait without complaint until their mother returns, and they enjoy the special meal when it is ready.

In general, barrio men spend very little time with their families. They are at home only briefly during the day, and even then their attention is often absorbed by business and the society of other men. Men are sometimes affectionate and playful with their children (especially the youngest) and often show pride in them before visitors. They are occasionally asked by their wives to discipline unruly sons. However, the only children who interact at all intensively with their fathers are boys of 12 years and over. Boys of this age work in the fields every day and begin to participate with the other men of the compound.

Similarly, barrio women are occupied almost full time with their primary responsibility—the provision and preparation of food for the family. When they are not busy in the kitchen, they are relaxing—always with hands at work—with other women in their own courtyard or a neighboring one, or they are chatting with others while selling fruits in the market. The youngest child and the oldest daughter receive more attention from their mother than any of her other children. A nursing infant must be attended to by his own mother whenever she is present, and, in addition to routine care, he receives many expressions of love, both verbal and physical. The oldest daughter, on the other hand, needs little care but much instruction. The mother teaches her to fulfill the feminine role by example, often calling her from play to watch some operation in order that she may learn to perform it. As the oldest daughter learns more and more of the appropriate role behaviors, she comes to interact with her mother and the other women of the compound as a woman among women.

Neither men nor women are often found playing with children. Thus children between infancy and young adulthood spend their days apart from adults for the most part. However, their play is often imitative of adult role behavior. They are content to watch adults at work and to be near them without doing anything else. They are happy, especially when very young, to perform little tasks for the adults around them. The daily routine in the barrio belongs to adults, and children observe it and practice it, first playfully and later in earnest, until they too are grown.

The Voices of Time

Edward T. Hall

Time talks. It speaks more plainly than words. The message it conveys comes through loud and clear. Because it is manipulated less consciously, it is subject to less distortion than the spoken language. It can shout the truth where words lie.

I was once a member of a mayor's committee on human relations in a large city. My assignment was to estimate what the chances were of non-discriminatory practices being adopted by the different city departments. The first step in this project was to interview the department heads, two of whom were themselves members of minority groups. If one were to believe the words of these officials, it seemed that all of them were more than willing to adopt non-discriminatory labor practices. Yet I felt that, despite what they said, in only one case was there much chance for a change. Why? The answer lay in how they used the silent language of time and space.

Special attention had been given to arranging each interview. Department heads were asked to be prepared to spend an hour or more discussing their thoughts with me. Nevertheless, appointments were forgotten; long waits in outer offices (fifteen to forty-five minutes) were common, and the length of the interview was often cut down to ten or fifteen minutes. I was usually kept at an impersonal distance during the interview. In only one case did the department head come from behind his desk. These men had a position and they were literally and figuratively sticking to it!

The implication of this experience (one which public-opinion pollsters might well heed) is quite obvious. What people do is frequently more important than what they say. In this case the way these municipal potentates handled time was eloquent testimony to what they inwardly believed, for the structure and meaning of time systems, as well as the time intervals, are easy to identify. In regard to being late there are: "mumble something" periods, slight apology periods, mildly insulting periods requiring full apology, rude periods, and downright insulting periods. The psychoanalyst has long been aware of the significance of communication on this level. He can point to the way his patients handle time as evidence of "resistances" and "transference."

Different parts of the day, for example, are highly significant in certain contexts. Time may indicate the importance of the occasion as well as on what level an interaction between persons is to take place. In the United States if you telephone someone very early in the morning, while he is shaving or having breakfast, the time of the call usually signals a matter of utmost importance and extreme urgency. The same applies for calls after 11:00 P.M. A call received during sleeping hours is apt to be taken as a matter of life and death, hence the rude joke value of these calls among the young. Our realization that time talks is even reflected in such common expressions as, "What time does the clock *say*?"

An example of how thoroughly these things are taken for granted was reported to me by John Useem, an American social anthropologist, in an illuminating case from the South Pacific. The natives of one of the islands had been having a difficult time getting their white supervisors to hire them in a way consistent with their traditional status system. Through ignorance the supervisors had hired too many of one group and by so doing had disrupted the existing balance of power among the natives. The entire population of the island was seething because of this error. Since the Americans continued in their ignorance and refused to hire according to local practice, the head men of the two factions met one night to discuss an acceptable reallocation of jobs. When they finally arrived at a solution, they went en masse to see the plant manager and woke him up to tell him what had been decided. Unfortunately it was then between two and three o'clock in the morning. They did not know that it is a sign of extreme urgency to wake up Americans at this hour. As one might expect, the American plant manager, who understood neither the local language nor the culture nor what the hullabaloo was all about, thought he had a riot on his hands and called out the Marines. It simply never occurred to him that the parts of the day have a different meaning for these people than they have for us.

On the other hand, plant managers in the United States are fully aware of the significance of a communication made during the middle of the morning or afternoon that takes everyone away from his work. Whenever they want to make an important announcement they will ask: "When shall we let them know?" In the social world a girl feels insulted when she is asked for a date at the last minute by someone whom she doesn't know very well, and the person who extends an invitation to a dinner party with only three or four days' notice has to apologize. How different from the people of the Middle East with whom it is pointless to make an appointment too far in advance, because the informal structure of their time system places everything beyond a week into a single category of "future," in which plans tend to "slip off their minds."

Advance notice is often referred to in America as "lead time," an expression which is significant in a culture where schedules are important. While it is learned informally, most of us are familiar with how it works in our own culture, even though we cannot state the rules technically. The rules for lead time in other cultures, however, have rarely been analyzed. At the most they are known by experience to those who lived abroad for some time. Yet think how important it is to know how much time is required to prepare people, or for them to prepare themselves, for things to come. Sometimes lead time would seem to be very extended. At other times, in the Middle East, any period longer than a week may be too long.

How troublesome differing ways of handling time can be is well illustrated by the case of an American agriculturalist assigned to duty as an attaché of our embassy in a Latin country. After what seemed to him a suitable period he let it be known that he would like to call on the minister who was his counterpart. For various reasons, the suggested time was not suitable; all sorts of cues came back to the effect that the time was not yet ripe to visit the minister. Our friend, however, persisted and forced an appointment which was reluctantly granted. Arriving a little before the hour (the American respect pattern), he waited. The hour came and passed; five minutes—ten minutes—fifteen minutes. At this point he suggested to the secretary that perhaps the minister did not know he was waiting in the outer office. This gave him the feeling he had done something concrete and also helped to overcome the great anxiety that was stirring inside him. Twenty minutes—twenty-five minutes—thirty minutes—forty-five minutes (the insult period)!

He jumped up and told the secretary that he had been "cooling his heels" in an outer office for forty-five minutes and he was "damned sick and tired" of this type of treatment. This message was relayed to the minister, who said, in effect, "Let him cool his heels." The attaché's stay in the country was not a happy one.

The principal source of misunderstanding lay in the fact that in the country in question the five-minute-delay interval was not significant. Forty-five minutes, on the other hand, instead of being at the tail end of the waiting scale, was just barely at the beginning. To suggest to an American's secretary that perhaps her boss didn't know you were there after waiting sixty seconds would seem absurd, as would raising a storm about "cooling your heels" for five minutes. Yet this is precisely the way the minister registered the protestations of the American in his outer office! He felt, as usual, that Americans were being totally unreasonable.

Throughout this unfortunate episode the attaché was acting according to the way he had been brought up. At home in the United States his responses would have been normal ones and his behavior legitimate. Yet even if he had been told before he left home that this sort of thing would happen, he would have had difficulty not *feeling* insulted after he had been kept waiting forty-five minutes. If, on the other hand, he been taught the details of the local time system just as he should have been taught the local spoken language, it would have been possible for him to adjust himself accordingly.

What bothers people in situations of this sort is that they don't realize they are being subjected to another form of communication, one that works part of the time with language and part of the time independently of it. The fact that the message conveyed is couched in no formal vocabulary makes things doubly difficult, because neither party can get very explicit about what is actually taking place. Each can only say what he thinks is happening and how he feels about it. The thought of what is being communicated is what hurts.

AMERICAN TIME

People of the Western world, particularly Americans, tend to think of time as something fixed in nature, something around us and from which we cannot escape; an ever-present part of the environment, just like the air we breathe. That it might be experienced in any other way seems unnatural and strange, a feeling which is rarely modified even when we begin to discover how really differently it is handled by some other people. Within the West itself certain cultures rank time much lower in over-all importance than we do. In Latin America, for example, where time is treated rather cavalierly, one commonly hears the expression, "Our time or your time?" "*Hora americana, hora mejicana?*"

As a rule, Americans think of time as a road or a ribbon stretching into the future, along which one progresses. The road has segments or compartments which are to be kept discrete ("one thing at a time"). People who cannot schedule time are looked down upon as impractical. In at least some parts of Latin America, the North American (their term for us) finds himself annoyed when he has made an appointment with somebody, only to find a lot of other things going on at the same time. An old friend of mine of Spanish cultural heritage used to run his business according to the "Latino" system. This meant that up to fifteen people were in his office at one time. Business which might have been finished in a quarter of an hour sometimes took a whole day. He realized, of course, that the Anglo-Americans were disturbed by this and used to make some allowance for them, a dispensation which meant that they spent only an hour or so in his office when they had planned on a few minutes. The American concept of the discreteness of time and the necessity for scheduling was at variance with this amiable and seemingly confusing Latin system. However, if my friend had adhered to the American system he would have destroyed a vital part of his prosperity. People who came to do business with him also came to find out things and to visit each other. The ten to fifteen Spanish-Americans and Indians who used to sit around the office (among whom I later found myself after I had learned to relax a little) played their own part in a particular type of communications network.

Not only do we Americans segment and schedule time, but we look ahead and are oriented almost entirely toward the future. We like new things and are preoccupied with change. We want to know how to overcome resistance to change. In fact, scientific theories and even some pseudo-scientific ones, which incorporate a striking theory of change, are often given special attention.

Time with us is handled much like a material; we earn it, spend it, save it, waste it. To us it is somewhat immoral to have two things going on at the same time. In Latin America it is not uncommon for one man to have a number of simultaneous jobs which he either carries on from one desk or which he moves between, spending a small amount of time on each.

While we look to the future, our view of it is limited. The future to us is the foreseeable future, not the future of the South Asian that may involve centuries. Indeed, our perspective is so short as to inhibit the operation of a good many practical projects, such as sixty- and one-hundred-year conservation works requiring public support and public funds. Anyone who has worked in industry or in the government of the United States has heard the following: "Gentlemen, this is for the long term! Five or ten years."

For us a "long time" can be almost anything—ten or twenty years, two or three months, a few weeks, or even a couple of days. The South Asian, however, feels that it is perfectly realistic to think of a "long time" in terms of thousands of years or even an endless period. A colleague once described their conceptualization of time as follows: "Time is like a museum with endless corridors and alcoves. You, the viewer, are walking through the museum in the dark, holding a light to each scene as you pass it. God is the curator of the museum, and only He knows all that is in it. One lifetime represents one alcove."

The American's view of the future is linked to a view of the past, for tradition plays an equally limited part in American culture. As a whole, we push it aside or leave it to a few souls who are interested in the past for very special reasons. There are, of course, a few pockets, such as New England and the South, where tradition is emphasized. But in the realm of business, which is the dominant model of United States life, tradition is equated with experience, and experience is thought of as being very close to if not synonymous with know-how. Know-how is one of our prized possessions, so that when we look backward it is rarely to take pleasure in the past itself but usually to calculate the know-how, to assess the prognosis for success in the future.

Promptness is also valued highly in American life. If people are not prompt, it is often taken either as an insult or as an indication that they are not quite responsible. There are those, of a psychological bent, who would say that we are obsessed with time. They can point to individuals in American culture who are literally time-ridden. And even the rest of us feel very strongly about time because we have been taught to take it so seriously. We have stressed this aspect of culture and developed it to a point unequaled anywhere in the world, except, perhaps, in Switzerland and north Germany. Many people criticize our obsessional handling of time. They attribute ulcers and hypertension to the pressure engendered by such a system. Perhaps they are right.

SOME OTHER CONCEPTS OF TIME

Even within the very borders of the United States there are people who handle time in a way which is almost incomprehensible to those who have not made a major effort to understand it. The Pueblo Indians, for example, who live in the Southwest, have a sense of time which is at complete variance with the clock-bound habits of the ordinary American citizen. For the Pueblos events begin when the time is ripe and no sooner.

I can still remember a Christmas dance I attended some twenty-five years ago at one of the pueblos near the Rio Grande. I had to travel over bumpy roads for forty-five miles to get there. At seven thousand feet the ordeal of winter cold at one o'clock in the morning is almost unbearable. Shivering in the still darkness of the pueblo, I kept searching for a clue as to when the dance would begin.

Outside everything was impenetrably quiet. Occasionally there was the muffled beat of a deep pueblo drum, the opening of a door, or the piercing of the night's darkness with a shaft of light. In the church where the dance was to take place a few white townsfolk were huddled together on a balcony, groping for some clue which would suggest how much longer they were going to suffer. "Last year I heard they started at ten o'clock." "They can't start until the priest comes." "There is no way of telling when they will start." All this punctuated by chattering teeth and the stamping of feet to keep up circulation.

Suddenly an Indian opened the door, entered, and poked up the fire in the stove. Everyone nudged his neighbor: "Maybe they are going to begin now." Another hour passed. Another Indian came in from outside, walked across the nave of the church, and disappeared through another door. "Certainly now they will begin. After all, it's almost two o'clock." Someone guessed that they were just being ornery in the hope that the white men would go away. Another had a friend in the pueblo and went to his house to ask when the dance would begin. Nobody knew. Suddenly, when the whites were almost exhausted, there burst upon the night the deep sounds of the drums, rattles, and low male voices singing. Without warning the dance had begun.

After years of performances such as this, no white man in his right mind will hazard a guess as to when one of these ceremonial dances will begin. Those of us who have learned now know that the dance doesn't start at a particular time. It is geared to no schedule. It starts when "things" are ready!

. . .

Thousands of miles away from the reservations of the American Indian we come to another way of handling time which is apt to be completely unsettling to the unprepared visitor. The inhabitants of the atoll of Truk in the Southwest Pacific treat time in a fashion that has complicaed life for themselves as well as for others, since it poses special problems not only for their civil and military governors and the anthropologists recording their life but for their own chiefs as well.

Time does not heal on Truk! Past events stack up, placing an ever-increasing burden on the Trukese and weighing heavily on the present. They are, in fact, treated as though they had just occurred. This was borne out by something which happened shortly after the American occupation of the atoll at the end of World War II.

A villager arrived all out of breath at the military government headquarters. He said that a murder had been committed in the village and that the murderer was running around loose. Quite naturally the military government officer became alarmed. He was about to dispatch M.P.s to arrest the culprit when he remembered that someone had warned him about acting precipitously when dealing with "natives." A little inquiry turned up the fact that the victim had been "fooling around" with the murderer's wife. Still more inquiry of a routine type, designed to establish the place and date of the crime, revealed that the murder had not occurred a few hours or even days ago, as one might expect, but seventeen years before. The murderer had been running around loose in the village all this time.

A further example of how time does not heal on Truk is that of a land dispute that started with the German occupation in the 1890's, was carried on down through the Japanese occupation, and was still current and acrimonious when the Americans arrived in 1946.

Prior to Missionary Moses' arrival on Uman in 1867 life on Truk was characterized by violent and bloody warfare. Villages, instead of being built on the shore where life was a little easier, were placed on the sides of mountains where they could be better protected. Attacks would come without notice and often without apparent provocation. Or a fight might start if a man stole a coconut from a tree that was not his or waylaid a woman and took advantage of her. Years later someone would start thinking about the wrong and decide that it still had not been righted. A village would be attacked again in the middle of the night.

When charges were brought against a chief for things he had done to his people, every little slight, every minor graft would be listed; nothing would be forgotten. Damages would be asked for everything. It seemed preposterous to us Americans, particularly when we looked at the lists of charges. "How could a chief be so corrupt?" "How could the people remember so much?"

Though the Truk islanders carry the accumulated burden of time past on their shoulders, they show an almost total inability to grasp the notion that two events can take place at the same time when they are any distance apart. When the Japanese occupied Truk at the end of World War I they took Artie Moses, chief of the island of Uman, to Tokyo. Artie was made to send a wireless message back to his people as a demonstration of the wizardry of Japanese technology. His family refused to believe that he had sent it, that he had said anything at all, though they knew he was in Tokyo. Places at a distance are very real to them, but people who are away are very much away, and any interaction with them is unthinkable.

An entirely different handling of time is reported by the anthropologist Paul Bohannan for the Tiv, a primitive people who live in Nigeria. Like the Navajo, they point to the sun to indicate a general time of day, and they also observe the movement of the moon as it waxes and wanes. What is different is the way they use and experience time. For the Tiv, time is like a capsule. There is a time for visiting, for cooking, or for working; and when one is in one of these times, one does not shift to another.

The Tiv equivalent of the week lasts five to seven days. It is not tied into periodic natural events, such as the phases of the moon. The day of the week is named after the things which are being sold in the nearest "market." If we had the equivalent, Monday would be "automobiles" in Washington, D.C., "furniture" in Baltimore, and "yard goods" in New York. Each of these might be followed by the days for appliances, liquor, and diamonds in the respective cities. This would mean that as you traveled about the day of the week would keep changing, depending on where you were.

A requisite of our own temporal system is that the components must add up: Sixty seconds have to equal one minute, sixty minutes one hour. The American is perplexed by people who do not do this. The African specialist Henri Alexandre Junod, reporting on the Thonga, tells of a medicine man who had memorized a seventy-year chronology and could detail the events of each and every year in sequence. Yet this same man spoke of the period he had memorized as an "era" which he computed at "four months and eight hundred years' duration." The usual reaction to this story and others like it is that the man was primitive, like a child, and did not understand what he was saying, because how could seventy years possibly be the same as eight hundred? As students of culture we can no longer dismiss other conceptualizations of reality by saying that they are childlike. We must go much deeper. In the case of the Thonga it seems that a "chronology" is one thing and an "era" something else quite different, and there is no relation between the two in operational terms.

If these distinctions between European-American time and other conceptions of time seem to draw too heavily on primitive peoples, let me mention two other examples—from cultures which are as civilized, if not as industrialized, as our own. In comparing the United States with Iran and Afghanistan very great differences in the handling of time appear. The American attitude toward appointments is an example. Once while in Tehran I had an opportunity to observe some young Iranians making plans for a party. After plans were made to pick up everyone at appointed times and places everything began to fall apart. People would leave messages that they were unable to take so-and-so or were going somewhere else, knowing full well that the person who had been given the message couldn't possibly deliver it. One girl was left stranded on a street corner, and no one seemed to be concerned about it. One of my informants explained that he himself had had many similar experiences. Once he had made eleven appointments to meet a friend. Each time one of them failed to show up. The twelfth time they swore they would both be there, that nothing would interfere. The friend failed to arrive. After waiting for forty-five minutes my informant phoned his friend and found him still at home. The following conversation is an approximation of what took place:

"Is that you, Abdul?" "Yes." "Why aren't you here? I thought we were to meet for sure." "Oh, but it was raining," said Abdul . . .

If present appointments are treated rather cavalierly, the past in Iran takes on a very great importance. People look back on what they feel are the wonders of the past and the great ages of Persian culture. Yet the future seems to have little reality or certainty to it. Businessmen have been known to invest hundreds of thousands of dollars in factories of various sorts without making the slightest plan as to how to use them. A complete woolen mill was bought and shipped to Tehran before the buyer had raised enough money to erect it, to buy supplies, or even to train personnel. When American teams of technicians came to help Iran's economy they constantly had to cope with what seemed to them an almost total lack of planning.

Moving east from Iran to Afghanistan, one gets farther afield from American time concepts. A few years ago in Kabul a man appeared, looking for his brother. He asked all the merchants of the market place if they had seen his brother and told them where he was staying in case his brother arrived and wanted to find him. The next year he was back and repeated the performance. By this time one of the members of the American embassy had heard about his inquiries and asked if he had found his brother. The man answered that he and his brother had agreed to meet in Kabul, but neither of them had said what year.

Strange as some of these stories about the ways in which people handle time may seem, they become understandable when they are correctly analyzed. . . . [This] will provide a key to unlock some of the secrets of the eloquent language of culture which speaks in so many different ways.

Body Ritual Among the Nacirema
Horace Miner

The anthropologist has become so familiar with the diversity of ways in which different peoples behave in similar situations that he is not apt to be surprised by even the most exotic customs. In fact, if all of the logically possible combinations of behavior have not been found somewhere in the world, he is apt to suspect that they must be present in some yet undescribed tribe. This point has, in fact, been expressed with respect to clan organization by Murdock

(1949:71). In this light, the magical beliefs and practices of the Nacirema present such unusual aspects that it seems desirable to describe them as an example of the extremes to which human behavior can go.

Professor Linton first brought the ritual of the Nacirema to the attention of anthropologists twenty years ago (1936:326), but the culture of this people is still very poorly understood. They are a North American group living in the territory between the Canadian Cree, the Yaqui and Tarahumare of Mexico, and the Carib and Arawak of the Antilles. Little is known of their origin, although tradition states that they came from the east. According to Nacirema mythology, their nation was originated by a culture hero, Notgnihsaw, who is otherwise known for two great feats of strength—the throwing of a piece of wampum across the river Pa-To-Mac and the chopping down of a cherry tree in which the Spirit of Truth resided.

Nacirema culture is characterized by a highly developed market economy which has evolved in a rich natural habitat. While much of the people's time is devoted to economic pursuits, a large part of the fruits of these labors and a considerable portion of the day are spent in ritual activity. The focus of this activity is the human body, the appearance and health of which loom as a dominant concern in the ethos of the people. While such a concern is certainly not unusual, its ceremonial aspects and associated philosophy are unique.

The fundamental belief underlying the whole system appears to be that the human body is ugly and that its natural tendency is to debility and disease. Incarcerated in such a body, man's only hope is to avert these characteristics through the use of the powerful influences of ritual and ceremony. Every household has one or more shrines devoted to this purpose. The more powerful individuals in the society have several shrines in their houses and, in fact, the opulence of a house is often referred to in terms of the number of such ritual centers it possesses. Most houses are of wattle and daub construction, but the shrine rooms of the more wealthy are walled with stone. Poorer families imitate the rich by applying pottery plaques to their shrine walls.

While each family has at least one such shrine, the rituals associated with it are not family ceremonies but are private and secret. The rites are normally only discussed with children, and then only during the period when they are being initiated into these mysteries. I was able, however, to establish sufficient rapport with the natives to examine these shrines and to have the rituals described to me.

The focal point of the shrine is a box or chest which is built into the wall. In this chest are kept the many charms and magical potions without which no native believes he could live. These preparations are secured from a variety of specialized practitioners. The most powerful of these are medicine men, whose assistance must be rewarded with substantial gifts. However, the medicine men do not provide the curative potions for their clients, but decide what the ingredients should be and then write them down in an ancient and secret language. This writing is understood only by the medicine men and by the herbalists who, for another gift, provide the required charm.

The charm is not disposed of after it has served its purpose, but is placed in the charm-box of the household shrine. As these magical materials are specific for certain ills, and the real or imagined maladies of the people are many, the charm-box is usually full to overflowing. The magical packets are so numerous that people forget what their purposes were and fear to use them again. While the natives are very vague on this point, we can only assume that the idea in retaining all the old magical materials is that their presence in the charm-box, before which the body rituals are conducted, will in some way protect the worshipper.

Beneath the charm-box is a small font. Each day every member of the family, in succession, enters the shrine room, bows his head before the charm-box, mingles different sorts of holy water in the font, and proceeds with a brief rite of ablution. The holy waters are secured from the Water Temple of the community, where the priests conduct elaborate ceremonies to make the liquid ritually pure.

In the hierarchy of magical practitioners, and below the medicine men in prestige, are specialists whose designation is best translated "holy-mouth-men." The Nacirema have an almost pathological horror of and fascination with the mouth, the condition of which is believed to have a supernatural influence on all social relationships. Were it not for the rituals of the mouth, they believe that their teeth would fall out, their gums bleed, their jaws shrink, their friends desert them, and their lovers reject them. They also believe that a strong relationship exists between oral and moral characteristics. For example, there is a ritual ablution of the mouth for children which is supposed to improve their moral fiber.

The daily body ritual performed by everyone includes a mouth-rite. Despite the fact that these people are so punctilious about care of the mouth, this rite involves a practice which strikes the uninitiated stranger as revolting. It was reported to me that the ritual consists of inserting a small bundle of hog hairs into the mouth, along with certain magical powders, and then moving the bundle in a highly formalized series of gestures.

In addition to the private mouth-rite, the people seek out a holy-mouth-man once or twice a year. These practitioners have an impressive set of paraphernalia, consisting of a variety of augers, awls, probes, and prods. The use of these objects in the exorcism of the evils of the mouth involves almost unbelievable ritual torture of the client. The holy-mouth-man opens the client's mouth and, using the above mentioned tools, enlarges any holes which decay may have created in the teeth. Magical materials are put into these holes. If there are no naturally occurring holes in the teeth, large sections of one or more teeth are gouged out so that the supernatural substance can be applied. In the client's view, the purpose of these ministrations is to arrest decay and to draw friends. The extremely sacred and traditional character of the rite is evident in the fact that the natives return to the holy-mouth-men year after year, despite the fact that their teeth continue to decay.

It is to be hoped that, when a thorough study of the Nacirema is made, there will be careful inquiry into the personality structure of these people. One has but to watch the gleam in the eye of a holy-mouth-man, as he jabs an awl into an exposed nerve, to suspect that a certain amount of sadism is involved. If this can be established, a very interesting pattern emerges, for most of the population shows definite masochistic tendencies. It was to these that Professor Linton referred in discussing a distinctive part of the daily body ritual which is performed only by men. This part of the rite involves scraping and lacerating the surface of the face with a sharp instrument. Special women's rites are performed only four times during each lunar month, but what they lack in frequency is made up in barbarity. As part of this ceremony, women bake their heads in small ovens for about an hour. The theoretically interesting point is that what seems to be a preponderantly masochistic people have developed sadistic specialists.

The medicine men have an imposing temple, or *latipso*, in every community of any size. The more elaborate ceremonies required to treat very sick patients can only be performed at this temple. These ceremonies involve not only the thaumaturge but a permanent group of vestal maidens who move sedately about the temple chambers in distinctive costume and headdress.

The *latipso* ceremonies are so harsh that it is phenomenal that a fair proportion of the really sick natives who enter the temple ever recover. Small children whose indoctrination is still incomplete have been known to resist attempts to take them to the temple because "that is where you go to die." Despite this fact, sick adults are not only willing but eager to undergo the protracted ritual purification, if they can afford to do so. No matter how ill the supplicant or how grave the emergency, the guardians of many temples will not admit a client if he cannot give a rich gift to the custodian. Even after one has gained admission and survived the ceremonies, the guardians will not permit the neophyte to leave until he makes still another gift.

The supplicant entering the temple is first stripped of all his or her clothes. In every-day life the Nacirema avoids exposure of his body and its natural functions. Bathing and excretory acts are performed only in the secrecy of the household shrine, where they are ritualized as part of the body-rites. Psychological shock results from the fact that body secrecy is suddenly lost upon entry into the *latipso*. A man, whose own wife has never seen him in an excretory act, suddenly finds himself naked and assisted by a vestal maiden while he performs his natural functions into a sacred vessel. This sort of ceremonial treatment is necessitated by the fact that the excreta are used by a diviner to ascertain the course and nature of the client's sickness. Female clients, on the other hand, find their naked bodies are subjected to the scrutiny, manipulation and prodding of the medicine men.

Few supplicants in the temple are well enough to do anything but lie on their hard beds. The daily ceremonies, like the rites of the holy-mouth-men, involve discomfort and torture. With ritual precision, the vestals awaken their miserable charges each dawn and roll them about on their beds of pain while performing ablutions, in the formal movements of which the maidens are highly trained. At other times they insert magic wands in the supplicant's mouth or force him to eat substances which are supposed to be healing. From time to time the medicine men come to their clients and jab magically treated needles into their flesh. The fact that these temple ceremonies may not cure, and may even kill the neophyte, in no way decreases the people's faith in the medicine men.

There remains one other kind of practitioner, known as a "listener." This witch-doctor has the power to exorcise the devils that lodge in the heads of people who have been bewitched. The Nacirema believe that parents bewitch their own children. Mothers are particularly suspected of putting a curse on children while teaching them the secret body rituals. The counter-magic of the witch-doctor is unusual in its lack of ritual. The patient simply tells the "listener" all his troubles and fears, beginning with the earliest difficulties he can remember. The memory displayed by the Nacirema in these exorcism sessions is truly remarkable. It is not uncommon for the patient to bemoan the rejection he felt being weaned as a babe, and a few individuals even see their troubles going back to the traumatic effects of their own birth.

In conclusion, mention must be made of certain practices which have their base in native esthetics but which depend upon the pervasive aversion to the natural body and its functions. There are ritual fasts to make fat people thin and ceremonial feasts to make thin people fat. Still other rites are used to make women's breasts larger if they are small, and smaller if they are large. General dissatisfaction with breast shape is symbolized in the fact that the ideal form is virtually outside the range of human variation. A few women afflicted with almost inhuman hypermammary development are so idolized that they make a handsome living by simply going from village to village and permitting the natives to stare at them for a fee.

Reference has already been made to the fact that excretory functions are ritualized, routinized, and relegated to secrecy. Natural reproductive functions are similarly distorted. Intercourse is taboo as a topic and scheduled as an act. Efforts are made to avoid pregnancy by the use of magical material or by limiting intercourse to certain phases of the moon. Conception is actually very infrequent. When pregnant, women dress so as to hide their condition. Parturition takes place in secret, without friends or relatives to assist, and the majority of women do not nurse their infants. ·

Our review of the ritual life of the Nacirema has certainly shown them to be a magic-ridden people. It is hard to understand how they have managed to exist so long under the burdens which they have imposed upon themselves. But even such exotic customs as these take on real meaning when they are viewed with the insight provided by Malinowski when he wrote (1948:70):

Looking from far and above, from our high places of safety in the developed civilization, it is easy to see all the crudity and irrelevance of magic. But without its power and guidance early man could not have mastered his practical difficulties as he has done, nor could man have advanced to the higher stages of civilization.

3 / Culture and the Concept of Normality

Introduction

It is obvious that there are great differences in behavior among people in the same society as well as great differences among societies. The fundamental problem posed in this chapter is how does one decide what constitutes typical or normal behavior within a group, and what does this imply about the concept of the abnormal? Anthropologists confront such questions in an acute form over and over again. Frequently their "gut reaction" to what they observe in the field is a queasy sensation known as "cultural shock." Some of this is based on the feeling that *much* of what they see is somehow atypical, abnormal, or downright "bad."

Take, for example, variations in drinking patterns. Though not all societies drink intoxicating beverages, in those that do there has evolved elaborate cultural patterns concerning appropriate and inappropriate contexts. There are also theories of why some individuals may drink outside appropriate bounds as defined by the culture. In our society we call such people "alcoholics" and have evolved an elaborate set of beliefs and myths as well as practices that are highly patterned in terms of our customary response to such people. In addition, culture even provides the pattern of behavior for the alcoholic himself. Group response to drinking varies widely over the world. For example, the Navaho frequently become aggressive and engage in fighting and other types of aggression when intoxicated. The Mixtec, on the other hand, drink themselves politely and cheerfully into insensibility while drinking in groups. Are these patterns equally normal?

Experiences such as vomiting also are highly culturally patterned. In our own society we view nausea and vomiting as undesirable and uncomfortable, and in both belief and practice we view it as an involuntary response having to do with our physical state. We may attribute it to something we ate or to some experience such as sea-sickness or air-sickness. Among the Zuñi vomiting is seen as pleasurable, and is under voluntary control. During special ceremonies in Zuñi, bowls are passed among the group and each person voluntarily vomits into the bowl and perceives the experience as pleasurable.

Benedict has provided one of the most insightful and sensitive studies on the variety among societies as to what is defined as abnormal behavior on the part of the individual. Her contribution focuses much more on psychological characteristics of groups and individuals. She documents the important point that what might be judged as abnormal or psychotic behavior in one context may be seen as normal and appropriate behavior in another culture context. She goes through a variety of behaviors that have sometimes been thought of as abnormal such as trance, catalepsy, divination, homosexuality, acquisitiveness, aggressiveness, etc. In the variety of cultures that she examines she shows that each of these behaviors may be viewed from a perspective that would define them either as normal and appropriate or as abnormal and inappropriate.

One pervasive theme of Benedict's article, in accord with the anthropological notion of "cultural relativity," is that prior to the careful study of a particular group, we cannot assume *anything* about either the substantive definition of abnormality or the response to it on the part of the group. There is no physical or mental state that qualifies as absolutely abnormal in a cross-cultural survey. By implication, one possible concept of normality that can be applied cross-culturally is a statistical one, empty of specific descriptors and free from value-judgments. That is, studying a particular community one could describe as "normal" (or "most normal") that which is observed most often—the most common occupation, the most usual way of obtaining a spouse, etc. By contrast, the "less normal," is definable as the least common behaviors— whatever form they may take and irrespective of whether they are approved of by either the anthropologist or his informants.

Benedict's carefully-considered position includes the notion of "abnormals of extreme fulfillment of the cultural type"; that is, persons whose behavior and status fall at the "upper" extreme of their societies, according to the local valuation of them. Though they play conspicuous and, often, useful roles in their societies, they are as abnormal as those at the very bottom of the social order, statistically speaking.

There is a recurrent motif in Western history and literature to the effect that there may be dynamic affinities between the "lowest" and "highest" extremes of behavior that go far beyond mere similarity in terms of their respective frequencies. Hence, for example, there is the phenomenon of persons who pass "from rags to riches" and, sometimes, back to rags again; or those who, like Augustine, leap from the status of great sinner to that of a great saint.

The second article in this chapter, an excerpt from an essay by the French social anthropologist, Claude Lévi-Strauss, provides considerable insight into the psyche of an honored abnormal. Lévi-Strauss analyzes the sequence of events which leads Quesalid from an initial cynical and contemptuous opinion of *shamanism*, and of the "tricks" that he himself uses as an apprentice, to a gradual "conversion" to a crusader's zeal on behalf of his calling. In part, then, it is a processual analysis of a man's passing from a very low to a very high evaluation of himself and his profession. But it is also clear that even in mid-career Quesalid was still acutely aware that only a very fine line separates an honorable practice from a damnable one, great success from shameful failure. Incidentally, Quesalid was a Kwakiutl, so the epic and sometimes tragic events recounted from his career took place in the dramatic social setting sketched by Benedict for the Kwakiutl.

There is another major theme in the Lévi-Strauss article which, to a certain extent, runs counter to an incidental comment by Benedict. She comments about the possibility that persons "sham" or "simulate" abnormal behavior when such behavior is rewarded. Though the comment, in context, is qualified, it does hint of ethnocentric values that crop up often in Westerners' accounts of outstanding individuals—particularly of shamans, magicians and other esoteric practitioners.

A Western analyst may concentrate on, and deplore, the "tricks" used by a shaman in more serious circumstances without realizing that the shift in circumstances may give such tricks merely a secondary, supporting role in the proceedings. This is roughly comparable to treating a Western physician's "bedside manner," also a body of learned psychological techniques, as though it were a straightforward, exploitative "con job."

Parker's study of the wiitiko psychosis, which he characterizes as "a bizarre form of mental disorder involving obsessive cannibalism," illustrates another of the novel implications of the conception of behaviors as falling along an uninterrupted continuum. As Parker puts it, his analysis of certain typical features of Ojibwa personality and cultural setting is intended to "yield a view of the wiitiko psychosis, not as a complete and qualitative departure from normal personality, but as an outgrowth . . . from it." (Compare this with the description, in the preceding chapter, of the Yąnomamö, among whom a "normal" wife-beating may lapse into homicide.)

Parker's approach is similar to that of Freud, who was one of the first to insist that there is, indeed, "method in madness," that the components of gross psychopathology are simply exaggerated manifestations of the minor, manageable psychopathologies of everyday life in a Western society. However, there is a fundamental difference in "cultural phrasing," in focal subject matter, between the Western and the Ojibwa settings. The strong emotional ambivalence, the taboos and anxieties which attach to *sexuality* in our society are centered, instead, upon the obtaining and eating of *food* among the Ojibwa.

Parker pursues his multi-faceted analysis through details of child-rearing and sex role training, political and economic organization, and other features of Ojibwa culture and ecology. We note, in particular, the presence of a series of myths and fairy tales that are grim indeed. These shared cannibalistic fantasies and the knowledge that they have been acted out in the past provide the Ojibwa with an explicit pattern for behaving when normal patterns fail.

Examples so far include concepts of normality and abnormality in cases where the contrasts are fairly sharp and where the abnormal behavior in question is considered definitive of the person (as *being* a shaman, a wiitiko, etc.). But there are many occurrences which temporarily interrupt a person's normal behavior without necessarily causing him to be redefined as generally abnormal. Transitory conditions of illness or disablement, mourning, anxiety about bewitchment and the like, elicit responses from the community that give the anthropologist further information about the restorative and preventive resources available for adapting to day-to-day exigencies. Since such conditions sometimes, through persistence or repetition, "escalate" from the status of nearly-normal to chronically abnormal, the observer may see acted out a whole series of interactions which would not be likely to come up in conversations with informants.

There are illustrations of such responses in many of the readings in this book. Among the most fully-developed are those by O'Nell and Selby (Chapter Four: illness), Dole (Chapter Six: mourning), Evans-Pritchard (Chapter Seven: misfortune), and Beattie (Chapter Eight: family dispute). The next two articles in this chapter—both drawn from Mexican community studies—focus on illness from two perspectives.

Romney and Romney provide a cultural inventory of the wide variety of beliefs and behaviors available to the members of a Mixtec Indian community for preventing, counteracting, describing, and explaining a range of ailments. One primary function of folk medical concepts and terminologies is simply that of providing a familiar name and explanation for every ailment encountered, thereby reassuring the sufferer and others that treatment is feasible and, in fact, already begun in the act of diagnosis.

The article illustrates clearly two features characteristic of non-Western medical traditions. One of these is common to both primitive and peasant outlooks; namely, the fact that what we distinguish as organic diseases vs. psychological disturbances are not sharply distinguished or not distinguished along the same lines.

The second feature has to do with the "layer cake" composition of the system, built up from beliefs and practices from a variety of other traditions. In this article, we find such juxtapositions as the following: (1) aboriginal Mesoamerican beliefs and practices involving the use of the sweat bath; (2) Renaissance (Conquest) Hispanic usages, such as the hot/cold conceptual scheme; (3) West African (via West Indies) influences, represented by doll-and-pin sorcery; and (4) modern Western medicines and practices. Such layering is usually most evident in peasant communities; though it is safe to assume that the same kinds of borrowing, generally on a smaller scale and at a slower rate, occur in primitive societies as well. It should be added that the members of a community do not seem to feel that these elements are incongruous with one another (as, say, a Western physician would).

Fabrega and Metzger narrow their focus specifically to a study of psychological disturbances, as they are conceptualized and treated in a small Hispanic community in southern Mexico. They note that the local system of beliefs and practices is maintained not merely because it "is flexible enough to include all kinds of disturbances encountered," but also because members of the community have occasion to see their most influential representatives apply the system in specific cases. Such acts reaffirm the validity of the system from time to time.

They also emphasize another finding which would hold true of virtually all small non-Western (or, in this case, slightly-Westernized) communities; namely, that private misfortunes such as illness rapidly become matters of public concern and action. In their conclusion Fabrega and Metzger point out that this supportive response by the group—as contrasted with the traditional Western practice of isolating the physically and mentally ill—accords with the goals of modern psychiatry. And, in fact, anthropologists working in other communities have, on occasion, discovered practices which seemed to them somewhat in advance of Western psychiatric beliefs and practices.

Edgerton and MacAndrew in the final selection of the chapter, entitled "The Possibility of Friendship," provide a particularly interesting example of a dyadic relationship that includes people who are thought of as abnormal. It is a poignant case study in situational relativity—this time in a special subcultural niche (the mental institution) that contrasts sharply with the general U.S. culture that surrounds it. Under these circumstances a variety of interpersonal relationship which we think of as common and basic to normal human relationships—namely, friendship—stands out as an exception to the behavioral norms of the institution.

Anthropology and the Abnormal
Ruth Benedict

Modern social anthropology has become more and more a study of the varieties and common elements of cultural environment and the consequences of these in human behavior. For such a study of diverse social orders primitive peoples fortunately provide a laboratory not yet entirely vitiated by the spread of a standardized worldwide civilization. Dyaks and Hopis, Fijians and Yakuts are significant for psychological and sociological study because only among these simpler peoples has there been sufficient isolation to give opportunity for the development of localized social forms. In the higher cultures the standardization of custom and belief over a couple of continents has given a false sense of the inevitability of the particular forms that have gained currency, and we need to turn to a wider survey in order to check the conclusions we hastily base upon this near-universality of familiar customs. Most of the simpler cultures did not gain the wide currency of the one which, out of our experience, we identify with human nature, but this was for various historical reasons, and certainly not for any that gives us as its carriers a monopoly of social good or of social sanity. Modern civilization, from this point of view, becomes not a necessary pinnacle of human achievement but one entry in a long series of possible adjustments.

These adjustments, whether they are in mannerisms like the ways of showing anger, or joy, or grief in any society, or in major human drives like those of sex, prove to be far more variable than experience in any one culture would suggest. In certain fields, such as that of religion or of formal marriage arrangements, these wide limits of variability are well known and can be fairly described. In others it is not yet possible to give a generalized account, but that does not absolve us of the task of indicating the significance of the work that has been done and of the problems that have arisen.

One of these problems relates to the customary modern normal-abnormal categories and our conclusions regarding them. In how far are such categories culturally determined, or in how far can we with assurance regard them as absolute? In how far can we regard inability to function socially as diagnostic of abnormality, or in how far is it necessary to regard this as a function of the culture?

As a matter of fact, one of the most striking facts that emerge from a study of widely varying cultures is the ease with which our abnormals function in other cultures. It does not matter what kind of "abnormality" we choose for illustration, those which indicate extreme instability, or those which are more in the nature of character traits like sadism or delusions of grandeur or of persecution, there are well-described cultures in which these abnormals function at ease and with honor, and apparently without danger or difficulty to the society.

The most notorious of these is trance and catalepsy. Even a very mild mystic is aberrant in our culture. But most peoples have regarded even extreme psychic manifestations not only as normal and desirable, but even as characteristic of highly valued and gifted individuals. This was true even in our own cultural background in that period when Catholicism made the ecstatic experience the mark of sainthood. It is hard for us, born and brought up in a culture that makes no use of the experience, to realize how important a role it may play and how many individuals are capable of it, once it has been given an honorable place in any society.

Some of the Indian tribes of California accorded prestige principally to those who passed through certain trance experiences. Not all of these tribes believed that it was exclusively women who were so blessed, but among the Shasta (10) this was the convention. Their shamans were women, and they were accorded the greatest prestige in the community. They were chosen because of their constitutional liability to trance and allied manifestations. One day the woman who was so destined, while she was about her usual work, would fall suddenly to the ground. She had heard a voice speaking to her in tones of the greatest intensity. Turning, she had seen a man with drawn bow and arrow. He commanded her to sing on pain of being shot through the heart by his arrow, but under the stress of the experience she fell senseless. Her family gathered. She was lying rigid, hardly breathing. They knew that for some time she had had dreams of a special character which indicated a shamanistic calling, dreams of escaping grizzly bears, falling off cliffs or trees, or of being surrounded by swarms of yellow jackets. The community knew therefore what to expect. After a few hours the woman began to moan gently and to roll about upon the ground, trembling violently. She was supposed to be repeating the song which she had been told to sing and which during the trance had been taught her by the spirit. As she revived her moaning became more and more clearly the spirit's song until at last she called out the name of the spirit itself, and immediately blood oozed from her mouth.

When the woman had come to herself after the first encounter with her spirit she danced that night her first initiatory shamanistic dance, holding herself by a rope that was swung from the ceiling. For three nights she danced, and on the third night she had to receive in her body her power from her spirit. She was dancing, and as she felt the approach of the moment she called out, "He will shoot me, he will shoot me." Her friends stood close, for when she reeled in a kind of cataleptic seizure, they had to seize her before she fell or she would die. From this time on she had in her body a visible materialization of her spirit's power, an icicle-like object which in her dances thereafter she would exhibit, producing it from one part of her body and returning it to another part. From this time on she continued to validate her supernatural power by further cataleptic demonstrations, and she was called upon in great emergencies of life and death, for curing and for divination and for counsel. She became in other words by this procedure a woman of great power and importance.[1]

It is clear that, so far from regarding cataleptic seizures as blots upon the family escutcheon and as evidences of dreaded disease, cultural approval had

---

[1] In all cultures behavior which is socially rewarded attracts persons who are attracted by the possibility of leadership, and such individuals may simulate the required behavior. This is as true when society rewards prodigality as when it rewards catalepsy. For the present argument the amount of shamming is not considered though it is of obvious importance. It is a matter which cultures standardize quite as much as they standardize the type of rewarded behavior.

seized upon them and made of them the pathway to authority over one's fellows. They were the outstanding characteristic of the most respected social type, the type which functioned with most honor and reward in the community. It was precisely the cataleptic individuals who in this culture were singled out for authority and leadership.

The availability of "abnormal" types in the social structure, provided they are types that are culturally selected by that group, is illustrated from every part of the world. The shamans of Siberia dominate their communities. According to the ideas of these peoples, they are individuals who by submission to the will of the spirits have been cured of a grievous illness—the onset of the seizures—and have acquired by this means great supernatural power and incomparable vigor and health. Some, during the period of the call, are violently insane for several years, others irresponsible to the point where they have to be watched constantly lest they wander off in the snow and freeze to death, others ill and emaciated to the point of death, sometimes with bloody sweat. It is the shamanistic practice which constitutes their cure, and the extreme physical exertion of a Siberian seance leaves them, they claim, rested and able to enter immediately upon a similar performance. Cataleptic seizures are regarded as an essential part of any shamanistic performance (8).

A good description of the neurotic condition of the shaman and the attention given him by his society is an old one by Canon Callaway (6, pp. 259 ff.) recorded in the words of an old Zulu of South Africa:

The condition of a man who is about to become a diviner is this; at first he is apparently robust, but in the process of time he begins to be delicate, not having any real disease, but being delicate. He habitually avoids certain kinds of food, choosing what he likes, and he does not eat much of that; he is continually complaining of pains in different parts of his body. And he tells them that he has dreamt that he was carried away by a river. He dreams of many things, and his body is muddied (as a river) and he becomes a house of dreams. He dreams constantly of many things, and on awaking tells his friends, 'My body is muddied today; I dreamt many men were killing me, and I escaped I know not how. On waking one part of my body felt different from other parts; it was no longer alike all over.' At last that man is very ill, and they go to the diviners to enquire.

The diviners do not at once see that he is about to have a soft head (that is, the sensitivity associated with shamanism). It is difficult for them to see the truth; they continually talk nonsense and make false statements, until all the man's cattle are devoured at their command, they saying that the spirit of his people demands cattle, that it may eat food. At length all the man's property is expended, he still being ill; and they no longer know what to do, for he has no more cattle, and his friends help him in such things as he needs.

At length a diviner comes and says that all the others are wrong. He says, 'He is possessed by the spirits. There is nothing else. They move in him, being divided into two parties; some say, "No, we do not wish our child injured. We do not wish it." It is for that reason he does not get well. If you bar the way against the spirits, you will be killing him. For he will not be a diviner; neither will he ever be a man again.'

So the man may be ill two years without getting better; perhaps even longer than that. He is confined to his house. This continues till his hair falls off. And his body is dry and scurfy; he does not like to anoint himself. He shows that he is about to be a diviner by yawning again and again, and by sneezing continually. It is apparent also from his being very fond of snuff; not allowing any long time to pass without taking some. And people begin to see that he has had what is good given to him.

After that he is ill; he has convulsions, and when water has been poured on him they then cease for a time. He habitually sheds tears, at first slight, then at last he weeps aloud and when the people are asleep he is heard making a noise and wakes the people by his singing; he has composed a song, and the men and women awake and go to sing in concert with him. All the people of the village are troubled by want of sleep; for a man who is becoming a diviner causes great trouble, for he does not sleep, but works constantly with his brain; his sleep is merely by snatches, and he wakes up singing many songs; and people who are near quit their villages by night when they hear him singing aloud and go to sing in concert. Perhaps he sings till morning, no one having slept. And then he leaps about the house like a frog; and the house becomes too small for him, and he goes out leaping and singing, and shaking like a reed in the water, and dripping with perspiration.

In this state of things they daily expect his death; he is now but skin and bones, and they think that tomorrow's sun will not leave him alive. At this time many cattle are eaten, for the people encourage his becoming a diviner. At length (in a dream) an ancient ancestral spirit is pointed out to him. This spirit says to him, 'Go to So-and-so and he will churn for you an emetic (the medicine the drinking of which is a part of shamanistic initiation) that you may be a diviner altogether.' Then he is quiet a few days, having gone to the diviner to have the medicine churned for him; and he comes back quite another man, being now cleansed and a diviner indeed.

Thereafter for life when he achieves possession, he foretells events, and finds lost articles.

It is clear that culture may value and make socially available even highly unstable human types. If it chooses to treat their peculiarities as the most valued variants of human behavior, the individuals in question will rise to the occasion and perform their social roles without reference to our usual ideas of the types who can make social adjustments and those who cannot.

Cataleptic and trance phenomena are, of course, only one illustration of the fact that those whom we regard as abnormals may function adequately in other cultures. Many of our culturally discarded traits are selected for elaboration in different societies. Homosexuality is an excellent example, for in this case our attention is not constantly diverted, as in the consideration of trance, to the interruption of routine activity which it implies. Homosexuality poses the problem very simply. A tendency toward this trait in our culture exposes an individual to all the conflicts to which all aberrants are always exposed, and we tend to identify the consequences of this conflict with homosexuality. But these consequences are obviously local and cultural. Homosexuals in many societies are not incompetent, but they may be such if the culture asks adjustments of them that would strain any man's vitality. Wherever homosexuality has been given an honorable place in any society, those to whom it is congenial have filled adequately the honorable roles society assigns to them. Plato's *Republic* is, of course, the most convincing statement of such a reading of homosexuality. It is presented as one of the major means to the good life, and it was generally so regarded in Greece at that time.

The cultural attitude toward homosexuals has not always been on such a high ethical plane, but it has been very varied. Among many American Indian tribes there exists the institution of the berdache (12, 15), as the French called them. These men-women were men who at puberty or thereafter took the dress and the occupations of women. Sometimes they married other men and lived with them. Sometimes they were men with no inversion, persons of weak sexual endowment who chose this role to avoid the jeers of the women. The berdaches were never regarded as of first-rate supernatural power, as similar men-women were in Siberia, but rather as leaders in women's occupations, good healers in certain diseases, or, among certain tribes, as the genial organizers of social affairs. In any case, they were socially placed. They were not left exposed to the conflicts that visit the deviant who is excluded from participation in the recognized patterns of his society.

The most spectacular illustrations of the extent to which normality may be culturally defined are those cultures where an abnormality of our culture is the cornerstone of their social structure. It is not possible to do justice to these possibilities in a short discussion. A recent study of an island of northwest Melanesia by Fortune (11) describes a society built upon traits which we regard as beyond the border of paranoia. In this tribe the exogamic groups look upon each other as prime manipulators of black magic, so that one marries always into an enemy group which remains for life one's deadly and unappeasable foes. They look upon a good garden crop as a confession of theft, for everyone is engaged in making magic to induce into his garden the productiveness of his neighbors'; therefore no secrecy in the island is so rigidly insisted upon as the secrecy of a man's harvesting of his yams. Their polite phrase at the acceptance of a gift is, "And if you now poison me, how shall I repay you this present?" Their preoccupation with poisoning is constant; no woman ever leaves her cooking pot for a moment untended. Even the great affinal economic exchanges that are characteristic of this Melanesian culture area are quite altered in Dobu since they are incompatible with this fear and distrust that pervades the culture. They go farther and people the whole world outside their own quarters with such malignant spirits that all-night feasts and ceremonials simply do not occur here. They have even rigorous religiously enforced customs that forbid the sharing of seed even in one family group. Anyone else's food is deadly poison to you, so that communality of stores is out of the question. For some months before harvest the whole society is on the verge of starvation, but if one falls to the temptation and eats up one's seed yams, one is an outcast and a beachcomber for life. There is no coming back. It involves, as a matter of course, divorce and the breaking of all social ties.

Now in this society where no one may work with another and no one may share with another, Fortune describes the individual who was regarded by all his fellows as crazy. He was not one of those who periodically ran amok and, beside himself and frothing at the mouth, fell with a knife upon anyone he could reach. Such behavior they did not regard as putting anyone outside the pale. They did not even put the individuals who were known to be liable to these attacks under any kind of control. They merely fled when they saw the attack coming on and kept out of the way. "He would be all right tomorrow." But there was one man of sunny, kindly disposition who liked work and liked to be helpful. The compulsion was too strong for him to repress it in favor of the opposite tendencies of his culture. Men and women never spoke of him without laughing; he was silly and simple and definitely crazy. Nevertheless, to the ethnologist used to a culture that has, in Christianity, made his type the model of all virtue, he seemed a pleasant fellow.

An even more extreme example, because it is of a culture that has built itself upon a more complex abnormality, is that of the North Pacific Coast of North America. The civilization of the Kwakiutl (1–5), at the time when it was first recorded in the last decades of the nineteenth century, was one of the most vigorous in North America. It was built up on an ample economic supply of goods, the fish which furnished their food staple being practically inexhaustible and obtainable with comparatively small labor, and the wood which furnished the material for their houses, their furnishings, and their arts being, with however much labor, always procurable. They lived in coastal villages that compared favorably in size with those of any other American Indians and they kept up constant communication by means of sea-going dug-out canoes.

It was one of the most vigorous and zestful of the aboriginal cultures of North America, with complex crafts and ceremonials, and elaborate and striking arts. It certainly had none of the earmarks of a sick civilization. The tribes of the Northwest Coast had wealth, and exactly in our terms. That is, they had not only a surplus of economic goods, but they made a game of the manipulation of wealth. It was by no means a mere direct transcription of economic needs and the filling of those needs. It involved the idea of capital, of interest, and of conspicuous waste. It was a game with all the binding rules of a game, and a person entered it as a child. His father distributed wealth for him, according to his ability, at a small feast or potlatch, and each gift the receiver was obliged to accept and to return after a short interval with interest that ran to about 100 per cent a year. By the time the child was grown, therefore, he was well launched, a larger potlatch had been given for him on various occasions of exploit or initiation, and he had wealth either out at usury or in his own possession. Nothing in the civilization could be enjoyed without validating it by the distribution of this wealth. Everything that was valued, names and songs as well as material objects, were passed down in family lines, but they were always publicly assumed with accompanying sufficient distributions of property. It was the game of validating and exercising all the privileges one could accumulate from one's various forbears, or by gift, or by marriage, that made the chief interest of the culture. Everyone in his degree took part in it, but many, of course, mainly as spectators. In its highest form it was played out between rival chiefs representing not only themselves and their family lines but their communities, and the object of the contest was to glorify oneself and to humiliate one's opponent. On this level of greatness the property involved was no longer represented by blankets, so many thousand of them to a potlatch, but by higher units of value. These higher units were like our bank notes. They were incised copper tablets, each of them named, and having a value that depended upon their illustrious history. This was as high as ten thousand blankets, and to possess one of them, still more to enhance its value at a great potlatch, was one of the greatest glories within the compass of the chiefs of the Northwest Coast.

The details of this manipulation of wealth are in many ways a parody on our own economic arrangements, but it is with the motivations that were recognized in this contest that we are concerned in this discussion. The drives were those which in our own culture we should call megalomaniac. There was an uncensored self-glorification and ridicule of the opponent that it is hard to equal in other cultures outside of the monologues of the abnormal. Any of the songs and speeches of their chiefs at a potlatch illustrate the usual tenor:

Wa, out of the way. Wa, out of the way. Turn your faces that I may give way to my anger by striking my fellow chiefs.

Wa, great potlatch, greatest potlatch.[2] The little ones[3] only pretend, the little stubborn ones, they only sell one copper again and again and give it away to the little chiefs of the tribe.

Ah, do not ask in vain for mercy. Ah, do not ask in vain for mercy and raise your hands, you with lolling tongues! I shall break,[4] I shall let disappear the great copper that has the name Kentsegum, the property of the great foolish one, the great extravagant one, the great surpassing one, the one farthest ahead, the great Cannibal dancer among chiefs.[5]

I am the great chief who makes people ashamed.
I am the great chief who makes people ashamed.
Our chief brings shame to the faces.
Our chief brings jealousy to the faces.
Our chief makes people cover their faces by what he is continually doing in this world, from the beginning to the end of the year,
Giving again and again oil feasts to the tribes.

I am the great chief who vanquishes.
I am the great chief who vanquishes.
Only at those who continue running round and round in this world, working hard, losing their tails,[6] I sneer, at the chiefs below the true chief.[7]
Have mercy on them![8] Put oil on their dry heads with brittle hair, those who do not comb their hair!
I sneer at the chiefs below the true, real chief. I am the great chief who makes people ashamed.

I am the only great tree, I the chief.
I am the only great tree, I the chief.
You are my subordinates, tribes.
You sit in the middle of the rear of the house, tribes.
Bring me your counter of property, tribes, that he may in vain try to count what is going to be given away by the great copper-maker, the chief.
Oh, I laugh at them, I sneer at them who empty boxes[9] in their houses, their potlatch houses, their inviting houses that are full only of hunger. They follow along after me like young sawbill ducks. I am the only great tree, I the chief.

[2] The feast he is now engaged in giving.
[3] His opponents.
[4] To break a copper, showing in this way how far one rose above even the most superlatively valuable things, was the final mark of greatness.
[5] Himself.
[6] As salmon do.
[7] Himself.
[8] Irony, of course.
[9] Of treasure.

I have quoted a number of these hymns of self-glorification because by an association which psychiatrists will recognize as fundamental these delusions of grandeur were essential in the paranoid view of life which was so strikingly developed in this culture. All of existence was seen in terms of insult.[10] Not only derogatory acts performed by a neighbor or an enemy, but all untoward events, like a cut when one's axe slipped, or a ducking when one's canoe overturned, were insults. All alike threatened first and foremost one's ego security, and the first thought one was allowed was how to get even, how to wipe out the insult. Grief was little institutionalized, but sulking took its place. Until he had resolved upon a course of action by which to save his face after any misfortune, whether it was the slipping of a wedge in felling a tree, or the death of a favorite child, an Indian of the Northwest Coast retired to his pallet with his face to the wall and neither ate nor spoke. He rose from it to follow out some course which according to the traditional rules should reinstate him in his own eyes and those of the community: to distribute property enough to wipe out the stain, or to go head-hunting in order that somebody else should be made to mourn. His activities in neither case were specific responses to the bereavement he had just passed through, but were elaborately directed toward getting even. If he had not the money to distribute and did not succeed in killing someone to humiliate another, he might take his own life. He had staked everything, in his view of life, upon a certain picture of the self, and, when the bubble of his self-esteem was pricked, he had no interest, no occupation to fall back on, and the collapse of his inflated ego left him prostrate.

Every contingency of life was dealt with in these two traditional ways. To them the two were equivalent. Whether one fought with weapons or "fought with property," as they say, the same idea was at the bottom of both. In the olden times, they say, they fought with spears, but now they fight with property. One overcomes one's opponents in equivalent fashion in both, matching forces and seeing that one comes out ahead, and one can thumb one's nose at the vanquished rather more satisfactorily at a potlatch than on a battle field. Every occasion in life was noticed, not in its own terms, as a stage in the sex life of the individual or as a climax of joy or of grief, but as furthering this drama of consolidating one's own prestige and bringing shame to one's guests. Whether it was the occasion of the birth of a child, or a daughter's adolescence, or of the marriage of one's son, they were all equivalent raw material for the culture to use for this one traditionally selected end. They were all to raise one's own personal status and to entrench oneself by the humiliation of one's fellows. A girl's adolescence among the Nootka (16) was an event for which her father gathered property from the time she was first able to run about. When she was adolescent he would demonstrate his greatness by an unheard of distribution of these goods, and put down all his rivals. It was not as a fact of the girl's sex life that it figured in their culture, but as the occasion for a major move in the great game of vindicating one's own greatness and humiliating one's associates.

In their behavior at great bereavements this set of the culture comes out most strongly. Among the Kwakiutl it did not matter whether a relative had died in bed of disease, or by the hand of an enemy, in either case death was an affront to be wiped out by the death of another person. The fact that one had been

[10]Insult is used here in reference to the intense susceptibility to shame that is conspicuous in this culture. All possible contingencies were interpreted as rivalry situations, and the gamut of emotions swung between triumph and shame.

caused to mourn was proof that one had been put upon. A chief's sister and her daughter had gone up to Victoria, and either because they drank bad whiskey or because their boat capsized they never came back. The chief called together his warriors. "Now I ask you, tribes, who shall wail? Shall I do it or shall another?" The spokesman answered, of course, "Not you, Chief. Let some other of the tribes." Immediately they set up the war pole to announce their intention of wiping out the injury, and gathered a war party. They set out, and found seven men and two children asleep and killed them. "Then they felt good when they arrived at Sebaa in the evening."

The point which is of interest to us is that in our society those who on that occasion would feel good when they arrived at Sebaa that evening would be the definitely abnormal. There would be some, even in our society, but it is not a recognized and approved mood under the circumstances. On the Northwest Coast those are favored and fortunate to whom that mood under those circumstances is congenial, and those to whom it is repugnant are unlucky. This latter minority can register in their own culture only by doing violence to their congenial responses and acquiring others that are difficult for them. . . .

· · ·

Behavior honored upon the Northwest Coast is one which is recognized as abnormal in our civilization, and yet it is sufficiently close to the attitudes of our own culture to be intelligible to us and to have a definite vocabulary with which we may discuss it. The megalomaniac paranoid trend is a definite danger in our society. It is encouraged by some of our major preoccupations, and it confronts us with a choice of two possible attitudes. One is to brand it as abnormal and reprehensible, and is the attitude we have chosen in our civilization. The other is to make it an essential attribute of ideal man, and this is the solution in the culture of the Northwest Coast.

These illustrations, which it has been possible to indicate only in the briefest manner, force upon us the fact that normality is culturally defined. An adult shaped to the drives and standards of either of these cultures, if he were transported into our civilization, would fall into our categories of abnormality. He would be faced with the psychic dilemmas of the socially unavailable. In his own culture, however, he is the pillar of society, the end result of socially inculcated mores, and the problem of personal instability in his case simply does not arise.

No one civilization can possibly utilize in its mores the whole potential range of human behavior. Just as there are great numbers of possible phonetic articulations, and the possibility of language depends on a selection and standardization of a few of these in order that speech communication may be possible at all, so the possibility of organized behavior of every sort, from the fashions of local dress and houses to the dicta of a people's ethics and religion, depends upon a similar selection among the possible behavior traits. In the field of recognized economic obligations or sex tabus this selection is as nonrational and subconscious a process as it is in the field of phonetics. It is a process which goes on in the group for long periods of time and is historically conditioned by innumerable accidents of isolation or of contact of peoples. In any comprehensive study of psychology, the selection that different cultures have made in the course of history within the great circumference of potential behavior is of great significance.

Every society,[11] beginning with some slight inclination in one direction or another, carries its preference farther and farther, integrating itself more and more completely upon its chosen basis, and discarding those types of behavior that are uncongenial. Most of those organizations of personality that seem to us most incontrovertibly abnormal have been used by different civilizations in the very foundations of their institutional life. Conversely the most valued traits of our normal individuals have been looked on in differently organized cultures as aberrant. Normality, in short, within a very wide range, is culturally defined. It is primarily a term for the socially elaborated segment of human behavior in any culture; and abnormality, a term for the segment that that particular civilization does not use. The very eyes with which we see the problem are conditioned by the long traditional habits of our own society.

It is a point that has been made more often in relation to ethics than in relation to psychiatry. We do not any longer make the mistake of deriving the morality of our own locality and decade directly from the inevitable constitution of human nature. We do not elevate it to the dignity of a first principle. We recognize that morality differs in every society, and is a convenient term for socially approved habits. Mankind has always preferred to say, "It is morally good," rather than "It is habitual," and the fact of this preference is matter enough for a critical science of ethics. But historically the two phrases are synonymous.

The concept of the normal is properly a variant of the concept of the good. It is that which society has approved. A normal action is one which falls well within the limits of expected behavior for a particular society. Its variability among different peoples is essentially a function of the variability of the behavior patterns that different societies have created for themselves, and can never be wholly divorced from a consideration of culturally institutionalized types of behavior.

Each culture is a more or less elaborate working-out of the potentialities of the segment it has chosen. In so far as a civilization is well integrated and consistent within itself, it will tend to carry farther and farther, according to its nature, its initial impulse toward a particular type of action, and from the point of view of any other culture those elaborations will include more and more extreme and aberrant traits.

Each of these traits, in proportion as it reinforces the chosen behavior patterns of that culture, is for that culture normal. Those individuals to whom it is congenial either congenitally, or as the result of childhood sets, are accorded prestige in that culture, and are not visited with the social contempt or disapproval which their traits would call down upon them in a society that was differently organized. On the other hand, those individuals whose characteristics are not congenial to the selected type of human behavior in that community are the deviants, no matter how valued their personality traits may be in a contrasted civilization.

The Dobuan who is not easily susceptible to fear of treachery, who enjoys work and likes to be helpful, is their neurotic and regarded as silly. On the Northwest Coast the person who finds it difficult to read life in terms of an insult contest will be the person upon whom fall all the difficulties of the cul-

[11]This phrasing of the process is deliberately animistic. It is used with no reference to a group mind or a superorganic, but in the same sense in which it is customary to say, "Every art has its own canons."

turally unprovided for. The person who does not find it easy to humiliate a neighbor, nor to see humiliation in his own experience, who is genial and loving, may, of course, find some unstandardized way of achieving satisfactions in his society, but not in the major patterned responses that his culture requires of him. If he is born to play an important role in a family with many hereditary privileges, he can succeed only by doing violence to his whole personality. If he does not succeed, he has betrayed his culture; that is, he is abnormal.

I have spoken of individuals as having sets toward certain types of behavior, and of these sets as running sometimes counter to the types of behavior which are institutionalized in the culture to which they belong. From all that we know of contrasting cultures it seems clear that differences of temperament occur in every society. The matter has never been made the subject of investigation, but from the available material it would appear that these temperament types are very likely of universal recurrence. That is, there is an ascertainable range of human behavior that is found wherever a sufficiently large series of individuals is observed. But the proportion in which behavior types stand to one another in different societies is not universal. The vast majority of the individuals in any group are shaped to the fashion of that culture. In other words, most individuals are plastic to the moulding force of the society into which they are born. In a society that values trance, as in India, they will have supernormal experience. In a society that institutionalizes homosexuality, they will be homosexual. In a society that sets the gathering of possessions as the chief human objective, they will amass property. The deviants, whatever the type of behavior the culture has institutionalized, will remain few in number, and there seems no more difficulty in moulding the vast malleable majority to the "normality" of what we consider an aberrant trait, such as delusions of reference, than to the normality of such accepted behavior patterns as acquisitiveness. The small proportion of the number of the deviants in any culture is not a function of the sure instinct with which that society has built itself upon the fundamental sanities, but of the universal fact that, happily, the majority of mankind quite readily take any shape that is presented to them.

The relativity of normality is not an academic issue. In the first place, it suggests that the apparent weakness of the aberrant is most often and in great measure illusory. It springs not from the fact that he is lacking in necessary vigor, but that he is an individual upon whom that culture has put more than the usual strain. His inability to adapt himself to society is a reflection of the fact that that adaptation involves a conflict in him that it does not in the so-called normal.

Therapeutically, it suggests that the inculcation of tolerance and appreciation in any society toward its less usual types is fundamentally important in successful mental hygiene. The complement of this tolerance, on the patients' side, is an education in self-reliance and honesty with himself. If he can be brought to realize that what has thrust him into his misery is despair at his lack of social backing he may be able to achieve a more independent and less tortured attitude and lay the foundation for an adequately functioning mode of existence.

There is a further corollary. From the point of view of absolute categories of abnormal psychology, we must expect in any culture to find a large proportion of the most extreme abnormal types among those who from the local point of view are farthest from belonging to this category. The culture, according to its major preoccupations, will increase and intensify hysterical, epileptic, or paranoid symptoms, at the same time relying socially in a greater and greater degree upon these very individuals. Western civilization allows and culturally honors gratifications of the ego which according to any absolute category would be regarded as abnormal. The portrayal of unbridled and arrogant egoists as family men, as officers of the law, and in business has been a favorite topic of novelists, and they are familiar in every community. Such individuals are probably mentally warped to a greater degree than many inmates of our institutions who are nevertheless socially unavailable. They are extreme types of those personality configurations which our civilization fosters.

This consideration throws into great prominence the confusion that follows, on the one hand, the use of social inadequacy as a criterion of abnormality and, on the other, of definite fixed symptoms. The confusion is present in practically all discussions of abnormal psychology, and it can be clarified chiefly by adequate consideration of the character of the culture, not of the constitution of the abnormal individual. Nevertheless, the bearing of social security upon the total situation of the abnormal cannot be exaggerated, and the study of comparative psychiatry will be fundamentally concerned with this aspect of the matter.

It is clear that statistical methods of defining normality, so long as they are based on studies in a selected civilization, only involve us, unless they are checked against the cultural configuration, in deeper and deeper provincialism. The recent tendency in abnormal psychology to take the laboratory mode as normal and to define abnormalities as they depart from this average has value in so far as it indicates that the aberrants in any culture are those individuals who are liable to serious disturbances because their habits are culturally unsupported. On the other hand, it overlooks the fact that every culture besides its abnormals of conflict has presumably its abnormals of extreme fulfillment of the cultural type. From the point of view of a universally valid abnormal psychology the extreme types of abnormality would probably be found in this very group— a group which in every study based upon one culture goes undescribed except in its end institutionalized forms.

• • •

The baldest evidences of cultural patterning in the behavior of unstable individuals is in trance phenomena. The use to which such proclivities are put, the form their manifestations take, the things that are seen and felt in trance, are all culturally controlled. The tranced individual may come back with communications from the dead describing the minutiae of life in the hereafter, or he may visit the world of the unborn, or get information about lost objects in the camp, or experience cosmic unity, or acquire a life-long guardian spirit, or get information about coming events. Even in trance the individual holds strictly to the rules and expectations of his culture, and his experience is as locally patterned as a marriage rite or an economic exchange.

The conformity of trance experience to the expectations of waking life is well recognized. Now that we are no longer confused by the attempt to ascribe supernormal validity to the one or the other, and realize how trance experience bodies forth the preoccupations of the experiencing individual, the cultural patterning in ecstasy has become an accepted tenet.

But the matter does not end here. It is not only what is seen in trance experience that has clear-cut geographical and temporal distribution. It is equally true of forms of behavior which are affected by certain unstable individuals in any group. It is one of the prime difficulties in the use of such unprecise and casual information as we possess about the behavior of the unstable in different cultures, that the material does not correspond to data from our own society. It has even been thought that such definite types of instability as Arctic hysteria (14) and the Malay running-amok were racial diseases. But we know at least, in spite of the lack of good psychiatric accounts, that these phenomena do not coincide with racial distributions. Moreover, the same problem is quite as striking in cases where there is no possibility of a racial correlation. Running amok has been described as alike in symptoms and alike in the treatment accorded it by the rest of the group from such different parts of the world as Melanesia (11, pp. 54–55) and Tierra del Fuego (7).

The racial explanation is also ruled out of court in those instances of epidemic mania which are characteristic of our own cultural background. The dancing mania (13) that filled the streets of Europe with compulsively dancing men, women, and children in mediaeval times is recognized as an extreme instance of suggestibility in our own racial group.

These behaviors are capable of controlled elaboration that is often carried to great lengths. Unstable individuals in one culture achieve characteristic forms that may be excessively rare or absent in another, and this is very marked where social value has been attached to one form or another. Thus when some form of borderline behavior has been associated in any society with the shaman and he is a person of authority and influence, it is this particular indicated seizure to which he will be liable at every demonstration. Among the Shasta of California, as we have seen, and among many other tribes in various parts of the world, some form of cataleptic seizure is the passport to shamanism and must constantly accompany its practice. In other regions it is automatic vision or audition. In other societies behavior is perhaps closest to what we cover by the term hystero-epilepsy. In Siberia all the familiar characteristics of our spiritualistic seances are required for every performance of the shaman. In all these cases the particular experience that is thus socially chosen receives considerable elaboration and is usually patterned in detail according to local standards. That is, each culture, though it chooses quite narrowly in the great field of borderline experiences, without difficulty imposes its selected type upon certain of its individuals. The particular behavior of an unstable individual in these instances is not the single and inevitable mode in which his abnormality could express itself. He has taken up a traditionally conditioned pattern of behavior in this as in any other field. Conversely, in every society, our own included, there are forms of instability that are out of fashion. They are not at the present time at least being presented for imitation to the enormously suggestible individuals who constitute in any society a considerable group of the abnormals. It seems clear that this is no matter of the nature of sanity, or even of a biological, inherited tendency in a local group, but quite simply an affair of social patterning.

. . .

REFERENCES

BOAS, F., "The social organization and the secret societies of the Kwakiutl Indians." *Rep. U. S. Nat. Mus. for 1895*, 1897, pp. 311–738.

———, "Ethnology of the Kwakiutl" based on data collected by George Hunt. *Bur. Amer. Ethnol., 35th Ann. Rep. to the Secretary of the Smithsonian Instit.* 2 vols. (Washington: Govt. Print. Office, 1921), pp. 1481.

———, "Contributions to the ethnology of the Kwakiutl." *Columbia Univ. Contrib. Anthrop.*, Vol. 3. (New York: Columbia Univ. Press, 1925), pp. vi + 357.

———, "Religion of the Kwakiutl." *Columbia Univ. Contrib. Anthrop.*, Vol. 10. Vol. II. (New York: Columbia Univ. Press, 1930), pp. vii + 288.

BOAS, F., and HUNT, G., "Kwakiutl texts." *Mem. Amer. Mus. Natur. Hist.: Jesup North Pacific Expedition*, Vol. 3. (Leiden: Brill; New York: Stechert, 1905), pp. 532.

CALLAWAY, C. H., "Religious system of the Amazulu." *Publ. Folklore Soc.* (London, 1884) 15., pp. viii + 448.

CORIAT, I. H., "Psychoneuroses among primitive tribes." In *Studies in abnormal psychology*, Ser. 6. (Boston: Gorham (n.d.), pp. 201–208.

CZAPLICKA, M. A., *Aboriginal Siberia. a study in social anthropology*. (Oxford: Clarendon Press, 1914), pp. xiv + 374. (A convenient summary.)

DEWEY, J., *Human nature and conduct: an introduction to social psychology*. (New York: Holt, 1922), pp. vii + 336.

DIXON, R. B., "The Shasta." *Bull. Amer. Mus. Natur. Hist.*, 1907, 17, pp. 381–498.

FORTUNE, R. F., *Sorcerers of Dobu*. (New York: Dutton, 1932), pp. 346.

GRINNELL, G. B., *The Cheyenne Indians*. (New Haven, Conn.: Yale Univ. Press, 1923), pp. vi + 358.

HECKER, J. F. C., *The black death and the dancing mania*. (Trans. from the German by B. G. Babbington.) (New York: Humboldt, 1885), pp. 47.

NOVAKOVSKY, S., "Arctic or Siberian hysteria as a reflex of the geographic environment." *Ecol.*, 1924, 5, pp. 113–127.

PARSONS, E. C., "The Zuñi La'mana." *Amer. Anthrop.*, 1916, 18, pp. 521–528.

SAPIR, E., "A girl's puberty ceremony among the Nootka." *Trans. Roy. Soc. Canada*, 1913, 7 (3rd ser.), pp. 67–80.

The Sorcerer and His Magic
Claude Lévi-Strauss

Quesalid (for this was the name he received when he became a sorcerer) did not believe in the power of the sorcerers—or, more accurately, shamans, since this is a better term for their specific type of activity in certain regions of the world. Driven by curiosity about their tricks and by the desire to expose them, he began to associate with the shamans until one of them offered to make him a member of their group. Quesalid did not wait to be asked twice, and his narrative recounts the details of his first lessons, a curious mixture of pantomime, prestidigitation, and empirical knowledge, including the art of simulating fainting and nervous fits, the learning of sacred songs, the technique for inducing vomiting, rather precise notions of auscultation and obstetrics, and the use of "dreamers," that is, spies who listen to private conversations and secretly convey to the shaman bits of information concerning the origins and symptoms of the ills suffered by different people. Above all, he learned the *ars magna* of one of the shamanistic schools of the Northwest Coast: The shaman hides a little tuft of down in the corner of his mouth, and he throws it up, covered with blood, at the proper moment—after having bitten his tongue or made his gums bleed—and solemnly presents it to his patient and the onlookers as the pathological foreign body extracted as a result of his sucking and manipulations.

His worst suspicions confirmed, Quesalid wanted to continue his inquiry. But he was no longer free. His apprenticeship among the shamans began to be noised about, and one day he was summoned by the family of a sick person who had dreamed of Quesalid as his healer. This first treatment (for which he received no payment, any more than he did for those which followed, since he had not completed the required four years of apprenticeship) was an outstanding success. Although Quesalid came to be known from that moment on as a "great shaman," he did not lose his critical faculties. He interpreted his success in psychological terms—it was successful "because he [the sick person] believed strongly in his dream about me." A more complex adventure made him, in his own words, "hesitant and thinking about many things." Here he encountered several varieties of a "false supernatural," and was led to conclude that some forms were less false than others—those, of course, in which he had a personal stake and whose system he was, at the same time, surreptitiously building up in his mind. A summary of the adventure follows.

While visiting the neighboring Koskimo Indians, Quesalid attends a curing ceremony of his illustrious colleagues of the other tribe. To his great astonishment he observes a difference in their technique. Instead of spitting out the illness in the form of a "bloody worm" (the concealed down), the Koskimo shamans merely spit a little saliva into their hands, and they dare to claim that this is "the sickness." What is the value of this method? What is the theory behind it? In order to find out "the strength of the shamans, whether it was real or whether they only pretended to be shamans" like his fellow tribesmen, Quesalid requests and obtains permission to try his method in an instance where the Koskimo method has failed. The sick woman then declares herself cured.

And here our hero vacillates for the first time. Though he had few illusions about his own technique, he has now found one which is more false, more mystifying, and more dishonest than his own. For he at least gives his clients something. He presents them with their sickness in a visible and tangible form, while his foreign colleagues show nothing at all and only claim to have captured the sickness. Moreover, Quesalid's method gets results, while the other is futile. Thus our hero grapples with a problem which perhaps has its parallel in the development of modern science. Two systems which we know to be inadequate present (with respect to each other) a differential validity, from both a logical and an empirical perspective. From which frame of reference shall we judge them? On the level of fact, where they merge, or on their own level, where they take on different values, both theoretically and empirically?

Meanwhile, the Koskimo shamans, "ashamed" and discredited before their tribesmen, are also plunged into doubt. Their colleague has produced, in the form of a material object, the illness which they had always considered as spiritual in nature and had thus never dreamed of rendering visible. They send Quesalid an emissary to invite him to a secret meeting in a cave. Quesalid goes and his foreign colleagues expound their system to him: "Every sickness is a man: boils and swellings, and itch and scabs, and pimples and coughs and consumption and scrofula; and also this, stricture of the bladder and stomach aches. . . . As soon as we get the soul of the sickness which is a man, then dies the sickness which is a man. Its body just disappears in our insides." If this theory is correct, what is there to show? And why, when Quesalid operates, does "the sickness stick to his hand"? But Quesalid takes refuge behind professional rules which forbid him to teach before completing four years of apprenticeship, and refuses to speak. He maintains his silence even when the Koskimo shamans send him their allegedly virgin daughters to try to seduce him and discover his secret.

Thereupon Quesalid returns to his village at Fort Rupert. He learns that the most reputed shaman of a neighboring clan, worried about Quesalid's growing renown, has challenged all his colleagues, inviting them to compete with him in curing several patients. Quesalid comes to the contest and observes the cures of his elder. Like the Koskimo, this shaman does not show the illness. He simply incorporates an invisible object, "what he called the sickness" into his head-ring, made of bark, or into his bird-shaped ritual rattle. These objects can hang suspended in mid-air, owing to the power of the illness which "bites" the house-posts or the shaman's hand. The usual drama unfolds. Quesalid is asked to intervene in cases judged hopeless by his predecessor, and he triumphs with his technique of the bloody worm.

Here we come to the truly pathetic part of the story. The old shaman, ashamed and despairing because of the ill-repute into which he has fallen and by the collapse of his therapeutic technique, sends his daughter to Quesalid to beg him for an interview. The latter finds his colleague sitting under a tree and the old shaman begins thus: "It won't be bad what we say to each other, friend, but only I wish you to try and save my life for me, so that I may not die of shame, for I am a plaything of our people on account of what you did last night. I pray you to have mercy and tell me what stuck on the palm of your hand last night. Was it the true sickness or was it only made up? For I beg you have mercy and tell me about the way you did it so that I can imitate you. Pity me, friend."

Silent at first, Quesalid begins by calling for explanations about the feats of the head-ring and the rattle. His colleague shows him the nail hidden in the head-ring which he can press at right angles into the post, and the way in which he tucks the head of his rattle between his finger joints to make it look as if the bird were hanging by its beak from his hand. He himself probably does nothing but lie and fake, simulating shamanism for material gain, for he admits to being "covetous for the property of the sick men." He knows that shamans cannot catch souls, "for . . . we all own a soul"; so he resorts to using tallow and pretends that "it is a soul . . . that white thing . . . sitting on my hand." The daughter then adds her entreaties to those of her father: "Do have mercy that he may live." But Quesalid remains silent. That very night, following this tragic conversation, the shaman disappears with his entire family, heartsick and feared by the community, who think that he may be tempted to take revenge. Needless fears: He returned a year later, but both he and his daughter had gone mad. Three years later, he died.

And Quesalid, rich in secrets, pursued his career, exposing the impostors and full of contempt for the profession. "Only one shaman was seen by me, who sucked at a sick man and I never found out whether he was a real shaman or only made up. Only for this reason I believe that he is a shaman; he does not allow those who are made well to pay him. I truly never once saw him laugh." Thus his original attitude has changed considerably. The radical negativism of the free thinker has given way to more moderate feelings. Real shamans do exist. And what about him? At the end of the narrative we cannot tell, but it is evident that he carries on his craft conscientiously, takes pride in his achievements, and warmly defends the technique of the bloody down against all rival schools. He seems to have completely lost sight of the fallaciousness of the technique which he had so disparaged at the beginning.

The Wiitiko Psychosis in the Context of Ojibwa Personality and Culture

Seymour Parker

The wiitiko psychosis, a bizarre form of mental disorder involving obsessive cannibalism, has been reported by many investigators for the area between Lake Winnipeg and Labrador. The illness is associated mainly with the Cree and Ojibwa Indians who inhabit Canada's forested northland. Although this mental disturbance has been reported for both sexes, it usually afflicts males who have spent varying periods alone in the frozen forest in an unsuccessful hunt for food. The initial symptoms are feelings of morbid depression, nausea, and distaste for most ordinary foods, and sometimes periods of semi-stupor. Gradually, the victim becomes obsessed with paranoid ideas of being bewitched and is subject to homicidal (and occasionally suicidal) thoughts. He feels that he is possessed by the wiitiko monster, a fierce cannibalistic being, to whose will he has become subjected. The conviction of the existence of a wiitiko monster itself is not evidence of pathology, since this is a socially shared belief among the

Ojibwa. If the illness progresses beyond this stage, the individual begins to see those around him (often close family members) as fat, luscious animals which he desires to devour. Finally, the wiitiko sufferer enters a stage of violent homicidal cannibalism. It is commonly thought that once this stage is reached and the person has tasted human flesh, the craving will not leave him and he must be killed. Accounts of the progress of the illness can be found in the writings of Hallowell (1934), Landes (1937b), and Cooper (1933a). Unfortunately, none of these investigators had an opportunity to obtain detailed and reliable life history data about an actual wiitiko victim.

Although there exist descriptive accounts of the disorder and extensive literature concerning the personality structure and culture of the Ojibwa Indians, there has been little attempt, thus far, to understand the wiitiko illness as a function of the individual's total participation in his society and the peculiarities of Ojibwa culture. Landes accounts for the wiitiko illness in terms of an exaggeration of an ever-present and objective fear of starvation among the Ojibwa. She states that "hunger-anxiety is a fundamental emotion which *windigo* sufferers have seized upon for the path of their deviation" (Landes 1938b:214). Thus, to this observer the illness reflects an exaggeration of a normal anxiety, conditioned by objective determinants in the environment. A similar etiological explanation is offered by Cooper (1933a) who derives both the psychosis and the wiitiko folklore from the prevalent environmental conditions (i.e., periodic food scarcity). Hallowell (1934) does not deal directly with the etiology of wiitiko, but does feel that the symptoms of obsessive cannibalism and private pathological phantasies are given form by Ojibwa cultural beliefs in the existence of a cannibalistic wiitiko monster.

The etiological explanations given by Landes and Cooper raise a number of problems. The first (noted by Landes herself) is that the neighboring Eskimo and Athabascan-speaking peoples are neither prone to this disorder (Honigman 1954:381–382) nor do they believe in possession by a fierce cannibalistic monster. It is probable that we are dealing here with something more complex than a simple environmental causation. In addition, the explanations do not aid in understanding the accompanying symptoms such as anxiety, depresssion, and paranoid and homicidal ideation. Finally, none of these explanations is related to the personality dynamics of the Ojibwa individual. In a critique of the writings of the "cultural psychoanalysts," Abram Kardiner (1933) noted that the crucial point in understanding the development of the neurotic problem is to see how environmental pressures interact with personality structure.

The objective of this paper will be to understand the wiitiko psychosis, not merely as a bizarre reaction to severe environmental pressures, but as a form of pathological adjustment of the modal Ojibwa personality to such pressures. In all societies the socialization process demands a price in terms of the peculiar anxieties and tensions that it engenders. These anxieties are, in a manner of speaking, the price that is paid for "normal" adjustment to the cultural practices and values in the society. Ultimately, any etiological analysis of a mental disorder cannot be disassociated from a consideration of normal personality structure in the particular society (Hallowell 1934). The author hopes that this discussion will yield a view of the wiitiko psychosis, not as a complete and qualitative departure from normal personality, but as an outgrowth (albeit a pathological one) from it.

• • •

THE EARLY SOCIALIZATION OF THE OJIBWA INDIVIDUAL

Most of the accounts of the first stage of life of the Ojibwa individual point to a rather permissive handling of the small baby. Peter Grant (1890:322–323) observed that parents felt great joy upon the birth of a child, especially a boy. However, both sexes were treated with equal care and affection. The child was swaddled in a blanket and, at the age of one month, placed in a portable cradleboard where he was in almost constant contact with the mother. The cradleboard was discarded when the child was able to crawl. However, even prior to this, he was often taken out and permitted to lie on a blanket or was fondled by adults. The child had free access to its mother's breasts whenever it cried and was not usually weaned before the age of two to four years. Other accounts corroborate this picture of a rather mild and pleasant infancy period (Densmore 1929:51; Jeness 1935:90; Landes 1937a:13). There is no evidence of deprivation or trauma in the early child-rearing practices.

Aside from socialization techniques, other cultural institutions of the Ojibwa have important implications for personality development in this early period. The structural isolation of the nuclear family in the kinship system results in the young child having but minimal contact with significant adults other than his mother (and occasionally his grandmother). In addition to the structural isolation of the family, it is also geographically isolated during the greater part of the year when the family is out alone in its hunting territory. The absence of the wider kin group and mother surrogates, and the frequent absence of the father from the home while hunting, magnify the importance of mother for the satisfaction of the child's needs. His dependence on this central figure is greatly intensified.

Although the first few years of life are characterized by considerable affection and permissiveness, a rather sudden and drastic change occurs between the ages of three and five (Landes 1937b:117). At this time, the socially shared anxieties and values of the group begin to impinge directly on the youngster. These people consider themselves to be so near the bare subsistence level that the child, in his untrained state, is regarded as a liability both to himself and to the group. His lack of supernatural power is conceptualized as an "emptiness" and "void" that must quickly be "filled" by means of rather severe training. Strong efforts are made to wean the child from his dependent state. Overt affectionate behavior by the parents toward the child is withdrawn, and the latter is prodded to assume many aspects of adult behavior. In order to harden their bodies, children had to bathe in a lake or river at the beginning of each month until the freeze-up. In the winter they ran naked to a mark on the ice or are driven out into a snow storm and rubbed with snow (Jeness 1935:94). A male child of three or four years old is given a feast to which seasoned hunters are invited. On these, and similar occasions, he is goaded to become a "man" and a great hunter. Soon after this first feast, he is taken out by his mother who teaches him how to set traps, and later by his father who lends him tools and acquaints him with the rules of hunting. At the age of nine, the boy is allowed the use of specially assigned hunting grounds—by twelve he is often a competent hunter with his own grounds, distant from those of his father. Already, he must remain away from home for long periods, hunting in the silent frozen forest. He returns for short periods, in order to give his catch to his sister, who prepares food for him and makes his clothes—very much as his mother does for his father.

One of the major institutions in Ojibwa society is the vision quest, which enables the child to overcome his omnipresent vulnerability and emptiness (i.e., lack of power). When boys reach the age of four to six years, they are often forced to abstain from one meal a day "at intervals that are graduated according to the fanaticism of his parents" (Landes 1938b). He is besieged by his parents, particularly by his mother and grandmother, to go without food in order "that you may learn what to do with your life" (Landes 1938b:3). If the child refuses to accept the fast imposed on him, he may be cuffed, denied food by his parents, and have his face rubbed with charcoal. By the time he reaches eight, he may be required to fast for two meals a day, every other day, for many weeks throughout the winter months. Whereas the father acts as a guide and teacher, it is usually the mother who prods and spurs her son on to abstain from food, to strive for visions, and to be a great hunter. It is interesting in this connection to note that the withdrawal of food is the most common technique used by adults to punish the disobedient child. At an early age the child is impressed with the association of the withdrawal of food and the withdrawal of parental affection and punishment. Other punitive techniques used by the mother to "help the child grow up" involve threats of separation if he does not conform.[1] The mother might warn the child that he will be taken away by an animal, or by the ghost of a dead person. He is even told, in hushed whispers, that the wiitiko monster will come to take him if he is bad (Guinard 1930).

The big test of endurance comes at puberty. The boy is left alone in the forest for a few days without food and is expected to remain there until he is able to communicate with the supernatural by means of a vision. Ojibwa myths are replete with accounts of the intense suffering and pain that accompany the vision quest. This valued achievement signifies the boy's securing of his own power and represents the fact that he is no longer dependent on other people. He has achieved a prime goal of Ojibwa socialization—self-reliance.

• • •

. . . It is hypothesized that in this society food (or its absence) is associated with the possibilities of power and security on one hand, and inadequacy, pain, and rejection on the other. These two ideas represent the opposite sides of the same coin. In this society "to be seriously hungry is a confession of defeat and a source of shame" (Landes 1937c). The child is impressed early with a mythology involving the dangers of starvation. He is constantly given to understand that his own worth depends on becoming a great hunter and securing abundant food. He learns that obtaining food is the fruit (and proof) of supernatural aid. At the tender age of three or four the child is spurred and prodded by his parents to deny himself food in order to secure "power." In some respects the associations with food and eating may be comparable to those associated with sex in Western society. Just as the sexual urges of a child in our society frequently become linked with fear of rejection by parents and a danger to self-

[1]Such threats must be particularly traumatic to the child brought up in the relatively isolated nuclear family. An important factor that usually serves to pare down the magnified parental image is absent in this society. In many societies peer group interaction helps to fulfill this important socialization function. Because the Ojibwa family lives alone in its hunting territory for most of the year, children's peer groups are relatively weak.

esteem, the Ojibwa child soon learns to associate food transactions with the possibility of rejection, anxiety, feelings of inadequacy, and the anticipation of danger. In both cases, a biological urge that was originally accompanied by anticipations of pleasure, becomes associated with a painful and anxiety-provoking sensation. Frustrations involving food, through the process of stimulus generalization, become part of, and reinforce the broader dependency frustration (Rado 1956:326). This may lay the basis for a masochistic development (Kardiner 1939:71). The idea of the importance of food and eating is closely related, psychodynamically, to frustrated dependency needs. Clinical evidence, in our own society, indicates that a need for support and dependency is often represented in dreams by eating or even the fear of being eaten (Kardiner 1939:222).

• • •

. . . The competitive emphasis in the thinking of the Ojibwa is noted by Ruth Landes: "Each person goes out by himself, never thinking of others except to wonder if they will get the jump on him" (Landes 1937c). She also notes their strong desire for supremacy that sometimes assumes "startling forms." For example, during the games that are sometimes played in the summer villages, the winner is actually in danger of his life, for he encroaches upon the self-regard of the loser. "A man is ashamed not only to be defeated by an opponent but also to be outshone by a partner" (Landes 1937c). Hallowell (1955:181) states that one of the primary concerns of Ojibwa individuals is how they rank in power with others—"Is he more powerful than I, or am I more powerful than he?" In a sense, the executive agent of self-esteem and security is removed to a position external to the self. While this is universally true, to some extent, the degree to which it is dynamically operative in this society appears to be outstanding.

THE OJIBWA ADULT AND HIS SOCIAL INSTITUTIONS

The characterization of the pre-adult Ojibwa has indicated particular predispositions to react to the impact of the physical and social environment. We are now prepared to look at the behavior of the adult. Although most of the neighbors of the Ojibwa (i.e., Eskimos, Plains Indians) may be described as individualistic and self-reliant, one is impressed with the exaggeration of these qualities in this group. Their economic and political institutions demonstrate a strong individualism, with but minimal development of cooperative techniques. The major economic activity of hunting involves the isolation of the nuclear family during the winter months. The scarcity of game makes it difficult for more than one family to draw sustenance from a fairly extensive hunting territory. Ownership of the hunting grounds is strictly private, and the exclusive rights of use are fiercely guarded. "This territory cannot even be crossed without permission under pain of death at sight. This absoluteness of individual ownership excludes even the closest relatives" (Landes 1937b). The inheritance of property depends on the predilection of the individual and does not follow any strong traditional prescriptions.

In the late spring, the family moves into a temporary "village" with a few other families. The families may vary from year to year and each nuclear family inhabits a separate household. The political organization of these villages is loose and flexible. There are no regularly constituted chiefs or councils, no organized policing system or military organization. In the past, the most powerful men were the shamans, who were consulted on various matters. Temporary leaders were appointed for given tasks, such as raiding or trading. If a man was not in accord with the decision of the leader (or temporarily appointed council of elders), he could either withdraw from the activity or leave the village. Nobody was forced to conform. Barnouw (1950:16) comments that "every man was for himself or for his own family, and there were few activities which linked the isolated families together." Trees used to obtain sugar sap in the spring were individually owned and worked. Likewise, fishing and berrying involved no co-operative endeavors. Only in the harvesting of the wild rice in the fall did a man and wife regularly cooperate with each other.

Religion has been aptly termed as the "Rorschach of society." This is true insofar as the institution allows wide latitude for the projection of attitudes derived from social experiences. Man's conception of the nature of the supernatural forces, and his relationship to them, often reflect the basic psychological constellations derived from relationships with his fellow men. The projective nature of religion provides an opportunity to explore personality dynamics in the society.

. . .

Aside from this "diagnostic" aspect of religion, what are its psychological functions for the Ojibwa individual? Does not the dependency relationship between man and the supernatural in this society serve to satisfy some of the dependency needs of the former? The answer to this question is rather complicated and cannot be answered with an unqualified "yes." The relationship with the supernatural is a double-edged sword. On the one hand, it is true that insofar as success in individualized achievement confirms the potency of the vision, the Ojibwa individual feels that powerful supernatural beings have taken him under their special protection. Here is one of the few situations in which dependency cravings and their satisfaction can be given overt expression and societal legitimation. However, it has also been observed that the great emphasis placed by parents on the vision quest as a very private achievement stresses to the maturing child that human beings can be of no fundamental aid to him. . . .

Studies of the psychodynamics of dependency indicate that frustrated and unsatisfied dependency cravings often result in repressed rage (Rado 1956:219, 326; Glover 1956:24). Is there any evidence of such feelings toward the Ojibwa supernaturals? The literature is suggestive, rather than conclusive, in this regard. Cooper (1933b) quotes an early account which notes that these people were normally obsequious to their "bad" God (i.e., wiitiko). In misfortune, they would sing to him, imploring his mercy. In health and prosperity they would likewise sing to him in an attempt to stay in his good graces. However, when they were under the influence of alcohol, they would be furious with him and run out of their tents and fire their guns in order to kill him. . . .

Other indirect evidence that supports the above speculation is found in the attitudes toward the shamans—who have been granted power and the favor of the supernaturals and to whom the Ojibwa individual confesses his sins in order to be cured from an illness. The shamans are the earthly representatives of supernatural power and also are individuals on whom one is often forced to be dependent. For the most part these individuals are regarded with suspicion because of the evil and dangerous qualities attributed to them. It is also interesting to note that during the "vision" experience, the Ojibwa often perceive the supernatural in the shape of an animal that they desire to kill (Landes 1938a). In this connection, it should be remembered that the wiitiko sufferer also sees his potential victims in the form of animals that he desires to kill and devour. From the data presented thus far it seems reasonable to conclude that the Ojibwa are basically ambivalent toward all persons or supernatural beings on whom they are dependent (i.e., parents, shamans, and supernatural beings). They desire help and nurturance, but at the same time anticipate danger and pain. They are overtly obsequious toward these objects, yet feel considerable anger toward them.

The above discussion raises the problem of the meanings of phantasies of devouring. Previously it was noted that phantasies of devouring or of being devoured often occur in individuals whose dependency needs are being frustrated. Both of these types of ideation may represent the desire to become one with the object from whom one desires dependency satisfactions. There is also clinical evidence to indicate that cannibalistic phantasies are associated with hostile and sadistic impulses toward the object of dependency (Glover 1956: 85; Kardiner 1939:224). Thus, oral phantasies may represent a desire to consummate and perpetuate the relationship with the object of dependency or to destroy this object. Actually, the degree to which the phantasies of the dependent person will take on an aggressive character is related to the extent to which his social relationship prevents or allows him to satisfy his dependency needs. The dependent and aggressive phantasies are often two sides of the same coin. Some of the observations of Abram Kardiner on cannibalistic phantasies are pertinent to this discussion:

The "fear of being eaten up" is a constellation often found in individuals in a helpless state. The derivation of the cannibalistic impulse from frustrated dependency is, however, not a direct one. The phases are as follows: An observation confirmed by everyday experience is that "love can turn to hate." Because of its frequency, this observation does not offend common sense. Of similar character is the observation that an inability to trust another object to satisfy certain emotional cravings leads to the perception of being injured by that object, whereupon active steps in the form of aggression against the object are taken. The form of aggression derives its character from the nature of the impulse in question. The frustrated impulse leads to the perception of the object doing the negative of the wish to depend on the object; the wish to eat the object becomes the fear of being eaten. It is this perception against which an aggressive attitude is taken—"I eat you up" (Kardiner 1939:224).

It becomes clearer how the loved one (and needed one) can also be the hated and threatening one. These seemingly contradictory attitudes toward the object of dependency (i.e., desire to perpetuate it and the desire to obliterate it) represents a psychodynamic conceptualization of an important focus of tension between the Ojibwa individual and his society.

Aggressive intent associated with biting and devouring is given overt representation in some of the cultural practices among the Ojibwa. Hallowell quotes Father LeJeune, an early observer of the Ojibwa, as saying: "So enraged are they against everyone who does them an injury, that they eat the lice and other vermin that they find upon themselves, not because they like them, but only, they say, to avenge themselves and to eat those that eat them" (Hallowell 1955:140). Here the idea is clearly expressed that "I want to eat (i.e., obliterate, destroy) you because you intend to eat me." It is noteworthy that the means used to express aggression against an annoying stimulus is to devour it. Another interesting oral aggressive mechanism found in Ojibwa behavior involves the punishment of an adulterous wife. A husband might vent his hostility on an unfaithful wife by cutting or biting off her nose (Kinietz 1947:135).

The elaboration of food rituals among the Ojibwa may provide a means of gauging the degree to which food and eating are laden with anxiety (Kardiner 1939:220). There is ample testimony by students of Ojibwa society concerning the proliferation of food rituals. If the pregnant woman does not observe numerous food taboos, her child will be afflicted with various deformities (Higler 1936). There are countless respect observances toward animals. Feasts are held after the first game of the season is killed, on naming ceremonies, and for postmenstrual purification (Landes 1937a:137). If a hunter did not make a food offering to the supernatural after killing a bear, he might be killed by a bear on future hunts. To waste food, or to misuse it in any way, brings swift supernatural vengeance (Cooper 1933b:58). Bread, meat, or wild rice are ritually thrown into the fire or placed in some other appropriate spot (Bernard 1929). Food is given to the recently deceased from a dish used by various relatives on festive occasions. Also, the widow or widower, during the year of formal mourning, carries the dish of the deceased spouse and eats from it. In the case of the death of a widowed parent, one of the children performs this ritual. This was known as "eating with the dead" (Kinietz 1947:149). Cooper (1933b:77) reports that in the hierarchy of the Ojibwa supreme beings the "food manitu" was supreme.

Anxiety about witchcraft is widespread in Ojibwa society. An individual suspects not only his neighbors and distant kin, but also close relatives (Landes 1938b:36). Often the shaman who is most suspect is a blood relative and housemate. An early missionary stated that he rarely saw a dying Ojibwa who did not feel that he had been bewitched (Hallowell 1946). Failure in hunting is almost invariably considered to be the result of black magic practiced by neighbors or kin. Hallowell (1946) states that, according to Ojibwa beliefs, if one is failing in the pursuit of a livelihood, "it is somebody's fault." Thus, failure in hunting signifies much more than the physical danger of starvation—it carries with it the additional anxiety of feeling subject to the hostility and rejection of others. It is intimately related to an individual's feelings of social acceptance, ego-esteem, and power. Witchcraft beliefs contribute to the further elaboration of individualism and social "atomism" observed in the economic and political institutions.

THE MYTHOLOGY OF THE OJIBWA

• • •

The following is an outline of a very interesting series of myths, repeated with minor variations in both the Schoolcraft and Jones collections:

A father returns to his tent each evening to find that his sons have been crying. They appear neglected and hungry. When asked why they are in this sad state, the children tell him that they are being neglected by their mother. The hunter discovers that his wife leaves the children alone as soon as he leaves the home and has sexual relations with her (snake) lover. The father kills his wife (by chopping her up or by decapitation) and then goes away. Before departing, he tells his children that their mother will follow them in order to kill them and gives them food and advice on how to elude her. He is subsequently killed by the vengeful spirit of the mother. Then begins a melodramatic chase, with the two small children fleeing the pursuing "dead" mother who wants to kill them. In some versions, she cries to them that she only wants to give them suck, but they "know" that this is not her real intention. In one particularly gruesome version of the tale the younger child weeps when his mother is killed and goes to her decapitated corpse in an attempt to suck milk from her dead breasts. As he does this, her eyes roll and finally the head begins to chase both sons. The boys refer to the head of their mother as a wiitiko cannibal monster who wants to devour them. Finally, the pursuing mother is destroyed and the children remain unharmed.

Insight into the child's resentment and phantasies about being "pushed" to maturity is found in one of the above tales in which the mother attempts to get the small boys away from the tent so that she can carry on her clandestine love affair. She urges them to go into the forest to hunt because "it is not manly to stay around the lodge," and warns them that they will not grow up to be great hunters if they tattle to their father.

．　．　．

Resentment arising from being forced to fast is a very common theme in Ojibwa mythology. Father, mother, and grandmother (or "old woman") are about equally implicated in the numerous stories concerning a small boy who is forced to fast for his vision or to perform an impossibly difficult task. After intense suffering, the child revenges himself on his kinsmen by homicide and cannibalism, by turning into a bird and flying away (despite the tears and entreaties of his parents), or by dying (and leaving his parents brokenhearted and remorseful). In a group of closely related tales, a small male child is stolen by an animal or by Toad Woman while he is left alone (i.e., neglected) by his mother. Usually the mother feels bad and finally manages, by various ruses, to get her son back.

Although overt expression of dependency needs is stringently discouraged in this society, it is interesting to find that such expressions are by no means uncommon in the myths. . . .

．　．　．

A FURTHER CHARACTERIZATION OF THE OJIBWA ADULT PERSONALITY

．　．　．

There is considerable agreement in the writings of Hallowell and others on some of the other outstanding characteristics of the Ojibwa. The aspects of their personality that have been commented on most frequently are the prevalence of a high level of interpersonal hostility, an oblique (or indirect) way of expressing this hostility, hypersensitivity to insults, exaggerated pride, and the frequency of "paranoid"[2] reactions. Hallowell brings considerable evidence to bear on the existence of a high level of interpersonal hostility. He also comments on the characteristic means of expressing these feelings: "It can be understood that such care is taken to avoid offending others in such small matters of daily life, that the Saulteaux are even more careful to avoid any open expression of anger in face to face relationships. An overt expression of anger or aggression of any sort in this society is tantamount to a challenge to a duel by sorcery, since there is no institutionalized form for settling such matters in any other way. . . . If retaliation is sought it is always by some covert means" (Hallowell 1956). Given the high level of hostility, plus a predisposition to handle it in this manner, it is not unexpected that oblique mechanisms such as malevolent sorcery and gossip are rife.

· · ·

The widespread belief in malevolent sorcery provides an additional motivation for the repression (and suppression) of hostility. It has been observed in clinical practice that the repression of hostility (or of any other strong impulse) often leads to the creation of anxiety and feelings of defenselessness. Figuratively speaking, the ego has lost its command of an important mechanism with which to manipulate, or resist attack from, the social environment. The perception of the environment as threatening and hostile varies directly with the feeling of defenselessness and vulnerability. In the case of the Ojibwa, this perception is buttressed by the objective dangers stemming from the physical environment (e.g., starvation) and the institutionalized behavior of the group (e.g., sorcery, competitive individualism, etc.). Under such conditions, the development of "over-sensitivity" and "paranoid" ideation becomes understandable.

· · ·

THE WIITIKO PSYCHOSIS

. . . The early and severe emphasis on self-reliance and individualism leads to unsatisfied dependency cravings and repressed hostility. Personality structure and social institutions both curtail and negatively sanction any direct attempts to satisfy either of these needs. As a result, the adult Ojibwa treads the precarious and narrow path between his quest for affection (support, nurturance, etc.) and his desire to give vent to an overpowering rage. He consequently fears failure to live up to the rather narrow and rigidly defined masculine role, but also fears the social rejection and envy that come with outstanding achievement and success.

In her discussion of the wiitiko psychosis, Landes notes that women are relatively free from this illness. It is interesting that those women who were subject to its symptoms usually experienced a "masculine" training and ethos during their childhood and adolescence (Landes 1938a). This confirms the impression that the severe conditioning and social role requirements of the male in this society are related to the wiitiko disorder. It has been noted that men who have

[2] I use "paranoid" as a descriptive personality trait. There is no implication here of psychopathology.

experienced prolonged failure in hunting are particularly vulnerable. Reports of the illness mention, as common symptoms, a period of deep depression, sometimes preceded by a violent and abusive mood (Landes 1938b:215). Finally, there develop well defined paranoid fixations and cannibalistic behavior.

The close association of pathological symptoms with failure in hunting brings to mind the previous discussion of hunger and failure among Ojibwa males. This failure provokes intense anxiety, not only because it threatens starvation, but also because it is loaded with the dangers of a drastic loss of self-esteem. Failure in hunting not only means that "I have no food," but also that "I have lost my power," "I am empty and worthless." To the objective fear of starvation is added the powerful anxiety of ego obliteration. It has been mentioned that a failure of supernatural power indicates that "someone is practicing evil magic against me." This belief illustrates that supernatural rejection is the psychological equivalent of being rejected by significant others in the social environment. It is a dramatic and ultimate frustration of dependency needs. It is the Achilles heel of the Ojibwa. Most discussions of the relationship of the wiitiko psychosis and the "fear of starvation" have emphasized the manifest fear, but have failed to note the importance of the anxiety stemming from the latent (or symbolic) meaning of the situation to the Ojibwa individual.

The depressive state is occasionally preceded by feelings of being persecuted, and even overt abusiveness or violence. The production of rage is a usual concomitant of a severe frustration of dependency needs in the dependent individual. I have already elaborated on the mechanism which accounts for this rage and the paranoid feelings.[3] What is unusual here is that the individual now begins to express his rage and aggression in a *direct and overt manner*. Pathology is indicated by a failure of the normal defense mechanisms (buttressed by social institutions) to divert the expression of hostility into institutionalized channels.

In many cases, overt signs of violence or rage are not present and the initial symptoms consist of a prolonged depression accompanied by nausea and loss of appetite and occasional periods of semi-stupor. Psychoanalytical studies of depression indicate its close association with an actual or threatened withdrawal of love, nurturance, and support. Subjectively, it is usually felt as an intense loss of self-esteem, worthlessness, and feelings of vulnerability (Rado 1928).

The rage generated by frustrated dependency needs is turned inward and is experienced as melancholic depression. The depressive symptoms also represent a mechanism for regaining love and support.[4] Common techniques used by the dependent person for regaining love are self-punishment, expiation, and self-abasement. Symbolically, he humbles himself before the object of his dependency and begs for forgiveness and nurturance. This masochistic technique

[3]Kardiner presents clinical evidence from our own society to indicate that the paranoid individual is also characterized by frustrated dependency needs and an intense rage which he projects onto his environment (1939:429).

[4]It is probable that the vision seeking experience itself represents one of the institutionalized means used by the Ojibwa for escaping from depression and doubts of self-worth. Given the values and social consensus in this society concerning the efficacy of the vision, this technique for resolving depression cannot be regarded as a neurotic mechanism. It is an effective technique provided by the culture for dealing with anxiety and thus facilitates normal social role performance.

for obtaining help and nurturance has already been encountered in the discussion of Ojibwa religion and mythology. Probably the intensity of the depression at this stage of the illness results from the conflict between the coercive rage directed toward the object of dependency and the submissive fear generated in the superego of the dependent person (Rado 1951). It should be noted that, in this depressive stage, the normal defenses against the overt expression of aggression are still intact. The illness is often arrested at this point and the individual recovers without any further pathological development.[5]

Finally, we come to the full blown psychotic symptoms involving fixed paranoid delusions and cannibalistic behavior. The victim feels that he has been possessed by the spirit of a cannibalistic wiitiko monster (as a result of malevolent witchcraft) and that he must serve the appetite of the wiitiko as his own (Landes 1938a). The Ojibwa picture this monster as an immense being, full of rage, fury, and anger, and possessed of superhuman strength. Landes (1937b) suggests that the omnipotent and fierce qualities of this being may be a projection, by the Ojibwa, of their fear of starvation onto a predatory wiitiko "and so arises the picture of his rage and passion." Doubtless the passion of the monster is exaggerated by the intensity of the objective fear of starvation. However, I feel that this explanation is inadequate for two reasons. First, actual or even threatened starvation is not invariably part of the situation of the wiitiko sufferer. Second, other peoples who also face periodic starvation (i.e., the Eskimo) do not experience possession by such a fierce cannibalistic ogre. In line with the previous analysis, I suggest that the *prototype* of the wiitiko monster is the mother figure, who is a major agent of dependency frustration in early life. The basis for the predisposition that later results in the phantasy of a persecuting monster is established in the early socialization process, particularly in the mother-son relationship. It is cultivated and given definite form by the cultural belief in such a monster. In the adult Ojibwa, it is more fruitful, heuristically, to think of the wiitiko monster as a phantasy figure symbolizing the wider circle of significant others who continue to frustrate the dependency cravings of the adult and constitute threats to his vulnerable self-esteem. The previously cited quotation of Abram Kardiner, dealing with the transformation of the nurturing object into the persecuting object is pertinent to the understanding of this symptom. As a defense against the fear of being "eaten" (i.e., becoming completely powerless or having his ego obliterated), which is represented subjectively by feelings of being possessed and forced to serve the wiitiko, the individual desires to eat (i.e., obliterate) his persecutor. When faced with a severe failure (e.g., failure in hunting), the individual feels abandoned and worthless. For the wiitiko victim, the usual masochistic devices to insure dependency satisfaction, and the normative cultural channels for an oblique expression of hostility, no longer suffice to relieve anxiety and depression. Under these conditions, the dam (constituted by

[5]One can only speculate about the meaning of the "gastric" symptoms (i.e., refusal to eat various foods and nausea) that often accompany this depressive stage. It may be that the refusal to take (or to keep down) food represents a mechanism used by the outraged dependent individual to avenge himself on the frustrating agent. It is similar to some types of suicidal motivation in our society. It is noteworthy that there is a belief among the Ojibwa that an inability to digest food is a sign of approaching death. It is also possible that cannibalistic phantasies begin at this time foreboding the full blown psychotic urges. This might give rise to feelings of guilt and disgust associated with food intake in this prepsychotic phase.

ego defenses) is shattered and the repressed cravings for the expression of dependency and aggressive needs burst forth. The depressive conflict between the rebellious rage and the submissive fear is resolved. If this interpretation is correct, then the psychotic symptoms serve, at the same time, to allay dependency cravings (by becoming one with the object of dependency) and to aggress against this frustrating object (by killing and eating it). The psychotic aspect of this behavior consists not of the dependent and aggressive feelings in themselves, but in the failure of the normal personality and institutional defenses and the resultant overt expression of hitherto repressed or socially channelized impulses.

Unfortunately we do not have any reliable data on the prevalence or the distribution of the wiitiko illness. Landes (1937c) states, impressionistically, that "insanity is recognized and comparatively common among the Ojibwa." None of the other writers on the subject even venture such a vague guess about its prevalence. Aside from many other difficulties, the problem arises as to the range of pathological behavior that should be included under this condition. Landes (1937c) classifies as wiitiko all insanities in this society. Others, such as Hallowell and Cooper, also maintain that the illness need not necessarily include cannibalistic behavior. In all probability this condition is a cultural variation of what we regard as schizophrenia.

• • •

I have tried to show how an early personality predisposition is elaborated and even exaggerated by the cultural institutions and values among the Ojibwa. The dependency frustration is not something that automatically perpetuates itself as a result of an early fixation. Rather, it is something that is nurtured and developed by the day-to-day competitive emphasis and self-reliant isolation imposed by adult institutional life. Likewise, the danger of direct and overt expressions of hostility cannot be fully explained (psychodynamically) without an understanding of the role of malevolent sorcery and the precarious economic existence of the Ojibwa. The role of early personality development lies in its tendency to set limits to the possible alternative modes of reacting to the stresses and strains of adult life. Why a particular mode is adopted, however, can rarely be understood without recourse to the current life situation. To elucidate the early development of a personality trait does not suffice to explain the reasons for its perpetuation or its current function in the social and psychological equilibrium of the individual.

REFERENCES

BARNOUW, VICTOR, "Acculturation and personality among the Wisconsin Chippewa." *American Anthropological Association Memoir* 72, 1950.

BERNARD, SISTER M., "Religion and magic among the Cass Lake Ojibwa." *Primitive Man* 2:52–55, 1929.

COOPER, JOHN M., "The Cree wiitiko psychosis." *Primitive Man* 6:20–24, 1933a. "The northern Algonquian supreme being." *Primitive Man* 6:41–111, 1933b.

DENSMORE, FRANCES, "Chippewa customs." *Bureau of American Ethnology Bulletin* 86, 1929.

GLOVER, EDWARD, "Selected papers on psycho-analysis." Vol. 1 (New York: International Universities Press, 1956).

GRANT, PETER, "The Saulteux Indians about 1804." In *Les bourgeois de la compagnie du Nord-Ouest*, Louis Rodrigue Masson, ed. (Québec: A Coté et cie, 1890).

GREEN, ARNOLD, "Culture, normality, and personality conflict." *American Anthropologist* 50:225–237, 1948.

GUINARD, J. E., "Wiitiko among the Tête-de-Boule." *Primitive Man* 3:69–71, 1930.

HALLOWELL, A. IRVING, "Culture and mental disorder." *Journal of Abnormal and Social Psychology* 29:1–9, 1934. "The social function of anxiety in a primitive society." *American Sociological Review* 6:869–881, 1941. "Some psychological characteristics of the northeastern Indians." In *Man in Northeastern America*, Frederick Johnson, ed. (Andover: Papers of the Robert S. Peabody Foundation for Archeology, 1946). "Myth, culture, and personality." *American Anthropologist* 49:544–556, 1947. "Values, acculturation, and mental health." *American Journal of Orthopsychiatry* 20:732–743, 1950. "Culture and experience." (Philadelphia: University of Pennsylvania Press, 1955).

HILGER, M. INEZ, "Chippewa customs." *Primitive Man* 9:17–24, 1936.

HONIGMANN, JOHN J., *Culture and personality* (New York: Harper & Row, 1954).

HORNEY, KAREN, *The neurotic personality of our time* (New York: W. W. Norton and Co., 1937).

JENNESS, DIAMOND, "The Ojibwa Indians of Parry Island." *Bulletin of the Canada Department of Mines 78.* (Ottawa: National Museum of Canada, 1935).

JONES, WILLIAM, "Ojibwa texts." 2 vols., T. Michelson, ed. *American Ethnological Society.* (New York: G. E. Stechert and Co., 1919).

KARDINER, ABRAM, "The relation of culture to mental disorder." In *Current problems in psychiatric diagnosis*, Hoch and Zubin, eds. (New York: Grune and Stratton, 1933). *The individual and his society.* (New York: Columbia University Press, 1939.)

KINIETZ, W. VERNON, "Chippewa village; the story of Katikitegon." *Cranbrook Institute of Science Bulletin 25.* (Bloomfield Hills, Mich., 1947).

LANDES, RUTH, "Ojibwa sociology." *Columbia University Contributions to Anthropology 29.* (New York: Columbia University Press, 1937a). "The Ojibwa of Canada." In *Cooperation and competition among primitive peoples*, Margaret Mead, ed. (New York: McGraw-Hill, 1937b). "The personality of the Ojibwa." *Character and Personality* 6:51–60, 1937c. "The abnormal among the Ojibwa Indians." *Journal of Abnormal and Social Psychology* 33:14–33, 1938a. "The Ojibwa woman." *Columbia University Contributions to Anthropology 31.* (New York: Columbia University Press, 1938b).

MASLOW, A. H. and B. MITTELMANN, *Principles of abnormal psychology.* (New York: Harper and Row, 1941).

RADO, SANDOR, "The problem of melancholia." *International Journal of Psychoanalysis* 9:420–436, 1928. "Psychodynamics of depression from the etiologic point of view." *Psychosomatic Medicine* 13:51–55, 1951. *Psychoanalysis of Behavior.* (New York: Grune and Stratton, 1956).

SCHOOLCRAFT, HENRY ROWE, *Indian legends from algic researches and historical and statistical information respecting the Indian tribes of the United States*, M. L. Williams, ed. (East Lansing: Michigan State University Press, 1956).

Disease and Curing

A. Kimball Romney and Romaine Romney

Illness is common in the barrio. Although some of it is chronic (for example, rheumatism, certain types of dysentery, and malaria among those men who have worked in hot country), much illness is seasonal. The winter months bring colds and flu with their complications (earache, eye inflammation), especially among children. Measles strike yearly in the heat of the spring before the rains begin, and here again children are the principal victims. In the rainy summer months intestinal diseases are common. Barrio people recognize the seasonal distribution of kinds of illness to some extent by their tendency to lay the blame for an epidemic on the weather. For example, one woman explained the occurrence of much illness one summer by saying that in the previous year the rains had come earlier, and so by June the water was no longer muddy and there was little sickness. The association of muddy water and sickness in her thinking seems likely. April and May are said to be good months for taking a purgative, perhaps to prepare for the dangers of summer. Again, measles is said to occur at about the same time each year, when the sun is so hot that it heats the blood and produces a rash as the heat seeks a way out of the body.

Although the weather helps to explain the widespread occurrence of illness in the barrio, the illness of an individual is usually thought to have much more specific causes. Some few conditions—for example, wounds, burns, poison ivy, and malaria—are believed to be caused by the physical agents with which they are associated in Western medicine. Poison ivy is contracted by touching or being near the plant, and malaria comes from the bite of a mosquito in hot country. Most diseases, however, are assigned causes of other kinds. In order of importance, these include: (1) disturbed emotional states such as fear and anger, (2) ritual contamination, (3) magical seizure by sorcery, and (4) improper diet or regimen. Supplementing these categories in the explanation of individual illness is the belief in differential susceptibility to illness. Susceptibility is increased by abnormal bodily conditions brought about by exertion, excessive sweating, body exposure, wounds or blows, as well as by the conditions of pregnancy, parturition, menstruation, and menopause. Weakness may also be due to extreme youth or to old age. The illness of a particular individual is interpreted in the light of his condition (weakness or strength) and his recent experience, as well as his symptoms.

Fright is "like a heat in the stomach," taking away the appetite and producing fever, sleeplessness, and general apathy. It may follow a fall, especially a fall into water, or the unexpected sight of a snake, or any other event which produces fear or shock. (Among these other events is the sight of aggression, "seeing some person kill another person, or seeing someone else pushing somebody from behind into the water.") Anger as well as sometimes causing illness and sometimes death is also believed to cause pain in childbirth and miscarriage in those who are weak for one reason or another. One type of weakness which is relevant here is an overabundance of bile or, rather, a tendency for the bile to be discharged readily into the stomach or the liver. The danger of illness following anger is greatest before breakfast because the bile sack is fullest then. It is considerably less after eating, for then food supports the sack, and the bile is less likely to be released. Another type of weakness is due to pregnancy, which entails the danger of pain or miscarriage. Still another is due to menstruation, which makes the pores hollow due to loss of blood.

Ritual contamination may cause excessive crying in an infant, illness (fever and vomiting), or bodily deformity. It comes from a number of sources. One of the most common is the evil eye. People who have unusually bright, staring, or hypnotic eyes are thought to cause illness or harm merely by looking at another person. It is possible for this person to contaminate the individual unconsciously as he (or, more frequently, she) admires him, but some cases of evil eye are said to have been deliberately caused by a witch. Infants are particularly vulnerable to the evil eye, especially when they are sleeping and hence defenseless. Another kind of contamination is *mal aire*, a term which includes two rather different concepts. One is simply evil air, which may enter the body and cause illness. Gas in the intestines is interpreted as "air inside" and is a cause of worry and loss of appetite In many barrio people. Night air is evil, and people go outdoors at night rarely and then with nose and mouth covered by the rebozo or serape.

The second concept translated as *mal aire* is a dark shape which may be encountered at night. This shape frightens the victim, and fright is formally the cause of the resulting symptoms. However, the symptoms—fainting, dizziness, "absence of breathing," half-consciousness—are quite different from the usual result of fright. The same symptoms are reported for the result of an encounter with the *tabayuku*, or owner of the earth. The *tabayuku* appears only to men, and always in the shape of a woman—the particular woman whom the man is thinking about at the moment, whether wife or lover or someone else. The *tabayuku* takes the victim to her cave and kisses him. She offers the victim many wonderful things—all the things he has wanted—and asks that the victim pay her for them with a kiss. Afterward the victim returns home half-crazed, and unless he is cured, he may die.

Evil air also emanates from the body of a dead person. It can cause a swelling on the back of the head of a newborn infant if either he or his mother is exposed to it.

Sorcery can cause insanity as well as other forms of illness. It is sometimes used by one person who is angry with another. The person who bears the grudge does not do the witchcraft himself. Instead, he hires a witch in el Centro or, more often, in one of the neighboring towns. (There are said to be no witches in the barrio.) The witch may steal the soul of the victim by sending out his *nagual*, or animal counterpart, and illness results. Alternatively, the witch may make a small figure of wax or clay in the shape of the victim and stick cactus spines into it. The figure may have an opening where the stomach would be, into which is placed the stub of a candle previously used at a wake. The witch buries this figure near the victim's house at night in order to cause his illness.

Improper diet or regimen can cause a great variety of illnesses, and diet is considered so important to well-being that those barrio people who consult the town doctor usually ask him to prescribe a special diet for the patient in addition to the medication he suggests. Proper diet is defined in terms of a complex of ideas that attributes hotness or coldness to foods. These attributes do not seem to be consistently related to the actual temperature of the material. For example, meat, fat, chocolate, and mangos are hot foods, while water is cold, and *papauza*, dry toasted tortilla, and aguardiente are apparently neutral or "refreshing." Neither the hot nor the cold condition is good or bad in itself. Rather, good health depends on equilibrium between the internal condition of the individual and the condition of things which affect him. Illness may result from adding hot to hot or cold to cold; taking a warm bath in hot weather or a cold bath in cold weather may produce headache and fever. Similarly, it may follow an excess of hot foods; it is said that people in Copala, who eat "nothing but mangos," suffer greatly from diarrhea. Illness may also come as a result of mixing hot and cold in a particular way; one can develop pains in the arms after grinding chocolate if one washes in water. Anger is especially likely to cause illness if one eats hot foods (pork, fat) while in the hot condition or if one bathes, turning one's hot condition suddenly to cold. As might be expected, the wrong type of food can also aggravate illness which already exists. It is bad for a sick person to drink either cold water or hot liquids; so he is given lukewarm water exclusively.

The hot-cold complex is important, then, not only in diagnosis but also in the treatment of illness. Avoidance of the type of food which caused the illness is one aspect of curing. Another is the administration of cooling or refreshing foods or herb baths, when the illness is regarded as a hot one. Diarrhea is treated by avoiding all hot foods and by eating refreshing or neutral fruits and dry tortillas. A person with a cold may be given a sponge bath in aguardiente mixed with mentholatum and camphor, or mentholatum and candle wax may be applied to his throat, temples, and the sides of his nose. Mejoral, a patent pain-killer, is considered refreshing and may be given in small quantities to children with colds. Fainting and nausea may be treated by application of a cooling herb, *ruda*, to the back of the neck and by drinking a mixture of lemon and bicarbonate of soda. Dizziness after an encounter with *mal aire* or the *tabayuku* is treated by blowing aguardiente from the mouth all over the patient's body and by applying a great number of herbs—*ruda* and myrrh and others. Anger-caused illness and illness due to fright are treated in much the same way. In the case of measles, several steps in the treatment participate in the hot-cold complex in different ways. First, a mixture of aguardiente and mexcal is blown over the patient's body to cool the skin and bring the rash to the surface. He is protected from wind, which might shock the body and drive the rash inward. (When the heat represented by the rash stays inside, the patient usually dies.) Then, some days after the rash has appeared, he is given a sweat bath. Barrio people explain that the heat of the sweat bath is a refreshing heat.

The sweat bath, which is used in combination with various herbs for fevers of other kinds and for rheumatism as well as for measles, is administered in a more or less permanent structure in the courtyard or house of the patient. Some barrio households have a *baño de refresco*, a sweat bath built of adobe, but most build a *baño de toro*, a temporary structure, when it is needed. The *baño de toro* is made by arching bamboo poles to form a framework some 6 feet long and 3 feet high. The framework is placed over a fireplace built with four adobes set in a square. A fire is built in the fireplace, and rocks the size of a softball are piled on top of it. The rocks are allowed to heat for several hours; in the meantime, small leafy branches (brought from the river) are tied together in bunches to form dusters. Finally, the framework is covered with several layers of mats, and the patient and his helper (a woman relative or a professional curer) go inside. Behind a blanket which covers the doorway to the bath, they undress. Water is thrown onto the rocks so that steam rises from them. Then the helper brushes the patient well with the bunch of branches for 20 minutes or more. On emerging from the bath, the patient wraps in a blanket and lies down. He should be given only warm water to drink, but he can have anything to eat that he wants. The sweat bath may be repeated several times at two-day intervals before the cure is considered complete.

In addition to herbs, patent medicines, and baths, a number of rituals are employed in curing illness. Illness caused by the evil eye is sometimes diagnosed by examining the inside of an egg for telling signs, and it can be cured only by the touch of the person who caused the contamination. In other types of illness in children, the patient may be taken to church for an *evangelio*, a short and simple service in which the priest reads scripture over the head of the child, and a candle is lighted. (Evangelio may also be read for children who are not ill as a prophylaxis.) There is some indication that the professional curers of the barrio use rituals or prayers in curing. It would be surprising if the belief in illness caused by fright (*espanto*) were not accompanied by some kind of ritual to retrieve the soul of the patient from the spot at which it was lost, for this combination of beliefs is common in Middle America and, indeed, occurs elsewhere in the Mixteca. Some curers are said to know how to suck foreign objects (inserted by witches) out of the patient's body. Divining the outcome of illness by means of an egg is also reported. The egg is rubbed on the afflicted part of the body and then stood on end. A small piece of incense is placed on top and lighted. If the heat of the burning incense breaks the egg, it is expected that the patient will die.

Ritual means are also taken to prevent illness. Babies often wear a pointed shell on a cord around their necks to prevent coughs. They can be protected from contamination caused by the presence of death and from spells cast by witches by a bag of selected herbs which the mother wears tied around her waist.

Curing may be attempted by members of the patient's immediate family, in the first instance. Herb remedies for simple illnesses are widely known, and aspirin is often bought in local stores. Often, also, the patient is given no medication at all but is allowed to rest and is given little food until the disease goes away of its own accord. Illness which is vague (e.g., headache, slight fever, listlessness) and not alarming in its symptoms may be tolerated by the patient and the family for days or even weeks. At some point, which differs in each household, the illness is defined as serious and treatment is begun. Home remedies and store-bought medicines are usually tried first, and it is when they have no effect that a professional curer is sought.

The barrio has several professional curers, all of them women who also serve as midwives. Their methods include the rituals described above, and it is they who apply the more elaborate herb baths required in cases of fright and anger. If the illness is judged to be caused by witchcraft, a witch from a neighboring community may be called in to cure it.

Local *curanderas* charge less and are generally more trusted than the town doctor, but barrio people occasionally consult the doctor. A resident doctor in Juxtlahuaca is a rarity, the only ones in recent years having been recent graduates doing their six months of required social service. To a considerable extent, they share the feeling of el Centro people toward the Indians and behave toward them in much the same way. Barrio people who visit the doctor are likely to be examined briefly or not at all and to be sold medication at greater than usual cost. Nevertheless, some families take their sick members there when the illness defies local treatment and they have the money. Frequently they ask for injections, one of the services that only the doctor can perform. While injections have the confidence of some barrio people, others fear them. It is rumored that the recent death of a barrio child was caused by one of the doctor's injections.

Praying to the saints may be an adjunct to any cure for an illness. An ill person may go to the church where the statues of the saints are kept and make a special prayer on an individual basis to the particular saint. The typical procedure would be for the individual to light a candle for the saint and to make an informal prayer to him. In a few cases, an individual would go to the priest and ask for a special mass or service. The practice of promising a saint a special mass if he will cure an illness is also known, although very rarely used. On the whole, the part played by the saints in curing is a nominal one and is primarily an adjunct to other methods.

Although illness is an everpresent concern in the barrio, it does not seem to be a dominant one. People make an effort to avoid illness by eating properly and behaving prudently (avoiding anger, aggression, and ritual contamination). When they become ill, they tend to wait patiently until they are well again. If the illness is severe or of long duration, they attempt to cure it—first by the means which are nearest at hand and least expensive, next by means which are thought more certain but also cost more, and, finally, by any means at all up to a given economic limit. Death, when it comes in spite of everything that has been done, is seen as a loss but also as an end to suffering, and it is accepted "if God wishes it."

Psychiatric Illness in a Small
Ladino Community

Horacio Fabrega, Jr. and Duane Metzger

Primitive or folk medicine traditionally has been a subject of interest to both anthropologists and psychiatrists.[1] Many anthropological and psychiatric studies

[1]See, for example: W. H. R. Rivers, Medicine, Magic, and Religion, (London: Kegan Paul, Trench, Trubner, 1924). F. E. Clements, "Primitive Concepts of Disease," (Univ. of Calif.,

have focused on the medical beliefs of various primitive societies.[2] In many settings disease classification is known to be a result of conceptions of etiology that include naturalistic and supernaturalistic premises, and the meanings of disease to individuals have been shown to be quite different across cultural and subcultural groups.[3] Studies of this type have both intrinsic scientific interest and considerable practical value to public health.[4] In published reports dealing with folk medical systems, however, there is little direct reference to psychiatric illness. This omission may reflect the unified way in which disease seems to be construed and modeled in certain preliterate settings, in which there appears to be no necessary distinction (social, moral, or medical) between afflictions of the "body" and of the "mind." In places where psychiatric illness may actually be viewed differently—for example, as more threatening or mysterious—than other diseases, the absence of published reports emphasizing these differences may reflect the reluctance of informants to be interviewed about psychiatric illness, perhaps because concern with it generates anxiety. There are studies, of course, which have dealt specifically with conceptions about psychiatric illness in primitive societies.[5] The emphasis of folk psychiatric studies, however, usually is on therapeutic practices or on the unusual symptoms and syndromes that are found in certain settings.[6]

Investigators who study folk medical systems appear to regard disease generically and to emphasize formal and semantic features of beliefs. There appears to be little interest in studying how the sick person is regarded by others or what his role is in the community. Usually, there is a neglect of the sociopsychological implications and concomitants of illness generally and of the sick person specifically. This position is in contrast to studies in our own culture: Here, the attitudes and conceptions of persons regarding physical and psychiatric illness

---

Publications) in *Amer. Archeology and Ethnology* (1932) 32:185–252. R. Redfield and M. P. Redfield, *Disease and Its Treatment in Dzitas, Yucatan,* Contribution to Amer. Anthropology and History No. 32, (Washington, D.C.: Carnegie Inst., 1940). E. H. Ackerknecht, "Problems of Primitive Medicine," *Bull. History Medicine* (1942) 11:503–521.

[2]See, for example: D. B. Silver, "Zinacanteco Shamanism," thesis submitted to Harvard Univ., June, 1966. R. N. Adams, *An Analysis of Medical Beliefs and Practices in a Guatemalan Indian Town* (Guatemala: Instituto de Nutricion de Centro America y Panama, 1953). L. B. Glick, "Medicine as an Ethnographic Category: The Gimi of the New Guinea Highlands," *Ethnology* (1967) 6:31–56.

[3]See: L. Saunders, *Cultural Difference and Medical Care,* (New York: Russell Sage Foundation, 1954). A. Rubel, "Concepts of Disease in Mexican-American Culture," *Amer. Anthropol.* (1960) 62:795–814. E. Freidson, "Client Control and Medical Practice," *Amer. J. Sociology* (1960) 65:374–382.

[4]C. E. Taylor and M. Hall, "Health, Population, and Economic Development," *Science* (1967) 157:651–657. G. M. Foster, "Relationship Between Theoretical and Applied Anthropology: A Public Health Program Analysis," *Human Organization* (1952) 11:3–16.

[5]See, for example: R. B. Edgerton, "Conceptions of Psychosis in Four East African Societies," *Amer. Anthropol.* (1966) 68:408–425. G. Devereux, "Primitive Psychiatry," *Bull. History Medicine* (1940) 8:1194–1213; "Primitive Psychiatry II," *Bull. History Medicine* (1942) 11:522–542. M. Gelfand, "Psychiatric Disorders as Recognized by The Shona," in *Magic, Faith, and Healing,* edited by A. Kiev, (New York: Free Press of Glencoe, 1964), pp. 156–173.

[6]See, for example: P.-M Yap, "Mental Diseases Peculiar to Certain Cultures. A Survey of Comparative Psychiatry," *J. Mental Science* (1951) 97:313–327. A. Kiev, "The Study of Folk Psychiatry," in *Magic, Faith, and Healing,* edited by A. Kiev, (New York: Free Press of Glencoe, 1964), pp. 3–35. S. Parker, "The Wiitiko Psychosis in the Context of Ojibwa Personality and Culture," *Amer. Anthropol.* (1960) 62:603–623; "Eskimo Psychopathology in the Context of Eskimo Personality and Culture," *Amer. Anthropol.* (1962) 64:76–96.

have been reported,[7] and investigations have focused on some of the social transactions and family adjustments involving the ill person that take place prior to the seeking of care or hospitalization.[8] Little is known about such matters in a "primitive" sociocultural setting. These social concomitants of illness are relevant to psychiatry, since they lead to greater understanding of how human disease is socially patterned and handled by the immediate group. Besides having descriptive value, however, emphasis on the sociocultural correlates of illness allows one to draw inferences about how disease is related developmentally to environmental circumstances, and such information can clarify the natural history of a disease. Field studies dealing with the social concomitants of illness also furnish background information that can be used in subsequent analytical epidemiology studies.

METHODOLOGICAL PERSPECTIVE

Currently, one of the central concerns of anthropology, both conceptually and methodologically, is to obtain accurate descriptions of a group's cognitions in a particular domain. In some investigations the methods of linguistics are used to specify the native conceptual categories that partition a domain of interest (botany or kinship, for example). The formal ordering of a group's relevant cognitions begins with the use of an independent coding scheme which structures the universe represented by the respondent's set of labels pertaining to the domain of interest. By means of this map or independent classificatory system, it is possible initially to delineate the native categories and eventually to determine the ordering principles of the informant's conceptual space. This method of analysis ultimately yields the semantic components of the concepts labeled by the informant's language terms. Providing that the behavior of the respondent in areas relevant to the domain can be predicted accurately by means of hypotheses derived from the cognitive system, the validity of the system is considered high although the conjectured ordering principles may not coincide with those that the respondent actually holds. This study is patterned after semantic approaches of this type[9] in the sense that it makes an attempt to

[7]S. H. King, "Beliefs and Attitudes About Mental Disease," in *Perceptions of Illness and Medical Practice*, edited by S. H. King, (New York: Russell Sage Foundation, 1962), pp. 134–159. F. R. Crawford, G. W. Rollins, and R. L. Sutherland, "Variations in the Evaluation of the Mentally Ill," *J. Health and Human Behavior* (1960), 1:211–219, and (1961) 2:267–275.

[8]See, for example: E. L. Linn, "Agents, Timing, and Events Leading to Mental Hospitalization," *Human Organization* (1961) 20:92–98. Carroll A. Whitmer and C. Glenn Conover, "A Study of Critical Incidents in the Hospitalization of the Mentally Ill," *Social Work* (1959) 4:89–94. M. Hammer, "Influence of Small Social Networks as Factors on Mental Hospital Admission," *Human Organization* (1963–1964) 22:243–251. J. A. Clausen and M. R. Yarrow, "Paths to the Mental Hospital," *J. Social Issues* (1955) 11:25–32.

[9]See, for example: C. O. Frake, "The Ethnographic Study of Cognitive Systems," in *Anthropology and Human Behavior*, (Washington, D.C.: Anthropol. Soc. of Washington, 1962), pp. 72–93. W. H. Goodenough, "Cultural Anthropology and Linguistics," in *Report of the Seventh Annual Round Table Meeting on Linguistics and Language Study*, edited by P. L. Garvin; Monogr. Series on Language and Linguistics, No. 9, (Washington, D.C.: Georgetown Univ. Press, 1957). A. F. C. Wallace, "Culture and Cognition," *Science* (1962) 135:351–357; "The Problem of the Psychological Validity of Componential Analysis," in *Formal Semantic Analysis*, edited by E. A. Hammel, Publication of *Amer. Anthropol.* (1965) 67, No. 5, Part 2;

delineate the meaning others share about a domain and is not concerned with the particular truth-functions of the formulations or conclusions of the native system.[10] To express this in another way, this report attempts to portray the meaning of the domain from the point of view of the inhabitants themselves—that is, what they think about psychiatric illness and psychiatrically ill persons. Although "meaning" is used here in the sense of what someone consciously believes and reports verbally, inferences about the feelings that appear to accompany the verbal reports are offered. Some social circumstances and experiences believed to be important correlates of the beliefs are discussed, but no attempt is made to search for meanings not verbally acknowledged by the social group.

RESEARCH SETTING AND TECHNIQUES

The study we are reporting on here was conducted in Tenejapa, a small town in the highland portion of the state of Chiapas in Mexico, in an area almost entirely populated by Indians. These Maya Indians live in units which surround the valley city of San Cristobal de las Casas, the economic and commercial center of the region. The Maya of Chiapas comprise a nucleus of some 175,000 Indians living in *municipio* units distributed about San Cristobal. These Indian *municipios* resemble townships—they are territorial and political subdivisions of the state, each consisting of a central town and surrounding countryside. The major-

229–248. W. C. Sturtevant, "Studies in Ethnoscience," in *Transcultural Studies in Cognition,* edited by A. K. Romney and R. G. D'Andrade, Publication of *Amer. Anthropol.* (1964) 66, No. 3; 99–131.

[10]This ethnoscientific method contrasts sharply with the approach often followed in other studies dealing with primitive medicine. In such studies, the categories and procedures of a system that is reflected in informants' statements are examined in terms of similarity or validity vis-à-vis the scientific perspective which is regarded as real ("actual"). (See E. H. Ackerknecht, "Natural Diseases and Rational Treatment in Primitive Medicine," *Bull. History Medicine* (1946) 19:467–495; "Contradictions in Primitive Surgery," *Bull. History Medicine* 1946) 20:184–187. That type of approach entails assessing either the "correctness" of the principles of disease classification or the "medical value" of the therapeutic maneuvers that are used. When viewed from such a perspective, the statements that comprise the domain are found to be logically interrelated. The premises used for reaching conclusions are formulated in statements which when judged empirically or scientifically are considered either true or false. They can entail formulations that involve people, animals, physical or natural happenings, spirits, or "magicoreligious" themes (myths or "metaphysical premises"). The classic ideas of B. Malinowski (*Magic, Science and Religion,* (London: Sheldon Press, 1926), pp. 19–84), A. R. Radcliffe-Brown (*Structure and Functions in Primitive Society,* (London: Cohen and West, 1952), pp. 133–177), and E. E. Evans-Pritchard (*Witchcraft, Oracles and Magic Among the Azandes,* (Oxford: Clarendon Press, 1937) appear relevant both to this approach and at this level. For purposes of clarification, it is important to emphasize that this particular analytic approach is not used in this report, although occasional statements may be found which reflect it. Another approach often used in the study of the conceptualizations of a group or individual is that which seeks to explain the belief—that is, to explain "why" it is held. Implicating an underlying conflict or psychological mechanism as the reason for the existence or development of a belief is an example of this approach. When a different (e.g., unconscious) "meaning" is attributed to the belief, this particular approach is usually being followed. (See G. Devereux, *Mohave Ethnopsychiatry and Suicide: The Psychiatric Knowledge and the Psychiatric Disturbances of an Indian Tribe,* (Washington, D.C.: Smithsonian Inst., Bureau of Amer. Ethnology Bull. 175, 1961.) Since the goal of the method used in this report is to obtain accurate and self-contained descriptions of a group's cognitions, the procedure of invoking a meaning that is external to the native system will not be followed.

ity of the Indians live in rural hamlets that are scattered throughout a *municipio*. The town is the governmental and ceremonial focus and, in addition, is important as a trading center for the Indians.[11] Tenejapa is one such Indian *municipio* and is also the name of the *municipio's* central town.

The town is populated by what are locally called Ladinos—people of mixed descent, whose main language is Spanish, who dress in essentially Western clothing, and who are culturally oriented to Western as opposed to indigenous values. Tenejapa (Ladino population about 450) is only 30 miles from San Cristobal de las Casas (population 25,000), but it is nevertheless isolated because of limited communication and transportation. Most Ladino residents of Tenejapa support themselves by farming, raising chickens and pigs, and by trading with the Maya Indians who reside in the township and visit the town.

Field studies having an ethnographic focus (involving both Indians and Ladinos) had been conducted over the past seven years in this *municipio* by one of the authors (DM). This allowed him easy access to four representative residents of Tenejapa who served as principal informants for this study. These Spanish-speaking Ladino males were born and had always lived in Tenejapa, and had cooperated in previous ethnographic studies with the anthropologist. Only two of the informants had completed six years of primary education. It is important to stress that both the past educational experience and current life pattern of each of the informants provide them with only a marginal understanding of current developments in medicine and other basic and applied sciences.[12]

Much of the data for this study was gathered by means of interviews using a technique of ethnographic investigation and description that is in the process of development.[13] The procedures employed were largely those of systematic elicitation of responses from informants, and they can be briefly characterized as directed toward discovering native-language questions which regularly and successfully constrain informant responses to a limited set. Questions which are adequate in this sense are termed frames, and the regularly associated answers are called responses. The frame and responses constitute a unit in the description, and such units may be seen to be related to each other in a variety of

[11]Indian inhabitants of each *municipio* speak a distinct dialect of Tzotzil or Tzeltal, possess a distinctive style of dress, and have local customs that differ in varying degrees from those of their neighbors. The very elaborate socioreligious hierarchy of Zinacantan has been described and analyzed in: F. Cancian, "Informant Error and Native Prestige Ranking in Zinacantan," *Amer. Anthropol.* (1963) 65:1068–1075; *Economics and Prestige in a Maya Community: The Religious Cargo System in Zinacantan*, (Stanford Univ. Press, 1965). E. Z. Vogt, *Los Zinacantecos*, (Mexico, D.F. Instituto Nacional Indigenista, 1966). "Structural and Conceptual Replication in Zinacantan Culture," *Amer. Anthropol.* (1965) 67:342–353. A similar system exists in Tenejapa. This hierarchy consists of ranked series of *cargo* positions in a ceremonial ladder. To pass through this ceremonial ladder a man must serve a year at each level. The subsistence system in these Maya communities is based upon crops of maize, beans, and squash grown in farms that are located in the highlands. The diet is supplemented by chicken and beef, eaten especially on ritual occasions. For further details dealing with the ecological and ethnographic features of these communities, see Vogt, above.

[12]For a descriptive and historical background for some of the relevant conceptions that are common in this region, see G. Aguirre-Beltran, *Medicina y Magia*, (Mexico: Instituto Nacional Indigenista, 1963).

[13]D. G. Metzger and G. E. Williams, "Some Procedures and Results in Study of Native Categories: Tzeltal 'Firewood'," *Amer. Anthropol.* (1966) 68:389–407; "A Formal Ethnographic Analysis of Tenejapa Ladino Weddings," *Amer. Anthropol.* (1963) 65:1076–1101.

ways within the description as a whole. Starting with a shared framework of communication (Spanish was used exclusively), the initial goal is to search for the specific and relevant frames in the domain of interest, namely, psychiatric illness. These frames are used in the subsequent elicitation process when choices, contrasts, and cognitive boundaries are sought.[14]

The interviews were all conducted in the homes of the informants. Initially, most of the data was collected by the formal eliciting procedures. Informal interviews were also held and informants were asked to relate general information pertaining to instances of psychiatric illness they had seen or learned about. Subsequently, repeated group interviews were held with three of these informants. These group interviews will be analyzed in future publications, but they provided some of the background data used in this report.

NATIVE CONCEPTIONS

Locura

When discussing psychiatric illness in general, the Ladinos have a variety of expressions to denote the person who evidences the disturbed behavior. (In each case, English meaning approximations are given in parentheses.) Most likely he will be called un loco, or said to have locura (he is crazy, mad, or insane). Terms that seem to convey humorous ridicule are safado, chiflado, or le patina ("he is nuts" or "he has a screw loose"). Esta fuera de mente seems to be a more formal expression that conveys a sense of gravity and concern or sympathy ("he has a mental disorder," "he's got a nervous condition"). All of these descriptive labels and phrases seem to refer to persons who display very disordered behavior, for when informants are asked how these disorders are manifested or are asked to give reasons for the application of the descriptive label in a specific instance, some of the answers are as follows: He talks to himself, has strange facial mannerisms and gestures, stares at the sky or street, tears his clothes, does not attend to his physical appearance, wanders about aimlessly, often disrobes, can be very violent, is unpredictable, does not carry on meaningful conversations, or urinates and defecates openly showing no concern or restraint. A loco can be either alterado or calmado (agitated or calm). Usually, in the same person the condition oscillates between these two extremes. It is believed that as "the sun starts going down," the disturbance becomes more turbulent and grossly bizarre.

The person suffering from locura is said to feel no pain, to experience no distress in very cold climates, to acquire extra strength as a result of being "mad," to eat raw food, to not sleep, to not think, to be unable to comprehend or recognize people or natural happenings, to lack moral sensibilities, to lack responsibility, and to be impulsive. Some disturbed individuals are said to be "rabid," like wild animals. In virulent forms of locura the person is said to be endiablado, which literally means he is possessed of or by the devil or at least has taken on the attributes of a devil.

[14]For a more extensive review of this procedure, see Metzger and Williams, Op. cit.

Other Kinds of Psychiatric Illness

More extended discussions and less formal eliciting procedures reveal that several other types of psychiatric illness are recognized in Tenejapa besides *locura*. Some of the behavior manifestations of the person who is *loco* and some comments about the nature of *locura* are said to apply to other types, briefly described as follows:

(1) *Desorientado*. A person so described or labeled is able to relate and communicate effectively and manifests some order and organization in his life pattern—that is, he sleeps and eats regularly according to a schedule, recognizes others, and maintains continuous interpersonal relations. He is usually able to support himself at least marginally by carrying out simple tasks. He is regarded as abnormal because of his tendency to be unpredictable and absentminded, and to evidence socially inappropriate behavior. He may not answer questions, or at times he may smile or act foolishly. If employed to carry out a menial task, he has to be carefully watched or supervised because he is distractable and unable to maintain attention and sustained effort. At social gatherings he manifests his inappropriate behavior by inability to participate in the shared meaning of the occasion, foolishness when the occasion demands solemnity, or use of obscene language in the presence of women.

(2) *Atrabancado*. This word is used to label someone who persistently shows a tendency toward impulsiveness and abruptness in his social relations. He is able to be socially independent and self-supporting. When assigned a task, however, his hyperactivity and general restlessness lead him to overlook important details or to terminate the job before it is properly done. He appears unable to regulate his behavior and modify output in order to coordinate it with earlier behavior sequences of shifting demands. Though *desorientado* and *atrabancado* can be used descriptively to refer to particular actions of persons not necessarily regarded as disturbed or abnormal, they are also used as nominal form-class concepts denoting a type of psychiatric illness.

(3) *Tonto* or *Idiota*. These terms refer to persons who are grossly deficient in cognitive faculties. They are said to be unable to comprehend or communicate, but otherwise manifest no bizarreness, agitation, or unpredictability; they attend to biological needs only in a rudimentary way.

(4) *Nervioso*. This term denotes individuals who are able to work and be self-supporting, and who usually manifest sound judgment. It is the nature of their emotional life that is regarded as abnormal, for they are said to be excitable, hyperactive, tense, and impulsive. One who is prone to aggressive outbursts, or one who constantly worries or is overly sensitive, is said to be *nervioso*.

Beliefs About the Etiology of Psychiatric Illness

The following remarks are some of the replies to the Spanish frame inquiring about the cause of the condition of *locura*: (1) Trauma to the head can lead to *locura* because it "disconnects the organs of the mind." (2) Hereditary defects. (3) Injury during the delivery process can damage or traumatize the child and injure his mind. (4) Insufficient sexual contact. With regard to males, it is said that when "maturity" first becomes manifest by a change in the individual's voice, it is imperative that the boy start having heterosexual relations to insure a normal development. Fathers will normally give their sons this advice and frequently secure a woman for this purpose. Failure to do this means that "material" accumulates, spills over into one's system, and can cause mental and bodily damage that can result in *locura*. (5) Excessive sexual activity depletes the male of vital material, and this weakens his mental constitution. Seminal material is considered the "finest and purest essence of the blood," and insufficient amounts can weaken and disorganize an individual. (6) Masturbation. It is said that masturbating to ejaculation entails a fourfold loss of sexual products as contrasted with intercourse. In addition, because it is unnatural and mechanical, it can likewise be harmful. The importance of sexual themes in the etiology of psychiatric illness seems to be limited to males; females are regarded as passive and more sacred and are never discussed vis-à-vis sexuality. (7) Malevolent action against the person manifesting the disturbance. Any social altercation can prompt someone who feels that he has suffered an injustice to obtain the services of a person who can cause psychiatric illness. These intermediary agents can be either *hechiceros, brujos,* or *espiritistas malignos* (persons in a pact with the devil). Though they can resort to several mechanisms to bring on the illness, most often they use *bebedizo,* which is applied to food or drink and has a particular capacity to bring on acute psychiatric illness, often of the "violent" type, which can culminate in death. It should be emphasized that contained in any "cause" of *locura* is the implied belief that either directly or indirectly it is the result of diabolical activity. (8) Inadequate or insufficient food can weaken the "constitution" and eventually lead to psychiatric illness. "Heavy" meals, and food containing excess vitamins, salt, or "heat" can also have a deleterious effect on the mental constitution. (9) A cold air or draft. (10) Excessive exertion. (11) Implicit in several of the above, but also explicitly regarded as capable of bringing on psychiatric illness, is *una impresion fuerte* (a strong impression or emotional experience). A sudden fear, a disappointing business failure, excessive "love passion," and the abrupt acquisition of a great quantity of money are some of the examples cited. Any strong subjective experience, in fact, seems to be regarded as potentially dangerous to one's mental health. The experience takes possession of the *cerebro* (this word can imply both mind and brain), and can disorganize it and compromise the person's behavior and thinking. Related to this point appears to be the belief that persisting worries of any type and excessive intellectual work or study can bring on *locura*. (12) *Una sugestion* (literally, a suggestion, being taken in by someone, or being overcome by an idea). Emphasis here apparently is on an idea or conception (emotional concomitants being secondary) that "grasps the mind" and can then control or rule the person and impair his autonomy or capacity for independent thought and action. Some overlap between this item and items 7 and 11 is acknowledged. It is imperative that an individual be strong and have confidence in his thoughts and perceptions in order to be able to resist impressions and suggestions. (13) Insufficient social stimulation is believed to result in *locura*, and those who lead isolated lives and work and live in the fields are particularly prone to develop psychiatric illness. Contact with other people is needed to develop one's brain and mind and to enable him to acquire normal living habits.

OBSERVATIONS AND COMMENTS ON NATIVE CONCEPTIONS

The attitudes and opinions of the informants about persons suffering from *locura* suggest that the disturbed person is regarded as if he were not "human." In addition, emphasis is placed on grossly bizarre, socially inappropriate and disorganized characteristics, which seem to imply a regressed and psychotic individual with marginal or absent "contact." It can be inferred that, in general, the psychiatrically ill person is regarded as being dangerous and is much feared, though because of his irrationality, absence of understanding, and impulsiveness, he is not blamed and frequently is pitied. Psychiatrically ill persons are believed to possess no souls or to have fallen out of grace with God. It is said that among the Maya Indians of the region, persons whose behavior is judged to be disturbed are often assumed to be witches and are consequently killed. No instance of this belief, or of an execution for this reason in the Ladino population of Tenejapa, was elicited.

The features used in the classification of the various psychiatric illnesses suggest that Ladinos use primarily interactional and social criteria to classify persons who manifest maladaptive behavior. In other words, it seems that it is the manner of and capacity for conducting structured and group-validated interpersonal relations that are used as criteria in judging if someone is normal or suffering from a psychiatric illness. Even with those who are regarded as ill because of their possession by or close involvement with spirits, the illness is recognized and labeled because of its constraint on social relationships, and not necessarily because the person expresses unusual beliefs or because he claims unusual perceptions. Judging adequacy or normality by behavioristic criteria, Ladinos appear to implicitly regard one who manifests this maladapted behavior as reflecting or containing attributes of the mysterious and uncertain. This belief in turn, which we shall discuss below, appears to account for the anxiety and fear Ladinos display when they talk about or deal with the psychiatrically ill person.

Central to all considerations of health and illness is the notion of a person's *consistencia* (consistency, one's inner substance). It is a construct that appears to denote bodily material. Proper diet, rest, and exercise are conducive to the development of a *consistencia fuerte* (strong consistency), which protects one and makes him less vulnerable to illness. If pathogenic circumstances surround a person and he does not succumb to illness, this is attributed to his strong consistency. On the other hand, if one has a *consistencia debil* (weak consistency), even slight exposure to noxious factors can lead to serious illness. Regardless of what is believed to have caused *locura, consistencia* is inevitably used as an explanatory (intervening) concept. There is also the belief that conformance with religious and ethical principles protects the individual as he engenders love and respect from God and his fellow man. The obverse—immoral conduct and violation of the group's validated rules—leads to supernatural displeasure and personal animosities and jealousies which prompt retaliation, either directly through God, devil, or angered neighbors, or indirectly through *hechiceros* or *brujos* (roughly, sorcerers or witches).

The General Domain of Psychiatric Illness

When lengthy and unstructured discussions are held with informants on the subject of psychiatric illness, very often the conversation turns to interpretations of experience involving considerations of spirits, devils, individuals in a pact with the devil, and malevolent doings by others alone or through the intermediation of *hechiceros* or *brujos*. Careful analysis of verbal reports reveals that very often psychiatric illness is thought to occur as a direct result of *espiritus* or *actos del diablo* (devil's doings). In addition, even when very "naturalistic" explanations or causes of psychiatric illness are given (such as an accident involving a blow to the head), the devil is thought to have acted indirectly (for instance, by distracting the afflicted person). The classic description by Evans-Pritchard of witchcraft among the Azande can be consulted as an illustration of the general tendency to invoke the devil as an intervening variable in the causation of psychiatric illness.[15] For the Ladino of Tenejapa, stories of persons seeing or talking to spirits or even the devil are common. A report of this type, though frightening, is regarded as a veridical experience and is not questioned. Should someone show undue concern and preoccupation about spirits and talk of fearing possession by them, however, it is then likely others will say he has been "affected" by these spirits and that he may be suffering from early manifestations of *locura*. It may then be thought that his illness (*locura*) was actually caused by the spirits, though the reality of his contact with the spirits would not be doubted. In other words, the existence of spirits does not seem to be questioned; they are known to communicate with people. They usually are seen or heard at night or when a person is alone, and invariably within a context that is associated with profound anxiety. Discussions focused on this topic also produce considerable anxiety, and it appears that spirits and devils are relegated to the domain of experience that is labeled mysterious, threatening, and dangerous. Consequently, it is the psychiatrically ill person's relative preoccupation with this facet of his life and the absence of appropriate anxiety or feeling of eeriness about it that appear to underlie the judgment that he is suffering from *locura*. In addition, it is also believed that spirits can cause *locura* by taking possession of an individual. Preoccupation with spirits is taken as evidence of incipient possession by them and "madness." Whether a particular manifestation is regarded as the result of a normal belief or any other culturally sanctioned interpretation of experience, as opposed to a pathological symptom, is determined not so much by content or structure as it is by its relationship to a social context or by the manner in which it is reported.[16]

It should be stressed that beliefs and experiences involving the intervention of supernatural agents, both benign and malignant, in daily affairs are common in this social group and are not exclusively associated with notions of psychiatric illness. Sorcerers are sought to "win" a person or to promote a love affair, and formulas and potions are available for this kind of activity. Activity of this type is never openly discussed; who uses the sorcerer, and the identity of sorcerers are carefully guarded secrets. A prominent set of beliefs concerns the return of the dead and the possibility of communicating with deceased persons. Most people can report a personal incident, or one involving relatives, in which a deceased loved one was seen. When a Ladino dies in Tenejapa, a filled glass of

[15]See Evans-Pritchard, *op. cit.*
[16]A. F. C. Wallace, "Cultural Determinants of Response to Hallucinatory Experience," *Arch. General Psychiatry* (1959) 1:58–69. E. A. Weinstein, *Cultural Aspects of Delusion: A Psychiatric Study of the Virgin Islands*, (New York: Free Press of Glencoe, 1961).

water is kept near his bed for ten days so that the spirit may drink should it become thirsty. Accounts of *naguales* (beings who frequent the night in animal form) are common, as are stories of diabolical persons with "supernatural" abilities and capacities, who can deceive, trick, or injure one. It is never clear in fact who may *not* be in a current pact with the devil. Also, what may be classified by an observer as incidents that are associated with strong emotional and subjective concomitants—such as anxiety, awe, suspicion, sadness, fear—are often labeled as examples of "suggestions" or "effects" that involve or are caused by evil spirits or magical agents. In summary, diabolical influences, spiritism, and the supernatural in general are all very real to the Ladino and affect him frequently and in a variety of ways. This dimension of his life is regarded as threatening, dangerous, and mysterious. The conceptions that Ladinos have about a disturbed person or about psychiatric illness per se also involve this dimension. It is as if the *loco* or *locura* personified in a very grotesque and forceful way this frightening aspect of the Ladino's life experiences.

Factors Affecting the Report of Beliefs

When informants are questioned concerning their stated conceptions of psychiatric illness, very often it appears as if they lacked an explanatory mechanism that could account for the development of the disease. In other words, what appears to be a very condensed belief or statement is offered as the cause of *locura*. For example, masturbation, diabolical activity, or an emotional experience will be said to bring on *locura*. The informant will not volunteer information that will systematically relate the "cause" to the *locura*. On first impression, the informant's statements regarding how *locura* develops might suggest that Ladinos have no systematic etiological explanation. But it would be more accurate to say that their explanation of psychiatric illness is inadequate from the standpoint of the observer, who relies on different explanatory premises and principles that he "feels" or "knows" are correct. Confidence in an explanation or mechanism is obviously a very subjective matter and, consequently, relative to the needs and capacities of the individual and group. Almost invariably, when informants were probed further to explain how the particular cause eventuated in the *locura*, they would manifest some incoherence, uncertainty, and, in general, behavior clinically consistent with anxiety. Usually, the ultimate basis offered in support of a belief or explanation about the cause of *locura* was a communication or social transaction with an important other person, often a relative or what could otherwise be called an authority figure. A simple and direct example of this is, "I was told by my uncle that X is what caused his *locura*," or "I knew Y about him [the patient], and Don Ramon told me Y causes loss of mind." We concede, of course, that psychological certainty entails a trusting commitment of some kind, and perhaps citing authorities is a universal response when persons are pushed for an explanation. What we are emphasizing here is the apparent readiness of Ladinos to rely on the judgments of others for the resolution of the questions that arise about specific instances of psychiatric illness. In other words, despite a system of beliefs and conceptions that is flexible enough to include all kinds of disturbances encountered, the basis for the certainty communicated by informants (when questioned about their conception of psychiatric illness) seemed to be not in the belief or cognitive system per se, but rather in its application by a significant other person in the specific instance.

Social Correlates of Illness

Tenejapa is a small and isolated town where individuals live in constant and direct contact with each other. The residents, of course, have had long-standing relationships with each other, and a strong sense of group identity unites them. Important happenings in San Cristobal or nearby smaller towns are known to all even though they may not directly concern the people of Tenejapa. Ladinos have friends and relatives residing throughout neighboring communities, and the information gained by one person on a business or social trip to another community is brought back and discussed by all. Within Tenejapa also, events that may initially involve only a few quickly become public. Private experiences or misfortunes are rare, since reports of most events are quickly transmitted and shared.[17] Perhaps because of this, psychiatric illness, or any kind of illness for that matter, is something everyone experiences vividly.

When a person becomes ill and suffers pain or traumatic mutilation, or manifests grossly disturbed and disorganized behavior, he is not usually isolated in an institution (i.e., hospitalized).[18] Instead, he continues to live in Tenejapa and the family attempts to cope with the disability in the home. Other residents witness and share the suffering and quickly learn about the disease and its consequences. Very frequently, an attempt is made to help the family cope with the concomitants of the illness. Neighbors volunteer advice or food and other related services. This sharing promotes direct experience of, and participation in, the effects of disabling illness. Also, the chronically ill (e.g., epileptics in poor control) live in the town and their exacerbations are often witnessed or learned about. When the condition of a chronically ill person deteriorates, or, in general, when any acute illness breaks out, it is often friends and relatives that will first treat the sick. Later, if this fails, they may help the family travel by horseback or truck to a nearby town to see the "right" herbalist, spiritualist, or doctor. Moribund persons are helped, fed, and cared for by family and relatives; friends will often take turns in relieving the family of burdens. The day-to-day status of a dying person is usually known to all residents of Tenejapa. When death comes, the funeral and social events that follow involve most of the residents of the town and seem to be powerful emotional experiences for all. Mourning becomes a group affair and experience. Details of the loss and of the witnessed pain and suffering are shared, discussed, and reexperienced.

[17]For a description of some of the ways in which inhabitants of other Ladino towns gain information originally of a private nature, see J. C. Hotchkiss, "Children and Conduct in a Ladino Community of Chiapas, Mexico," Amer. Anthropol. (1967) 69:711–718.

[18]Hospitalization is, of course, sometimes resorted to, but only in very rare circumstances, when family and local measures fail. Hospitals, staffed by physicians, in San Cristobal or Tuxtla Guttierez (the capital of the state of Chiapas) may be used. What little use is made of a hospital, clinic, or physician seems to be related primarily to the Ladino's felt need for diagnosis (or advice or prescriptions). The idea of using a hospital for short- or long-term treatment or for convalescence seems to have almost no currency. These factors relate to the values associated with the family, and the meanings attached to separations from the family and features of Western scientific medicine generally. For example, patients with broken bones may be "hospitalized" in the home of a well-known bone setter, but it is likely that a spouse or relative will "stay in" with the sick person. Hospitalization for psychiatric illness was reported, but this was unusual and occurred in cases of extreme social disorganization. The general point emphasized here is what might be termed the "tolerance" that exists with regard to pain and illness, and the extent to which illness and symptoms are woven into the social life of the community—psychiatric illness and symptoms included.

The consequence of this general closeness and sharing is that severe illness, psychiatric illness included, is something about which the informants "know" a great deal and have very strong feelings. Thus, in the broadest sense, the "treatment" of psychiatric illness is something in which all residents seem to participate. They either help take the patient or family to the chosen therapist or bring the latter to the town. In addition, since in most cases the ill person stays in the town, it is the residents who "restrain" or contain the behavior when it exacerbates. An acute agitation or disorganization is thus handled by the group; and when the acuteness subsides, social adjustments are required and made in the group for "preventive" reasons. Psychiatry as "practiced" in this community, then, very much involves the group. The *loco* is cared for and looked after by the town residents. He is fed and often clothed by others, and, should he wander away, he will be brought back by a friend or somebody who knows of his "condition." The excesses of a *nervioso* are tolerated; should he drink too much, he will be encouraged to stop. When relating to him on a social occasion, the townspeople will make careful attempts not to provoke him. All residents share knowledge about who is *loco, atrabancado,* or *idiota;* who needs care and must be looked after; and what is the most socially expedient way to relate to those who are ill or vulnerable.

CASE ILLUSTRATION

This case history is presented as translated from a verbatim report by an informant.

The Señora which I am about to refer to is called Y. Sixty years old, single, born in Huixtan and living in this town of Tenejapa for approximately some thirty-five years. Her physical and moral conditions have in the past always been normal. This lady is my neighbor and I have observed some faults in her mentality. This lady had her parents, a brother, and a sister. The father died first, then all there was left was the mother, one sister and one brother, and remained like that for a long time. Afterwards, the mother died, about a year later the brother died. The two sisters were left, but they did not get along. Then the sister looked for work and moved out of the house.

The lady stayed in the home and when she found herself alone she started to get lonely. She started to change physically and morally and it was observed that she had points of madness, her actions were contrary to normal [the normal behavior]. When this lady started with her madness, she could not sleep nights. All she did was talk during the nights about things without meaning [meaningless things], suddenly, she would start singing or shouting. In short, to do things without any sense. Then she started losing weight since she didn't cook her meals and ate when she pleased [ate at all hours]. This lady became pale and thin. The relatives tried to give her food, but she would not accept it. Sometimes some of the neighbors of this lady would take her some meager things to eat. Like you would say, bread, milk, coffee; but everything was useless, she did not accept [she would not eat]. She very often avoided talking to us and to other neighbors. She would not act the way she used to. She started conversing with herself during the day and as time went by, her talking increased, a thing that at night made it impossible for her to sleep, and in her conversations, she always talked about the dead brother and of her mother, and in this way she spent all her nights. Some people would take her some things to eat and she would not eat them because she would say they could be poisoned and that is why they could not help her, and also, Mr. X would take her some medicines and the lady would make Mr. X take it first and she would ask him if the medicine didn't have something in it and that is why she wanted him to take it first. When she was talking, she would lock herself in her home and it was impossible to go in and talk to her.

Considering the state of madness by which said lady was going through, the relatives tried to see that she become cured, they went to the clinic that is run by the nuns and immediately they came to the house to treat the lady Y, but it resulted that she did not let herself be treated. In studying the fact that this lady would not let herself be treated, some people were of the opinion that they should speak with the priest and maybe through him she would let herself be treated, including taking some nourishment. In fact the priest came to the sick lady's home, but it happened that he found the doors locked. The priest could not go inside the house. Considering that the lady is the only one that lives in her house and that her relatives live apart, by such concept, they could not have realized at what time the lady had locked herself in her home. As a result, certain people were of the opinion and said that it would be interesting to climb through the attic and observe if the lady was inside her house—and that is the way they went about it. When the person went inside the house through the attic he said, "Here she is, in bed lying down on her stomach." Then the priest said, "Come down and open the doors so we can go in and see if she is dead." The person that went inside the house to open the doors was frightened because he had observed that near her bed the lady had knives and machetes, and he was afraid that she was going to attack him. Finally, the priest and one of the sick lady's relatives went inside the house. When she realized that these people were inside her home, she became furious and tried to reach the knives she had by her bed; but immediately they grabbed her by the arms and detained her. At that moment they tried to force some medicine down her and immediately some food. Then the priest procured some holy water and blessed the place and with that she started calming down.

Then the sister, who is all right, would send her food at the proper hours [so that she would eat on time] and little by little she stopped conversing with herself and then she started going over to the neighbors' homes to spend the night. She would come to one house one night and another house the next. The neighbors would ask her why was she asking for lodging, and she would answer that it was because somebody wanted to murder her. The neighbors would ask her who, and she would say, "Some bandits that want to steal my belongings." And the people who would lend their homes to her would lament themselves because she would always carry a knife when she went to sleep, and also she had "head" lice. Those were the two things that would worry them because with the knife she could kill them. What if the madness would hit her, she could get off the bed and finish them [kill them], and the lice they could catch, and they would pray to God that she would not come [to their homes] at night, and they would sometimes close their homes early so that when she arrived she would find the house locked and she wouldn't come in, and maybe she would go to another house for that night.

Still, as a result of the attention she started receiving, little by little she regained her reasoning, and she improved in about three months after the time she became sick. Now lately it has been observed that this woman Y, that possibly she has disregarded her meals, possibly because of some circumstances, and suddenly it is observed that the madness wants to come back. It is considered that her madness comes because of the lack of nourishing meals—what is commonly called debility [weakness] of the brain.

This case summary illustrates some of the features of the social context and the social implications of psychiatric illness in this community. Illness is made a social affair, and the care of the psychiatrically ill is initiated and carried out by neighbors and important leaders of the community using measures that have local meaning. Some of the current attitudes, foci, and goals of "community psychiatry" could be said to be embodied and applied in this setting. In other words, an instance of psychiatric illness in the town leads community leaders and residents to intervene with the intention of resolving what perhaps is felt to be a crisis situation in the community. The goal of the intervention is restoration of social functioning and the elimination of social isolation and withdrawal, and this is initially attempted directly by trying to meet the physical and psychosocial needs of the sick person. He is not segregated or institutionalized. Actions and responses of residents carry the implication that the "patient" will remain an integral part of the community, and spontaneous "treatment and rehabilitation" efforts are made. This pattern of coping with a crisis involving psychiatric illness stands in contrast to that adopted in Western civilization.[19]

In a broader and more humanistic perspective, it would seem that a real concern for the ill person and a desire to be of help to him play an important role in the community involvement. It is acknowledged that an analysis of the implications of this kind of social intervention is an exceedingly complex matter and is in many ways beyond the scope of this presentation. In general, the above case summary, as well as the related substantive issues dealt with earlier in the paper, suggests that some of the current focal concerns of psychiatry and the emphasis on community mental health are not necessarily accompaniments of only Western scientific knowledge or of attitudes about the saliency of methods of treatment based on this knowledge.

[19]M. Foucault, *Madness and Civilization: A History of Insanity in the Age of Reason,* (New York: Pantheon Books, 1965).

On the Possibility of Friendship
Craig MacAndrew and Robert Edgerton

Of the relationships that are so much a part of everyday life, few have resisted agreed definition, much less adequate explanation, more successfully than has the phenomenon of "friendship." There are almost as many definitions of friendship as there are definers, and whether friendship is attributed to "complementary need satisfactions" or to "perceived similarity of values and personality," whether it is seen as an essentially instrumental form of role performance or as an attenuated or diverted sexual relationship, few would seriously recommend that our understanding of the relationship goes much beyond the programmatic. Concerning friendship, then, there is as Rangell (1963) suggests, a need for basic case descriptive material:

It is astonishing how little has been written in the psychoanalytic literature on this most frequent of all human relationships. The references which do exist are generally glancing, scanty and en passant. (p. 3)

Nor is this dearth of case material in any way peculiar to the psychoanalytic literature. While there is information of sorts available on the criteria people proffer in answer to such questions as "Why do you like Smith?" etc., descriptive studies of the phenomenon as it manifests itself over its temporally extended course are virtually nonexistent.

What follows is a case study of an enduring friendship between two severely retarded institutionalized males whose IQ's place them within the "imbecile" range. Because persons at this level of mental retardation are commonly held to possess only the barest rudiments of those qualities which are taken to be peculiarly human, the present case report will perforce concern itself, albeit by indirection, with the very *possibility* of friendship.

THE FRIENDS

Lennie and Ricky are patients at Pacific State Hospital, a large public institution for the mentally retarded. Lennie is a 28-year old male who is both spastic and epileptic. He suffers from frequent epileptic seizures (grand mal) and, as a severe spastic, his speech, ambulation and general motor control are severely impaired. On three psychological evaluations conducted over the past ten years, Lennie's IQ has consistently measured either 31 or 32. He is extremely frail of build, and his angular features are characterized by an intensity of expression which erroneously suggests that he is constantly in pain.

Ricky is a blind 33-year old male with Von Recklinghausen's disease. He, too, suffers a marked disability of gait; his speech, however, while grossly limited, is not quite so severely impaired. Although Ricky's IQ was moderately higher in childhood—at ten years of age, his IQ was found to be 53—it has remained between 34 and 40 over the past 20 years. In contrast to Lennie, Ricky is pudgy, round of face and typically relaxed in appearance. His perennial good humor is remarkably contagious, an effect which is in no small measure responsible for his status as a ward favorite.

Considered independently of their relationship, neither Lennie nor Ricky is remarkable. Other patients at this hospital, and at other institutions for the mentally retarded for that matter, present essentially similar constellations of pathology and of deficit. Their relationship to each other, however, is *not* commonplace—it is an extraordinarily intense and pervasive friendship. As the official ward notes repeatedly record, "These two patients are inseparable." Indeed, their relationship is so all-encompassing and so durable that it is unique in the institution.

Ricky was institutionalized in 1940 at the age of 10; Lennie was institutionalized some 13 years later at the age of 18. A few months after Lennie's admission he was transferred to the ward where Ricky had been living for the previous 3½ years. Within a very short period of time after Lennie's arrival on the ward (staff recollections on this point are vague but univocal), their relationship began. Lennie was then 18 and Ricky was 23. There is agreement that prior to his meeting with Lennie, Ricky had never before established close ties with another patient; indeed, he is remembered as having been withdrawn, suspicious and fearful prior to this period. We know that within six months after Lennie's arrival on the ward they had developed a conspicuous friendship, the intensity and pervasiveness of which are said to have remained constant over the 10 years which have subsequently elapsed. That their relationship has literally been devoid of change over this period is scarcely credible, but there is agreement to a man among members of both the professional and the non-professional staff that the essential features of the relationship have been amazingly stable throughout its 10-year history. Thus, although the relationship as described here is based upon observations made over the period of 1962 to 1964, it should be borne in mind that the pattern we shall attempt to document is a long-enduring one.

A TYPICAL DAY

Lennie and Ricky sleep in adjacent beds among more than 80 fellow patients in a large dormitory on Ward Y.[1] All patients are awakened at 6:15 each morning. While most remain in bed as long as possible, Lennie and Ricky typically get up immediately. Upon arising, Ricky goes into the dayhall and sits alone (although blind, he is quite capable of finding his way around the ward unaided), while Lennie, still in his pajamas, obtains clean clothes from the clothes bin for both of them. While Ricky dresses himself quickly, Lennie, whose every movement is an awkward and difficult struggle for control over his cerebral palsied fingers and limbs, is much slower. In desperation Lennie will occasionally request and receive Ricky's assistance in tying a shoelace or fastening a difficult button.

• • •

Continuing now with the daily routine, they enter the dining room before the other patients (an administrative dispensation for their disability) and sit at a table together. Their breakfasts are very shortly brought to them, at which point Lennie examines the meal and informs Ricky of the composition of their morning fare. As a rule, soon after they have begun to eat, other patients begin to enter the dining room. Since seating facilities are limited, some of these patients usually share the same table with Lennie and Ricky. Because certain of the patients who join them take advantage of Ricky's blindness by attempting to remove food from his tray, Lennie takes it upon himself to protect his friend from such thievery. He slaps or strikes the hand of any would-be thief or, if he finds the situation beyond his control, he calls for a staff member. . . .

Unless the weather is inclement, they are allowed to go outside where they usually sit—often for hours at a time—on a wooden bench near the main entrance to the ward. As they sit together on this bench, their world takes on new

---

[1] The patients on Ward Y are extremely retarded ambulatory adult males whose IQ's fall in the lower range of those labeled idiot and imbecile. While details of the patient population and of the ward itself are not essential to our presentation, the interested reader will find an account of these and related matters in an earlier paper by the present authors (MacAndrew and Edgerton, 1964).

dimensions. They talk, observe, interpret and speculate with a contagious gusto, their words punctuated by bursts of laughter, sweeping gestures and a near total lack of self-consciousness. Their conversation is memorable: it is virtually without interruption; it is lively; it is accompanied by dramatic facial expressiveness; and to the outsider, it is almost completely incomprehensible. Indeed, even ward employees who have supervised them for years can understand but snatches of what they say to each other. When attempting to communicate with an outsider, both patients can, with effort, speak more distinctly. When talking to each other, however, their speech has much the flavor of a private language—not literally a private one, of course, but rather a phonetic distortion of English which, while similar to, is more exaggerated than, the speech patterns common to the severely cerebral palsied. While Lennie's ability to articulate English is very limited, Ricky has learned to understand most of what Lennie says and when talking to him has come to modify his own speech to correspond to Lennie's vocal pattern. The peculiar character of their conversation is accentuated by the fact that Lennie speaks in a rapid-fire, high pitched whine and Ricky in an excruciatingly slow, deep bass.

Their conversation ranges over a surprisingly rich variety of topics: reminiscences of prior events, such as last year's trip to the county fair (an annual excursion of great moment to all patients); the detailed comings and goings of the ward staff such as the fact that Mr. Smith is off duty and is probably at home watching TV; the doings of other patients such as the fight yesterday in which one patient pushed another down and hurt him; . . . .

They also monitor the passing scene with intense and detailed concern. Lennie is characteristically acutely aware of the goings on around him and spends considerable time in telling Ricky what he sees—clouds, passersby, birds, cars, trains, airplanes, and the like. There are occasions, however, when Lennie forgets his friend's blindness, as, for example, during their most recent trip to the County Fair where the sight of so many different animals caused him to call excitedly, "Ricky, look at the animals!" At times, interest flags somewhat and Lennie will keep Ricky abreast of such less momentous happenings as the progress of an ant as it passes their bench—a happening which sometimes holds their concerted attention for prolonged periods of time. On such occasions, if the ant stops, Lennie may prod it with a stick, and Ricky will ask urgently, "What's he doing now, Lennie?" At other times Lennie's running commentary on the world around him will cease, and Ricky will request that his reports continue.

• • •

When the weather keeps Lennie and Ricky inside, their time is spent somewhat differently. This is not, however, because their intensely private relationship is significantly diluted by the close proximity of so many others; they construe the profoundly retarded patients on the ward only as nuisances to be avoided, and the staff members are usually too busy to concern themselves with them much beyond occasional passing greetings. In addition to their own general conversation and Lennie's running commentary on the passing scene, the two friends may watch TV together. The audio portion is enjoyed by both, and Lennie, in an occasional phrase, explains what is happening on the screen. They also "read" pictorial magazines together; Ricky turns the pages (always, but for no apparent reason, backwards) and Lennie looks at the pages and describes and/or passes judgment ("Good," "No like that," etc.) upon what he sees. In a single session they may go through several magazines in this fashion. When Lennie tires of giving his comments, Ricky stops turning the pages, and the magazine session comes to a natural conclusion. . . .

Before lunch, Lennie and Ricky may do some "work" on the ward. Their regular assignment consists of washing and drying the dozen or so chrome and plastic couches in the dayhall and TV room. In accomplishing this task, a marked division of labor is readily apparent. While Ricky waits, Lennie, working very slowly and carefully, wipes a couch with a rag dipped in a pail of soapy water. Ricky then feels the couch to see where it is wet and drys it off. Sometimes Ricky asks Lennie that he be allowed to do the washing—a request which Lennie typically honors. Since Ricky cannot see the couch, Lennie assists him on these occasions by providing him with a running feedback. When Ricky finishes, Lennie dries the wet couch, and without saying anything, cleans the spots that Ricky misses. While the job is scarcely performed with great efficiency, it is really neither intended nor expected that they do a perfect job; the administrative intent is rather that the task provide them with some sense of responsibility and accomplishment. The success of this work policy is evidenced by the desire of both patients to do the "important" job of washing. Nor is the job an effortless ritual. It is actually quite difficult and tiring for them as they must bend, stoop and kneel in its performance. Indeed, there are days in which its prestigious character is overweighed by its onerous physical demands, and on such days Lennie and Ricky show themselves not to be devoid of guile—they may profess fancied infirmity or simply absent themselves from the area when the work hour approaches.

After lunch, which proceeds much as did breakfast, Lennie and Ricky sit outside and talk for a short while before Ricky is required to attend the institution's special training sessions for the blind. Thus, shortly before 1:00 p.m. on each weekday afternoon, Lennie (voluntarily) leads Ricky to his classroom which is located some 500 yards from the ward, and usually remains at the school with him until the class ends. . . .

On reaching the ward they retire to the bench outside the main entrance and remain absorbed in their own conversation until they are called for dinner. Afternoon visitors may stop to greet the pair as they enter the ward and, if these visitors are familiar, both patients will recognize them—Ricky is, incidentally, surprisingly adept at the recognition of voices—and return a cheerful greeting. Should additional conversation ensue, Lennie does most of the talking. Ricky, however, must almost always interpret Lennie's words to an outsider; he listens to Lennie, sometimes asks him to repeat some portion of what he has said, and then "translates." If the visitor is a stranger, Lennie and Ricky evidence a marked reticence to speak. Neither will volunteer information and Ricky in particular may become visibly quite anxious. The significance of Lennie's protective or buffer role for Ricky is readily apparent at such times.

• • •

Bedtime is at 9:00 p.m. and after brushing their teeth and changing into bedclothes, they dutifully retire to their adjoining beds, usually at the same time. Neither has problems sleeping.

SOME SIGNIFICANT FEATURES OF THE FRIENDSHIP

Sharing is clearly the most noteworthy feature of the relationship between Lennie and Ricky. We have already documented the pervasiveness with which the two patients share each other's time, perceptions and interests. In comparable degree, they share material things as well. Thus, for instance, should Ricky be given some peanuts or candies by someone on the staff, he will automatically share his gift with Lennie, or, if Lennie is not with him, he will save a share for him until he returns. Lennie behaves in identical fashion. While Ricky has no known living relatives, Lennie does, and he regularly shares their presents of food, clothing, and toilet articles with his friend. Additionally, Lennie's parents regularly provide him with small sums of money with which he finances their regular visits to the canteen. Nor is their sharing contingent upon their physical proximity. On those occasions in which Lennie is allowed to go home on visits for a couple of days or more, he regularly buys a supply of candy and other snacks for Ricky before leaving. Here too, Ricky reciprocates as best he can. Recently, for example, while Lennie was home for a visit, the entire ward went on an off-grounds barbeque picnic and Ricky carefully wrapped and saved a portion of everything served, brought it back to the ward, and presented it to Lennie when he returned. And when Ricky does obtain some money— usually through the sale of a basket he has woven in school—he evidences a generosity towards Lennie which is every bit the equal of Lennie's generosity towards him.

• • •

This leads to a second notable feature of their relationship—the almost complete absence of hostility, bickering or open quarreling. This lack of acrimony is the more remarkable in view of the almost continuous interaction between the two patients; they are seldom separated, the opportunities for conflict are many, yet they are rarely at odds with each other. On infrequent occasions, however, they do quarrel. At such times, Lennie will stalk away pettishly, but his anger is only momentary, and on his return they resume their doings without any visible sign of lingering acrimony. . . .

While such conflict is exceedingly rare, neither Lennie nor Ricky is hesitant to express his displeasure either with other patients or with one or another of the employees. Lennie berates, shoves, kicks or strikes patients who annoy him or who infringe upon what he takes to be either his or Ricky's rights. Although temperamentally more placid and thus less quick to rile than Lennie, Ricky too will defend against any attack upon their real interests by punching or kicking the transgressor. While Ricky is extremely sensitive to teasing, his annoyance is particularly apparent when Lennie is not around. When teased on such occasions he has indiscriminately attacked both patients and employees by punching, kicking, biting and tearing at their clothing. The point to be made is that since neither Lennie nor Ricky is a passive, vegetative person, bereft of emotion and aggressive inclination, the singular lack of conflict in their relationship can hardly be explained on such grounds.

Quite the contrary, with each other they become paragons of demonstrative concern and affection. They greet each other with huge smiles, they talk and joke together with obvious delight, and they repeatedly evidence their continuing regard for each other's well being. When they are together their faces and hands become expressive, and even Ricky's blind eyes become sparkling and alive. In contrast, when either is alone, this pervasive delight gives way to an impassive, somber withdrawal. Examples of the affectionate concern each has for the other are abundant in the happenings of an ordinary day: Ricky responds to Lennie's epileptic seizures or falls by cradling his head and gently patting him until he recovers; as they sit together, Lennie sometimes rests his head on his friend's lap and dozes—and sometimes Ricky will nap leaning against Lennie's shoulder; . . . But the most persuasive evidence of their mutual affection comes from their simple everyday comments, as when Lennie says to no one in particular, "I like Ricky best," or as one regularly asks the other toward the end of a day, "Did you like this day?"

Clearly then, the relationship between Lennie and Ricky is neither parasitic nor exploitive in nature. Neither friend dominates the other—each initiates certain actions and follows in others; each is capable of expressing, and in fact does express, his own sometimes discrepant interests and preferences, and each makes decisions that are binding upon the other. In a word, there is a remarkably equalitarian character about the relationship, with each party depending on, and receiving, sustenance from the other, in a context of overriding mutual benefit. While already mentioned, we could emphasize here that the relationship between Lennie and Ricky has always been rigidly exclusive. Although both are acquainted with many of their fellow patients throughout the hospital, neither Ricky nor Lennie seeks to establish any sort of friendship with these patients; in fact, they regularly rebuff their friendly advances, thus consciously avoiding sustained interaction with them. Indeed, even when Lennie is home on a visit, Ricky typically remains by himself, neither seeking nor accepting friendly contacts with other patients.

We would finally note that their relationship is in no way overtly sexual. Despite its duration and intensity, there is no evidence whatever that there has ever been any form of overt sexual contact between Ricky and Lennie. Staff members whose combined experience spans the full ten years of the relationship, insist that sexuality has never entered into the relationship. Nor is there any reason to doubt the honesty of these reports, for these same employees freely admit to the existence of overt homosexual relations between other patients on their ward. Administrative corroboration of the non-sexual character of their relationship is found in the fact that while the hospital's policy requires that close patient relationships be broken up by physical separation whenever overt homosexual activity occurs, the hospital records which span the ten-year period of their friendship contain numerous entries to the effect that they are inseparable.

We have outlined what we take to be the principal characteristics of a highly improbable, strikingly pervasive and intense friendship between two severely retarded young men. Hopefully, we have provided sufficient detail to convince the reader that this long enduring and highly elaborated relationship is indeed a *friendship* of a highly human order. The existence of such a relationship between two persons of such enfeebled intellect must be counted as compelling testimony to the essentially human character of even the most retarded among us.

That relationships such as this are so rare in the larger population is, perhaps, a commentary on many things.

REFERENCES

MACANDREW, C., and EDGERTON, R. "The everyday life of institutionalized idiots." *Human Organization*, 23, 312–318, 1964.

RANGELL, L. "On friendship." *J. Amer. Psycho-anal. Assn.*, 11, 3–54, 1963.

4 / Roles and Statuses

Introduction

The focus in this chapter is upon cultural patterns that arise when people interact among one another. In all societies there are situations in which individuals relate to each other in culturally-patterned social relations. This general topic merges imperceptibly into the next chapter where we talk about the patterns of family life, and discuss one way in which people interact as members of subgroups within the culture.

The concepts of *role* and *status* are basic to a discussion of this chapter and the one which follows immediately. *Status* refers to an individual's *position* in a society. For example, the President of the United States is a *status* position irrespective of the individual who occupies the position. The concept of *role*, on the other hand, refers to the actual *behavior* of an individual who is occupying a given *status*. The analogy of a stage play may help make these notions more concrete. The manuscript of a play specifies the various *statuses*. During the performance, actors individually occupy these *statuses* and are said to be performing *roles*, which may be performed with various degrees of appropriateness.

As an individual goes through his daily routine he occupies a variety of statuses and performs a variety of roles. In our own society status is sometimes used to refer to all of the statuses that an individual occupies. For example, we refer to an individual as having high general status if he occupies a series of important, specific statuses. He may, for example, be chairman of several boards of corporations, president of a university, and the holder of a Nobel Prize. For the sake of clarity we refer to such general statuses as prestige, and we would describe such a person as having high prestige. We will reserve the word status to refer to a single position.

In Chapter Eight on "Patterns of Conformity and Control," we will discuss the ways in which a culture exerts pressure on the individual to appropriately perform the *roles* of the various statuses that he occupies.

Cultures vary as to their mechanisms for assigning appropriate statuses and roles. Linton (1936) has made the distinction between *ascribed* and *achieved* status. *Achieved* statuses are those which are generally acquired through individual effort and competition. *Ascribed* statuses are assigned to individuals on the basis of inheritance or inherent qualities. An example of an *achieved* status in our own society would be the President of the United States. An example of *ascribed* status would be the Queen of England. To become President of the United States, great individual effort is involved in achieving the strenuous and tension-ridden status of top public servant. In the case of the Queen of England, the position is inherited on the basis of family kinship and there is no choice in the matter of enjoying the prerogatives and comforts of the inherent position. An example of an *ascribed* status based on inherent differences would be that of male or female. Differences in age provide inherent qualities for the ascription of certain statuses. All societies ascribe certain statuses on the basis of inherent sex difference, although each culture uses its own unique and individual elaborations in assigning such statuses. Some of the roles and statuses that vary on the basis of sex are illustrated by selections in this chapter, while others are elaborated further in the following section on the family and sex.

Hamamsy's article, "The Role of Women in a Changing Navaho Society", portrays a phenomenon that seems odd at first glance—the liberation of Navaho *men*. The Navaho are *matrilineal*, which means that most property is held and inherited by women; and *matrilocal*, which means that a groom normally goes to live with his wife and her family after marriage. He traditionally played a somewhat subordinate role in that household, which is oriented around his wife and children and her kinsmen who live in an *extended* family. In the event that the marriage dissolves, the female retains the house and all property.

However, in recent decades a "patrilineal" government policy that put the ownership of land in the hands of men, combined with indirect influences stemming from the U.S. economy, have altered radically the traditional situation. As you will see, the roles and statuses of both men and women have been altered too fast for the Navaho to "catch up" yet. This is, in part, because ascribed roles and statuses—such as those defined by sex—are inherently harder to redefine. It is difficult, consciously, to recognize that the traditional notion of what a man or woman "is" no longer fits the realities of life very closely.

In their careful analysis of "susto" or fright, a psychological disturbance which is common in a Zapotec Indian community in Mexico, O'Nell and Selby illustrate another form of liberation from a sex role. In this case, however, the route of escape is an institutionalized one, and the escape is usually only temporary.

In these Indian communities, by contrast with the Navaho, it is normal for the wives to move into the husband's extended family. Subordinated to her mother-in-law, the woman leads a very constricted life, unable to withdraw from tense relationships in the ways that her husband is permitted to do—e.g., by going off to work on a plantation for the season or simply by getting drunk. According to O'Nell and Selby this probably accounts for their much higher susceptibility to *susto*, a melancholic condition which is locally accepted as a valid "medical" excuse for temporarily receiving special attention and neglecting the normal demands of woman's role.

The status and role of begging in the analysis by Fabrega turns out to revolve around a series of primary dyadic relationships between two individuals—the beggar and the client. It is interesting to note that these are recognized statuses and that most of the encounters are between a single beggar and a single client at any given time. The description is from a town in Southern Mexico and one might compare it to our own society in which more developed institutions organize social welfare functions on the basis of larger groups rather than patterning them around dyadic encounters.

Fabrega explores at length the stigmatized role of the beggar, the behaviors and strategies involved in this role, and the feelings of beggars and of patrons. In some respects, especially for beggars with no visible handicap, this particular role may require a certain amount of dramatization if it is to succeed. Fabrega notes that "when walking, they typically crouch and lean forward. This mode of presentation appears to constitute a facet of a social role. . . ." Though it sounds like a paradox in light of the ordinary usage of the term, the low status of beggar is, in technical usage, an *achieved* one. No one is born to this status; one can become a beggar only by working at it.

In the final reading, Hotchkiss gives us a close look at the children and their conduct in Chiapas, Mexico. He notes that most anthropologists, if they pay attention to children at all, tend to view them as adults-in-the-making; that is, they concentrate on the preparation of children for *adult* roles (e.g., see Parker's article in Chapter Three).

Perhaps it is precisely their low social "visibility" as non-persons which allows children to play rather special and important roles in the community Hotchkiss studied. Adults in this Mexican town are rather formal in their interpersonal relationships and place a high value on privacy and secrecy. However, children generally have ready access to neighbors' homes and bring back news about what they have seen and overheard. This and related roles that substitute for face-to-face encounters between the adults involved fall on the borderline between overt and covert patterns; the roles are not defined nor acknowledged, but everyone knows pretty well what is going on. However, because of their anomalous, out-of-focus nature, such roles are not correlated with a clear-cut status.

REFERENCES

LINTON, RALPH, *The Study of Man* (New York: Appleton, 1936).

The Role of Women in a Changing Navaho Society

Laila Shukry Hamamsy

INTRODUCTION

Most of the work on which this paper is based was done in 1951–52 in the Fruitland Irrigation Project in San Juan County, at the northwestern corner of New Mexico. The project area has a thirteen-mile boundary along the southern bank of the river, which is settled on the north by Mormons and other white farmers. The area at that time included 2,500 acres of irrigated land divided into 205 farms and assigned to 191 family units (Sasaki 1950). The nearest urban center is the predominantly white town of Farmington, just off the reservation.

Although the area has long been inhabited by Navaho farmers and owners of livestock, the development of the irrigation project dates from 1933 when the land was surveyed for the purpose of establishing farm tracts. These tracts were assigned in ten-acre lots to original residents and to applicants from other parts of the reservation.

Particular aspects of Fruitland's position made it useful for the purposes of this study. There is directed social change in the form of government programs, including the irrigation project itself. Further, Fruitland is on the edge of the reservation and is in continuous interaction with the neighboring white society. It is also a well-defined geographic and social unit. Finally, there was available a great deal of data gathered by the research team of the Cornell University Southwest Project which had been working in the area since 1948.

Data for the present study were gathered by the author during a 17-week residence in the Fruitland area in 1951 and 1952, and preceding that, during a three-week residence at Navaho Mountain, a more traditional settlement than that represented by Fruitland. Methods of collecting data were primarily those of participant observation and informal open-ended interviews. They were chosen because of the limited time of residence and because the relationship between the author and the residents rapidly became one of friendship, which seemed to make difficult the role of formal interviewer. Additional sources of data were the field notes of other research workers of the Southwest Project, Indian Service reports and documents, and anthropological literature on the Navaho.

TRADITIONAL ECONOMIC AND SOCIAL ORGANIZATION

The economic and social organization here termed traditional is that which developed after 1868 when the Navaho returned to the southwestern location after a four-year forced exile. It is informal and loosely knit in comparison to that of many other Indians, for example, the Pueblo; and there are local variations due to differing degrees of contact with other groups, historical accidents, and geographic conditions. A general pattern, however, is fairly evident and even today many conform to it. Kluckhohn and Leighton (1946) estimate conformity in livestock regions at 85 percent.

The Navaho traditionally live in widely scattered matrilocal family groups (extended families). Within each group, each nuclear family lives in a separate hogan. The extended family is usually composed of an older woman, her husband, her unmarried children, her married daughters, and the daughters' husbands and children. Some families have additional but secondary shelters at summer pasture lands.

Raising livestock and subsistence farming are the major economic activities. In these, and in the management of the hogan, there is a division of labor between men and women, each assuming significant functions. Men are generally responsible for the horses and cattle, women for the sheep and goats. Women carry the main burden in the running of the hogan, including the making of clothing, but men are responsible for the leather and silver work. Blanket weaving is a common pursuit of the women, and baskets and pottery are made by a few.

The smallest and most important unit of social and economic co-operation is the nuclear family, but in the frequent times of heightened activity such as harvest and planting, all members of the group in an area may help each other. On the other hand, in some regions the extended family operates as a unit. The sheep of all members of the family will be pooled under the direction of the matron of the household, and are herded by the group's young men and women.

The ownership and use of property and livestock is generally subject to control by the extended family, although individuals and nuclear families may be owners in fact. Only personal property such as jewelry and cash is not under such control. Economically, the women fare equally with or better than the men, since they are the usual owners of sheep, a major property, and since they can earn cash through their weaving. In addition, inheritance is through the women, and daughters and nieces often receive the same as or more than the male relatives.

The father is the formal head of the family, but the mother and children make up its stable core. The man moves frequently between his family of orientation and his family of procreation, since he has obligations to both. In contrast, the woman remains with her family of orientation, in her own extended family group. Within this group, and in her own nuclear family, she usually has as much or more influence than her husband. She often makes the decisions in the family's financial affairs, even if the goods involved were originally the husband's individual property. "The general tendency, even in spite of the theoretical power of the avunculate, is for sons, brothers and husbands to consult the maternal head of the house and to respect her opinion" (Reichard 1928:53). Children count descent through the mother and are considered to belong to her and her clan.

The one social function of the family that is usually left to the men is that of relations with the world outside the group, but here too, women can play a part if they choose.

All members of the extended family participate in the raising and training of children. The mother has the day-to-day responsibility for their care and discipline. Maternal uncles have important teaching and disciplinary functions. The father's relationship to the children, on the other hand, is mainly affectional. As the young grow into adult life, they remain under the social control of the family, since they are dependent on the goodwill of parents and relatives for their economic survival and social acceptance.

Marriages are usually arranged by parents and relatives, most importantly the maternal uncles, and are frequently made for economic and social reasons. The groom provides a bridal gift, often livestock and household utensils, and these become the property of the bride. Newly wed couples live near the wife's family, and there is constant visiting of the young woman and her children with the family matron. The husband is excluded from such contact by a taboo forbidding a man to look upon his mother-in-law. The son-in-law's position is a subordinate one in the extended family household and he is closely supervised by his father-in-law. One groom was told: "Your folks have turned you over to us. You don't belong over there any more. You are here now, to take care of the bride's property" (Dyk 1947:109–110). The young married woman, on the other hand, enjoys security and assistance with her household and family tasks from the close relatives surrounding her. Her family protects her if her husband is abusive, and she retains her property and her children in case the marriage fails.

If the marriage is successful and productive, the husband and wife may establish a more independent hogan and may separate their flocks from the family herd, thus becoming the nucleus of a new extended family group. If the marriage dissolves, as is frequent, it is the husband who suffers dislocation and financial loss. Leighton and Kluckhohn (1947:83) estimate that only one woman in four reaches old age with her original husband. Desertion is the most common cause of family dissolution, more frequent even than death. The husband is forced out of his home, to return to his family of orientation or to a new wife's hogan, and his property usually remains with his former wife.

Beyond the extended family, the next unit of social organization is the outfit: a group of related extended families who co-operate in larger economic, social, and religious functions. Groups of outfits occupying specific localities are organized into bands with recognized leaders. There is also a clan organization which is chiefly important as a regulator of marriage choices. There is no indigenous centralized tribal organization.

NEW ECONOMIC POSITION

The drastic changes introduced into the traditional Navaho economic pattern within the last twenty-odd years have had direct effects on women's economic position and on the value of their work, and are, we suggest, important among the forces that are redefining the role of Navaho women today.

Most Navaho have been subject to a slow economic decline and to the accompanying need for new sources of income, notably wage work. In Fruitland the economic picture is particularly sharp. It is an area in which the greatest changes have been made in traditional agriculture and herding patterns. Being a border community, the residents are nearer to work opportunities and more enticed than Indians in the interior by employment opportunities in the white world "outside." Both of these factors have direct effects on the Navaho woman's economic position.

Two aspects of the land policy initiated in 1933 are relevant. First, only married men were originally eligible for land, and only on the condition that they made proper use of it. Women and children, traditionally important owners of land, were thus barred in the beginning from ownership. They could become owners only through inheritance or other transfer from the male assignees. Further, the threat that the government might "take away" the land if it were used improperly introduced an uncertainty not existing in traditional ownership patterns.

The second aspect of the changing economy is less direct. It is that few families manage to make a living from farming alone, or even in combined farming and livestock operations. Most of them are forced to seek additional income. The most available source is in the white communities at Fruitland's border. The economic result of this is that the Navaho woman's family may have more "cash" than formerly, but it is provided by the man of the house. Both of these are elements foreign to traditional organization, and their effect will be discussed in some detail later.

The extent to which this new economic picture applies in Fruitland can be indicated briefly. Crop report estimates obtained from the Farm Management Supervisor of the Fruitland Project reveal that in the summer of 1951 about 69 percent of 191 families had under assignment between six and fifteen acres, and earned a generously estimated yearly income of less than $900. Only nine families owned between 25 and 33 acres (the maximum holding) and averaged $1,774. Livestock holdings are limited by government regulation and by the lack of good range vegetation. In 1952, 69 individuals held sheep-permits, but they stocked only 61 percent of the sheep their permits allowed them.

On the other hand, the dependence of the Fruitlanders on wage work has increased. In 1952, the author interviewed 38 families and found that of the 32 men in these, all but two had at some time engaged in off-reservation or government work. The two exceptions are men who have large acreages and are successful farmers. There were 43 able-bodied women in this same group of families, but only 11 of them had ever engaged in wage work. Of these, only four were married women living with their husbands. The others were widowed or divorced.

When the women do find work, they are usually poorly paid in comparison with the men. There are a few openings in government institutions such as schools and hospitals, but the major sources of employment are in such areas as seasonal agricultural work, restaurants, and domestic service. The men, on the other hand, find their major employment opportunities in such relatively better paid fields as railroads, agriculture, lumbering, construction and road work, and oil, military, and mining operations, in that order of importance.

SOME EFFECTS OF NEW ECONOMIC POSITION ON SOCIAL PATTERNS

All of the traditional units of Navaho social organization still function in Fruitland, but significant changes are taking place in the relative importance of family units. The importance of the independent biological family is increasing, while the influence of the extended family and of larger units lessens. There is also a strong tendency away from matrilocality. Some men and women still share farm and home tasks and the responsibility for children, but many men are frequently not at home to do their share. Finally, the economic responsibilities of the family fall less on the family as a unit, and more on the male head of the independent nuclear family.

Fruitland residence patterns in 1952 show a trend away from matrilocality. Of 36 families studied, there were only five older families acting as heads of extended family units. There were 13 younger couples living as part of these extended groups, but 12 of these were in patrilocal residence. The remaining 18 families lived independently on their own plots; five of them near, but not as part of the husband's family; five near the wife's family, and eight not near families of either spouse. The five families living near the wife's family were cases in which daughters had married outsiders.

In families where subsistence farming and herding are still major occupations, men and women share the tasks. But many women have been forced by their husbands' absences in wage work to take over many of the farm chores that traditionally belong to men. Thus:

In the summer time [according to one informant] she comes and stays at Fruitland in order to take care of the farm. Her husband stays at Shiprock and visits on weekends. Her husband helps on the farm, does the carrying of heavy things, while she does all the rest.

Women without husbands and living away from an extended family find it difficult to maintain their farms. One woman told an interviewer:

My boy has been working outside and I have to irrigate my farm all by myself. Sometimes my neighbors, who belong to the same clan come and help, but most of the time I work it all myself.

Some in this position give up their land:

After her husband's death, she found that she could not take care of the farm, so she gave it to her son and moved next to her daughter.

Women still have major responsibility for housework and the care of children, but housework takes little time. Laundry is meagre and cooking has become simplified and less time-consuming as the women adopt processed foods. Care of the children is less demanding since only the preschool children are constantly at home. The older children are in school, some in day schools and some in off-reservation boarding schools. The traditional craft of weaving has become impossible with the decline of sheep flocks.

This changing pattern toward independent families and less housework affects the women in a number of ways. Mothers of preschool children, while usually not over-worked, lack the support that other members of the extended family could provide. They have the continuous care of the children and if they leave home to visit or shop, must either take the children with them or hire a baby-sitter. Many complain that they feel tied down. They also lack the guidance and assistance in training and discipline that older members of the family could provide.

The women who have no children, or only older children, have little to do. Many are bored or restless:

Before getting married, Elizabeth worked in a cafe in town. She had stopped "to have a rest." She is bored with home, however, and would like to go back to work again. "I hate to stay at home. There isn't much to do."

A few of the women do try to find wage work; many seek diversion in the nearby town, and others in visiting friends and relatives:

I asked: "What does Mary do all day?" Her aunt said, "Nothing. She just takes care of her baby. She comes to visit me and she goes to visit my mother, that's all."

Economically, the wives are generally dependent on their husbands, but the men are often erratic and irresponsible providers. Cash, as was noted above, traditionally the property of an individual owner, is still considered by many men to belong solely to them, with the result that many women are frequently without economic support. One old man told an interviewer:

The Navaho people who work for wages don't put any money in the bank. They spend everything and at the end, they don't have any money to take care of the needs of other members of the family. They will spend all their money on cars sometimes, but they won't have enough money to eat and buy clothes for the children.

Some women do manage to get part of their husbands' earnings. The following comment by one who does, suggests that she feels her husband to be an exceptionally considerate provider:

My husband give me money. Sometimes he cash check and give me money. Many times he give me all of it. . . . He is good that way. He don't go and spend all his money like some do.

In a few families interviewed by the author, both husband and wife have wage work. In most of these, however, each pays his own way, even in recreational expenses such as an evening in town.

The poorest women in Fruitland are generally the middle-aged and old women who have no male providers. They frequently have no economic support except the relatively inadequate welfare aid. Under traditional conditions these women would be well off; they might be managers of large extended family units, or at least respected female relatives with secure positions within the family group.

"OUTSIDE" INFLUENCES ON TRADITIONAL SOCIAL PATTERNS

Through increasing contact with the white world, the Navaho have become familiar with new goods, new ways of doing things, new forms of recreation, and a number of new problems. Many Navaho now own cars, radios, stoves, washing machines, and other modern durable goods. Some build frame or stone houses to replace the traditional and inexpensive hogans. The desire for these new things makes many women urge their men to greater effort in finding wage work, often with the result that the women become still more alone on the farm and in the home. In addition, these new products and ways are rapidly replacing traditional bases for determining prestige and standards of living. The direct effect of this on the women is that they become less important for the family standards and prestige, while the men, as the wage earners, become much more so.

Traditionally, religious ceremonies, dances, fairs, family visiting, and family parties were major forms of recreation. Women, it may be noted, have important functions in most of these. The frequency of these events, particularly the larger and more organized forms, is now diminishing, and no new forms of recreation have developed on the reservation to replace them. Instead, there is an increasing tendency, especially among younger Navahos, to seek amusement in the urban white center off the reservation. To get there, however, the women usually have to depend on the men—for the ride to town and the money to spend. Once in town, men and women frequently seek separate entertainment. For the women this may be going to the movies, eating in restaurants, drinking, shopping, meeting friends, and window-shopping. One man described his family's trip to town: "I'm happy, and my family is happy. I take a couple of drinks, my wife goes shopping."

"Outside" educational patterns are replacing the traditional home education in the skills of home-making, farming, and herding. While this newer education, which is under government direction, is available to both boys and girls, it is frequently the boys of the family who receive the better and longer training. Many girls are taken out of school early to help at home. Since school-learned skills and the ability to speak English are important factors in earning and social abilities, the girls are often disadvantaged. The author found only a few families in which the wife was better educated than her husband, and in some of these families she was a strong member and family spokesman, a position roughly comparable to that of the wife in a traditional family group.

Many of these new ways can be further traced for their effect on family relationships and family harmony. Differences in education, of course, are an important source of conflict between generations of a family, as well as between members of a single generation. The increasing amount of disposable income and the increasing desire for purchased goods means increasing occasions for family conflict over how wages will be used. For example: "M. B. was reported to the police by his wife who is having a difficult time because M. B. does not bring home his checks" (Field Notes). Drunkenness, wife-beating, infidelity, and jealousy are marked causes of discord in the Fruitland area. Drunkenness is reported to be the most common cause of friction, and it is often a contributing factor in other conflicts: "Suspicion of infidelity of marital partners appears to be especially marked at Fruitland because of easy access to town and liquor. Whenever men or women are away over night they are immediately suspected of having had an affair" (Sasaki 1950:89).

CHANGING SOCIAL ORGANIZATION OF THE FAMILY

Relationships within the family are changing. The father, because of his importance as breadwinner, and because of the change from matrilocal to neolocal or patrilocal residence arrangements, is becoming more indispensable to the family for its economic and social well-being, and at the same time he is frequently away from home. The wife, therefore, still has the daily responsibility for running the house and for the care and training of the younger children. Both mother and father lose influence, however, as the children grow and undertake school education. Frequently the parents find themselves in an ambivalent position toward these children. Many favor white education, and want their children to embrace white ways:

The son told me that his father . . . [felt] the main thing was to get an education, so the white man could not cheat him.

Another father told an interviewer that:

He was anxious for them [the children] to learn a little English and a trade because things were going to get tougher for the Navahos if they don't have a trade.

At the same time, parents find themselves ineffectual in the face of their children's greater education and rejection of traditional customs. Lacking economic and social control, they have little effect against rebellion. Girls frequently express revolt through sexual adventures, which result in the further problem of illegitimate children. Traditionally such children were absorbed into the large, loose framework of the extended family, but today both the unmarried mother and her children may be without economic or social support.

The growing independence of the young carries over to marriage customs, and increasing marriages are contracted without parental consent. The author knew twelve Fruitland couples who had married within the last ten years. Eight of these married through personal choice and only four through parental arrangement. All of the women in the first group were educated to the extent that they spoke English, and seven of them had worked for wages before marriage. Of the four in the latter group, only one was sufficiently educated to speak English. Even in traditionally arranged marriages, the groom's gift has undergone a change. Frequently, he no longer gives livestock or household utensils, but instead a cash payment.

The position of the daughter-in-law in a patrilocal extended family unit (and to some extent in an independent nuclear family) needs special mention for the marked contrast it provides with that of the daughter-in-law in the traditional matrilocal residence. In a patrilocal unit, the young married woman has to live closely and interact frequently with people who do not embrace her as one of them. Her mother-in-law, the head of the woman's division of the extended family, exercises authority over her without at the same time offering her protection and emotional security. A possessive mother-in-law is in fact often a rival for the young husband's attention. In such rivalry, the daughter-in-law is in a weak position, and even lacks the protection provided by a mother-in-law taboo. The young woman's main, and possibly only, defense in such rivalry lies in her personal influence over the husband.

Conflicts occur frequently in such situations. When mild, they take the form of verbal battles, with gossip a strong weapon. In more serious cases, the young woman can be forced from her home alone, or with her husband if her influence over him is strong. In either case, she suffers dislocation and the loss of economic security and opportunity that she may have enjoyed as part of the extended family. When there is a marked degree of difference in the education of the older and younger women, there are occasions for additional and serious conflicts. Again, it is a struggle which the daughter-in-law, alone in the family group, is likely to lose. Such conflicts arise over education of the children, health measures, the family's manner of living, recreation, and related matters.

In virtually every kind of family organization today, most conflicts that result in divorce or desertion by the husband mean economic and social disorganization and loss of prestige for the women and children. If the family has been in patrilocal residence, the woman and children are frequently forced to leave their homes. In neolocal residence, deserted wives, while possibly retaining their houses, lose economic support. They sometimes return to the wife's family, but this often imposes an economic burden on her people. Other solutions are the finding of a new husband, or moving to town in search of employment. This move is likely to result in minimal economic security, at best, and more often in unemployment, drunkenness, and sexual promiscuity.

The nine cases of divorce known to the author in Fruitland suggest the extent to which women's position in broken marriages has changed. Six of the nine cases resulted in the woman's leaving home. Only two of these women returned to live with their own relatives; the other four left Fruitland and went to the nearby urban white center. In three cases the men left the family. Two of these were families in matrilocal residence and the wives, although not suffering dislocation, did suffer economic hardship, since they had been economically dependent on their husbands' wages.

CONCLUSION—EVALUATION OF THE NEW POSITION OF NAVAHO WOMEN

The preceding summary of life in Fruitland today suggests that there are three aspects of the woman's role that have been adversely affected by the recent social and economic changes there: her economic position, the significance of her function within the family, and her sense of security and bargaining position in family interaction. The last of these is largely a result of the first two.

Although the Fruitland society, in gross calculation, has gained economically from the recent industrial development in the San Juan Valley, a close examination shows that while the men have been compensated for the loss of their traditional sources of livelihood, the women have not been directly compensated in any way. In wage work most men find an adequate substitute for the declining livestock economy. As far as women are concerned, in losing their sheep, they have lost their economic independence. There are few job opportunities for them, and their duties in the home make it impossible for most of them to seek work outside.

This economic dependence of woman is aggravated by the fact that the wants of their families have increased considerably. To obtain the goods and services of white society, the women have to depend upon the industry and good-will of the wage earners—the men. Some women do benefit from what their husbands earn, for there is beginning to develop a definition of the husband's role as economic provider. But there are many instances in which the traditional attitude toward cash is still operative and is applied with a vengeance. Middle age bestows prestige and wealth on the Navaho woman of traditional society, especially if she is fortunate enough to have a large female progeny. In contrast, the poorest category of women in Fruitland are the middle-aged women without male providers.

In assessing the significance of woman's functions in Fruitland today as against those of traditional society, the following questions may be asked: How valuable are her social and economic activities, and how personally rewarding? Can the performance of these be a means for the attainment of status in the prestige hierarchy of society?

Traditionally, every member of the family performs significant tasks that contribute to the survival of the whole unit. The woman, as the central figure in the home, assumes functions there that are indispensable to the economic and social well-being of her family. She is also well equipped to handle most phases of an important economic activity—sheep-raising. The accumulation of wealth is possible for both men and women. As wealth spells prestige among the Navaho, this means that woman's labor and industry are important in determining the status of the family on the prestige ladder of the community.

In Fruitland, the division of labor still follows convenience, and convenience decrees that women perform most of the tasks in and around the house. But the home has been shorn of much of its economic and social significance, and has been largely deserted by the men and older children. The importance of women's functions has declined accordingly. Wage employment is for most families the only means for acquiring processed goods and the newer prestige symbols such as cars and modern homes. It is the men who make these acquisitions possible, and who are therefore mainly responsible for determining the social and economic status and the prestige of the family.

Although women no longer have equal economic opportunities and rewards, they still have the traditional functions of child-bearing and rearing. Are these personally satisfying? Many younger women express dissatisfaction. Mothers in independent residence complain of being tied down by their children, and school-trained women who worked prior to marriage describe home life as confining and dull. In addition, children are no longer social and economic assets. For women who have no children, homemaking offers unproductive leisure, boredom, and restlessness. Farm work is seasonal, and housekeeping takes little time. Weaving is no longer a possible leisure-time activity.

The woman's sense of security and her position within the family have been affected by these changes. The absence of the support of close relatives and the lack of economic opportunities that traditional organization provides, have threatened her sense of economic and social security. And the very facts of her dependence and the diminished significance of her functions have greatly lowered her bargaining position in family interaction. The pertinent questions here are: Which marriage partner can function more adequately without the other? And, who suffers most in case of disagreement that breaks up the family?

When we compare the traditional economic organization to that which is evolving in Fruitland, we find that the woman has become more dependent on the man for her economic and social well-being, and correspondingly, she is much less indispensable to her husband for his well-being. In case of a disagreement that results in a split of the family, she is the one who suffers most, both economically and socially. Thus, the majority of women find themselves relegated to a very minor position of power in the family arena, unless they manage through some personal influence or advantage to counteract the disadvantages of the weak bargaining position offered by the emerging culture.

We conclude, then, that the changing economic position and social organization of the Navaho today are adversely affecting the women. They are losing their economic independence, the satisfactions and rewards that accompany their functioning, and their security and power within the family.

Navaho men are adjusting to the changing conditions by increasingly adopting the life and culture of the white world, but the women are being left stranded on the reservation. Much that was economically and socially important there has become out-moded and discarded, and little has so far evolved to fill the void resulting in the lives of the women. We cannot assume that this is a final, stable position. What direction the women's lives will take depends on where the women see their opportunities; whether life on the reservation can be revitalized and made more satisfactory, or whether the women will follow their men into the world outside. Many of the forces that have helped to shape the changes outlined in this paper continue to be effective and will continue to influence the role of women: government agricultural and service programs, the continually emerging cash economy, school education, and, not least, the continuing culture of the Navaho, which acts as a sieve through which other forces must pass.

REFERENCES

DYK, WALTER, A Navaho autobiography. (New York: Viking Fund Publications in Anthropology, No. 8, 1947).

KLUCKHOHN, CLYDE and DOROTHEA LEIGHTON, The Navaho (Cambridge: Harvard University Press, 1946).

LEIGHTON, DOROTHEA and CLYDE KLUCKHOHN, Children of the people (Cambridge: Harvard University Press, 1947).

REICHARD, GLADYS, Social life of the Navajo Indians with some attention to minor ceremonies (New York: Columbia University Press, 1928).

SASAKI, TOM T., "Technological change in a Navaho farming community: a study of social and psychological change." Thesis: Cornell University, 1950.

Sex Differences in the Incidence of Susto in Two Zapotec Pueblos: An Analysis of the Relationships Between Sex Role Expectations and a Folk Illness

Carl W. O'Nell and Henry A. Selby

Susto is a name frequently given to an illness widely reported in Hispanic America. Because of its obvious affinity to specific cultural patterns and because the condition falls beyond the pale of orthodox medical practice, *susto* is classed as a folk illness (Rubel 1964). . . .

. . . In wakefulness, the *susto* sufferer is listless, depressed, and timid, usually exhibiting a loss of interest in his customary affairs, and frequently complaining of poor appetite and loss of strength. In sleep, the patient is restless, often complaining of troublesome dreams or other manifestations of sleep disturbance. One of the more consistently encountered folk beliefs is that the *asustado* (sufferer from *susto*) has lost his soul to a malignant spirit and that the patient's cure rests upon the recovery of the soul through specific treatments or rites performed by a curing specialist.[1]

The majority of anthropological contributions to the subject of *susto* have been descriptive. Recent work (Clark 1959; Foster 1959; Gillin 1948) suggests that the condition probably serves a psycho-social function in certain cultural settings. The contribution of Rubel (1964) is particularly valuable, not only because it attempts an orderly description of the phenomenon—its symptomatology and folk etiology—but especially because it presents an array of hypotheses which can be considered for empirical research.

Having learned in the course of our field work in two Zapotec communities in Oaxaca, Mexico, that *susto* was commonly experienced in both villages, we were encouraged to undertake a collaborative study of this folk illness as a psycho-social phenomenon. Using Rubel's work as a point of departure, we developed an hypothesis linking sex role performance to the incidence of *susto*. Each of us worked independently, collecting the necessary field data in his selected village, O'Nell in San Marcos Tlapazola and Selby in Santo Tomas Mazaltepec.

THE VILLAGES

The villages are each about one hour's drive by automobile from the city of Oaxaca. San Marcos Tlapazola lies to the southeast and Santo Tomas Mazaltepec to the northwest of the capital. Both are old foundations. Santo Tomas Mazaltepec is clearly pre-Columbian in origin, and it appears in the list of towns originally allotted to Cortez (Iturribaria 1955: 75). The antiquity of San Marcos Tlapazola is not as clearly documented, although Spanish archives currently stored in the local *palacio*, dealing with civil and religious administrative affairs, support the probability that it was a settled community at the time of the arrival of the Spaniards.

The pre-conquest histories of the two pueblos are divergent, evidenced by the fact that San Marcos Tlapazola speaks a Valley dialect, and Santo Tomas Mazaltepec a Sierra dialect. Events since the Spanish conquest have tended to produce convergence. The two villages share approximately the same ecological conditions, subsistence patterns, social organization, and general cultural form. Despite their proximity—they are about 42 kilometers from each other[2]—there

---

[1]Either male (*curanderos*) or female (*curanderas*) curers are sought to alleviate this condition in various places in Oaxaca. However, residents of San Marcos Tlapazola insist that only women are effective as curers of *susto* in their community. This preference was not noted for Santo Tomas Mazaltepec.

[2]Estimated from a map of Oaxaca produced by Cecil R. Welte (Mapa de las localidades del Valle de Oaxaca, segun el censo de poblacion de 1960, Oaxaca, 1965).

is no direct contact between them. For our purposes, then, they represent two independent cases within the same cultural area.

In describing their experiences with or knowledge of *susto*, the people in San Marcos Tlapazola and Santo Tomas Mazaltepec evidenced close agreement. Reports of symptomatology, folk etiology, and courses of treatment were essentially consistent between the two communities. Commonly reported symptoms closely approximated those making up the syndrome described by Rubel (1964).

A few variations will illustrate regional and individual differences which conceivably could be of importance in cross-regional studies of *susto*. These variations tended to be in the nature of additional symptoms, i.e., unexpected complaints offered in addition to, rather than in place of more commonly reported symptoms. Loosely ranked in order of the frequency with which they were reported, these symptoms were fever, muscular pains, complexion changes, nausea, other stomach or intestinal upsets, and vertigo. One person gave intense thirst as a *susto* symptom; another listed rectal bleeding.

There is also a widespread and interesting belief that in stubborn cases the assistance of a *medico* (orthodox medical practitioner) may be efficacious. Strongly implicit in this belief, however, is the notion that the powers of the native curer are paramount in soul recovery and that the medical doctor assists only in strengthening the body by supplying vitamins and other medicines. Also deserving of mention, because it is consistent with similar beliefs elsewhere in Hispanic America, is the belief that unless cured, *susto* culminates in death.

THE PSYCHO-SOCIAL FUNCTION OF SUSTO

• • •

Following Rubel (1964), we made the basic assumption that *susto* represents an important culturally and socially sanctioned avenue of escape for an individual suffering from intra-culturally induced stress. *Susto* was assumed to be the result of an individual's self-perceived failure to meet a set of culturally established expectations in a role in which he had been socialized. Although not fundamental to the design of our study, we made the further assumption that the *susto* experience provides a person and his social group with mechanisms for the eventual social reinstatement of the individual.

Once a person is labeled *asustado*, an important shift obviously occurs in his relationship to others. Normal role expectations are relaxed to a greater or lesser extent and a new repertoire of behavior becomes appropriate. The *asustado* becomes temporarily what Goffman (1958: 95–96) would call a "nonperson"—a person who by virtue of his relaxed social situation can act without reference to the detailed codes that normally bind his behavior. The disease condition provides a psychological respite—a moratorium in normal role performance. This shift in role is conceived to be the basic function of *susto* as a psycho-social phenomenon. The culture provides a channel of escape for the relief of psychological stress engendered within the cultural framework.

Of no less importance, either to the individual or society, are the processes of rehabilitation and reintegration which ultimately will reunite the individual to his group (Parsons and Fox 1948). The treatment of the sufferer involves a temporary change of status which of itself may signal the beginning of rehabilitation. By village standards, considerable time and money are expended upon the *asustado*. More importantly, perhaps, he frequently becomes the focus of a great deal of sympathetic understanding, especially within his own extended family group. The treatment thus constitutes a form of reassurance that the sufferer is, in fact, an important member of the extended family.

From Bateson's (1958) point of view, the development of *susto* constitutes a signal that schism within the extended family had gone too far for the affected individual to tolerate. Treatment is the process whereby the schism is resolved and the sufferer is reincorporated into the group.

We do not, of course, assume that *susto* represents the only mechanism of escape in the face of stress generated through self-perceived role inadequacy. General health conditions, temperamental tendencies, personality traits, situational variables, and other factors conceivably must all be assumed to have a bearing upon whether a given person develops *susto* when confronted with role stress or whether some other avenue of relief from stress becomes manifest. Our assumption is merely that, once it is developed, *susto* presents us with a measure of role stress.

Cognizant of all the preceding assumptions, but focusing upon the assumption that *susto* is the result of emotional stress engendered through a self-perceived failure to meet a set of social expectations regarding sex role performance, we have formulated the following hypothesis: *The sex which experiences the greater intra-cultural stress in the process of meeting sex role expectations will evidence the greater susceptibility to susto.*

SEX ROLE DIFFERENCES

Male-female sex role differences hinge fundamentally upon the differential socialization of boys and girls. Parents in the two communities often indicate that boys are more delicate than girls in infancy with the observable result that boys are more freely indulged. The factual basis for this alleged delicacy is difficult to validate with our data, but it agrees with findings in our own and other cultures that male infants are subject to higher mortality rates than are female infants (Scheinfeld 1958). It may simply reflect a prevailing tendency to prefer male offspring to female offspring.

From some point early in childhood girls learn that they are more restricted than boys. A small sample of mothers in Santo Tomas Mazaltepec (N = 6) indicated that boys require greater indulgence than girls because they are eventually due to experience greater liberty. Although parents in San Marcos Tlapazola were less explicit on this point, very young boys were more frequently observed moving about freely in the *calles* near their homes than were young girls.

In middle childhood both sexes are expected to perform certain simple duties, such as carrying small bundles and running errands. Observation seems to indicate that boys frequently escape punishment for dalliance on errands, whereas girls may be severely reprimanded or punished for similar dalliance. Responsibilities of child care are preponderantly allotted to girls, although boys do not escape such duties, especially if there are no girls in the household.

Young boys are permitted, even encouraged under certain conditions, to manifest aggressive behavior, whereas girls rarely exhibit aggressive tendencies and run the risk of punishment if they do exhibit them. This is particularly evident in teasing behavior and the maltreatment of small animals.

Prepubescent and adolescent girls are expected to learn and master many tasks the counterparts of which occur much later for boys. At an age when a boy is just learning how to direct a plow and drive oxen, a girl may be married, pregnant, and responsible for an adult woman's tasks of food preparation.

These differences in socialization are but reflections of the differential sex-role expectations of mature men and women. A woman should be constantly at work caring for her house, her children, her mother-in-law, her husband, or tending to her pottery making. In contrast, a man is expected to rest periodically because his work is deemed to be harder. If a woman appears idle she is suspected of being a gossip. Except for infidelity, this is the worst offense a woman can commit since it tends to disrupt communal harmony.

A woman is expected to control herself. In Santo Tomas Mazaltepec a woman's loss of composure is associated with temporary possession of *mal de ojo* (evil eye). In San Marcos Tlapazola it may indicate that the woman is incapable of presenting a proper spiritual defense against malignant forces which may harm her or her family. In either circumstance an angry mother is frequently held accountable for illness in her children. The ideal woman is enduring and patient. Men, too, are expected to control themselves, but if a man seriously loses his temper it is often assumed that he is justified in doing so.

A woman must be submissive and give no indication of rebelliousness (actually women learn to get their way by the practice of guile). Ideally, men do not rebel either, but they have at their disposal many more ways of making their wishes known or effecting their own plans.

The Zapotec woman in these communities is allowed virtually no freedom of sexual expression, and she must tolerate her husband's infidelities as long as he does not publicly proclaim a rupture in their marital relations. Men, on the other hand, enjoy a distinct sexual advantage in being able to exploit women other than their wives. Cognizant of the intricacies of this situation, men show extreme jealousy of their wives. The slightest suspicion of infidelity grants a man license to beat his wife. Unaccompanied women do not move about freely in either village. Men frequently say, "Women have no vices because they do not go out in the streets." It would be more correct to say, "Women do not go out in the streets so that there will be no suspicion of vice."

Residential patterns after marriage also complicate a woman's sex role expectations as compared to those for men. In both Santo Tomas Mazaltepec and San Marcos Tlapazola it is customary for the young bride to move to her husband's family. In Santo Tomas Mazaltepec residence is 75 percent patrilocal, i.e., with the husband's parents. In San Marcos Tlapazola it is 78 percent patrilocal.[3]

Currently some girls marry as early as fourteen years of age.[4] Although the

[3]These percentages were higher in the past (cf. Murdock 1960: 13). In San Marcos Tlapazola, however, 35 per cent of all households are nuclear family residential units.

[4]A small number of informants in Santo Tomas Mazaltepec reported marriages at from six to eight years of age, and the customary age for the marriage of girls in previous generations was reported to be from ten to twelve years of age. When this occurred it meant that the young girl, still immature, went to live with her husband's family. Such a girl slept with her mother-in-law until she was sufficiently developed to sleep with her husband. During this maturation period the young girl was socialized in her wifely role under the close supervision of her mother-in-law. Older informants who had experienced this pattern reported that they went to their husbands' houses ignorant of sex, nervous at leaving their family of orientation, feeling abandoned, exploited, and intimidated. Young husbands during the same period of maturation neither changed their residence nor were they so closely

vast majority of marriages are contracted within the village, girls move into a new extended family setting. The emotional effect of changing residential patterns at marriage may be considerable. The new bride is subject to the authority not only of her husband but also of his mother and father, and in effect she may find that she has to obey many other persons as well. To be sure, the authority of her father-in-law or husband's older brother may be indirect, it is nevertheless felt and in actuality may outweigh the authority of her husband.

The mother-in-law is usually the key figure with whom the new bride has to contend. The young girl may literally be under the surveillance of her mother-in-law from dawn until dusk. The prevailing ethic brooks no disrespect or disobedience to the mother-in-law, and neither beatings, tongue lashings, nor "sweat-shop" work conditions constitute grounds for non-compliance. Ordinarily mothers-in-law are strict, much stricter than mothers. Boys continue to work with their fathers and brothers even after marriage. Young men, married or unmarried, have considerable freedom of movement and in their leisure meet with friends in the *calles* or the *cantinas.*

Children represent a positive value in these communities. Sterility is regarded as a very unfortunate condition and is feared by married couples since it means that in old age they will not have the assistance of adult children. The major responsibility of any married woman is the bearing and rearing of children. If the union is sterile, the onus of sterility is commonly placed on the woman, although some people realize that men as well as women can be sterile. Child mortality in the two villages is high—conservatively estimated at about 40 percent of all births. Stillbirths are frequent, and in such cases little if any public recognition is given to the fact that pregnancy has even occurred. For children who have survived the first year of life, however, death is viewed as a tragic occurrence, and someone, nearly always the mother, is held responsible for the tragedy. (In neither village did we observe the resignation to the death of young children which has been reported for other parts of Meso-America.) The grave responsibilities associated with having children and the uncertainties which surround it constitute a potential source of deep emotional stress weighing more heavily upon women than upon men.

It seems quite clear that women must conform to a tighter set of role expectations than men. Moreover, they have fewer ways of reducing anxiety over role performance. The role expectations of the male more readily allow him to shift responsibility from his shoulders than is true for the female. If his crops do poorly, he may blame the weather or a malevolent agent, but if the woman fails in her household tasks or in the care of children she alone is to blame. Similarly men are freer than women to engage in strategic retreat from uncomfortable situations. A man under emotional stress may relieve his anxieties by going to his *milpa* (corn field) for a day, on a trading expedition for a week, or, if necessary, to the *fincas* (plantations) in the hot country for a prolonged period of work. Women, with extremely few exceptions, cannot practice comparable forms of social withdrawal. Finally, men can retreat into an approved state of irresponsibility, the most frequent and obvious being that of drunkenness. The

---

supervised. Older and freer than their wives, they were permitted the adolescent license of running with a *palomilla* (gang) and gaining such sexual experience as could be found.

TABLE 1

Reported Attendance at Cuelgas *in Santo Tomas Mazaltepec: Differential Response by Sex*

	Attend	Do not attend	Total
Men	26	4	30
Women	12	13	25
Total	38	17	55

Result: $x^2 = 7.2; p < 0.01$ (1 df).

borracho (drunk), even when he proves to be a nuisance, is treated with exceptional tolerance. People are also willing to concede that he may have his reasons, and there are many situations in which this method of escape is socially sanctioned.

Young women are effectively barred by community pressures from using drunkenness as an escape from responsibility. And older women, who enjoy increased status[5] and greater freedom from restraint in their use of alcohol, find the occasions which they can use alcohol with impunity fewer in number and kind than those open even to younger males.

Two additional measures of differential sex role expectations support our other ethnographic observations. The first of these measures freedom of social participation; the second measures cognitive evaluation.

In Santo Tomas Mazaltepec drunken fiestas lasting three to five days are customarily celebrated in honor of a person's saint's day (called *cuelga* or *dia del onomastico*). These are socially sanctioned occasions when participants are permitted relatively free expression of aggression and affective feelings. We interpret them as opportunities for the relief of emotional stress. The frequency of *cuelga* attendance by men and women, obtained from a sample of 55 individuals in Santo Tomas Mazaltepec, revealed a statistically significant difference between the sexes (see Table 1).

If our assumption about the *cuelga* as a sanctioned means of stress relief is correct, it appears that men are significantly freer to avail themselves of this avenue of escape than women are. However, one must be cautious in making the broad assumption that the *cuelga* operates uniformly as a mechanism for relief from stress for the two sexes. It may be that young married women find attendance at *cuelgas* stressful.[6]

[5]Upon becoming a *suegra* (mother-in-law) a woman's status changes appreciably in both communities. The status of mother-in-law brings with it not only respect, deference, and obedience from daughters-in-law but also some relaxation of the disabilities and restrictions associated with the feminine role. At its fullest expression it brings with it a privilege of drunken license and ribaldry approximating that of a senior male.

[6]Women who attend these fiestas in Santo Tomas Mazaltepec may actually be subjected to increased stress by the fact of their attendance. Although older women may participate rather freely in the festivities, younger women are expected to remain in the background, sitting discreetly to one side if not working in the kitchen. If a man wishes to dance with a woman other than his wife, he requests this privilege of her husband. Women fear such requests because they may raise suspicion and ire in their husbands. The wife of a jealous man is in danger of a beating on such an occasion.

TABLE 2

Differential Response by Sex Concerning Which Sex Experiences Greater Comfort in the Life Situation (San Marcos Tlapazola)

	Men do	Women do	Both equal	Total
Men	13	5	7	25
Women	16	2	7	25
Total	29	7	14	50

The second measure is one of the cognitive evaluation of comfort in the life situation. Fifty individuals in San Marcos Tlapazola—25 men and 25 women—were asked which sex, in their opinion, finds life more comfortable. The results are reported in Table 2.

Both men and women agree that life is more comfortable for men than it is for women. We find the agreement between the sexes on this matter interesting in view of the fact that it supports descriptive ethnographic data gathered largely by observation with data of an evaluative type from a sizable sample of informants.

DIFFERENTIAL SUSCEPTIBILITY TO SUSTO

Since women appear to experience greater intra-cultural stress than do men in the process of meeting sex-role expectations in both San Marcos Tlapazola and Santo Tomas Mazaltepec, our hypothesis would lead us to anticipate that they would reveal greater susceptibility to *susto* than men. Susceptibility to *susto* is defined as the relative proportions of individuals of each sex reporting *susto*.

The data were gathered first in San Marcos Tlapazola from a sample of 30 individuals—fifteen males and fifteen females. They were commonly sought in context with other data, the rationale being that people might not respond readily if confronted by direct questions regarding their experiences with *susto*. In the course of gathering other data, respondents were asked about their personal experiences with *susto* when it seemed convenient to do so. The questions followed a generalized pattern, though they were not always phrased in exactly the same terms for all respondents. They were first presented in Spanish in most cases but frequently had to be repeated in Zapotec. The respondent was first asked whether or not he had experienced *susto* at any time in his life. Then his approximate age at the time of each experience and its duration were recorded. If they wished to do so, respondents were allowed to give details of their experiences concerning symptoms, precipitating causes, etc., but such data were not actively solicited. The ethnographer indicated an equal interest in negative and positive responses to guard against bias.

It was found that most people showed no obvious reluctance to answering questions about their experiences with *susto*. Consequently some persons—both men and women—were approached directly with these questions. In such cases the investigator made it known that he was interested in various health problems in the village and would appreciate any help the respondent might give him by answering a question or two about his experiences with *susto*.

For each individual it was noted whether or not he or she had experienced *susto*. The case was considered positive if an individual reported having had such an experience, regardless of the number and intensity of the experiences reported. An individual was regarded as a negative case if he reported no such experience. A chi square (χ^2) test was made of the individual responses. The χ^2 difference between men and women was 2.14 (1 df.) Though not significant at the .05 level, this result was encouraging; 67 percent of the women reported some experience with *susto* as compared to 40 percent of the men.

Two modifications were made in the method for Santo Tomas Mazaltepec. First, it was felt that a random sample was necessary to control for latent bias. Second, it was decided to take a slightly larger sample. Accordingly, a sample of 40 persons—twenty males and twenty females—over twenty years of age was

TABLE 3

Relative Proportions of Males and Females Reporting Susto
in San Marcos Tlapazola

	One or more times	Never	Total
Men	6 (40%)	9 (60%)	15
Women	10 (67%)	5 (33%)	15
Total	16	14	30

Result: $\chi^2 = 2.14$; $p > 0.10$ (1 df).

randomly made of the entire native population of Santo Tomas Mazaltepec. Each respondent was asked directly, i.e., not in connection with other data, whether or not he or she had ever experienced *susto*. The number of experiences, the ages at which they had occurred, and the duration of each were recorded for each respondent.

A chi square (χ^2) test was run on these data, and the result $\chi^2 = 5.22$ (1 df) was significant, $p < 0.025$. In Santo Tomas Mazaltepec 55 percent of the women sampled indicated that they had experienced *susto* at some time in their lives as compared to 20 percent of the men (see Table 4).

TABLE 4

Relative Proportions of Males and Females Reporting Susto
in Santo Tomas Mazaltepec

	One or more times	Never	Total
Men	4 (20%)	16 (80%)	20
Women	11 (55%)	9 (45%)	20
Totals	15	25	40

Result: $\chi^2 = 5.22$; $p < 0.025$ (1 df).

CONCLUSIONS

We feel that these two independent tests of our hypothesis serve to support our basic assumption that *susto* represents an important culturally and socially sanctioned mechanism of escape and rehabilitation for persons suffering from intra-culturally induced stress resulting from failure in sex-role performance. The ethnographic evidence encountered in the two villages indicated that women stand the greater likelihood of experiencing role stress both because their sex roles are more narrowly defined than are those for men and because fewer outlets for escape from stress are open to them in this culture. Consistent with this is our evidence on differential susceptibility, indicating a markedly higher incidence of *susto* among women than among men.

. . .

REFERENCES

BATESON, G., *Naven.* 2nd ed. New York, 1958

CARRASCO, P., "Pagan Rituals and Beliefs Among the Chontal Indians of Oaxaca." *Anthropological Records* 20:07–117, 1960.

CLARK, M., *Health in the Mexican-American Culture.* Berkeley, 1959.

FOSTER, G. M., "Relationships Between Theoretical and Applied Anthropology: A Public Health Program Analysis." *Human Organization*, 11:5–6, 1952.

———, "Relationships Between Spanish and Spanish-American Folk Medicine." *Journal of American Folklore* 66:201–247, 1953.

GILLIN, J., "Magical Fright." *Psychiatry* 11:387–400, 1948.

GOFFMAN, E., *The Presentation of Self in Everyday Life.* Edinburgh, 1958.

GUITERAS HOLMES, C., *Perils of the Soul.* New York, 1961.

ITURRIBARIA, J. F., *Oaxaca en la historia.* Mexico City, 1955.

KELLY, L., *Folk Practices in North Mexico.* Austin, Texas, 1965.

MURDOCK, G. P., *Social Structure in South East Asia.* Chicago, 1960.

PARSONS, T., and R. FOX, "Illness, Therapy and the Modern Urban American Family." *Journal of Social Issues* 8:31–44, 1952.

RUBEL, A. J., "Concepts of Disease in Mexican-American Culture." *American Anthropologist* 62:795–815, 1960.

———, "The Epidemiology of a Folk Illness: Susto in Hispanic-America." *Ethnology* 3:268–283, 1964.

SCHEINFELD, A., "The Mortality of Men and Women." *Scientific American* 198:22–27, 1958.

Begging in a Southeastern Mexican City

Horacio Fabrega, Jr.

The purpose of this report is to present ethnographic material dealing with a type of deviant behavior, the phenomenon of begging as observed in a small city in southeastern Mexico. Using an analytical framework derived from the fields of behavioral science and medicine, I will examine the behavior which constitutes begging and will explore some of the social and psychological characteristics of beggars as persons. Emphasis will be given to the mode of presentation of the beggar and to the attitudes and perceptions that people have of him, and an attempt will be made to understand the many interrelated factors that account for the existence of begging and beggars in his region. Important and somewhat unique functions appear to be served by this type of social activity.

RESEARCH SETTING

The study was conducted during May through July of 1969 in the valley city of San Cristobal de las Casas, located in the highland portion of the state of Chiapas in southeastern Mexico. San Cristobal, with an approximate population of 25,000, is the principal center for a hinterland in which live about 175,000 Indians of Mayan descent. These are divided into several different social groups, each characterized by a distinct dialect, mode of dress, and a separate territorial unit termed a *Municipio*. The persons who reside in San Cristobal itself are termed Ladinos,[1] they speak Spanish fluently, wear western clothing, and are identified with the values and institutions of the Mexican national government. Culturally, they are distinct from the Mayan Indians who frequent the streets of San Cristobal during the daylight hours. These distinctively dressed Mayans come to the large market to sell their agricultural or homemade products or to purchase items from the various commercial establishments.

Even when compared with other regions in the Republic of Mexico, San Cristobal and its surrounding *municipios* are striking in their degree of poverty. There are no major industries in the city and little municipal revenue is derived from cattle or the harvesting of such agricultural items as the fruit, cotton, sugar, and coffee which account for the relative prosperity of other cities in Chiapas. The Indians instead are engaged in a subsistence system based upon crops of maize, beans, squash and a few green vegetables grown in farms located in the highlands.

San Cristobal manifests many of the features included by Sjoberg (1960) in his

[1] It should be noted that Professor Moscoso (1963: 5–38), using essentially racial criteria, divides the resident population of San Cristobal into two principal groups: the Ladino who "has white skin, . . . wavy hair, straight nose—if male, heavy bearded—small mouth, etc." and the *mestizo*, also called *cruzado* (literally, "crossed") resulting from the "fusion of the White with the Indian." Most American anthropologists, however, refer to these two groups by the term "Ladino" and I will adopt such a terminology in this paper.

characterization of the pre-industrial city.[2] Animate power, for example, is the principal form of energy used to perform work. Electricity is available, but used mainly to operate a few household appliances and for lighting. Since there are no large-scale industries, there are no managers nor assembly line workers. Craftsmen exist, and they participate in every phase of the manufacture of a particular article. They also sell their products and regulate the quality of their own work. San Cristobal in large part depends on the food and other raw materials that are brought from the hinterland and in turn serves as the principal marketing center for the surrounding area.

The internal arrangement of the city is similar to that described for other preindustrial cities, with narrow streets and low and crowded buildings. Residential and commercial activities are frequently conducted in the same structure. Sections of the city, called *barrios*, are relatively well demarcated socially and economically, with each *barrio* containing a population homogeneous in income and social status. Typically, the poorer sections of San Cristobal are located at the periphery or outskirts of the city, and it is here that the beggars live. Social status boundaries in San Cristobal are restricted though permeable, and status distinctions can be observed in speech, dress, and personal mannerisms. A small elite, which includes persons in the high positions of government, religion, education, and some of the professions, exercises considerable power and visibly commands much respect in social dealings. The middle class is small.

A number of characteristics of San Cristobal, as well as its relation to the surrounding region, help explain the prominence of beggars in this city. First of all, the relative lack of employment opportunities and the absence of institutional and regulatory agencies for dealing with the indigent means that needy persons are largely forced to rely on informal means of support. Residents of San Cristobal cite the pleasant climate of the highlands as an important factor in attracting persons, including the very needy, to the city; many beggars, in fact, acknowledge a preference for San Cristobal for its climate. Large numbers of beggars also come to San Cristobal because the political authorities are relatively tolerant of them—an indication of the city's generosity and long tradition of charity. San Cristobal, it is to be emphasized, is the most prominent religious center in this region. It has served as the seat of the Catholic bishopry since 1544 and hence has a long history of exercising important formal and informal religious functions. (Trens 1957; Castillo Tejero 1961: 207–219; Flores Ruiz 1961: 233–245). These functions have always included helping the poor and needy and have indirectly encouraged the activity of beggars. Residents, in discussing this religious aspect of life in San Cristobal, proudly refer to the fact that there are eighteen Catholic churches within the confines of this relatively small city.

The unique economic and social functions that San Cristobal performs for the surrounding *municipios* must be considered in explaining the prominence of beggars who are of Indian descent. Because the city is continually used for commerce (both buying and selling) and occasionally for medical purposes by the surrounding Mayan Indians, San Cristobal has become identified as a place with resources to which Indians can turn for help and support. In earlier cen-

[2]For a more comprehensive perspective on the socio-ecological features of settings such as San Cristobal, see Sjoberg (1960) and Kahl (1959).

turies, San Cristobal served as a key center for the Spanish settlers who conquered and ruled the highland region. When the Chiapas area became part of the Mexican nation, federal agencies involved in promoting assimilation of the Indian were housed in San Cristobal, and the city continues to exercise political power over the *municipios*, for officials supervising Indian civil affairs either live in or look to San Cristobal for authority.

. . .

In summary, even though the perceptions of residents in this general region is that San Cristobal is a place that can offer help, the city really has few material resources. In addition, no social welfare agencies for dealing with the needy exist; hence, needy persons must rely on informal means of support. A growing population coupled with limited available land hastens the generally prevailing rural-to-urban migration, but San Cristobal's lack of industry offers little solution to the employment needs of Ladino and Indian alike. Begging as an activity, then, can be viewed as an economic necessity as well as the result of traditions associated with the city's religious and political functions for the hinterland. . . .

RESEARCH METHODS

The behavior of beggars was systematically observed in those parts of San Cristobal where begging activity is prominent. This observation took several forms, from casual inspection at a distance to participation in interactions with beggars as a potential client. Ecological units of the city (the market, the plaza, etc.) were observed and attempts were made to evaluate the nature of the begging activity in these units. Besides noting descriptive features of begging behavior (i.e., posture, verbal exchanges, type of donations requested, etc.), the density of beggars and the amount of time they spent begging in any one locale was noted. In addition, Ladino residents of the city served as general informants and, through unstructured interviews, provided information dealing with their conceptions and attitudes towards beggars and begging behavior. This material was used to delineate the dominant social view or bias regarding this activity. Also, with the help of three Ladinos of the lower economic bracket who served as principal informants, a group of beggars was asked to furnish life histories.

. . .

. . . The number of beggars at any one period of time is difficult to determine since (1) they are distributed over a large area (2) they differ in hours of begging and in degree of visibility, and (3) their total number is constantly changing. Thus, it was not possible to systematically sample the beggar population. Nevertheless, we believe we were able to obtain information from a large and representative group. . . .

FINDINGS

General Characteristics of Beggars. It should be stated at the outset that by far the majority of those interviewed were not natives of San Cristobal. Most beggars, in other words, had migrated to the city, either from the surrounding *municipios*, from other regions of Chiapas or, in some cases, from other states of Mexico. The group of beggars studied was almost equally divided between Ladino and Indian. The group was partitioned on the basis of age and then cross-classified by ethnic background and sex. Males predominated (75%), while females constituted 40 percent of the Ladino category, but only 10 percent of the Indian. Roughly one-third of the Indians fell in each of the three age categories (young, middle aged, old), and the pattern was essentially the same with the Ladinos, although there were slightly more older Ladinos. There was a tendency for males to be in the younger age categories and a stronger tendency for females to fall in the oldest age category. Finally, the group of beggars was divided into two mutually exclusive subgroups on the basis of whether a visible physical deformity or handicap was present. Close to 60 percent of the overall group had a visible physical handicap. Compared to Ladinos, a somewhat larger proportion of Indians demonstrated a physical handicap. The male subgroup had a larger proportion of persons with a physical handicap than did the female, and there was a moderately strong association between age and the presence of a handicap, with 75 percent of the "young" as compared to 40 percent of the "old" age categories showing a physical handicap.

. . . Certain factors account for the small proportion of females in the sample: (1) females in Mexico and in Latin America generally have less social autonomy than males and there is strong social censure against the presence of young females on the streets (Diaz-Guerrero 1955: 411–417); (2) domestic work is often available for women in San Cristobal; and (3) most Indian females are more conservative than males and are less likely to leave their hamlets. As noted earlier, the females in the sample were predominantly old Ladinas, and a large proportion demonstrated clinical evidence of depressive illness.

We can summarize these data by classifying the beggars in this study as follows: (1) those with an obvious physical deformity or disability who were severely impaired (e.g., double amputees, the totally blind, deaf-mutes, etc.); (2) those with physical deformities and handicaps that were less disabling (e.g., single amputations, contractures, partial blindness, deafness); (3) those who claimed a medical illness and appeared ill (e.g., appeared weak and emaciated, had obvious swellings of the extremities, demonstrated a continuous cough and other physical diagnostic evidence of lung disease, etc.); (4) those who claimed illness but did not appear ill; (5) those with prominent symptoms of psychiatric disability (e.g., psychosis, chronic alcoholism, depression); and (6) those who were elderly and claimed to have no living relatives. These categories were not, of course, mutually exclusive. Many beggars who had an obvious medical illness, for example, were quite old and had no living relatives, and a large portion of the elderly beggars without visible evidence of somatic disease, but claiming illness, were persons with symptoms of depression or schizophrenia.

Reasons for Begging. Our subjects invariably cited two conditions as leading them to beg. The first was their inability to support themselves by working because of medical handicap, illness, old age, or simply weakness. It is, of course, not easy to establish the validity of a person's assertion that he is unable to work, but the majority of the beggars interviewed had evidence of either a prominent physical disability or a chronic medical disease. Approximately one-fifth of the subjects were without a physical disability and appeared able-bodied and healthy. The majority of these, however, were in the "old" category. Another one-fifth of the subjects, although demonstrating a physical handicap that limited their ability, were nonetheless capable of some kinds of work. It should be remembered, however, that for both of these types of persons, the old and the moderately impaired, the availability of jobs in San Cristobal is severely restricted.

The second factor that subjects reported had led them to beg for a living was the lack of living relatives or friends who were willing and able to offer help. About three-quarters of the sample reported having no contacts with relatives (parents, siblings, or spouses), and this was usually because the relatives had died. The remaining quarter maintained some relationship with relatives but stated that they were not able to obtain economic support from them.

Knowing the social conditions in this region, individuals in these circumstances (i.e., ill, old, poor, and without a family) have the options of seeking exclusive support from the Church, obtaining medical care through hospitalization, or asking for custodial care in the home for the aged. These alternatives, however, are not usually realistic ones. The first two, because of the limited economic resources of the region, offer at most only short term support. Hospitals, for example, are understaffed, lack space and facilities, and can only give acute or emergency medical care. The Church is able to provide support for only a small proportion of the needy and then only irregularly. The home for the aged is also understaffed and limited in facilities, and has the additional liability of being overcrowded and having a long waiting list. Almost all beggars stated that they had considered or tried these various options but had found them unsatisfactory because food was scarce and inconstant, personnel appeared uninterested and were not attentive, living conditions were inadequate, and the like. Begging provided them with a less uncomfortable existence.

• • •

It was very clear that, for a substantial proportion of the persons interviewed, begging provided important psychological and social benefits in addition to offering a means of physical support. The dread of loneliness and the fear of death were frequently expressed and, as mentioned, most beggars were homeless and many significantly depressed. The loneliness and isolation that permeated their lives were often reflected in preoccupations with acquiring monetary savings which were to be used for burial, and with a dread of dying alone and not being found. For these lonely and isolated persons, taking to the streets offered continual exposure and some contact with others. The value of a donation given on a regular basis to this type of person far exceeded economic considerations; it served as an indication that someone understood and gave the beggar the feeling that he or she had contacts who were concerned, if not friends who cared. All indications are that beggars also derived considerable emotional support from others of their kind. In rare instances, this was actualized in the form of strong personal relationships, but in most cases it seemed to involve feelings of identification and implicit understanding derived from occasional associations with other beggars.

For a few persons, choosing to become a beggar could be viewed as analogous to what in Western medical settings is termed sociopathic or psychopathic behavior. Such persons appeared strong and able-bodied and capable of obtaining regular employment in San Cristobal itself, in nearby more industrialized cities or in plantations located in the region. They decided to beg because this represented a somewhat easier way of obtaining support and also enabled them to live in San Cristobal. In deliberately misrepresenting their social and physical circumstances enacting the deportment of a sick, disabled and needy individual, they were making socially fraudulent claims on the city's residents in order to obtain economic benefits.

Social Perceptions Related to Begging. In San Cristobal the person who begs in order to support himself is called a *limosnero* (from *limosna*, meaning "alms"). . . .

Residents place individual *limosneros* in one of two groups. The first is composed of those who are seen as truly needy and deserving, which usually means that they have a serious deformity or handicap and consequently are unable to work. Such persons are believed to be entitled to beg and deserving of help and support. They merely have to display or make reference to their deformity in order to establish legitimacy and obtain a *limosna*. Such an exchange is very likely to be punctuated by a statement that contains religious symbols or has religious overtones. Some residents place aged persons in this first class of beggars.

In the second group are those *limosneros* who either feign a handicapped condition or appear normal on casual inspection. The second group, in other words, consists of persons who are believed able to work. They are said to beg because of laziness and weakness. Implicit in this derogatory response is the conviction that life is difficult and that a person has the obligation and responsibility to work and be self-sufficient. Any suspected reluctance to meet this rather basic human requirement is censured. Even illness, it is often said, does not excuse a person from meeting this requirement unless, of course, the illness is severe enough to be called *una enfermedad de cama* (literally, "a bed illness").

Further probing, however, brings out other important considerations that point to the complex set of attitudes persons in San Cristobal have towards *limosneros*. Residents know that some diseases and pathological conditions (e.g., anemia) that are not associated with "visible" manifestations may nevertheless produce "legitimate" weakness and lassitude. They also know that medical treatment requires both economic means and social support (family or institutional). A person is regarded as deserving of a *limosna* if he can convince others that he has this type of condition and also lacks treatment resources. Consequently, *limosneros* without highly visible signs of disability and deformity depend on their style of self-presentation and on controlling information about themselves in order to be successful (Goffman 1959). In other words, besides explicitly appealing to religious sentiments, their demeanor and behavior while begging must accomplish two objectives: first, it must communicate a support of the prevalent norm regarding self-sufficiency and independence ("I should work and take care of myself like others do"); at the same time, it must explain and justify their failure to do so by the usual socially prescribed means ("but I can't because I am sick and to get treatment I need your help").

The Behavior of Limosneros. Most male *limosneros* go about unshaven and barefoot, wearing ragged and dirty old clothing. Those that are able to walk do so slowly, in a labored fashion that emphasizes a sense of weakness and a lack of well being. When walking, they typically crouch and lean forward. This mode of presentation appears to constitute a facet of a social role and an attitude of humility and degradation. A certain percentage of *limosneros* are, of course, constrained to adopt this demeanor because of physical reasons. Women wear long black or gray dresses, shawls which cover most of the head or face, and carry baskets wherein they place their donations. A demeanor of labored effort and weakness is again always depicted, and the impression usually is one of austerity, deprivation, and pathos.

As mentioned earlier, a request for *limosna* is usually made in statements that appeal to religious and ethical emotions, refer explicitly to the beggar's disability, and list the reasons for his inability to work. The stereotypy of these statements suggests that the communication is predominantly a symbolic one, as opposed to being referential.[3] Diminutive and depreciative forms are typically used in these statements e.g., *una limosnita* ("small alms"), *soy un pobrecito* ("I am a small poor one"), *un favorcito* ("a little favor"), and the like.

Not all beggars, however, make explicit verbal requests. It is possible, in fact, to classify *limosneros* according to the degree of physical activity or directness shown in their begging deportment. Some, invariably those with the most visibly striking handicaps, do not search out clients, but merely place themselves on the sidewalk of a commercial street. There they quietly sit or stand without requesting help or otherwise verbally acknowledging a need. An empty plate or cup is set aside for passers-by to deposit their contributions. Other *limosneros*, also those with serious deformities, crawl or otherwise intrude themselves into the immediate physical proximity of a potential donor. There they clearly expose their deformity and perhaps look at their donor, moving on only after an alm is volunteered or overtly denied.

Implicit in these nonverbal exchanges is the mutually shared conception that complementary rights and obligations are involved. The very nature of these encounters points to the existence of governing rules of conduct that seem to bind the *limosnero* with his donor in a tacit contract. *Limosneros* feel entitled and expect to receive help; conversely, residents experience an obligation to provide this help in the form of alms (Gouldner 1960: 161–178). The existence of these implicit and binding rules, of course, contributes to the resentment and guilt that residents experience when approached by *limosneros*.

A more active and intrusive *limosnero*, usually one without a serious deformity or medical handicap, searches out passersby and verbally solicits alms. Still others knock on the door of someone's home or enter a commercial establishment to ask for food, money, or clothing. There appears to be an inverse relationship between the extent and obviousness of a *limosnero's* handicap or disability and the degree of physical activity that he manifests while soliciting help.

Besides differing in their manner of soliciting help, *limosneros* also differ in what they solicit. The majority explicitly ask for a *limosna*, or alm, but some accept only money. Those who are willing to receive food carry a basket for storing and transporting these donations. During a day they may receive a few tortillas, a small portion of cooked or uncooked beans, chile, eggs, salt, sugar, vegetables, and occasionally a piece of meat. Clothes, such as old shoes or worn-out trousers, are also solicited, as well as medicines and herbs.

---

[3]For a deeper appreciation of the way in which context and circumstances affect language use, see Herbert Blumer, "The Methodological Position of Symbolic Interactionism" in Herbert Blumer (1960: 1–60); Harold Garfinkel (1964: 225–250); and Dell H. Hymes (1962: 13–53).

Most *limosneros* "borrow" a place to live and sleep in someone's house, but some stay in the streets. Those borrowing a place sleep in a corridor or patio; common or shared toilet facilities are denied them. They typically take to the streets in the early morning hours, as is the custom for most residents of San Cristobal, after a light breakfast that includes a cup of coffee which they themselves prepare on a "borrowed" fire. They spend the daylight hours in the streets and return "home" just before nightfall. Later in the evening they typically prepare a meal using the elements collected during the working day, a meal that they may share with other *limosneros* staying in the same home or with friends. Any socializing or other forms of private behavior (as opposed to their public role behavior as *limosneros*) is manifest after hours.

Beggars ordinarily go out daily, although a large proportion reserve Sundays as a day of rest. During the week on any one day, they tour different segments of the city, shift locations, and alternate neighborhoods and establishments in order to "avoid becoming a regular nuisance to others." About two-thirds of the *limosneros* interviewed confined their begging activity to San Cristobal. Most of the Ladinos in this group were female. Indians in this group who had remaining relatives or who owned houses in their *municipios* and hamlets usually returned there about every two or three weeks. These Indian *limosneros*, in other words, belonged to households which were located in nearby hamlets, although they actually spent a greater portion of their time in San Cristobal. The remaining one-third of the *limosneros* interviewed (mostly Ladino males but including some male Indians) regularly visited other nearby cities, including Guatemala, where they likewise assumed the role of a *limosnero*. These itinerant beggars typically alternated and shifted among cities. Of them, it can properly be said that they were residents of the region, not just of San Cristobal. Very few beggars were permanently domiciled, and as mentioned, of those who were, almost all were female.

SOME SOCIAL AND PSYCHOLOGICAL IMPLICATIONS OF BEGGING

It is difficult to establish the denotative features of the term *limosnero*. Descriptively, for example, the behavior of *limosneros* is not unique or even unusual in San Cristobal. Members of religious orders in San Cristobal regularly feed and clothe persons who otherwise do not solicit additional help. Nuns are frequently seen in the street soliciting contributions to help the needy. Both Ladinos and Indians ask for help and favors (either money, food, or work) during times of crisis. Requests of this latter type may be more frequently made to relatives and close friends, but they can extend beyond these groupings. In addition, there exist persons who persistently ask for and, in fact, are totally supported by the help of closed social networks consisting of kin and friends.

The term *limosneros*, which residents state refers to public and indiscriminate begging as the principal if not sole means of support, does not strictly apply to the persons mentioned above, even though the behavior in question is analogous. Related to these considerations is the *pobre vergonzante* (roughly speaking, one too proud to acknowledge his need) which is applied to a person (usually of higher social background) who needs, repeatedly seeks out, and accepts help from others but only under conditions that overtly deny that a request or donation is involved. Such a person, for example, is given a loan he knows he is not expected to repay, may be "requested" to perform a small piece of work and be paid in advance a sum that clearly surpasses what the work is worth, or may at regular and specified intervals of time "show up" for a friendly talk or visit at noon and subsequently be "invited for lunch."

The actual behavior of *limosneros* in San Cristobal then, is not, strictly speaking, unique since there are analogous phenomena which even residents of the city readily acknowledge are related to the activity of *limosneros*. An additional set of observations suggests that the term *limosnero* refers primarily to a social role that has unique connotations. Although a large proportion of *limosneros* spend their entire working day soliciting and entreating others for direct and non-remunerative help, some *limosneros* are willing to perform circumscribed and menial tasks for which they are given token payment. The work in question is not contracted, but viewed by the giver as a justification for his contribution. In the market, for example, some *limosneros* are easily coerced into carrying a heavy bundle to a specified location, or in other contexts they may be commanded to clean a cornfield. Similarly, a known *limosnero* may show up and beg for permission to perform a needed function (e.g., clean a garden, wash the sidewalk, sweep the patio, etc.) as an exchange for his alm. Although such persons are working, they are working under dramatically asymmetrical conditions. They never lose the designation of *limosnero* and they continue to be differentiated socially. Relatively menial activities such as these are performed by non-*limosneros* under a binding contractual agreement that implies reciprocal rights and duties.

Just as there are beggars who will perform a specified piece of work for pay, there are some persons who will beg in between regular jobs or during periods of underemployment. Many persons, for example, contract for work in the lowland coffee plantations. When their work is completed, they may return to San Cristobal to wait for an indeterminate period before finding another contract. During this period they may dress poorly and beg in the streets. Because they behave as do other *limosneros*, the fact that they ordinarily work is overlooked in everyday social dealings; they are therefore classified as *limosneros*.

The begging behavior of *limosneros* is, then, not strikingly discontinuous from what is often observed in San Cristobal, and many individual *limosneros* do not restrict their self-supporting activities entirely to begging. Nevertheless, *limosneros* are clearly differentiated socially in San Cristobal. Were one to select a set of identities that would distinguish a *limosnero*, it would include reference to the fact that the person so labeled maintains an existence by indiscriminately seeking others out and asking for their help without repaying. These particular identities, however, appear to constitute only necessary conditions for the application of the label *limosnero*. Even the physical and bodily attributes of a *limosnero* are not critical elements that serve to differentiate him, for disability, ragged clothing and unclean appearance are not typical of all *limosneros*, nor are they limited to persons so labeled. . . .

· · ·

The stigma attached to being a *limosnero* is easily documented. Almost all individual *limosneros*, for example, report having experienced shame when they began to beg, and the great majority continue to be embarrassed. Most *limosneros* beg only away from their home town or city for fear of being seen by people they know. Residents of San Cristobal usually refer to *limosneros* regardless of their age, sex, or background by means of the informal personal pronoun *tu* ("you") and overtly describe their status as a socially inferior and reprehensible one. The generally held view is that being identified as a *limosnero* is a disgrace and engaging in this type of behavior connotes a "loss of face" (*pide descaradamente*—literally, "asks without face; or *se descaro*, "he removed his face"). *Limosneros* are not usually allowed inside the living quarters of a person's home because they are regarded as physically and socially unclean. Should a *limosnero* request a place to sleep, he is likely to be offered the kitchen or the corner of an outside corridor or patio. Social interactions with *limosneros* are abrupt and superficial, suggesting that they are regarded as non-persons or token, persons. Publicly, *limosneros* are either ignored or related to nonverbally. . . .

The manner in which *limosneros* are viewed is not limited just to considerations of stigma and disgrace, however. Residents frequently expressed resentment and antagonism when questioned about *limosneros*. These feelings seemed to be generated in part by the knowledge that some *limosneros* were manipulative and dishonestly misrepresented their circumstances. These particular *limosneros* were seen as engaged in a form of borderline criminal activity. Remember that charity and concern for others, in this very Catholic city, are both valued traits. The behavior enjoined could be said to approach that of an ideal norm. It is, in fact, the existence of this type of norm that enables "legitimate" *limosneros* to obtain support. Violation of this legitimacy by some beggars accounts for some of the antagonism voiced towards *limosneros*. In addition, of course, all *limosneros* are continually testing and making economic demands on the resident population. Coupled with the sense of obligation that residents feel to help the poor and needy, these demands, although part of the interactional formula, still prove irritating. Lastly, *limosneros* especially the "legitimate" ones, are advertising socially undesirable and unpleasant facets of life in San Cristobal, namely, its poverty and lack of social welfare agencies. The latter fact especially disturbs many residents at the same time that it contributes to their feeling of obligation to render assistance.

An additional but related set of factors helps to clarify the rather complex way in which *limosneros* are viewed. First of all, *limosneros* are constant reminders of the vicissitudes that life can bring. Even though San Cristobal residents may not know a particular *limosnero* personally, they know that illness, deprivation, and isolation are the preconditions that usually lead a person to beg. Residents have had experiences, direct or indirect, with persons who have had these difficulties, and *limosneros* no doubt awaken or reawaken fears that a similar fate might befall them. Furthermore, as reported elsewhere (Fabrega and Metzger 1968: 339–351), in Ladino towns and perhaps in folk communities generally, the phenomena of illness, death and by extension, social crises of any type, are not discontinuous from regular and recurrent social activity. The concomitants of such events, which include suffering, pain, types of deformity and medical disability, as well as social and economic deprivations, are always visible. The small size of the communities and the tradition of closeness and sharing require that residents become personally involved with the consequences of deprivations and crises. These communities lack regulatory social welfare agencies and services to isolate, remove, or resolve behaviors of this type, so town residents must cope with them directly.

Visibly deformed or sick persons often migrate to San Cristobal from these small, folk communities to obtain more substantial help. Since they are not accustomed to concealing their disability in social interactions, they make little attempt to do so in the city. In the folk or village community, "uncontrolled" interactions are the rule. In an urban setting, however, such behavior is viewed differently; persons in the city are less accustomed to this public display of disability and deprivation. Greater social distance exists between residents in the city than in the towns from which a large proportion of *limosneros* come. Moreover, *limosneros* manifestly display and use their disability in order to elicit support. The encounter between this type of "real" *limosnero* and his potential client in the city thus involves making immediately evident a spectacle that the urban resident is not, and does not want to be, intimately associated with. Consequently, the city resident is likely to experience an encounter with a visibly handicapped or impoverished *limosnero* as unpleasant and anxiety provoking. What is more, this type of *limosnero* is making overt demands on a person he does not personally know, a person who is not bound to him by friendship or family ties. There exists, in other words, little opportunity for identifying with the specific life condition of a *limosnero*. The preceding factors are alike in making it difficult for a client to feel comfortable when approached by a *limosnero* and seem, in part, to account for the feelings of antagonism and avoidance that San Cristobal residents express towards *limosneros*.

In conclusion, it can be said that a clearly defined set of characteristics attach to most San Cristobal *limosneros*. The life circumstances of these persons, which often include medical disability, economic deprivation, and social isolation, make them dependent on others. Hoping to obtain more substantial help than that provided them in village communities by informal means, they migrate to the city. This ecological setting, however, besides lacking adequate preventive medical knowledge and facilities, does not provide welfare services that can help them adapt to their disabilities. Agencies that can offer meaningful social, economic, or medical rehabilitative support simply do not exist. In many ways, these people are forced to beg in order to subsist. It is likely that some *limosneros* attain a better life as a consequence of this migration. Those residents of San Cristobal who support the indigent and the disabled beggar by means of donations constitute an informal welfare system. The social identity that is earned by a person making use of this system, however, perpetuates and perhaps increases his isolation and contributes to feelings of estrangement, alienation, and self-derogation accompanied by the stigma of being deviant.

REFERENCES

BECKER, HOWARD S., *Outsiders*. (New York: The Free Press, 1963).

BLUMER, HERBERT, "The methodological position of symbolic interactionism." In *Symbolic Interactionism Perspective and Method*, ed. Herbert Blumer. (New Jersey: Prentice-Hall, 1960), pp. 1–60.

CAPLOW, THEODORE, "The social equality of Guatemala City." In *Studies in Human Ecology*, ed. George A. Theodorson. (New York: Harper and Row, 1961), pp. 331–348.

COLBY, BENJAMIN and P. L. VAN DEN BERGE, "Ethnic relations in Southeastern Mexico." *American Anthropologist* 63:772–792, 1961.

DIAZ-GUERRERO, ROGELIO, "Neurosis and the Mexican family structure." *American Journal of Psychiatry* 1,12:411–417, 1955.

ERIKSON, KAI T., "Notes on the sociology of deviance." In *The Other Side: Perspective on Deviance*, ed. Howard S. Becker (New York: The Free Press, 1964), pp. 9–21.

FABREGA, HORACIO, JR. and DUANE METZGER, "Psychiatric illness in a small Ladino community." *Psychiatry* 31:339–351, 1968.

GARFINKEL, HAROLD, "Conditions of successful degradation ceremonies." *American Journal of Sociology* 61:420–424, 1956. "Studies of the routine grounds of everyday activities." *Social Problems* 11:225:250, 1964.

GOFFMAN, ERVING, "The moral career of the mental patient." *Psychiatry* 22:123–142, 1959. *The Presentation of Self in Everyday Life.* (New York: Doubleday and Company, 1959). *Stigma.* (New Jersey: Prentice-Hall, 1963).

GOULDNER, ALVIN, "The norm of reciprocity: a preliminary statement." *American Sociological Review* 25:161–178, 1960.

HOLLAND, WILLIAM R., *Medicina Maya en los Altos de Chiapas.* (Mexico, D. F.: Instituto Nacional Indigenista, 1963).

HYMES, DELL H., "The ethnography of speaking " In *Anthropology and Human Behavior.* (Washington D.C.: Anthropology Society of Washington, 1962), pp. 13–53.

KAHL, JOSEPH A., "Some social concomitants of industrialization and urbanization." *Human Organization* 18:53–74, 1959.

LEMERT, EDWIN M., *Social Pathology.* (New York: McGraw-Hill, 1951). "Human Deviance," *Social Problems and Social Control.* (New Jersey: Prentice-Hall, 1967).

MOSCOSO, PRUDENCIO P., "El complejo Ladino en los altos de Chiapas. Memoria de la Academia Nacional de Historia y Geografia," *Bulletin* 194:5–38. (Mexico D.F.: Universidad Nacional Autonoma de Mexico, 1963).

REDFIELD, ROBERT, *The Folk Culture of Yucatan.* (Chicago: University of Chicago Press, 1941).

RUIZ, EDUARDO FLORES, "Sociologia historica de Ciudad Real." In *VIII Mesa Redonda San Cristobal la Casas, Chiapas: los Mayas del Sur y sus Relaciones con los Nahuas Meridionales.* (Mexico. D.F.: Instituto Nacional Indigenista, 1961), p. 233–245.

SCHEFF, THOMAS J., *Being Mentally Ill: a Sociological Theory.* (Chicago: Aldine Press, 1966).

SJOBERG, GIDEON, *The Preindustrial City Past and Present.* (New York: The Free Press, 1960).

TEJERO, NEOMI CASTILLO, "Conquista y colonizacion de Chiapas." In *VIII Mesa Redonda San Cristobal Las Casas, Chiapas: Los Mayas del Sur y sus Relaciones con los Nahuas Meridionales.* (Mexico, D. F.: Sociedad Mexicana de Anthropologia, 1961), pp. 207–219.

TRENS, MANUEL B., *Bosquejos Historicas de San Cristobal Las Casas.* (Mexico, D.F.: H. Camara de Diputados, 1957).

VAN DEN BERGHE, PIERRE L. and BENJAMIN N. COLBY, "Ladino-Indian relations in the highlands of Chiapas, Mexico." *Social Forces* 40:63–71, 1961.

Children and Conduct in a Ladino Community of Chiapas, Mexico

John C. Hotchkiss

For secrets are edgéd tools,
And must be kept from children and from fools.
        John Dryden, Sr. Martin Mar-all, II, ii.

I

As children grow up in the town of Teopisca in Chiapas, Mexico, they are called upon to perform important tasks in the innocuous guise of running errands for adults, who are either unwilling or unable to do them for themselves. These tasks are spying and entering encounters that would involve the loss of face or endanger one's self-respect. Probably everywhere the young are a potential resource to be exploited in these ways because they possess incomplete selves, are "nonpersons," or are "profane" (Goffman 1958: 95–96). An adult does not have to act toward children in the same way as he does toward his peers, and socially, children can get away with things that an adult cannot. The importance of privacy and secrecy in the social life of Teopisca provides the clue to the significance of the roles that children play.

By viewing some acts of children as integral to certain aspects of social relations among adults, a perspective emerges that departs from the usual studies of socialization of the young. Most studies of child-rearing emphasize the characteristics of the adult culture and examine how a child moves into it. Investigators have studied child-training practices, mechanisms of cultural transmission, learning processes, the formation of personality, and dimensions of affect as these are found at different stages of the developing child in specific cultural milieus. There is also a growing body of literature that explores and tests, cross-culturally, general theories regarding "the different patterns of child rearing and subsequent differences in personality" (Whiting 1964).

With few exceptions do we find statements that regard children as integral to the role system of a community. To be sure, a functional argument is commonly made that rites of passage involving children not only do something for the child, but also validate the status of his parents. (I have interpreted the baptism fiesta of Teopisca in this way: the infant, especially the first-born son, provides a symbol for his parents that is communicated to others by a fiesta, which thereby validates a new status for the parents [Hotchkiss 1963].) And, in another context, there are statements that the presence of children may facilitate conduct between adults. An example is provided by Goffman:

We can understand, then, why a male's comment to a child can be employed as a way of initiating contact with the woman accompanying the child. Dogs, of course, being even more profane than children, provide another classic bridging device to their masters [1963:126].

Reo Fortune, in the life-cycle chapter of his monograph on the Dobu, provides a description of the socialization process that explicitly considers the growing child as a functionary in the adult social system (1932: 273–279). Dobuan children receive early training in magic and the use of charms, and are taught the significance of secrecy regarding them. The child moves from an understanding of "baby charms" to the "real ones of adult life" and is "well versed in his obligation of keeping magic secret." It is recognized that a child between seven and 12 knows about any of his family's magic business involving accusation of sorcery, so that those who might feel accused "obtain a kinsman or a close friend to try to 'pump' the small boy of the family that summoned in the diviner."

Again, the boy is a good confidant and go-between in the most private of love affairs. Just because the boy is not personally involved in adult life he is made use of as a bribed spy and confidant in affairs of the heart, of magic, and of the underground war of the black art [1932:276].

The central concern of Barker and Wright in their study of children in a midwestern town of the United States is with psychological aspects of children's behavior; however, they stress the importance of children's participation in the social life of Midwest:

... to keep Midwest functioning, children were essential both as performers and as members, spectators, and customers of settings. Children and adolescents did not often occupy the roles of house guests who had to be entertained, or of slightly daft characters who required special arrangements "to keep them busy." A modern Pied Piper would have left Midwest not only distraught, but crippled economically and socially [1954:121].

It is my aim in this paper to specify the ways in which the children of Teopisca may likewise be said to keep the town from being crippled socially. That children fulfill important economic functions will not be emphasized here—it is their role in community conduct that I treat.

II

Teopisca is a town of 3,600 people located on the Pan-American Highway 21 miles southeast of San Cristobal Las Casas in the central highlands of Chiapas, Mexico. The elongated, grid-patterned central area of the town is in the middle of a small valley, and at the edge of the valley against the hills are outlying neighborhoods (*barrios*). These barrios are separated from the central grid area by cultivated fields, at distances that range from one-quarter to three-quarters of a mile, but they are considered part of the town.

In this overwhelmingly Indian region of Chiapas, Teopisca stands out as one of the few Ladino towns. Its Ladino traditions are of considerable depth, reaching back into colonial times. This Ladino population is socially stratified; and in identifying most of the lower class, ethnic considerations come into play, for many of these families are descendants of immigrants from the neighboring Indian community of Huistan who came to Teopisca during the land-reform turmoils of 1914–1917. Their descendants are ladinized today, but because in many situations their ethnic background is still remembered, I use the label "ladinized Indians" to refer to them. (In this paper, I shall refer to "high status" families, "low status" families, and "ladinized Indian" families. Where I am not specific, or refer to "Teopiscanecos," my remarks apply to families and children of all statuses.) Most of the ladinized Indians live in the barrios, where their ancestors first settled, although through the years some have taken up residence in the side and back streets of the central grid area of the town.

• • •

Although the economic activity of the town is predominantly agricultural, Teopisca is the location of an important subregional commercial center for the small-scale, local exchange of immediate consumption goods. . . .

The vast majority of Teopiscanecos are Roman Catholic. Although there is no resident priest, a priest from San Cristobal visits town almost every Sunday, and his masses are well attended by families of the middle and high statuses. Most of the ladinized Indians are indifferent to the religious activity that is centered at the main church, but carry on vigorous periodic Catholic ceremonials in their own barrio chapels. The priest never participates in these religious affairs of the barrios.

Spanish is the language of the town, and for most people the only one they speak. A few people of the older generation of immigrants can speak Tzotzil, a Mayan language, but these people are also bilingual and use Spanish most of the time. Children growing up in the barrios today learn only Spanish.

III

In this community where diversions are few, conversation with others is in itself a pleasurable pastime. . . . Restrictions governing public contact between the sexes are not strict in Teopisca; men and women may strike up conversations together in stores, on the street, and in the plaza. The festive occasions for celebrating saints and the fiesta held in homes for baptisms, weddings, birthdays, and wakes are particularly apt for sociability.

Conversation with others is important in order to obtain information. Decisions that affect the Teopiscanecos' conduct of day-to-day affairs depend upon their knowledge of fellow townsmen. Who has corn to sell, and at what price? Who is a good curer? Who is a reliable worker to hire? From whom may I borrow? Who would be willing to help me sponsor a fiesta? These are some of the questions that people ask themselves about others.

Useful information about others, however, is obtained in contexts that most often are not neutral, that is, in affectively charged conversations with others— gossip. Useful information about someone is conveyed along with evaluations of him. New bits of information are continually added to a body of knowledge, a dossier, that a person has for each of many of his fellow townsmen.

Information about oneself that becomes a topic of general gossip has escaped one's control. It might be used in ways that are damaging to one's reputation. A Teopiscaneco is concerned about his reputation because he knows that in his face-to-face encounters with others, the image of self that he presents must be congruent with his reputation, which nearly everyone in town has knowledge of or holds an opinion about.

With this concern, we can expect to find that people take measures to ensure some degree of secrecy in order to minimize the revelation of information about themselves. The methods that they employ in order to avoid or minimize contact with others are to be understood, first of all, as holding strategies and as protection against the inevitable. Complete isolation is, of course, impossible, nor is it desirable.

The physical arrangements of dwellings and the rules of access to the confines of the home provide a great deal of protection. Unless one is formally invited, a visit to another's home requires an explicit reason or excuse. Secrecy about the domestic establishment of higher status families is maintained by their high adobe walls. Although their houses are placed abutting the sidewalks, the doorways allow access only to the counters of the stores, and windows remain stoutly shuttered. Only when someone within a house has a specific purpose for looking out are the shutters opened. Fences of boards and thick hedges surround the homes of the lower status families. The wattle-and-daub houses of the poor have no windows (although a small peephole for looking out is often found), and the houses are oriented inward, with the doorway facing away from the street or path so that activity in the adjacent patio may go unobserved. High status families have inner patios and gardens, where only the most intimate guests are permitted; few get beyond the store, although an occasional visitor is politely escorted as far as the living room. The living room in these larger homes is seldom lived in, is standardized in its appointments in order to give away little information, and is well spruced up at all times in order to convey positive impressions.

Compare the means of domestic secrecy of Teopisca with this example from India:

The irregular high, rain-furrowed mud walls which faced us might have been mistaken for a deserted fortress. No dooryards, no windows were there to give glimpses of family life. Nothing but blank walls and more walls, so joined that it was often difficult to tell where one man's house ended and his neighbor's began [Wiser and Wiser 1963:1].

• • •

When in public, Teopiscanecos use conventions that seem designed for personal privacy. First of all, the most common greeting when passing on the street, "see you later" (*despues*), is the usual signal to terminate a conversation, and thereby does not allow one to be initiated. If a person is bold enough to probe, the standard reply is "I'm on my errand" (*Voy a hacer mi mandado*).

Women of all statuses, when venturing into public, wear a full shawl (*rebozo*), which is draped over the head and shoulders and reaches well below the waist. The rebozo always covers the shopping basket or whatever is being carried. In covering the head, it can be manipulated to restrict exposure of the face, especially from the sides.

Children and Conduct in a Ladino Community of Chiapas, Mexico **177**

A few women are reluctant to be seen in public at all: the only time they leave the confines of their houses is to attend mass at the church. A common explanation by Teopiscanecos for this retiring behavior is that these women's husbands are "jealous" (celosa) of them, this implying that the women may attract suitors if they are visible in public. The exchange operations required by these women's households are carried out, in part, by children. In discussing the social ecology of a village in Greece, where women rarely penetrate the "market place" (aghora), Friedl reports that children have a similar role:

... the world of the aghora, and indeed, the public world of the village, is a male world penetrated sporadically by children of both sexes. . . . Little girls up to the age of twelve or fourteen, alone or with their brothers, may be sent to the aghora on errands, but older girls and women will venture into the area only to pass through it on their way to church or to the fields. I have seen a young mother from the eastern end of the village, when she heard the calls of a tomato vendor, walk to the edge of the aghora area. She stood some two hundred feet from the tomato wagon, shouted to the pedlar to ask what his prices were, and then waited in the same spot until she could send a passing child to buy her tomatoes for her [1962:12].

Both the women of Vasilika, who should not enter the aghora to shop, and the Teopiscaneca who is reticent to enter public places rely upon the young, who have not yet learned to be concerned with the norms that govern the conduct of their elders.

Children, then, are not subject in the same way as adults to conventions that ensure privacy, and they can also be used to breach the walls of secrecy. The child who brings a condolence message to a family where there has been a death is sent by his parents not only to express his family's sympathies, but by this ruse to gain access to a household's inner or "back region" (Goffman 1958), where he can act as a spy. Children can gain access to a private, family-sponsored fiesta to which their parents are not invited by virtue of the laxness of the occasion; they can join their juvenile friends inside and later report to their families what they have seen. Children are always underfoot in situations like these, and adults act as if they were not there—an attitude that Goffman points out is widespread in situations where "nonpersons" are physically present (1958: 95–96).

But how, it may be asked, can this be possible? Certainly a Teopiscaneco is aware that what his own children are capable of doing, the children of others are equally competent to do, and that they may be directed in the same fashion against him. Indeed, there are things that a child from another household is not allowed to see. Wife-beating and intrafamilial quarreling, sexual relations, any act of theft, and the bounty of stealing must be kept from children's eyes. Also, a drunken person is hidden away from sight as well as circumstances permit. A man of the house where I lived was kept locked in a back room during the difficult period of sobering up after his annual binge. A fugitive from justice will remain hidden: a youth accused of many thefts fled town and then returned secretly to his home, where he hid in a hole in the ground and escaped discovery by the police, who made periodic searches of his home. Therefore, evidence of things that can be severely damaging to one's reputation are kept from children.

That is, one avoids allowing a child to see things that are a "complete story" and need little or no additional analysis by his parents in order for them to understand its meaning. There is less concern about information that a child may obtain in bits and pieces—and there is no effective defense against its revelation anyway.

IV

I now turn to discuss the responsibilities of children of Teopisca and the roles they perform that are related to adult concerns with secrecy and privacy.

In later childhood (the ages of five or six to adolescence), children in Teopisca are considered to be capable of reasoning, and are consciously taught tasks that are useful and anticipatory for adult life. Children readily adapt to this training and become competent and responsible in a variety of tasks. A girl of six can be left in charge of younger brothers and sisters, with her mother confident that if an emergency arises, the girl will know what to do or know where to turn for help. In a family of agriculturalists, a ten-year-old boy is a significant economic asset. He knows practically all the necessary agricultural skills and performs them in a way limited only by his physical ability. Although there is early differentiation according to sex in the socialization of the young, both boys and girls over the ages of five or six are called upon to run all types of errands.

Performing an errand is directly instrumental and frees another member of the household to do other things. The following are the most common errands: walking to a store to purchase items for the household, walking to a spring or common well to fetch water, taking the day's supply of corn to the mill to be ground, going to the plaza and selling products or vending them from door to door, walking to a house to summon a person or to deliver a message on behalf of someone of the household to adults of another.

Prior to embarking upon an errand, a child is given specific instructions regarding products, prices, and the quality of merchandise. An older child can be told to shop around for possible bargains on his own initiative. When selling goods, he is told what minimum price to accept. On all errands there are possibilities that a child will meet other children or adults and can learn from them things that may be quite irrelevant to the purpose of the errand. Therefore, a child is briefed on a wide variety of topics that are items of information for adults:

"Find out where Maria went yesterday."
"See if Don Jose is still drunk."
"Find out if it is true that the Martinezes have bought a new radio."
"See if Alberto has returned home yet." (On the suspicion that he is implicated in a recent murder and has fled town.)
"See if they have Agustina's chicken."

A child is normally sent on several errands a day. It is common practice for housewives to make repeated small purchases for immediate needs rather than make one trip to buy supplies for one or two days. Children of a household can therefore provide an intermittent monitoring service, and information that may be missed on one trip can be picked up on another.

Children and Conduct in a Ladino Community of Chiapas, Mexico **179**

When a child returns from an errand, he is extensively interrogated by an adult of his household to find out what the child has learned. I have seen several women who shared a compound household drop what they were doing and rush over to a returning girl and, all at once in great animation, bombard her with questions. Some adults are more constricted in their enthusiasm, however, and let a child spin his own tale of what he saw and learned. This kind of parental attention given to a youngster for performing errands is obviously rewarding to him and takes out the onerousness of what otherwise might be a chore. The child becomes expert at observation, even though he may not be expert in his ability to carry out fully the role of spy.

It must be remembered that there is risk in exposing a child to possible encounters in public while on an errand, for a child may be accosted by questions about his own family and unwittingly be a "double agent." Although he may be adept at warding off queries that could be damaging to his elders, a child is in a double bind because his training to respect adults makes it hard for him not to reply in some satisfactory way to them. Children have not always learned when it is appropriate to lie. Even though parents can emphasize to a child that he must not disclose information about themselves, at this stage of his development these instructions are in conflict with other things that he has been taught.

While freeing his mother for another task, a child on an errand may also free her from a social encounter that she wants to avoid. The young, as "nonpersons," can be exploited to perform "face-work" for adults (Goffman 1955). In Teopisca a woman feels shame and is embarrassed if she has to reveal information regarding her state of poverty to others, which might be construed in ways that would be disadvantageous to her when she needs to borrow a small supply of corn. Rather than face a borrowing encounter herself, she sends a child to her neighbor to make the request. A child is sent to pay back an old debt, and thereby preserves the front of his father, which would be threatened if the father made repayment personally. In situations such as these, the adults concerned can later meet each other without fear of references to these episodes. The acts were performed by children and are over and done with.

Tact is a recognized element in the proper mutual involvement of persons in Teopisca, and children are essential sometimes to its preservation (Goffman 1958: 132–133, 146–150). In the situations cited above, the efforts of the child in preserving face for his parent would be wasted if the adults had to square their accounts person to person. A high status man will send a child to convey a message to a subordinate and thereby avoid the risk of embarrassing the subordinate by making an unannounced visit himself. Summonses between families of equal status, too, are commonly made by children: "My father would like to talk to you." The summoner thereby displays tact in not intruding upon the privacy of the summoned.

Other status-specific attributes of self are involved in the child's performance of face-work for his parents. A woman of high status who has been impoverished by widowhood or a broken marriage and who must sell products of her own making, such as bread or sweets, cannot be seen sitting among women beneath her station in the plaza market place or go herself from door to door vending her wares. She calls upon a son or daughter who has not yet developed class consciousness to do these things.

As children grow closer to adolescence, they become increasingly reluctant to be used by adults in these ways. Adolescents continue to run errands to help their parents in a strict economic sense, but their usefulness as spies comes to an end as they lose the license that they possessed when younger. They make explicit complaints about having to perform someone else's face-work. They plead that a younger brother or sister should do it (if one is available), and they refuse on grounds of shame or embarrassment. These are arguments that adults understand. As one enters adolescence, one begins to share with adults some of the basic concerns of self, and one's assertions of self-autonomy terminate one's performance of these nonperson roles.

V

. . .

Unlike a complex urban society, where an individual enjoys respite in the exposure of self by his movement through many disparate situations, Teopiscanecos must live out their lives in a type of setting characterized by Pitt-Rivers as a place where ". . . people greet each other when they pass even if they are not acquainted; . . . everyone knows everyone whom everyone else knows; . . . [and] gossip is more powerful than the law" (1957: 5). To be sure, each adult in Teopisca is not personally acquainted with all other adults of the town; this is precluded by the size of the community and the wide range of status differentiation that obtains. Nevertheless, Teopisca is the community of identification that nearly all share for all of their lives. Some members of the higher status families maintain extracommunity affiliations with high status people elsewhere in the region, and within the town a person may affiliate with others on the basis of occupation, residential propinquity, status position, kinship, or fictive kinship ties. Although these affiliations provide the primary pegs for a person's identity, the fact remains that the community as a whole is the field of exposure of the self and the arbiter of reputation.

. . . [R]eputation cannot be treated lightly. While gossip is important as a source of instrumental information, it takes on special importance under conditions like those of Teopisca. It is a necessary evil. "Necessary" is my evaluation of gossip as a source of news. "Evil" is the evaluation of gossip made by Teopiscanecos themselves. They do not like it, and the notorious gossips of town are avoided and despised. One could muster evidence specific to the social groupings of Teopisca and interpret gossip in a manner congruent with Gluckman's argument that gossip functions to maintain the unity of groups (1963: 307–316), but I choose to stress another aspect of gossip, which is relevant for my discussion of children and secrecy.

Gossip can be damaging to one's reputation. Reputation affects or influences a person's conception of self, which in turn affects how he presents himself to others. This presentation of self in encounters with others must be creditable, and one of the sources of credit is reputation. "Reputation" is the body of knowledge, attitudes, and opinions held by others about a person. From the vantage point of ego, one's reputation is potentially the property of everyone else in the community. One is never sure who knows what about oneself, and how they might use what they know. It is wise, therefore, to minimize the exposure of information about oneself.

My discussion has focused upon two strategies whereby the revealing of information about oneself can be minimized. One strategy is to strive to maintain secrecy. This strategy is applied to ensure a good reputation, and is accomplished by remaining behind the walls of one's home and hiding shopping baskets under one's rebozo. This latter act may seem trivial, but I want to emphasize that it isn't for a Teopiscaneca. The purchase of a large quantity of bread by a ladinized Indian woman may signal a party (*fiesta*) to which some of her neighbors may not have been invited. Frequent purchases of meat may provoke envy on the part of others, which can lead to gossip about one's extravagance.

The second strategy is to strive to maintain privacy. (I am restricting "privacy" to "self-privacy.") Information about oneself that can become public knowledge can be revealed in any direct encounter with another. In Teopisca we find the defenses of the street greetings that do not allow an extended conversation to begin and the manipulation of the rebozo about the head and face in order to avoid recognition.

Counterparts to these defensive strategies include the use of children to obtain information about others and the sending of children upon errands. Acts by children can be viewed as implementing other protective measures essential in the system of conduct: when children are called upon to perform face-work for adults, they are helping to maintain fictions. The truth may be known, but a face-to-face acknowledgment of it by the adults is too painful for them to bear. A child go-between may indeed be aware of the truth, and the adult also may know that the child knows, but the adult does not have to behave toward the child in the delicate manner required if he were confronted with another adult. Tact is thus preserved by a child, say, acting as summoner. A child marketing products preserves the public status of his mother, for whom this activity might be severely demeaning. A child negotiates a petty loan, which would be an embarrassing task for his parents to do. And although an adult realizes that a child who enters his premises on an errand may be spying, in the face engagement the adult is not made uncomfortable because in dealing by definition with a nonperson, he knows nothing can go amiss in the interaction. And besides, the adult can interrogate the child about the latter's family without compunction.

• • •

REFERENCES

BARKER, R. G., and H. F. WRIGHT, *Midwest and its children*. (Evanston, Ill.: Row Peterson, 1954).

FORTUNE, REO, *The sorcerers of Dobu*. (New York: E. P. Dutton and Co., 1932).

FRIEDL, ERNESTINE, *Vasilika: a village in modern Greece*. (New York: Holt, Rinehart and Winston, 1962).

GLUCKMAN, MAX, "Gossip and scandal." *Current Anthropology* 4:307–316, 1963.

GOFFMAN, ERVING, "On face-work: an analysis of ritual elements in social interaction." *Psychiatry* 18:213–231, 1955. *The presentation of self in everyday life*. (University of Edinburgh: Social Sciences Research Center Monograph 2, 1958). *Behavior in public places*. (New York: Macmillan-Free Press of Glencoe, 1963).

HOTCHKISS, JOHN C., "Variations in the family fiesta among Ladinos and Indians: a study in acculturation in Chiapas, Mexico." Paper read at the annual meeting of the American Anthropological Association, November 21, 1963, in San Francisco, California, 1963.

PITT-RIVERS, JULIAN, "The closed community and its friends." *Kroeber Anthropological Society Papers* 16:5–15. (Berkeley, California, 1957).

WHITING, BEATRICE, ed., *Six cultures: studies of child rearing.* (New York: John Wiley and Sons, 1964).

WISER, WILLIAM, and CHARLOTTE WISER, *Behind mud walls: 1930–1960.* (Berkeley and Los Angeles: University of California Press, 1963) rev. ed.

5 / Families and Sex

Introduction

All cultures and societies include as part of their cultural patterns internally organized groups to mediate between the individual and his total culture. These groups are sometimes referred to as institutions and include such things as the family, political organizations, churches, etc.

If one takes a worldwide perspective, the most universal and fundamental cultural grouping is the family. It is within the family that many basic cultural functions are typically performed. It is the family that usually has the primary function of caring for the physical well-being of infants and young members of the society. The family operates as the first and most pervasive agent for teaching the child the basic cultural patterns that will be required of him as a fully participating member of the culture. Even in societies where there are highly-elaborated institutions, like schools, outside the family, the preliminary cultural training takes place within the family. The family is also typically a major economic unit that cares for its members' needs. In many societies it is also the responsibility of the family to provide for the care of its aged and infirm members.

In the history of the West there has been a gradual decline in the importance of the family, with many of its earlier functions taken over by schools, welfare agencies and other special-purpose institutions. This development has been accompanied by child-rearing practices that prepare a child from an early age to transfer his interests and loyalties from the family to other persons and groups and to operate independently and successfully in an individualistic society. Even so, the family is still the setting in which the child acquires skills, attitudes and aspirations that will shape his entire life; and for children and adults alike it holds a vital place as an emotional base, the distinctive roles of which (e.g., sexual and parental) make meaningful the many roles played outside the family.

In non-Western communities the family and related groups of kinsmen are even more central in the society. In some areas the family is so dominant that the society is labelled a "familistic society." Child-rearing practices condition the child to think of his developing ego and life career as inseparable from that of the family. The network of kinship, especially the terms and relationships within the family, provide the chief model for the child's experience of the world. Divinities, animals and other men relate to one another in terms of kinship roles like fathers, grandmothers, or children. Strangers who cannot be fitted into one of these roles are not likely to be understood or trusted.

In some societies a thorough understanding of local family patterns can be the key to understanding much that goes on. Anthropologists have a difficult time obtaining an accurate, insider's view of life in non-Western communities. This is true even when most households are made up of a monogamous, nuclear family (parents and their children), as in the U.S. In many cases the households and families themselves are complicated, from a Western point of view, by such practices as polygyny (more than one wife) or polyandry (more than one husband), by the co-residence (in a so-called "extended" family) of married brothers and their respective nuclear families, by co-residence of married children with unmarried siblings and their parents, or by any number of other variants. Each variant is characterized by different patterns of stresses and satisfactions.

In the first reading in this chapter Spiro raises a basic question: "Is the Family Universal?" Spiro begins by providing a handy summary of cross-cultural definitions of family and marriage, and then goes on to argue that they do not exist in this form in the Israeli *kibbutzim* that he studied. His argument that this "constitutes an exception to the generalization concerning the universality of the family" seems convincing enough, but the setting of his study is so extraordinary that this exception seems essentially to "prove the rule." That is, it suggests that a radical and intentional restructuring of the whole of a society may be necessary in order to displace familiar family and marriage patterns.

In "Sex Roles and Economic Change in Africa," LeVine tries to account for observed differences in sex roles and male/female dominance within a region where many general features of family and marriage are fairly uniform. Many of the societies in this region, Africa south of the Sahara, are patrilineal, i.e., names, privilege and inheritance are passed down from male to male. This is frequently attended by the practice of patrilocality, which means that newlyweds live with the husband's kinsmen rather than the wife's. Under these circumstances, wives are likely to be treated as subordinate outsiders, necessary to perpetuate the lineage and to help with domestic work but who have few claims upon the wealth and affection of lineage members. LeVine contends that this is frequently still true of women in East and South Africa, where "the traditional supports for their subordination and the rewards accruing to occupation of a clearly defined social position appear to have remained effective." In West Africa, however, male dominance backed up by patrilineal organization, though still maintained in appearance, has been largely undercut and, in some cases, reversed. LeVine looks for the explanation mainly along economic lines, comparing the economies of the regions both before and after they came under Western influence.

The liberation of women among one of these West African groups, the Kofyar, is the subject of Netting's article on "Marital Relations in the Jos Plateau of Nigeria." Again, the women derive much of their informal power through economic activities, making the male emphasis on the ceremonial activities that they reserve to themselves seem somewhat hollow and wishful. In addition, there are certain customary alternatives available to Kofyar women as wives that blunt the impact of the patrilineal system. In particular, they may divorce themselves from a husband and his patriline relatively easily. As Netting notes, "they move into the married state gradually and unceremoniously, and they may leave it in the same way." This association of casual marriage with casual divorce characterizes a number of societies, Western and non-Western.

Stoodley's article acquaints us with a peasant society whose settlements surround the capital of the Philippines. As with many once-primitive populations subject to heavy Western influence (for over three centuries in this case), the Tagalogs live in relatively large barrios and orient many of their relationships along territorial instead of kinship lines, emphasizing neighborly relations with whoever happens to live nearby. As it happens, however, many of the members of these barrios are, in fact, kinsmen; so the two bases of interaction frequently reinforce one another.

When he turns to the analysis of kinship terminology, Stoodley points out that the Tagalogs use many terms that are sex-neutral, suggesting an equal status for males and females alike. This he finds confirmed in other areas of their society, including the lack of either patri- or matri-lineality in family organization. Instead of structuring lines of authority according to sex, the Tagalogs focus heavily on relative age and birth order.

Is the Family Universal?

Melford E. Spiro

INTRODUCTION

The universality of the family has always been accepted as a sound hypothesis in anthropology; recently, Murdock has been able to confirm this hypothesis on the basis of his important cross-cultural study of kinship. Moreover, Murdock reports that the "nuclear" family is also universal, and that typically it has four functions: sexual, economic, reproductive, and educational. What is more important is his finding that no society "has succeeded in finding an adequate substitute for the nuclear family, to which it might transfer these functions" (1949: 11). In the light of this evidence there would be little reason to question his prediction that "it is highly doubtful whether any society ever will succeed in such an attempt, utopian proposals for the abolition of the family to the contrary notwithstanding" (p. 11).

The functions served by the nuclear family are, of course, universal prerequisites for the survival of any society; and it is on this basis that Murdock accounts for its universality.

Without provision for the first and third [sexual and reproductive], society would become extinct; for the second [economic], life itself would cease; for the fourth [educational], culture would come to an end. The immense social utility of the nuclear family and the basic reason for its universality thus begins to emerge in strong relief [p. 10].

Although sexual, economic, reproductive, and educational activities are the functional prerequisites of any society it comes as somewhat of a surprise, nevertheless, that all four functions are served by the same social group. One would normally assume, on purely a priori grounds, that within the tremendous variability to be found among human cultures, there would be some cultures in which these four functions were distributed among more than one group. Logically, at least, it is entirely possible for these functions to be divided among various social groups within a society; and it is, indeed, difficult to believe that somewhere man's inventive ingenuity should not have actualized this logical possibility. As a matter of fact this possibility has been actualized in certain utopian communities and it has succeeded within the narrow confines of these communities. The latter, however, have always constituted subgroups within a larger society, and the basic question remains as to whether such attempts could succeed when applied to the larger society.

Rather than speculate about the answer to this question, however, this paper presents a case study of a community which, like the utopian communities, constitutes a subgroup within a larger society and which, like some utopian communities, has also evolved a social structure which does not include the family. It is hoped that an examination of this community—the Israeli *kibbutz*—can shed some light on this question.

A *kibbutz* (plural, *kibbutzim*) is an agricultural collective in Israel, whose main features include communal living, collective ownership of all property (and, hence, the absence of "free enterprise" and the "profit motive"), and the communal rearing of children. *Kibbutz* culture is informed by its explicit, guiding principle of: "from each according to his ability, to each according to his needs." The "family," as that term is defined in *Social Structure*, does not exist in the *kibbutz*, in either its nuclear, polygamous, or extended forms. It should be emphasized, however, that the *kibbutzim* are organized into three separate national federations, and though the basic structure of *kibbutz* society is similar in all three, there are important differences among them. Hence, the term *kibbutz*, as used in this paper, refers exclusively to those *kibbutzim* that are members of the federation studied by the author.[1]

As Murdock defines it (p. 1), the "family":

is a social group characterized by common residence, economic cooperation, and reproduction. It includes adults of both sexes, at least two of whom maintain a socially approved sexual relationship, and one or more children, own or adopted, of the sexually cohabiting adults.

The social group in the *kibbutz* that includes adults of both sexes and their children, although characterized by reproduction, is not characterized by common residence or by economic co-operation. Before examining this entire social group, however, we shall first analyze the relationship between the two adults in the group who maintain a "socially approved sexual relationship," in order to determine whether their relationship constitutes a "marriage."

Murdock's findings reveal that marriage entails an interaction of persons of opposite sex such that a relatively permanent sexual relationship is maintained and an economic division of labor is practised. Where either of these behavior patterns is absent, there is no marriage. As Murdock puts it (p. 8):

Sexual unions without economic cooperation are common, and there are relationships between men and women involving a division of labor without sexual gratification . . . but marriage exists only when the economic and the sexual are united in one relationship, and this combination occurs only in marriage.

In examining the relationship of the couple in the *kibbutz* who share a common marriage, and whose sexual union is socially sanctioned, it is discovered that only one of these two criteria—the sexual—applies. Their relationship does not entail economic co-operation. If this be so—and the facts will be examined in a moment—there is no marriage in the *kibbutz*, if by "marriage" is meant a relationship between adults of opposite sex, characterized by sexual and economic activities. Hence, the generalization that, "marriage, thus defined, exists in every known society" (p. 8), has found an exception.

A *kibbutz* couple lives in a single room, which serves as a combined bedroom-living room. Their meals are eaten in a communal dining room, and their children are reared in a communal children's dormitory. Both the man and the

[1] The field work, on which statements concerning the *kibbutz* are based, was conducted in the year 1951–1952, and was made possible by a postdoctoral fellowship awarded by the Social Science Research Council.

woman work in the *kibbutz*, and either one may work in one of its agricultural branches or in one of the "service" branches. The latter include clerical work, education, work in the kitchen, laundry, etc. In actual fact, however, men preponderate in the agricultural branches, and women, in the service branches of the economy. There are no men, for example, in that part of the educational system which extends from infancy to the junior-high level. Nor do women work in those agricultural branches that require the use of heavy machinery, such as trucks, tractors, or combines. It should be noted, however, that some women play major roles in agricultural branches, such as the vegetable garden and the fruit orchards; and some men are indispensable in service branches such as the high school. Nevertheless, it is accurate to state that a division of labor based on sex is characteristic of the *kibbutz* society as a whole. This division of labor, however, does not characterize the relationship that exists between couples. Each mate works in some branch of the *kibbutz* economy and each, as a member (*chaver*) of the *kibbutz* receives his equal share of the goods and services that the *kibbutz* distributes. Neither, however, engages in economic activities that are exclusively directed to the satisfaction of the needs of his mate. Women cook, sew, launder, etc., for the entire *kibbutz*, and not for their mates exclusively. Men produce goods, but the economic returns from their labor go to the *kibbutz*, not to their mates and themselves, although they, like all members of the *kibbutz*, share in these economic returns. Hence, though there is economic co-operation between the sexes within the community as a whole, this co-operation does not take place between mates because the social structure of this society precludes the necessity for such co-operation.

What then is the nature of the relationship of the *kibbutz* couple? What are the motives for their union? What functions, other than sex, does it serve? What distinguishes such a union from an ordinary love affair?

In attempting to answer these questions it should first be noted that premarital sexual relations are not taboo. It is expected, however, that youth of high-school age refrain from sexual activity; sexual intercourse between high-school students is strongly discouraged. After graduation from high school, however, and their election to membership in the *kibbutz*, there are no sanctions against sexual relations among these young people. While still single, *kibbutz* members live in small private rooms, and their sexual activities may take place in the room of either the male or the female, or in any other convenient location. Lovers do not ask the *kibbutz* for permission to move into a (larger) common room, nor, if they did, would this permission be granted if it were assumed that their relationship was merely that of lovers. When a couple asks for permission to share a room, they do so—and the *kibbutz* assumes that they do so—not because they are lovers, but because they are in love. The request for a room, then, is the sign that they wish to become a "couple" (*zug*), the term the *kibbutz* has substituted for the traditional "marriage." This union does not require the sanction of a marriage ceremony, or of any other event. When a couple requests a room, and the *kibbutz* grants the request, their union is *ipso facto* sanctioned by society. It should be noted, however, that all *kibbutz* "couples" eventually "get married" in accordance with the marriage laws of the state—usually just before, or soon after, their first child is born—because children born out of wedlock have no legal rights, according to state law.

But becoming a "couple" affects neither the status nor the responsibilities of either the male or the female in the *kibbutz*. Both continue to work in whichever branch of the economy they had worked in before their union. The legal and social status of both the male and the female remain the same. The female retains her maiden name. She not only is viewed as a member of the *kibbutz* in her own right, but her official registration card in the *kibbutz* files remains separate from that of her "friend" (*chaver*)—the term used to designate spouses.[2]

But if sexual satisfaction may be obtained outside of this union, and if the union does not entail economic co-operation, what motivates people to become "couples"? It seems that the motivation is the desire to satisfy certain needs for intimacy, using that term in both its physical and psychological meanings. In the first place, from the sexual point of view, the average *chaver* is not content to engage in a constant series of casual affairs. After a certain period of sexual experimentation, he desires to establish a relatively permanent relationship with one person. But in addition to the physical intimacy of sex, the union also provides a psychological intimacy that may be expressed by notions such as "comradeship," "security," "dependency," "succorance," etc. And it is this psychological intimacy, primarily, that distinguishes "couples" from lovers. The criterion of the "couple" relationship, then, that which distinguishes it from a relationship between adults of the same sex who enjoy psychological intimacy, or from that of adults of opposite sex who enjoy physical intimacy, is love. A "couple" comes into being when these two kinds of intimacy are united in one relationship.

Since the *kibbutz* "couple" does not constitute a marriage because it does not satisfy the economic criterion of "marriage," it follows that the "couple" and their children do not constitute a family, economic co-operation being part of the definition of the "family." Furthermore, as has already been indicated, this group of adults and children does not satisfy the criterion of "common residence." For though the children visit their parents in the latter's room every day, their residence is in one of the "children's houses" (*bet yeladim*), where they sleep, eat, and spend most of their time.

More important, however, in determining whether or not the family exists in the *kibbutz* is the fact that the "physical care" and the "social care" and the "social rearing" of the children are not the responsibilities of their own parents. But these responsibilities, according to Murdock's findings, are the most important functions that the adults in the "family" have with respect to the children.

Before entering into a discussion of the *kibbutz* system of "collective education" (*chinuch meshutaf*), it should be emphasized that the *kibbutz* is a child-centered society, *par excellence*. The importance of children, characteristic of traditional Jewish culture, has been retained as one of the primary values in this avowedly antitraditional society. "The Parents Crown" is the title given to the chapter on children in an ethnography of the Eastern European Jewish village. The authors of this ethnography write (Zborowski and Herzog 1952: 308):

Aside from the scriptural and social reasons, children are welcomed for the joy they

---

[2]Other terms, "young man" (*bachur*) and "young woman" (*bachura*), are also used in place of "husband" and "wife." If more than one person in the *kibbutz* has the same proper name, and there is some question as to who is being referred to when the name is mentioned in conversation, the person is identified by adding, "the *bachur* of so-and-so," or "the *bachura* of so-and-so."

bring beyond the gratification due to the parents—the pleasure of having a child in the house. A baby is a toy, the treasure, and the pride of the house.

This description, except for the scriptural reference, applies without qualification to the *kibbutz*.

But the *kibbutz* has still another reason for cherishing its children. The *kibbutz* views itself as an attempt to revolutionize the structure of human society and its basic social relations. Its faith in its ability to achieve this end can be vindicated only if it can raise a generation that will choose to live in this communal society, and will, thus, carry on the work that was initiated by the founders of this society —their parents.

For both these reasons the child is king. Children are lavished with attention and with care to the point where many adults admit that the children are "spoiled." Adult housing may be poor, but the children live in good houses; adult food may be meager and monotonous, but the children enjoy a variety of excellent food; there may be a shortage of clothes for adults, but the children's clothing is both good and plentiful.

Despite this emphasis on children, however, it is not their own parents who provide directly for their physical care. Indeed, the latter have no responsibility in this regard. The *kibbutz* as a whole assumes this responsibility for all its children. The latter sleep and eat in special "children's houses"; they obtain their clothes from a communal store; when ill, they are taken care of by their "nurses." This does not mean that parents are not concerned about the physical welfare of their own children. On the contrary, this is one of their primary concerns. But it does mean that the active responsibility for their care has been delegated to a community institution. Nor does it mean that parents do not work for the physical care of their children, for this is one of their strongest drives. But the fruits of their labor are not given directly to their children; they are given instead to the community which, in turn, provides for all the children. A bachelor or a "couple" without children contribute as much to the children's physical care as a "couple" with children of their own.

The family's responsibility for the socialization of children, Murdock reports, is "no less important than the physical care of the children."

The burden of education and socialization everywhere falls primarily upon the nuclear family. . . . Perhaps more than any other single factor collective responsibility for education and socialization welds the various relationships of the family firmly together [p. 10].

But the education and socialization of *kibbutz* children are the function of their "nurses" and teachers, and not of their parents. The infant is placed in the "infants' house" upon the mother's return from the hospital, where it remains in the care of nurses. Both parents see the infant there; the mother when she feeds it, the father upon return from work. The infant is not taken to its parents' room until its sixth month, after which it stays with them for an hour. As the child grows older, the amount of time he spends with his parents increases, and he may go to their room whenever he chooses during the day, though he must return to his "children's house" before lights-out. Since the children are in school most of the day, however, and since both parents work during the day, the children—even during their school vacations—are with their parents for a (approximately) two-hour period in the evening—from the time that the parents return from work until they go to eat their evening meal. The children may also be with their parents all day Saturday—the day of rest—if they desire.

As the child grows older he advances through a succession of "children's houses" with children of his own age, where he is supervised by a "nurse." The "nurse" institutes most of the disciplines, teaches the child his basic social skills, and is responsible for the "socialization of the instincts." The child also learns from his parents, to be sure, and they too are agents in the socialization process. But the bulk of his socialization is both entrusted, and deliberately delegated, to the "nurses" and teachers. There is little doubt but that a *kibbutz* child, bereft of the contributions of his parents to his socialization, would know his culture; deprived of the contributions of his "nurses" and teachers, however, he would remain an unsocialized individual.

As they enter the juvenile period, pre-adolescence, and adolescence, the children are gradually inducted into the economic life of the *kibbutz*. They work from an hour (grade-school students) to three hours (high school seniors) a day in one of the economic branches under the supervision of adults. Thus, their economic skills, like most of their early social skills, are taught them by adults other than their parents. This generalization applies to the learning of values, as well. In the early ages, the *kibbutz* values are inculcated by "nurses," and later by teachers. When the children enter junior high, this function, which the *kibbutz* views as paramount in importance, is delegated to the "homeroom teacher," known as the "educator" (*mechanech*), and to a "leader" (*madrich*) of the inter-*kibbutz* youth movement. The parents, of course, are also influential in the teaching of values, but the formal division of labor in the *kibbutz* has delegated this responsibility to other authorities.

Although the parents do not play an outstanding role in the socialization of their children, or in providing for their physical needs, it would be erroneous to conclude that they are unimportant figures in their children's lives. Parents are of crucial importance in the *psychological* development of the child. They serve as the objects of his most important identifications, and they provide him with a certain security and love that he obtains from no one else. If anything, the attachment of the young children to their parents is greater than it is in our own society. But this is irrelevant to the main consideration of this paper. Its purpose is to call attention to the fact that those functions of parents that constitute the *conditio sine qua non* for the existence of the "family"—the physical care and socialization of children—are not the functions of the *kibbutz* parents. It can only be concluded that in the absence of the economic and educational functions of the typical family, as well as of its characteristic of common residence, that the family does not exist in the *kibbutz*.

INTERPRETATION

It is apparent from this brief description of the *kibbutz* that most of the functions characteristic of the typical nuclear family have become the functions of the entire *kibbutz* society. This is so much the case that the *kibbutz* as a whole can almost satisfy the criteria by which Murdock defines the "family." This observation is not meant to imply that the *kibbutz* is a nuclear family. Its structure and that of the nuclear family are dissimilar. This observation does suggest, however, that the *kibbutz* can function without the family because it functions as if it, itself, were a family; and it can so function because its members perceive each other as kin, in the psychological implications of that term. The latter statement requires some explanation.

The members of the *kibbutz* do not view each other merely as fellow citizens, or as co-residents in a village, or as co-operators of an agricultural economy. Rather do they view each other as *chaverim*, or comrades, who comprise a group in which each is intimately related to the other, and in which the welfare of the one is bound up with the welfare of the other. This is a society in which the principle, "from each according to his ability, to each according to his needs," can be practised not because its members are more altruistic than the members of other societies, but because each member views his fellow as a kinsman, psychologically speaking. And just as a father in the family does not complain because he works much harder than his children, and yet he may receive no more, or even less, of the family income than they, so the *kibbutz* member whose economic productivity is high does not complain because he receives no more, and sometimes less, than a member whose productivity is low. This "principle" is taken for granted as the normal way of doing things. Since they are all *chaverim*, "it's all in the family," psychologically speaking.

In short, the *kibbutz* constitutes a *gemeinschaft*. Its patterns of interaction are interpersonal patterns; its ties are kin ties, without the biological tie of kinship. In this one respect it is the "folk society," in almost its pure form. The following quotation from Redfield (1947) could have been written with the *kibbutz* in mind, so accurately does it describe the social-psychological basis of *kibbutz* culture.

The members of the folk society have a strong sense of belonging together. The group ... see their own resemblances and feel correspondingly united. Communicating intimately with each other, each has a strong claim on the sympathies of the others [p. 297]. ... the personal and intimate life of the child in the family is extended, in the folk society, into the social world of the adults. ... It is not merely that relations in such a society are personal; it is also that they are familial. ... the result is a group of people among whom prevail the personal and categorized relationships that characterize families as we know them, and in which the patterns of kinship tend to be extended outward from the group of genealogically connected individuals into the whole society. The kin are the type persons for all experience [p. 301].

Hence it is that the bachelor and the childless "couple" do not feel that an injustice is being done them when they contribute to the support of the children of others. The children *in* the *kibbutz* are viewed as the children *of* the *kibbutz*. Parents (who are much more attached to their own children than they are to the children of others) and bachelors, alike, refer to all the *kibbutz* children as "our children."

The social perception of one's fellows as kin, psychologically speaking, is reflected in another important aspect of *kibbutz* behavior. It is a striking and significant fact that those individuals who were born and raised in the *kibbutz* tend to practise group exogamy, although there are no rules that either compel or encourage them to do so. Indeed, in the *kibbutz* in which our field work was carried out, all such individuals married outside their own *kibbutz*. When they are asked for an explanation of this behavior, these individuals reply that they cannot marry those persons with whom they have been raised and whom they, consequently, view as siblings. This suggests, as Murdock has pointed out, that "the *kibbutz* to its members *is* viewed psychologically as a family to the extent that it generates the same sort of unconscious incest-avoidance tendencies" (private communication).

What is suggested by this discussion is the following proposition: although the *kibbutz* constitutes an exception to the generalization concerning the universality of the family, structurally viewed, it serves to confirm this generalization, functionally and psychologically viewed. In the absence of a specific social group—the family—to whom society delegates the functions of socialization, reproduction, etc., it has become necessary for the entire society to become a large extended family. But only in a society whose members perceive each other psychologically as kin can it function as a family. And there would seem to be a population limit beyond which point individuals are no longer perceived as kin. That point is probably reached when the interaction of its members is no longer face-to-face; in short, when it ceases to be a primary group. It would seem probable, therefore, that only in a "familial" society, such as the *kibbutz*, is it possible to dispense with the family.

REFERENCES

MURDOCK, G. P., *Social structure.* (New York: Macmillan, 1949).

REDFIELD, R., "The folk society." *The American Journal of Sociology* 52:293–308, 1947.

ZBOROWSKI, M. and E. HERZOG, *Life is with people.* (New York: International Universities Press, 1952).

Sex Roles and Economic Change in Africa

Robert A. LeVine

Cross-cultural variations in the relative position of the sexes have long attracted the serious attention of anthropologists. From the nineteenth-century theorists who posited matrilineal and patrilineal stages in cultural evolution,[1] through Mead's (1935) dramatic presentation of sex-role reversals in three New Guinea tribes, to attempts by British anthropologists to show that degree of matrilineality or patrilineality determines beliefs concerning conception (Richards 1950) and marital stability (Gluckman 1950), respectively, there has been an emphasis on

[1] Cf. Murdock (1949: 184–185) for a discussion of the hypothesis of the priority of the matrilineate as put forward by Bachofen and his followers from 1861 onwards.

the roles of men and women as explanatory variables in the analysis of cultural behavior.

In recent years it has become clear that terms like "matrilineal," "patrilineal," "matriarchal," and "patriarchal" are too general to do justice to the complex variations in sex roles which ethnographers have described. Roles may be differentiated by sex within each of the major institutional aspects of the social system: the family, the economy, the political system, the religious system, etc., and the patterns in one aspect may not be consistent with those of another. To give an example in terms of sex status, it is not difficult to imagine a society in which women play an important part in family decision-making but are discriminated against in the occupational sphere. Furthermore, even within the area of kinship, it appears that the general outlines of a descent system—as given in the terms "matrilineal," "patrilineal," and "bilateral"—are poor indices of sex status or position. Thus there are some patrilineal societies in which women have higher relative status than their counterparts in some matrilineal societies, due to structural factors such as residence and property rights which are more important in status placement than the method of establishing genealogical connections. Thus, if one is interested in the psychological or behavioral impact of cross-cultural variations in sex roles, it is necessary to specify the aspects of sex-role structure which are to be examined. In this paper I propose to examine two divergent patterns of change in the occupational roles of men and women, and their effects on behavior in husband and wife roles.

There are some conspicuous uniformities throughout the agricultural societies of sub-Saharan Africa in the traditional division of labor by sex and the husband-wife relationship. Among most of these peoples, men clear the bush and do other annual heavy tasks, while women have the larger share of routine cultivation. Women carry the heavy burdens, usually on their heads, while men occupy their leisure with a variety of prestigeful and important activities: cattle transactions (where there are cattle), government, and litigation. Thus women contribute very heavily to the basic economy, but male activities are much more prestigeful and require less routine physical labor. In husband-wife relations, the male is ideally dominant. Polygyny is extremely widespread in these societies, and the plurality of wives often augments the husband's power in the marital relationship. His power is buttressed further in those many groups in which the wives reside with their husband's kin group rather than their own. Within the domestic economy of the polygynous family each wife, living in her own house, tends to constitute a separate unit of production, regardless of whether she concentrates on agriculture or trade.

Thus African women have less prestigeful occupations than their husbands and are often subordinated to them in the family in consequence of polygyny, patrilocality, and the ideal of male dominance; nevertheless, women play essential and semi-autonomous roles in the labor force as producers and distributors of goods. Furthermore, the typical African woman thinks of herself as a cultivator or trader as well as wife and mother; her occupational role is part of her self-image. Since her occupational involvement is so great, it might be expected that changes in the economy would affect her behavior in family roles.

Within this generalized picture of sex roles in the agricultural societies of Africa there are traditional variations, some of which have been magnified in the course of recent socio-economic change. The contrast of interest here is that between the Bantu agricultural peoples in Kenya and South Africa and certain Nigerian societies. All of these groups of people could be described as "patrilineal" in the usual sense of the term, but differing patterns of economic development have so magnified the traditional differences between them that they provide a striking and instructive instance of contrast in sex roles.

In Kenya and South Africa the agricultural tribes had little occupational specialization or other forms of economic differentiation, and there were no indigenous markets. When European settlement came to both areas, the plantations, industries, cities, and governmental organizations established by the Europeans employed large numbers of Africans. A pattern of labor migration developed, with rural African men leaving home to work far away for a period of years, returning occasionally on vacation, and eventually retiring in their rural homes. Most frequently, though not always, they leave their wives and children behind to continue the agricultural work and maintain the husband's claim to his share in the patrimonial land. The South African government has deliberately fostered this pattern in order to prevent large permanent settlements of Africans in the city, but the similar development in Kenya indicates that it is not simply a function of government regulation. For most of the African migrants in these areas, the rural ties are economically indispensable as well as highly valued in emotional terms; furthermore, the cities do not provide sufficient accommodation for their families. Thus many of the rural areas are depleted of young adult males; it has been estimated, for example, that half of the married women in Basutoland have absent husbands (Sheddick 1953: 15). In other South African groups like the Tswana and Pondo, old surveys (Mair 1953: 20–27) report 40 to 50 percent of the adult men under 45 absent from their rural communities; the proportion is likely to be even higher nowadays. A similar though less extreme situation exists in the densely populated areas of central and western Kenya.[2]

Labor migration has not resulted in a drastic restructuring of sex-role norms in these rural communities but rather in an accentuation of traditional tendencies. Men were always more mobile and less bound to routine tasks than women, as well as having greater control over property, and this is even more the case under contemporary traditions. Many tasks in which men formerly participated are now relegated exclusively to their wives and children. The men have retained their rights in land and livestock, and they also control the cash income derived from their employment and the sale of cash crops. While the absence of the men unquestionably loosens the control they once had over their wives' activities, the women who remain behind cannot be said to have gained in status relative to men—unlike those South African women who take employment in the cities.

The situation of the rural woman under these conditions can be illustrated from my own data on a Gusii community in western Kenya (LeVine and LeVine 1963). Here the women now do almost all the cultivation—from breaking ground with hoes to harvesting—for most crops, tasks which they once shared with men. In addition they milk the cows, formerly a masculine prerogative, and try to keep an eye on the herding done by preadolescent boys who have re-

---

[2]In North Nyanza District of western Kenya, Wilson (1956) found an average of 45 percent of adult males absent because of employment. The situation is likely to be the same in the Kikuyu and Kamba areas of central Kenya where labor migration is an old, established pattern.

placed young men in this job. The domestic chores of fetching water, gathering firewood, grinding grain, cooking, and child care remain feminine responsibilities, and the married women can look only to their children for assistance.

What is the emotional reaction of the married woman to this burdensome load of responsibilities? From the Gusii evidence, it seems that her children become the ultimate victims of their mother's excessive work burden. In a statistical comparison with mothers from five societies outside Africa, the Gusii mothers were highest on "emotional instability," i.e., "the degree to which mothers shift unpredictably from friendly to hostile moods" vis-à-vis their children (Minturn, Lambert, et al. 1964). Observation of these mothers indicated that this shifting is related to their work load and fatigue at particular times of day and seasons of the year, which makes them more irritable and hostile with their children than they would otherwise be. The Gusii mothers were also least tolerant, among the six societies, of their children becoming angry when scolded, and most likely to punish a child for this. They were second highest on intensity and frequency of physical punishment. All of this supports the interpretation that these mothers are expressing in their relationship with their children aggression derived from the frustrations of their heavy work load.

Despite their daily frustrations, the indications are that the Gusii women, and other African women who share their situation, find some emotional comfort in their status in society that they might not receive in a more independent role. The traditional supports for their subordination and the rewards accruing to occupation of a clearly defined social position appear to have remained effective. Although this is hard to prove, some evidence concerning the Zulu in South Africa, who have been immensely affected by labor migration, may be relevant. A study by Scotch (1960) of blood pressure among rural and urban Zulu shows numerous relations between social conditions producing stress and the frequency of elevated blood pressures among those affected by the conditions.

One finding of this study is that among rural as well as urban Zulu, the separated and widowed women, who have become family heads involuntarily, have a significantly higher frequency of elevated blood pressure than married women. Scotch (1960: 1007) explains this in terms of the reluctance of Zulu women to assume the role of family head. Another way for a Zulu woman to become emancipated from her traditionally subordinate role is to become a working woman in the city. Although both men and women living in the city have a higher frequency of elevated blood pressure than rural residents, the rural-urban differential is much greater for women. This is explained by the author (Scotch 1960: 1003–1006) in terms of the more clearly defined role of women in the rural community. These findings point to the conclusion that the traditionally institutionalized role of the Zulu woman, despite its currently arduous character, still affords her less stress than a more independent role in the family and domestic economy. I would presume that this is equally true among other groups of East and South Africa where similar socio-economic changes have taken place.

Along the Guinea Coast and in the interior of West Africa, in contrast to the eastern Africa groups I have been discussing, a more specialized and differentiated economy existed prior to European contact. From the viewpoint of this discussion, its most important distinctive feature was the existence of indigenous markets in which women played a role as market traders. There was no substantial settlement of Europeans in West Africa. But under European administration, with the establishment of internal peace and the development of overseas trade, marketing activities increased, offering new opportunities to women as well as men. In some areas, these opportunities augmented the mobility and economic autonomy of women, causing drastic changes in the husband-wife relationship.

A dramatic example of such a change has been presented by Nadel (1952) for the Nupe of northern Nigeria. In traditional Nupe society, female trading—especially itinerant, long-distance trading—was ideally limited to childless women, whose sexual laxity while away from their husbands was regarded as permissible. In fact it appears that some child-bearing women also carried on this type of trade even in those days. As economic activity grew under British rule, an increasing proportion of mothers became itinerant traders. In the early 1930's Nadel found that many Nupe women were contributing a larger share of the family income than their husbands, who were often poor farmers. Furthermore, to quote Nadel (1952: 21):

Husbands are often heavily in debt to their wives, and the latter assume many of the financial responsibilities which should rightly belong to the men as father and family head such as finding bride-price for sons, paying for the children's education, bearing the expenses of family feasts, and the like. This reversal of the institutionalized roles is openly resented by the men, who are, however, helpless and unable to redress the situation.

Nupe men accuse these trading women of sexual promiscuity, label them as immoral, and talk nostalgically about the "good old days" when such behavior was unknown. Moreover, all witchcraft is attributed to women, with the official head of the women traders believed to be head of the Nupe witches. Men are never accused of witchcraft, are often seen as its victims, and have an exclusively male secret society which "by threats and torture, 'cleanses' villages of witchcraft." Nadel supports his linkage of the resented economic role of women to the witchcraft beliefs by pointing out that the neighboring Gwari tribe, who are closely related to the Nupe and similar in most aspects of culture, have much less trading activity and do not recognize a sex distinction in witchcraft attribution.

Another illustration of change in a Nigerian society is reported for the Ibo of Afikpo in eastern Nigeria (Ottenberg 1959). Before European contact, the women made pots, traded, and farmed, but the men controlled most of the income, performed the prestige activities of yam farming and slave trading, and limited the mobility of their wives because of the prevalence of warfare. Under the Pax Britannica, mobility became possible and trading increased. Most importantly, however, a new crop—cassava—was introduced. The men regarded it with disdain, preferring to farm their prestigeful and ritually important yams. The women were allowed to grow cassava between the yam heaps and to keep the profits for themselves. As time went on, this despised crop eliminated the annual famine before the yam harvest and attained a high and stable market value. The Afikpo women became capable of supporting themselves and their children without aid from their husbands, and nowadays they even rent land independently for cassava cultivation. Once a woman becomes self-supporting in this way, she can say, in the words of an elderly Afikpo woman, "What is man? I have my own money" (Ottenberg 1959: 215). Afikpo husbands have found it increasingly difficult to keep their wives at home in their formerly subordinate position.

We do not have data on the emotional reactions of Afikpo men to the new-found independence of their wives, but there is some relevant evidence from other Ibo groups where the economic advancement of women has gone much farther, particularly in market trading. In the Ibo town of Onitsha, noted for its wealthy and independent women, there is a developing publishing industry, producing pamphlets in English written by men for male readers. Conspicuous among these publications is a literature of masculine protest, with titles such as "Beware of Women," "Why Men Never Trust Women" (a novel), and "The World is Hard," subtitled "Wife Brought Leprosy to Her Husband after Communicating with a Secret Friend." These pamphlets, both fictional and hortatory, portray women as avaricious, scheming, and immoral creatures who poison their husbands for financial gain and betray them at will. The introductions to these works often contain statements like the following from "Beware of Women":

When you travel to other continents of the world, you will see that women of that parts behave better and more lovely than our mongerish African Women. Our women know nothing than to pretend, to talk lies, to trick and say "give me money" if you don't give them the money your word will be ignored. They don't know how to serve, to obey, to love, to pet, and to talk truth. They are rather licensed liars. Only very few are fair. In order to discipline them this little but effective booklet has been produced.

Men are exhorted in dozens of pamphlets to have as little as possible to do with women in order to protect their health and achieve financial success.

A final illustration from Nigeria comes from the Yoruba people, whose women are perhaps the most independent in Africa.[3] The Yoruba case is particularly interesting because it appears that their traditional sex-role arrangements allowed women a more autonomous economic role and a higher degree of mobility than the other groups we have been discussing, although change has proceeded in the same direction. The role of woman as independent market trader is and has long been highly institutionalized. Yoruba men attribute witchcraft to women, but their masculine protest lacks the naïve quality of surprise that is reported for the Nupe and the Ibo. Despite the overt signs of deference, wives are expected to be economically independent, quick to divorce their husbands if they find a more advantageous match, and generally difficult to control.

The Yoruba men manifest two tendencies other than simple hostility toward women which may be related to this long-standing pattern of feminine independence. One is a widespread and intense preoccupation with impotence. Many married men report experiencing impotence, others fear it, and it is an extremely common topic of conversation. Medical practitioners are besieged by impotent men seeking cures.[4] The other tendency is the occurrence of male

[3] The author carried out field work among the Yoruba in 1961–62 and 1963 with the support of grants from the National Institute of Mental Health (M-4865), the Ford Foundation Child Development Project of the University of Ibadan Institute of Education, and the University of Chicago.

[4] In the report of their psychiatric study in western Yorubaland, Leighton et al. state, "The worst thing that can happen to a man, we were told, is not to be potent" (1963:50),

transvestism in ritual and cultural fantasy. The donning of female clothing and/or hair styles is required of male priests in several cults on ceremonial occasions, and, in addition, there is a male masquerade cult in one part of Yorubaland which requires all its members to dress as females for its annual festival.[5] Outside of ritual, professional male transvestite dancers wearing European dresses tour the villages and provide a popular entertainment. Yoruba folklore contains male pregnancy tales, one of which was made into a popular song, recorded by a famous band, and requested frequently on the disc-jockey shows of the Ibadan and Lagos radio stations during the period of field work.

These fragments of disparate evidence suggests that among the Yoruba the alteration of traditional sex roles has reached the stage where men are not simply resentful of female independence but feel emasculated by it and envy it. Whether the manifestations of envy in transvestism arise from the boy's perception of his mother or the husband's feelings about his wives remains an open question.

CONCLUSIONS

All the societies discussed had a traditional ideal of male domination in the husband-wife relationship. Where, as in the East and South African societies, the pattern of labor migration has allowed continued control by husbands of the larger share of family income while placing an increasing burden of work on the wives, the traditional ideal has not been challenged. Thus, though the overworked women may become irritable and punitive with their children, they do not acquire a sense of deprivation concerning their status in society. Where, as in the Nigerian societies mentioned, economic development has, through the

---

and "Men are greatly concerned with potency" (1963: 153). Their survey of 170 men in community settings revealed 19 percent who reported a current potency problem (1963: 243). For the 76 men of the same sample who were rated as suffering from clear-cut psychological disturbance, the figure was 40 percent (1963: 253). The lack of comparable figures for other groups and of evidence that the potency problems were psychogenic in origin restricts the drawing of definite conclusions from these data; at this point all we can say is that this epidemiological survey appears to confirm independently the present author's impression that impotence is a distinctively serious source of concern for Yoruba men.

[5]See Beier (1958) and Prince (1964). Prince (1964: 109–110) states:
Men join the cult because of impotence, because their wives are barren or because of other diseases or misfortunes caused by witchcraft. . . . During the annual festival, the men masquerade as women, wearing women's clothes and flaunting prominent bullet-like breasts. Some look grossly pregnant. . . .
During my interview with the Gelede elders, two or three old crones several times poked their heads in the window to correct and scold the men. I had never before witnessed such an attitude of officiousness and arrogance on the part of women during my interviews with elders of other cults or with healers. It seemed to be part of the general picture of the cult as dominated by the "mothers," that is, the witches. As one of Beier's informants told him, "Gelede is the secret of women. We the men are merely their slaves. We dance to appease our mothers."
As with impotence, so in the case of transvestism among the Yoruba, the lack of comparable evidence from other groups makes definite conclusions difficult. Ritual transvestism certainly is not limited, in Africa or elsewhere, to societies in which the status of women is equivalent to that of Yoruba women. The conspicuousness of Yoruba transvestite practices to several independent observers, however, suggests that the pattern may be a more pervasive element in their culture than in others.

expansion of their traditional marketing role, allowed wives to attain independent and sometimes greater incomes than their husbands, the ideal of male domination in marital relations has been seriously challenged. Then men in these societies experience intense relative deprivation which results in their hostility to women, feelings of sexual inadequacy, and envy of women, all of which have cultural expressions. These divergent outcomes are determined by the degree of perceived deviation from the traditional ideal of male domination characteristic of most African societies. The general validity of this analysis remains to be tested in systematic research.

REFERENCES

BEIER, U., "Gelede Masks." *Odu* 6:5–23, 1958.

GLUCKMAN, M., "Kinship and Marriage among the Lozi of northern Rhodesia and the Zulu of Natal." *African Systems of Kinship and Marriage*, ed. A. R. Radcliffe-Brown and D. Forde, pp. 166–206. (London: 1950).

LEIGHTON, A., *et al., Psychiatric Disorder among the Yoruba.* (Ithaca: 1963).

LEVINE, R. A., and B. B. LEVINE, *Nyansongo: A Gusii Community in Kenya, Six Cultures: Studies of Child Rearing*, ed. B. B. Whiting, pp. 15–202. (New York: 1963).

MAIR, L. P., "African Marriage and Social Change." *Survey of African Marriage and Family Life*, ed. A. Phillips, pp. 20–27. (London: 1953).

MEAD, M., *Sex and Temperament in Three Primitive Societies.* (New York: 1935).

MINTURN, L. M., W. W. LAMBERT, *et al., Mothers of Six Societies.* (New York: 1964).

MURDOCK, G. P., *Social Structure.* (New York: 1949).

NADEL, S. F., "Witchcraft in Four African Societies: An Essay in Comparison." *American Anthropologist* 54:18–29, 1952.

OTTENBERG, P. V., "The Changing Economic Position of Women among the Afikpo Ibo." *Continuity and Change in African Cultures*, ed. W. R. Bascom and M. J. Herskovits, pp. 205–223. (Chicago: 1959).

PRINCE, R., "Indigenous Yoruba Psychiatry." *Magic, Faith and Healing: Studies in Primitive Psychiatry Today*, ed. A. Kiev, pp. 84–120. (New York: 1964).

RICHARDS, A. I., "Some Types of Family Structure Amongst the Central Bantu." *African Systems of Kinship and Marriage*, ed. A. R. Radcliffe-Brown and D. Forde, pp. 207–251, (London: 1950).

SCOTCH, N. A., "A Preliminary Report on the Relation of Sociocultural Factors to Hypertension among the Zulu." *Culture, Society and Health*, ed. V. Rubin. *Annals of the New York Academy of Sciences* 84:xvii, 1000–1009, 1960.

SHEDDICK, V. G. J., *The Southern Sotho.* (London: 1953).

WILSON, G., "Village Surveys: Bunyore, Nyangori, Maragoli, Tiriki, Boholo." Unpublished manuscript, 1956.

Marital Relations in the Jos Plateau of Nigeria: Women's Weapons: The Politics of Domesticity Among the Kofyar

Robert McC. Netting

The social position of African women is one of those compelling topics that allow the anthropologist to confront an invidious generalization and slay the stereotype of feminine oppression and subservience. He (or often she) can point out the variation in female roles and respect in neighboring societies (Talbot 1915: 96–97) and show by a wealth of examples that divergence from a Western ideal of womanhood does not necessarily imply a lower satus (Paulme 1963: 4). But Evans-Pritchard (1965: 41) has reminded us that any clarification of the status of women must be based on "imponderables" as well as on objective criteria. The following consideration of Kofyar women is an effort both to define criteria and to weigh some of the imponderables that figure in one version of the battle of the sexes.

The Kofyar are intensive agriculturalists living in dispersed settlements on the edge of the Jos Plateau in northern Nigeria. The women of this society have few institutionalized roles in political life or in patrilineal kin groups; they marry virilocally so that about seventy-seven percent live away from their native villages; they do not own land or major productive tools; they are regularly excluded from performances of most ritual including sacrifices, prayer, and divinations; and yet they appear to wield a large measure of power in the society. They do not do this just in terms of influence, persuasiveness, cajolery, and universal feminine wiles, nor are they the aged whisperers behind the throne who have been noted in the huts of some African chieftains. Rather they are self-assured, independent women who give the impression of knowing what they want and how to get it. The question then is how women who lack lineage office or support, most kinds of property, and religious authority can protect their interests so effectively.

Perhaps I should not have subtitled this paper "the politics of domesticity." It implies a mixing of levels between the home where conflicts can be privately reconciled through kin ties and sentiments and the public arena where competing interests are revealed and community decisions of policy are hammered out. But Lucy Mair, to whom we owe this distinction, also noted that conflict and competition begin within the family (1962: 10). The household may indeed deal with its own quarrels, but the *behavior* involved may be political. If the family and the household can be considered a social system, there is no doubt that Kofyar women participate in the "formulation and execution of binding or authoritative decisions" and that they "allocate valued things among two or more persons" (Easton 1959: 226). Male-female conflicts are seldom acted out in public, but when they are, a set of far-reaching rights of women are publicly *recognized* and incorporated in jural proceedings. These rights apply chiefly to economic goods and to the marriage bond.

Valued economic goods are used, owned, and manipulated by Kofyar women with considerable freedom. Certain major types of property do not belong to women in the sense that they may be permanently occupied, alienated, or inherited, but female rights of use are clearly marked. A Kofyar adult wife may demand a house of her own. It nothing suitable is vacant in the homestead, her husband must build her a hut. Since traditional Kofyar women's houses are elaborate two-storied, mud-domed structures (Netting 1968a), this may involve the spouse in several months of work plus extra expense if an expert builder is hired. Once ensconced in such a house, the wife may cook and feed her children in secret, admit selected guests for drinking, and store her grain and valuables. If a tin door is present, the key is hers. A woman should receive some farming land from her husband, and if none is available, she may borrow or rent a field from a relative or friend. When a husband dies, his widow and children may continue to inhabit his homestead and use its resources for as long as they wish.

Perhaps more important are the goods women actually own. Crops produced in a woman's fields, groundnuts, sweet potatoes, vegetables, and even late millet may be distributed according to her desires. She may choose to use a portion to feed her family, but if she decides to sell all at the market, her husband cannot interfere. If a husband is unwise enough to appropriate some of his wife's food, she may demand its return and carry the case to court, where male judges may try to placate her and end by awarding her compensation considerably in excess of the amount stolen.

Women have other sources of income. They go on their own initiative to collect raffia palm leaves, firewood, and other sylvan produce. These they sell directly at markets. They raise animals, especially chickens but also dogs, goats, and even cows. Some of this domestic stock may be kept at home while the rest is given out to friends in an offspring-sharing arrangement. Manufactured items make perhaps the largest contributions to the female exchequer. During the dry season, quantities of cotton thread, grain-storage baskets, and clay pots are produced by women for sale. Every Kofyar woman knows how to brew, and beer always finds a ready market (Netting 1964). Enterprising women may buy grain or engage working parties to farm millet for them. The risk and the proceeds belong entirely to the woman who has made the beer. She malts, grinds, cooks, and ferments the brew in her own home and sells it there or at market.

Thus women both have cash on hand and speedy access to more. Seven budgets I collected gave annual expenditures of £1/14–£7/19 and averaged £3/17/1. Though this is only a little more than a third of male expenditures in the same village, women have fewer obligations to meet. They do not contribute to bride wealth, they pay no tax, and they need not purchase tools. Much male wealth is tied up in houses and land, which is not easily convertible, so that females often seem both more solvent and financially more liquid. Women have cash reserves and can pay for what they want—usually cloth, beer, salt, condiments, and adornments. Men are often reduced to borrowing cash from women. Repayment is assured by threats of legal action or, if the debtor is a close relative, refusal of all future requests for loans. A husband's rights over property of his wife are strictly defined—in the event of divorce, he gets half her chickens (because they fed on his grain) and half her groundnuts (because she farmed with his hoe).

Women also retain a large measure of control over their labor. Kofyar intensive agriculture requires a heavy labor input and full mobilization of the household work force (Netting 1968b: 122–136). Women and men do the same tasks, hoeing, weeding, and harvesting side by side. A wife is the full partner of her husband in productive and maintenance activities. A husband needs his wife's contribution but he cannot compel it. A village chief who went on an errand with me one day was surprised and pleased to find that his three wives had continued to work on the homestead field in his absence. Obviously the choice was theirs. If a woman wishes to work on her own gardens, visit her parental home, or go about her own business, her husband cannot command her to do otherwise. The only time I ever saw women publicly censured for not working was when some individuals did not appear for a neighborhood thatching bee. They were scolded and ultimately fined, but the sanctions were imposed solely by other women.

The question remains, however, as to why masculine prerogatives are not more frequently asserted. Kofyar men are self-sufficient, tough, and stubborn. I believe that of the valuable things a woman controls, the most significant is herself, rights to her coresidence, her economic services, and her body. She may not originally assign these rights, but has the power to deny them. Marriage partners are always in short supply among the Kofyar. Every man would like to be a polygynist, but only a minority at any one time ever makes it. In a total of 489 families in a census of 15 villages, the average number of adult wives per husband was 1.75. The average per village ranged from 1.29 to 2.47 (see Table 1) and correlated well with relative village wealth. Fifty-five percent of the Kofyar men in the sample had one wife, and six percent had four or more. In the total sample population of 2,587, the average ratio of males to females was 1:1.395.

Bride wealth is substantial, and comparisons of pre-1930, 1930 to 1950, and 1950 on indicate that it has not significantly changed over time. Since the institution of Native Authority courts, about nine out of ten cases have been concerned with divorce and bride wealth. The Kofyar claim that in the days of feuding warfare men postponed marriage until their thirties when their prime fighting years were over. Now that men marry in their early twenties and women about a year after the menarche, wives are objects of even greater competition and emphasis on early betrothal has increased.

Conventions governing marriage do not seem at first glance to give women much of a voice. As girls they are warned not to become pregnant in their father's house (gam koepang) and may be beaten if caught in compromising circumstances with a boy. The fault in such cases is the girl's, and in some villages her father is liable to a fine. The offending daughter is married off in embarrassed haste, sometimes with reduced bride wealth. Marriages are arranged by the fathers of bride and groom, but they clearly require the girl's consent and that of her mother. Her acceptance of courtship gifts during adolescence indicates her continued willingness to be married. A boy and a girl who are engaged, or who want to be, may tease each other, conduct elaborate verbal fencing, and intrigue through mutual friends. Marriage is celebrated with only a perfunctory dance of the women resident in the groom's neighborhood. Even after it is held, the bride is expected to move back several times for varying periods to her father's homestead. A girl can put off marriage, and if the groom loses patience he may send his friends to capture her. There is great kicking and screaming, storms of abuse, and small battles between women relatives of the girl and female lineage mates of the groom who are helping to carry her off. This satisfying hullabaloo usually ceases when the captured bride (who was undoubtedly expecting it) is safely immured in a house of the groom's lineage. However, if the girl is really opposed to the match, she may go on weeping and struggling for a few days, by which time everyone is convinced of her feelings and she is allowed to return home peaceably.

Kofyar women do not actively resist marriage in most cases, but they feel in no sense bound to stay married. They move into the married state gradually and unceremoniously, and they may leave it in the same way. Divorce frequencies as indicated in Table 2 suggest that about forty-four percent of all adult women have been divorced at least once. To leave her husband, a woman merely goes

TABLE 1

Kofyar Marriage Patterns

Area/Village	Adult married men	Adult married women	Average wives per husband	No. of men with			
				One wife	Two wives	Three wives	Four or more
Latok Hills							
Mangbar	37	50	1.35	26	9	2	—
Dep	31	40	1.29	23	7	1	—
Gonkun	22	30	1.36	15	6	1	—
Koepal	16	21	1.31	13	1	2	—
Bong	49	69	1.41	36	7	5	1
Kofyar Hills							
Kofyar	61	115	1.89	33	15	7	6
Longsel	25	47	1.88	10	9	5	1
Pangkurum	25	55	2.20	8	8	5	4
Kopfuboem	16	26	1.63	11	2	1	1
Bogalong	50	101	2.02	18	17	13	2
Buumdagas	15	37	2.47	3	7	3	2
Kwa Plains and Foothills							
Dunglong	74	151	2.04	31	27	9	7
Mer	28	40	1.43	19	7	—	2
Korom	16	29	1.81	7	6	2	1
Wudai	25	45	1.80	14	5	4	2
Total	489	856	1.75	267	133	60	29
(% of total)				(55)	(27)	(12)	(6)

out to collect firewood or attend market and never returns home. She may go to her parents or directly to another man who has expressed an interest in marrying her. The beginning of the rainy season sees a veritable spate of women leaving their husbands. The rationale is that they wish to farm where they will be eating next year. This incidentally deprives their husbands of female labor when they need it most for cultivation. A husband cannot keep his wife from leaving or bring her home by force. A physical attack on the wife stealer by the deserted husband is a punishable offense. He must deal with her father, brother, or guardian, enlisting the support of her relatives in persuading the woman to return.

Bride payments, say the Kofyar wearily, are never complete. To stay in the good graces of in-laws, one must not only hand over an initial sum but one is forever subject to requests for loans (unrepaid), demands for hospitality (with beer *and* meat), and generalized sponging. If the husband wishes to retain his wife, he must satisfy her father or risk having him actively promote the woman's divorce and remarriage. Bride wealth unequivocally transfers only rights in a woman's offspring, and not all of those. Children belong to the husband who has paid bride wealth, and in former times the first one or two children born to a runaway wife (*la wa*, 'the child of going away') were returned to this man and affiliated to his kin group. What could not be purchased or contracted for were permanent rights of cohabitation and cooperation with a woman. Neither husband, kin, or village friends could keep her in a marriage she disliked. Pressure might be brought to bear by the former husband's withdrawal of a wife from one of the new husband's lineage mates, but it was agreed that nothing could prevail on a really determined woman.

Before the establishment of government courts, a woman who ran away permanently cost her husband any bride wealth he had paid. It was nonreturnable, and he could only hope, much as in the case of secondary marriage (Smith 1953), that she would someday come back to him. Bride wealth in these circumstances was often paid gradually and at intervals as the marriage appeared more permanent. A wife who leaves her husband is not felt to be necessarily in the wrong nor must she state grounds for divorce. In modern courts, she says only that she has "had enough" of the marriage and wants out. She is not fined or censured and pays only minimal costs, usually provided by her new spouse. The real reason for divorce may be less clear, but a survey of thirty-eight divorces in which women would discuss the matter showed twenty cases due to barrenness or to the death of children. Refusal of the husband to pay her kin was mentioned six times and quarreling five. Table 3, based on the reproductive history of a sample of divorced women in two villages, shows that a total of eighty-six percent left marriages in which they had been childless or in which their children had died, while only fourteen percent left living children behind them (for similar findings see Baker 1954: 372, 451). Thus a husband stands in more or less continuous danger of losing his wife. His best efforts may not be sufficient to secure her return, and he may be left with the long thankless tasks of (1) trying to get return of his bride wealth, which may necessitate further litigation, (2) trying to find another wife when most females are either betrothed or married, and (3) in the meantime performing in addition to his own chores the female jobs of fetching water, grinding, cooking, and child care.

If a Kofyar woman does not wish a divorce but is dissatisfied with her mar-

TABLE 2

Kofyar Divorce

Village	Married women with no divorces	Women with one divorce	Women with two divorces	Women with three or more divorces	Total women
Bong	46 (61%)	17 (22%)	10 (13%)	3 (4%)	76
Kofyar	29 (53%)	10 (18%)	9 (16%)	7 (13%)	55
Mangbar	37 (54%)	26 (38%)	4 (6%)	1 (1%)	68
Total	112 (56%)	53 (27%)	23 (12%)	11 (5%)	199

TABLE 3

Divorce and Childlessness

Village	Total no. divorces	No. after childless marriage	No. after loss of children (miscarriage, still-birth, early death)	No. after living children produced
Bong	64	31 (48%)	26 (41%)	7 (11%)
Kofyar	42	23 (55%)	11 (26%)	8 (19%)
Total	106	54 (51%)	37 (35%)	15 (14%)

riage, she has another alternative. She may take a *chagap*, a legitimate lover or cicisbeo who sleeps with her in her husband's homestead and with the knowledge and tacit consent of her husband. The relationship may be with a married or unmarried man and is based on mutual attraction and affection. It is not considered adultery (*wat neer*, 'stealing the vagina') or wife-stealing, and a husband who demurs is considered a selfish man and accused of "having no shame." One household head who stripped and drove out a man caught sleeping with his wife was a figure of fun. A woman who took a lover without her husband's permission would perhaps be judged by her neighbors and fined a chicken. A husband who discovered his spouse's clandestine affair might merely remark mildly that he would not stop the pair and why shouldn't they be open about it and sleep together properly inside the homestead. It is possible that a wife might be jealous of her husband's *chagap*, but even if a quarrel ensued between the two women, the extramarital relationship would not be mentioned.[1]

A wife may take a lover after being married a matter of six months. The lover usually comes from the same village and may be a near neighbor. He is no threat to the husband because there are strong sanctions against stealing the wife of a village coresident. He has no rights to any children born to the woman, even if he is known to be their genitor. A woman's husband and her lover may

[1] The ever-piquant relativity of morals is demonstrated by the shock and repulsion registered by Kofyar women over the behavior of Fulani youths at a dance who copulated promiscuously with unmarried and immature girls, did not ask permission of the girl's father or fiancée, and went to the open fields for love making. On the other hand, a sophisticated member of Roman society, when told of the Kofyar *chagap* relationship, remarked with enthusiasm, "My, how very civilized."

even cooperate in trying to get her back if she runs away to another village. The relationship may continue for years with the lover bringing occasional gifts and being especially entertained whenever the wife makes beer. He may visit her once or twice a week, and his schedule is arranged so as not to conflict with that of the husband.

For a woman who is barren or has ceased to become pregnant, the chagap relationship offers certain advantages. She may enjoy the attentions of one or several lovers and use their gifts and assistance in the economic endeavors to which she increasingly turns her hand. Every woman would like children, which give her higher value in her husband's eyes, status in the community, and a guarantee of care in her old age. If she has no children, she may still become an influential figure by accumulating wealth and engaging in extramarital liaisons. A fertile woman, however, has less time for crafts and trade and is prohibited from having a lover during pregnancy. There is also a two year postpartum period of nursing when she has no sexual relations at all. Of twenty women in one village who had legitimate lovers, fourteen were childless and two had just conceived for the first time.

In things that matter to a Kofyar woman, she retains considerable control. Where she lives, when she works, and with whom she sleeps are subject to her own choice. She cannot be ordered to work, restricted in economic matters, regulated in extramarital affairs, or constrained from changing spouses. Her value to husband, lover, and indeed the whole community is high, and she can allocate this value in such a way that potential conflicts are settled in her favor. The Kofyar contend that every man wants wives and that no male would ever initiate a divorce. A woman can realize herself through the alternate paths of children and the home or through wealth and lovers.

If women's weapons are so potent, what do men do to keep their self-esteem and maintain a semblance of dominance, which they regard as desirable? There are very few important factors in the division of labor that distinguish the sexes. Few tasks demand superior physical strength or endurance. A man and his wife are equal partners in production. There is little overt social subordination, and male domineering is met by loud, public arguments from the distaff side. A man is left with precious few prerogatives and limited practical authority. His position is vulnerable, particularly to a wife's decision to leave him. Recent changes have, if anything, further eroded male status by depriving him of the warrior role while increasing market opportunities for his spouse. With the growing importance of cash, differences in physical strength and aggressiveness may become less socially significant. In 1961, a series of named and roughly age-graded male agricultural work groups were flourishing in Bong village. They specialized in rapid, competitive hoeing of large bush fields. They had completely disappeared by 1966, some of their recreational aspects and all their popular interest having been taken over by contribution clubs. Members put stipulated sums into a pool, which was then presented to each of them in turn at a festive beer party. Women who could pay the contributions were admitted on an entirely equal footing with men. The objective circumstances of female economic and marital independence and a blurred division of labor do not emphasize sexual distinctions or differences in social power, and I would suggest that Kofyar males assert their distinctness and their claim to social superiority largely in symbolic terms.

The sexual dichotomy is repeatedly stressed in more or less arbitrarily assigned conceptual oppositions. The right hand and the right side (*gan wu mis*) are considered masculine while the left are feminine, indicating relative strength. To go to the left means to go wrong, and to give something with the left hand is an insult. Women are to walk ahead of men on the path so that men can keep an eye on their wives. One of three binary oppositions used in interpreting divinatory signs is male vs. female. Traditionally Kofyar men wore a loin cloth or skin while married women wore bunches of leaves suspended fore and aft from a string around the waist. Older men and especially diviners might tie on a sheepskin (*naar*) so that it hung from waist to knees in back. It is said that when short cloth kilts were first introduced for women, a prominent chief strongly objected on the grounds that it made women look like men, and "Can a woman divine?" Women do not go hunting, an activity Kofyar men value highly although it is largely rewarding as sport rather than in game. Whatever meat is secured should be brought back home and shared with the family. The only exception to this rule is the eating of hares' ears by men in the bush. They insist that the morsels are especially tasty and salty, and in order to avoid giving a portion to women they maintain the transparent fiction that hares actually have no ears.

These rather minor symbolic signposts are multiplied and elaborated in magic and religion. Women cannot enter the sacred grove that belongs to each lineage. They may not prepare or partake of ritual meals and sacrifices. They may not doctor illnesses or perform curing ceremonies. Divination is a uniquely male occupation. Lineage and clan prayer meetings and grave libations exclude women. Certain granaries may not be entered by women, and their dangerous state during menstruation prohibits them from preparing food for their husbands or coming in contact with his medicines. The antifeminist bias is most clearly apparent in the periodic announcements of the *kum or*, 'the shouting spirit.' Men go secretly by prearrangement to the hilltops at night and utter a growling roar in which are audible certain warnings to women. They are told, for instance, to return home promptly from beer drinks so as to prepare food for their husbands. At the first sound, women are enjoined to enter their huts and leave whatever food they were cooking on pain of illness. Women appeared to observe these rules, but they showed no particular anxiety over the voice of the spirits. Perhaps they were merely going along with the game. It appeared to me that the village males were resorting to a "supernatural" medium for conveying commands that they could not utter to their wives' faces in the light of day. An unbecoming spirit of revenge may also be present in the diagnosis by a man of serious female illness as due to *mang riin*, 'the taking of her shadow,' usually by a spurned lover.

Even in this masculine forest-preserve of symbols, women are not wholly at a disadvantage. Though cut off from most ritual activity, they may undergo possession, trembling and thrashing, and speak in the voice of a dead father or brother, demanding the performance of an expensive funeral commemoration ceremony (*maap*). This condition, called *nazhi*, may also grant them second sight and allow them to chew unharmed on a poisonous cactus. Women's accusations of witchcraft or confessions of witch practices are as frequent and carry as much weight as those of men. Even in the singing of abusive songs at harvest time, when men poke fun at the baldness of women's genitals, women reply verse for verse, deriding the swollen scrotum of men and using gourds and sticks in spirited pantomime. Women's sexual appetite is said to be the equal of men's, and it is perhaps noteworthy that the physical position for Kofyar intercourse is side-by-side rather than male superior.

Though it appears that males erect a considerable symbolic edifice in search of sexual identity and status, it is not clear just how well they succeed. Perhaps a folktale best illustrates the male dilemma. Rumor has it, according to the story, that one of the wives of God has a penis. God, who closely resembles a typically nonauthoritarian Kofyar village chief, decides to brew beer and invite all the people to see for themselves. Each of his wives appears in turn, exposes herself, and says, "Do you see me with a penis? I have your thing," i.e., a vagina. At last the tenth and most recent wife of God is summoned. She responds slowly, getting out of bed, descending from her upper room, rattling her bracelet as she pauses at her round house door. The audience calls her repeatedly and waits with mounting impatience and suspense. Only God knows that the woman once had a penis which he himself in intercourse uprooted and got rid of. The woman finally pokes her head out of the entrance hut, but God snatches her back into the house and the people are left staring. The tale concludes abruptly with the curiosity of the onlookers unsatisfied and the sex of God's wife ambiguous.

When Kofyar men are confronted with the very real weapons of women, as they must be daily in the domestic round, their elaborate shields of institutionalized symbols prove to be a poor defense. The male can only fall back on his physical difference, the seat of what is known in Nigeria simply as his "power." At least he has what no woman can hope to possess, his manhood, his penis. But behind this brave assertion whispers the psyche of his society, the mythic presentiment, that perhaps she has that, too.

REFERENCES

BAKER, T. M., "The social organization of the Birom." Unpublished Ph.D. dissertation, University College, London, 1954.

EASTON, DAVID, "Political anthropology." In Biennial review of anthropology. B. Siegel, ed. (Stanford: Stanford University Press, 1959).

EVANS-PRITCHARD, E. E., The position of women in primitive societies and other essays in social anthropology. (London: Faber and Faber, 1965).

MAIR, LUCY, Primitive government. (Harmondsworth: Penguin Books, 1962).

NETTING, ROBERT McC., "Beer as a locus of value among the West African Kofyar." American Anthropologist 66:375–384, 1964. "Kofyar building in mud and stone." Expedition 10(4):10–20, 1968a. Hill farmers of Nigeria: cultural ecology of the Kofyar of the Jos Plateau. (Seattle: University of Washington Press, 1968b).

PAULME, DENISE (ed.), Women of tropical Africa. (Berkeley: University of California Press, 1963).

SMITH, M. G., "Secondary marriage in Northern Nigeria." Africa 23:298–323, 1953.

TALBOT, D. AMAURY, Woman's mysteries of a primitive people, the Ibibios of southern Nigeria. (London: Cassell, 1915).

Some Aspects of Tagalog Family Structure
Bartlett H. Stoodley

This is a study of the Tagalogs, a specific linguistic group in the Philippine Islands; the provinces of Laguna, Rizal, Bulacan and Bataan, which surround the chartered city of Manila, are the Tagalog provinces. . . .

• • •

The typical and traditional Tagalog family lives in a rural or semirural barrio. A barrio is adequately described in the 1939 Census of the Philippines:[1] "The barrio usually consists of from ten to 1,000 houses. Ordinarily, these houses are located very near each other, forming a small village, although in some cases the barrio may comprise several small settlements locally known as sitios. Typically the barrio is separated from another by rows of rice paddies or other areas, although there are a considerable number of barrios closely adjacent to each other. The centrally located barrio and the one in which the municipal building is located is known as the población."

. . . Out of the 338 barrios in the province of Bulacan, 252 have populations of less than 1,000, and only thirty-two have populations of over 2,000. The largest barrio is under 6,000. Malalos, the largest municipality, numbers 38,000, but it is composed of forty-five barrios ranging in size from 325 to 3,500. This population distribution is characteristic of the other Tagalog provinces with the exception of Rizal, which runs a little larger.

Barrio and family are closely related. Family members may have obligations to the barrio group. For instance, at the time of the barrio fiesta, individuals are appointed to arrange for a mass, to direct the procession of the local sacred image, to procure the blessing of the fields, to decorate the plaza and prepare for the dance and the presentation of the traditional play. Although there is at least one *teniente del barrio* who is the only legally recognized political officer in the barrio, he must divide his traditional authority with the respected elders in the barrio in matters having to do with its good. Each barrio has at least one *sari-sari* [small general] store.[2] The owner is usually a woman. She buys fish and rice and vegetables at the local market early in the morning and sells them to the local housewives on her return. These occasions furnish opportunity for daily gossip, bantering, and restrained haggling. The sari-sari store owner is expected to "carry" indigent barrio residents. Co-operative groups are drawn from the barrio for house-building and for the cultivation of the rice fields.

Family members also have obligations to the neighbors. No definite geograph-

[1]Volume II, p. 48. This paper does not have application to family types in the Manila metropolitan area where, of course, industrialization and urbanization are having their greatest effects. The writer proposes to investigate the Manila area to test hypotheses suggested by this paper.

[2]The *sari-sari* store is a familiar landmark in the barrio. Besides fish and rice, the store carries cigarettes and soft drinks. It is usually a center of communication, and profit seldom exceeds a few pesos weekly.

ical limits define neighbors, yet the Tagalogs have definite customs of obligation to them. These obligations are not so much new obligations as they are re-enforcements of obligations which may exist generally. For instance, one owes an obligation to lend food to a barrio member, one owes a greater obligation to a neighbor, and the greatest obligation to a kin. So, in the case of weddings one has obligations to the barrio at large, but these obligations are intensified in the case of neighbors and more intensified in the case of kin. Obligations to neighbors are real obligations; they are not permissive or based on friendship ties. However, as we said, they attach to rather vague geographical limits and so, at these limits, there is some room for personal preference.

The strong framework of reciprocal rights and duties that both join and divide the barrio is provided by pervasive kinship relations. Barrio obligations, neighbor obligations, and kin obligations are woven into a solid web and are often quite indistinguishable from each other. For Ego and spouse, the kinship group includes any identifiable blood relative of either of them. These relatives may be living in the same barrio with Ego and spouse, or they may be at some distance. Obligations of economic and moral support and general differential treatment exist toward these kin, although distance may make them inoperative. Within this symmetrical kinship system there exists an "operating" family composed of those members of the kin group actually living together in one household. The most frequent household composition in the barrio studied[3] was the nuclear or conjugal arrangement of husband, wife, and children, although there was a sprinkling of parents, brothers and sisters, nephews and nieces, grandchildren and one "liberation" child.[4] More affluent families may number as many as fifteen members. A specific Tagalog family is a rather adventitious unit, and we can get a clearer picture of the family structure by considering the roles available for occupancy.

Kinship terminology furnishes a few insights. There is no Tagalog equivalent for "in-law," and most terminology makes no distinction between relations of Ego and relations of Ego's spouse, either on the same level or on ascending or descending levels. Where this distinction becomes important, Tagalogs make it by referring, for instance, to mother's brother or father's sister. We find the same multilineality here that Parsons refers to with reference to the American "middle class" family (Parsons 1954: 177). However, there are some important exceptions to this which point not to any favoring of one side of the family, but to role relationships in a given household.

Married persons distinguish terminologically between their own brothers and sisters and their brothers- and sisters-in-law. There are six terms given below for brothers and sisters. The Tagalog word for brother-in-law is *bayaw* for sister-in-

---

[3]The barrio research was concentrated in Cruz na Ligas. It had a population of about 600 persons and was located about 15 kilometers from Manila. At the beginning of the study, Cruz na Ligas was quite effectively isolated from Manila. Only a carabao path led into the barrio. The barrio members themselves felt bound to the población of Marikina by ancient ties although Marikina was as far away as Manila and could only be reached by a long walk through rice fields to the nearest bus line. Some social change was in progress in Cruz na Ligas at the beginning of the study. Additional lines of communication with Manila were opened when a rough road was completed into the barrio, and shortly after the study was finished the barrio was electrified.

[4]There is surprisingly little bitterness among Filipinos over the numerous unwed mothers left by departing GIs. Filipinas left on the docks were described as "hanggong pier."

law, *hipag*. Likewise, they distinguish between their own parents and their parents-in-law. *Ina* and *ama* are mother and father; *biyenan* refers to both mother-in-law and father-in-law.

Tagalogs employ sex-neutral kinship terms much more than we do. The following kinship words of this nature are in general use: *asawa*, spouse; *apo*, grandchild; *kapatid*, sibling; *bata*, child; *manugang*, older boy or girl; *pamang-kin*, nephew or niece; *pinsan*, cousin; *biyenan*, mother- or father-in-law; *anak*, son or daughter. To make a sex designation, the Tagalogs add "na lalaki" (male) or "na babae" (female).

This seems to point to an equivalent social evaluation of male and female. Other data confirm such an hypothesis. No invidious distinctions are made with reference to either sex, and both have equal social status. This may be profitably compared with the history of "woman" in the Western world, where historically that sex has had marked inferiority of status. Although there is a strong male preference in institutional Catholicism, this influence, although exerted for 300 years, has had only localized effect on Filipinos. The Filipinos also have not developed institutionalized male and female "principles"; they do not consider the sexes as harboring separate significances. When sex distinctions are made, they point to important role distinctions. . . .

We conclude from this brief terminological discussion that the Tagalog family, or *mag-anak*, is symmetrically multilineal, that neither female nor male roles are likely to be dominant, and that effective family roles are provided for a family extended to three generations in the direct line and to brothers and sisters, on both sides, and their spouses and children collaterally. This picture conforms to the expectations of Tagalogs themselves.[5] The very symmetry of kinship relations hinders the realization of the "ideal family" within one household. Friction between "in-laws" would be maximized. The "nipa hut," which is the typical dwelling, can accommodate an impressive number. Cooking is often done outdoors, and washing is always done there. Furniture may consist of a table, a long bench, and a chair or two. Sleeping mats are extended on the split-bamboo flooring at night and rolled up in the morning. Eating is unceremonial and often done outdoors. The "functions" of the home are therefore at a minimum. Even so, the nipa hut could hardly be "stretched" to include children, spouses of children, and children's children. Arrangements of this sort may be made for a brief period of time, but new nipa huts are cheap and enduring and there is usually ample room in a barrio for the construction of new ones. Accordingly, newly married couples are encouraged and helped to construct their own lodging as soon as possible. A recalcitrant bride or groom, who feels that he or she has been unjustly forced into marriage by the parents, may obtain revenge by continuing to live with them after the marriage. However, this habit of splitting into conjugal groups at marriage does not affect the essential structure of the Tagalog family. Role relations continue according to the traditional pattern, but instead of being carried out within the household they are carried out through a continuous pattern of interkin visiting. It is immaterial whether a newly married pair lives with or near the bride's family or the groom's family. Which side of the family occupies the effective family roles may therefore depend on the accident of location. Most marriages take place, however, between persons living in the same barrio.

[5] The Civil Code also confirms this view. See Civil Code of the Philippines, Article 226.

According to what little evidence is available, there was traditionally a kind of "bilateral indifference" in naming. There were no surnames and a child might be identified as "the first child of" either the mother or the father. The Spanish required the use of surnames and imposed a patronymic system. The present Civil Code requires a married woman to use her husband's name, although she may also employ her own first name and surname. In barrio practice, a married woman is known by a diminutive such as Sela, Juling, Tinay, Chitong, etc. More formally she is known by her maiden name.

There is also multilineal inheritance of property. This applies not only to personal property, but to real property or to the right to work real property. As a result of this system, rice fields have been divided into small parcels which are often widely separated. Parcels of land may also be given to boys or girls upon marriage, and in such a case the location of the household may depend on easiest access to the rice fields. The right of testamentary disposition of property is recognized by the Civil Code, but children are one class of "compulsory heirs" and they are entitled to the "legitime" or one half of the "hereditary estate of the father and of the mother."[6] Division of the legitime and division by intestacy are the same. Equal shares are given to the children without distinction by age or sex, and these provisions only re-enforce the practice.

Tagalogs carry on practices with reference to the ownership and inheritance of land which antedate the Spanish conquest, and title through the Spanish crown was superimposed upon this network of custom. The result was to require the Tagalog traditional "owner" to pay rent to a Spanish overlord. Land tenure provisions under the American administration did not improve the situation, and peasant unrest in the Philippines reflects the wide discontent of the Filipino tenant.

Certain basic features serve to further outline the structure of the Tagalog family. There is considerable "consciousness of kin" extending to relatives outside the mag-anak. It is important that a person is a "third cousin of my mother" or "my father's relative from Samar." As many kin as possible attend weddings and funerals and are present at barrio fiestas. A newly married couple should visit those kin on both sides of the family who were unable to attend the wedding. Although there are strong patterns of neighbor visiting, there are even stronger patterns of kin visiting. If one is in good financial circumstances, his kin to any degree are likely to come to live with him. Room must be made for them, and they have the obligations of being in need of the aid and of being grateful for it. They should help with the household duties while present. Although money and personal and real property is individually owned kin have strong claims to it. A married person in comfortable circumstances may be hard put to keep his own possessions, for they are subject to the claims of his kin and also of his spouse's kin. Such claims are instituted through the spouse who is blood kin.

There are very strong affectional bonds between the consanguine members of the mag-anak. Children are highly prized and continuously indulged during the first two or three years. Grandparents on both sides, brothers and sisters of the married couple, older siblings, neighbors and friends, all vie with the mother and father in holding and fondling the baby. The child is permitted to nurse at

---

[6]See Civil Code of the Philippines, Article 888.

any time and place. Toilet training is extremely relaxed; the split-bamboo floor is a convenient disposal unit. There are no observable reactions of aversion to feces.[7] Although strong cathectic bonds are formed with the mother, bonds of almost equal intensity are formed with aunts, grandparents, and older siblings. Solidary relations with brothers and sisters are especially remarkable. It is not unusual for a married man or woman to prefer the company of his brothers and sisters to the company of the spouse, and this is not generally interpreted as a reflection on the relations between the spouses.

Authority is structured by birth order among siblings regardless of sex, and affection tends to be structured inversely to authority, i.e., in reverse birth order. After a child is about three years old he is expected to conform to the demands of others, and he becomes subject to a rather complicated system of authority. All older siblings have authority over all younger ones, with institutionalized emphasis being placed on the authority of the oldest boy or girl. We may term this a "ladder" type of authority if we think of each rung of the ladder as representing a chronological period of one year. A sibling is subject to the authority of any sibling above him on the ladder, but the more rungs that separate him from the other sibling, the more extensive the authority. Siblings who are separated from other siblings by enough rungs of the ladder may employ corporal punishment. Older children may have a right to slap younger ones if the age difference is sufficient. We discovered occasionally that younger siblings felt resentful against older siblings because of some physical punishment that had been administered. The resentment was not explained by any feelings of innocence or that the punishment was excessive, but by the opinion that the older sibling was not enough older to give such a punishment. Younger siblings have a "right of appeal" to the parents and to other siblings older than the one exercising the authority, and orders are often effectively countermanded in this way. The oldest son or daughter has a special increment of authority, as mentioned above, and this carries over in part to the spouse of the oldest child. Younger siblings are expected not only to obey their older siblings, but also to show respect to them.

There is a large gap between the authority of siblings and that of the parents. Children are expected not only to be obedient and respectful to their parents, but also to show reverence to them. Upon leaving or returning to the home after more than a routine journey, the children are expected to kiss the hands of their parents or press their parents' hands to their foreheads while bowing before them. This appears to be a pre-Spanish trait with Spanish reenforcement. When the children grow up and marry, the obligation to show respect remains unchanged, but the duty of obedience is softened to a duty of consultation.

It should be noted that the authority given to children is general or diffuse. It applies to all family affairs, making allowance for the age of siblings who exercise it. This type of diffuse authority attaches to parents, of course, and also to the roles of aunts and uncles. More distant kin derive authority from their special position as kin, combined with a society-wide allocation of authority and respect according to age. Omitting the allocation of sexual rights, it follows that any two members of a Tagalog kin group can function as a family. An older sibling, for instance, is able to exert satisfactory authority and control over a younger sibling when the two are separated from the rest of the family group.

[7]This suggests fundamental differences in personality structure from the typical "anal" type.

In one instance at the University of the Philippines, a houseboy "from the province" was suspected of stealing a typewriter. He had a slightly older sister also working in the vicinity. She terminated his employment and required him to live in the house where she worked. He was practically under "house arrest" until his case was terminated, when his sister sent him back to the province. The writer had two houseboys who were brothers, aged 22 and 18. The elder supervised the younger in his work and social life, contributed to his education, and felt the obligation to continue this unless the younger brother married or until he finished his education.

Authority is allocated about equally between parents both with reference to children and to family matters in general. The history of the Tagalog family in this regard offers an interesting comparison with the American "middle-class" family. While the American family has a patriarchal background extending back some thousands of years and has only recently developed equalitarian features, the Tagalog family has a long pre-Spanish history of equalitarianism and only developed patriarchal aspects under the cultural influence of the Spanish. This latter influence was re-enforced by the wide and enthusiastic acceptance of Catholicism. A theoretical prerogative is assigned to the husband and attached to a modicum of social distance, and is probably most effective with children. A majority of Filipino children reported that they respected their fathers more than their mothers, but explanations written into answers showed the children meant that they "ought" to respect their fathers more than their mothers, rather than that they actually did so. This prerogative does not provide any effective dominance over the wife, however. The Civil Code of the Philippines, which takes quite a hand in family matters, does not grant a prerogative to the husband in all matters, but it does provide that " . . . the father and mother jointly exercise parental authority over their legitimate children who are not emancipated. In cases of disagreement, the father's decision shall prevail, unless there is a judicial order to the contrary." The "judicial order" refers to another section of the Code which provides for the establishment of a family council. This section is worth quoting, since it indicates one solution to the problem of reaching decisions when the parents are interdependent peers by ancient custom. Articles 252, 253, and 254 of the Civil Code provide: "The Court of First Instance may, upon the application of any member of the family, a relative, or a friend, appoint a family council, whose duty it shall be to advise the court, the spouses, the parents, guardians and the family on important family questions. The family council shall be composed of five members who shall be relatives of the parties concerned. But the court may appoint one or two friends of the family. The family council shall elect its chairman and shall meet at the call of the latter or upon order of the court." The typical barrio family is not aware of this provision, and in any event has no means to resort to it. Disputes, bickerings, and even open quarrels between husband and wife are "normal," and chicanery and deceit are sometimes employed. All these are the tools of decision. If they fail, there are many lines of influence bearing on husband and wife from brothers and sisters, uncles, aunts, and parents which may tip the scales.[8]

[8]The husband is often the loser in this struggle, from which arises the Tagalog-American slang phrase, "under the *saya*" (skirt), which indicates the loss of all initiative to a woman. It is quite possible that a significant pattern of concubinage in the Philippines is in part a protest by the male to domination in the home.

The above sketch of authority allocation in the Tagalog family would suggest that strong authoritarian patterns would develop, but this is not the case. The division of authority results in the would-be authoritarians falling out among themselves. There are checks and balances in authority in that parents may restrain each other, and parents and other siblings may restrain siblings. An oldest boy or girl approaching maturity may even act as a partial check on the authority of the parents. An attitude questionnaire now being analyzed by the writer indicates that Filipinos place authority within a framework of "law" or "right" on which the authority depends for its existence.

There is another strong corrective in this pattern. The affectional "design" with reference to children tends to run counter to the distribution of authority. Children will report that their mothers love each youngest child the most. They explain it on the basis that childbirth is a dangerous thing and the mother is grateful to each new child for sparing her life. It is an institutionalized expectation that the mother, and possibly the father, will favor the younger children over the older children. In addition, the siblings themselves are expected to conform to the same affectional "design." As a result, children with the least authority influence tend to possess the most affectional influence. They can "get around" their parents and older siblings and wheedle them into subjection.

An extended family structure and strong authority patterns culminating in the parents would indicate the probability of an arranged marriage pattern. It is true that parents are expected to have a strong influence in the choice of a marriage partner, but a type of romantic love is also institutionalized in the Tagalog group. A type of Tagalog love-song known as *kundiman* gives evidence of a romantic love complex at the folk level a couple of centuries ago. This pattern probably had pre-Spanish roots but at an early date it became quite indistinguishable from the Spanish type, imported from medieval Europe. Since premarital chastity was not stressed in the pre-Spanish culture, it is probable that the dominant influence of Spanish culture on the romantic love complex was to "spiritualize" it. This may have been a stabilizing influence on Tagalog family structure, for the Spanish introduced the idea of chivalric renunciation and thus made romantic love consistent with parental prerogative in the choice of a marriage partner. The beloved was frequently renounced in just this manner. José Rizal, the national hero and martyr, is an example of such a renouncing child.

Since the advent of the Americans, the American version of romantic love has tended to supersede the Spanish, even in remote barrios, and thus a point of strain has been introduced. For Tagalogs interpret the American version as meaning that the swain is entitled to marry the beloved even against parental resistance. Tagalog parents have been slow to surrender their rights in this matter, and a marked trend toward elopement has developed. In view of the structure of the Tagalog family, elopement is a serious matter, and formalized procedures for elopement are already developing. Elopement "works" because it reduces any hope the parents may have had of making a "better" marriage for the girl. However, to minimize the enmity of the girl's parents and the disgrace to the girl, the eloping couple ordinarily stays at the home of some cooperating kinsman. It is unthinkable in Tagalog psychology that the eloping couple should be socially severed from the rest of the family. On the other hand, the elopement is a serious breach of the obedience due to the parents. A "go-between" having social standing and influence with the parents may have to work for a long time before a reconciliation is effected. Even then the offending couple will have to appear before the girl's parents and submit to such punishment as they may inflict.

The life-cycle in the Tagalog family offers some points of comparison with the American family. Children are socialized not only by the mother and father but also by the entire kin group. There is little or no distinction between the socialization of boys and girls until the age of ten or eleven. Severe corporal punishment is institutionalized, but there is also a high degree of emotional security. Most punishments are given for disrespect and disobedience.[9] Toilet training is highly permissive. Household chores are divided among the children. Both boys and girls are expected to do housework, including cooking; if there are no girls in the family, the household chores will fall to the boys. But if there are girls, they are expected to take a larger share of the work, and the boys are "emancipated" a little earlier. There is much time for play. Boys and girls play together much of the time in an unorganized and random fashion. However, in the barrio studied by the writer, the boys play marbles with each other and practice shots on the basketball court on the plaza if they can get hold of a rubber ball they use for the purpose. Marbles are usually not played for "keeps." Basketball does not get to be a "game" until a boy is in his teens.[10] The smaller boys take turns trying to get the ball in the basket, or they try to keep the ball away from each other. Often they forget the basket and run around through the lanes of the barrio with the ball, but this is not seen as any departure from the game. Rules for play are loosely made and often disregarded; the emphasis is on expression and "fun," and not on winning.

Parents are strict at times and flexible at other times, sometimes "rational" and sometimes impulsive. This is an institutionalized norm. Among all members of the family there is considerable emotional "build-up" and "drain-off," and this again is a norm. It is subject, however, to the gradations of authority and the respect and obedience attached to these gradations. In a society where there is institutionalized emphasis on "expressiveness," the meaning of emotional displays may be quite different from the same displays in a different type of society. Among the Tagalogs, emotional build-up and discharge is a legitimized procedure, and is found continuously in interactive situations. It is usually not the result of aggressive drives and directed against someone but is an expression of personal virtuosity. Other individuals may be keyed to similar pyrotechnic displays or they may view it in silence or with exclamations of appreciation. A great deal of emotional expressiveness is therefore possible within the parent-child relationship, or the husband-wife relationship, without threatening its solidarity.

There are no institutionalized *rites de passage* at puberty for either boys or girls. As puberty approaches, boys are more and more emancipated from house-work and tend to go in gangs. They may be involved in minor escapades. This

---

[9]It should be noted that severe corporal punishment is associated with marked emotional solidarity between parents and children.

[10]"Game," that is, with a structure of rules such as that reported by Piaget. The data suggest that the stages reported by Piaget would not appear the same in the Philippine setting. I venture the hypothesis that the "co-operative" stage extends through the years eleven and twelve, during which years Piaget observed the development of the codification stage. See Jean Piaget, *The Moral Judgment of the Child*, (N. Y.: Harcourt Brace Jovanovich, 1932).

trend does not present the dynamic aspects of a "youth culture," but a response to the lack of any social definition at that time. After puberty the boy is expected to start courting, and he also spends more and more time with groups of male adults who gather around the barber-shops or the sari-sari stores.

The parents of a newly married pair retain the respect, even reverence, that is due to parents, but there is a radical shift in authority. The parents lose the decisive authority they formerly held. In its place, they retain the milder authority that is the prerogative of age throughout the society. After marriage the wishes of the parents on both sides of the family should be treated as requests rather than commands. Thus in theory the newly married pair become the new heads of the family. In practice, it takes increased age, experience, and a separate place of abode, all acting interdependently, to consolidate this new position.

A seriousness and dignity is attached to the position of male head of the Tagalog family which is related to borrowings from Spanish family patterns and to Catholic influence and also to pre-Spanish social structure, where the male head was important in tribal councils. At the present time this is an empty symbolism, but it produces reserve in the family head and a motivation to "live up" to the position. This is an impediment to the introduction of universalistic occupational norms in the Philippines, since the family head must in a sense start at the top, i.e., take a job which has prestige consistent with his dignity. One cumbersome way of resolving this dilemma is by acquiring some educational badge of status and then taking any lucrative occupational position, whether or not it is related to the presumed competency. LL.B. degrees have the highest prestige.

In this regard, "red tape" is an interesting fetish. Governmental bureaus are full of it but, for the Filipino, red tape is a ceremony for status demonstrations. After such a demonstration the Filipino official is very likely to brush all red tape aside and get down to business with surprising directness.

The position of male head, then, represents a cul de sac since it lacks any effective prerogative in the family system and any generally available method of legitimizing status outside of the family. To fill the vacuum, many male heads resort to ritualistic acts of dignity and affectations of importance. As a terminal position, the role of the Tagalog male head is comparable to that of the married female in the American family. It has been pointed out by Parsons (1942: 604), Komarovsky (1946: 184), and others that the American middle-class female receives a discontinuous socialization in that she learns to prize the competitive struggle for success and prestige which are "built into" the occupational system. At the same time she is expected, at least traditionally, to look upon marriage and family life as a terminal adult goal. An analogous situation faces the Filipino male. His socialization is discontinuous in the sense that the cooking and housework he performs as a boy furnish little or no technical or emotional preparation for the vestigial and symbolic aspects of "headship."

Formerly, the role of household head carried prestige and responsibility. In pre-Spanish social organization the male head belonged to a council of males with important influence in tribal matters. In this group, the chief was but "primus inter pares." This political function of the role was lost under the Spanish. It is impossible to follow the development of this role through the intervening time, but it is clear that, under the Spanish, both secular and religious influence combined to add prestige, authority, and even primacy to the role. But, as I have pointed out, the strong equalitarian relations between the sexes prevented the prestige and authority from being more than ritualistic. No socialization of the male prepares him for gratification in such a role. The advent of industrialization and American ideals of success and competition have only compounded the difficulty, for these ideals are consistent with pre-Spanish ideals in style and are part of the general social environment in which all Filipinos grow up. The Filipino male head is then scarcely "rewarded" by his vestigial prestige. In an analogous manner, we see that the American middle-class female is likely to be less than fully rewarded by the available gratification of the mother-wife role. The idealization of "mother" in the culture furnishes a kind of nonfunctional prestige analogous to the same type of prestige in the role of the Filipino male head.

The Tagalog female, on the other hand, learns the duties and skills which are later important to her as a wife and mother. The goals to which she learns to aspire are available to her as an adult, and education is not likely to alter her attitudes. In the socialization of children, the similar socialization of both sexes among the Tagalogs means that the boy's socialization is skewed in the direction of the system that is "functional" for girls, while the opposite tends to be true in American society.

The Tagalog girl has a rich selection of gratifications available to her in adulthood. The female head is the house manager and the spiritual advisor to the children. At first she does the housework herself, but this is not onerous. Women obviously enjoy the opportunities for gossip and banter that exist in the washing groups. In any event, the work is apportioned to the children as they grow up. The female head supervises the gatherings of kin on special occasions such as weddings and funerals, and she is adept at manipulating the political elements at work within the extended family and the larger kin group. She has a strong influence on the marriages of her children and, in an advisory capacity, she influences the families of her sisters and brothers and the marriages of their children. She plans adept choices of comadres and compadres ["godparent"] to advance the family fortunes. The female head is also the traditional family treasurer, and the income of the husband is turned over to her. Her judgment in money matters is generally relied on. In terms of consistent socialization and terminal rewards, the Tagalog female is in a position comparable to that of the American male. There is an additional element of consistency in the female Tagalog pattern. There is no shift from a youthful particularistic orientation to an adult universalistic orientation; the Tagalog female's orientation to social objects throughout her lifetime is particularistic.

What effects are industrialization and urbanization having on the Tagalog family? The Tagalog male has a strong "quality" orientation. He sees the "society" as a system of permanent positions having increments of power and allocations of perquisites, and also certain obligations to other positions such as kinship. The position of the rice farmer has neither power nor prerequisites, but it is traditionally respectable. It has not become evident to the Tagalog male that "business" jobs have either power or prerequisites and, furthermore, in terms of the influential Spanish attitude, they are hardly respectable. The position of lawyer is respectable by Spanish standards and is close to the seat of power. Most Tagalog lawyers do not practice law; they simply are lawyers, and should be addressed by that title. Under the Spanish, the Tagalogs learned that the government was a very important place to be. Most Tagalog male heads would like to be politicians, or have politicians for compadres, or at least be "next" to politicians. Under these circumstances ritualistic inefficiency is "normal" in the Philippines, and the pluming of one's status feathers is more important than the accomplishment of a task. The orientations of Tagalog males are slowly undergoing change and the symbolic aspects of the male headship will gradually disappear, but this should not disrupt the family structure.

A more severe strain on the family occurs as achievement values from the United States bite into the obligations of brothers and sisters to look after the family group and to provide support and even education for younger siblings. The educational preparation and individual achievement of older siblings is thus curtailed. However, there are factors that lessen this strain. The marked permissiveness with reference to household composition aids the mobility of the household unit. Tagalog families can be found around the Manila area in all kinds of fragmented combinations. Kin who are not male family heads can therefore undertake to fill positions wherever job opportunities exist. The strain focuses at the point where funds from employment must be used for the support of the kin group rather than for the advancement of the wage earner himself. The gradual breakdown of family obligations at this point would have far-reaching and disorganizing effects on the structure of the Tagalog family.

Unmarried women have obligations of family support much the same as men, and they are frequently employed. Married women are also working in increasing numbers. The Census of the Philippines lists 12,267 women working in the field of manufacturing in the province of Bulacan, as compared with 8,256 men. The bulk of the men are employed as laborers, although there is a fair sprinkling of tailors, shoemakers, butchers, carpenters, blacksmiths, etc. Proportionally there are far fewer women laborers. The largest categories for women are modistes [hat-makers] (3,653) and embroiderers (3,140). In commerce there are 8,430 women listed to 4,586 men; this is mostly small retail trade. There are 2,954 sari-sari store female proprietors compared with 980 men; there are 124 female proprietors of haberdashery and dry goods stores to 13 male proprietors. The income of women from employment matches the earning of men up through the 1,800 peso bracket. Men are over-represented in the higher brackets, but it is probable that these higher incomes are in large measure earned by individuals with Spanish and Chinese ethnic backgrounds.

• • •

. . . The writer's observations suggest that Filipinos do not think of nepotism in the same manner that Americans do. Nepotism per se is not condemned. There is, however, a strong emphasis on the social obligations of the position, whether or not it was obtained by nepotism. This in turn raises the possibility that in Filipino society, nepotism controlled by institutionalized norms may develop technical efficiency. The American insistence on universalistic norms is theoretically more efficient, but in practice this efficiency is mitigated by networks of particularistic arrangements.

The structure of the Tagalog family also favors the competence and interest of the woman. The mobility aspect of the family is pertinent here, but the family structure also makes possible the "liberation" of at least some females from family roles. Due to the variety of family personalities with which children continuously interact, the mother is not exclusively cathected by them. Strong cathexis is distributed among aunts, grandmothers, sisters, and female cousins. Among this group, therefore, there exists the possibility of occupational selection, with females left in the family group distributing themselves as necessary to "compensate" for vacant family roles. Women can be expected to compete more and more with men in the occupational structure. However, this need not increase the strain within the Tagalog family, for traditionally there is considerable leeway in the family for a struggle for "power." Also, the extended family system tends to prevent family status from being as closely bound up with occupational status as it is in the United States.

REFERENCES

LIKERT, RENSIS, "A technique for the measurement of attitudes." *Archives of Psychology* 140:5–55, 1932.

KOMAROVSKY, MIRRA, "Cultural contradictions and sex roles." *American Journal of Sociology*, Vol. LII, No. 3, 184–189, 1946.

KROEBER, A. L., *Anthropology*. (New York: Harcourt Brace Jovanovich, 1923).

PARSONS, TALCOTT, "Age and sex in the social structure of the United States." *American Sociological Review*. Vol. 7, 604–616, 1942. *Essays in Sociological Theory*. (Glencoe: The Free Press, 1954).

PARSONS, TALCOTT, R. F. BALES and E. A. SHILS, *Working Papers in the Theory of Action*. (Glencoe: The Free Press, 1953).

6 / Rites of Passage

Introduction

Within a single culture it is typical for the most dramatic ceremonies and cultural elaborations to develop around the major transitions in the lifecycle of an individual, such as birth and death. From the point of view of the culture, such transitions affect the group structure in that they involve the addition or subtraction of individuals from the group. In a similar but less dramatic fashion, changes in status such as from child to adulthood are also important events from both the groups' and the individual's point of view. The group, therefore, develops rituals to publicly announce and dramatize these events that are so critical to both the individual and the group. In the literature, the rituals that mark these transition points are called rites of passage.

Such rituals, which are elaborated around the individual's new status symbolize to him that the group is interested in his welfare, and are important in giving an individual in a complex society a sense of social cohesion rather than one of isolation or alienation.

In 1909 Arnold van Gennep, a Belgian anthropologist, published the classic treatise entitled *Les Rites de Passage* (transl., 1960).

Rites of passage are rites intended to "move" a person or group from one "location" to another, or from one status/role to another, within a society's "structural space"—e.g., from the status/role of "unmarried man" to that of "married man," from childless bride to mother, from undergraduate to graduate. Van Gennep showed that such a rite, or ritual cycle, can generally be analyzed into three phases: 1) rites of separation; 2) rites of transition; and 3) rites of incorporation.

The general purpose of these rites in the first phase is to detach the celebrant from a particular status/role and to sever or, at least lessen, his ties with those among whom he has played the role in question. The emotional tone of such a "send-off" may be joyous or sad or a fusion of the two in "sweet sorrow"; the parting may focus on a single, symbolic moment—as when a father "gives away" his daughter at marriage—or it may be elaborate and extended. In any case, one message communicated to the celebrant and others in attendance is that, at the very least, a "little death" has occurred.

Van Gennep noted that the three phases of a rite of passage may not necessarily be equally elaborated, adding that rites of separation frequently dominate funeral ritual. In a chapter devoted to the subject, he offers the generalization that "persons for whom funeral rites are not performed . . . are the most dangerous dead. They would like to be reincorporated into the world of the living, and since they cannot be, they behave like hostile strangers toward it" (1960: 160). Compare this with Kluckhohn's observation, in the articles that follow, that among the Navaho "every item in the funeral ritual is intended to prevent or cajole the deceased from returning to plague his relatives." The Navaho do, in fact, perform minor rites to memorialize the deceased—symbolically reincorporating their "good parts" into the society of the living—but the overall emphasis is clearly on divorcing the dead from the living; and Kluckhohn shows why this is so by describing and analyzing their beliefs about death and the afterlife.

Van Gennep also pointed out that the celebrant's passage from one position to another in social space is frequently punctuated and symbolized by the physical act of crossing a threshold or passing through a portal (or bridal bower, triumphal arch, etc.), especially in the bustling, ritually-impoverished urban scene. In traditions richer in ritual, the transitional phase may be greatly elaborated, with the celebrant suspended in a social limbo between the "no longer" and the "not yet."

Kloos' account of female initiation among the Maroni River Caribs (on the N. E. coast of South America), exhibits the full cycle of a rite of passage. As is usual in rituals that move a person from the status of child to that of adult, the greatest elaboration comes in the transitional phase. Hence, the Maroni Carib girl, at first menstruation, is *separated* fairly abruptly from her normal routines and social contacts. Then, for a period of eight days (it used to be a full month), she lives in a kind of social limbo, ungroomed and dressed in old clothes, restricted in diet and sleeping at a distance from her family. At the end of this period there is a rite (burning cotton in her hands) that symbolizes her new duties as a woman, followed by a feast to celebrate her re-entry into society. Kloos suggests that the occurrence of female initiation may be most common in societies in which the girl continues to live in her parental household after marriage. The ritual leaves no place for conflicting opinions about when she ceases to be a child and ceases to be treated like one.

In the article by Dole we see a ritual cycle which terminates at different points for the mother and father of the dead infant. The first farewell, consisting of the interment of the body and the burning of its possessions, is attended by the whole community. The parents then enter a transitional period represented by a week of mourning. When the corpse is removed from the grave and cremated, the father makes a dramatic and prescribed gesture expressive of his willingness to reincorporate the dead baby into the community; but he is restrained, and shortly afterwards he returns to a normal frame of mind. The mother, however, continues to mourn for several more days until, by an act of endocannibalism, she symbolizes even more dramatically the reincorporation of the deceased—in greatly altered form—into the memory of the society into which he was born.

In the final article, "Rebirth in the Airborne," Melford S. Weiss makes an explicit application of the rites of passage framework to the training of a U.S. paratrooper.

REFERENCES

VAN GENNEP, ARNOLD, The Rites of Passage, trans. by Monika Vizedom (Chicago: University of Chicago Press, 1960).

Conceptions of Death
Among the (Navaho)
Clyde Kluckhohn

. . .

Whatever the ultimate causes of the conviction in an existence beyond the grave may be, it is certain that such doctrines and rituals have promoted the psychological adjustment of individuals and the integration and survival of societies. A funeral is a symbolic assertion that a person is important not only to his immediate relatives but to the whole group. The belief that the soul is not destroyed with the body usually implies a continuation of the individual's potency beyond the mortal life-span.[1] Indeed, the careful attention to ritual detail is less frequently envisaged as a triumphant affirmation of immortality than as a necessary instrument for protecting the living against the malignant powers of the dead. Rites are also a means of reintegrating the family and the larger group after the disruption caused by the loss of one of its members.

. . . [O]ne can hardly consider immortality, in the strict sense, as a pan-human concept. Almost all peoples have conceived of some continuation, of something that was not extinguished with the last beat of the heart. But this is not invariably felt to be permanent. A gradual extinction is often portrayed, or a sudden annihilation after so many generations or other fixed period. When the soul is thought to be imperishable, personal immortality does not necessarily follow. The soul-stuff may be merged with that of others or in natural forces.

. . .

Many values and motivations that we are wont to think of as inevitably attached to the notion of immortality are in fact local in time and space. This emerges from careful consideration of any cultures that are apart from the Western and, specifically, the Judeo-Christian tradition. Those of the Navaho, . . . in the American Southwest will do as well as any. Much, though not all, of what may be said of these beliefs relating to the afterlife would apply to many other American Indian life-ways. . . .

. . .

. . . The Navaho believe that life begins when wind enters the body through its orifices (particularly the ears) or when Changing Woman places a tiny bit of soul-substance in the infant's head just after birth. The question as to whether

---

[1] A somewhat different emphasis is found in Hindu and Buddhist thought, for, according to these views, even if the soul is reborn, it will be reborn as a different individual, even in some cases as a member of a different species. Some doctrines state that the greatest blessing is to continue to exist without taking individual form. Certain specialists assert that the soul-stuff that goes through reincarnations is not considered an individual soul but rather a part of the universal soul seeking release from any definite form or forms by attaining union with its source.

this soul existed before this is not raised. Most Navahos feel that a stillborn infant or a fetus lacks a soul. They say you can see the trail of the first death in the whorls of the fingertips.

Death is the end of all good things to the Navahos. They have no belief in a glorious immortality. Existence in the hereafter appears to be only a shadowy and uninviting thing. The afterworld is a place like this earth, located to the north and below the earth's surface. It is approached by a trail down a hill or cliff, and there is a sandpile at the bottom. Deceased kinfolk, who look as they did when last seen alive, come to guide the dying to the afterworld during a journey that takes four days. At the entrance to the afterworld old guardians apply tests to see if death has really occurred.

Death and everything connected with it are horrible to The People. Even to look upon the bodies of dead animals, except those killed for food, is a peril. Dead humans are put away as soon as possible, and with such elaborate precautions that one of the greatest favors a white person can do for a Navaho is to undertake this abhorrent responsibility.

This intense and morbid avoidance of the dead and of everything connected with them rests upon the fear of ghosts. The other Earth Surface People who have fearful powers—witches–are also very terrible, but they are, after all, living beings who can be controlled in some measure and, if necessary, killed. Ghosts are, as it were, the witches of the world of the dead, a shadowy impalpable world altogether beyond the control of the living.

Most of the dead may return as ghosts to plague the living. Only those who die of old age, the stillborn, and infants who do not live long enough to utter a cry or sound do not produce ghosts, and for them the four days of mourning after burial need not be observed, since they will not be injurious to the living. Otherwise, any dead person, no matter how friendly or affectionate his attitude while he was living, is a potential danger.

A ghost is the malignant part of a dead person. It returns to avenge some neglect or offense. If a corpse has not been buried properly, if some of his belongings that he wished interred with him have been held out, if not enough animals have been killed at his grave, or if the grave has been disturbed in any way, the ghost will return to the burial place or to his former dwelling.

Ghosts appear after dark or just before the death of some family member, in human form or as coyotes, owls, mice, whirlwinds, spots of fire, or indefinite dark objects. They are usually dark or black. They may change form or size before one's eyes or make recognizable sounds (as of familiar birds or animals) and noises of movement. Whistling in the dark is always evidence that a ghost is near. Since ghosts appear only at night, adult Navahos are afraid to go about in the dark alone, and all sorts of night shapes and sounds are fearful.

Ghosts may chase people, jump upon them, tug their clothes, or throw dirt upon them. Their actions not only are frightening in themselves but also are omens of disaster to come. When a Navaho thinks he has seen a ghost or when one has appeared in his dreams, he is sure that he or a relative will die unless the proper ceremonial treatment is successfully applied.

The Navahos always document their seeing of ghosts with actual sensory evidence: large or unusual tracks, a bit of owl feather in a strange place, a fire that is unaccounted for. Missionaries and physicians sometimes speak as if the reports of ghosts were strictly comparable to the hallucinations and delusional experiences of the mentally unbalanced. Such a judgment overlooks the part played by cultural tradition (as opposed to the individual's "mentality") in interpreting the evidence of the senses.

As Hallowell has written (1938, p. 38):

... psychologically, the actual order of reality in which human beings live is constituted in large measure by the traditional concepts and beliefs that are held.... Indians are able to point out plenty of tangible empirical evidence that supports the interpretation of the realities that their culture imposes upon their minds.

Night in the Navaho country is huge; in every direction there is silence, and strange forms and shadows sometimes give a start to those who have not been brought up to believe in ghosts. But if you *have* been reared on ghost lore, then you have a readymade scheme for interpreting, for elaborating from an actual sensory experience. Almost all people believe what they find others believing—those others with whom they identify themselves. White men also believe many things on authority, not because they themselves have seen the evidence and worked out the theory from first principles themselves.

• • •

Navaho thinking accords with the Greek epigram, "Death is evil; the Gods themselves have judged it so." Mythology pictures the Navaho supernaturals as fearing death. The mortality of human beings is sometimes rationalized in myth on the ground that otherwise the earth would become too crowded. But the solace of beneficent divine purpose is lacking. On the contrary, dying either is regarded as due to an experimental caprice of some divinity or is explained as the daily payment demanded by the Sun for carrying out his travel.

Death is evil, and the dead are feared. Every item in the funeral ritual is intended to prevent or cajole the deceased from returning to plague his relatives. The corpse's property is deposited with him, but this is no spontaneous gesture of affection nor a disinterested desire to promote well-being in the afterworld. Navaho lore teaches that any stinginess on the part of the living will bring swift and terrible retaliation.

It is significant that the living are most vulnerable to the ghosts of their own relatives. Indeed, if a ghost appears in or near a crowd, only the relatives will be sensitive to the apparition. There is little or no dread of the spirits of those long gone. Navaho thought is not clear whether this is because souls gradually cease to exist or because ghosts lack motivation to return from ghost-land after the relatives they have known in life have also disappeared from the surface of the earth.

This focus of anxiety upon the ghosts of known relatives is most plausibly explained by Opler's (1936) theory developed to understand similar belief and behavior among two Apache tribes. On the one hand, there is vehement mourning for the dead and, in most cases, genuine evidence of grief. On the other hand, there is exaggerated terror that the beloved relatives will return to take a living person back with them or at least bring severe "ghost sickness." Opler points out that physical survival demands the closest sort of cooperation in the family group. Feelings of antagonism and resentment must ordinarily be severely suppressed during life, for open conflict and competition would threaten the successful carrying out of subsistence activities. Yet the behavior of drunken Apaches and Navahos plainly evidences the intensity of submerged feelings of hostility toward some close relatives. Hence ghosts may be understood as projections of the largely unconscious hate and distrust that the living have felt toward dead members of the intimate family circle. Sentiments at death are best described as mixed. The positive side comes out in tears and the melancholy sense of loss. The negative side is expressed in fearful dreams and fantasies of ghost apparitions.

One of the reasons that Navaho conceptions of life after death are much less clearly formulated than other aspects of their religious beliefs is the reluctance to discuss anything connected with death or the dead. Only when some individual believes himself victimized by a ghost but feels a need to consult a diviner for more precise information as to which ghost is troubling him and what the diagnosis for ceremonial treatment is, does one hear unforced statements of Navaho theory.

Fear, however, is not the whole story. I have heard more than one Navaho utter the substance of Confucius' famous question, "We do not know life, how do we know death?" As the Navahos say, "These things are hidden from us." The Navahos accept the inevitability of dying, but in a religion that almost entirely lacks revelation and prophecy the afterlife is defined only by a few vague statements in the traditions of the people. Moreover, the whole of Navaho implicit philosophy maintains that it is this life that counts—partly on the ground that living here and now may be rich and satisfying, partly because such notions as there are of the next world portray it as a rather vague, misty, unexciting place. A very old man once explained his traveling around so much in this way: "I want to move around while I can. Soon I'll be dead and I won't be able to. I'll have to take a long rest."

A more positive note is sometimes struck in the statements of older Navaho intellectuals. It is said that for the living to be much concerned with death and the afterlife is both unwise and unhealthy. Indeed, Navaho religion considers such preoccupation to be symptomatic of psychic or organic illness, though the ordinary Navaho's interpretation would find the cause in the supernatural visitation of a ghost. Yet there is a deep current in Navaho thought that is congruent with Spinoza's proposition, "The free man thinks about nothing so little as about death, his wisdom consisting in the contemplation, not of death, but of life."

Navaho eschatology is almost entirely consistent in affirming that a "wind" or "breath" leaves the body at death for a spiritland, although I have heard a few Navahos say something like this: "We used to believe that. Now we think when you die you stay dead." The spirit-land is most often located to the north (which is the fearsome direction to the Navaho). Sometimes it is placed to the west. It is usually said to be beneath the surface of this world and is often identified with the land from which the Holy People emerged in mythological times. Some accounts depict ghost-land as continually cloudy or shrouded in darkness; others describe it as a barren, desert place. Activity seems to be almost nonexistent according to some informants; other accounts suggest that dead Navahos farm, hunt, and carry out the other pursuits of terrestrial life, including ceremonials. A few informants consider that only the souls of animals and insects go below, while human souls have a home above ground. The dominant picture, though, is that of returning to an interior, dark place ("the dark earth"). The psychoanalyst will surely find here a standardized unconscious fantasy of return to the womb.

The Mohave Indians distinguish four soul-substances, but many Navahos speak of two. One of these appears to reside permanently in spirit-land. The other is variously described as lingering (at least for many years) about the grave or as moving back and forth between spirit-land and the homes of the living, often in the skin of a coyote, mouse, or owl. Some informants appear to distinguish between the fate of the good and evil incorporeal parts of the person. Only the evil leaves the spirit-land to return to the earth as a ghost. Some informants maintain that the good part of the soul goes to four different places, depending upon the time of day when a person dies. A few say that none of the good lives on after death.

There is conflicting lore with respect to the appearance of the dead. The dead leave their skins but are still portrayed as taking with them whatever they were dressed in. The gruesome aspect of the corpse itself is seldom mentioned. Ghosts are almost never seen in human form, although there are a few cases of apparition of skeletons. On the other hand, myths speak of spirits as combing their hair and painting their faces red. Those who have visited the netherworld in dream, coma, or unconsciousness readily recognize their relatives. In the opinion of Father Berard Haile, the best Navaho scholar, a spirit living without bodily form would be inconceivable to the Navaho. One myth affirms that women in the "dark place" will cease to have menstrual periods and to bear children.

The Navaho, then, do not yearn for immortality. They accept some form of continued existence as probable, but the prospect is more accepted than welcomed. It should be noted explicitly that Navaho dead are not thought of as joining their divinities. The divinities are in entirely separate places. Nor can the unacculturated Navaho regard the Christian belief in the resurrection of the body with anything but horror. This is almost certainly the reason that the two Ghost Dance movements that swept the western United States in the nineteenth century were rejected by the Navaho. As Hill says (1944, p. 525):

For the Navaho with his almost psychotic fear of death, the dead and all connected with them, no greater cataclysm than the return of the departed ... could be envisioned. In short, the Navaho were frightened out of their wits for fear the tenets of the movement were true.

• • •

Every culture, as Max Weber showed, must provide orientations to such inescapable problems as death. The answers which the cultures of southwestern Indians give to this question may seem to imply the philosophy of Stevenson's phrase, "Take everything as it comes in a forlorn stupidity." I personally prefer Malinowski's verdict: "In short, religion here assures the victory of tradition and culture over the mere negative response of thwarted instinct."

Female Initiation Among the Maroni River Caribs

Peter Kloos

In her article on female initiation rites (1963) Judith Brown demonstrates the relationship between these rites (or at least the nonpainful form) on the one hand, and matrilocal residence and economic importance of women on the other. With regard to matrilocal residence she argues that

female initiation rites will occur in those societies in which the young girl continues to reside in the home of her mother after marriage. The purpose of the rites appears to be an announcement of status change both to the initiate and to those around her, made necessary because she spends her adult life in the same setting as her childhood [1,963:841].

Her hypothesis is statistically confirmed.

With regard to the second factor she argues that when the economic contribution of women in a particular society is important, then a need is felt to assure their competence. Again her hypothesis is confirmed, but less convincingly so, the correlation being lower. Against the background of these cross-cultural results I shall describe and discuss the female initiation rite of the Maroni River Caribs. These Caribs are close relatives of the Barama River Caribs (see Gillin 1939), who are used by Judith Brown in testing her hypotheses. Gillin, however, gives no detailed description of the rite itself (see Gillin 1936: 72).

THE MARONI RIVER CARIBS

The Maroni River Caribs are a group of Amerindians living mainly at the mouth and lower course of the Maroni and Mana rivers. There are other, smaller, groups on the rivers Oyapock, Cottica, and Iracu. In all they number about 1500 and constitute a group in that they are relatively isolated—by distance, dialect, and physical appearance—from other Caribs in northwest Surinam (on the rivers Saramacca, Coppename, Wayombo, Tibiti, and Suriname) and interact more with members of their own group than with the Western Caribs. My fieldwork has been carried out mainly in the villages of Christiaankondre and Langaman-kondre, with a total population of just over 500. Present-day economy in these villages is a mixed one. Fishing and agriculture (shifting cultivation with bitter manioc as main crop) are of primary importance, while hunting and collecting are secondary. A considerable part of the fish caught is sold in the markets of Albina and St. Laurent-du-Maroni (French Guyana), or in Surinam's capital, Paramaribo.

Although the villages are of fair size, a few hundred inhabitants as a rule, their structure is simple and their pattern of settlement is uniform. The spacious houses, not much more than a palm-leaf thatched roof on six or eight poles, are built in clusters, separated by secondary forest and small manioc plots. The clusters are strung along the river bank, forming a long but narrow inhabited strip. Residence is as a rule uxorilocal; with about seventy-five percent of the women beginning married life within their own domestic group. (see Table 1)[1] Thus each house cluster generally includes the residences of a married couple (and their unmarried children) plus their married daughters (with their husbands and children); each nuclear family possesses its own house. After a few years a couple may move near the parents of the husband (for instance when he is the only or the eldest son).

Apart from this localized kinship group, there are only two others, the bilateral personal kindred and the sibling group; there are no unilineal groups. In marriage there is a preference for a classificatory cross-cousin and marriage is monogamous. Most of the villages have a government appointed chief (kapitein), who has—at least in the Surinam villages—two assistants (bastiaan or ba:sia). Chieftainship is of little importance however.

The only division of labor is between men and women. The men fish and hunt and do the heavier work in the garden, like clearing. Building a house and making basketry and household utensils in general is likewise men's work. The women prepare food. Above all this means the toilsome production of manioc

TABLE 1

Residence at the Beginning of Marriage (Initial Residence) and Present Residence of Fifty-Five Married Women in Christiaankondre, Related to Age Group

| Age group | Initial residence | | Present residence | |
	In her original domestic group	Otherwise	In her original domestic group	Otherwise
Above median age (34)	20	7	10	17
Below median age (34)	22	6	20	8
Totals	42	13	30	25

cakes from the poison-containing tubers. For these she harvests, peels, washes, and grates the tubers, presses the pulp to extrude the poison, fetches firewood, and bakes the big cakes. Cooking fish is a minor job compared with this. Also, although few women nowadays make pottery, every woman spins cotton for the hammocks.

The division of labor, however, is not rigid. Often a wife goes fishing with her husband or lends a hand when he is building a new house. And her husband

[1] I give these data without further comment and refer to the analysis of residence in The Maroni River Caribs, Chapters 4 & 5. In Table 1 the question is only "did (or does) a woman live in the domestic group in which she grew up." I divided the population into two age groups, using median age of the women to distinguish between young and old. However, differences between first and second marriages are ignored. The data are restricted to Christiaankondre. One couple is omitted; it is an older couple that lives alternatively in Christiaankondre and in another Carib village.

doesn't regard it as below him to peel manioc or even to give some aid in knotting a hammock. Involving both men and women, but falling under a woman's responsibility, is the important task of making alcoholic drinks from manioc (*kasi:li*[2] from pulp, *pa:ya* and *pa:yawa:lu* from slightly burned manioc cakes). Although a woman is expected to do any service her husband requires, her position is certainly not inferior. Inside and outside her own house a woman expresses her thoughts and wishes as an equal partner.

An important institution in the life of the children is the mission school. (The Caribs have for a long time been at least nominally Roman Catholic.) It was founded in 1925 as a simple elementary school (a so-called *boslandschool*, 'bushschool'). In 1958 it was converted into a normal elementary school according to Surinam law (*gewoon lager onderwijs*). Virtually all children attend school, although at any moment ten to twenty percent of the children may not be present. The school is also a stepping stone to Paramaribo, and many children go to Paramaribo even before they finish the school in their village. The Caribs feel, rightly so, that their school is not as good as a school in town and try to send their children, boys as well as girls, to Paramaribo. In 1967 about twenty-five percent of the children between six and fifteen did not live in the village, because they were at school in Paramaribo, Albina, or St. Laurent-du-Maroni.

THE INITIATION RITE FOR GIRLS

The Carib rite conforms to the definition given by Judith Brown (1963: 836). It consists of "ceremonial events, mandatory for all girls." This rite is "celebrated between their eighth and twentieth year"—in fact, among the Caribs at the age of nearly thirteen,[3] because it is a cultural elaboration of the first menstruation. It does "not include betrothal or marriage customs"—although among the Caribs marriage follows soon after the first menstruation. In Carib society the rite is the affair of an individual girl. As soon as it is discovered that a girl is bleeding her mother makes her a small room in the house where she can tie her hammock or she is given the upper part of the house (*su:la*, attic). There she has to stay eight days.[4] Also her mother constructs near the house a small shelter in which the girl can wash herself. She is not allowed to go the river or to the forest. A girl who discovered that she was menstruating for the first time during Mass was allowed to go home; however, a girl who discovered this when she was with her parents in the garden on the other side of the river was not allowed to cross the river and had to stay in a small shelter near the garden.

---

[2]A note on orthography: /ï/ an unrounded close back vowel; /l/ is a flap; /:/ I use in accordance with Hoff (1968) to indicate a long vowel; /ŋ/ is a nasal. I did not indicate that all consonants but the flap are palatalized when they follow the /i/, like the /s/ preceding the /i/, unless the consonant is also followed by the /i/.

[3]Six reliable ages in years and months: 11/7, 12/6, 12/9, 12/11, 13/4, 13/7 (average 12 years and 9 months).

[4]The Caribs say *aiti de*, using Creole language. Ahlbrinck (1931:323) wrote that a girl is confined for one month (one moon month). My informants too said that one month was customary in the past. The same shortening may be noted in certain funeral customs. A few months after a death a feast was given, *omaŋgamo*. This feast is nowadays often called an *aiti de* and is given on the eighth day after the day of death. The eighth day is in Creole thinking important and the Caribs took it over.

If such a shelter is not available a girl returns to her house as soon as possible and without special precautions.

The reason given for staying home and especially for avoiding the river is that the waterspirit, *oko:yumo*, cannot stand the smell thought to be connected with female reproductive processes, such as menstruation.[5] The Caribs say *tïbo:le man*, 'she smells.' And should she come near the river (or even a well), *oko: yumo* would carry her away.

In a popular story it is told that once, not so long ago, a girl having her first menstruation was in her mother's house. Her mother went to the garden but warned the girl that, should a man come to the house, she was not allowed to come down. After the mother left a man *did* come. He induced the girl to come down and follow him to the river where he gave her a present, a golden neck-lace, and sent her back to her mother, who was crying because she understood that the waterspirit had taken away her daughter. The man—*oko:yumo* in dis-guise—warned the girl not to tell about her visit to *oko:yumo's* realm, nor about the origin of the necklace. Her friends however, very curious, made her drunk and in her drunkenness she told everything—and disappeared (i.e., died).

Also the spirit of the forest, *ima:wale*, is a menace to the girl, but less so than the waterspirit.

This carrying away is a manner of speaking; *oko:yumo* causes illness or even death. (I do not know of any case of a girl dying during the menarche; I have, on the other hand, cases in which death of a child was attributed to *oko:yumo* because the father travelled just after the birth of his child or because its mother came near the river).

To be unattractive to *oko:yumo* the girl dresses in old clothes and does not comb her hair. She is left alone as much as possible, though at night she often has a younger sister as companion if she sleeps alone in a house. Also her diet is restricted. She lives mainly on porridge made from manioc cake (*sa:mu:lu*) and on small species of fish (*pata:ka, mi:so*). There are some individual varia-tions in things forbidden, but in general she should not eat big things—no large fish, no meat from big animals like the tapir (*maipu:li*). Smaller animals are al-lowed. Fruits, especially sweet fruits, are forbidden, and likewise sugar and sugarcane. Eating big fish or animals results in a large belly; eating sweet fruits and sugar results in rotten teeth or in eczema around the mouth. If she eats rice her hair will become white. After eight days many girls look rather emaciated, as a result of the food restrictions.

The only activity allowed during seclusion is spinning cotton; indeed, a girl is obliged to do so. She has to make cotton in order to make a hammock, not for her own use, but for her father, brother, or another person. Should she keep the hammock for her own use, she would become a lazy woman. A woman who can make a cotton hammock—the Caribs, although in other respects quite de-pendent upon industrial products sleep exclusively in home-made cotton ham-mocks—is a respectable woman. At present, with seclusion reduced from one month to eight days, no girl succeeds in making enough cotton to make a ham-mock. The obligation to spin cotton remains however.

[5]There are five categories of persons who are especially vulnerable to an attack by the waterspirit *oko:yumo*: a girl having the menarche and in general all menstruating women; a woman who has delivered a child; a newborn child; its father; its older sibling; cf. Kloos 1970.

Toward the eighth day the mother of the girl makes the native manioc drink, normally pa:yawa:lu. She invites an old man and an old woman—people who have a reputation of industriousness—to come to her house early in the morning of the eighth day. A woman who is often invited to such an occasion is the wife of the old chief of Christiaankondre, la:limo. She is about seventy, but still seems to be possessed by a passion for working. The only moments when she is at leisure are when she is playing a little with one of her numerous offspring. Her daughters, granddaughters, and great granddaughters often visit her, but while they are having a chat, the old woman remains busy. Her nickname is tranga man or tranga pi:pi, 'strong man' or 'strong grandmother' (tranga and man are Creole). She is reputed to have said once during a feast that she was strong and could work like any man.

These old people come to the house before sunrise. The mother of the girl keeps ready some bits of cotton fluff, while her father collected the day before a bowl with large ants, yu:ku.[6] First the girl takes a bath in the little shelter near the house. Then the old woman takes a bit of cotton, lays it on the open hand of the girl and sets fire to it. Not to be burned the girl throws it from one hand to the other until it is burned. This is repeated many times. This is taken to mean that in the future her hands should never be at rest but constantly moving and busy. The old man takes the bowl (pa:lapi) with ants, takes the girl by her arms, and puts her hands into the bowl. These large and fiercely biting ants remind her that she, being an adult woman, should be industrious like the ant. In many cases also individual ants are taken from the bowl and allowed to bite the girl behind the knee and on the arm.

She is not allowed to show pain. If a girl does show pain it does not affect her future capabilities. But, it is said, she shall be old before her age. In the rite the emphasis is not on the endurance of pain, yet pain may play a role. A young girl of almost thirteen, who can have her menarche at any moment is regarded as a lazy girl. This is discussed in her presence, and it is said that it shall not be sufficient in her case that she puts her hands in a bowl with ants, rather she will have to lie down in a hammock filled with them.

During these ceremonial acts only the members of the nuclear family of the girl and the old persons are present. The presence of other persons is avoided. Should a lazy person be present it is felt that his laziness might be transmitted to the girl.

Now the girl is dressed by her mother in a new kami:sa (loincloth); her face, legs and arms are painted; and she is adorned with necklaces, bracelets, ear-rings, etc. Fully decorated she stays the rest of the day in her hammock. Only when she is completely dressed up for the feast the guests arrive. There are no special invitations, but everyone knows that in that particular house the manioc beverage has been made and that everyone is welcome. There is no special attention for the girl, though some women give a special greeting to her and comment on her being an adult woman now.

The course of the feast does not differ from other feasts. After some time someone fetches one or two drums, dance songs are sung and people dance. Most visitors become, like the family of the girl, more or less intoxicated and the feast stops abruptly when the drink is finished. The girl does not participate, although some allow such a girl to drink a little.

[6]yu:ku. probably Neoponera commutata (Dr. D. C. Geijskes, personal communication).

In a certain number of cases actual behavior deviates from the pattern described above. First, it seems that the rite itself is changing, probably degenerating and disappearing. We have already noted that the period of seclusion was shortened from one month to eight days. Further, in many cases no ants are used (some men say that particular ant is rare nowadays; the truth is that they don't take the trouble to go and look for them). Many girls argue that those girls who have had the menarche in Paramaribo (being at school) and were not subjected to the rite are not lazier than other girls who were. Second, there are circumstances in which the normal pattern does not fit very well. In the case of an ill girl the rite was completely omitted, because she was thought too weak. In the case of a girl whose grandmother died a few days before the final symbolic acts, she received the burning cotton on the seventh day and in a very hasty manner. No ants were used, no feast was given.

After the feast a girl resumes her work in the household, but not before she has washed her hands to get rid of the smell. She grates some manioc, washes her hands with it, and throws it away. She now resumes her tasks and is allowed to take her daily baths in the river again. In the weeks that follow she receives some instruction. Most of it she knows already but a few things, like making of pottery are now taught. "She knows already, but not yet very well," it is said, and, "It won't do any harm if everything is repeated." Instruction includes information about taking care of a man and about sexual intercourse, but she knows about that, too.

A second menstruation receives no special attention. A girl is expected to know what to do and what to avoid. She can take care of herself, dresses again in an old loincloth, does not take her bath in the river, and avoids contact with men (she does not cook, she does not touch man's tools, for instance. Washing her hands with grated manioc again is the symbolic end of the monthly menstrual period.

A girl having her first menstruation is an *imï:ndapo*, 'she who is bleeding' (from *mï:nu*, 'blood,' *mï:nda*, 'to bleed'). Between first and second menstruation she is an *imï:ndase:na*; the suffix *-se:na* after a verb forms a substantive 'someone (occasionally something) whom befell recently that which is expressed in the verb.' After the second menstruation she is an *imï:ndamase:na*, *-ma-* indicating completeness. In adult women menstruation is indicated with the word *no:mo*, e.g., *no:mo man*, she is *no:mo*, 'she is menstruating.'

The initiation means a change in the girl's life—it certainly is an announcement of status change—but not an abrupt one. A girl of ten or so already cooperates with her mother (younger than ten if she is the eldest girl in a household). She helps in making manioc cakes (peeling and grating, though not baking), in caring for her younger siblings, in washing clothes, and in other activities. However, she is allowed to play with other children, also with boys of her age, to roam in her local group, and to be idle part of the day. After initiation this behavior is no longer thought correct; she has to behave like an adult woman, working and staying at home. When she has no other things to do she ought to spin cotton, like a good, industrious woman. Her marriage chances depend upon her capacities and her inclination to work. If she is alone in her parent's house and a visitor comes, she is expected to receive him like her mother should do. The initiation is the official sign of a behavioral change, visibly taking place in a few months time. It also changes her school behavior. Premenstruation girls already stay home often—for instance when a mother goes to the garden and asks her daughter to look after the preschool children. After the menarche almost all girls leave school and become fully incorporated in a household's economy. Girls who are in Paramaribo or elsewhere at school often come back to the village. (This happened a few years ago more often than at present.) These girls, too, soon become full-fledged members of the household. For a few years after initiation a girl has her place in the household of her father and mother. There is some sexual experimentation (girls of this age are closely, but not always effectively, guarded, especially by their mothers), and after a few years she forms her own family. Typically a woman gives birth to her first child when she is fifteen or sixteen. However, the change from family of orientation to family of procreation again is not abrupt. Normally a boy lives for a few months in the house of his father-in-law before building a house for himself and his wife. This house being in the vicinity of the girl's parents, a young woman spends a good deal of her time in her mother's company, even in her mother's house. Her mother helps her planting the first garden. Together they go into the forest to fetch firewood. Often a young woman processes her manioc in her mother's house, using her mother's instruments. Only when a woman's daughters get married and her own mother dies does this orientation change.

DISCUSSION

In many, perhaps most, ethnographic reports the various phenomena described are not seen as isolated items but as causally related elements. Statements about these causal relations are often not verified, verification being not always possible with data from one society only. It is here that cross-cultural research steps in and affirms or rejects such a statement (as far as the limits of comparative methodology allow). Cross-cultural research is thus fed back to ethnographical research.

With the evident symbolism of industriousness in the Carib ritual in mind—spinning of cotton but not for own use, the use of ants, burning of cotton in always busy hands, the avoidance of lazy persons, and the recruitment of industrious, experienced elders—it does not require much fantasy to assume a relationship between the existence of female initiation and the economic importance of women in Carib society. But without comparative data such an assumption cannot be more than a plausible hypothesis. Ethnography is full of such assumptions, often regarded as truths, because they are plausible. Many of them have never been verified, many also are probably untenable in the face of comparative research, and quite a few have been proven to be untenable.

In the present case, backed by cross-cultural comparative research, I am, I think, allowed to say that the Caribs practice female initiation *because* women in their society play an important (economic) role and *because* women tend to remain in the group in which they grew up until well after the beginning of marriage. I am also allowed to interpret the symbolism as expressions of female importance. But still I have to be careful! How easy it is to add to the list of symbols the early rising on the eighth day. In fact, it fits the relationship quite well (at least according to our ideas, and in a large degree also to Carib ideas) but it is not much more than that. Considering that in Carib society *all* ritual and ceremonial activity of crucial importance takes place very early in the morning, I presume that the early rising in female initiation is connected to this phenomenon rather than to industriousness, of women in particular.

According to Brown (1963), the second factor determining female initiation is uxorilocal residence. The cross-cultural results might have been even more impressive had residence been seen in a processual perspective. The Barama River Caribs, for instance, are classified as neolocal (although with matrilocal alternative) and consequently do not support the hypothesis. Gillin, however, wrote that a boy lives some time in a girl's house. He has to show that he is a hunter, that he can build a house and clear a garden, in short, that he is able to support his wife. "[A man and his wife] usually live in the girl's settlement until the birth of the first child. Later they *may* move elsewhere" (Gillin 1936: 75; italics mine). From the point of view of the argument underlying Brown's hypothesis, the Barama River Caribs fully support the hypothesis. Gillin offers no statistical data. Data about the Maroni River Caribs can be found in Table 1. This flaw in the demonstration is probably owing to the use of the World Ethnographic Sample to validate the hypotheses. In the same issue of the *AA* as the Brown article, such dangers inherent in the World Ethnographic Sample were expressed in the context of another piece of cross-cultural research, likewise based on the W.E.S. "Not having the opportunity to make a complete factor-analysis of the ethnographic sources one is tempted to use the not always appropriate categories of the W.E.S." (Kloos 1963: 861). This very circumstance is the reason that I doubt the validity of the test of the "economic importance" hypothesis (see Brown 1963: 850). The hypothesis is validated ($p = .05$) but the correlation is not particularly high. I doubt the result less than the method, and I would not be amazed if another method of establishing the relative contribution to subsistence gave a clearer relationship. (Judith Brown herself stresses the weakness of the method used.)

Finally, how do the Caribs explain the rite? In so far as they have thought about it, they refer to the woman's economic role. Between residence and the experience of the rite they fail to see any connection. For them the rite is good in itself, first of all. Second, it is regarded as a means to secure the fulfillment of an adult woman's role.

REFERENCES

AHLBRINCK, W. G., *Encyclopaedie der Karaiben.* (Amsterdam: Verhandelingen der Koninklijke Akademie van Wetenschappen, nieuwe reeks, deel 1931) XXVII, 1.

BROWN, JUDITH K., "A cross-cultural study of female initiation rites." *American Anthropologist* 65:837–853, 1963.

GILLIN, J., "The Barama River Caribs of British Guiana." Papers of the Peabody Museum 14, 1936.

HOFF, B. J., *The Carib language* ('s Gravenhage: M. Nyhoff, 1968).

KLOOS, P., "Matrilocal residence and local endogamy." *American Anthropologist* 65:854–862, 1963. "Search for health among the Maroni River Caribs. Etiology and medical care in a 20th century Amerindian group in Surinam." *Bÿdragen tot de taal-, Land- en volkenkunde* 126:115–141, 1970.

————, "The Maroni River Caribs of Surinam." *Assen: Van Gorcum*, 1971.

Endocannibalism Among the Amahuaca Indians

Gertude Dole

The eating of human flesh by human beings has been extremely widespread. It has apparently been practiced all over the world by peoples on all levels of cultural development.

The purpose and meaning of the practice may differ radically according to the social relation that exists between the body consumed and the person who eats it, that is, according to whether the subject eaten belongs to the in-group or the out-group. Hence, this dichotomy serves as a useful device for classifying the numerous instances of cannibalism. If an enemy or other person outside the local or kin group is eaten, the custom is referred to as "exocannibalism"; the term "endocannibalism" refers to the practice of consuming members of one's own group (Steinmetz, 1896, p. 1). Another rare type of cannibalism that has been reported is the eating of one's own flesh. The Iroquoian Indians of New York and Canada are said to have forced prisoners to swallow pieces of their own flesh (Hrdlička, 1911 p. 201). This type might be termed "autocannibalism."

For the purpose of the present study both exocannibalism and endocannibalism will be further divided into two types according to whether their functions are biological or supernatural. These two types are (1) gastronomic, in which the subject is eaten for its food value, and (2) ritual or magical, in which the spirit is absorbed.

Gastronomic endocannibalism has occurred in civilized and primitive societies alike, arising out of dire need for food. Scarcity of food has not infrequently forced arctic peoples, for example, to eat members of their own groups. And from the pioneer days of the United States, we recall the Donner Party for the fact that its members resorted to endocannibalism because of hunger.

In contrast to hunger endocannibalism, the ritual type is usually restricted to uncivilized peoples. At the time the great voyages of discovery took place, Europeans had very little acquaintance with cannibalism. When Spanish and French explorers in the Antilles discovered that the Carib (or Caniba) Indians ate their slain enemies and captives, they were horrified and adapted the name of these natives to refer to the practice (Humboldt, 1853, v. 3, p. 214; Barcia, 1880). The conquistadors and the missionaries who followed them were determined to stamp out this "bestiality" wherever they came across it, and as a result of their tireless efforts the custom has been abandoned by most of those who formerly practiced it. One group in South America that has had very little contact with Whites and has maintained the custom to this day is the Amahuaca of eastern Peru.

The Amahuaca are a very small population of Panoan-speaking Indians who live in very small settlements along the border of southeastern Peru and western Brazil. They depend about equally on hunting and horticulture for their livelihood. Their staple crop is maize, but some sweet manioc and other crops typical of the tropical forest are raised. Amahuaca material culture is exceedingly simple. Steel tools were introduced by pioneers of the rubber and lumbering industries some 70 years ago, but until that time only stone axes and wooden clubs or tortoise-shell hatchets were used to clear the land for gardening.

During recent field work among the Amahuaca a death occurred in a polygynous extended family, and the following is a description of the funerary rites that took place on that occasion.

THE AMAHUACA FUNERARY CEREMONY

An infant died in the night. When this fact was discovered at dawn, the little corpse was flexed and wrapped in its mother's skirt and a blanket. The bundle was firmly bound with bast. The mother of the infant, Yamba Wachi, took the bundle and wailed over it as she sat on the floor of her house. Tears flowed, and her eyes swelled. Occasionally she wiped mucus from her nose.

A grave was prepared immediately in the middle of Yamba Wachi's house floor. It was dug by a young man, Hawachiwa Yamba, who was Yamba Wachi's prospective son-in-law. Except for two young boys, all of the people of the community attended the burial. All the adults sat or stood quietly near Yamba Wachi, while the children roamed in and out of the house at will. When the grave had been dug as deep as Hawachiwa Yamba could reach with his arm, he gently took the bundle from the mother, placed it in one of her cooking pots, and adjusted another pot over it in the grave. He tucked some of Yamba Wachi's palm-leaf mats tightly around the pots in such a way as to prevent dirt from falling into the lower one and pushed loose dirt into the grave to cover the pots.

Then Yamba Wachi searched out and burned a few rags, corncobs, and an old hammock that had been in contact with the baby before its death. Still wailing, she sat down again and with a smooth pebble pounded the surface of the grave lightly with slow even strokes until it was quite even and firm. When this was finished, she swept the dirt floor and threw out the refuse. She then returned to her place beside the grave and continued to wail intermittently throughout the rest of that day and for about ten days thereafter.

One week after the date of burial, the corpse was cremated. Early in the morning Hawachiwa Yamba and four other young men cut a large quantity of very hard dry firewood. They also split Yamba Wachi's grinding trough into long sticks. These sticks and the rest of the firewood were piled up carefully, leaving a depression in the middle for the burial vessels. Hawachiwa Yamba lighted the funeral pyre. He and one of his helpers opened the grave with machetes and removed the two burial pots, taking care not to open them. Nevertheless the odor of decaying flesh escaped as Yamba Wachi took the vessels fondly in her arms and wailed over them, caressing the lower one.

At this point Yamba Wachi's husband, Maxopo, approached her beside the grave, put one hand on the vessels, and began to wail with her. Although he had previously shown no grief, he now generated tears, and mucus dripped from his nose. After a short time Hawachiwa Yamba took the burial pots from Yamba Wachi. He quickly dumped the decaying remains into a third pot in which he had broken a small hole in the base, covered this pot with another, and placed them on the flaming pyre. When they had finished doing this, Maxopo suddenly dashed toward the fire with hands outstretched as if to retrieve the corpse. His gesture was apparently a part of the ritual and was anticipated by the helpers, who joined in restraining him. They all crouched in a huddle near the fire and chanted and wailed loudly as the fire blazed.

When the fire had burned for about an hour, Hawachiwa Yamba lifted the charred remains with a long pole and shook them. Rib bones, calcined and white, were seen separated from one another. However, charred flesh still clung to the rest of the skeleton. The remains were stirred, and wood was placed in the pot to finish burning the flesh. After about an hour and a half longer, the flesh was entirely consumed. The pot was removed from the fire and soon Yamba Wachi, still wailing and weeping, began to slowly and laboriously pick out of the cremation pot the tiny bits of whitened bones that remained with the hot coals and ash.

Maxopo ceased to wail. He brought out a bowl of cornmeal and chatted and joked with Hawachiwa Yamba as they sat together and ate cornmeal. Yamba Wachi, on the other hand, continued to wail and search for bits of bones for about four hours. Finally she arose and put the cremation pots, together with the ashes, into the open grave and covered them with the loose dirt from the grave. She scooped up the charcoal from the funeral fire bed and put it into a carrying basket, which she lifted onto her back with a tumpline. She carried the basket down the hill to the river and put the charcoal into the water. This ended the day's ceremony, which had lasted nine hours.

Yamba Wachi continued to wail intermittently a few more days, holding the bowl of bones on her lap. During this time her adult son cut a new grinding trough for her. When the trough was finished she ground some corn and made gruel. Into this she mixed the bone powder and drank the mixture.

In the Amahuaca funerary ceremony, the primary concern of the participants is to appease the spirit of the deceased while it is at hand by expressing affect to it. When the body has been disposed of, the spirit is thought to disappear also. But until this is accomplished, there is some anxiety lest the spirit of the deceased cause trouble, as it "hangs around wanting to kill someone." The prescribed way for the closest relatives to express concern to the spirit is by weeping. As one observer commented with reference to the Cashinahua, who are closely related to the Amahuaca, "The more one moans and sobs, the better the deceased's shade is appeased. The depth of one's sorrow can be measured by the length of the mucus hanging from one's nose" (Tastevin, 1925, p. 34). The mother continued to mourn until she had consumed the last vestiges of the infant, whereupon her attitude changed radically, as had her husband's earlier. She became voluble and happy, with no suggestion of her bereavement.

DISCUSSION

Amahuaca endocannibalism is not an isolated phenomenon in South America. It was reported among most of the Panoan peoples in the Ucayali valley. Among three of these groups the funerary rites are restricted to consuming pulverized bones or ashes as among the Amahuaca (Carvalho, 1931, pp. 230, 254; Izaguirre, 1922–29, v. 2, pp. 246–47; Villanueva, 1902, p. 67). But ten other Panoan groups consumed the flesh of their dead, five of these going so far as to kill the sick and aged for this purpose (Espada, 1889–92, v. 27, pp. 84–85; v. 30, p. 133;

Figueroa, 1904, p. 118; Izaguirre, 1922–29, v. 1, p. 227; v. 9, pp. 41, 104; v. 12, pp. 445–46; Oppenheim, 1936, p. 148; Tastevin, 1925, p. 34).

Endocannibalism occurred somewhat less frequently among peoples outside the area occupied by the Panoans. Nevertheless many instances have been reported throughout the continent among peoples of Marginal, Tropical Forest, and Circum-Caribbean culture types. It does not appear likely therefore that its occurrence in South America can be related to the influence of any restricted group of people or correlated with culture level. Nor does the pattern of its distribution lend itself to an interpretation through the concept of age area. Hence we must look for other factors to explain its occurrence and distribution here.

The meanings of customs as expressed by those who practice them, although frequently mere rationalizations, sometimes yield clues to the function and development of those customs. Let us consider, then, the meaning of endocannibalism expressed by the Amahuaca and other Panoan peoples.

As we have already seen, among the Amahuaca consuming of the pulverized bones of the deceased is apparently an attempt to banish the spirit. The Conibo cremated the corpse in order to prevent the spirit from reoccupying the body and drank the ashes in order to forget the dead (Espada 1889–92, v. 30, p. 133). The reason given by the Remo and Cashinahua for consuming the remains was to put the dead to rest (Carvalho, 1931, pp. 254, 227). Another report on the Cashinahua indicates that the deceased was mourned to appease the spirit and that when the body had been eaten, the spirit would fly away to the west (Tastevin, 1925, p. 34). For these people, eating the flesh was clearly a duty and a disagreeable one. The shaman is said to have forced everyone in the group to eat a piece of the roasted corpse, and everyone went to a secluded corner to eat his piece "with much weeping for the dead man and the sad lot of humanity" (Tastevin, 1925, p. 34). The Capanahua's reason was "piety," or a desire to honor the dead (Izaguirre, 1922–29, v. 41).

But in spite of the obvious supernatural element in Panoan funerary endocannibalism, some of the data indicate that there is also a gastronomic aspect to the practice. The Capanahua, for example, roasted the body "like game," and it is said that they found this food agreeable, drinking the blood as we drink wine (Izaguirre, 1922–29, v. 9, p. 41). The Cashibo ate their old people with delight (Bastian, 1878, v. 2, p. 761). They and the Mayoruna killed the old and sick, the Mayoruna doing so before they could grow thin (Izaguirre, 1922–29, v. 12, p. 445–46; Martius, 1867, v. 1, p. 430). Figueroa's (1904, p. 118) description of their endocannibalism suggests a thorough confusion of the supernatural and gastronomic elements.

When a parent, son, or other relative dies, they weep, and then, between floods of tears, they cut him into pieces; they boil the flesh or roast it and eat it as fresh meat; the rest they smoke to be eaten on other days. They usually place the entire corpse on a fire, where they remove small pieces of meat from it as it is roasting, and eat between wails and weeping, which they mix with the mouthfuls, until the deceased is entirely eaten. . . . They save the heads until they are full of worms in the orifices and brains, and they eat these for they like them very well mixed with chili pepper.

A Mayoruna man on the point of death made explicit the gastronomic value of the practice. He had fallen gravely ill while away from home. Expecting to die shortly, he was loudly bemoaning not his illness but the thought that he would be interred and would thus be eaten by worms; he would have preferred, according to ancient custom, to serve as food for his relatives instead (Osculati, 1850, pp. 210–11).

Other peoples have expressed the same reasons as those voiced by Panoans, and demonstrate a similar confusion of practical and supernatural objectives. (See, e.g., Roth, 1915, p. 158; Sumner, 1906, pp. 331–33; Sumner and Keller, 1927, v. 2, pp. 1237–39.) In eastern Amazonia, among the Botocudo, the flesh of a dead child was eaten "with tenderness" by its mother (Waitz, 1859, v. 3, p. 446). Other Tapuya peoples believed that the soul would live again in the eater (Anonymous, 1874, p. 297), and that the deceased could not be preserved in any better way than inside their relatives (Herckman, 1934, p. 25). A Camacan mother ate her dead infant because it had come from her body and should return to it, being a prize too precious to leave to the worms (Castelnau, 1850, v. 4, p. 382).

A frequent reason given for consuming human remains is that the good qualities of the deceased will thereby be transmitted to the eater. In the northwest Amazon area the Cubeo expressed this belief succinctly by saying that in this way they incorporated all the energy of their forebears (Coudreau, 1884, v. 2, p. 173). An instance of flesh endocannibalism reported in Colombia is suggestive. It is said that funeral feasts were "the only time the Sae ever tasted meat" (Kirchhoff, 1948, p. 390).

Another consideration that may be of significance in the development of endocannibalism is warfare. Among many peoples, including Panoans, the eating of the flesh of one's own people was associated with warfare. The Comobo and Ruanahua, for example, were said to kill and eat people who were old and unable to serve for war (Izaguirre, 1922–29, v. 1, p. 277). Endocannibalism was associated with warriors also among the Indians of Bonda on the north coast of Colombia in the 16th century. Here the liquids derived from drying a corpse over a slow fire were drunk by the most valiant warriors (Reichel-Dolmatoff, 1951, p. 92). Even among some groups that practiced only the bone-ash type of cannibalism there is a suggestion that it had been associated with warfare. For example, the Island Caribs were said to have practiced it for the purpose of absorbing the spirit and valor of the dead (Koch, 1899, p. 84), and later abandoned the practice because they had no more warriors (La Borde, 1886, p. 253).

The possibility of a functional relation between endocannibalism and warfare is strengthened by a high correlation of these two phenomena. The Panoans were at war with one another at the time of the first White contact and, elsewhere in South America, warfare was most intense in those areas where flesh endocannibalism occurred. Moreover, many groups practiced both revenge and funerary cannibalism, and the forms of the former custom resembled those of the latter.

The available data suggest that the eating of flesh is an early phase of ritual endocannibalism, and that the drinking of ground bones is a ritual survival of the simpler form. If this is so, consuming the flesh of one's relatives becomes more understandable as a custom adapted from revenge cannibalism.

I have noted the gastronomic aspect of flesh endocannibalism. It may be that a need for meat is another significant factor in the development of endocannibalism. (Of course, warfare and hunger do not necessarily operate independently; rather it might be expected that they reinforce each other.) In spite of repeated denials of the relevance of hunger to ritual endocannibalism, this question has never been adequately investigated. The reports of ritual endocannibalism record an established custom that has been perpetuated through predilection for human flesh or supernatural beliefs or both. Neither its inception nor the conditions which gave rise to it are described. Valuable data on this question may soon be supplied by a group of Indians (Pacaás Novos) in western Brazil, recently publicized by the magazine O Cruzeiro (March 3, 1962). These Indians are described as starving and at war with their Indian neighbors and with Whites. They eat the flesh of both enemies and relatives because of hunger and lack of other food.

REFERENCES

ANDREE, R., Die Anthropophagie. (Leipzig, Germany, 1887).

ANONYMOUS, "Die Götter den wilden Indianer in Brasilien." Globus. 25: 296–298, 1874.

BARCIA, R., Primer Diccionario General Etimológico de la Lengua Española. (Barcelona, Spain, 1000).

BASTAIN, A., Die Culturländer des Alten America. 3 vols. (Berlin, Germany, 1878).

CARVALHO, J. B. DE., "Breve noticia sobre os indígenes que habitam a fronteira do Brasil com o Perú." Boletim do Museu National. 7: 225–256,1931.

CASTELNAU, F. DE., Expédition dans les Parties Centrales de l'Amérique du Sud. 6 vols. (Paris, France: 1850).

COUDREAU, H. A., La France Equinoxiale. Voyage à Travers les Guyanes et l'Amazonie. 2 vols. (Paris, France: 1886–87).

FIGUEROA, F. DE., Relación de las Misiones de la Compañía de Jesús en el País de los Maynas. (Madrid, Spain: 1904).

HERCKMAN, E., Manuscript reproduced on pp. 14–28 in "Os Tapuias do Nordeste e a Monografía de Elias Herckman." Revista do Instituto de Ceará. 48: 7–28, 1934.

HRDLICKA, A., "Cannibalism." F. W. Hodge, Ed., Handbook of Indians North of Mexico. Bureau of American Ethnology, Bulletin 30. (Washington, D.C.: 1911), 1: 200–201.

HUMBOLDT, A. VON., Personal Narrative of Travels to the Equinoctial Regions of America during the Years 1799–1804. 3 vols., 1853.

IZAGUIRRE, B., Historía de las Misiones Franciscanas y Narración de los Progresos de la Geografía en el Oriente del Perú . . . 1619–1921. (Lima, Peru: 1922–29).

JIMENEZ DE LA ESPADA, M., ed., "Noticias auténticas del famoso río Marañón." Bol. soc. Geográf. Madrid. pp. 26–30, 1989–92.

KIRCHHOFF, P., "The Guayupe and Sae." J. H. Steward, Ed., Handbook of South American Indians. Bureau of American Ethnology, Bulletin 143. (Washington, D.C.: 1948), 4: 385–391.

KOCH, T., "Die Anthropophagie der südamerikanischen Indianer." Intern. Archiv. Ethnograph. 12: 78–110, 1899.

LA BORDE, FATHER DE., History of the Origin, Customs, Religion, Wars, and Travels of the Caribs, Savages of the Antilles in America. Tr. from the French by G. J. A. Bosch-Reitz. Timehri. 5: 224–254, 1886.

LINNE, S., Darien in the Past. Elanders Boktryckeri Aktiebolag. (Göteberg, Sweden: 1929).

LOEB, E., "Cannibalism." *Encyclopaedia of the Social Sciences*. 3: 172–173, 1930.

MARITIUS, C. F. P. v., *Beiträge zur Ethnographie und Sprachenkunde Amerika's zumal Braziliens*. 2 vols. (Leipzig, Germany: 1867).

METRAUX, A., "Mourning rites and burial forms of the South American Indians." *America Indigena*. 7(1): 7–44, 1947.

———, "Warfare, cannibalism, and human trophies." J. H. Steward, Ed., *Handbook of South American Indians*. Bureau of American Ethnology, Bulletin 143. 5: 383–409, (Washington, D.C., 1948).

OPPENHEIM, V. *Notas ethnographicas sobre os indígenas do Alto Juruá (Acre) e valle do Ucayali* (Perú). Ann. acad. Brasil. Sci. 8: 145–155, 1936.

OSCULATI, G., *Esplorazione delle Regioni Equatoriali*. (Milano, Italy: 1850).

REICHEL-DOLMATOFF, G. *Datos Historico-Culturales sobre las Tribus de la Antigua Governación de Santa Marta*. (Instituto Etnológico del Magdalena, Santa Marta. Bogotá, Colombia: 1951).

ROTH, W. E., *An Inquiry into the Animism and Folk-lore of the Guiana Indians*. Bureau of American Ethnology, Bulletin 30. (Washington, D.C.: 1915), pp. 103–386.

SCHAAFFHAUSEN, H., "Die Menschenfresserei und das Menschenopfer." *Arch. Anthropol.* 4: 245–286, 1870.

STEINMETZ, R. S., 1896. "Endokannibalismus." *Mittheilungen der Anthropologischen Gesellschaft in Wien*. 26: 1–60, 1896.

SUMNER, W. G., *Folkways*. (Boston, Mass.: Ginn and Co., 1906).

——— and A. G. KELLER, *The Science of Society*. 4 vols. (New Haven, Conn.: Yale University Press, 1927).

TASTEVIN, C., "Le fleuve Murú. Ses habitants—Croyances et moeurs kachinaus." *La Géographie*. 44: 14–35, 1925.

THOMAS, N. W., "Cannibalism." *Encyclopaedia Britannica*. 5: 184–185, 1910.

VILLANUEVA, M. P., *Fronteras de Loreto*. Lima, Perú: Imprenta y Librería San Pedro, 1902).

WAITZ, T., *Anthropologie der Naturvölker*. Vol. 3.(Leipzig, Germany: 1859).

Rebirth in the Airborne

Melford S. Weiss

The structural criteria of special purpose (military), sex (male), and age (adult), all emerge from this study of induction into the airborne. Melford Weiss describes the rituals one must go through in order to move from civilian status to that of paratrooper. The training period includes elements of superstition magic, and ceremony, and is compared to similar rites in non-Western cultures.

When an American paratrooper first learns to jump, he does more than step out of an airplane. He steps into a new way of life. Furthermore, his training even takes note of this major transition in his life in a formal ceremonial manner. This training period—marked by pomp and circumstance, superstition and ritual—is what anthropologists refer to as a *rite of passage.*

Rites of passage are universal features of complex as well as simple societies. They mark critical changes in man's life cycle, such as birth, death, and initiation. The paratrooper training program can best be understood as an initiation, a form of entry into an elite group. The process is interwoven with magical and symbolic ritual practices. In one training unit for example, each time the trainees enter the airplane, the jumpmaster draws a line on the ground in front of the entrance hatch with the toe of his boot. Each prospective jumper then stomps upon the line before entering the airplane in order to ensure a safe landing. Whether or not they actually believe in the practice (many do not) is of decidedly less importance than the fact that this ritual serves to bind the group together.

A paratrooper's training ends in a ceremonial climax. At the close of training it is customary in some military units to reenact the jumping procedure in a fashion symbolic of rebirth. Newly qualified paratroopers are invited to a "prop blast" at the noncommissioned officers' club. There a wooden model of an airplane has been hastily rigged. The new initiates line up in jump formation inside the plane. They jump and land facing the jumpmaster, their instructor. He hands each a loving cup full of "blast juice." This must be quaffed within the count of "1000, 2000, 3000," the time between an actual jump from a plane and the opening of the chute. Failure to drain it to the dregs within the allotted span is called a "malfunction," the term for chute failure. The process must be repeated, perhaps three or four times, till success is achieved. Then the initiate is ritually one with his fellows.

INITIATION RITES

Rites of passage vary in different cultures, but according to Arnold Van Gennep a typical rite has three stages:

—*separation* from the former group or state;
—*transition* to the new;
—and finally, *incorporation.*

In birth and death rites, for example, separation is emphasized most: "The Lord giveth, the Lord has taken away." In the case of paratrooper training the transitional phase is most important. The paratrooper rite described here is a composite of training programs of many groups from World War II to the present time.

The paratrooper school is inside a compound surrounded by barbed wire and guarded by sentries. In this compound the trainee is fed, trained, and occasionally entertained. He is allowed to go out in the evening but usually does so in the company of other troopers. Fraternization with the nonparatrooper world is not encouraged, but separation from the former civilian environment is only partial.

The transitional phase usually lasts three weeks. During the last week the candidate makes five practice jumps which mark stages in his progress toward final acceptance. Not all the jumps are equally important—the first and fifth are most significant.

Paratrooper training is officially a secular affair. But certain superstitious practices which are interwoven show that, in the broadest sense, it is also a religious rite. From the beginning of the transition period the trainees are subjected to continuous periods of anxiety. Since they are all volunteers with a strong emotional investment in success, these stresses serve to bind them more closely to one another and to the group they seek to enter. So do the "magical" devices they learn to use to relieve anxiety. These include the wearing of charms and fetishes, such as a girl friend's picture above the heart, a pair of sweat socks worn on a previous successful jump, or a replica of the "trooper wings" placed inside a boot.

Use of "sympathetic magic" is fostered by the paratrooper mythology to which the trainee is exposed during this stage. The following examples of paratrooper tales illustrate elements of both *mana* (a spiritual force independent of persons or spirits which explains success, excellence, and potency when these qualities are not otherwise explainable) and *taboo* (a prohibition based upon the assumption that disastrous consequences can be averted if certain acts are not performed):

He was a jinx and was always present at any accident. I would never jump with him in my line. I once touched him before I was about to jump and pretended to be sick in order to avoid jumping that day. Nobody laughed at me when I told them the real reason.

A master jumper told this story: "When I was a youngster, I felt that should I ever lose my original set of wings I could never jump again. They had a natural magic about them which protected me. When I went home I put them in the bottom drawer of my mother's dresser. I knew they would be safe there!"

Legend maintains that the paratrooper compound is off limits, and one myth relates the unhappy story of the intoxicated soldier from another unit who tried to sneak into the compound and was found next morning with his face severely scratched. The soldier claimed that he was attacked by a small bird and then passed out. But paratroopers claim that the bird was in fact the "screaming eagle," the totemic symbol of the 101st Airborne Division.

During the transition period myth and magic help the trainee to identify with paratroopers in general and share their *esprit de corps*. This becomes a formidable force as airborne units are made up entirely of volunteers. Thus a man becomes a paratrooper by choice and remains one all his military life unless he disobeys a direct order to jump. As in the case of other select military units, paratroopers are bound to one another by pride in a common history and system of training. They consider themselves superior to all other such groups—

not only in their military virtues, but in their vices as well. A paratrooper is supposed to be able to outdrink, outbrawl, and outwhore any other member of the armed forces.

THE JUMPOUT DROPOUT

Systems of initiation depend for their success upon how much the candidate wants to belong to the group. Sometimes, in the case of paratrooper training, he may not want to badly enough. A young man may decide he does not care to spend his active life plunging out of airplanes with nothing but the silkworm's art for support. Since all trainees are volunteers, this is technically no disgrace. All he has to do is request reassignment.

But because of the problem of preserving group morale the dropout is usually eliminated with almost indecent haste. Many instructors feel that to let him hang around will spread the "rot," and other failures or jumping accidents may result. When a would-be dropout says he wants out at the end of a training day, he is more than likely to be called to the orderly room during the next morning's formation. By the time the other trainees return from their midday meal he will have left the training area forever, usually to spend a month's KP duty in some nonelite holding company. For example one dropout said:

I was scared and I knew it. I dared not let the others know, but I did not think I could hide it very long. We were listening to a master jumper telling us about his first jump and my stomach got queasy and I was sick. I told my sergeant I wanted out. I left the very next day.

If a trainee should quit during the training day, particularly with a public fuss, more brusque tactics may be used. One would-be paratrooper reports:

I was fed up with this bastard. I made a scene and cursed the Army and shouted that you can shove the paratroopers. I yelled, "I quit." My training NCO rapidly approached me, ripped the patch from my shoulder, and cut the laces of my jump boots.

In some primitive societies those who fail the tests of manhood may be killed outright. The ripping of the patch and the cutting of the laces serves the same function symbolically. It signifies the separation of the dropout from his companions and thus binds the group more closely together, as does the knowledge that the failure is headed for KP or some other nonstatus duty.

As noted before, the transitional phase of paratrooper training has substages. These occur mainly after the first and fifth (last) practice jump. After the first there is no ceremony, but there is a change in the relationship between the trainees and the seasoned paratroopers. As soon as the jumping experience has been shared, the trainee begins to be treated with at least a modicum of respect by his instructors. Conversation in the barracks becomes less guarded. Before any mention of "spilling silk" or "flying a streamer" was avoided. Now jokes about jumping accidents and chute failures are freely bandied about.

The fifth jump is marked by a definite ritual. After the first four the trainee rolls his own chute. After the last he hands it to the platoon sergeant, who rolls it for him and places it in the supply truck. Then the NCO shakes his pupil's hand, congratulates him, and in some cases invites him to use his, the sergeant's, given name. This reversal of roles marks acceptance into the group. The same evening this is confirmed at a party at the enlisted men's club, usually off limits to officers. The paratroopers-to-be, including officer candidates, are invited to join in the drinking and usually do.

The whole transitional period in paratrooper training closely parallels initiation rites in both Western and non-Western societies. During this stage the initiate learns the formulas, gestures, and chants of the brotherhood. These include a paratrooper prayer and a paratrooper song. The latter is a gruesome chant in which the paratrooper verbalizes, jokingly, his fear of sudden and gory death. It is sung to the tune of "The Battle Hymn of the Republic":

Is everybody ready? cried the Sergeant, looking up.
Our hero feebly answered yes, as they stood him up.
He leapt right out into the blast, his static line unhooked.
O he ain't gonna jump no more!

There was blood upon the risers, there were brains upon the chute,
His intestines were a dangling from his paratrooper boots;
They picked him up still in his chute and poured him from his boots;
O he ain't gonna jump no more!

CHORUS: Glory gory what a helluva way to die!
Glory gory what a helluva way to die!
Glory gory what a helluva way to die!
O he ain't gonna jump no more!

WINGS AND A THREE-DAY PASS

After transition comes incorporation in two stages—an official ceremony and the unofficial "prop blast" described earlier. The official ceremony is a colorful affair in the tradition of most military rituals. It marks the end of the rigorous training and is a welcome climax to weeks of agonizing tension. It takes place the day after the final (fifth) practice jump. The men in the training unit line up in alphabetical order; uniforms are smartly pressed, faces agonizingly clean shaven, and hair close cropped. They stand at attention while the post band plays the national anthem, followed by "Ruffles and Flourishes." The division flag flies just beneath Old Glory.

The men bow their heads as the post chaplain reads from the Bible. After a congratulatory speech the training commandant presents each man with his diploma. The division commandant passes through the ranks, reviews the troops, and pins "wings" to each man's chest. The chaplain delivers the closing benediction. The band continues to play military music as the men now assemble by training platoon and proudly march by the reviewing stand. As the soldiers reach the stand, they are saluted by the senior officers, and the new troopers return the salute. The men are then dismissed and given a three-day pass.

Many features of this ceremony have symbolic significance. The new paratrooper is being initiated into a special brotherhood within the military forces of an American, predominantly Christian, society. The chaplain's benediction gives the ceremony "divine sanction" and links it, however tenuously, with the prevailing Christian religion. The "American heritage" is reflected by the American flag and the national anthem. The polished boots, clean shaves, and close haircuts set up the image of the "clean-cut, all-American boy." The rest of the rite is military, with calculated differences. The marching, the salute, the respect for rank, and the three-day pass remind the paratrooper that he is a member of the armed forces. But the jump-school graduation certificate and the "wings" belong only to paratroopers and serve as permanent marks of that status.

The brotherhood of all troopers is symbolized by the formation itself. While the platoon is the standard military unit, on this one day the men line up in alphabetical order. This wipes out platoon distinctions and incorporates all the men in a pan-paratrooper sodality. Being saluted first by their superiors, against military protocol, shows the "troopers" that they now occupy a coveted status in the military.

Although the training NCO's are not required to attend, they are present throughout the ceremony. At the close they rush to congratulate the new members and welcome them into the brotherhood. The new status of the members has now been recognized and sanctioned by military society. With the evening's "prop blast" and its symbolic reenactment of the jumping process, the rite of passage is complete. The initiate is now wholly separated from his past life and "reborn" into a new, select brotherhood and a new way of life.

7 / Witchcraft, Mysticism, and the Supernatural

Introduction

The human invention and continual reinvention of supernaturals represents an attempt to deal with the as yet unknowable. Anthropologists have collected a bewildering variety of synonyms and euphemisms for various concepts that contain supernatural or unknown qualities. These include magic, ghosts, ancestor worship, witchcraft, divination, voodoo, totemism, symbolism, mana, taboo, ritual, myth, religion, god, the occult, etc. Most anthropological reports of cultural elaborations of these concepts and beliefs seem to miss the excitement and depth of feeling that the participants must share in their ceremonies. One of the authors, for example, had read about Navaho ceremonies long before doing his first field work which happened to be among the Navahos. He was little prepared when he observed his first three-day ceremony for the profound depth of feeling shared by the Navaho during the ceremony. These emotional and even mystical feelings were contagious, and he found it a profound experience. It was, of course, impossible to detect whether his mystical experience had anything to do with theirs, but he would venture to guess that almost any human being would have deep feelings during the course of such an experience.

Given their cultural history of codified theology and antiritual biases, early anthropologists tried for a long time to "translate" what they heard and saw in other societies into the relatively dry, logical medium to which they were accustomed. Faced with what often seemed like fragmented, untidy, oral traditions, these anthropologists were likely to sort out the motifs that "made sense" and to fill in the "gaps" by resort to "logic" or by asking informants leading questions. Many "primitive" concepts of gods, souls and other such very Western entities were created by just such encounters between anthropologist and informant. And ritual also was generally regarded by the anthropologist as nothing more nor less than beliefs translated into action, which would be about like saying that the only thing important about a ballet is the formal knowledge that it communicates.

The results obtained by this naive method of "translation" were frequently as unsatisfying as they were inexact. Lewis Henry Morgan, the most famous U.S. anthropologist of his generation, probably spoke for most of his colleagues when he stated in 1877 that:

Religion deals so largely with the imaginative and emotional nature, and consequently with such uncertain elements of knowledge, that all primitive religions are grotesque and to some extent unintelligible (quoted by Waal Malefijt, 1968:91).

Most of the writings in this tradition, though patronizing, were benign enough in their impact. Their overall message was congruent with the 19th century doctrine of "liberal paternalism": Primitives are childlike and uninformed but educable. In 1921 the French philosopher and "armchair" anthropologist, Lucien Lévy-Bruhl, published a book translated under the title *Primitive Mentality* that unintentionally created a scandal for which many have still not forgiven him. His book was generally taken—or mistaken—as scientific proof that "the natives" really *do* have inferior minds. What Lévy-Bruhl did, in effect, was to sum up all the tough-minded analyses of the old tradition and to argue, more cogently than his predecessors, that the whole gamut of primitive magico-religious beliefs is quite systematic and contrasts consistently with a civilized worldview. In particular, he maintained that the primitive beliefs included in his wide-ranging citations implied little or no respect, on the part of primitives, for the "law of contradiction" of Aristotelian logic:

...A mind like this...will admit both that the sexual act is the ordinary condition of conception, and at the same time declare that conception may occur without it (1966:441).

The impact was dramatic. Within two years of its publication in French, an English translation appeared. The "prelogical mentality" of primitive man became a slogan for racists; and Lévy-Bruhl became the scapegoat.

Lévy-Bruhl's book certainly contains passages that sound illiberal when taken out of context; although many of them have parallels in Christianity and other religious traditions—e.g., the notion of impregnation by either natural or supernatural means in the quotation above. And it is clear on careful reading that his aim was not to put down primitives but, on the contrary, to demonstrate the distortions produced when analysts thoughtlessly impose Western concepts of logic and reality upon non-Western beliefs. As he wrote in his concluding paragraph: ". . . our thought cannot assimilate them with what it knows as its 'ordinary' objects. It therefore despoils them of what there is in them that is elementally concrete, emotional and vital" (1966: 447).

In 1937 Evans-Pritchard published a now-classic work entitled *Witchcraft, Oracles and Magic among the Azande*, from which the first article in this chapter is excerpted. As he confided to one of his students (Pitt-Rivers, 1971: xi–xii), "the book is a critique of Lévy-Bruhl's theories of how natives think; yet Lévy-Bruhl is mentioned only in a single footnote."

The rebuttal is mainly along two lines. First, Evans-Pritchard emphasizes that among the Azande, a rather large group with settlements on both sides of the Sudan-Congo Republic border, witchcraft beliefs do not have the awesome, mystical overtones that Lévy-Bruhl attributed to the mentality of primitives in general. On the contrary, it is the witchcraft of our *own* history that seems especially "weird" by comparison with Zande notions. Except in cases of extreme misfortune, when it becomes the idiom of paralegal accusation or of philosophical speculation, a casual mention of witchcraft as the cause of misfortune conveys about as much information and excitement as our casual references to "bad luck." When farmers in the U.S.A. or in Zandeland attribute a poor crop to bad luck or witchcraft, respectively, the main message is simply that there has been a poor crop.

However, when the Azande must come to grips with a grave misfortune, to wrestle a brute event into intellectual and moral alignment with their view of the world, a characteristic difference between such notions as witchcraft vs. bad luck emerges clearly, for they are not content to cut short their speculations, as Westerners are conditioned to do, with the "scientific"—and fatalistic— verdict that a particular tragic event is simply by chance, or accidental, or a sheer random event. Rather, they insist on making sense of it, making it meaningful—socially, morally, emotionally and, not least of all, *logically*. Hence, to what we, as well as they, see as two coinciding sequences of ordinary, natural causes: (1) a family seeking shade under a granary; (2) a granary collapsing because termites have weakened it, the Azande add a third variable to account for the fact that the two natural sequences coincide, and tragically. This third and crucial cause is the ill-will of another person, determining the event by psychic means which seem mystical to *us* but seem perfectly natural and familiar to the Azande. Evans-Pritchard implies, then, that starting from a cultural premise that "witchcraft participates in all misfortunes," the Azande are as consistently and insistently logical as we in explaining and evaluating the events of their lives—possibly even more logical and consistent, if one were to look critically at some of the vagaries that shape our accounts of misfortune . . . the "mental cruelty" of a spouse, the "temporary insanity" of a homicide.

In the next two articles we again encounter worldviews in which no outstanding event is considered to be accidental, where every such event is scrutinized for its hidden implications for interpersonal relations in the community.

Bohannan, in her report on the Tiv of northern Nigeria, indicates what is gained by this emphasis on social interaction. She notes that the Tiv's concept *tsav* ('effective volition') can be used to explain any and every event or trait of character, including *both* good and bad. This has been found to be true of many such systems of belief—as it is, incidentally, of the Christian concept of God's will or the Freudian concept of libido—and, accordingly, it is the *specific* uses to which this idiom is put, day by day, and the relationships between accusers and accused that promise to be of greatest interest. As she puts it: ". . . where unusual affluence as well as unusual misery are all manifestations of the working of *tsav*, the only important questions can be whose *tsav*, to what degree, and to what end."

When the Tiv describe a man as being a 'man of tsav' they indicate that he is a man who stands out and bears watching. Everyday attributions of *tsav*, which can imply either use or abuse of the power, gradually shape public consensus as to whether a particular man is mainly good—and deserving of support—or mainly bad—and, therefore, to be avoided and censured. In the precolonial past this censure was expressed by forcing "men of tsav" to undergo an ordeal by poison, an act which had explosive implications for the restructuring of the community, since it inevitably removed (through death) a certain percentage of the dominant, elderly males from community affairs and increased the relative influence of other, younger males. In other words, the act constituted a traditional and decisive mechanism of controlled revolt against established authority. The British administration outlawed this "drastic social surgery" on humane grounds; and it is difficult to argue that they should have decided otherwise. Yet it seems apparent that the removal of this "check and balance" mechanism had, in this part of Tivland, resulted in a social and psychological atmosphere that might be described as "social pathology."

Lindenbaum's article focuses on the South Pacific. Here we find an essentially similar system of beliefs, where "all maladies result from some form of socially disapproved action." However, there is one vital difference between the way that the Tiv and the South Fore societies "map" the distribution of harmful, mystical influence. For the Tiv, as we saw, this influence indicated *internal* dissatisfactions and traditionally led to a purge among competing males. The South Fore, by contrast, conceive of mystical harm as always originating *outside* the local group. Accordingly, a "deteriorating situation" among the South Fore tended to draw the members of the local group into closer cooperation, followed by the severing of ties or the initiation of outright warfare with the neighboring group that was suspected of causing their troubles.

In "Gosiute Peyotism" Carling Malouf describes a church-like religion centering upon the veneration and use of peyote. Malouf cites early reports indicating that the Gosiute have known about the psychedelic drug for some time, although only a few individuals had used it. The present two cults arose as a result of activities by "missionaries" from the Ute and Sioux. One important effect of these formalized cults with their group ritual was to bring greater unity to a group that formerly had been atomized. Even the presence of two different cults does not cross-cut this new unity, since the two congregations are careful not to schedule their services for the same time; and members of one cult occasionally participate in the services of the other cult.

REFERENCES

EVANS-PRITCHARD, EDWARD, EVAN, *Witchcraft, Oracles and Magic Among the Azande* (Oxford: Clarendon Press , 1937).

LÉVY-BRUHL, LUCIEN, *Primitive Mentality*, trans. by Lilian A. Clare. (Boston: Beacon Press, 1966).

PITT-RIVERS, JULIAN A., *The People of the Sierra*, 2nd. ed. (Chicago: University of Chicago Press, 1971).

WAAL MALEFIJT, ANNEMARIE DE, *Religion and Culture* (New York: Macmillan, 1968).

Witchcraft Explains Unfortunate Events

E. E. Evans-Pritchard

It is an inevitable conclusion from Zande descriptions of witchcraft that it is not an objective reality. The physiological condition which is said to be the seat of witchcraft, and which I believe to be nothing more than food passing through the small intestine, is an objective condition, but the qualities they attribute to it and the rest of their beliefs about it are mystical. Witches, as Azande conceive them, cannot exist.

The concept of witchcraft nevertheless provides them with a natural philosophy by which the relations between men and unfortunate events are explained and with a ready and stereotyped means of reacting to such events. Witchcraft beliefs also embrace a system of values which regulate human conduct.

Witchcraft is ubiquitous. It plays its part in every activity of Zande life; in agricultural, fishing, and hunting pursuits; in domestic life of homesteads as well as in communal life of district and court; it is an important theme of mental life in which it forms the background of a vast panorama of oracles and magic; its influence is plainly stamped on law and morals, etiquette and religion; it is prominent in technology and language; there is no niche or corner of Zande culture into which it does not twist itself. If blight seizes the groundnut crop it is witchcraft; if the bush is vainly scoured for game it is witchcraft; if women laboriously bail water out of a pool and are rewarded by but a few small fish it is witchcraft; if termites do not rise when their swarming is due and a cold useless night is spent in waiting for their flight it is witchcraft; if a wife is sulky and unresponsive to her husband it is witchcraft; if a prince is cold and distant with his subject it is witchcraft; if a magical rite fails to achieve its purpose it is witchcraft; if, in fact, any failure or misfortune falls upon any one at any time and in relation to any of the manifold activities of his life it may be due to witchcraft. Those acquainted either at firsthand or through reading with the life of an African people will realize that there is no end to possible misfortunes, in routine tasks and leisure hours alike, arising not only from miscalculation, incompetence, and laziness, but also from causes over which the African, with his meager scientific knowledge, has no control. The Zande attributes all these misfortunes to witchcraft unless there is strong evidence, and subsequent oracular confirmation, that sorcery or one of those evil agents which I mentioned in the preceding section has been at work, or unless they are clearly to be attributed to incompetence, breach of a taboo, or failure to observe a moral rule.

When a Zande speaks of witchcraft he does not speak of it as we speak of the weird witchcraft of our own history. Witchcraft is to him a commonplace happening and he seldom passes a day without mentioning it. Where we talk about the crops, hunting, and our neighbors' ailments the Zande introduces into these topics of conversation the subject of witchcraft. To say that witchcraft has blighted the groundnut crop, that witchcraft has scared away game, and that witchcraft has made so-and-so ill is equivalent to saying in terms of our own culture that the groundnut crop has failed owing to blight, that game is scarce this season, and that so-and-so has caught influenza. Witchcraft participates in all misfortunes and is the idiom in which Azande speak about them and in which they explain them. Witchcraft is a classification of misfortunes which while differing from each other in other respects have this single common character, their harmfulness to man.

Unless the reader appreciates that witchcraft is quite a normal factor in the life of Azande, one to which almost any and every happening may be referred, he will entirely misunderstand their behavior towards it. To us witchcraft is something which haunted and disgusted our credulous forefathers. But the Zande expects to come across witchcraft at any time of the day or night. He would be just as surprised if he were not brought into daily contact with it as we would be if confronted by its appearance. To him there is nothing miraculous about it. It is expected that a man's hunting will be injured by witches, and he has at his disposal means of dealing with them. When misfortunes occur he does not become awe-struck at the play of supernatural forces. He is not terrified at the presence of an occult enemy. He is, on the other hand, extremely annoyed. Some one, out of spite, has ruined his groundnuts or spoiled his hunting or given his wife a chill, and surely this is cause for anger! He has done no one harm, so what right has anyone to interfere in his affairs? It is an impertinence, an insult, a dirty, offensive trick! It is the aggressiveness and not the eerieness of these actions which Azande emphasize when speaking of them, and it is anger and not awe which we observe in their response to them.

Witchcraft is not less anticipated than adultery. It is so intertwined with everyday happenings that it is part of a Zande's ordinary world. There is nothing remarkable about a witch—you may be one yourself, and certainly many of your closest neighbors are witches. Nor is there anything awe-inspiring about witchcraft. We do not become psychologically transformed when we hear that someone is ill—we expect people to be ill—and it is the same with Azande. They expect people to be ill, i.e., to be bewitched, and it is not a matter for surprise or wonderment.

But is not Zande belief in witchcraft a belief in mystical causation of phenomena and events to the complete exclusion of all natural causes? The relations of mystical to common-sense thought are very complicated and raise problems that confront us . . . Here I wish to state the problem in a preliminary manner and in terms of actual situations.

I found it strange at first to live among Azande and listen to naive explanations of misfortunes which, to our minds, have apparent causes, but after a while I learned the idiom of their thought and applied notions of witchcraft as spontaneously as themselves in situations where the concept was relevant. A boy knocked his foot against a small stump of wood in the center of a bush path, a frequent happening in Africa, and suffered pain and inconvenience in consequence. Owing to its position on his toe it was impossible to keep the cut free from dirt and it began to fester. He declared that witchcraft had made him knock his foot against the stump. I always argued with Azande and criticized their statements, and I did so on this occasion. I told the boy that he had knocked his foot against the stump of wood because he had been careless, and that witchcraft had not placed it in the path, for it had grown there naturally. He agreed that witchcraft had nothing to do with the stump of wood being in his path but added that he had kept his eyes open for stumps, as indeed every Zande does most carefully, and that if he had not been bewitched he would have seen the stump. As a conclusive argument for his view he remarked that all cuts do not take days to heal but, on the contrary, close quickly, for that is the nature of cuts. Why, then, had his sore festered and remained open if there were no witchcraft behind it? This, as I discovered before long, was to be regarded as the Zande explanation of sickness. Thus, to give a further example, I had been feeling unfit for several days, and I consulted Zande friends whether my consumption of bananas could have had anything to do with my indisposition and I was at once informed that bananas do not cause sickness, however many are eaten, unless one is bewitched. . . .

Shortly after my arrival in Zandeland we were passing through a government settlement and noticed that a hut had been burnt to the ground on the previous night. Its owner was overcome with grief as it had contained the beer he was preparing for a mortuary feast. He told us that he had gone the previous night to examine his beer. He had lit a handful of straw and raised it above his head so that light would be cast on the pots, and in so doing he had ignited the thatch. He, and my companions also, were convinced that the disaster was caused by witchcraft.

One of my chief informants, Kisanga, was a skilled wood carver, one of the finest carvers in the whole kingdom of Gbudwe. Occasionally the bowls and stools which he carved split during the work, as one may well imagine in such a climate. Though the hardest woods be selected they sometimes split in process of carving or on completion of the utensil even if the craftsman is careful and well acquainted with the technical rules of his craft. When this happened to the bowls and stools of this particular craftsman he attributed the misfortune to witchcraft and used to harangue me about the spite and jealousy of his neighbors. When I used to reply that I thought he was mistaken and that people were well disposed towards him he used to hold the split bowl or stool towards me as concrete evidence of his assertions. If people were not bewitching his work, how would I account for that? Likewise a potter will attribute the cracking of his pots during firing to witchcraft. An experienced potter need have no fear that his pots will crack as a result of error. He selects the proper clay, kneads it thoroughly till he has extracted all grit and pebbles, and builds it up slowly and carefully. On the night before digging out his clay he abstains from sexual intercourse. So he should have nothing to fear. Yet pots sometimes break, even when they are the handiwork of expert potters, and this can only be accounted for by witchcraft. "It is broken—there is witchcraft," says the potter simply. . . .

In speaking to Azande about witchcraft and in observing their reactions to situations of misfortune it was obvious that they did not attempt to account for the existence of phenomena, or even the action of phenomena, by mystical causation alone. What they explained by witchcraft were the particular conditions in a chain of causation which related an individual to natural happenings in such a way that he sustained injury. The boy who knocked his foot against a stump of wood did not account for the stump by reference to witchcraft, nor did he suggest that whenever anybody knocks his foot against a stump it is necessarily due to witchcraft, nor yet again did he account for the cut by saying that it was caused by witchcraft, for he knew quite well that it was caused by the stump of wood. What he attributed to witchcraft was that on this particular occasion, when exercising his usual care, he struck his foot against a stump of wood, whereas on a hundred other occasions he did not do so, and that on this particular occasion the cut, which he expected to result from the knock, festered whereas he had had dozens of cuts which had not festered. Surely these peculiar conditions demand an explanation. Again, if one eats a number of bananas this does not in itself cause sickness. Why should it do so? Plenty of people eat bananas but are not sick in consequence, and I myself had often done so in the past. Therefore my indisposition could not possibly be attributed to bananas alone. If bananas alone had caused my sickness, then it was necessary to account for the fact that they had caused me sickness on this single occasion and not on dozens of previous occasions, and that they had made only me ill and not other people who were eating them. Again, every year hundreds of Azande go and inspect their beer by night and they always take with them a handful of straw in order to illuminate the hut in which it is fermenting. Why then should this particular man on this single occasion have ignited the thatch of his hut? I present the Zande's explicit line of reasoning—not my own. Again, my friend the wood carver had made scores of bowls and stools without mishap and he knew all there was to know about the selection of wood, use of tools, and conditions of carving. His bowls and stools did not split like the products of craftsmen who were unskilled in their work, so why on rare occasions should his bowls and stools split when they did not split usually and when he had exercised all his usual knowledge and care? He knew the answer well enough and so, in his opinion, did his envious, backbiting neighbors. In the same way, a potter wants to know why his pots should break on an occasion when he uses the same material and technique as on other occasions; or rather he already knows, for the reason is known in advance, as it were. If the pots break it is due to witchcraft.

We must understand, therefore, that we shall give a false account of Zande philosophy if we say that they believe witchcraft to be the sole cause of phenomena. This proposition is not contained in Zande patterns of thought, which only assert that witchcraft brings a man into relation with events in such a way that he sustains injury.

My old friend Ongosi was many years ago injured by an elephant while out hunting, and his prince, Basongoda, consulted the oracles to discover who had bewitched him. We must distinguish here between the elephant and its prowess, on the one hand, and the fact that a particular elephant injured a particular man, on the other hand. The Supreme Being, not witchcraft, created elephants and gave them tusks and a trunk and huge legs so that they are able to pierce men and fling them sky high and reduce them to pulp by kneeling on them. But whenever men and elephants come across one another in the bush these dreadful things do not happen. They are rare events. Why, then, should this particular man on this one occasion in a life crowded with similar situations in which he and his friends emerged scatheless have been gored by this particular beast? Why he and not someone else? Why on this occasion and not on other occasions? Why by this elephant and not by other elephants? It is the particular and variable conditions of an event and not the general and universal conditions that witchcraft explains. Fire is hot, but it is not hot owing to witchcraft, for that is its nature. It is a universal quality of fire to burn, but it is not a universal quality of fire to burn *you*. This may never happen; or once in a lifetime, and then only if you have been bewitched.

In Zandeland sometimes an old granary collapses. There is nothing remarkable in this. Every Zande knows that termites eat the supports in course of time and that even the hardest woods decay after years of service. Now a granary is the summerhouse of a Zande homestead and people sit beneath it in the heat of the day and chat or play the African hole game or work at some craft. Consequently it may happen that there are people sitting beneath the granary when it collapses and they are injured, for it is a heavy structure made of beams and clay and may be stored with eleusine as well. Now why should these particular people have been sitting under this particular granary at the particular moment when it collapsed? That it should collapse is easily intelligible, but why should it have collapsed at the particular moment when these particular people were sitting beneath it? Through years it might have collapsed, so why should it fall just when certain people sought its kindly shelter? We say that the granary collapsed because its supports were eaten away by termites. That is the cause that explains the collapse of the granary. We also say that people were sitting under it at the time because it was in the heat of the day and they thought that it would be a comfortable place to talk and work. This is the cause of people being under the granary at the time it collapsed. To our minds the only relationship between these two independently caused facts is their coincidence in time and space. We have no explanation of why the two chains of causation intersected at a certain time and in a certain place, for there is no interdependence between them.

Zande philosophy can supply the missing link. The Zande knows that the supports were undermined by termites and that people were sitting beneath the granary in order to escape the heat and glare of the sun. But he knows besides why these two events occurred at a precisely similar moment in time and space. It was due to the action of witchcraft. If there had been no witchcraft people would have been sitting under the granary and it would not have fallen on them, or it would have collapsed but the people would not have been sheltering under it at the time. Witchcraft explains the coincidence of these two happenings.

The Frightened Witch

Laura Bohannan

Most of the Tiv, whom it has been my fortune to know well, I have liked and respected. I could not like Shingir, and the respect that his abilities when sober, forced from me was greatly diminished by his behavior when drunk. Nevertheless, of all the 600-odd people in that particular lineage area, only one man, Anyam, was as able as Shingir and yet more sober in his habits. Anyam, however, was not wholly sane.

Furthermore, neither Shingir, nor the community of which he was the head, is typical, since a general terror of witchcraft is as rare in Tivland[1] as witches are common. The prevalence of witchcraft in Shingir's land was proven to the Tiv by the unusual prevalence there of serious illness. The virulence of the witchcraft, and the absence of any powerful men of good will, was proven to them by the unusually great number of deaths in the community. The insatiability of the witches was proven by the frequency of epidemics, mainly of smallpox, and the hate of the witches for each other by the fact that not even the most powerful escaped unscathed. Everyone was suspicious. Almost everyone was under suspicion. Everyone was afraid. Those who could went away. Those who stayed, drank too much and fell to quarrelling when they tried to joke. Their fear was obvious. All Tiv who saw it and who knew anything of the situation—as neighbors, traders, or visiting relatives—expressed both astonishment and a certain horror in speaking of it. It was also a situation that because of its very rarity attracted my interest.

These same circumstances were also responsible for much of my interest in Shingir: the abnormality of the situation almost painfully focused the attention of his people upon him and his deadly rival Anyam. Unquestionably the most powerful two men in the community, and the most feared, everything they did was watched. People who knew Shingir well agreed on one point: he was a man grossly misjudged, whether for good or for ill, by the rest of the world. Therefore, I shall try to show him here as he was seen by four of the people most concerned with him: Ahuma, his crony; Anyam, his greatest enemy; Kusugh, his main heir; and Mfaga, his senior wife. Finally, because all these people were trying to influence me in my opinion of Shingir, I shall begin by sketching my own relationship with him.

Finding a good working site had been a fairly simple matter in the densely populated and relatively sophisticated areas of southern Tivland. In the north, it was rather more difficult.

"If you want to see all the old ceremonies, and find a lot of witches," Tiv from the southern and central lineages advised, "go down there. They still do all the things our grandfathers did, for they sit in the bush, away from everything that's happening." Close friends sometimes added, "They're dirty. They have no respect and no manners. You won't find anyone to talk to; they run away from Europeans—they don't know the mine recruiting stopped years ago. You wouldn't like it there."

---

[1]Tivland lies in the Northern Provinces of Nigeria, on both sides of the Benue River, some 140 miles from its confluence with the Niger, extending approximately from about 6°30' N. to 8° N. and from 8° E. to 10°. There are about 800,000 Tiv, among whom there are surprisingly slight differences in language, manners, and custom from one to another of the eight lineage segments which compose the tribe. Perhaps the most important variations are the shifts, from south to north, of (1) high to low population density (from as much as 550 per square mile to as little as 25, or less, per square mile), and (2) of what may very loosely be described as the worldly sophistication of the south and the unpolished, unsecular north.

Certainly people did disappear at the approach of a European and carriers. After a few days walking, I was immediately prejudiced in Shingir's favor because his was the first homestead that our arrival did not disrupt. Not only were Shingir's people there, they gathered around to look and talk. Shingir himself suggested a longer visit, and when I remarked that I was looking for a spot in which to settle and build some huts, for which I would pay, he made me welcome.

"Look at us," Shingir waved his hand round his homestead. "Some of our wives are even living in the storage huts." Indeed, there were 139 men, women and children crowded into the 41 huts that formed Shingir's homestead circle.

All Tiv homesteads form a series of concentric rings, usually circular but often oval or even irregular, to avoid a muddy depression or some other natural inconvenience. The outermost ring consists of the gardens devoted to tobacco, vegetables, and herbs for spice and medicine. Just within is the ring of storage huts, all round structures of mud with tall thatched roofs, some on stilts for grain, others low and half underground for the storage of yams and other root crops. Every married woman normally has her own granaries, located just behind her sleeping hut. These large round sleeping huts form the next ring, and every married woman with a child is entitled to one. Here she cooks. Here she and her children sleep. The innermost circle is formed by the reception huts, one to each married man, set just in front of the huts of his wives. Here he receives visitors, has ceremonies performed, and here too the whole family gathers on rainy days.

All these rings are concentric about a large open yard, preferably containing one or two large shade trees. In this yard men meet on important occasions, dances are held, story tellers perform on moonlit evenings, children play, and women gossip. It is the heart of the homestead. In this regard, Shingir's homestead was indeed an exception, for it faced in upon an evil-smelling corral occupied by Shingir's fifteen head of cattle. The people of his homestead had little space for themselves.

But no one did anything about it. None of the men was building a hut for his new wife, nor even repairing a tumble-down reception hut. Everyone agreed that the homestead must be moved, but no one could agree where to move it. It lay on the path up from the river, between two slight hills, a site that compressed the homestead into a rather narrow oval. It also lay too near the river. During the rains, the lower part of it, where Shingir's huts lay, was flooded and all of it became intolerably muddy. Shingir thought it would be quite enough if the homestead were gradually shifted uphill. He would start by building at the highest end, the rest would then follow suit until all were back in the same position relative to each other. Everyone else in the homestead wished to move away altogether. Since I wished to build just uphill from the rest of Shingir's homestead, almost precisely on his chosen spot, Shingir found my presence convenient. In the long run, I would have built his huts for him just where he wanted them.

Shingir had other reasons for making me welcome. As Native Authority head (or taregh, in Tiv) of a fairly large lineage segment, he felt obliged to entertain visiting Europeans. Some months later, after a beer drink, he confided that he felt himself in the administration's black books and wished me to give a good report of him. More immediately, he wanted medicine for himself and his people: the illness within Shingir's homestead, with its dirt and its cattle, was notorious even locally. The nearest dispensary was a day's walk by the direct route, passable only during the dry season. Even then, few people considered going there until they were too ill to walk. For all practical purposes they were without the benefit of so much as first aid which was all I could offer, but even that proved not to be much in itself when babies sat down in fires, neglected sores ate down to the bone, and unwashed cuts became severely infected. Shingir found me useful. I found him a ritual expert, willing to give me a front seat at the many ceremonies he was called upon to perform and able to give me much information about what I had seen and he had done.

Nevertheless, our continued association proved a great strain on both of us. Shingir could never be sure I would be around to witness only his more commendable actions, nor, clearly, was he ever quite sure how to behave towards me. Sober, he vacillated irritatingly between sham servility and spurious bonhomie. Drunk—and during the height of the beer drinking season in the rains, he was customarily drunk five days out of seven—he bullied my servants, and, according to his mood, tried to bully me or to become overly familiar. Several times he tried to get me to drink with him from the same beer calabash, my mouth adjoining his, a Tiv indecency between man and woman.

My servants hated him, feared him, and profoundly respected his ceremonial knowledge, of which they frequently made use when they or their wives were ill. Like myself, they suffered from Shingir's lack of manners and from his inability to understand a hint. We all learned to eye Shingir's approach, to discover whether to welcome or avoid him. If his stocky, corpulent figure came straight towards my hut, if there was a slight stamp in his walk, if the large togalike cloth which elders wear was decently in place, and if he leaned firmly on his spear, then I went to greet him. On such occasions he had come to tell me the news, to ask for medicine, to invite me to a ceremony, or to discuss with me the ritual of a ceremony he had just taken me to witness and the background of kinship and personalities against which it had taken place. On such occasions, I was grateful both to and for Shingir. I had known several elders who knew more about fetishes and their ritual, but none who could explain them as well.

Shingir did not, however, always come in this manner or for these purposes. As many as four or five days of the seven-day beer-brewing week, he was more than a little drunk by mid-morning. Then, when he stumbled slightly, when his toga swung open, when he held his spear like a yoke across his shoulders, and when the flesh on his face seemed to hang loose, I knew he would be overly familiar with me and extortionate in his demands to my servants. All of us would retreat behind closed doors, hoping that Shingir was merely following the path that led through our cluster of huts either in search of more beer or going home to sleep.

Whenever Shingir, drunk, made for the kitchen, a very few moments brought one of my servants to the door to ask me to rid them of Shingir. Shingir helped himself too freely to my supplies and to their belongings. I would go reluctantly. At the sight of me, Shingir would call out, "Can't you wait for me to come to your door?" and roar delightedly at his own jest. When he laughed, the wen on his neck between ear and chin, shook in its pendulous fold of flesh like a golf ball in jelly. With considerable difficulty—he was, after all, my host—I would pry him from my kitchen and see him home. I did not want Shingir to make my servants' life intolerable, nor did I want him handling my food and my cooking utensils. In addition to some sort of skin trouble, Shingir had gonorrhea, very common in Tivland. From the look of the sores he had showed me, I suspected that he had syphilis as well, rare as that disease is among a people who suffer yaws.

There were awkward moments with Shingir, but we were too useful to each other not to try to forget them as quickly as possible. Eventually, as he began to understand that I did not enjoy a carouse, he again turned to Ahuma in his more jovial moods and these difficulties occurred less frequently.

Shingir and Ahuma were boon companions and particular cronies. Both of them relished their food and their beer, showed the world a bluff and hearty face, and enjoyed the heat of shouted argument. Ahuma was also a knowledge-able elder, with a considerable command of ritual, which he was seldom asked to perform, and a shrewd man, whose shrewdness often just failed of its mark. He was consistently Shingir's ally, and occasionally, one of his greater embar-rassments.

It was Shingir who had seen that Ahuma had been named tax collector. Ahuma's first collection coincided with a series of complaints that tax had been twice collected. A few people said that they had two sets of receipts to show for it, and turned them over to Shingir to keep until the District Officer came on tour. These receipts were accidentally eaten by a goat, and Shingir told the complainants that, in the absence of proof, it was no use even mentioning the affair to the District Officer. The victims retired to sulk, while the countryside laughed at their gullibility.

Ahuma's second collection showed no such irregularities. Unfortunately, he did not feel himself able to carry such a weight of pennies and shillings and changed the entire sum into paper money, which Shingir quite providentially had in his possession at that moment. Ahuma and the money fell into the river. Ahuma nearly drowned. The money had wholly disintegrated by the time the box containing it had been recovered. Shingir, who had witnessed this luckless event, supported Ahuma's tearful story to chief and administration. Nevertheless, Ahuma lost his job. In spite of this, however, there still clung to him the not inconsiderable prestige of having been tax collector. Certainly people felt, and Shingir frequently said, that Ahuma had reason to be grateful to him for the whole affair. Consequently, whenever Ahuma was discovered trying to conceal anything from Shingir, Shingir complained loudly over his friend's ingratitude, even while he showed how very much afraid he was that Ahuma might desert him for Anyam. This fear of treachery underlay Shingir's frequent rages at Ahuma, and his quite astounding willingness to swallow insult and trickery once he could surely attribute both to Ahuma's purely personal greed. I first saw this aspect of their relationship in the developments that followed one of the most elaborate series of rituals I had ever watched Shingir perform.

On this occasion the entire lineage in the person of its elders and homestead heads had been summoned to Ahuma's for the performance of curative ceremo-nies for one of his married daughters. Shingir, as the most influential elder with the command of the necessary fetishes, performed the ceremony. As part of the ritual, the sacrificial chickens are eaten by all the elders of the lineage who have control of those particular fetishes (akombo, in Tiv). In this case, there were eight such men, including Shingir. The rest of us were given a purely secular feast: yam porridge provided by the father's household, and meat provided by the girl's husband (who also furnished the chickens and money for the ceremony). Everyone thus has a strong interest in the generosity of the son-in-law; I have known the elders to veto such a ceremony until a larger animal had been provided for the feast. On this particular occasion, the goat paraded before us all could scarcely fail to please for it was large and fat. Nevertheless, the elders were slow to approve it. In Tivland many a man knows his neighbor's livestock and younger children equally well. This goat was Ahuma's, not a new one brought by the son-in-law. Ahuma, leaning across me to Shingir, announced in the stage whisper of politeness, "My son-in-law had no suitable animal. I sold him one. He brought the money." Everyone's face cleared, and the ceremony proceeded.

The next morning, Shingir went off to a beer party and returned within a bare half hour. Ahuma's half-brother had just whispered in his ear that the son-in-law had not merely brought money; he had brought a fat sow, far more valuable than the goat that Ahuma had foisted off on the elders. Shingir, angry at Ahuma for having tried to cheat him and half annoyed because it had been so poor an attempt, went after Ahuma while the men of his homestead searched for the pig.

Only Kusugh, Shingir's heir and his father's brother's son, stayed behind—to explain the event to me: Ahuma tries to do everything that Shingir has done, but "Ahuma bungles. Then Shingir is very angry and forces Ahuma to make reparation. When a fool does a wicked thing everyone can see that it is indeed evil, and then everyone remembers who else has committed such an act, and finds that act evil even when it was done by a clever man who made it seem well done at the time."

Kusugh looked around to make sure no one was listening. He never opposed Shingir publicly, though this was not the first time he had "explained" his actions to me. "You have heard of Ahuma and the tax money that was destroyed. He was a fool, and still has no money. How do you think he paid his witness? And what made Ahuma think of it? Shingir was once keeping some bank notes for someone; they fell into the fire and were burnt. But it was not very much money, and it was the money of a man without influence, not the government's."

Whatever Kusugh might have added was cut off by the noisy approach of the pig, reluctantly dragging at the end of a grass rope tugged by an excited youngster. It was soon followed by Shingir, Ahuma, and most of the elders who had been at the beer drink. Only Anyam was absent.

They paused in my courtyard. "This is the pig," Shingir accused, "that we should have eaten. It was brought to Ahuma for us, and he hid it. And where?" Shingir was angry now, and perturbed. "At Anyam's." It was to Anyam, Shingir's rival and his enemy, that Ahuma had apparently turned.

Ahuma recognized the issue. "Yes, I hid the pig, but I meant to send it across the river where you wouldn't find it. Not to Anyam's." He spoke with a rare sincerity that convinced us all. "Anyam met my son on the path; he took the pig from him, forcibly, and said he'd keep it for me. Where do I stand in this land? With you, Shingir? Or with Anyam? Let the boy tell you himself."

As Ahuma's son told in detail of his meeting with Anyam, Shingir grew slowly less tense. At the end of the story, he was relaxed enough to listen almost sympathetically to Ahuma's claim that the sow was about to farrow and therefore should not be slaughtered.

"Very well," said Shingir, "we will wait and see. Meanwhile, let the sow remain in the care of my senior wife, where we may all watch it. If there is no litter, we will eat the sow. If there is a litter, we will eat them all."

Ahuma shouted his claim to the litter, thereby conceding the sow, and a noisy argument followed it to its new quarters. It was uproar without acrimony. The two men were still allies, united against Anyam. To maintain that alliance, each would forgive the other much.

Anyam was Shingir's opposite in every respect: a small-boned man, tall and nervous, a clairvoyant, and in his youth a diviner. Everyone, my servants included, described his manner and appearance as that of Tiv in the time of their fathers. Anyam wore his hair in a short pigtail; his face was scarred with the old-fashioned raised welts, and he wore earrings that looked like black shoe buttons. He was a soft-spoken man, one who rarely drank or jested. He had command of even more fetishes than Shingir, and was considered his only rival in witchcraft. People who spoke of Shingir as a witch generally used the euphemism, "he knows things." Anyam was bluntly called a "man of tsav," when he was not outright dubbed "one of the mbatsav."

One cannot long speak about Tiv without speaking of tsav. In its most concrete form, tsav is a witchcraft substance on the heart, a fatty sac on the pericardium, the presence or absence of which may be established by a postmortem operation. During a man's life, however, the presence of the substance, and hence the power of witchcraft, can only be assumed. It is so assumed wherever a man's fortunes and behavior reveal the ability, power, talent, and force of personality which both are tsav and manifestations of tsav.

Is a person in any way outstanding, if only as a singer, dancer, hunter? He has some tsav, though perhaps only a little. Is a man healthy, possessed of a large family and prosperous farms? He is a "man of tsav," or he could not have warded off the envy of others either in its physical or mystical expression. Is a man solitary? Are his dependents few and ill? Have there been many deaths in his family? Then he is either a victim of the mbatsav, who are the men of tsav joined together for good or evil, or, quite possibly he is himself one of the mbatsav and the cause of these misfortunes. Where fortune as well as misfortune, where the attainment of political and social influence as well as near-ostracism for abnormality of personality or of habit of life, where unusual affluence as well as unusual misery are all manifestations of the working of tsav, the only important questions can be whose tsav, to what degree, and to what end.

Tsav is effective volition. A man of tsav wills death, and the cause of death is his agent, be that cause disease, a falling tree, or a chance arrow. No one in Tivland dies a natural death, for it is considered "natural" for man to go on living. Death then is always due to witchcraft, and the funeral is largely concerned with establishing whose witchcraft and why. Usually the witch is found to be a man of prominence, hence certainly a man of tsav, who had a well-known grudge against the deceased. And here, as far as acts of the day are concerned, the matter rests. If any vengeance is taken, it is taken mystically, and appears only when the death of the witch or one of his relatives—of old age, illness, or whatever cause—is found at the funeral to have been willed by a relative of some victim of the witch.

A man of *tsav* may also will and effect the health and welfare of his land and his people. Here the fetishes (*akombo*) of the Tiv and his knowledge of their ritual are his agents. In a very narrow sense, these fetishes are magical forces, the emblems of which may be plants, stones, celts, corn cobs, almost anything. They are non-human forces, established at creation by the Heavens (*Aôndo*), which also gave the Tiv the means—ritual knowledge—and the power—*tsav*— to manipulate these forces. Neither *tsav* nor these forces are good or bad in themselves, though both are dangerous. They are ability and instrument; the moral quality attaches to their use.

Most of these fetishes, the "small fetishes," affect individuals. The great fetishes, on the other hand affect the fertility, prosperity, and health of entire social groups. While the small fetishes, the minor magical forces, are maintained in full strength by sacrifices of chickens or goats and the concomitant performance of the appropriate ritual performed by a single man, the great fetishes demand the sacrifice of a human life and the performance of ritual by the men of *tsav* of the community concerned. Thus the world cannot prosper without death, and even in their approved role the *mbatsav* cause death. Thus, too, when a pleasant, wholly unimportant adult or a child dies when there are no obvious incidents that might have furnished motive for the death of that individual, then it is assumed that that individual was killed by the witches in concert as the wholly legitimate sacrifice to the great fetishes, the victims of which preferably are persons of minor social importance. But if there are too many such deaths, this explanation no longer serves.

Sometimes, for not all men are good or work together for the common benefit, the *mbatsav* engage in struggles for power. Then they kill not only for necessity and the land, but to weaken each other. Such a situation is "known" to exist when there is much illness in the land, when people die, and when eventually the land itself refuses to bear its crops. Then there is no remedy but to summon all the people of the land to drink sasswood that the evil may die.[2] Today, with this rather drastic social surgery effectively forbidden by the British government, people can only run away or sit out the witches' feud to the end, until only one remains alive and master. This possibility is one of the great cautionary myths of the Tiv, usually told to remind the elders, as the *mbatsav* or witches, of the dangers of a warfare which leaves a land desolate and the conqueror without people. A few men say their grandfathers actually lived through such a battle. The people among whom I lived believed themselves in this situation; they labeled Anyam a witch interested in killing for his own ends, and gave Shingir the bare benefit of the doubt.

Yet, of the two, I found Anyam the more congenial, simply because he was

[2]The bark of sasswood (*Erythrophleum guineense*) is highly poisonous, causing symptoms of depression of the circulation, difficulty of breathing, vomiting, and convulsions, the latter resulting from the direct action on the medulla centre. Drunk as an infusion, Tiv occasionally use it as medicine to cause convulsions, but only when they consider the alternative certain death (as for example to induce the afterbirth when it has not appeared thirty-six or forty-eight hours after birth). Its most common use was in ordeal, either individual or mass. In such ordeals, the innocent drink the infusion, vomit, and live; the guilty are unable to vomit and die.

reserved and quiet where Shingir was boisterous and apparently without self-restraint. On the other hand, Shingir could talk well and freely. Anyam would not converse. He would answer questions, and occasionally a direct question would set him off, propounding his views with near fanaticism. He was not a man with whom one could be at ease.

One day when I had found him alone in his reception hut hafting a dagger, nothing I could say drew more than a grunt from him. Nevertheless, since everyone else was drinking beer, I sat on determined to get at least a rest from my walk before I left. Eventually Anyam put aside his work and took up his pipe. I lit a cigarette and had all but finished it, still in silence, before Anyam had finished shredding tobacco and had tamped it into the pipe. As he scrabbled through the ashes for a coal, he spoke, "Once you asked me the names of all my ancestors and of all the children they begot. Where are they all?"

"You have said," I spoke cautiously, not sure to what Anyam was leading, "that your father's eldest brother's children left here, long ago, and are sitting in the bush."

Anyam made no response.

"The rest," I said rather blankly, "are dead."

A glow of hate lit Anyam's eyes and smouldered in his voice. "Dead. All of them. Even my mother's sons. Killed."

"Shingir?" I ventured.

"Shingir." In Anyam's mouth, the name was an expletive. "Shingir! Yes, but it was I, I who killed them, so that I might become great in the land. Like my father. While he lived, we had the greater power, and Shingir was afraid. Now that he is dead, Shingir is trying to kill me. Shingir has already killed those who came between him and what he desired. We have both killed that we may be strong. Now I can protect my own. Now I am as strong as Shingir, but Ahuma still fears. Soon all the land will know my strength."

Tsav is nourished by its exercise, or, in Tiv idiom, by the witch's feeding upon human flesh. Anyam was saying that he had fed his own power of witchcraft upon those under his control that it might quickly wax strong enough for him to turn it upon his enemy. In one sense, he had merely forestalled the death of his dependents at Shingir's hands, an alternative that would have left him just as deprived of followers but without any increment in his own strength as a witch. Nevertheless, Anyam's insistence that he himself killed by witchcraft was abnormal. Normally a Tiv always accuses someone else.

Anyam continued to explain himself. "You ought to know with what sort of man you are dealing. Shingir speaks with a double tongue that deceives many Europeans. I have thrown many times," he laid his hand on his divining apparatus, "and I see, though it is hard to tell about Europeans, that your heart is turned edgewise against Shingir, but that you have no grudge against me. We, the witches of this land, have not met by night since you came, and we shall not meet again until you go. That we decided when you came here. Yet the great owls are heard by night. [Anyam named the species of owl known to be one of the metamorphoses of the witches when they go to warn their victims] and since I have not gone out, it must be Shingir. You have the ability to bear this knowledge, and I want you to know the meaning of what happens in this land while you are here. Then, when you leave, you may tell the District Officer."

"It is useless to speak to the District Officer of witchcraft, Anyam. You know it."

"I know it," said Anyam. "If the Europeans of the government were men with hearts to understand these matters, they might make us all drink sasswood. But that they have forbidden. There is nothing to stop the witches now." The notion amused Anyam. "Tell them that Shingir eats the tax money, that he does not speak truly about the law cases from this land. Tell them of any of the matters to which they do not close their eyes and their ears, then you and I will soon be rid of Shingir. Once he no longer has the government's backing, I can swing the rest of the witches, whom he influences by day, and then I can kill him."

Anyam picked up his dagger and weighed it in his hand somberly. "Shingir plays the fool, drinking beer with the youngsters. He is a man of many quarrels, a noisy man, not one who discusses affairs slowly and quietly and heals the land. He is spoiling the land; he has killed my people, and I shall kill him. Help me in this, and you will do well."

Both Shingir and Anyam were feared as witches. But Anyam was also feared as one fears those who may suddenly become wholly mad. It was, I think, this fear that kept followers from him. Certainly, on the one occasion I saw Anyam publicly open in his enmity to Shingir, it was Shingir that we all followed.

It was at one of the beer drinks Anyam so rarely attended. When the second calabash started around, Shingir, mellow with beer, reminded us all that the well-being of his land and his people was his heart's only desire. He invariably did so, and everyone in earshot invariably made the proper response, chorusing, "You speak well, Shingir."

Before we could turn the conversation, Anyam's voice stopped us all. "Your land is spoiled, Shingir, and your people are dead. Where is Tar? Where is Ndor?"

Shingir was silent. The rest of us sat, not knowing where to look.

Anyam's catalogue of the dead was long, and, though he paused after each name, Shingir found nothing to say. When Anyam finally ceased, Shingir blundered from his seat, down the path out of the homestead, strangely deflated. After some moments we all followed him. Anyam was wrapt in meditation and seemed to want none and nothing of us. It was only later, much later, that Shingir began to roar about "that liar" and to regain firmness of flesh and feature.

Shingir was not widely credited with most of the dead Anyam had named. Yet, even to my knowledge, almost everyone believed that Shingir had killed the three men who had stood between himself and the homestead headship. Certainly those who would discuss such matters with me unanimously attributed the unhealthy state of the people in Shingir's homestead to Shingir's powers of witchcraft, and cited the situation as proof of a reign of fear. Nevertheless, there *were* people in Shingir's homestead, quite a lot of people. Indeed, it was one of the largest I have known in Tivland. Anyam's was nearly empty. The homesteads of "evil" witches are usually empty, and illness in the homestead testifies to their wickedness. Why, then, these people stayed was one of the great riddles of Shingir's position as a witch.

Kusugh, who would almost surely be Shingir's successor to the homestead headship, was during Shingir's lifetime, his right hand man. He was a smooth-skinned, well-spoken man in his late 40's, a man who was never quite in the foreground yet never quite overlooked. Shingir made great use of him, for Kusugh excelled in all practical arrangements, anything from getting a number of men out on the farms at about the same time to extracting further bride-wealth from penniless and goatless sons-in-law.

I had a great deal to do with Kusugh myself. If anything went wrong with my huts, or with supplies of food, water, and firewood, it was to Kusugh that I turned, and Kusugh always solved my difficulties. Many of the elders discussed their farms and their livestock with Kusugh. But no one ever asked his opinion on those matters that lay within the province of the elders, and Kusugh never volunteered any opinion on such matters. If anything of importance came up in Shingir's absence, he always followed the absolutely correct procedure: soothe everyone just enough to keep them from blows until the matter can be decided by the right person, Shingir.

I was never able to discover what Kusugh thought of Anyam. I very soon realized, however, that Kusugh both hated and feared Shingir, though at first I had few "facts" to support this impression: a single remark by Kusugh's wife, that she had once run away from Shingir's only to return when she discovered that Kusugh was "afraid to settle elsewhere," and my own awareness of how much of what I knew to Shingir's discredit was first learned from Kusugh.

It was Kusugh who had brought my full attention to Shingir's refusal to help Ugele, a man widely liked as a pleasant companion and respected as an in-dustrious farmer. Ugele was one of those unfortunates who had been given curative doses of antimalarials while he was in the British army. Consequently, when he returned to his home, he was subject, as few adults among the Tiv are, to acute attacks of malaria. He was often quite seriously ill, and I had given him medicine, enough to break the fever. Shingir had flatly refused to prescribe any herbal remedies, to perform any ritual, or to have the cause of Ugele's illness investigated by a diviner. Such behavior could only mean that it was Shingir who was willing Ugele's illness.

It was Kusugh who had informed me that Agum, another member of the homestead and a great mimic and song-maker, used to hold Shingir up to ridicule in his songs. Traditionally such songs must avoid the libelous: they must be either true or impossible. Shingir had not really minded the song referring to what he did when he changed himself into a boar at night. No one can do such a thing. Moreover, the boar in the song was a most potent and aggressive animal. Shingir did object to the verses about burnt bank notes, sticking to his friends against the prosecution of the British government, and holding his tongue when provoked by Anyam. Worst of all, if common knowledge of the events and the occasion and manner of the singing hadn't plainly shown the satiric intent of the verses, one might have sworn they were meant as praise songs. There is no reason not to repeat praise songs, and since Agum's had good tunes, they were widely sung. After the death of Anyam's father, when Shingir became powerful in the land, Agum came down with smallpox and barely survived. From that time, Shingir was not mentioned in Agum's singing, "for the next time, Shingir will kill him." Smallpox is one of the most blatant manifestations of potent witchcraft. Public opinion concurred with Kusugh's interpretation of Agum's illness.

It was Kusugh who mentioned in the same breath that Shingir commanded the great fetishes which demand life and that too many of the children borne by the wives in the homestead had died. Uvia, Shingir's brother's son, was the only survivor of the ten children his mother had borne. Infant mortality in Tivland is high. In Shingir's homestead it was so high that it attracted the attention of the Tiv. They considered it unnatural. Kusugh had even implied that Shingir had taken far more lives than he could possibly need unless he were involved in a flesh debt.

It is believed that witches sometimes share the flesh of their human victims in mystical feast with other witches, generally of lesser power, who are then under obligation to return the feast. Once such a chain of indebtedness starts in a community, there is, and can be, no end to the deaths needed to continue the feasting, any more than there is ever an end to any of the chains of gift-giving and counterfeasting on any level. Such a situation is believed to exist whenever two features of every day life are prominent: when there are more deaths in a community than the normal rationale of witchcraft can satisfactorily explain and when an unpopular man is able to impose his will on others and become very influential. Both these conditions certainly existed here. But I still could not see why the people did not adopt the usual Tiv remedy of going away and leaving the witch in isolation. A Tiv can always flee to his mother's people for protection.

I asked Kusugh. He turned, as though he had long been waiting for an opportunity to speak: "Our mother's kin *do not* protect us. Ugele's mother's people sent him back. Agum's mother's people sent him back. Uvia's mother's people sent him back. And mine made me return. All of us who are here have been sent back. That is how we know there is a flesh debt, and that is how we know where Shingir has his flesh debts. Through them he controls not only this land, but all those about us where otherwise we might find refuge. There is no escape for us. There is no escape for the land, for Anyam and Shingir are both killing us. Only if we, the younger men who are not witches, could rise up and force every elder in this land to drink sasswood, then it would end. And then the District Officer would kill us. Why were we here when you came? If you had come to take us to the mines, you would have taken us away from Anyam and Shingir. Why did we want you to stay? The witches would not meet at night while you were here. Why do we still want you to stay? Who of us has died since you came? Not one of us. But the land has been spoiled, and when you go we will die again, those of us who do not please Anyam and Shingir. Both men have killed to obtain power, nor will they cease to kill and kill—Anyam, until he holds this land in the palm of his hand, Shingir until he is able to hold the land undisputed."

Kusugh saw little hope for the land. He himself hoped to survive by doing as little as possible to attract envy while making himself necessary to those whom he feared. Most of the men in Shingir's homestead were pursuing the same course.

Only among the women was I able to find anyone with a real affection for Shingir. Some quality in his personality seemed to arouse in them a peculiar mixture of pity and trust, spiced with a suggestion of sexual attraction. Even Kusugh's wife did not dislike him. Those of Shingir's fifteen wives who had been with him for more than ten years were very fond of him. Although some of the younger ones seemed to prefer his absence to his presence, they all stuck by him. In his turn, Shingir provided well for them; they had large farms, good clothes, and comparatively many trade utensils. He was indulgent with them, demanding rather less than the normal respect a Tiv wife shows her husband, not noticing if they drank too much, and not suspicious of their trips to visit relatives.

Shingir's senior wife, Mfaga, fussed over his food and worried about his health. Long after I had convinced Shingir that I could not cure his ailments, Mfaga continued to ask me to treat him. "He is ill. It is not because of his age that he can no longer beget children. Give me medicine for him, medicine to heal him, not just medicine for beer headaches." But I had only aspirin to give her.

"You cannot know Shingir," Mfaga once told me. "You have never seen him when he was not ill and afraid at heart. To know him, you should have known him long ago, when I bore him our first child. Then the land was at peace. Anyam's father was alive, and the land prospered. None then could hoe a farm so well as Shingir, nor dance so well. None was so well liked, and none so admired. Then, even then, Anyam, whose heart was black with envy of those who had farms, and livestock, and wives, and children, and friends, even then Anyam hated Shingir. We four who know him, we were married to him then, before Anyam's father died." She stared into the fortunate past.

"And when he died?"

"Then Anyam was free to do evil. He fed the evil within him on the lives that lay in the palm of his hand, his mother's sons and his father's. And so the land began its dying, and we began to know fear. Then, when the water came," she was speaking of the great smallpox epidemic, the marks of which were on children of 10, on adults, and in genealogies, "we, the people of Shingir also died. Kusugh said Shingir was killing us to feed his own power; he lied. I saw Shingir weep when his brothers died, and I know that Anyam was too much for him. I also was afraid, but it was not Shingir that I feared. Anyam! Anyam! Who gave Shingir that wen upon his neck? Who has made him unable to beget children? Do you know how fear can rot the heart of a man? And yet, with fear in his heart, he tries to protect us. There is death in the land, and war at night, but while Shingir yet lives we will remain. Look. Look out that door. In this homestead you can hear the voices of children and the laughter of women, smell the smell of cooking food, and hear the voices of men. But in Anyam's homestead there is nothing to hear; there is only silence."

Not long ago, I had a letter from one of my servants. He wanted some money for a goat for a ceremony for his second wife. At the end of the symptoms and the request came the news: "Taxes are spoiling the land, and there has been no rain for the crops, but everyone you know is alive and well. Except Shingir. Anyam was the stronger, and Shingir is dead."

I sent goat money by the next post, partly in memory of faithful service, partly because his wife's illness had begun during that most unhealthy season at Shingir's, and quite irrationally because Shingir was dead and I had never really liked him. I still don't like him, even in retrospect, though I wonder if I haven't wronged him. Aggressive, loud-mouthed, careless of his person, drunken, bluff in manner, and underhand in dealing—yes. But also a man trusted by his wives, though feared by his relatives. A man without friends, but capable of holding some followers and convives. Above all, a sick and frightened man who believed, as every Tiv there believed, that he was engaged in a deadly duel with a man evil at heart and strong in witchcraft. I find myself sorry for his land, sorry that it was Anyam who conquered.

Sorcery and Structure
in Fore Society
Shirley Lindenbaum

In their introduction to *Gods, Ghosts and Men in Melanesia*, Lawrence and Meggitt consider the problem of why sorcery is an important institution in some societies and not in others. They note, for instance, that it is an obsession in Dobu and among the Tangu but is rarely used among the Mae Enga and the Ngaing. They look to the socio-political sphere for an explanation and suggest that sorcery can be demonstrated at work in at least two types of society: those with fluid and those with stable local organizations.[1] Among the former they suggest, following Hogbin, that "sorcery accusations are a necessary means of easing tension between individuals who lack the security of membership in solidary groups."[2] As examples of such societies they list Dobu, Tangu, Garia, and Huli. Among the latter, with stable local organizations, they note that these are "based on permanently settled descent groups or congeries of such groups which, in the absence of wars for territorial or other economic aggrandisement, can preserve their identity only by mutual suspicion, rivalry, and hostility. Sorcery accusations act here both as an important medium for expressing enmity and as an excuse for initiating warfare, which is ultimately the most effective means of relieving feelings of aggression."[3] Among examples of this second type of local organization they list the Kuma and the Kainantu peoples (Kamano, Jate, Fore, and Usurufa).

I am concerned here to explore the obsessive interest in sorcery manifested by one of the Kainantu peoples, the South Fore. There are two ways of approaching the problem. On the one hand, South Fore residential mobility gives rise to sorcery accusations among individuals who lack the security of membership in solidary groups. Yet these accusations also appear to preserve the identity of their groups by mutual suspicion, rivalry, and hostility leading to a kind of

[1] P. Lawrence and M. J. Meggitt, p. 17.
[2] *Ibid.*
[3] *Ibid.*

warfare unrelated to territorial acquisition. It could be said from this that South Fore local organization is based on fluid groups in the guise of descent groups, qualifying them for a place in both types of society outlined by Lawrence and Meggitt. I prefer to interpret the situation as an indication that the South Fore are wrongly classified and belong instead to the first type of society, that based on fluid local organization. I would also say that this type of social system may give rise to sorcery accusations which are produced both as an expression of insecurity among co-residents and as a political means by which social groups express their identity.

SOUTH FORE SOCIETY

The South Fore have ample fertile land for a small population. With a density at an average of 33 persons per square mile (compare central Enga with an average of 120 per square mile, and in places exceeding 300),[4] their political problems are not focussed on restricting the access of outsiders to group resources. Rather, the opposite is the case, how to maintain group strength for defense against aggressive neighbors. A South Fore parish[5] therefore readily admits newcomers and provides them with fertile land.

Indeed, the Fore may always have had ample land resources. Their mythology is not that of conquerors; it suggests instead the adaptation of a people to a new environment, of small bands of original settlers who filter into new territory, seek out water sources, and settle in scattered locations to build houses and plant gardens. They identify plants and trees as they encounter them and take group names from clumps of trees or other topographical features wherever they settle. Men of Wanitabe parish, for example, say that their ancestors planted their first gardens by a local stream (wani=water, tabe=big); the men of Kume, by a kume (Garcinia) tree, and the men of Kalu by the kalu (Elaeocarpus) tree.

Subsistence is based on the cultivation of sweet potato, taro, yam, sugarcane, winged bean, and a variety of other vegetables, indigenous ("pitpit"—Setaria sp.) and introduced (beans, corn, tomatoes). The amount of land under Imperata grass and wild canes is not extensive when compared with the denuded slopes around Goroka, and much forest land still remains. This fact would support Watson's view that Highlands horticulture in this area is a relatively recent innovation,[6] and certainly many Fore stories describe men hunting for possums, birds, cassowaries, and rodents, and women catching frogs. Diamond also reports a discriminating system of zoological classification, and he notes that, although the Fore today subsist largely on cultivated vegetables, a few genera-

[4]M. J. Meggitt, 1967, pp. 20–35.

[5]An account of South Fore political organization can be found in Glasse and Lindenbaum, pp. 308–26. There three important structural units are examined: the parish, the section, and the line. For this paper, it should only be noted that the parish refers to the largest aggregate with a distinct political identity. It is a coalition of factions united for security and defense. The section is a subdivision of the parish and is a residential rather than a genealogical unit. The section is also the effective political and jural unit. The line, the smallest subdivision of the parish, is a genealogical unit. Its name indicates its place of origin. Every parish contains enclave lines which originated in other parishes, and which, if they wish, enjoy dual residential and gardening rights.

[6]J. B. Watson, 1965a, pp. 295–309; 1965b, pp. 438–50.

tions ago they may have depended more heavily on wild animals and plants. He suggests that the detailed classification of animals represents "an economic relict of disappearing food habits."[7]

Social relationships, both large-scale political associations and the dyadic relationships of kinship, are characterized by a degree of flexibility and expediency which allows for constant adjustment to changing situations and demands. Individuals and groups readily find refuge in distant parishes by right of kinship, friendship, or military alliance. The need for kinsmen may be met by appropriately redefining a relationship. Compared with the high value Central Enga, for instance, place on agnation as the primary basis for recruiting male members of groups, the South Fore exhibit what might be described as a cavalier attitude toward genealogical relatedness.

There are several aspects to this kind of fictional kinship. Firstly, Fore adopt infants belonging to classificatory kin and co-residents. The transaction is of economic benefit to all concerned.[8] They also permit the occasional adoption of a young Fore boy by the Kamano or Keiagana people to the north in return for a place of transit and hospitality on the journey to Kainantu or Goroka. Secondly, they create needed kinsmen if a person in the appropriate category is not close at hand or if a number of extra kinsmen are desired to extend exchange relationships. A mechanism exists for fabricating such relatives,[9] most of whom are mother's brothers or sisters—relatives who provide the basic commodities, women and food. Thirdly, there are categories of people who in a sense function like kinsmen, in that they provide essential support. Their services are recognized from time to time throughout life and at death with a special payment. Age mates are one such category,[10] another are wagoli (wa=man, agoli=base, root). Wagoli were allies in wartime, and their territories are always considered places of refuge. They are roots to which new branches may attach themselves.[11] Wagoli of one generation become kinsmen in the next.

The obverse of this attitude toward the value of relationships holds true. Real kinsmen who live at too great a distance, or who for some other reason do not fulfil expected obligations, gradually become less important, and in a sense the tie lapses.[12]

The social system then allows a flexible manipulative approach to personal and group relationships. Within a fixed framework, the components may be advantageously reordered and redefined. It is a social system in which true kinsmen are supplemented or replaced by fictional kinsmen, and in which the status of other categories of people is elevated by redefinition in recognition of the services they provide.

---

[7]J. Diamond, p. 1104.

[8]As an example, one adopting father gave food worth $14 to the mother's father and brothers, their due payment for the fruit of the marriage. He also gave some pay to his wife's brothers, as if his wife had indeed produced the child. He expects a small reciprocal payment of food from both parties. He also expects to receive a large portion of the child's bride price to repay him for his lifetime care of the child.

[9]R. M. Glasse, 1969, p. 30.

[10]A discussion of Fore age mates will be found in Lindenbaum and Glasse, pp. 165–73.

[11]R M. Glasse and S. Lindenbaum, p. 311. I am indebted to Graham Scott, Summer Institute of Linguistics, for his assistance in helping to sort out many linguistic tricks and puzzles.

[12]R. M. Glasse and S. Lindenbaum, p. 322.

Such a system has both strength and weaknesses. While the parish may incorporate newcomers to boost strength, the repeated change in composition robs the group of a sense of solidarity. In the course of a lifetime, any man may reside in a number of parishes and support the activities of each host group in turn.[13] In wartime some segments within a single parish therefore regard each other with suspicion because of their ties with kinsmen and former co-residents. In present-day affairs this status ambiguity among parish members is reflected in sorcery beliefs and accusations.

SORCERY AND ILLNESS

Analysis of material from an ethno-botanical collection, of ethnographic statements, and of observed behavior indicates that the South Fore classify illnesses in a consistent and systematic way. There are two major categories of disease: defined and distinguished by beliefs about causation. In the first place, there are certain maladies caused by the malicious actions of men against men; these diseases result from acts of sorcery.[14] Other diseases are not caused by the evil machinations of men and are therefore not attributed to sorcerers. They are believed to be brought about instead by nature spirits inhabiting the trees, vines, bamboos, water, or rocks in the spirit places associated with the parish of residence. They may also be caused by the ghosts of the recently dead belonging to the parish of residence, or they may result from violations of social rules and expectations among co-residents.[15]

Some details of the beliefs concerning the activities of sorcerers, the clinical manifestations of sorcery-caused ailments, and the appropriate course of action will serve to indicate the logic in the classification system.

SORCERY-CAUSED ILLNESS

Fore are distracted by the frequent occurrence of a degenerative disease of the central nervous system called *kuru*, a word meaning trembling, fear.[16] It is uniformly fatal, has an average duration of a year, and a yearly rate of incidence throughout the entire region of 1% of the population (higher in South Fore).[17] Despite more than a decade of intensive enquiry, no cure for the disease has been found, and locally it is still believed to be the result of sorcery.

The sorcerer is said to steal some physical particle intimately associated with the victim—who is usually a woman[18]—such as food remnants, fragments of a

[13]*Ibid.*

[14]The morpheme *kio* ("poison" in pidgin) is often present in the name of a disease caused by such a technical act. I am using sorcery here as Evans-Pritchard defined it for the Zande. It operates directly through spells, rites, and medicines. It is conscious, voluntary, taught, and may be bought. This attitude toward religion as a technology to be used for practical ends is typically Melanesian. See Lawrence and Meggitt, p. 18.

[15]This sub-category could be regarded as resulting from the action of one man against another. However, the Fore consider the cause of the illness here to be the wrongful behaviour of the victim. In the case of sorcery, no such attitude of guilt is assumed by the victim. This is discussed again later.

[16]*Kuru* literature is voluminous.

[17]M. P. Alpers, pp. 65–82.

[18]A recent article by R. Hornabrook and D. Moir notes that since 1957 there has been a progressive rise each year in the number of men who have died of *kuru*.

skirt, hair, nail clippings, or excrement. With certain leaves and a sorcerer's stone he makes a bundle, tying the components together with vines. There may be some variation in procedure, but he always makes a bundle enclosing a marginal particle taken from the victim. He then utters a spell. Beating the bundle with a stick, he calls the victim by name and says, "I break the bones of your legs, I break the bones of your feet, I break the bones of your arms, I break the bones of your hands, and finally I make you die."[19] He then places the bundle in muddy ground, and as the bundle rots, so the victim's health deteriorates. Progressive motor incoordination is in fact the clinical course of the disease.

A second example concerns *karena*, a category of diseases of the respiratory system including tuberculosis, emphysema, and other lengthy delibitating diseases, particularly of the aged. *Karena* is in fact the word for "old person." In this case it is believed that the sorcerer places a certain crushed stone in a small length of bamboo tube suitable for a man's pipe. He carries this to the victim's garden and slips it through the fence. The victim feels the desire to smoke, sees the bamboo, puts his tobacco in it, and as he smokes, the poison passes into his body.[20] Some *karena* sorcerers are said to use another method. They place the poison in the victim's drinking water or food. He feels internal pains and his stomach is said to be on fire. He has a fever and his breathing comes fast. After this initial manifestation of the disease, any future illness will probably kill him, though it would be insufficient to harm a healthy person.

A third example concerns the illness known as *nankili*. Here the sorcerer is thought to sharpen pig, cassowary, or possum bones (*kili* means "little needles") and fold them into certain leaves. He smokes his pipe, calls the name of the victim, and blows smoke across the bundle. The nails fly from the bundle into the body of the victim, who falls ill with sharp chest and body pains.

How are sorcery-caused ailments to be avoided? Since Fore fear the hostile acts of other men, they take care not to give the sorcerer the materials he needs. People hide their hair or nail clippings and make use of deep pit latrines.[21] When women move from an old to a new house they take particular care not to leave behind old fragments of clothing. Women, after parturition in the seclusion huts set aside for menstruation and childbirth, wash blood from the placenta and throw it into the latrine. They scrape the ground where the blood fell to remove any trace and burn the child's umbilical cord, stirring it among the ashes of the fire until it is undetectable.

During periods of hostility between adjacent parishes men guard the water holes at night to prevent enemy sorcerers from contaminating them. When the incidence of *kuru* in one hamlet is high the members may close off the foot track leading through it, thus depriving travellers of the opportunity to pick up food remnants between their toes.

Despite these various kinds of preventive behavior, however, people still fall ill, and in particular many women succumb to *kuru*. There is a variety of cures,

[19]Another description of *kuru* sorcery can be found in R. Berndt, pp. 218ff.

[20]There is no one-to-one correlation of indigenous disease categories and those of Western medicine. It is interesting to note, however, that the implication of *karena* sorcery is that smoking may be hazardous to health.

[21]The first missionary to visit the neighboring Awa people had to take South Fore with him to show the Awa how to construct pit latrines.

the essential part of all of them is divination to reveal the identity of the sorcerer. The commonest method makes use of possum meat. The victim's husband, together with several kinsmen, age mates, or male co-residents, place hair clippings of the victim in a length of bamboo tube. Then into another tube the diviner pushes some freshly killed possum flesh. Striking one bamboo against the other, he calls out the name of the suspect. Then he puts the bamboo of possum meat in the fire. If it remains uncooked, this is proof of the man's guilt.

At this point of the inquiry the victim may die. The husband, still harboring strong misgivings, may invite the local group of an acquitted man to come and eat and smoke in peace. He gives the visitors tobacco to smoke and a meal of vegetables prepared in a communal earth oven. If on returning home one of the visitors falls ill, the victim's ghost is said to have unmasked him at last. Divination may also be carried out on the day of mourning before the corpse is interred.[22] Visitors are invited to attend a ceremony in which they have to approach the corpse one by one. A sudden release of fluid by the corpse indicates the guilt of the man close by at the time. His companions may be unaware that they have been harboring a sorcerer. The members of one parish section called to undergo an investigation felt the need to provide themselves with supernatural protection before they left home. They performed a rite to prevent the public disclosure of any unconfessed sorcerer. If the day's proceedings had resulted in an exposure they indicated that they would not condemn the man. Rather, they would have been angry with him for placing them in a position of danger by allowing them to attend.

In most cases, however, the search takes place while the victim is still alive. A suspect may be called to attend a court hearing[23] at the victim's hamlet, where he always arrives with a company of kin and supporters, about ten in all, the war party of old. Accusers and accused sit in opposed groups, the orators on each side alternating in a debate that lasts from mid-morning till late afternoon. At the end of the day if the conflict remains unresolved the visitors depart without an offer of food. There may have been some temporary catharsis, however, in a battle fought with words.

Of the three kinds of sorcery described,[24] most activity is stimulated by cases of *kuru* and *karena*. Both diseases threaten group survival and viability; one threatens the reproductive powers of the group, the other the group leadership. *Nankili*, however, is rarely fatal, and the emphasis is on cures and treatment rather than on identification.

ILLNESS NOT CAUSED BY SORCERY

A spirit-caused ailment, *mai'ena biyei* (literally, "that ground over there hit him"), may be the result of a pregnant woman's touching a certain tree, vine, or other spirit-inhabited object in the reserved parts of the forest of her husband's parish.[25] The infant is then born deaf or blind and is referred to as *mai yagala*,

---

[22]In the past the body may have been eaten. See R. M. Glasse, pp. 748–54.

[23]For a discussion of informal court hearings see R. Berndt and C. Berndt.

[24]Fore have beliefs concerning many other kinds of sorcery. See R. Berndt, pp. 213ff. These examples have been selected to illustrate three kinds of theory of causation.

[25]Stands of forest thought to be inhabited by spirits should be left uncut. In fact, men sometimes do remove bamboos or vines from them without apparent harm.

"ground or spirit child." Again, a man may have a stiff neck or he cuts his foot with an axe. Relief is gained by his revisiting the forest area, finding the offended tree, and making a gift of money and food. He hangs a string of shells on the branches and rubs the trunk with pig fat. He should also take along a medicinal meal of cooked pork bespat with *ni* (*Commelinaceae tradescantia*)[26] and afterwards eat it.

It should be noted that infants born with gross physical deformities are not treated in this way. Monstrous births are considered an offense to the entire community, and their occurrence causes a community-wide schism. Men hold the women responsible for the affront. They believe they have been polluted and seclude themselves in order to perform purificatory rituals similar to those for youths at initiation. The women kill the malformed infant and also withdraw.[27] The abomination has threatened the dividing line between human and non-human beings, and the men respond by uniting to exhibit the most basic of social boundaries, that of men against women in a hierarchical arrangement.

Ghost-caused ailments may occur if a man removes vegetables or cuts a banana tree or sugarcane from the gardens of someone recently deceased. The harvest should remain as a sign of mourning, and the ghost punishes those who behave without sufficient respect. It enters the body of the offender, or one of his close kinsmen, causing weakness, nausea, and fainting spells. The sick person may be cured by a "smoke man," a specialist magician who sits beside him smoking. The magician sees the angry ghost and blows it out with the smoke. The victim must then visit the grave with a libation of pig's blood.

The final category of ailments concerns the infringement of social rules amongst the living. If a man cuts down someone else's tree, his son or daughter may fall ill, or blemishes may appear on the child's neck or face. To effect a cure, he must offer the owner compensation in goods or money. Appeased, the latter spits medicinal plants and barks on the child's skin or gives him a meal of pork with *ni*.

These three categories thus have several things in common. Encroachments against nature spirits, or against ghosts of the recently dead, or against neighbors must be made good by some kind of compensation; the spirit or ghost receives food, the angry person material payment. The victim is then restored to health. There is a Melanesian quality in the therapy—the notion of compensation for injury, with its emphasis on equality and a return to the *status quo*. It resembles judgments in indigenous court cases where fines are estimated to equal just the amount of damage.[28] In addition, the notion of bribery, of persuasiveness accompanied by a gift, resembles the behavior among allies in time of war and the social manipulations common in everyday affairs.

[26]*Ni*, like pig fat, is believed to have magical reviving powers. It is frequently used in rituals and men spit it on food given to children of the parish section to protect them from disease. *Ni* is a wild plant, deriving its strength from its association with the bush spirits. See Barrau, p. 132.

[27]Women also kill one of twins.

[28]As an example, children playfully left large rocks on a road where a tractor was to pass. The trailer was uncoupled, and the pin broke. The driver and his crew that evening held a court hearing and fined the parents of each of five children $2. After a moment's consideration the crew returned the $10 to the parents, demanding instead sweet potatoes and yams worth $10. Thus they solved an immediate practical problem for themselves and forced the culprits to do unpleasant work carrying vegetables from the gardens in the chill of dusk. An air of good humor and satisfaction surrounded the whole affair.

Further comment can now be made about some other features of the system of classification. Dangerous diseases that usually cause death are ascribed to sorcery. These are also a threat to important groups in the society, the women who insure its continuity, and the men who protect it. Minor ailments among adults, and the sickness and death of children belong to the non-sorcery category.

A second characteristic of the system relates to the ascription of guilt. All maladies result from some form of socially disapproved action. In the case of sorcery, the action comes from the evil machinations of outsiders, enemies in another parish or parish section. Sorcery allegations thus appear to be statements about the relationships of men residing in different groups. Non-sorcery ailments, however, place guilt inside the group where its location is known and therefore does not require detection. Minor illnesses result from wrongdoing by the victim himself, or a close kinsman, and concern his relationship with his group's land, former members of the group, or neighbors. Thus, the assignment of the origin of a minor illness appears to involve a statement about group membership, rules of behavior, and common responsibilities.

Although minor ailments are in fact ascribed to some kind of breach by a group member, fear of illness does not appear to operate as a sanction regulating behavior in any important way. Central moral issues—adultery, theft, and the destruction of property—are handled by direct action. Infringements result in beatings, court hearings, compulsory compensation, or temporary withdrawal of group privileges.[29] Beliefs about ailments not caused by sorcery therefore do not appear to be strong mechanisms for social control. The classification system itself indicates where the danger to the group lies; minor ailments involving little dangers (or big dangers to children) require little cures and adjustments. Minor ailments concern social challenges that do not threaten group unity or integrity (of which the Fore have little), and the treatments can therefore be carried out at home. Sorcery discussions, however, are statements about severe ailments involving major dangers to the group. The treatment demands intergroup action.

Sorcery accusations also do not appear to be mechanisms of social control;[30] rather, sorcery beliefs operate as an expression of present political reality. Acts of preventive medicine, such as the refusal to eat food in another parish, or the extra care taken with food leavings in some places rather than in others, express the social distance between the men in the groups concerned, the current degree of friendship or mistrust. The location of a sorcery challenge indicates the extent of mutual loyalty felt by a group of co-residents. Sometimes the challenge is issued across parish borders, and sometimes it occurs between sections of the same parish; in either case, it signals possible political separation.

This history of the relationships among the three present parishes of Waisa, Wanitabe, and Yagareba illustrate the process. About 25 years ago some men of Wanitabe lived at Waisa, where they had taken refuge during war. The two groups worked together in harmony until the death of several of the Wanitabe leaders unsettled the remainder. Wanitabe accused sorcerers at Waisa of de-

---

[29] A young boy hit his sister. His elders placed a ban on his portion of pork from the girl's bride price. When the marriage day arrived those who had imposed the sanction relented, but the youth as a point of honour refused to accept the meat.

[30] R. Berndt, p. 220, makes a similar observation.

pleting their numbers, and after short battle, they and their families moved to their present ground adjacent to Yagareba. From 1961 to June, 1963, men of Wanitabe and Yagareba appeared to be living together without stress. They combined to sponsor communal feasts when the demands of kinship and friendship required. At that time they spoke of their relationship as that of "brother parishes." Then in 1963, both groups suffered heavy losses from *kuru*.[31] By 1970, Wanitabe and Yagareba regarded each other as enemies, and sorcery accusations flashed back and forth across the borders. Three Wanitabe men are currently serving gaol sentences on sorcery charges brought against them by men of Yagareba. The current atmosphere of hostility and suspicion is so acute that normal social congress between the two groups has ceased.[32] No visits may be made by any individual into the territory of the other, unless a specific invitation is issued ahead of time, for the two groups are still tied to each other by the mutual economic obligations of kinship. Recipients attend such kinship payments with the greatest wariness and are obviously ill at ease. Some fail to go at all, though they have been notified. Their share of food and valuables is delivered to them by recognized emissaries.

Sorcery challenges between previously allied parishes, or between different sections of one parish, are thus an indication of incipient fission. In the past, confrontations were followed by warfare and the migration of the defeated section. Now, appeals are made to the courts, and if migration is not feasible, social separation follows.

Although sorcery challenges may redefine the boundaries of a unit so that it foregoes previous alliances, there is a limit to the extent of shrinkage. Feelings of uncertainty may at times occur at close range, among members of one section, but here it is no longer politic to identify the suspect. A migrant from the North Fore who had resided since early manhood with a certain section of Yagareba parish was provoked by the imminent death of his wife from *kuru*. He made an undirected plea into the night for any guilty sorcerer residing with him in the same hamlet to undo his evil work and free the woman. His speech indicated that he believed that the sorcerer was indeed within hearing and that the attack was a slight to both himself and his wife for their services, he as warleader, she as a provider of food. Yet he was not in a position to identify anyone; political behavior at the level of the parish section is directed at attempts to widen rather than to diminish membership.

CONCLUSION

The nature of the South Fore social system, which facilitates the improvising of individual and group relationships, contributes to mutual mistrust among men at close range. Although the parish section freely admits outsiders to boost group strength, the very presence of newcomers and previously unrelated people in turn gives rise to suspicion, particularly in times of stress. Thus when a section member succumbs to a major illness the loss endangers the viability of the group because of its small scale. The presence of *kuru*, a widespread and

---

[31]Census records indicate that seven Wanitabe women and five Yagareba women and one Yagareba youth died of *kuru* in 1963.

[32]R. M. Glasse noted the change in 1969 and referred to it as a state of "social quarantine". R. M. Glasse, 1970, p. 211.

uncontrollable disease, gives rise to realistic fears for survival, which are expressed in terms of assault by sorcerers.

South Fore discussions about sorcery are part of a larger preoccupation with disease. Statements about the cause of an illness, besides being attempts to explain misfortune, are also statements about the structure of the society, the dangers to which its composite units are exposed, and the measures that can be taken to protect those units. Little dangers come from within; big dangers from without. If the origin of a minor ailment is located within a small residential group, the members are in agreement about mutual loyalties and more or less confident of their powers to insure them. If the origin of a major ailment comes from outside the smallest viable political unit, resolution of a misfortune of this order is a major political demand, and may require strong supernatural aid. Since South Fore society offers no more enduring mechanisms, group boundaries are increasingly defined and protected by ritual and metempirical argument in place of outright warfare.

Thus, the society does not appear to offer its members a strong basis for common loyalty, and sorcery discussions are an obsession. Accusations are a means of easing tensions among mutually unrelated people who reside together. They also have a political role as a mechanism by which social groups define themselves.

REFERENCES

ALPERS, M. P., "Epidemiological Changes in Kuru, 1957 to 1963," National Institutes of Neurological Diseases and Blindness Monograph No. 2, pp. 65–82, 1966.

BARRAU, J., "L'Humide et le Sec: An Essay on Ethnobiological Adaptation to Contrastive Environments in the Indo-Pacific Area," Peoples and Cultures of the Pacific, P. Vayda (Ed.), pp. 113–32, 1968.

BERNDT, C., "Socio-cultural Change in the East Central Highlands of New Guinea," Southwestern Journal of Anthropology, Vol. 9, pp. 112–38, 1953.

BERNDT, R., Excess and Restraint: Social Control Among a New Guinea Mountain People, Chicago, 1962.

DE LEPERVANCHE, M., "Descent, Residence and Leadership in the New Guinea Highlands," Oceania, Vol. XXXVIII, pp. 134–58, 163–89, 1967–68.

DIAMOND, J., "Zoological Classification System of a Primitive People," Science, Vol. 151, No. 3714, pp. 1102–04, 1966.

DOUGLAS, M., Purity and Danger: An Analysis of Concepts of Pollution and Taboo, New York, 1966.

EVANS-PRITCHARD, E. E., Witchcraft Oracles and Magic Among the Azande, London, 1937.

GAJDUSEK, D. C., "Kuru," Transactions of the Royal Society of Tropical Medicine and Hygiene, Vol. 57, pp. 151–69, 1963.

GAJDUSEK, D. C., "Definitive Bibliography on Kuru in New Guinea," National Institutes of Neurological Diseases and Blindness, Bethesda, 1965.

GLASSE, R. M., "Cannibalism in the Kuru Region of New Guinea," Transactions of the New York Academy of Science, Series 11, No. 29, pp. 748–54, 1967.

GLASSE, R. M., "Marriage in South Fore," *Pigs, Pearlshells, and Women: Marriage in the Highlands of New Guinea*, R. M. Glasse and M. J. Meggitt (Eds.), Englewood Cliffs, 1969.

GLASSE, R. M., "Some Recent Observations on *Kuru*," *Oceania*, Vol. XL, pp. 210–13, 1970.

GLASSE, R. M., and LINDENBAUM, S., "South Fore Politics," *Anthropological Forum*, Vol. 2, pp. 308–26, 1969.

HOGBIN, H. I., *Social Change*, London, 1958.

HORNABROOK, R. W., and MOIR, D. J., "*Kuru:* Epidemiological Trends," *Lancet*, Vol. 2, pp. 1175–79, 1970.

LANGNESS, L. L., "Some Problems in Conceptualisation of Highlands Social Structures," *American Anthropologist*, Vol. 66, Pt. 2, pp. 162–82, 1964.

LAWRENCE, P., and MEGGITT, M. J. (Eds.), *Gods, Ghosts and Men in Melanesia*, Melbourne, 1965.

LINDENBAUM, S., and GLASSE, R.M., "Fore Age Mates," *Oceania*, Vol. XLIX, pp. 165–74, 1969.

MEGGITT, M. J., *The Lineage System of the Mae Enga of New Guinea*, New York, 1965.

MEGGITT, M. J., "Patterns of Leadership Among the Mae Enga of New Guinea," *Anthropological Forum*, Vol. 2, pp. 20–35.

WATSON, J., "From Hunting to Horticulture in the New Guinea Highlands," *Ethnology*, Vol. 4, pp. 295–309, 1965a.

WATSON, J., "The Significance of a Recent Ecological Change in the Central Highlands of New Guinea," *Journal of the Polynesian Society*, Vol. 74, pp. 438–50, 1965b.

Gosiute Peyotism
Carling Malouf

At the present time there are two distinct peyote cults among the Gosiute, each of which claims to be the orthodox method.[1] One of these is known as the Tipi Way, and the other is known as the Sioux Way, or Western Slope Way. Both are basically of Plains origin but have undergone some modifications.

• • •

The Gosiute have at least been aware of peyote since 1907 when Ralph V. Chamberlain was making an ethnobotanical study among them, but there was no

[1]The Gosiute are a Shoshone speaking people who live in western Utah on two reservations. In 1936 there were 151 persons registered with the Indian Service at Deep Creek and 39 on the Skull Valley reserve.

organized ritual in its use.[2] According to Hayes, "There were less than a dozen users before 1925."[3] My own informants were very indefinite about these dates, but sometime between 1925 and 1928 the peyote movement gained momentum among the Gosiute and a cult of the Sioux Way was organized at Deep Creek. The ritual, paraphernalia, and organization were borrowed from the Utes with whom the Gosiute are in close contact. Thus, many persons from many different groups have all contributed to the formation and structure of the Gosiute peyote cults. The Tipi Way was likewise borrowed from the Utes but not before several "peyote missionaries" had made an impression.

Meetings are held by both groups about four or five times a month, depending on the season. During the fall, when nearly everyone is out picking pine nuts, only one or two meetings may be held. American holidays, illnesses, etc., are the chief occasions in which meetings are held. Efforts are made by the two cults to avoid having meetings on the same night, or within a few days apart. Meetings held on holidays may call for special variations in procedure, for example, on Memorial Day the Tipi Way people lay flowers along the altar. These flowers are usually made of crepe paper and are similar to those placed on the graves. Holiday, or week end meetings are usually held in a tipi, or tent while those held in cabins are ordinarily just family affairs. Sometimes, members and officials of the Tipi Way may travel to Skull Valley, a distance of about eighty or ninety miles to the east, to attend a meeting if one has already been scheduled by the Sioux group at Deep Creek.

Meetings of the Tipi Way at Deep Creek are held in an old army squad tent, although a tipi is much more desirable. Members of the Tipi Way in Skull Valley have a large twenty foot tipi which they have used since 1936. The Deep Creek Sioux Way also possesses a tipi.[4] When a small attendance is anticipated, particularly when a meeting is being held by a family for a sick person, the ceremonies may be held in a cabin. It is necessary that the entrance of the tipi, or tent face toward the rising sun, hence, I was told that most modern cabins built by the Indians have their doorways facing the east "because a man does not know when he may have to have a meeting in his home." However, even the cabins built in pre-peyote days have their doorways toward the east. Apparently, the custom is old but the meaning and significance of it has changed to conform to new ideology.

An altar, in the shape of a crescent moon, is made of wet sandy material to give it rigidity.[5] It may also be mixed with some cement to give it permanence. The size varies from four to six feet in length and usually has a maximum height of five to six inches. A line is drawn along the curve from one tip to the other

[2]Ralph V. Chamberlain, The Ethno-botany of the Gosiute Indians (Proceedings of the Academy of Natural Sciences, Philadelphia, 1911). Information included here is from a verbal statement made in 1940.

[3]Hayes, op. cit., p. 34.

[4]Hayes makes a statement concerning the use of tipis among the present day Gosiute: "It is interesting to note that a people, who in aboriginal times never used a tipi, and seldom, if ever, saw one, should feel that the ceremony is not complete without it." Hayes, op. cit., p. 35. The Tipi Way at Deep Creek do not feel they can afford to purchase the canvas to make a tipi and are using the tent until they can obtain the material. The present tent was swapped by a white man for a sack of pine nuts.

[5]One person who had recently returned from a meeting among the Utes at Myton, Utah, had observed an altar made of red sand and seemed enthusiastic about this new innovation in altar making.

and "it represents the path of life." A small depressed area on the top of the crescent serves as a resting place for the chief peyote. It remains there during the entire meeting. Surrounding the altar and extending in parallel lines to the entranceway is a "willow rope." Participants sit outside of the area enclosed by this "rope." A pile of charcoal is placed to the east of the crescent moon altar. Live coals are added to this pile from time to time by the fire chief when directed to do so by the leader. The coals are furnished from a small fire built in the apex of four sticks piled in the usual V-shape, the arrangement being identical to that described by La Barre for the typical Plains rites.

If the meeting is held in a cabin, special precautions are necessary against the dangers of fire. In this case, an apron, made of the same material as the crescent moon, is extended in front of the altar. The hot coals are placed upon this apron. A kerosene lamp is used in lieu of a fire but the usual V-shape pile of sticks, unlighted, is placed to the east of it. A fire is made outside with four more sticks, also piled in a V-shape, and it is from here the fire chief obtains live coals. All furniture is removed from the cabin when it is used for a peyote meeting. A stick about two feet long and two inches thick is placed between the arms of the V-shape fire sticks and it is used for lighting cigarettes. Before the exercises commence the fire is lighted with a very brief ceremony.[6]

Meetings usually commence about nine p.m. Participants line up outside the tipi with the officials in the front of the line and the women in the rear. They are usually dressed in simple but neat clothing and provide themselves with a blanket to sit on and to wrap around their shoulders whenever its gets chilly. Participants seat themselves in the usual manner with the drummer to the leader's right, the cedar man to his left, and the fire chief facing the leader on the opposite side of the room. The fire chief is the only person that does not always circumscribe the altar when entering the room. When the leader directs him to replenish the coals on the charcoal pile, he may sometimes do so without necessarily passing clockwise around the altar.

After everyone is seated, the leader takes out his equipment and lays it on the ground between himself and the altar. He then removes a peyote disk that had been placed on the depression on the altar earlier in the evening and puts the chief peyote in its place. Thus, the meeting is officially in progress. A bedding of sage brush (Artemesia tridentata) is provided on the depression upon which the chief peyote rests.

The equipment furnished by the leader consists of a staff, a drum, two fans, a drumstick, a bird bone whistle, a peyote disk or chief peyote, and, if I may, a clock. The latter, however, was not essential but was useful.

• • •

Particular pride is taken in the care and possession of fans. Of the two provided by the leader one is used by him as a personal fan and the other is used by the singers with the staff. One of these fans, the Gosiute claimed, is the one

[6]Possibly a flint and steel set may be used for lighting the fire but I was not permitted to observe this stage of the ceremony. If a flint and steel set is used it offers an interesting contrast to both the aboriginal method of making fire, which employed a drill set, and the introduced European method of using matches. Another way of getting a light for the fire is to obtain coals from one already burning in the cooking shelter, or stove in an adjoining cabin.

originally presented to the Utes when the cult was first introduced to them. TW possesses a fan of eagle feathers that had been obtained in Texas. Still another fan in the possession of AJ has only seven feathers in it.[7] After midnight personal fans are unwrapped from silk handkerchiefs and are used by all participants to draw smoke from the incense toward themselves. They are also moved up and down in rhythm with the beating of the drum and the shaking of the rattle. Personal fans are not used by the singers.

A short prayer is given by the leader, who then produces a bag of Bull Durham tobacco and a bundle of paper. He passes the bag and paper bundle to the person to his left and commences to roll a cigarette. The bag is passed entirely around the room and all participants roll cigarettes. As the smoking progresses, the leader, and then each participant in clockwise order, prays for the cure of aches and pains, or any thing else that may be desired. Finally, the participants take a few puffs on their cigarettes, blow the smoke toward the altar, and put out the lighted end by spitting on it. The cigarettes are then gathered by the fire chief, who places them along the altar. At midnight the fire chief, among his other duties, replaces these cigarette butts at the altar tips at the end of "the path of life."

Next, a bundle of sage brush tips is passed around the room and each person breaks off some pieces, rubs them in his hands, inhales the fragrance, and then chews them. While these are being chewed, the participants spit in their hands and rub their bodies starting from the head and working on down toward the feet.

When these preliminaries are over, the cedar man is directed to place some incense on the coals. The leader stands up and passes a bag of peyote through the smoke incense four times. This bag is then passed around the room clockwise and each person takes four buttons. The meeting cannot continue until everyone has finished eating his first button.

The leader, accompanied by the drummer, sings the opening song. In this song the participants are supposed to be able to hear Peyote talking to them, provided they listen carefully. When the song is completed, the leader will take the drum from the drummer and will accompany the cedar man who sings four songs of his own choice. The instruments are then passed around the room and the participants, except the women, sing and play in the usual manner, each singing a series of four songs. The end of a song or chant is marked by a rapid and continuous shaking of the rattle by the singer and an increased tempo on the drum by the drummer.[8]

At 11:30 p.m. arrangements are made for the midnight exercises, and while these preparations are being made the participants are free to talk and even laugh. This freedom is supposed to relieve some of the psychological and

[7]A twelve feather fan, made in the manner described by La Barre is used here. The twelve feathers are sometimes interpreted as representing the twelve months of the year. They were obtained from a bird having twelve feathers in its tail, according to my informant. Mr. Elmer R. Smith, of the University of Utah, has obtained a myth from the Gosiute attributing the origin of the twelve months of the year to a quarrel between coyote and eagle; the latter wanted twelve months in the year, one for each feather in his tail, while the former wanted a month for each hair in his coat. Eagle flew away and because coyote could not catch him there have since been twelve months in the year.

[8]When asked why women did not sing in the meetings, the Gosiute invariably replied that they did so formerly but have discontinued the practice.

physiological strain incident to participation in a peyote meeting (I am rephrasing the informant's words here). At this time the fire chief changes the charcoal pile into a crescent moon just east of the regular sand altar. The cedar man places fresh incense on the newly arranged charcoal pile and the midnight water song is rendered by the leader.

The fire chief goes outside and obtains a bucket of water. A blanket is spread on the floor and the fire chief kneels upon it with the bucket between his knees. A sauce pan, to be used as a dipper, is placed by the bucket. The fire chief, who is still kneeling by the bucket, makes a motion with his hands as if drawing some of the incense toward the bucket and ceremoniously blesses the water. The leader prepares a cigarette and it is handed, together with the fire stick, to the fire chief by the cedar man. The fire chief takes four puffs on the cigarette, blows the smoke toward the altar, and prays. The drummer, and then the cedar man follow suit and the butt is placed at the altar tip.

The fire chief tips the bucket away from him and pours a portion of the water on the ground "to keep mother earth from drying up." The bucket and the dipper is passed around the room, beginning with the person south of the doorway, and each of the participants takes a drink. All of them sprinkle a little water on themselves and then pat their arms, body, and legs. The bucket is returned to the fire chief, who takes the last drink, then he takes the bucket outside.

After the water ceremony the leader and the cedar man go outside and the leader blows his whistle in the four directions and offers prayers. When they return, incense is placed on the coals and everyone stands, unrolls his or her silk handkerchief in which personal fans are kept, and holds it toward the altar as if drawing the smoke toward their body, and then they pat themselves. They sit down on their blankets; the instruments are put into circulation again; and the singing and praying continues as it did before midnight. Prayers and songs dominate all activities until about four a.m. Anyone can leave at the end of a series of four songs but someone must accompany him. If the instruments should be passed to a person who is praying, he is not disturbed until he has finished. The singing can then continue.

A coffee can is provided for participants to vomit in when anyone requires its use. (When requested it is not necessarily passed clockwise.) It is one of the duties of the fire chief to aid those persons unable to care for themselves and to keep the place clean.

When the dawn breaks in the east, the cedar man, or someone else who may be outside, comes in and says: "The Sun is coming up." The leader then sings the morning song and after its completion preparations are made for the morning water exercises. This ceremony is similar to that performed at midnight except that a woman, instead of the fire chief, blesses the water. The bucket is not taken out until after the breakfast, however. After the water ceremony the women are sent outside to get the ceremonial breakfast. They return with three pans, one of which contains corned beef, another pears or some other fruit, and the other corn. These may usually be commercial canned goods and are arranged in the following order away from the altar: corn, fruit, and corned beef.[9]

---

[9]Stewart, op. cit., states that the Gosiute sometimes use rice instead of corn. Canned sweet corn is all that I have ever seen used.

After a blessing the pans are passed around clockwise and each person partakes of the food. A spoon is provided in each pan for eating, although individuals may use a private dish and spoon if they prefer. When the pans have completed the circuit of the room, they are placed behind the altar in a reverse order, that is, with the corned beef closest to the altar and the fruit and corn following respectively.

The drum head is removed by the drummer after the breakfast and then he removes fourteen pieces of charcoal that had been placed inside. The meaning of these is not yet known to these people; all they profess to know is that it is a necessary part of the procedure. The charcoal pieces are placed along the charcoal moon. The drummer then holds the kettle up, drinks some of the water, and sprinkles a few drops on himself. The rest of the water is poured on the altar on the side toward the leader.

The crescent moon of coals is banked up against the sand moon by the fire chief, the food and water bucket is taken outside by the women, the chief peyote is removed by the leader and placed in his shirt pocket and the meeting is officially over. Candy may also be passed around at the conclusion of the ceremonies

A feast is given in the morning and visitors, in addition to the participants in the meeting, come as guests. While it is being prepared by the women, the men lounge around singing songs, or chatting with each other until the dinner is served.

The Sioux Way conducts a very similar meeting but there are many detailed differences. The Sioux Way, as far as I know, does not require a breakfast, the use of candy, or tobacco, and the basic songs are different. According to Omer Stewart, Sioux Way meetings are conducted without levity, and sometimes a velvet crescent altar may be used.[10]

The large majority of the Gosiute population are, at present, members of the peyote cults, the membership itself not being restricted to any particular generation.[11] Persons from fourteen to sixty-five years of age are actively engaged in peyote worship. Even babies may be given peyote tea.[12] Furthermore, the peyote believers do not restrict themselves to membership in any particular Way and will often participate in one or the other's meetings. When asked why he did this, one informant replied, "Same herb." Even the officials of the two cults will sometimes attend the other's meetings. The fact that the leader of the Sioux Way of peyotism among the Gosiute was recently elected head of the first tribal council in Gosiute history attests to the strength of the cults in the social life of these people and the favor they sustain.

To the Gosiute the chief function of peyote is the curing of sick and for supernatural guidance in political and economic activities. It is also noteworthy that a dependence is being made on peyote for education. One informant, for example, said he was sorry he had gone to school as Peyote would have told him everything necessary to know.

[10]Stewart, op. cit.

[11]It is difficult to determine which cult is strongest of the two at Deep Creek, or their respective memberships, as they are never static. That there is a competitive element existing between the two cults is also probable.

[12]In the early stages of a meeting a pan of peyote tea may be passed to the participants. Tea is also served to those too ill to eat. In one meeting the participants came into the cabin as they arrived, took a drink of tea, and went outside again for the line up.

Peyote is supposed to give many other benefits to believers. For example, one man was temporarily given the power to prophesy. He once predicted that the next day two "Ute boys" would come from Whiterocks. "Sure enough, the next day two Ute boys did come from Whiterocks." The informants voluntarily insisted that this man had not had any previous communication with the Utes.

"During a meeting a person's mind can leave his body and can travel anywhere. You may be sitting in one corner, pretty soon you may be sitting in another corner watching yourself sitting in the other. Peyote is not made by man, it just come up, like a tree. He speaks and understands all languages and is smarter than any man, hence, it does not matter what language is used to speak to him. If you want anything just ask Peyote and if you are sincere you will get it. It is necessary to work *with* Peyote to get best results. In peyote there is everything, good and bad. There is fire, water, humans, earth, plants, and even the soul. During a meeting it is up to the devout to seek out the good and leave the bad in the room in which the meeting is held. This room is not only a church, it is also our hospital."

Very often the peyote movement is conceived of as a slight variation of aboriginal shamanism in which Christian elements are considered mere apologetic tendencies, or as an actual combination of aboriginal shamanism and Christianity in which the elements of each can be pigeon-holed and studied. The peyote cults are also considered as primarily a means by which the Indian produces visions,[13] or used as a means of curing sickness.[14] Actually, peyotism should be considered as a movement in itself in which many factors, including curing, visionary, apologetic tendencies, etc., are all functionally interrelated and have all contributed to its widespread acceptance or rejection.

There are a few obvious Christian elements that appear in the Gosiute Tipi Way of peyotism. First, the prayers, although directed to Peyote, end with some words in which God, Mary, Jesus Christ, and finally Amen are included. The place of Mary in the mind of the cult is a problem. The words "Jesus Christ the Savior" appear in one Gosiute song. Second, the Bible is used to argue in favor of the existence of the cult, although it has no part in the ritual. One quotation, for example, is from the *New Testament: (Romans* 14, verses 2 and 3).

2. For one believeth that he may eat all things: another who is weak eateth herbs.

3. Let not him that eateth despise him that eateth not; and let not him judge him that eateth: for God hath received him.

A reasonable amount of caution should be taken in considering this use of the Bible as merely apologetic.

Probably, the missionaries, both Catholic and Protestant, that have labored among the Indians of Utah and contiguous States have made considerable impression on the Indian cultures. However, even the peyote cults seem to be closer in harmony with older beliefs and traditions. Such items as meeting at night, use of bird bone whistles, use of herbs for curing, doorway facing the east, and numbers four and twelve would certainly be clearer to a mind condi-

[13]Ruth Shonle, *Peyote—Giver of Visions* (American Anthropologist, Vol. 27, 1925).
[14]R. E. Schultes, *The Appeal of Peyote* (Lophophera williamsii) *as a Medicine* (American Anthropologist, Vol. 40, 1938).

tioned in Gosiute culture than would most Christian concepts. On the other hand, the Gosiute have accepted practices that may be aboriginal to some Indians but not to the Gosiute. These are the use of the tipi, water drums, fans (although eagle feathers were used by aboriginal shamans), gourd rattle, and possibly the clockwise ceremonial movement, the taking of a bath preceding participation in a religious meeting, and the possible use of a flint and steel set. Still other elements may be entirely foreign if not contrary to any previous Gosiute beliefs and practices. In aboriginal times the shaman, when curing a sick person, allowed his soul to go out and bring back the soul of his patient before it wandered too far away. At the present time not only the leader has this power but the souls of various individuals may wander about during a peyote meeting, regardless of their official standing in the church. Furthermore, the leader does not receive any special rewards or powers from the supernatural for his activities in conducting meetings. Shamanism had suffered a breakdown and Christianity was misunderstood. Peyotism, which combines the conception of Christianity with previous beliefs, plus many new concepts, which have not yet become stabilized within the culture concerned, offers itself as a movement which meets the cultural or psychological needs of various individuals. Even those rejecting the cult will, in one way or the other, be affected by its introduction.

As yet there have been no indigenous religious leaders with sufficient prestige to incorporate any major changes in Gosiute peyote concepts and rites, although there have been several prominent outsiders connected with its inception. Except for the addition of a few minor elements, and a failure to include some others, the Gosiute have borrowed the cults already "made to order." That is, the adjustments necessary to make the cults appealing to the Gosiute have been made elsewhere. This does not mean, however, that changes may not be made later.

While it is true that the cults themselves were borrowed from the Utes, contacts are not entirely restricted to these people. Various members frequently attend meetings at Fort Hall, Idaho, in Nevada, and other places. Omer Stewart has informed me that he attended a peyote meeting on the Ute reservation in which at least two Gosiute were present. Nevada Shoshone, including Ruby Valley peoples, and Northern Paiute frequently attend Gosiute meetings at Ibapah and Ben Lancaster himself has brought some of his followers to attend Gosiute ceremonies. Some Gosiutes attend Lancaster's Nevada meetings but others are refused admittance for fear they may spoil his own lucrative business by revealing that some of his extraordinary practices, such as collecting donations, are not orthodox. The Nevada cults have not made any impression, as far as I am aware, on the Gosiute.

Apparently, Oklahoma is a sort of Mecca for it is the desire of many cultists to some day visit the area. It is in Oklahoma that the cult is supposed to have originated. "In Oklahoma they know peyote and they know how to use it."[15] The Gosiute, incidentally, are also aware of the wealth the Oklahoma Indians have accumulated from oil holdings.

One member of the Tipi Way, DM, was the first to go to Oklahoma on a pilgrimage. Because of this feat, and because of his many other accomplishments and contributions in the cult, he was presented at a special meeting with a large

[15]Hayes, op. cit., p. 35 (from a quotation of Hayes' informant).

canvas tipi, made by the women, when he moved to Skull Valley from Deep Creek in 1936. Thus, the cult spread to Skull Valley. Both the Utes and the Oklahoma Indians enjoy high prestige among the Gosiute. In addition to these the Sioux Way also have additional respect for the Dakota, or Sioux Indians. For example, FS, one of the leaders of the Sioux Way at Deep Creek claimed that only the Sioux Indians were capable of interpreting the many pictographs in the mountains around Deep Creek. Advanced means of communication, automobiles, mail systems, radio, telegraph, etc., introduced by the white man, have made it possible for tribes over large distances to become very well acquainted. But it also makes the process of diffusion much more complex for the ethnographer to study.

Attitudes toward the cults vary among different Indians and whites living in the vicinity of the Gosiute reservations. At the present time, apparently, the majority of Indians are peyote participants. A few fight its spread. Others in the culture simply consider peyote as a dope, although, they themselves often attend meetings presumably for the effects of the intoxication. Still others ignore the movement entirely. Many Indians, however, see a definite value in its use. There were no statements given by informants that said participation would lead to insanity, a belief which is current among many opposers of peyotism in Nevada.[16]

To the whites, particularly those in the Indian Service and immediately concerned with the Gosiute, peyote seems a detriment to the Indians because it leaves them incapable of working for two or three days after a meeting. A few see some value in its use in that peyote members are prohibited from drinking alcohols. The Indians also recognize this value and the few members that drink enjoy little prestige. TJ, for example, has attended meetings at Fort Hall, Idaho, and other places, yet he is not a popular member of the cult. All his personality deficiencies cannot, of course, be attributed to his drinking but it serves as a useful argument by his acquaintances. "The Indians at Ely, Nevada" I was told, "do not have a peyote cult, hence, they are heavy drinkers." Perhaps the greatest value of peyote and the cult evolved around it is that it gives the Gosiute society a certain amount of coherence which tends to unify the group for the accomplishment of various objectives. Tribal unity, in what was aboriginally an atomistic society, is something the Gosiute have never yet enjoyed.

[16]Stewart, op. cit.

8 / Patterns of
Conformity and Control

Introduction

If one reviews the various cultural patterns illustrated up to this point, the question arises as to why members of various cultures came to conform to the cultural patterns that constitute their social heritage. Perfect conformity is never completely achieved in any society or culture. Generally, however, the vast majority of the members of all societies overwhelmingly conform to the totality of their cultural patterns, making non-conformity newsworthy. The study of these rare, noteworthy exceptions provides insight into the various mechanisms at work to produce conformity.

There are several explanations for conformity, and each explanation applies to different situations at different times. As we have emphasized in the earlier sections, various aspects of culture tend to be highly integrated and interrelated. The ways in which conformity is achieved provide us with a convenient point of departure for illustrating the interrelationships among various culture patterns. For example, in the last chapter we referred to the threat of ostracism as one possible way of bringing pressure to bear on the members of the society, to make them conform. An alternative method sometimes used in our own society is the use of physical force as exercised by designated legal agencies. Before delving into these more complex reasons and explanations for conformity let us turn our attention to some of the more obvious possibilities.

If we reflect back to Chapter Two and take a typical daily routine as a set of patterns, it is possible to conceive of these daily repetitive acts as simple habits in which conformity is simply the path of least resistance. For many of these simple customs we might assume that sheer economy of effort is sufficient to maintain patterns over a long period of time. For example, when brushing one's teeth, it is easier to follow an established practice rather than to make a decision each morning based on apparent need.

Simple suggestion may lead to some kinds of conformity. Dreams, for example, are a form of culturally patterned behavior. In various cultures adults continually suggest to children the form and content of their dreams. In such an example the process of suggestibility may go some distance in accounting for why the child would learn to dream in the same manner as the adults.

Anthropologists, philosophers and others have created elaborate and complex theories about conformity that go well beyond the rather simple examples discussed so far. For instance, beliefs about religion and illness can easily operate to bring enormous pressure on the individual to conform to the beliefs and practices of his culture. Christianity has preached that good acts will land one in Heaven, while evil acts may assign one to Hell and perdition. Such beliefs would tend to act on the individual to insure "good behavior," which is defined as conforming to the established norms.

In some societies children are taught that "bad behavior" may lead to illness. For example, while doing field work among the Mixtec in Mexico one of the authors encountered an example of this phenomenon and recorded it as follows:

294

It concerned a woman, whom we shall call Catalina, who supplemented her income by selling tortillas in the marketplace. All people who occupy space in the market are expected to pay a very small tax for the space they occupy there. One market day when Catalina was selling her tortillas, the tax collector came around to her place in the market to collect the tax. By mistake, he attempted to collect the tax a second time from her. She tried to explain that she had already paid her tax, and an argument of a very mild nature ensued. Shortly afterward, she confided to her friends in the market that she had felt very angry about this double imposition and that she did not feel well and was worried about having become so angry. She thereupon left the market in the afternoon and went home. She became increasingly ill during the evening and died about midnight. The cause of her death was attributed to the illness that was caused by her aggressive feelings. All of the people in the barrio accepted this as the explanation. The event was reported to the children and talked about in front of them and used as an object lesson for the importance of controlling one's feelings.

The well-internalized belief that anger or aggression can lead to illness and possibly death is a strong deterrent to placing oneself in a situation that may lead to anger or aggression. When the validity of such a belief is reinforced or demonstrated by actual deaths, as in the case of Catalina, it becomes a very potent deterrent to aggressive behavior and thoughts.

In the example quoted above we see an intimate relationship between theories of illness and pressure to conform. Some writers have distinguished between the concepts of "guilt" and "shame." They would refer to the above example as guilt, since the pressures of conformity were present internally within the individual and related to their own beliefs. In the case of shame, pressure to conform would be extended and would depend on others' being present who would bring to bear social approval or disapproval on an individual in order to obtain conformity. A person controlled primarily by shame would not steal in front of a policeman or disapproving parent, but might steal if he had no fear of discovery. A person controlled by guilt would refrain from stealing on the basis of his internal beliefs about the supernatural or beliefs about illness, even though there was no possibility that his transgressions would be discovered.

In the first article in this chapter, Lieban describes a Philippine community in which the diagnosis of illness frequently conveys an implicit moral warning, as is the case in many non-Western curing traditions (e.g., see Lindenbaum's article in Chapter Seven). An individual rendered vulnerable and suggestible by illness and anxiety may be "scolded," in effect, by being told that his illness stems from an encounter with an *ingkanto*—any of a number of mythical creatures that symbolize "alluring, but basically unattainable, wealth and power outside the barrios." This "lesson" is followed by curing activities which, aside from their medical effects, convey the message that the local community—represented by a respected member, the curer—remains attentive and supportive to the sufferer.

Hamer and Hamer, in discussing "Spirit Possession and its Socio-Psychological Implications Among the Sidamo of Southwest Ethiopia," illustrate a multi-purpose system of beliefs and actions. Spirit possession serves as a way to gain prestige for a Sidamo lacking other means (courage, wealth or skill in oratory), but it is by no means an easy or automatic route. The usual way of becoming possessed of a spirit is by inheritance, which passes specifically to the child "who has been most obedient and subservient to the possessed parent." Whether one claims to have inherited a spirit or to have suddenly been possessed by one (preferably one that is currently fashionable), it rests with the community to support or else reject these implicit claims to prestige and acceptance. In a final section of the article, which is not included here, the Hamers note how the same basic system finds different expression in three societies.

The next two readings, by Beattie and Epstein, both illustrate the general features of highly-personal, informal "courts" in Africa and New Guinea, respectively. The setting is comparable to a Western court in the sense that claimants are airing their complaints before a group of peers who will render a verdict, but beyond this the similarities give way to contrasts. For example, where Western law (in theory, at least) is indifferent to the status of claimants, the non-Western cases illustrated here take account of everything known about claimants in the process of reaching a decision. The disputes themselves—e.g., disrespect of a child towards a parent—are often of a personal kind and indicate a great degree of "fine tuning" in the meshing of individual behavior and public opinion. The most notable contrast, perhaps, is the definition of a satisfactory end-result. In our impersonalized tradition, the trial process ends with a verdict, rendering one side a winner and the other a loser. But this is neither feasible nor desirable in a community where all the parties to a dispute will continue to live close to each other and interact frequently. Under these circumstances, it is not surprising to find the trial process extended until, ideally, everyone is convinced that the good relations between the disputants have been restored. Even if some sort of penalty is involved there is an attempt to take the "sting" out of it; the Nyoro custom reported by Beattie is especially well-designed to do this.

Noyes, in the final article, surveys basic issues relating to the taboo of suicide. Among other things, Noyes suggests that the present-day tendency to classify suicide as an act of insanity may be a further source of anxiety to persons who experience suicidal impulses; in other words, it is a poor means of control. More generally, Noyes suggests that control of suicide by society (i.e., low frequency) seems to be correlated with social orders that produce a high degree of conformity and control in *all* aspects of behavior.

The Dangerous Ingkantos:
Illness and Social Control
in a Philippine Community
Richard W. Lieban

The growing liaison between medicine and the social sciences has been marked by increased interest in the relationship between illness and the state of society. Effects of this relationship may be looked for in psychological or physical symptoms of the individual reacting to social influences, or, conversely, as in this paper, attention may be directed to the consequences of individual illness for social organization.

Consideration of the pertinence of illness and therapy to problems of social control has occupied a prominent place in the work of Parsons, who has approached the subject in terms of role motivation and performance. Parsons (1951:29) sees a social system as requiring that those in the system are adequately motivated to role performances that may be necessary for maintenance or development of the system. According to Parsons (1951:431), illness can become involved in the "motivated processes of interaction," and he states:

> The fact that the relevance of illness is not confined to the non-motivated purely situational aspect of social action greatly increases its significance for the social system. It becomes not merely an "external danger" to be "warded off" but an integral part of the social equilibrium itself. Illness may be treated as one mode of response to social pressures, among other things, as one way of evading social responsibilities. But it may also ... have some possible positive functional significance.
> ... Participation in the social system is always potentially relevant to the state of illness, to its etiology and to the conditions of successful therapy ... (1951:431).

Using Parson's thesis as a point of departure, this paper will consider some medical aspects of social stability in a Philippine community. More specifically, I will be concerned with how beliefs about certain illnesses and their treatment may help offset influences which can divert or weaken adherence to traditional roles in the community.

The community discussed is Sibulan, a municipality on the island of Negros in the southern Bisayan islands. The area in question manifests a regional variation of the peasant culture found in other Christian lowland areas of the Philippines. In Sibulan some rice is grown, but small farming operations producing corn for subsistence and coconuts for the market predominate. There are some differences in wealth in the rural barrios of Sibulan, but essentially they are one-class settlements in which the standard of living is frugal, and most families have little cash for conveniences or indulgences produced in the world outside. Yet these people are aware of styles of life far more elaborate than their own.

Sibulan is immediately adjacent to Dumaguete, capital of Negros Oriental Province. Dumaguete is a port and commercial center for surrounding areas, and luxury goods are displayed in some of its stores. In the capital, a small professional, official, and business class has a standard of living substantially above that of the peasantry in the barrios. Dumaguete is, moreover, the site of a major Protestant-missionary university which retains some Americans on its staff and draws a number of others to Dumaguete as visitors. The rural barrios of Sibulan are also not far from coconut and sugar plantations in the province. Sibulan is traversed by the provincial highway, and while the light traffic on this road includes carabao carts and antique buses, occasionally an up-to-date automobile speeds by as a reminder that people of means live in the area.

In addition to the picture of affluence in their region which barrio people have, additional impressions of wealth are gained by those in the barrios who have travelled to Manila and other cities beyond the province. Images of life outside the Philippines are provided by mass communications media: motion pictures shown in Dumaguete or by mobile units in the countryside, newspapers and magazines which circulate in limited quantity in the barrios. In the case of foreigners, especially Americans, distance—social or geographical—lends enchantment, and foreign wealth which does exist is often magnified in the minds of barrio people. The view which the barrio population has of the discrepancy between its own poverty and outside wealth is an important aspect of the connection between illness and social control in the community which this paper will seek to establish.

Although Sibulan is a Catholic community, a number of non-Christian supernatural concepts are still prevalent there. Among the most important of these is a belief in what are called *ingkantos*, referring to spirits which can assume human form. Generally ingkantos remain invisible, but sometimes observers see them in dreams or visions. Ingkantos frequently inhabit trees and remote places, but they can be present anywhere. Some ingkantos are conceived of as only heads living in a mound of earth, others as dwarfs, giants, or a combination of human and fish. However, in most cases when ingkantos are seen, they appear as attractive Malaysian Filipinos, mestizos, or Caucasians who are most frequently thought to be American or Spanish. The majority of ingkantos seen by informants were described as having at least some Caucasian features. Ingkantos often are not only handsome or beautiful; they are very rich and powerful as well. They also are dangerous, and it is thought that contact with them may lead to illness or death. While the term ingkanto is Spanish in derivation, and beliefs about ingkantos strongly reflect contact between Filipinos and foreigners up to the present time, old Spanish accounts of culture in Negros indicate that features of the ingkanto concept already were existent early in the Spanish colonial period,[1] and some roots of the concept probably antedate the Spanish arrival in the Philippines.

[1] Povedano, an *encomendero* in Negros, described in 1578 local beliefs in spirits called *tumaos* as follows (Povedano 1954:16): "These spirits have wonderful habitations. They have magnificent buildings, good foods and all other luxuries enjoyed by wealthy people. They have even large boats plying from one ocean to another. And finally they are ready to defend their possessions from human intrusions by causing serious harms to the offender's life or property." Povedano (p. 16) said that to the ordinary eye the magnificent edifices of the tumao appear only to be trees or large boulders. He further discussed (pp. 16–18) how tumao might become romantically involved with human beings and how they could

Whatever its age, history, and metamorphosis, ingkanto lore still has a vivid place in contemporary life, and it is constantly replenished by accounts of those who are eyewitnesses to the appearance and behavior of ingkantos. The following is a case in point.

My informant was a man 22 years old. One evening the previous year he was walking to a friend's house, when out of the corner of his eye he saw three men with long white hair standing in the moonlight. When he directly faced them, they vanished, but as he turned his eyes back to the path in front of him, the figures reappeared to the side of him. He called to them, and when they did not answer, he ran home in fright. For the next two hours, he could hardly breathe, and the following morning he felt very weak. Then, he said, "as if in a dream," the three men of the night before appeared, and they told him that he should visit certain trees known as favorite abodes of ingkantos. The men said if he did this he would see beautiful women and enjoy himself. After he heard this, the young man ran out of his house, with his worried parents following him. He first went to a *dalakit* tree (*Ficus payapa* Blanco), where he saw a beautiful girl who appeared to him to be a mestiza.[2] Although there were other people with him by then, only he could see the girl, who was leaning out of the

---

make men sick by throwing particles at them that could penetrate the skin, ideas also held today about ingkantos, as described in the main body of the paper above. Povedano (p. 17) reported the belief that if a human being ate special food offered him by a tumao, he became a tumao, and there is a comparable contemporary notion concerning human relations with ingkantos.

Pavón quoted from what he called "a curious document of Father Francisco Deza, dated Ilog, in the year (16?)14" as follows (Ilog is identified in the document as a town in the Parish of Occidental Negros): "The Indios of this town say that the creatures called *tumao* are people like unto us, who if they wish to become invisible, are invisible; while if we wish to see them, we may if they wish, but if they do not wish we may not see them. Should one of those men take a fancy to an Indio woman, he flies away with her, and until he wishes to return her, no one can find her. The *tumao* always have good food, and are very cleanly folk. They make their homes in the dirt heaps called *bongsod*, and their houses look like little heaps of dirt. There they do no harm to any one. But if anyone does harm to them and breaks down the places where they live, then they return the harm done them by causing sickness to those who have caused harm to them. . . . They have the power of making an Indio like themselves after he has eaten their food (Pavón 1957:50–1)."

While in Sibulan and Dumaguete, I never heard the word tumao used to refer to ingkantos, or in any other connection, but I was unaware of the term at the time, so I did not question informants about it. Interestingly enough, Millington and Maxfield (1906), who collected folklore in Panay in 1904, wrote that there was a belief in that Bisayan area in *tamawos*, of whom it was said: "They live in mounds or elevated places in the fields. Their houses, which are generally on the inside of the mound, although sometimes built outside, are of metal or glass, and ordinarily invisible to mortals. Those who have seen them, and in each town there is usually at least one person who claims to have done so, say that the houses have the appearance of those inhabited by men, contain handsome furniture, and usually have in them beautiful young ladies who do their utmost to induce the child whom the tamawo has captured to partake of their food, since if a mortal once eats of their food he becomes for all time a tamawo like themselves."

[2] The importance of the association of ingkantos with trees in a Leyte area is discussed by Nurge (1958:1162–63). The idea that dalakit (*Ficus payapa* Blanco)—often called *baliti*—trees are the dwellings of ingkantos or other spirits is widespread in the Phillippines, in pagan and Moslem as well as Christian areas (e.g., see Fox 1952:310; 1954:246–7; Cole 1913:176; and Garvan 1931:197. Charles Warriner, in a private communication, notes that among the Maranao, a Moslem group in Mindanao, it is believed that the baliti tree is the favorite habitation of certain spirits).

window of a large brick building and wearing a shiny dress that looked as if it were made of gold. The girl was also wearing a gold wrist watch, much superior to his cheap watch. She looked at him and then said: "Let us exchange our watches." He replied that he could not trade because her watch was "too nice." With this, the girl and the building disappeared, and he went on to other trees, but he saw no more ingkantos. His mother and father then brought him home in a daze and sent for a *mananambal*, a folk healer. The mananambal rubbed the body of the patient with a special oil known for its supernatural properties, and he also performed a *palina*, a fumigation technique employed for the treatment of supernatural illnesses. In addition, the mananambal left him a prayer written on a piece of paper, and he was instructed to keep this with him at all times until he got well. For about a week after his encounters with the ingkantos, the patient felt depleted; he had difficulty eating, and he grew very thin. Then he gradually recovered his strength.

This case illustrates certain facets of human experiences with ingkantos and the aftermath of these experiences which are of prime concern in this paper.

First, attractive ingkantos generally are seen by human beings of the opposite sex, and sexual motifs often are expressed in relationships which people have with ingkantos, sometimes to the point where sexual intercourse with ingkantos is reported. However, the sexual factors in these experiences are closely associated with economic and power factors. In other words, ingkantos are enticing not only because they are physically attractive, but also because they are magnificently rich, and they hold out the promise of enabling their protégés to transcend the possibilities of ordinary existence. Those who have seen ingkantos describe their imposing houses or mansions, banquet food, peerless automobiles, watches, and other possessions. And ingkantos can tempt with power as well as wealth. Sorcerers in the area are said to derive part of their power from special relationships they have with ingkantos (Lieban 1960:130), and a healer told me that once she was approached in a dream by two male ingkantos who told her that if she left them regular offerings of food, her treatment of her patients would be successful and she would become rich. She was frightened and declined the opportunity.

Second, contact with ingkantos is usually followed by illness. In many instances, people may be unaware that they have had a brush with ingkantos until they become ill and their trouble is diagnosed as due to the spirits. Ingkantos usually remain invisible, and a human being may irritate or offend them unwittingly. In such instances, ingkantos may strike through object intrusion, and the patient is treated by a mananambal who seeks to extract the suffused particles from the victim. In other cases, such as that of the man described previously, an ingkanto may be seen. Such contacts may be fleeting or prolonged, single or repeated, and illness frequently ensues. There is no one illness attributed to ingkantos. Among the symptoms described to me for different cases were: boils or other skin eruptions, abdominal pains, body swelling, diarrhea, hemorrhaging, headache, earache, trembling, delirium, extreme fatigue, and stupor. Known or putative contact with ingkantos rather than symptoms of the patient seems crucial in the attribution of illness to ingkantos, and the same symptoms may be variously linked to contact with ingkantos or to other causes depending on prior experiences of the patient and the opinion of the diagnostician.

Third, illnesses which are believed to be the consequence of contact with ingkantos are treated by mananambal. There are hospitals and physicians in the provincial capital and a physician in the rural health clinic in Sibulan. A patient may seek modern medical treatment if it is felt that his illness stems from natural causes. However, illnesses of supernatural origin, such as those ascribed to ingkanto contact, are considered the province of mananambal in the barrios. The role of the mananambal is defined as one of service; he charges no fees and is generally compensated by small voluntary payments of cash or produce. (Cf. Pal 1956:432–33 and Arens 1957:121).

The etiology of illness discussed above, and the cultural and social contexts in which these concepts are found, suggest a relationship between illness and social control in Sibulan. To people of the barrios, ingkantos appear to represent, *inter alia*, glittering and inaccessible wealth and power beyond the local community. The individual who sees and interacts with an ingkanto can, through fantasy, bring temptation within reach, or succumb to it. However, such experiences are considered hazardous and often are thought to lead to illness or death. This pattern of thought and behavior associated with beliefs about ingkantos and their influence appears to support social equilibrium in the community by dramatizing and reinforcing the idea that it is dangerous to covet alluring, but basically unattainable, wealth and power outside the barrios. In this way, the value of accepting the limitations of barrio life and one's part in it is emphasized. Furthermore, if someone has a relationship with a dazzling ingkanto and becomes ill, it is the mananambal, a symbol of barrio service and self-sufficiency, who restores the victim to health and reality. Thus, one woman told of her seduction by an ingkanto, after which she became ill. She was cured by a mananambal, who after completion of the treatments gave her a prayer for protection against future trouble with the ingkanto. One night the same ingkanto returned in the most beautiful car she had ever seen and invited her to take a ride. At this point, she recited the prayer given her by the mananambal, and the ingkanto drove off shouting that if it had not been for the mananambal he would have had her. She said that she had never seen an ingkanto again after that.

If fantasies which transport the individual beyond the barrio milieu and consequences of such fantasies reflect centrifugal and centripetal influences on the community, the same can be said for actual migrations from Sibulan and their consequences. Some, especially younger people before they are married, go to Manila or other cities to find work. Most informants who had gone to urban centers and then returned to Sibulan said they were drawn to cities by the chance to earn money and buy clothes and other goods they wanted. Such migrants generally wind up as servants or laborers, or they cannot find work. Some remain in the cities, but others return to Sibulan and stress the difficulties and impersonality of the city in contrast to their own community. One informant who was unable to secure employment in Manila while there talked about the wonders of the city, but he also said that even if he had been able to find work in Manila he still would have returned to Sibulan because "if we are poor in Manila it is very hard." Another informant said that those who are destitute can get help in the barrio, but "in Manila no one will even give them a banana." While such a statement is a hyperbole, it does reflect a prevalent view, apparently based on experience, that rural barrios of Sibulan offer more security than cities do elsewhere.

To this point, discussion of the manner in which beliefs about illness caused by ingkantos contribute to the regulation of society has stressed control of unsettling foreign, modern, and urban influences on a folk community. However, the problem can be more broadly defined than this, in general terms of restraint of personal desires in behalf of social commitment. The desires may be created by the contact situation, as were those discussed above, or they may be inflated traditional wants. To illustrate how ingkantos can be involved with the latter, an informant mentioned that if one planted crops on land belonging to ingkantos, the harvest might be larger than usual, but one might get sick. Another informant told of how her husband when fishing for shrimp one time said in a light-hearted way that he wished he could catch all the shrimp in the stream. He soon caught a profusion of shrimp, but when he saw two ingkantos nearby, he hurried home, considerably frightened.

Examples of ingkanto lore such as these are indicative of an important theme in the community: greed is wrong and unwise. This is illustrated in what happens when a field is harvested. Often the farmer harvesting his crop is joined by a number of helpers, most of them from poorer households and most of them unsolicited. Although the majority of these helpers, called *manalabang*, usually are not needed, I never saw or heard of any of them being turned away, and each of them receives about one-eighth or more of what he harvests. Explanations of why a farmer should share his crop with supernumerary harvesters included: greed is not the custom in the community, grace should be shared with others, the goodwill of neighbors should be retained, and selfishness could earn one a curse.

These views reflect community pressures, by means of which part of an individual's wealth is siphoned off to kinsmen and neighbors. Such levelling tendencies seem to be characteristic of barrio social organization.[3] In this perspective, illnesses attributed to ingkantos can be seen as helping to reconcile the individual to social reality by demonstrating that it is a mistake to overindulge personal desires.

REFERENCES

ARENS, RICHARD, S. V. D., "The tambalan and his medical practices in Leyte and Samar islands, Philippines." *The Philippine Journal of Science* 86:121–30, 1957.

COLE, FAY COOPER, "The wild tribes of Davao district, Mindanao." *Field Museum of Natural History, Anthropological Series*, Vol. XII, no. 2, Chicago, 1913.

FOX, ROBERT B., "The Pinatubo Negritos: their useful plants and material culture." *The Philippine Journal of Science* 81:173–414, 1952. "Religion and society among the Tagbanuwa of Palawan Island, Philippines." Unpublished Ph.D. dissertation, University of Chicago, 1954.

GARVAN, JOHN M., "The Manobós of Mindanáo." *Memoirs of the National Academy of Sciences*, XXIII. First memoir, Washington, 1931.

LIEBAN, RICHARD W., "Sorcery, illness and social control in a Philippine municipality." *Southwestern Journal of Anthropology* 16:127–43, 1960.

[3] Lynch (1959:131), writing of a Bikol area in Luzon, says that typically a lower class person "has no surplus at all for any length of time, for if he should happen to have something extra in the way of food or money he will shortly give it away (every relative a bank, every friend a granary) or have it borrowed away if he delay."

LYNCH, FRANK, "Social class in a Bikol town." Research series, No. 1. *Philippine Studies Program*, Department of Anthropology, University of Chicago, 1959.

MILLINGTON, W. H. and BERTON L. MAXFIELD, "Philippine (Visayan) superstitions." *Journal of American Folklore* 19:205–11, 1906.

NURGE, ETHEL, "Etiology of illness in Guinhangdan." *American Anthropologist* 60:1158–72, 1958.

PAL, AGATON P., "A Philippine barrio." *University of Manila Journal of East Asiatic Studies* 5:333–486, 1956.

PARSONS, TALCOTT, *The social system.* (Glencoe: The Free Press, 1951).

PAVON, JOSE MARIA, "The Robertson translations of the Pavón manuscripts of 1838–1839. A—Stories of the Indios of this island (Negros)." Transcript no. 5-A. *Philippine Studies Program*, Department of Anthropology, University of Chicago, 1957.

POVEDANO, DIEGO LOPE, "The Povedano manuscript of 1578. The ancient legends and stories of the Indios Jarayas, Jiguesinas and Igneines which contain their beliefs and diverse superstitions." Translated and annotated by Rebecca P. Ignacio. Transcript no. 3. *Philippine Studies Program*, Department of Anthropology, University of Chicago, 1954.

Spirit Possession and Its Socio-Psychological Implications Among the Sidamo of Southwest Ethiopia

John and Irene Hamer

The Sidamo are a Cushitic-speaking people found in southwestern Ethiopia, about 150 miles south of Addis Ababa. . . .

In this paper we wish to consider the phenomenon of spirit possession among the Sidamo as it relates to the social structure and beliefs about disease therapy and religion. Possession among these people is related to certain concepts pertaining to supernatural power and the healing quality of spirits. It is believed that the spirits which possess individuals have been sent by Magāno, the sky god. Furthermore, all unexplainable illnesses are attributed by the possessed to the dissatisfaction of these supernatural beings, and only through their appeasement can sickness be alleviated.

An important aspect of the social structure is the ability of an individual to show his superiority in one or a combination of attributes involving wealth, oratorical ability, or bravery. In addition, there is a noticeable ascribed sexual difference in this superior status accorded males over females. A person with one or more of these attributes is considered to have the ability to influence the lives of others. Considering that in the struggle for power and prestige there must be losers, either by ascription or by failure to achieve through one of the three attributes, there must be some cultural means of alleviating the sense of failure if social unity is to be preserved. It is our contention that spirit possession provides such a psycho-cultural outlet.

SPIRITS

To appreciate the importance of spirits it is first necessary to see how the Sidamo conceptualize their position vis-à-vis the supernatural world. According to the religious mythology, the sky god creator was originally much closer to the people than he is today. It seems, however, that he became angry with mankind and returned to the sky, where he influences the course of events only in a distant and most indirect fashion. This sky god, Magāno, is seen as a punishing deity who seems in the main to be concerned with the giving and taking of life. Though they do not go so far as to suggest that Magāno sent the spirits, known as shatāna (sing. shatāni), to compensate for his aloofness, most informants were of the opinion that they had indeed been sent as his emissaries. The shatāna are thought to have an influence on such important aspects of everyday life as childbirth, health, and the reproduction of cattle. No specific form is ascribed to the shatāna, and the observer becomes aware of their presence only indirectly through the occurrence of unexplained illness, the dialogue which they carry on through the mouth of the possessed, and the jerking motion of the head and shoulders of the individual when the spirit enters his body.

The method of propitiating these spirits is analogous to that used in appeasing Magāno and the founders of the principal Sidamo clans. It is based on a pragmatic view of a supernatural world which people seek to manipulate for their own ends. Because Magāno is the most powerful of supernatural entities, people, despite his aloofness, occasionally promise him an animal sacrifice if he will make them wealthy, improve their ability to procreate, or cure certain illnesses. If their goal is achieved—there is no time limit for fulfillment—they make good the pledge. Such vows are known as tāno, and they occur much more frequently in the form of agreements between individuals and the deified founding ancestors of the principal clans. They may also take the form of a promise to make a prescribed sacrifice at one of the numerous sacred locations in the Sidamo country. Though the term tāno is not used in connection with the propitiation of shatāna, the procedure is obviously similar. Since these spirits are believed to have the ability to bring and alleviate illness, as well as to control reproduction, an individual may be able to manipulate their actions in his favor by offering a comparable form of reciprocity. For example, when a possessed person becomes ill, the shatāni is asked if it brought the illness; if it replies in the affirmative, the people agree to give it food if it will promise to heal the victim. When the spirit has fulfilled his end of the bargain, the men of the community gather to perform the ritual food offering.

The two oldest shatāna are conceptualized as the father and mother of all these beings. According to legend, some men who were hunting in the lowlands around Lake Abbaya came upon some unusual looking maize plants. On their return to the highlands they planted some of this maize, and in time it grew and was harvested. After people had eaten food prepared from the corn, many of them became seriously ill and some of them died. It was during this time of trouble that Abo, the father of the shatāna, appeared. After telling the people his name, which happens to be the same as that of one of the most respected and feared of the early clan founders, he indicated that illness and death came to them because they had taken his corn. He agreed, however, to cure the sick if the people would always call and feed him when they were ill. Some time after this the wife of Abo appeared and took the name of Iyo (the term for mother or old lady in Sidamo). In time Abo and Iyo acquired some fifteen sons and daughters, one or more of whom usually appear with their parents when they possess an individual. This story has a number of variations, but all of them involve the discovery of shatāna in or near a body of water and the ingestion of food which leads to an illness remediable only by calling and feeding the supernatural carriers.

Other shatāna have made their appearance since the conquest of the Sidamo by Emperor Menelik II in 1893.[1] Three spirits, Amabassa, Walde, and Adeli, are thought by informants to have come from the Amhara. At least seven other shatāna have originated with individual Sidamo since the second decade of this century. Finally, Borantiča, an important Arussi deity, is regarded by many Sidamo today as a shatāni.

It was possible to obtain information from 31 informants identifying the spirits which had possessed them or their close relatives. Among the spirits listed above, Abo, Iyo, four of their sons, and one of their daughters were mentioned most frequently, and the more recent shatāna least frequently. Some informants were of the opinion that females are more subject to possession than males, while others questioned any significant difference by sex. In our sample there were nearly as many men as women, thirteen as compared with sixteen, who indicated they were subject to possession. Both men and women reported that they were more often possessed by male than female shatāna.[2]

POSSESSION

Possession can be considered from the standpoint of its onset and associated illnesses, ritual procedures, and the intensity and duration of the phenomenon. Regardless of when they first appear to the individual, shatāna are always preceded by an illness. It was the opinion of all informants, and substantiated by 23 subjects with spirits, that illnesses cannot be related to specific shatāna. The four most frequently reported disorders for possessed individuals of both sexes involved complaints of the head and nose, malfunctions of the gastro-intestinal tract, fever, and rheumatic conditions. The high frequency of head, nose, fever, and intestinal disorders may be at least partially attributed to the contrasting heat, cold, and dampness of the highland environment, the lack of sanitary facilities, and the contact with malaria on journeys to the lowlands. Because of

[1]This was the period of the unification of the Ethiopian Empire under the Amhara ruler Menelik II, who led his armies in subduing the various tribes and states of the southwest.
[2]From the sample of sixteen women and thirteen men who are or have been subject to possession, it was determined that 72 percent of the spirits possessing women were male, while 28 percent were female. Of those possessing men, 70 percent were male and 30 percent female.

the expense of feeding *shatāna*, most informants reported that they initially resisted accepting possession. They nevertheless asserted unanimously that they began to get better, some even reporting complete recovery, as soon as they gave in and accepted the demands of the spirits.

The occurrence of a prolonged unexplainable illness is generally considered the first sign that a *shatāni* is seeking to possess an individual. Though the potential host at first resists possession, possibly for as long as several months, he eventually evinces a tendency to shiver and shake periodically. If one or both of his parents has been subject to possession, his kinsmen and fellow villagers become convinced that the spirit wishes to be acknowledged and to pass on to the child. Generally the parent has died before such a transference occurs, though we recorded one instance where an old man passed on a *shatāni* to his daughter before his death. It was difficult to establish the criteria by which *shatāna* are transmitted when both parents have been hosts, but informants were of the opinion that the more powerful spirit would be the one passed on. In anticipation of possession in such cases, the men of the village assemble after dark in the hut of the patient and call the *shatāni* to the accompaniment of drumming and hand clapping. When the spirit begins to speak through the mouth of the patient, it first accepts responsibility for causing the illness, alleging that it wants "the child" to become its new host. It refers to the possessed as a horse (forāsho) if he is male, or a mule (gāngo) if female, and asks for the same measure of care and attention as is accorded these animals, in return for which it promises to protect the steed from future illnesses.

In cases when the patient is not the descendant of a parental host, or where there is uncertainty as to the connection between the physical disorder and the intervention of *shatāna*, it is possible to consult an expert, called *količka*, who understands the supernatural world and can verify the presence of a spirit as well as suggest a song to be used in summoning it. Such an expert, nearly always a male, is known to possess a powerful spirit which he has acquired either from his father or through dreaming and divination. In the latter case, the *shatāni* has appeared to him in a dream on several occasions, demanding that he serve as its host or face the alternative of death, and the dream has been confirmed by sacrificing a cow and examining the veins of its stomach lining. The *shatāna* of *količka* are more powerful than those of ordinary mortals; as one of these experts explained, "The distinction between our possession and that of the non-*količka* is the difference between the expert and the amateur." Indeed, they are considered potent enough to permit their hosts to predict the future as well as to cure disease. A *količka* has the ability to communicate with his *shatāni* at any time, though night is generally preferred, by beating upon his drum and singing the appropriate summoning song. These specialists in the supernatural are viewed by the community with a mixture of awe and fear. They have the power not only to diagnose and cure illness but also to provide solutions to personal and communal problems; and they are noted for their dire predictions of famines, epidemics, and interpersonal conflicts. They are characterized by alternate periods of mysterious withdrawal from and close intermingling with other people.

Six of our seventeen subjects indicated that, after prolonged illness, they had consulted a *količka* to determine whether a spirit wanted to possess them. Four of the six had parents with spirits, and two did not. The diagnostic procedures of the *kolica* indicate that his role is primarily to provide confirmation of possession. His initial act is to summon his spirit, which, speaking through him, asks a series of leading questions about the client's illness and life history. What follows is dependent on the results of this dialogue and on how much the *kolica* knows of the client's background. If he is uncertain as to the cause of the illness, he may direct the client to return home and await the occurrence of a dream or make a sacrifice to his deceased father. If, on the other hand, he knows enough about the life of the client and his family, he may diagnose possession immediately. When sacrifice has been prescribed, and the client recovers, it is evident that a *shatāni* was not involved. When recovery does not follow, the first occurrence of a dream sends the client back to the *kolica*, who can now decide with confidence that a *shatāni* is involved. The specialist then teaches the client a song for calling spirits and advises him to return to his village, call the *shatāni*, and thereby determine its identity. For this service the client and his kinsmen provide him with a gift of money or food.

The procedure for calling a spirit does not differ with the sex of the host, but the actual calling is always done by men, generally the agnates of a man or the affines of a woman. The initial attempt and most subsequent efforts to contact a spirit are made at night. It was difficult to ascertain just how a prospective host, without the precedent of parental spirits as a guide, can determine which of the many *shatāna* is possessing him. Informants questioned on this subject invariably answered that there is no way of knowing the identity of a spirit until it begins to speak. Some individuals appeared to associate particular disease symptoms with a particular *shatāni*, but informants did not reveal any consensus about such a correlation. Also there seemed to be some tendency to make the power of the spirit the basis of selection. Six out of eight of our subjects whose possession was not hereditary were possessed by either Abo or Iyo, the father and mother of all spirits, or by recently recognized and hence powerful spirits.

When the men who are to do the calling gather in the hut of the neophyte host in the evening, their attitude is usually casual, and they spend much time discussing the events of the day before settling down to their serious task. If, however, the individual who is suspected of being possessed is very ill or in great pain, the approach to the matter may be less casual. The men begin with a general song for summoning *shatāna*.[3] If the patient is able, he joins in the singing and clapping. The time that it takes for the spirit to come varies; sometimes it comes within one or two hours after the men begin to sing, but in other cases it may be two or more evenings before it appears.

An ill person lies on a bed during the early stages of the procedure, but one

[3]Spirit songs are called *hiyāta*. Each has a leader and a chorus. The leader may compose the song as he sings, the only requirement being that the words must rhyme. The following example is used to call Golama:

Golē, golē — Golē is brave [chorus].
Golē, golē — To make songs difficult is to lead one to forget them.
Golē, golē — Matu was Donga's mother [a lady who was well known in the past as a host for Golama].
Golē, golē — Golē is brave.
Golē, golē — I have no place to stand and sing.
Golē, golē — Someone became angry [referring to the *shatani*] and destroyed the children.
Golē, golē — Golē is brave.
Golē, golē — Sing, otherwise you are only taking up space.
Golē, golē — Unless you sing what is the use of having so many people.

who is not suffering too much discomfort sits on a stool with the men, who are gathered around the fire. The spirit enters the head of the possessed and causes it to shake—at first gradually and then more violently until his whole body begins to shudder. It is believed that the spirit entering the head of the possessed rides him as one would ride a horse or mule. The sideways, to-and-fro motion of the head and shoulders does in fact resemble that of a rider traveling at a gallop. As the shaking becomes more pronounced, the neophyte may rise, move toward the fire, and quickly pick up and drop some hot coals. The men, however, catch him and return him to his seat beside the fire. Finally the spirit announces its presence through its host, either by making a whirring sound like an insect or simply speaking out. There follows a dialogue between the *shatāni* and one of the men who has been designated spokesman because of his knowledge of spirits:

Spirit: Why did you call me?
Spokesman: We called to find out if you had brought this illness to X.
Spirit: I brought this illness to X because I wish to possess him, and he has refused to accept me; I am hungry and he has not fed me.
Spokesman: Will you heal X if he feeds you?
Spirit: Yes, I will make him well if he will feed me.
Spokesman: Who are you and who is with you?
Spirit: I am Abo, and my wife Iyo and our children Golā and Lafissa are with me.

The spokesman may then ask what it is that the spirit wishes to be fed, and the latter may suggest the kind of food that it wishes to receive, at least once a year, if it is to keep the horse or mule in good health. Most informants reported that they had been instructed to feed their spirits an animal, such as a bull, ram, or a sheep, along with ensete flour, butter, and honey. A few stated that it was sufficient to provide only barley, butter, and honey at the annual feeding.

After the initial possession experience, the possessed has the spirits called only at the annual feeding, when their children or cattle are ill, or when they wish to give thanks for some auspicious occurrence such as the birth of a child. Except in emergencies, the calling procedure always requires singing and drumming by the adult male members of the community. The catalogue of *shatāna* songs is known to all, and during the course of an evening the men sing a number of general calling songs, climaxed by that associated specifically with the host's *shatāni*. If an unusual illness suddenly befalls a child of the possessed, and there is insufficient time for the men of the community to foregather, the spirit may be called by taking a special grass (*hortshā*), mixing it with butter and spices, and placing it on the head of the host. The latter then asks the spirit to enter and tell whether it has caused the child to become sick.

There is apparently no fixed time for the annual feeding. Some perform this ritual at the end of the rains in October, others when the barley is harvested in January, and still others whenever they happen to have the necessary food. The feeding is much less elaborate on occasions other than the yearly feast. The procedure involves putting a small piece of meat or a little honey ensete, or barley on the tip of an ensete leaf and placing it on the tongue of the host. Though the food goes into the mouth of the possessed, it is believed that it is actually consumed by the *shatāni*. Since a possessing *shatāni* is always accompanied by one or more spirits who are considered his kinsmen, and who often take turns with him in accepting blame for bringing illness, they must be summoned separately and fed in similar manner. The more powerful a *shatāni* is, the more "kinsmen" he is likely to have and the longer it takes to summon them.

As to the effect of possession on the individual, four out of ten informants reported that they lost consciousness when the *shatāni* first came upon them but became aware of what was going on as soon as it began to speak. The others, however, were completely cognizant of what was happening throughout the possession experience. The voice of a *shatāni* is recognized as being the same as that of the possessed, the only difference being that it is sometimes louder than usual and may be characterized by a noticeable hesitancy, almost a stutter. One woman stated that her spirit sometimes spoke in Gallenia,[4] though she herself claimed not to understand this language. A majority of the informants reported that the *shatāni* always speaks in an angry and indignant manner which seems quickly to exhaust the vitality of its steed. It was in fact observed that after its departure the host was usually drenched with perspiration and so exhausted that he needed several days to recover.

Spirits exhibit considerable variation in supernatural power, which the Sidamo attribute to the noticeable differences in the degree to which they influence the lives of the possessed. Generally, spirits are considered to be the most potent at their time of origin, but there have been cases of seizure by older spirits who are recognized as more than usually strong. It is an indication of a powerful possession if the possessed remains behind the bamboo partition which divides the dwelling during the ritual, rather than mingling with the crowd around the fire. Criteria for the potency of a *shatāni*, in addition to the number of its accompanying spirits, include its ability to force people other than family members to serve as its steed, its demands for large gifts, and the making of prophesies.

A person may have a dream in which a spirit appears in the form of a neighboring host and asks to be served and fed. If he ignores this request, he is likely to suffer a severe physical illness or temporary insanity. To recover his health he must then not only fulfill the demands made in the dream but also go to the neighbor's compound accompanied by his close paternal relatives to beg the spirit to release him. He should remain with the host for a period of from several days to a month providing such services as cutting wood, preparing food, or working in the garden. At the end of this time he is considered to be cured and goes home, but he must return periodically with a small token of food as a sign of continuing respect for the spirit. It is said that the majority of people who are either afraid of or actually subject to this temporary form of possession are women.

A less spectacular way for a spirit to show its power is by making extravagant demands for gifts other than food. The stronger the *shatāni*, the more frequent and difficult are these demands. At its first appearance it may request a separate house in which to be called and fed. Subsequently it may make demands for various types of rings, bracelets, buttons, or strings of cowrie shells. Sometimes

[4]This is a general term used to refer to words and phrases taken from the languages of the Arussi people in the north and the Gugi on the southern boundaries of Sidamo territory.

these items can be obtained by the possessed only after a prolonged search of the local markets.

A third indication of unusual power is the ability of a spirit to tell men who may consult its host why their cows are unfecund or women why they have been unable to bear children, and to prescribe a course of action to alter these conditions. If these directions bring results, the client is expected to bring a suitable gift as an expression of gratitude.

Traditionally, and even today for a majority of people, the only way to escape from a *shatāni* is through death. The spirit leaves its host just prior to his death, having indicated its intention to pass on to a favored child, who may be of either sex and who is alleged to be the one who has been most obedient and subservient to the possessed parent. Occasionally the spirit requests to be fed by both the possessed and this favorite child during the lifetime of the former.

Since World War II it has been possible to break the tie with one's *shatāni* by joining one of several European mission churches. When this happens, the spirits are believed to depart when the host stands before the congregation, renounces all *shatāna*, and professes a belief in Christian principle. Persons who experience this form of religious conversion acknowledge that they are motivated to do so through anticipation of a superior form of supernatural protection to be provided by Jesus Christ; they are convinced that they will never again experience the illness and pain formerly associated with their *shatāna*. Coincident with this belief, however, is a fear that to waver in the newly found faith or to neglect church duties is to invite the return of the *shatāna*.

Considering the socio-psychological functions of possession, it may seem strange that some persons should want to break their ties with a spirit. There is, however, always a certain amount of ambivalence toward accepting possession because of its association with ill health and the fear that if the spirit is not properly served the host will die. Moreover, unless others recognize the *shatāni* as powerful and are motivated to serve it, the feeding obligation can become expensive for the possessed and his immediate kinsmen.

SOCIAL STRUCTURE

The extent to which prestige is based on the power to influence others provides the key to understanding the relations between social structure and possession among the Sidamo. Since there is considerable sexual difference in the way positions of influence are structured, we may begin by examining the situation among men.

At all levels of organization in which males are involved, prestige is partially based on seniority in chronological age. Deference must always be shown by a younger to an older male. In childhood younger brothers are expected to serve and obey older brothers. Initiation into the age-grade system, which can happen at any time between early childhood and late adolescence, is merely a preliminary to the circumcision ritual, which confers elder status on the individual years later. For a man to become an elder and live to a very old age is to acquire as much prestige as it is possible to obtain by ascription.

Since however, there are many other males with similar ascribed positions at all age levels, a man must achieve status in some way if he is to distinguish himself. One traditional means of acquiring fame was to show unusual bravery in battle or in attacking and subduing a leopard, lion, or other ferocious beast. There are still some old men, and even a few younger ones, who have achieved fame by killing an Arussi tribesman in a border skirmish. The usual means of achieving renown and influence today, though, is through the acquisition either of wealth or of oratorical expertise. A man is considered wealthy if he has a large number of cattle or combines a smaller herd with extensive fields of ensete and coffee. It is our impression that skilled orators tend also to be wealthy.

For men who aspire to fame and social dominance, but for one reason or another have no talent as warriors, orators, or farmers, spirit possession provides an alternative opportunity for achieving status. A person with a powerful spirit may accumulate wealth from gifts, and he has the potentiality of attracting large audiences when he undergoes possession, even if he is completely ignored in the assembly of elders. In the villages where field work was conducted, three of the four men with spirits were considered to be poor farmers, to possess few livestock, and to be inadequate public speakers, and two of them were also alleged to be cowards. Moreover, it was reported by some of the older men that two out of three known originators of powerful spirits in the last fifty years had lived in poverty prior to their possession experience. Within a few years of the initial appearance of their shatāna, they became wealthy and achieved fame throughout Sidamo. The followers of Shiffa, the original "horse" of the spirits Galāmo Marāme, increased to the point that a large village of supplicants grew up around his residence.

Indirect evidence to the same effect was provided by informants who indicated that they wanted spirits so that people would serve them, or that they dismissed them when people stopped bringing food for the ritual feedings. One man frankly admitted that he had decided to become a Christian when he realized that he had few supplicants and was wasting much of his own property in feeding his shatāna.

The possession of women can best be understood by comparing their status with that of men. The Sidamo place so much stress on the importance of the male line and on patrilocal residence that a man, once he has paid bridewealth, has virtually absolute rights to the services and procreative potential of his wife. A woman has no rights of inheritance from her affines or agnates. Consequently, in her old age, if her husband is dead and she has no sons, she must either rely on generosity of her spouse's kinsmen or return to her own agnates, who may receive her reluctantly. During her marriage her husband may send her away at will and beat her whenever he pleases. She must always defer to him and his male agnates and must observe a variety of taboos; for example, she may not mention the name of her husband's father, she must avoid him and all his collateral male agnates, and she must look down at the ground when spoken to by a man. Even in their ritual greeting of men it is customary for women to demean themselves by referring to their position as of no more consequence than the earth upon which the men tread. The only aspects of a woman's role which serve to alleviate her subordinate position are her capacity for childbearing and the dependence of her husband upon her for food preparation and labor.

Since a man can never admit to accepting the opinion or advice of a woman, one of the few ways she has of commanding the attention of her male affines, or of achieving wider renown, is through spirit possession. In possession, it is not she but the spirit temporarily using her as a host who arrests the attention of the men in the community. Hence a woman who achieves fame as the "mule" of a powerful spirit does not constitute a threat to male feelings of status superiority. In the name of her *shatāni* she can make demands on her husband and his male agnates for food and presents which would not be appropriate to her role as a woman and a wife.

Though a husband and his male kinsmen may resent the expense and inconvenience of feeding the woman's spirit, they usually accept the obligation in order to prevent conflict that could lead to divorce and the consequent costs and effort of obtaining another spouse. Failure to feed a possessed woman's spirit, moreover, provides her with an excuse for being ill and thus unable to serve her husband. One female informant even told of having "given in" after being admonished by her *shatāni* to leave her negligent husband. The significance of this indirect form of feminine manipulation for a man of limited resources can be seen from the fact that women married to wealthy men do not have spirits. Marriage to a man of wealth is considered ideal, because it guarantees a woman enviable gifts of clothing, food, land, and animals. Less successful men are often aware that their wives use possession to exploit their fear of losing the bridewealth, which is not returnable at divorce, and many humorous stories of such forms of exploitation are current throughout Sidamo. Several informants related instances of men who had become so infuriated with the whimsical demands of their spouses' spirits that they managed, by means of severe beatings, to frighten their wives into foregoing possession.

As an interesting alternative to solitary possession, a husband and wife may have *shatāna* simultaneously. The spirits are quite different, and the wife usually precedes her spouse as a host by several years. According to informants, either the woman convinces her spouse that for both of them to have *shatāna* will provide increased protection for their children's health and greater fecundity for their cattle, or the husband decides that having a spirit of his own will insure his remembering to feed the one possessing his wife. Given the structural relationship of men vis-à-vis women, this latter explanation sounds like a rationalization on the part of males to justify to their agnates the feeding of a wife's spirit.

PSYCHOLOGICAL ASPECTS

Failure by men as warriors, orators, or farmers, and by women in making desirable marriages, does not provide a sufficient explanation for the possession phenomenon. Not all unsuccessful persons acquire spirits, and it is necessary to examine certain psychological variables to account for the selective aspects of possession and its association with illness. Such an approach requires a consideration of psychological dependency and of the personality attributes of a certain type of psychosomatic debility. Kardiner (1939: 32) has suggested the following definition for dependency:

It is a basic ego attitude necessary for survival in response to anxiety resulting from a feeling of helplessness, or to a feeling of limited resources, strength or ability. The attitude is one of soliciting support, help, or protection. In extreme instances, it is an actual wish that another person take over all responsibility for the subject's welfare.

More recently Sears (1963: 25–63), after comparing dependency tendencies in two samples of nursery-school children, has suggested that the development of this attribute differs along sexual lines. When parents promote dependent behavior in their daughters, the latter exhibit this tendency in the nursery-school setting, but Sears could find no relation between the encouragement of dependency in sons and their exhibition of this attribute in the nursery school. He nevertheless indicates that the encouragement of specific acts of dependency, not merely "generalized dependency," is likely to encourage dependent behavior in children of both sexes.

The frequency with which children sought help, physical contact, and close proximity with adults and peers, as well as their rather obvious attempts to gain attention in the home, community, and testing situations, led the authors to conclude that dependency is generally encouraged in Sidamo. This reliance on parental figures, usually promoted by praise and rewarded by extra food for compliance with adult demands, comes to an abrupt end for most youths at the time of their marriage. An exception is to be noted in the case of "favorite" children, who are found in many Sidamo families. Such children tend to be continually in attendance on their elders and to be unusually obedient, and they receive noticeably more food and more lavish displays of affection than do their siblings. When the favorite is the youngest son, he is expected to remain with or near his father, serving him until death. Even when the preferred son is not the youngest, and hence not expected to care for his father in the latter's old age, more than the usual amount of visiting and gift exchange occur between them.

In view of the dependency factor, it is not surprising that, when a parent has acquired a *shatāni*, it is the favorite son or daughter who becomes the host in the next generation. It was possible to obtain data on the approximate age at which spirit possession first occurred in fifteen such subjects—six males and nine females. All of the males first underwent possession at around the onset of middle age, i.e., well after marriage and at about the age when the death of their parents is to be expected. Two of them specifically indicated that they had dreamed, after the death of the parental host, that the spirit wanted them and had shortly thereafter become ill. For males, possession thus appears to provide a substitute for the dependency relationship previously exhibited toward parents. It enables them periodically to focus upon themselves the concern of their male agnates and other members of the community, thereby rewarding them for their dependency on their *shatāna* manifested in the ritual feeding of the latter.

For favorite daughters, it is not death which disrupts the dependency relationship with the parents, but rather marriage and removal to the village of the husband. Of our nine female subjects, one had her first possession experience prior to marriage, six at the time of their marriage, one four years after her marriage, and one after the birth of her children. The physical separation of married women from their parents is intensified by the reluctance of their husbands to permit them to return for visits. Under these circumstances, acquiring a spirit enables a woman periodically to attract dramatic attention from her husband and other men in the community, who are ordinarily indifferent to her emotional needs. Possession thus provides a similar outlet for dependency in women as in men.

An interesting exception is to be noted in the fact that favorite daughters of parental hosts who marry wealthy men rarely acquire *shatāna*. A possible explanation is that wives who serve well their successful husband tend to be indulged by the latter with clothing, cattle, food, housing, and favors for their children. Such women are not only respected and envied by those who have made less successful marriages but are amply rewarded for their submissive and faithful service to their spouses. In effect, their former dependency role *vis-à-vis* their parents is transferred to the husband.

Psychosomatic factors seem frequently to be involved in illnesses associated with possession. Of 23 subjects who reported their symptoms, ten mentioned severe rheumatic disturbances involving stiffness, swelling, and aching of the joints. They asserted that, after accepting possession, they were able to resume their normal activities almost immediately, even in cases where they had been confined to their beds for prolonged periods. All of them maintained, moreover, that they experienced no recurrence of their rheumatic pains as long as their *shatāna* were fed on demand by their male agnates and other adult males of the community.

This information is especially interesting in the light of a number of studies which have indicated a relationship between psychosocial factors and rheumatoid arthritis in modern industrial societies. These researches, though their findings have not always been consistent, nevertheless reveal a tendency for arthritic patients to be excessively concerned over separation from a key parent and to be unusually self-sacrificing and willing to serve others (King 1955: 287–302; Ludwig 1949: 339; Scotch and Geiger 1962: 1037–1067; Robinson 1957: 344–345). Another study (Cobb and King 1958: 466–476) goes so far as to indicate a connection between an arthritic condition and the stresses generated by frustrated occupational and educational ambitions. The rheumatic complaints of the Sidamo, with their postulated relationship to dependency and the striving for attention, reveal obvious similarities to the rheumatoid arthritis syndrome. Other illnesses associated with possession–gastro-intestinal disturbances, skin disease, fever, and head and nasal complaints—may also have a psychosomatic aspect, since rapid recoveries are similarly reported upon acceptance of the role of host to a spirit.

The state of helplessness that goes with disease tends to be rewarded by the community. Any form of sickness in Sidamo entitles the sufferer to an extraordinary amount of attention. Even in the case of a small child, kinsmen and friends of the parents from miles around congregate in the hut of the patient, bringing food and sharing it with him. This rewarding of dependency derives from childhood when parents regard the giving of food as the standard means of satisfying any attempt to attract attention or achieve closeness. To fail to respond with sustenance is tantamount to rejection, and is in fact employed by parents as a convenient form of punishment for small children. Since feeding has such important emotional connotations, it is not surprising that the Sidamo are reluctant to turn away strangers and even stray dogs who are hungry. If our hypothesis that possessed people show an unusual amount of dependency is correct, then it is understandable why the host of a spirit reverts to a state of helplessness characterized by conscious or unconscious somatic symptoms, and why *shatāna* complain of neglect which can only be compensated by feeding.

• • •

REFERENCES

CERULLI, E., Zar. Encyclopedia of Islam 4: 1217. London, 1934.

COBB, S., and S. H. KING, "Psychosocial Factors in the Epidemiology of Rheumatoid Arthritis." *Journal of Chronic Diseases* 7: 466–475, 1958.

HABERLAND, E., *Galla Süd-Aethiopiens.* Stuttgart, 1963.

KARDINER, A., *The Individual and His Society.* New York, 1939.

KING, S., "Psychosocial Factors Associated with Rheumatoid Arthritis." *Journal of Chronic Diseases* 2: 287–302, 1955.

LEIRIS, M., "Le culte des zars à Gondar." *Aethiopica* 3: 96–103, 1934.

——, *La possession et ses aspects théâtraux chez les Ethiopiens de Gondar.* Paris, 1958.

Ludwig, A. O., "Emotional Factors in Rheumatoid Arthritis: Their Bearing on the Care and Rehabilitation of the Patient." *Physiotherapy Review* 29: 338–350, 1949.

Messing, S., "The Highland-Plateau Amhara of Ethiopia." Unpublished Ph.D. dissertation, University of Pennsylvania, 1957.

——, "Group Therapy and Social Status in the Zar Cult of Ethiopia." *Culture and Mental Health,* ed. M. K. Opler, pp. 319–332. New York, 1959.

ROBINSON, C., "Emotional Factors and Rheumatoid Arthritis." *Canadian Medical Association Journal* 77: 344–345, 1957.

SCOTCH, N., and H. GEIGER, "The Epidemiology of Rheumatoid Arthritis." *Journal of Chronic Diseases* 15: 1037–1067, 1962.

SEARS, R., "Dependency Motivation." *Nebraska Symposium on Motivation,* ed. M. R. Jones, pp. 25–64. Lincoln, 1963.

SHACK, W., "Some Aspects of Ecology and Social Structure in the Ensete Complex in South-West Ethiopia." *Journal of the Royal Anthropological Institute* 93: 72–79, 1963.

TUCKER, A., and M. BRYAN, *The Non-Bantu Languages of North-Eastern Africa.* London, 1956.

Informal Judicial Activity in Bunyoro

J. H. M. Beattie

In most African societies there are more or less institutionalized ways of settling inter-personal disputes below the level of the formal court system. Since the informal judicial or arbitrative groups responsible for carrying out these procedures do not usually meet at regular times or places and do not keep written records, often little is known of their activities outside the small communities in which they function. The following short account of the Nyoro institution of 'councils of natives' or 'of neighbors' (nkurato [singular rukurato] z'enzarwa, or z'abatahi) may therefore be of some interest. In it I briefly consider the nature and size of the communities in which these councils operate, their composition, the kinds of disputes they deal with and their manner of dealing with them (giving a few examples), the ways in which Banyoro regard them, and, finally, their social significance and effectiveness.

Bunyoro, one of the great interlacustrine Bantu kingdoms of Uganda, is ruled (under the Protectorate administration, represented in Bunyoro by a district commissioner and two or three assistants) by a hereditary king, the Mukama, and a hierarchy of appointed territorial chiefs. These chiefs are of four ranks, usually rendered in English as 'county chiefs,' 'sub-county chiefs,' 'parish chiefs,' and 'village headmen.' The two higher categories of chiefs hold official courts, constituted under the Protectorate's Native Courts Ordinance. These courts, which have the powers and jurisdictions usual for native courts in British Africa, are not our concern in this article. But it is necessary to note that the authority vested in them and the possibility of recourse to them provide a constant background to the field of inter-personal village relationships.

Banyoro live in scattered areas of settlement, not in compact villages. Their homesteads usually occupy the slightly raised areas, migongo, which are marked off from one another by the streams and papyrus swamps characteristic of the country. Much of Bunyoro is unpopulated bush, but in the settled regions density is quite high, often over 100 to the square mile. A typical homestead consists of one or two mud-and-wattle houses round a central courtyard, sheltered by a banana grove and surrounded by food gardens, and rarely more than shouting distance from the home of at least one neighbor. It is a traditional Nyoro value that patrilineal kinsmen should live near one another, especially full brothers. Sometimes they do, but often they do not, and most men's neighbors and daily associates include unrelated persons as well as patrilateral and matrilateral kinsfolk and affines. At least as important as kinship for the composition of co-operating local groups (for example for house-building or communal cultivation) are the principles of neighborhood (butahi) and friendship.

The smallest territorial division of which Banyoro speak is a kyaro (plural byaro); literally 'a place where people stay.' A kyaro is not the same thing as a mugongo, for a mugongo may be uninhabited, or occupied by two or three byaro. Thus a kyaro may not be physically marked off from neighboring byaro, though if there is no intervening river or swamp there is generally a more or less perceptible interval of uncultivated land. Though the boundary of a kyaro implies no barrier to kinship and other face-to-face relationships of neighborhood, a kyaro is none the less a distinct social unit; it has a name, and its members see themselves as members of one kyaro as against the occupants of other neighboring areas. Finally, the kyaro is not coterminous with any administratively recognised political unit. The smallest 'official' division, the area of the mutongole chief or village headman, may contain two or three migongo and half a dozen or more byaro. A kyaro may contain anything up to fifty or sixty households, though the average is somewhat lower; the one which I knew best had forty-one households and it was considered quite a large one. The smallest political unit, the butongole, averages 150 to 200 tax-payers.

Banyoro, then, form a population of scattered cultivators. They live in homesteads which are separated from other homesteads by fields and gardens and fallow land but which are near enough for an alarm to be widely heard. They think about and express their every-day social relationships in terms of kinship, of affinity, and simply of neighborhood. The informal tribunals which we are about to consider cannot be properly understood unless they are seen in this context of neighborhood and neighborly obligation. Bunyoro quite explicitly attach a very high value to 'neighborliness';[1] they like to have other people living near them, to visit constantly, and especially to eat and drink with one another. Sociability and *kyaro* solidarity are the highest community values, and we shall see that one of the main functions of the informal judicial procedures which we are about to describe is to sustain these values and to restore them when they are breached.

Like other people, Banyoro get along pretty well with one another on the whole, but sometimes they do not. Disputes between individuals may arise from a variety of causes. They may arise over property (as in case of inheritance disputes, debt and theft), over women (as in cases of adultery and marriage troubles), over the custody of children, over cultivation rights and claims to land, and over all kinds of minor issues at beer parties and at other times. The hostilities which these differences bring about can be expressed in various ways. Thus disputes may (though they rarely do) lead to inter-personal violence; they may—and this is common—express themselves in mutual recriminations and abuse or, more seriously, in the practice or imputation of sorcery; and they may result in the destruction of property, typically by arson. Once disputes have arisen and have ceased to be reconcilable at the 'private' level, they can be dealt with 'judicially' in either of two ways. They may be settled through the superimposed native court system (they would in any case be so dealt with if the dispute had led to a homicide or serious injury), or they may be dealt with through an informal local tribunal, a *rukurato rw'enzarwa.*

This body consists simply of a group of neighbors summoned *ad hoc* to adjudicate upon the matter in issue. Membership of the group is not an office; there is no formal appointment to it, and it is not a 'standing committee' with permanent or semi-permanent membership. It only comes into existence when an aggrieved person causes it to be known that he has a dispute with another person which he wishes to be heard by a *rukurato rw'enzarwa*. When they are informed, neighboring householders who are available and interested will come along. Some may be specially invited, but any neighbor may drop in without invitation, so long as he is not on bad terms with the complainant. The only qualifications for active participation in the council are membership of the male sex and, ideally, headship of a household: age in itself is not important. It is to be noted that these councils are not clan councils or councils of agnatic kinsmen, though sometimes they may approximate to such. There are, of course,

[1] The following story is often told to illustrate this: "Once upon a time a man moved into a new neighborhood. He wanted to make a trial of the kind of neighbors he had, so this is what he did. In the very middle of the night he pretended to beat his wife, to see whether the neighbors would come to help her or not. But he did not really beat her; instead he beat a goat-skin, and his wife screamed and cried out that he was killing her. But no neighbors came to see what was the matter, and the very next day the man packed up and left that place with his wife and went to find somewhere else to live."

certain kinds of disputes (for example, in regard to inheritance) which are primarily the concern of a group of agnatic kinsmen. But even in such cases, where both the parties to the dispute are of the same clan, representation on the council which is to settle the matter is generally based no less on neighborhood than on kinship. In a dispute known to me in which a father accused his adult son of rudeness and neglect of traditional manners (the son had sat on a chair while eating in his father's company and had used a spoon instead of his fingers to eat millet porridge, the traditional food of Banyoro), the father summoned two or three unrelated neighbors as well as his own kinsmen to hear his complaint against his son. The basic pattern, then, is the same whether the dispute is between kinsmen or non-kinsmen: in both cases kinsmen and non-kinsmen of each party may be present, though naturally in a matter such as inheritance which primarily concerns a group of agnates it is likely that there will be a higher representation of patrilineal kin. But the point is that the distinction is one of degree: participation in these councils is seen as an obligation deriving from neighborhood (*butahi*) at least as much as from any sort of kinship link with either or both parties to the dispute.

Cases dealt with by *nkurato z'enzarwa* of which I have records fall into the following rough categories. First I list those types of cases which arose between kinsmen or affines. An adolescent or grown-up 'child' disobeying its father (thus a son was fined for refusing to marry the girl his father had chosen for him, thus making his father feel 'shame' in front of people); a son attempting to seduce one of his father's wives; a man behaving rudely or with unseemly familiarity towards his wife's parents; a man treating his wife badly (by failing to provide her with a proper house, or with adequate clothes, or by beating her excessively or without good cause); a wife failing in her duty to her husband (by being lazy, adulterous, drunken or disobedient). Issues which arose between unrelated persons included the following: cases of quarrelling, abuse and assault; imputing sorcery (*burogo*) to another person without grounds, or falsely accusing another person of any crime; committing adultery; theft of foodstuffs from a field or of small articles; failure to settle debts. Of course, the gravest offences such as homicide, rape, actual sorcery (as opposed to the mere imputation of it) or serious theft would be taken directly to the official native courts or (in cases which exceeded the powers of the native courts) directly to the district commissioner's court. Minor disputes which the *rukurato rw'enzarwa* failed to settle would also be taken to the chief's court of lowest instance, and so would cases in which either party to the dispute insisted upon it. We shall see that in fact neither would be likely to do so, and even if he did the native court would ordinarily want to know why the matter had not been settled locally in the *kyaro*.

It is convenient to present here detailed accounts of three actual cases dealt with by *nkurato z'enzarwa*, each of which illustrates one or more aspects of the kinds of procedure involved. The first two cases are between unrelated persons; the third is between a man and his wife.

In the first case, two men at a beer party quarrelled. An older man, Yonasani, who was drunk, insulted a younger man, Tomasi. Tomasi wished to fight with Yonasani, but other people who were present prevented him from doing so. However, he left the party early and waited on the path towards Yonasani's home, and when Yonasani passed he dealt him a severe blow on the head with a stick and fled, leaving him lying on the ground. But Yonasani knew who his assailant was, and the next morning he complained to Tomasi's father, and went with him to see Tomasi to find out what he had to say. Tomasi at first denied all knowledge of the affair, but when Yonasani said that he intended to take the case to the official chief's court Tomasi's father said that he and his son would agree to a hearing before a *rukurato rw'enzarwa*. Tomasi's father accordingly summoned about half-a-dozen neighbors to come and settle the case, and they met at an appointed hour in the latter's house. After a brief discussion it was agreed that Tomasi had struck Yonasani, and that he had done wrong to do so, for if he was aggrieved by Yonasani's behavior he should have brought a case against him, not beaten him. He was accordingly instructed to bring four large jars of banana beer and five shillings' worth of meat to Yonasani's house. A day was arranged, about a week later, and the beer and meat was duly provided. All the people who had been there when the case was heard were present, and Tomasi was told to serve the beer, and to choose somebody to roast the meat on the fire. "Then," in the words of an informant who was present, "we began to eat and drink, and everybody started to laugh and joke as they do at a wedding feast. Soon some people began dancing, and we accompanied them by singing and clapping our hands. By now Tomasi and Yonasani had become quite friendly as they used to be before, and were chatting with each other and calling each other by their *mpako* names.[2] And from that day to this the quarrel between them has been finished and they are quite friendly."

The second case also concerned two men. Yozefu, an elderly man, had accused Yakobo of burning his house, on the grounds that he knew that Yakobo hated him, and that his wives had seen him running away. But Yakobo proved an alibi, and he then accused Yozefu, before a *rukurato rw'enzarwa* containing among other neighbors the local village headman, of 'spoiling his name.' Here is a translation of Yakobo's (written) account of the affair:

Everyone present agreed that Yozefu failed in this case [literally 'the case defeated him']. So I asked the village headman to take us to the sub-county chief's headquarters, so that I could accuse him in the chief's court. But many of the people present said to me 'Yakobo, it would be better for you to allow him to pay a 'fine' of beer and meat, in accordance with our Nyoro custom of forbearance and good manners'. So I said, 'All right; in that case I shall go home, and if he comes to my house and begs my forgiveness I shall forgive him, but if he does not come I shall accuse him in the sub-county chief's court'. He came in the evening, after I had called in some neighbors to hear what should pass, and we told him that he should bring four jars of beer and a goat. He said that he would bring them in a week's time. On the day arranged I called all the people who had been at the first hearing of the case, and we waited for Yozefu to come. He came, bringing two pots of beer. Then the neighbors who were present said, 'Ho, Yozefu, what are you bringing beer here for? Are you coming to marry here or what?'[3] He replied that he had brought it because of having spoken badly of me by saying that I had burned his house, and he begged me to accept two jars of beer only, as he had not been able to get any more. I said that I would accept them, but I reminded him that it was only owing to my kindness that he was not in prison, and I warned him that if he committed a similar fault in the future I would certainly take

[2]The *mpako*, a term which may be roughly translated "praise-names", are of Nilotic origin, and in Bunyoro their use implies a combination of intimacy and respect.

[3]When a suitor formally presents himself at the home of his prospective bride's parents, he takes with him a present of four jars of beer and a goat.

him before the chief's court [omu bukama, literally 'to the kingship'; the superimposed state in contrast to the community]. So I and all the people there drank the beer, and we danced, and the matter was finished. But even now I am still not friendly with Yozefu, and he does not come to my home. In this case, Yakobo further explained, "we did not actually require Yozefu to bring a goat; when the neighbors who were deciding the case saw that he was sorry, and since they knew he was a poor man, they agreed that it would be enough if he brought six shillings' worth of meat instead, in order to sweeten the beer.

My third example is a dispute between a woman and her husband. Yuniya, the wife of Matayo, brought three complaints against him. She had been married to him for more than ten years, but had had no children by him. He had children by other wives from whom he had afterwards separated.

The case was heard in the house of one Petero, an educated man and a clerk in the District Office, who was a classificatory 'grandchild' (sister's daughter's son) of Yuniya. He was present at the hearing, but the head of the proceedings was Jemusi, who although only distantly connected with Yuniya had grown up in the same household with her. He took the place that her father would have occupied had he been alive. Also present were two middle-aged men, the sons of an older sister of Yuniya. All these persons counted as being on Yuniya's side. Matayo was accompanied by a friend, a fellow clansman but not a close relation. Two near neighbors of middle age, Paulo and Erisa, both of whom were householders and neither of whom was related to either party to the dispute, completed the assembly. One or two other neighbors dropped in and went away again from time to time. It is to be noted that the case was heard on the wife's 'home' kyaro, not the husband's; his home was on another mugongo, some miles away.

The rukurato, at which I was present, was held in the front room of Petero's house. Everybody sat around the room on chairs, except Yuniya who sat on the floor just on the other side of the doorway leading to the back of the house. She was only permitted to be there because she was a party to the dispute, and even then she was not allowed to sit actually in the room. She made three charges against her husband Matayo, an elderly and somewhat irascible looking person. First, she said, he had accused her of sorcery; when he had guests in the house and told her to prepare tea for them, he warned them not to drink it until she had drunk some first, lest it should poison them. Second, he had locked her out of their house when he went visiting, and had refused to let her come into his room. And third, he had driven out of the house and then assaulted Yuniya's younger brother George, who was Yuniya's father's heir and who had been living with his sister and her husband for the past three years, since he had no house of his own. When Matayo was invited to reply to these charges he admitted the first two, though not with a very good grace, but in reply to the charge of assault he alleged that the young man George had assaulted him first.

There was some discussion, for the most part fairly calm and restrained although Matayo occasionally showed signs of restiveness, and then Erisa, the younger of the two unrelated neighbors who had been called in, spoke. Matayo, he said, lost on all three counts. He had failed to produce any evidence that in all the years of their marriage Yuniya had shown any signs of being a sorceress. To shut her out of her own house showed very great contempt (bunobi bukooto *muno*) for her and was quite unjustified; a man's wife is the mistress of the house, the *mukama w'enju*, and he has no right to exclude her from it. Finally, he had done wrong to chase away Yuniya's brother; he was of her clan and indeed was his 'father-in-law' (*isezara*), for he was his father's heir, and to such a person respect is due. The other unrelated neighbor, Paulo, expressed his agreement with these findings. Then Erisa said that Matayo should bring a goat and four jars of beer to Jemusi (this is the standard penalty, though it may be reduced), and that Yuniya should return to her husband's home.

At this point, however, Yuniya interjected emphatically that she would never return to Matayo: "they will continue to accuse me of sorcery," she said. Erisa thereupon declared that in that case the bride-wealth which Matayo had paid for her would have to be returned to him. She agreed, but said that she would need some time to find it. It should strictly speaking have been repaid by George, the father's heir, but since he was a young man without resources, Jemusi, Petero and Yuniya herself would help to make it up. The amount concerned was about seven pounds. Matayo then said with considerable vehemence that he would not now have her back even if she wanted to return, as she and her brother had tried to choke him to death when he had told him to leave. Nor would he pay the goat and beer ordered. So Paulo, the elder of the two unrelated neighbors, said, "that means, then, that you wish to be finally separated from your wife." Matayo emphatically agreed, and throwing his dilapidated felt hat upside-down on the floor he declared with passion that he wanted neither her nor any other wife; all he wanted was his money back. Then Jemusi told Matayo and his friend that he would send them a letter when the money had been collected, so that they could come and fetch it. Matayo said that he would not come back here for the money; they should send it to him. Then he and his friend left (Paulo had left after the judgment had been given), and the rest of the people who had been present gradually drifted away.

These three cases exemplify the kinds of matters dealt with by *nkurato z'enzarwa* and the procedures involved. The initial action is always taken by the injured party. We noted that whether or not the disagreement is between related persons the procedure is the same, and unrelated neighbors are just as likely to be present at the hearing of a dispute between kinsmen as kinsmen of the parties concerned are likely to be present at the hearing of a case involving unrelated persons. Any male householder in the *kyaro* may be present; as we have seen, it is neighborhood rather than kinship which determines the composition of the council. Always the same kind of penalty is imposed; the defeated party is ordered by the *rukurato* to bring beer and meat (usually a goat) to be consumed by the disputants and the members of the *rukurato*. And the person who loses the case is expected to humble himself, not only to the man he has injured but to the whole assembly. Thus Yozefu had to speak humbly and apologetically to Yakobo, and when ribald jokes were made at his expense by the party assembled to receive him he had to submit without showing resentment. I was told that when judgment is given it is proper for both parties to kneel down and thank the *rukurato* for its decision, but this would not usually be done nowadays.

Banyoro themselves greatly value their institution of *nkurato z'enzarwa*. They regard its use as the proper and seemly way of dealing with inter-personal disputes in the *kyaro*. It would be 'unneighborly' to take a minor complaint to the chief's official court, *omu bukama*, and it is an act of grace and kindness on the part of the complainant to refrain from doing so. A brief example may illustrate this. Isoke was accused of adultery. The wronged husband was going to take the case to the native court, but (I quote from my informant):

Isoke, seeing that he might be imprisoned, quickly went and pleaded with the husband thus: 'Sir, I beg you that the fault which is being taken to the court may be returned to the neighbors (*omu batahi*) for settlement, so that I may be "fined" there. Perhaps you will help me in this way.' The injured husband agreed, and the case was taken to a *rukurato rw'enzarwa*, where it defeated Isoke, who was told to bring meat and beer, as is customary.

Banyoro themselves make the point that to settle a case in this way, and to impose the conventional penalty, is to express confidence in the man who has erred; it shows that he is still accepted as a member of the community, and the affair is settled in the community and not outside it. To send him to the official court would in a sense imply the community's rejection of him. In this connection Banyoro sometimes quote the saying 'you don't tell someone who is not of your own people what it is that he has done to annoy you' (*atali wawe tokumanyisa ekyakubihirrire*); that is, the very fact that the issue can be frankly examined and decided by an informal council of neighbors (and therefore by implication friends) shows that the offender is still accepted as a member of the *kyaro* community. If a dispute between neighbors can be settled in the *kyaro* that is the way it should be settled; it is a serious matter to take it to the 'Government,' where strangers will hear the case and where heavier penalties including imprisonment, may be imposed. This should only be done when settlement at the community level is seen to be impossible.[4]

Of course, the parties to a case dealt with by a *rukurato rw'enzarwa* are not always completely reconciled, and Banyoro realize this; we saw that Yosefu never really became friendly with Yakobo, and Matayo was not reconciled to his wife. But Yozefu had not been friendly with Yakabo even before the case was heard, and Banyoro do not expect *nkurato z'enzarwa* to work miracles. And in the case of Matayo what was accomplished was not a reconciliation but a settlement, the effecting of a divorce. In this latter case, when the marriage ceased to exist, the possibility of paying over the meat and beer also ceased to exist, for that payment could only take place within the framework of an existing relationship. Where that relationship was broken, there could be nothing there to mend.

Still less is it the primary aim of a *rukurato rw'enzarwa* to 'punish' a wrong-doer. Certainly the possibility that it may impose a penalty may exercise a deterrent effect, and this is acknowledged; Banyoro are not wealthy and beer and meat cost money. But this is secondary. If one suggests that the culprit is made to suffer by being compelled to spend his money on meat and beer, Banyoro reply: "Why should he be angry or hurt? He consumes his share of the things he buys, and he enjoys the feast just as much as the others do." The main object, then, appears to be to reintegrate the delinquent into the community and, if possible, to achieve reconciliation without causing bitterness and resentment; in

[4]In a number of contexts Banyoro contrast the community, with its stress on intimacy, friendship and neighborly co-operation, with the superimposed state, the *bukama*, which is the source of political authority and the agent of a power which derives from outside the local community.

the words of an informant, the institution exists 'to finish off people's quarrels and to abolish bad feeling.' In Bunyoro social attachment and solidarity are typically expressed in communal eating and drinking, and the joint feast in which the proceedings of the *rukurato rw'enzarwa* culminate may be seen, in one aspect, as a device for re-integrating the offender into the *kyaro* community. For not only does he have his share of the food and drink he has provided, but he is himself the host. And this is a praiseworthy thing; from a dishonorable status he is promoted to an honorable one. So the beer and meat are not a 'fine,' at least not in the usual sense of that term; for their significance is rehabilitative rather than penal. It is perhaps hardly necessary to point out that if the conventional penalty were to be commuted to a money payment (and there is happily no sign of this happening as yet) the institution of *nkurato z'enzarwa* would completely change its form, for a money payment cannot be eaten or drunk, and it would inevitably sooner or later be turned to private and not public good.

These informal councils, then, serve functions quite different from (though no less important than) those aimed at by the official court system, to which they may be regarded as in a sense complementary. It would be a serious error to represent them simply as clumsy, 'amateur' expedients for punishing wrongdoers or settling civil disputes at an informal, sub-official level. The main significance of the institution of *nkurato z'enzarwa* lies not in the fact that they impose penalties (for they have no power to enforce what they order), or even in their arbitrative functions in determining disputes on the purely interindividual plane. Their social importance lies rather in the efficacy with which they restore good relations when these have been disrupted. And they do this not only by achieving, if possible, a satisfactory settlement of the issue in dispute, but also (and most importantly) by re-integrating the errant individual into his community through a shared feast. After this bygones are supposed to be bygones, and it would be improper to make any further reference to the originating dispute. Of course *nkurato z'enzarwa* do not invariably succeed in achieving these purposes; it would be very remarkable if they did. But quite often they do, and so long as the common people of Bunyoro are concerned to retain the goodwill and co-operation of their neighbors, such informal tribunals will have an important part to play in village affairs. For they serve to express and maintain the basic community values of social solidarity and good neighborliness. And in doing so they express, as no other institution can, the common moral consensus, for in an integrated and healthy community the general harmony is the concern of all.

Dispute Settlement Among the Tolai

A. L. Epstein

INTRODUCTION

Of the various aspects of Melanesian culture that have engaged the attention of anthropologists, law at once stands out as one of the most neglected. There would appear to be a number of reasons for this state of affairs. In the first place, there has been the policy of the administering authorities in Papua and New Guinea. In many other colonial dependencies the official recognition and status accorded to native law and custom and, perhaps even more important, the provision for the administration of justice through formally constituted native courts, gave direct encouragement to the study of indigenous legal institutions. In support of this point, out of the vast literature on African customary law reference need only be made to the work of Schapera (1938) among the Tswana, of Cory (1953) among the Sukuma, or my own study (Epstein, 1953) of African urban courts on the Zambian copperbelt, all of which were undertaken in response to expressed administrative needs. Administrative policy in Papua and New Guinea has taken a different line. In Papua there was little or no specific legislative recognition or enforcement of custom, although as a matter of practice courts paid some heed to it; in particular, rights to native land were always recognized as being governed by custom. In New Guinea the situation was different again, and legislation provided that "the tribal institutions, customs and usages of the aboriginal natives . . . shall be permitted to continue in existence in so far as the same are not repugnant to the general principles of humanity." Yet as Lynch has recently pointed out, the picture of the degree of legal support given to custom has long been confused, and it was not until 1963 that the Native Customs (Recognition) Ordinance was introduced in an attempt to grapple with some of the issues. More strikingly, there has never been any formal provision for the setting up of native tribunals composed of indigenes and administering customary law. In these circumstances there has been little pressure from official sources for systematic research into the nature of indigenous legal systems.

Yet the lack of interest in New Guinea customary law, as reflected in the paucity of the literature on it, cannot be laid simply at the door of colonial administrators. Allowance must also be made for the social organization of indigenous communities and the way in which this encouraged anthropologists to approach the subject of law. The observation has been repeated *ad nauseam*, but it is no less relevant because of that: New Guinea societies are small in scale, fragmented, and essentially parochial; there is in the Territory nothing corresponding to the institution of kingship or chieftainship, widespread throughout Africa. There is a concomitant lack of judicial mechanisms comparable with our own or those described for many parts of Africa for the enforcement of law. . . . [I]f we regard courts of law as a specialized institution to decide disputes by reference to rules which are recognized as valid within the society, and in a given society find that there are no such bodies, we can still proceed to inquire what kinds of dispute arise within it and what measures are taken for their settlement.

• • •

. . . [T]he present paper has the more modest aim of presenting in preliminary fashion some of the data on disputes and their settlement recorded in the course of field work on the island of Matupit on the Gazelle Peninsula of New Britain.

DISPUTES: NATURE AND INCIDENCE

It must be noted at the outset that any attempt to relate contemporary observations of Tolai behavior to traditional practice immediately confronts a number of difficulties. For almost a century now the Tolai have had a particularly close and sustained experience of alien domination, and, although there is much in their way of life that remains recognizably traditional, it has to be assumed that the changed social environment can have left few of their institutions wholly unaffected. The nature of our sources on the pre-colonial and early post-colonial periods poses a further source of difficulty. For although the ethnographic literature on the Gazelle Peninsula is unusually rich by New Guinea standards, and much of the best in it presents material collected before the turn of the century, it is not always illuminating on the issues with which I am most concerned here.

Traditional procedures for redressing wrongs have been described briefly by Parkinson (1907: 60) and have also been touched on in a number of papers by Danks, a Wesleyan Methodist missionary who established a station at Kabakada in 1879. In his paper on shell-money among the Tolai, he (1887: 310–11) refers to the question of law and order, observing that, because of the lack of all constituted authority, simple and ordinary quarrels lead to serious ones. "There is no one man vested with power or authority who can say 'cease' when any quarrel has reached a certain stage. All peace is arranged by common agreement, mutual consent, not by personal authority." He follows this up by citing a couple of examples to illustrate the working of the institution known as *kamara*. At first glance his comments would seem to be belied by the brief account of the same institution provided by his fellow missionary, George Brown. According to Brown (p. 184), if a man has a knife stolen, and the thief is probably known or strongly suspected, but the injured party has no means of obtaining redress himself, then he goes to the chief's land and cuts down some ornamental shrub, or perhaps breaks a small portion of the chief's canoe. The chief is not angry for this damage, which is in any case nominal. The chief is then able to enforce a large payment from the thief for the trivial injury done to his property. Although Brown speaks here of chiefs, it is plain that he is not ascribing to those he so designates the judicial and other powers commonly associated elsewhere with the chiefly office.[1] In the absence of a developed system of courts, *kamara* served, as Seagle (p. 37) has correctly perceived, as a method of mobilizing public opinion against a powerful malefactor; at the same time, it would appear that the effectiveness of *kamara* depended upon the presence of some prominent and influential individual with whom the chain of destruction referred to in Danks's and Parkinson's accounts could be brought to a halt.

• • •

At the time of my field work that this system worked fairly satisfactorily is seen in the fact that so few cases arising within a local community were referred to the Court of Native Affairs. This provided at the time a court of first instance for the hearing of disputes between indigenes, and it was presided over by an administrative officer. In fact, most of its work concerned non-Tolai living in or around Rabaul, though it also dealt with cases involving Tolai litigants from different settlements or parishes; only rarely was a dispute at Matupit taken before the officer. More recently, specially trained Papuans and New Guineans have

[1] Thus in a later context (p. 228), referring to the theft by Matupi of various items from the steamer, Brown remarks that the chiefs had little power to compel restitution. For other similar comments on the status of Tolai "chiefs", see Danks (1887: 309, note) and Wawn (p. 10).

been appointed to serve as Local Courts Magistrates, but I have no material on the working of this new system.

Matupit in 1960 was made up of three villages, each represented on the Rabaul Native Local Government Council by its own Councillor. Throughout the course of my stay regular meetings convened by a Councillor were a feature of the island's social life. These gatherings were given over to the discussion of items emanating from or to be referred to the Council or matters touching more directly the government of the village. These tasks completed, led by the Councillor and his "committee," the assembled village turned its attention to the hearing of the night's cases. All told, in the course of a twelve month's stay in 1960–61, I obtained records, in greater or lesser detail, of more than 60 cases dealt with in this period before the village moot (*varkurai*).

What kinds of matter, then, were aired? If only for purposes of exposition, it is necessary to group the cases in some way. This task is not so easy as might appear at first sight. Thus it has been frequently shown (Bohannan) that a set of events which would give rise to a particular cause of action in one folk system might be differently construed in another. Again, some folk systems have more developed technical vocabularies than others. In the present instance, while the Tolai have terms for specific offences such as incest, theft, abduction, etc., they appear not to group cases within broader terminological categories. A more important consideration perhaps is that many disputes have so complex an etiology that it would be difficult to encompass the issues within any single rubric, folk or analytical. Finally, there is the related point that what are put forward as the overt issues may simply be the medium selected for ventilating more deep-seated grievances which cannot easily be declared publicly or of which the parties may not be consciously aware. In these circumstances the grouping of cases by subject matter adopted in Table I can only be regarded as offering some impression of the range and variety of disputes heard.

By far the largest single class of disputes turned on various kinds of claim over or in respect to land. I have examined a number of these cases in considerable detail in my book *Matupit*, and I say nothing more here about them save to remark that disputes over land revealed a structure of legal argument that was much less evident in other kinds of case. . . .

TABLE 1

Disputes recorded at Matupit, 1960–61, by subject-matter

Class of Dispute	Number of Cases
Land	22
Matrimonial	15
Theft	6
Debt	7
Breach of kinship obligation	5
Miscellaneous	8
Total	63

The category matrimonial includes here not only disputes between husband and wife but also cases concerned with marriage arrangements, bridewealth transactions, abduction, and the like. Discussing husband-wife relationships among the Tolai, Danks (1889: 293) has commented that "the very fact that nine-tenths of the quarrels in New Britain arise from jealousy of the women speaks volumes concerning the conjugal mistrust and infidelity which exist in these islands." The picture he presents is far removed from the one I formed. Certainly, jealousy (a varngu) did come up there as a recurrent theme: informants would refer to it quite spontaneously, saying "a mangana kavevet" (one of our characteristics), but such comments were more frequently heard in the context of competition between males striving for social and economic prominence rather than in the field of domestic relations as such. Of course, infidelity occurs at Matupit as elsewhere, but on the basis of my material it would never have occurred to me in the field to have attached the importance to it that Danks does. Indeed, coming to the Gazelle Peninsula against a background of field work in Central Africa, and a familiarity with the ethnographic literature of that area, I was repeatedly struck by the sharp contrast between what seemed to me the relative lack of strife in domestic relations compared to the disharmony so characteristic in contemporary tribal society in Northern Rhodesia (now Zambia). . . .

The earlier authorities on the Tolai make frequent reference to theft, possibly because, having introduced so many new commodities to the area, they themselves were frequently the victims of it (Deane, p. 26; Parkinson, 1887: 79–80; cf. the reference to Brown quoted earlier). Most of the cases I recorded were of a petty kind—taking produce from the gardens without the owner's permission or appropriating for one's own purposes someone else's property; these were readily settled by payment of compensation in cash or tambu. However, there was also a great deal of concern at the time about the prevalence of house-breaking and stealing within the village. This was said to be a novel development and was mostly attributed—with some justification—to a number of the younger people over whom the elders were no longer able to exercise their authority and control.

The cases I have classified as debt were again mostly straightforward, though a number of them revealed some of the difficulties and complications that can arise nowadays from modern business transactions. The next category of cases was more varied, and I have grouped them together mainly because they involved quarrels between close kin. Finally, I have included in a miscellaneous category instances of minor breaches of customary law (e.g., use of abusive language) or infringements of rules passed by the village assembly, such as failure to turn out for work in the cocoa gardens on the appointed day.

A HEARING

As I have already suggested, the conduct of a moot depends to a considerable extent on the subject matter of the dispute. But nearly all cases reveal the complex interplay of changing social circumstances and the persistence of customary usages and traditional values. To illustrate this process, and at the same time to convey some impression of the character of a varkurai, I propose in the remainder of this paper to consider a case that is representative of the kind that arises between kin.

The case was heard in Kikila and was introduced by a young woman called IaBaiai (D5). Sitting on a mat before the Councillor, Penias, who occupied a chair, and the members of his "committee," she explained that recently she had gone into hospital, and had left her children in the care of their grandmother IaTaunia (C5). Returning from hospital, she learned that IaTaunia had been complaining about the behavior of the children and had told them they should go and stay with their own maternal kin, who would look after them. IaTaunia, a woman close to 70 and long a widow, now intervened to say that she had told the children to make a fire so that they could roast some food, but they had simply ignored her. IaBaiai continued, remarking that whenever Esau (D4), her husband, came home bringing fish, coconuts, megapode eggs, or any kind of food she always gave a share to IaTaunia and her younger sister IaKatai (C2), also a widow. "I have never done anything wrong so far as the two sisters are concerned. I have always considered their living." IaTaunia, she went on, did not behave like IaKatai, for IaKatai's way was always good whenever she had to leave her children with her. At this IaTaunia retorted that she would look properly after her two true grandchildren (the children of IaLait (D2), who were of her own lineage or *vunatarai*). IaBaiai, incensed by this remark, replied angrily: "From the way she is speaking, you would think some stranger and not Esau had fathered my children."

Throughout these interchanges neither the Councillor nor any member of the "committee" made any attempt to intervene. IaBaiai continued with her story. Tiale (C6), an old man who had by now come to join her on the mat, had told

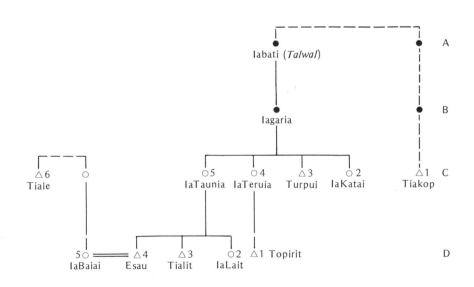

FIGURE 1.—DRAMATIS PERSONAE IN IABAIAI V. IATAUNIA.

her that IaTaunia was also complaining that she, IaBaiai, used IaTaunia's canoe to collect food just for herself and her children. Tiale supported this, and when IaTaunia asked why he had told IaBaiai this, he replied that it was because they were matrilateral kin (*barniuruna*).

Penias now spoke for the first time, asking IaTaunia why she had spoken in that way about the canoe. IaTaunia replied that she was afraid that her own canoe would wear out quickly. Esau had removed the outrigger from his own canoe, and there it just lay under his house. Now they used her canoe the whole time. Then IaBaiai had gone and told Esau what she had said about the canoe. Esau had become angry and told her that when she left his house he would give her back her canoe.[2] "When I heard what Esau said, I thought: so the house I sleep in I bought with my canoe. Very well, I will leave the house, and he shall return the canoe. Esau and his wife are always talking about me, wondering why I am always at them to sell a few things so as to accumulate *tambu* just as the Councillor has advised us."

Penias intervened again briefly to remark: "Yes. All of us should be strong so that we accumulate money and *tambu* to improve our living." IaTaunia then complained that recently when she had gone to sell slaked lime powder at Rabaul market IaBaiai had not helped her. IaBaiai replied that earlier they had worked together to prepare the lime and sell it. They had in fact made 100 fathoms of *tambu* with which to purchase a bride for Tialit (D3), a brother of Esau presently working on Buka. Then one day Tiakop (C1) had come on a visit from Talwat, a neighboring community, and she asked him if there was more lime available. He said there was. IaTaunia broke in: "I bought that lime from Tiakop with a little *tambu*. Anyway, Tiakop is not your maternal kinsman, I am true kin of Tiakop."

Esau meanwhile had been keeping in the background, sitting at the base of a house to the rear. Penias now asked him what he had to say about the canoe. He replied that the way IaTaunia was behaving, it was as though some entirely different woman had borne him. Now he wanted her to leave his house. Penias turned to IaTaunia: What was the reason you spoke so about IaBaiai's children that they should go to their own kin? There you were wrong. And what do you think about the canoe?

IaTaunia: My canoe will return to me and I shall leave Esau's house because of what he has just said.

Penias: And you, Esau, what do you think?

Esau: No, let her leave the house for her behavior towards me and the children is not good.

Penias: All right. Let us finish this quickly.

Committee: The "committee" here wants to make peace between you and not have you living apart.

Turpui (C3), one of the leading elders in Kikila, had hitherto been sitting apart. Now he stood up and addressed himself angrily to Esau. "So truly you are going to buy the house with the canoe? This canoe, you will pay for it, because you have used it to catch fish and all the time you have worked with it. Where is your love for your mother? Let us take this matter to the Government so that it judges you, for you have shown contempt for your own mother. The house is

[2]IaTaunia at the time was living in a house put up and formerly occupied by Esau. Esau and his wife now had another house nearby.

not a house of copper; it is just an old *kunai* house and it is perfectly all right that IaTaunia should stay there." Esau muttered: "All right, take it to the Government if you like."

At this point ToPirit (D1), who was on this occasion sitting on the "committee," spoke up. First he addressed IaTaunia quietly and coaxingly: "Well, Taunia, what do you think now?" She replied: "I have nothing to say. I want Esau to return my canoe." ToPirit turned to Esau: "Esau, let us think a little of those who bore us. We are not wild animals that live in the bush. When an animal gives birth, the offspring scatter and never return to help their mother. But we are not animals because the spirit of God rests within us. It is we people who matter. Esau, when you were a child IaTaunia cared for you, she fed and clothed you and brought you up until now you are married and have established your home. If IaTaunia behaves ill towards you, nevertheless, you should continue to help her. Take myself: I have many children and IaTaunia does not look after them. I do this myself. Now then, what do you say about the house? Remember, Esau, a canoe is not heavy, but IaTaunia is. What is a house? A house means a family, it means a mother and her children, but a canoe is just a piece of wood, of no importance. Will you look after IaTaunia?"

Esau remained silent, and ToPirit continued: "Do not spit upon her, for you came forth from her, not from a canoe. A canoe is one thing, a person something different. IaTaunia is now very old, she has again become like a child. Do not hurt her feelings with your talk. If a canoe should be damaged or lost, that is no matter, but if IaTaunia dies that does matter. Now you, IaTaunia, do not distress yourself about the house. If it falls into disrepair, Esau will build another for you. If he does not, he will stand before the *varkurai* again. As for your grandchildren, you should care for them properly, you should call for them to stay with you and give them things as you did before."

Penias now added a final few words. He said that Esau should look after the canoe and IaTaunia should continue to stay in the house. He asked Esau again what he had to say about the house. Esau now agreed that IaTaunia should continue to stay there. "Very well, let the case finish now. It is good that you should all be reconciled." A few days later the canoe was lying at its usual station at the *motonoi* and Esau was using it again with IaTaunia's permission.

We can approach the analysis of a dispute by asking what was at issue between the parties, how the issues were presented to the forum, and how the matter was finally resolved. In some cases the issues will be clear from the outset: the complainant can point to some specific breach of entitlement—for example, that the defendant stole his bicycle, seduced his wife, or planted crops on his land without permission—for which he seeks the appropriate redress. But in a small community where the parties to a dispute are neighbors and kin, that is to say where they are involved in sets of multiplex relationships that have been in being for some time, the matter may be more complex. In these circumstances the dispute tends to take the form of a series of grievances and counter-grievances, often of a more generalized kind; the evidence points not so much to a specific wrong or breach of entitlement for which there is an appropriate penalty or remedy but rather to the tension that has developed in a set of social relationships. So it was in the present case. IaBaiai began by complaining of her mother-in-law's failure to look after the grandchildren when they had been entrusted to her care. Gradually it began to appear that this was

only part of a more pervasive sense of grievance against IaTaunia, whose conduct was all the more reprehensible in that—so IaBaiai asserted—she herself
had always behaved as a model daughter-in-law. In support of this point IaBaiai
contrasted unfavorably IaTaunia's behavior with that of her sister IaKatai. When
IaTaunia retorted that she would only look after her true grandchildren, she
drew attention to the fact that the two sets of grandchildren belonged to different matrilineages. Technically this was correct, but in seeking to deny her
obligations to all those she called *tubugu* (my grandchild) she was clearly in the
wrong, as Penias was later to point out. On the other hand, neglecting one's
grandchildren is so unusual that for IaTaunia to affirm her own breach of the
norms of kinship was also to suggest that there were grievances on her side too.
She had, in fact, a number of complaints to bring against IaBaiai; but by far the
most serious of these seemed to relate to the use of the canoe. Yet from the
time this point was raised IaBaiai receded from the case, and what began to
emerge as crucial was the relationship between mother and son. The triangular
relationship of mother, son, and son's wife is always likely to provide a fertile
source of tension, and this tension can easily be aggravated in times of change
when the balance of the relationships is subtly altering. From the evidence of
some of my other case material it appears that nowadays there is a tendency for
some men to align themselves more closely with their wives than with their
mothers, producing a smouldering resentment on the part of the latter. In the
present instance clearly what rankled with IaTaunia was that when IaBaiai complained to Esau about his mother, Esau sided with his wife against her to the
extent of telling her to leave his house.

These points only emerge gradually as the hearing proceeds. What are the
characteristics of this mode of adjudication? One aspect that is immediately
striking is the minimal role of the Councillor and "committee," known as *tena
varkurai*. Of course this can vary considerably, depending on the nature of the
case and the personality and authority of the Councillor himself. Penias was well
liked and respected, but he hardly counted as an authoritative figure. Even so,
the procedure adopted on this occasion was not markedly different from that
followed at other hearings I attended at Matupit and in other Tolai settlements.
When someone wishes to raise a complaint, he informs the Councillor, who will
at the appropriate moment summon the village to assemble by blowing the
conch-shell. In this way he proclaims the jurisdiction of the moot. But at this
point resemblance between the role of *tena varkurai* and that of a bench of
judges as it is usually conceived ceases, so that to employ the term "judges" in
the context of a *varkurai* could be misleading. Avoiding any appearance of seeking to dominate or monopolize the proceedings, the task of Councillor and
"committee" is to maintain decorum and the conditions for orderly debate, to
hold the ring, so to speak, allowing the disputants to place their arguments
freely before the assembled village. So, as in the present case, the parties may
wrangle with one another without any attempt to call them to order. Again, the
tena varkurai from time to time put questions to the parties, but the questioning
does not amount to an interrogation or cross-examination as it would in an
African tribal court; taking the form "What do you think now?" or "What do
you say to that?," the questions are designed to elicit further information or
argument rather than to probe what has already been said. The underlying
assumption appears to be that only when grievances have been properly aired

on all sides can the path be opened up to reconciliation. In this connection the assembled villagers have an important part to play. Although they appear at first glance simply as an attentive audience immersed in the play unfolding before them, they are themselves actors in the piece, and by their reactions offer from time to time a judgement on the behavior of the parties. Seizing on such signals, Councillor and "committee" intervene at appropriate moments to try and persuade one or other of the parties to yield gracefully and so open the way to a settlement.

How, then, was a settlement reached in the present case? I have suggested that what lay at the core of the dispute was Esau's relations with his wife on the one hand and his mother on the other, and issue was joined when the matter of the canoe was introduced. Thereafter IaBaiai retired to the wings and it was Esau who was at the centre of the stage. At this point, had Esau taken a more conciliatory approach he might have won some public sympathy. But he was under considerable strain himself, and when he blurted out that IaTaunia should leave his house it was plain that he had put himself in the wrong: he had gone too far. Turpui, his maternal uncle and one of the acknowledged leaders in Kikila, was outraged and castigated him roundly. Turpui's suggestion that the matter be taken before the Government was spoken in the heat of anger; it was probably his way of saying that for such behavior Esau deserved to go to prison rather than a serious expression of intention. Such a course of action would have done nothing to heal the rift, and the "committee," having already indicated that it wished to see an end to the squabbling, did not pursue the point. In any case, Esau had been deeply shamed by Turpui's outburst, and, although he still mustered a show of defiance, he was now much subdued. The moment seemed ripe, therefore, for an attempt at reconciliation. ToPirit was in the best possible position to mediate. A "son" of IaTaunia and a "brother" of Esau, he was not an intimate party to the dispute, for he was of a different segment of the lineage. A man in his middle thirties, he had been playing an active part in village affairs for some time, and his views were listened to with respect. But in addition to the traditional status that he enjoyed, ToPirit was a senior clerk in one of the government departments in Rabaul. Thus he was also able to address Esau as a fellow member of the younger and more educated generation of Tolai. The address was couched in terms of an appeal to moral values to which all in the audience could be expected to subscribe and respond. ToPirit was a leading member of the local Seventh Day Adventist congregation, and some of his remarks seem to be strongly tinged by his Christian upbringing. Yet it also seems plain to me that he was speaking as a Tolai for whom traditional values still had a powerful meaning. Old women are notoriously difficult, he acknowledged, but one should make allowances for this. Soon she would be dead, he seemed to imply, and then it would be too late to make amends. In other contexts, including other *varkurai* I attended, mentioning the names of the dead could produce a profound emotional response. Here ToPirit, in suggesting that IaTaunia could shortly be expected to join the ranks of the ancestors, was making a final powerful emotive appeal which it would have been difficult for Esau to resist. He capitulated.

Earlier in the paper I cited Danks's comment that all peace is arranged by common agreement, mutual consent, not by personal authority. Analysis of the present dispute bears out the perceptiveness of his observation. It also provides evidence of the strong element of continuity in the legal aspect of Tolai culture, despite profound changes the Tolai have experienced in their social environment since Danks's day. Finally, I hope to have shown how settlement by consensus is in fact achieved. Confronted with such a mode of adjudication, some professional lawyers profess to find difficulty in understanding how it can offer the certainty and consistency which they see as a necessary ingredient of an acceptable legal system. They assert (Derham, p. 503) that decisions reached in this way are likely to result in variation in or departure from the established or recognized rules: "anything may be done that is in fact agreed to." I believe that such a view is based upon a misconception. So far as the dispute between IaBaiai and IaTaunia is concerned, it is evident that a settlement by consensus was achieved only because appeal was made to certain norms and values recognized and accepted throughout the community.

The case I have presented here illustrates the principle that the aim of every *varkurai* is the full airing of grievances and the reconciliation of the parties concerned. Reconciliation is not a mystical process: settlement can only be reached when the parties are persuaded that their behavior was not in conformity with the norms to which they themselves subscribe. In the present dispute the aim of the *varkurai* was achieved, at least temporarily. However, it should not be assumed that this always occurs or is achieved so readily. For present purposes I was able to treat the case as relatively self-contained, and so it was regarded at the hearing. In other cases, however, as Burridge (p. 770) has observed of disputes in Tangu, the specific issues which trigger off a particular incident cannot be considered as isolated acts, since each forms part of a complex of disappointments and grievances. Moreover, as in Tangu, the formal hearing of a dispute often provides more the occasion for what is essentially a contest between political rivals. On such occasions the parties in pressing their arguments appeal to the same body of customary law, but like litigants in our own system, each relies on different, though equally valid, principles or rules. In this event there may be a real difficulty in adjudicating between the opposing claims, and the result may be not a settlement by consensus, but a stalemate—the issues before the *varkurai* remain unresolved. Herein, of course, lies a major difference between a village moot and a court of law.

REFERENCES

AINSWORTH, J., *Report on Administrative Arrangements ... in the Territory of New Guinea*, Melbourne, 1924.

BLUM, H., *Neu Guinea und der Bismarck Archipel*, Berlin, 1900.

BOHANNAN, P., *Judgment and Justice among the Tiv*, London, 1957.

BROWN, G., *Autobiography*, London, 1908.

BURRIDGE, K., "Disputing in Tangu," *Amer. Anthrop.*, Vol. 59, pp. 763–80, 1957.

CORY, H., *Sukuma Law and Custom*, London, 1953.

DANKS, B., "On the Shell-money of New Britain," *J. Roy. Anthrop. Instit.*, Vol. 17, pp. 305–17, 1887.

DANKS, B., "Marriage Customs of the New Britain Group," *J. Roy. Anthrop. Instit.*, Vol. 18, pp. 281–94, 1889.

DEANE, W., (Ed.), *In Wild New Britain*, Sydney, 1933.

DERHAM, D. P., "Law and Custom in Papua and New Guinea," *University of Chicago Law Review*, Vol. 30, pp. 495–506, 1963.

EPSTEIN, A. L., *The Administration of Justice and the Urban African*, London, 1953.

EPSTEIN, A. L., "Injury and Liability: Legal Ideas and Implicit Assumptions," *Mankind*, Vol. 6, pp. 376–83, 1967.

EPSTEIN, A. L., *Matupit: Land, Politics and Change Among the Tolai of New Britain*, Canberra, 1969.

GLUCKMAN, M., *The Judicial Process Among the Barotse of Northern Rhodesia*, Manchester, 1955.

LYNCH, C. J., "Aspects of Political and Constitutional Development and Allied Topics," in Brown, B. J. (Ed.), *Fashion of Law in New Guinea*, Sydney, 1969.

MALINOWSKI, B., *Crime and Custom in Savage Society*, London, 1926.

NADEL, S. F., *The Nuba*, London, 1947.

PARKINSON, R., *Im Bismarck-Archipel*, Leipzig, 1887.

PARKINSON, R., *Dreissig Jahre in der Südsee*, Stuttgart, 1907.

POSPISIL, L., *Kapauku Papuans and their Law*, New Haven, 1958.

POWDERMAKER, H., *Copper Town*, New York, 1962.

SCHAPERA, I. *A Handbook of Tswana Law*, London, 1938.

SCHAPERA, I., "Malinowski's Theories of Law," in Firth, R. (Ed.), *Man and Culture*, London, 1957.

SEAGLE, W., *Quest for Law*, New York, 1941.

WAWN, W. T., *The South Sea Islanders and the Queensland Labour Trade*, London, 1893.

The Taboo of Suicide

Russell Noyes, Jr.

Suicide, like death, is a tabooed subject and a morbid topic not to be discussed except in the relative comfort of the context that considers it a sign of mental illness. It is for most persons unthinkable and unjustifiable. It remains a legal offense in only nine states but is frequently cited in insurance policies as a basis for excluding benefit payments to survivors and leads to refusal of religious funeral services in many instances. It implies an element of family disgrace, especially among Catholics, leading to attempts to hide the cause of death. Students of suicide even suspect that a number of suicides themselves seek to obscure their motivation by the use of methods which make death appear accidental. Often physicians find it difficult to ask some of their patients whether or not they have been contemplating suicide. Perhaps, however, the irrational responses of survivors and community to instances of self-imposed death are most revealing of the cultural attitude. Blame is frequently heaped upon the suicide's surviving spouse by his community, his neighbors, and his family—especially his in-laws. Cain and Fast noted in some instances actual finger-pointing and the phrase, "drove him to it" reverberating through community gossip.[1] They noted that such gossip, accusations, and ostracism often forced the spouse to move. Significantly, these authors remarked upon the "ferocity of guilt" in the survivors, which they laid first to the intentional, volitional quality of the act and thus the rage resulting from deliberate rejection by the suicidal individual. Secondly, they pointed to the survivors' feeling of responsibility for the suicide's death in the sense of not recognizing his torment and not relieving his anguish. Thus the suicide vengefully unleashes the fury of the survivor's conscience by crying through his violent act, "You killed me!"

Is not the physician doubly fearful of suicide? First, he shares the universal fear of death. But in addition to this fear, he has in death—whether by suicide or not—a professional enemy. It is that against which he unceasingly battles but against which he is finally powerless. In the face of death the traditional skills of his profession are rendered impotent and he may be confronted with the most bitter and agonizing suffering. He is sometimes inclined to share with his patients the view that death is unnatural and due to such supposed pathological processes as aging. Some physicians imbued with a faith in modern science wonder if death itself may not be a conquerable disease process.

What, then, of the consequences for the physician who not only fears death as does the rest of his culture but also dedicates his life to its avoidance? What happens to the physician who never quite fully anticipates his patient's suicide, whose guilt is increased by his belief that he should have prevented the loss of life, and who becomes, in many instances, an object of community blame as other survivors project their guilt upon him? It is not surprising that many a physician finds difficulty in conceiving of suicide other than as a product of psychosis or miscalculated gesture. He thus removes the patient from responsibility for his act and finds a measure of relief from his own anxiety. One prominent student of suicide stated, "There is no conceivable human situation which is unendurable or hopeless enough to drive a healthy man to death—neither mental anguish nor concentration camp torture, nor pregnancy out of wedlock, nor bankruptcy."[2] In divorcing health and suicide he expresses a value judgment shared by many members of the medical profession and reflecting an abhorrence of the individual who rejects one of the profession's basic tenets—life must be preserved and prolonged.

In contrast, Redlich and Freedman assert that the suicidal act is seen not only in psychotics but also in many neurotics and sometimes in relatively normal and mature persons. They go on to add, however, that closer examination reveals that "the so-called rational suicide in Western Culture, for example, in incura-

[1]Albert C. Cain and Irene Fast, "The Legacy of Suicide. Observations on the Pathogenic Impact of Suicide Upon Marital Partners," *Psychiatry*, 29:406–411, 1966.
[2]Stanley F. Yolles, "The Tragedy of Suicide in the U.S.," a talk delivered at George Washington University School of Medicine, October 1965. Public Health Service Publication No. 1558; p. 3.

able illness, often has irrational motivations. . . ."[3] One senses in the use of the word "irrational" a wish to exclude from prized reason behavior as loathsome as suicide. Shneidman and Farberow remark that one of the outstanding characteristics of the suicidal act is that it is illogical.[4] Nonetheless they describe one type under the heading of "normal logic," noting that the reasoning used is acceptable according to Aristotelian standards. Zilboorg stated, however, that ". . . pure reason and logic succeed at times in constructing an answer but it is an answer built on an emotional foundation." He remarked further that ". . . while we profess a great admiration for and pride in our reason, we actually— although indirectly—admit that it is one of the weakest tools in the armamentarium of man's endowments."[5] Thus suicide seems to be behavior that points, however unwilling we are to accept it, to the frailty of human reason. But in recognizing this tendency to relieve the suicide of responsibility for his rejection of life, one must ask whether a metaphysical problem has been simplified or reduced to one of clinical medicine. Does the physician while supporting his culture's values also perpetuate its fears?

Before examining the implications for the management of suicidal persons, an effort will be made to gain an understanding of the prevailing reaction to self-willed death by examining the attitudes of earlier periods and reviewing the psychodynamic explanation of the present-day attitude. It must be kept in mind that figures giving some accurate account of the actual practice of suicide did not become available until the nineteenth century so that one is limited in reviewing the history of suicide to the writings of authors who may express the view of but a single class and do not necessarily indicate the manner or extent to which certain attitudes of the times toward the act affected its expression.

PRIMITIVE ATTITUDE

In some primitive societies suicide was socially sanctioned as an acting out of the mourning process. From earliest times in many parts of the world there are records of customs which compelled widows to take their lives upon the death of their husbands. Among some Central Africans and Melanesians the wife was buried alive with her husband. Similarly, servants often followed their masters. A traveler to Peking as late as the fourteenth century saw female slaves and guards buried at the funeral of a Chinese emperor. Prominent in this type of suicide can be seen the primitive man's belief in immortality and the joining of spirits beyond the grave. Zilboorg has noted that civilized man has sublimated his need to identify with the dead by withdrawing from life and enshrouding himself in black.

One of the most prominent motives of suicides among primitive cultures was that of anger and revenge. Just as the child wishing revenge upon his parents following punishment may think of dying, saying to himself, "If I were dead, then you'd be sorry," so the primitive man acted out this motive. The nature of

[3]Frederick C. Redlich and Daniel X. Freedman, *The Theory and Practice of Psychiatry*, (New York: Basic Books, 1966), p. 550.

[4]Edwin S. Shneidman and Norman L. Farberow, "The Logic of Suicide," in *Clues to Suicide*, edited by Shneidman and Farberow, (New York: McGraw-Hill, 1957).

[5]Gregory Zilboorg, "Suicide Among Civilized and Primitive Races," *Amer. J. Psychiatry*, 92:1347–1369; pp. 1358, 1348, 1936.

the revenge expected varied from tribe to tribe and country to country. In northern Siberia the suicide relied upon his ghost to avenge his death; in southern India the task was left to tribal custom, for there the law of retaliation prevailed in the strictest sense. If a quarrel took place and a man tore out his own eye or killed himself, his adversary had to do the same, either to himself or one of his relations. A socialized current modification of this type of suicide is hara-kiri. The offended Japanese commits hara-kiri at the doorstep of the offender, who in turn is subjected by the community to social disfavor. One can note the influence of primitive logic operating in revenge suicide, a logic operative in the unconscious of Western man today as well.

Aside from such institutionalized forms, suicide was subject to taboo among primitive peoples, and it is to these ancient taboos one can trace the roots of fear and revulsion toward self-destruction in later times.

GOLDEN AGE OF SUICIDE

Writings from the classical age provide the first opportunity to study individual suicides and the influence of reason and philosophy upon the phenomenon. Throughout the age there was a growing acceptance of the act. According to Fedden,[6] several types were recognized. First, there were suicides for the sake of honor and dignity. This type included persons who sought to avoid the pain and ignominy of old age and disease. Behind such deaths was the belief in man as a noble animal which should not be reduced by such infirmities. Also of this type were suicides by women who wished to preserve their chastity and by warriors who refused to fall into the hands of the enemy. Thus, the Greek orator Demosthenes killed himself rather than fall into the hands of Antipater. A second type of suicide during the classical era was that involving love or the loss of love, and was similar to the suicide of mourning encountered among primitive peoples. Dido, for example, stabbed herself on her husband's funeral pyre, having sworn eternal fidelity to his memory. The dramatic end of Arria eclipsed that of other classical women who died for their husbands. Detected in an unsuccessful conspiracy against Claudius, her husband, Caecina Paetus, was condemned to death. He felt that suicide was his only dignified move, but a natural fear made him hesitate. Thereupon, Arria, to show him the way to liberty, seized his dagger and stabbed herself; dying, she handed the weapon to him with the famous words, *Paetus, non dolet,* "Paetus, it doesn't hurt." Finally, a sacrificial type suicide occurred, committed by one who believed that his own death would advance his cause, party, or family. Early Greek mythology describes Jocasta's suicide by hanging upon her discovery that her husband, Oedipus, was also her own son and her husband's murderer. Homer regarded this as a perfectly natural action to which no blame was attached. He felt it to be the only dignified way out of an intolerable situation. No other sacrifice could have absolutely proved her good faith and the taking of her own life was the only real atonement possible.

With qualifications, most classical philosophers seemed to believe that one was permitted to die if he did not wish to live. Thus the Stoic, Cynic, and Epicurean philosophies all led to the acceptance of suicide. There were two lines of

[6]Henry R. Fedden, *Suicide: A Social and Historical Study,* (London: Peter Davies, 1938).

thought in opposition, however. The first sprang from the Pythagorean doctrine which viewed life as a penitential journey, a discipline imposed by the gods, to which man must submit himself. From this viewpoint, suicide was a rebellion. Aristotle argued that the suicide, by casting aside social responsibility and obligation, committed an offense against the state. Thus he saw the suicide as one who deserted his post.

In the philosophies accepting suicide, there was emphasis on the importance of the individual and pronounced emphasis upon reason. Apparently, the increased importance of reason in classical times, and during the Renaissance as well, meant an increase in suicide or at least in its acceptance. According to the Stoic, man was unconquerable. The dignity of the human personality and the determination of the human will need never be sullied, for the door was always open and man's last and most faithful ally, death, would never desert him. Cried Seneca:

Foolish man, what do you bemoan, and what do you fear? Wherever you look there is an end of evils. You see that yawning precipice? It leads to liberty. You see that flood, that river, the well? Liberty houses within them. You see that stunted, parched, and sorry tree? From every branch liberty hangs. Your neck, your throat, your heart are all so many ways of escape from slavery. . . . Do you enquire the road to freedom? You shall find it in every vein of your body.[7]

Seneca himself, like a number of other philosophers, provided an example of the type of death he preached. Having fallen from the Imperial favor, he took the only course open to him and with his own hand forestalled Nero's vengeance. The most famous suicides of the ancient world were perhaps those of Mark Antony, who died for passion, and Cato, a Roman statesman dedicated to the maintenance of the liberty of the citizen and preservation of the traditional Roman virtues. When, during the decline of Rome, he realized that the values to which he had devoted his life were dead, he took his life and remained to the last unconquered.

ABSOLUTE CONDEMNATION

For most of the ancients suicide was honorable and consistent with their belief in the dignity of the individual man. During the next thousand years, however, through a gradual process, the suicide came at last to reside in the lowest circle of Dante's hell. The condemnation of suicide followed the decline in the importance of reason and the spread of Christianity. Early Christians, however, disregarded suicide completely. The Bible contains no condemnation of suicide though it records as many suicides as wars. Paul, in fact, classed self-destruction with other worthy but ineffectual approaches to grace: "Though I give my body to be burned and have not charity, it profiteth me nothing."[8] Prior to St. Augustine, Christian martyrs in untold numbers suffered voluntarily to testify to their faith and open the road to heaven.

But as the Church began to look upon the act as evidence that the person had

[7]Lucius Annaeus Seneca, *Moral Essays*, (New York: Putnam, 1928).
[8]I Cor. 13:3.

despaired of God's grace, an attitude similar to the primitive taboo toward suicide gradually permeated the Church, and suicide became one of the most sinful acts. According to theologians, even Judas had not sinned irreparably in betraying Christ; not until he committed suicide did he damn himself beyond recall. During this period suicide to preserve chastity, a well-established practice, became a concern of the Church. In the fourth century, St. Augustine first introduced arguments to the effect that "suicide is a detestable and damnable wickedness."[9] Augustine's principal argument was as follows: To kill oneself is to kill a man, therefore suicide is homicide; homicide is inexcusable and forbidden in the Ten Commandments. Strictures against homicide continued to flourish, but not until St. Thomas Aquinas, in the thirteenth century, were substantial arguments introduced in support of the Church's attitude. His arguments were that self-inflicted death was contrary to natural law and to charity, and, most importantly, that since man is God's property it is for Him to decide upon man's life or death.

Not only did suicide become a sin but also it became an object of punishment according to law. The suicide's property was confiscated and his body was subjected by custom to curious indignities. In England his nude body was dragged through the streets to its burial, which was done at night at a crossroads; a stake was driven through the heart in order to imprison the spirit and prevent its vengeful visitations upon the living. By the eighth century exceptions were being made for insane suicides, and prayers were said for those who were considered to have committed suicide through the vexations of the Devil. Despite the early compassion for the insane suicide, the mentally ill of the late Middle Ages who were regarded as possessed by the Devil were often burned for their own deliverance. Sprenger noted in the *Malleus Maleficarum* that these witches frequently "made away with themselves, or when they were hauled off to prison strung themselves up in their cells. . . ."[10] Finally, suicide reached its lowest point in the description in Dante's "Inferno," written in the thirteenth century. Guided across the river of boiling blood by Vergil, the poet encounters in the seventh circle of hell the souls of the suicides, which are there encased in thorny trees whose leaves are eaten by the odious Harpies. When the limbs of these damned are thus damaged the wounds bleed. Only as long as the blood flows are the souls of the trees able to speak, symbolizing the way in which in life they had found voice in their own blood.

RETURN OF REASON

The Renaissance and the Reformation marked a reassertion of individual responsibility and with it a spirit of rational inquiry. Questions regarding the meaning of life and death were scarcely asked, and when they were they were answered by the Church. With the rediscovery of classical learning and with the Reformation there was a resurrection of those ideas which had made suicide seem logical and socially possible. Absolute condemnation of suicide began to fall away and the more enlightened began to judge the act from a reasoned standpoint. At the same time Christianity continued to temper and overlay the

[9]Aurelius Augustinus, *De Civitatis Dei*, Book 1.
[10]Johann Sprenger and Heinrich Kraemer, *Malleus Maleficarum*, translated by Montague Summers, 1489.

old Stoic ideas. In eight tragedies Shakespeare provided fourteen suicides. The contemplation of the act by Hamlet is most familiar. In those soliloquies where Hamlet speaks of suicide his grounds for argument change, and as the play moves on his restraining motives apparently shift from the medieval Christian prohibitions to rational argument and fear of the unknown:

. . . who would fardels bear,
To grunt and sweat under a weary life,
But that the dread of something after death,
The undiscover'd country from whose bourn
No traveller returns, puzzles the will
And makes us rather bear those ills we have
Than fly to others that we know not of?[11]

Dryden also reflected the changing climate in *All for Love*, in which his attitude toward the suicides of Antony and Cleopatra is one of praise, pity, and admiration. As he says in the last line of the play: "No lovers lived so great or died so well." Of Antony's death he makes Cleopatra say, "thou alone wert worthy so to triumph," the implication being that suicide is the only fit and dignified end for so great a man.

With the arrival of the eighteenth century, a new phase of open discussion appeared. Among viewpoints favoring suicide the attitude of Hume was perhaps the most significant. He argued that it was not contrary to the law of nature nor of harm to society. He felt that the individual's contract with society was based on mutual benefit. Should society give him nothing or should it not make life tolerable, then he had every right to consider the contract void and to cut himself off. Besides, he argued, there could be little use to society in an unhappy man. Therefore, he said, let the unhappy lover, the outcast, and the old deserted parents depart from the world, which is for them but a desert.

Arguments in opposition to suicide were at first largely holdovers from earlier times. Voltaire, however, expressed a practical caution that young girls who propose to hang and drown themselves for love should not be so precipitate, for change is as common in love as in business. But eventually one of the most important arguments began to be heard—that concerning the interpersonal effects of most suicides in terms of responsibility evaded or guilt provoked. The parent, friend, or child left behind represented real stumbling blocks for philoophers who wished to establish the innocence of the self-destructive person. Madame de Stael added an argument giving recognition to the growth and maturational potential of life's crises. In effect she said that to escape from pain might be to escape from something that by its action could make one better and greater. Suicide would thus amount to a refusal to fulfill the possibilities of nature.

SUICIDE AND INSANITY

By the beginning of the nineteenth century, suicide had become a disgrace, and families were resorting to secrecy in order to prevent the scourge of gossip. When secrecy was not possible, families turned to what they felt to be a lesser

[11]*Hamlet*, Act III, Scene 1.

evil than disgrace—madness—for justification. Thus the association between suicide and insanity grew closer. Arguments for and against suicide began to be silenced as interest was shifted from the moral aspect to questioning of the cause. Statistics accumulated. As the self-destructive act increasingly became a sign of madness, all the superstitious fear of the mad attached itself to persons committing it. Suicide was also fitted into the then current theories of psychological medicine. Gall, for example, felt that the act occurred in people with thick craniums, and Cananis asserted that it was due to an excess of phosphorus in the brain. One voice, however, was unstilled—that of the romanticists, who ennobled and romanticized death. Self-imposed death became for them a brave and gracious approach to peace, a proof of sincerity and of unwillingness to temporize with the world. Death represented a mystical reunion with Nature. Suicide acquired heroic qualities and often became for them a fine ending and a worthy exit. The literature on suicide eventually reached such gigantic proportions that a bibliography compiled by Rost early in the twentieth century occupied a volume of almost 400 pages. Psychiatrists wrote scholarly and voluminous treatises on the subject, investigating and in some cases putting to statistical test the contention that suicide and insanity were related. Esquirol[12] claimed that all suicides were insane, while Kraepelin stated in his textbook that on the basis of his observation of rescued suicides only 30 percent offered symptoms of insanity.[13] Durkheim likewise collected considerable interesting data indicating that suicides were not necessarily insane; he pointed out convincingly that if suicide were etiologically connected with psychoses, one should expect cultures yielding a greater number of psychoses also to yield a greater number of suicides, but that he found the contrary to be true.[14] The valuable later contributions, especially from such psychoanalytic theorists as Freud, Zilboorg, and Menninger, point to the great variety and complexity of motivations. Sociologists have revealed as myths such common explanations as business or financial failure. The significant influence of cultural patterns and attitudes has been shown through a number of cross-cultural studies. The numerous interpretations point to the great diversity of the act and to the mystery which still surrounds it.

Thus the prevailing attitudes toward self-destruction may be traced through the major periods of recorded history of the Western world. Certain forms have received social sanction, even idealization; others have met absolute condemnation. Society's reaction has not always been what it is today, but the roots of the current lingering prejudice can be identified in primitive superstition. The emphasis on reason and the rise of individualism were trends which were accompanied by an increased acceptance or open consideration of suicide. Social attitude and personal belief have influenced both the motivation for suicide and the arguments for and against it. It remains to inquire further into the origin of the fear of suicide.

SOURCES OF FEAR

As mentioned before, suicide poses a threat to the living. In rejecting life, the

[12]Jean E. D. Esquirol, *Mental Maladies, A Treatise on Insanity*, a facsimile of the English edition of 1845, (New York: Hafner, 1965).

[13]Emil Kraepelin, *Clinical Psychiatry*, translated from A. Ross Diefendorf, 7th German edition, (New York: Macmillan, 1923).

[14]See footnote 2.

suicide seems to cast aside all that is meaningful or of value. Such an act stirs misgivings and makes us fearful of meeting that same despair in our own lives. The observer is also troubled by the ease with which obligations are thrust aside and loved ones are forsaken. Not only is the survivor of the suicide deserted, but also he is left with no object upon which to vent his resultant rage. Some authors have felt that an impulse toward suicide lies dormant within all human beings, attached to desires for escape, reunion, rebirth, or atonement; as these desires seek expression, they give rise to anxiety. It has also been suggested that the fear of suicide has an instinctual basis. Freud postulated a death instinct, a force which he felt dominated life and had as its goal the return to the organic state.

Perhaps most significantly, however, the fear of suicide, like that of death, appears to stem from a deep sense of responsibility for the act or, in other words, a feeling that one has killed another. Freud felt that suicide represented a retaliatory abandonment and an act whereby another person was almost always psychologically killed.[15] The primitive revenge suicide amply testifies to the aggressiveness of the self-destructive act. Some understanding may be derived from a look at the child's experience of death. Children regard it as a departure and a reversible casual event, but they never see it as occurring by accident or as a natural happening. In the face of the death of a parent, the child experiences resentment over having been abandoned but also feels himself responsible. This feeling of responsibility arises from death wishes toward the ambivalently loved parent, wishes which are felt to have the power of action. Thus the survivor's response to suicide, where there is a deliberate element to the death, is much greater. It should be emphasized that such ambivalence or, more specifically, repressed hostility is universal in human relationships. No matter how strong the love or affection for another, he remains in part a hostile stranger toward whom feelings of hate in some measure exist. In this connection Freud felt that man in his unconscious mind was by nature cruel and murderous, and unrestrained by those forces which prevent other animals from killing and devouring their kind.[16] Noting the frequency of wars, the existence of weapons having gigantic destructive power, and the ubiquitousness of crime, one cannot but consider such a statement as having some merit. It may be concluded that the fear of suicide has as its origin unconscious death wishes which create a fear of abandonment—abandonment by suicide.

IMPLICATIONS FOR MANAGEMENT

The attitude toward suicide that has evolved today is broad in its implications, especially in two general areas. The first involves physicians directly; the second often concerns physicians indirectly but is related to changing motivations for the self-destructive act.

Following a trend originating in the Middle Ages, the care of the suicidal has

[15]Sigmund Freud, "Notes Upon a Case of Obsessional Neurosis," pp. 293–383 in *Collected Papers*, Vol. 3, (New York: Basic Books, 1959). Sigmund Freud, "The Psychogenesis of a Case of Homosexuality in a Woman," pp. 202–231 in *Collected Papers*, Vol. 2, (New York: Basic Books, 1959).

[16]Sigmund Freud, "Thoughts for the Times on War and Death," pp. 288–317 in *Collected Papers*, Vol. 4, (New York: Basic Books, 1959).

increasingly been turned over to practitioners of the healing arts. Reluctantly accepted, this responsibility has been accompanied by a fearful approach and a tendency to conceive of suicide in terms of psychosis or miscalculated gesture. While the physician may intellectually avoid categorizing suicide so rigidly, he unwittingly finds himself falling back upon such reassuring explanations the closer the act comes to his own patient or family. No matter how the doctor may judge suicide, he is responsible for accurately predicting the serious suicidal attempt—society so charges him. If he fails to fully appreciate that there are warning signs that do not necessarily indicate impending or fully developed psychosis, he may err in his predictions. Of course, by far the most important indicators are the patient's own statements of his consideration of suicide, regardless of the integrity of his personality. In times of emotional stress death wishes and suicidal thoughts are so common that a complete and strenuous disclaimer can occasionally cause concern. The physician should be alert, for example to: (1) strong identification with or hope of rejoining someone deceased; (2) intense rage with avenues of expression blocked; (3) a marked degree of impulsivity; and (4) inexpressible grief. Of increasing seriousness are statements referring to plans for suicide, means for carrying it out should the desire become strong, and, of course, definite intention to kill oneself. Previous attempts also increase the likelihood of future ones, perhaps in part by establishing a pattern of reaction. The physician must inquire in great detail about the events preceding those attempts, and about the precipitating circumstances, the intent, and the result, in terms not only of the individual's response of guilt, relief, disappointment, and so forth, but also of the reaction of spouse, family, or friends. Was the response intense, and was it one of guilt, rage, or indifference? It is also often worthwhile to learn the response to suicidal ruminations. Has the patient been horrified, comforted, or restrained from action? The physician who tends to view self-destruction with fear, as an unthinkable, desperate act, may forget to ask himself such questions as, "What draws him to suicide?" and "What holds him back?" Such a listing of danger signals could be extended but perhaps the doctor should remind himself and take solace in the fact that one of suicide's characteristics remains a degree of unpredictability.

Perhaps the implications of the prevailing cultural attitude toward suicide become even more significant when one looks at the physician in his role as therapist. Here his anxiety may be reflected in his management of his patient. He may be led too readily to hospitalize the person who threatens to destroy himself, instead of giving him the curative personal relationship he is seeking; such action in some instances may deprive the patient of the opportunity to resolve a crisis by means of his own resources. Perhaps worse, the therapist's anxiety is communicated to the patient who is regarded as having suicide potential, and exerts a detrimental influence. First, communication is blocked and a barrier erected, supported by the anxiety of both physician and patient. No matter how we as physicians regard suicide, some persons at certain times feel that it is a very real possible solution to their life situation. As such it demands frank discussion. The therapist must have information concerning fantasied reactions of survivors, conception of death, and possible sources of identification with deceased family members or friends. He must gain some awareness of his patient's beliefs and philosophy of life. Such knowledge in part forms the basis for his prediction of the likelihood of suicide and in part forms the foundation for an understanding and commitment great enough to make the patient pause and weigh carefully his choice. Anxiety in the physician may interfere with his pursuit of this line of inquiry by making him fearful lest he suggest the very thing he seeks to prevent.

It is the self-evident duty of physicians to prevent suicide. In most instances there would be devastating consequences to family and friends if it were not avoided. In an equally large number of instances, those contemplating self-destruction adhere to religious systems of belief that themselves present objections to suicide. But when family or religious objections do not apply, does the physician have the right to impose his judgment in that which is a patient's own affair? In our society a doctor is often quite wrongly blamed for a suicide; in addition, he is vulnerable to an injury to his professional prestige and self-respect. Under these circumstances it is the rare physician who could be expected to step outside of and act with freedom from the limiting viewpoint of his time. As he makes the assessment that suicide is increasingly probable, his responsibility increases for communication of this knowledge to appropriate members of society so that steps can be taken to prevent it. But because of society's view of suicide, most physicians are probably restrained from communicating questions of a different sort which they might legitimately ask, namely, given the individual's system of values, could not the act of suicide under certain circumstances be adaptive or self-realizing for this particular person? The classical period provides dramatic examples of self-imposed deaths which were not only consistent with but also essential to the maintenance of a system of beliefs. A statement from a recent report dealing with medical practice and psychiatry supports this consideration: "Constructive rebellion or refusal to adapt to unacceptable situations may be the essence of good emotional health; sometimes even death may be, if the individual's value system experiences death as a maintenance of self."[17]

Hatred or revenge in suicide, a prominent motive, also often requires a special approach. Resentment stemming from real or fantasied disappointments is directed toward the spouse, family, and, not infrequently, the physician. Whether the potentially self-destructive individual is encouraged to proceed or held back from suicide often depends upon the degree to which he senses—often unconsciously—that the act would be effective in achieving the desired hurtful end. The point to be made is that the patient's family quite often encourages the patient in the direction of ending his life through attitudes both conscious and otherwise. Such an attitude may be one of rejection, but perhaps more often it is an ambivalent one. In such an instance the patient senses the vulnerability of his spouse or family member to feelings of guilt in the event of his suicide. The physician must maintain a lookout for these family forces seducing or prodding his patient toward taking his own life; if he senses their existence and believes he cannot alter them, the physician might attempt to separate his patient from them. The suicidal person is also fully aware that the therapist is especially vulnerable to feelings of guilt by virtue of his responsibility, involvement, and exposure to loss of prestige, and the patient may find this an additional impetus for seizing upon suicide for the expression of rage. It becomes

[17]Group for the Advancement of Psychiatry, *Medical Practice and Psychiatry: The Impact of Changing Demands*, Report No. 58, 1965; p. 335.

important, therefore, that the physician inform his patient, himself, and if necessary the patient's family that he cannot carry the entire burden of responsibility for the life of his patient. In so doing he may well reduce the risk that the patient will resort to the irreversible act.

The various cultural elements that have been prominent in the suicides of different historical ages—revenge, honor and dignity, sacrifice and faith, reunion with Nature—have affected the frequency of suicide, but, perhaps more importantly, they have determined the basic motivation or purpose of the act during different periods. In this connection it would appear that the element most prominent in the suicides of today is the primitive expression of revenge. Perhaps the suicidal act, forced into a kind of subterranean existence by the taboo attached to it, has been stripped of its more worthy elements. But is there inherent or potential value in this act or is suicide merely a holdover from less civilized societies? Just as man through his capacity to appreciate time is the only animal able to conceive of death, so also he may be the only one with the potential of ending life if he chooses. What is the significance of the choice which suicide seems to open to each human being? It has been said that unless a man can choose death he cannot truly commit himself to life. The classical era provided, at least among the philosophers and nobility, examples of thought and systems of belief with which the act of suicide was consistent. This was an age when the active consideration of suicide as a possibility increased the dignity of the individual man's existence and was an ennobling force. Is it not demeaning to preserve life at any cost, as though death were an enemy? Judgment of the act of suicide, however, is possibly of lesser concern than the welfare of society, which may be affected by the taboo. The current effort to prevent suicide, which weakens the suicide taboo by increasingly identifying the act as illness, may paradoxically result in a rise in its incidence. The possible rise in incidence, however, is not the only concern.

History reveals a close relationship between the attitude toward suicide, its frequency, and the type of social organization. In closely integrated, autocratic societies the incidence has been low and the attitude severe, whereas in more individualistic, democratic societies the reverse has been true. During the Middle Ages, when it is believed that suicide was rare, this most individual of actions must have seemed an affront to the authority of the Church. Much more lenient was the attitude of the ancients and romantics, who glorified the individual, his dignity, and his potentiality. The difference in incidence may be accounted for not only in terms of a prohibitive attitude existing in more rigid, less self-reliant societies, but also by the fact that in these societies authority, tradition, and custom have provided answers to life's problems and have shared its burdens. Society, in support of its basic organization, is perhaps forced to adopt a particular position with respect to this act.

In the final analysis only the surface is scratched by such considerations as these. Suicide, like other aspects of death, remains a mystery. Yet we may at least agree with Nietzsche that "The thought of suicide is a great consolation: by means of it one gets successfully through many a bad night."[18]

---

[18]Friedrich Nietzsche, "Beyond Good and Evil," p. 98 in *Complete Works*, Vol. 12, (New York: Macmillan, 1911).

9 / Culture Contact

Introduction

Up to this point in our description of cultural patterns the emphasis has been upon patterns of interactions in a single society taken in isolation. This is convenient for some purposes, but, of course, cultures do not exist in isolation. Rather, most cultural groups or societies face the question of how to devise patterns of successful or unsuccessful coexistence with other cultural groups. This chapter focuses upon cultural contacts among whole societies.

In simple cases, unfortunately, culture contact results in the annihilation of the weaker group. For example, the original people of Tasmania were systematically exterminated by the early European settlers, who wanted their land. Fortunately, not all contact results in such a final solution. In this chapter we attempt to illustrate the dynamics behind a variety of situations of culture contact in the hope of gaining some insight that might be used in facilitating greater tolerance and understanding in the future. In order to do this, we need to face certain widespread human characteristics.

As indicated previously, it seems to be a universal human characteristic to make value-judgments between good and evil. All humans are constantly making such evaluations, either consciously or unconsciously. For all humans it seems to be that the criteria of the ultimate good consist of their own patterns and practices of behavior, and any behavior that is different from their own usually is judged to be "bad." It is likely that the Europeans who slaughtered the Tasmanians and hunted them down like animals rationalized their behavior by defining the Tasmanians as nonhuman.

Since there is an infinite variety of cultural beliefs and practices around the world, it is impossible to know and understand even a significant fraction of the variety of human behavior. Therefore, a certain laziness in learning about others is unavoidable because of the amount we must learn in order to understand behavior that is very different from our own. In this connection we might recall Ruth Benedict's article on the abnormal and the normal in Chapter Three. This article could only have been written by an anthropologist who had spent enough time and study to appreciate that there is no single permanent absolute criterion that defines normal or abnormal. Benedict had trained herself to take perspectives outside her own cultural teachings. Learning to take a variety of perspectives is enormously difficult, so let us examine for a moment why.

Each cultural belief and practice that becomes well-established within an individual, because of his experience over the years, is internalized and learned at various levels. As one learns a practice as a child it may be a rather simple habit. If it is an important pattern we are eventually called upon to defend the practice to people slightly different from ourselves. Cultural practices take on additional levels of meaning as we defend them. We learn to give *intellectual* arguments in their defense. We gradually become emotionally attached to the patterns so that we learn them at an *emotional* level as well. Finally we attach *values* to the patterns. Since our own practices are involved, the value we attach to them is good rather than evil.

The tendency to take one's self as the center of the universe and to judge all cultural patterns in terms of one's own is frequently labeled "ethnocentrism" by the anthropologist. One of the aims, of course, in training other anthropologists is to attempt in a small way to break down such patterns of ethnocentrism in order to gain a more genuine understanding and insight into other cultures, as well as to gain respect and tolerance for differences. In the current chapter we have included a rather wide variety of reports of culture contact as well as a variety of responses.

In the first article Deloria discusses the topic of stereotypes. As an American Indian he is primarily interested in the stereotypes that he perceives among the rest of the culture concerning the American Indian. Stereotyping is one of the defenses used by people to avoid learning about others. They usually are gross generalities that avoid an understanding or appreciation of perspectives other than our own. Since our stereotypes of others are always different from our own patterns, they always imply an inferior image; they imply negative value and negative emotion and lack of intellectual understanding.

When cultures of very uneven technology and philosophy meet, it is possible to discern at least two quite radically different patterns of contact. If the culture with the lesser technology is not powerful enough to constitute a threat and does not possess gold or wealth worthy of plunder, one recurring pattern is for the more powerful culture to treat the weaker and poorer culture as dependents. In this situation the "conquering" culture attempts to provide schools and other welfare programs to take care of the non-threatening culture or group. This relationship may follow a period of violence or plunder and apply only to the remnant of a previously threatening or wealthy society.

In cases where the less technologically developed groups pose either a threat or have land or gold to plunder, contact usually results in violence. The stories of Cortéz and his plunder of Mexico, and Pizarro and his plunder of Peru are examples that come immediately to mind. In the conquest of the United States, culture contact was characterized by continual violence and plunder. In the United States, the land occupied by the Indians was cause for greed on the part of the conquerers. In the second article by Brown we have a description from an American Indian's point of view of one of the thousands of encounters between an American Indian group and the representatives of the ever-greedy culture of the white Americans.

In the third article of this chapter, Murphy shows that aggressive warfare is by no means a monopoly of the West in intercultural dealings. Although most such non-Western traditions were quelled by Western administrations—as among the Mundurucú themselves after 1912—there were once many such groups where fighting between villages or across cultural lines was carried far beyond mere defense. For example, the Yąnomamö (also a group from the interior of South America; see Chagnon's article in Chapter Two) still define themselves as fierce people and center much of their internal organization upon the prospect of an attack, delivered or received. We might note, by contrast, that certain other non-Western groups—e.g., the Eskimos—could not even understand the motives and dynamics of warfare, when first introduced to the notion. Murphy's analysis gives us a picture of headhunting among the Mundurucú—a South American group of tribes, a group whose motto could well be "In order to keep the peace we kill others."

The last selection by Bohannan illustrates the difficulties of understanding a point of view different from one's own. Her difficulty in communicating a story from her own culture to the Tiv is an excellent example of the anthropological concept of "cultural relativity." The concept refers to the fact that the interpretation of human behavior is relative to the cultural perspective from which it is viewed. Bohannan's preconceptions that certain types of human situations were universal and therefore understandable to everyone were dissolved. Her article documents her shock, amusement, and dismay at the totally different interpretations which the Tiv gave to *Hamlet*.

Stereotyping

Vine Deloria, Jr.

One reason that Indian people have not been heard from until recently is that we have been completely covered up by movie Indians. Western movies have been such favorites that they have dominated the public's conception of what Indians are. It is not all bad when one thinks about the handsome Jay Silverheels bailing the Lone Ranger out of a jam, or Ed Ames rescuing Daniel Boone with some clever Indian trick. But the other mythologies that have wafted skyward because of the movies have blocked out any idea that there might be real Indians with real problems.

Other minority groups have fought tenaciously against stereotyping, and generally they have been successful. Italians quickly quashed the image of them as mobsters that television projected in *The Untouchables*. Blacks have been successful in getting a more realistic picture of the black man in a contemporary setting because they have had standout performers like Bill Cosby and Sidney Poitier to represent them.

Since stereotyping was highlighted by motion pictures, it would probably be well to review the images of minority groups projected in the movies in order to understand how the situation looks at present. Perhaps the first aspect of stereotyping was the tendency to exclude people on the basis of their inability to handle the English language. Not only were racial minorities excluded, but immigrants arriving on these shores were soon whipped into shape by ridicule of their English.

Traditional stereotypes pictured the black as a happy watermelon-eating darky whose sole contribution to American society was his indiscriminate substitution of the "d" sound for "th." Thus a black always said "dis" and "dat," as in "lift dat bale." The "d" sound carried over and was used by white gangsters to indicate disfavor with their situation, as in "dis is de end, ya rat." The important thing was to indicate that blacks were like lisping children not yet competent to undertake the rigors of economic opportunities and voting.

Mexicans were generally portrayed as shiftless and padded out for siesta, without any redeeming qualities whatsoever. Where the black had been handicapped by his use of the "d," the Mexican suffered from the use of the double "e." This marked them off as a group worth watching. Mexicans, according to the stereotype, always said "theenk," "peenk," and later "feenk." Many advertisements today still continue this stereotype, thinking that it is cute and cuddly.

These groups were much better off than Indians were. Indians were always devoid of any English whatsoever. They were only allowed to speak when an important message had to be transmitted on the screen. For example, "many pony soldiers die" was meant to indicate that Indians were going to attack the peaceful settlers who happened to have broken their three hundredth treaty moments before. Other than that Indian linguistic ability was limited to "ugh" and "kemo sabe" (which means honky in some obscure Indian language).

The next step was to acknowledge that there was a great American dream to which any child could aspire. (It was almost like the train in the night that Richard Nixon heard as a child anticipating the dream fairy.) The great American dream was projected in the early World War II movies. The last reel was devoted to a stirring proclamation that we were going to win the war and it showed factories producing airplanes, people building ships, and men marching in uniform to the transports. There was a quick pan of a black face before the scene shifted to scenes of orchards, rivers, Mount Rushmore, and the Liberty Bell as we found out what we were fighting for.

The new images expressed a profound inability to understand why minority groups couldn't "make it" when everybody knew what America was all about—freedom and equality. By projecting an image of everyone working hard to win the war, the doctrine was spread that America was just one big happy family and that there really weren't any differences so long as we had to win the war.

It was a rare war movie in the 1940's that actually showed a black or a Mexican as a bona fide fighting man. When they did appear it was in the role of cooks or orderlies serving whites. In most cases this was a fairly accurate statement of their situation, particularly with respect to the Navy.

World War II movies were entirely different for Indians. Each platoon of red-blooded white American boys was equipped with its own set of Indians. When the platoon got into trouble and was surrounded, its communications cut off except for one slender line to regimental headquarters, and that line tapped by myriads of Germans, Japanese, or Italians, the stage was set for the dramatic episode of the Indians.

John Wayne, Randolph Scott, Sonny Tufts, or Tyrone Power would smile broadly as he played his ace, which until this time had been hidden from view. From nowhere, a Navajo, Comanche, Cherokee, or Sioux would appear, take the telephone, and in some short and inscrutable phraseology communicate such a plenitude of knowledge to his fellow tribesman (fortunately situated at the general's right hand) that fighting units thousands of miles away would instantly perceive the situation and rescue the platoon. The Indian would disappear as mysteriously as he had come, only to reappear the next week in a different battle to perform his esoteric rites. Anyone watching war movies during the 40's would have been convinced that without Indian telephone operators the war would have been lost irretrievably, in spite of John Wayne.

Indians were America's secret weapon against the forces of evil. The typing spoke of a primitive gimmick, and it was the strangeness of Indians that made them visible, not their humanity. With the Korean War era and movies made during the middle 50's, other minority groups began to appear and Indians were pushed into the background. This era was the heyday of the "All-American Platoon." It was the ultimate conception of intergroup relations. The "All-American Platoon" was a "one each": one black, one Mexican, one Indian, one farm boy from Iowa, one Southerner who hated blacks, one boy from Brooklyn, one Polish boy from the urban slums of the Midwest, one Jewish intellectual, and one college boy. Every possible stereotype was included and it resulted in a portrayal of Indians as another species of human being for the first time in moving pictures.

The platoon was always commanded by a veteran of grizzled countenance who had been at every battle in which the United States had ever engaged. The whole story consisted in killing off the members of the platoon until only the veteran and the college boy were left. The Southerner and the black would die in each other's arms singing "Dixie." The Jewish intellectual and the Indian formed some kind of attachment and were curiously the last ones killed. When the smoke cleared, the college boy, with a prestige wound in the shoulder, returned to his girl, and the veteran reconciled with his wife and checked out another platoon in anticipation of taking the same hill in the next movie.

While other groups have managed to make great strides since those days, Indians have remained the primitive unknown quantity. Dialogue has reverted back to the monosyllabic grunt and even pictures that attempt to present the Indian side of the story depend upon unintelligible noises to present their message. The only exception to this rule is a line famed for its durability over the years. If you fall asleep during the Late Show and suddenly awaken to the words "go in peace my son," it is either an Indian chief bidding his son goodbye as the boy heads for college or a Roman Catholic priest forgiving Paul Newman or Steve McQueen for killing a hundred men in the preceding reel.

Anyone raising questions about the image of minority groups as portrayed in television and the movies is automatically suspect as an un-American and subversive influence on the minds of the young. The historical, linguistic, and cultural differences are neatly blocked out by the fad of portraying members of minority groups in roles which formerly were reserved for whites. Thus Burt Reynolds played a Mohawk detective busy solving the crime problem in New York City. Diahann Carroll played a well-to-do black widow with small child in a television series that was obviously patterned after the unique single-headed white family.

In recent years the documentary has arisen to present the story of Indian people and a number of series on Black America have been produced. Indian documentaries are singularly the same. A reporter and television crew hasten to either the Navajo or Pine Ridge reservation, quickly shoot reels on poverty conditions, and return East blithely thinking that they have captured the essence of Indian life. In spite of the best intentions, the eternal yearning to present an exciting story of a strange people overcomes, and the endless cycle of poverty-oriented films continues.

This type of approach continually categorizes the Indian as an incompetent boob who can't seem to get along and who is hopelessly mired in a poverty of his own making. Hidden beneath these documentaries is the message that Indians really WANT to live this way. No one has yet filmed the incredible progress that is being made by the Makah tribe, the Quinaults, Red Lake Chippewas, Gila River Pima-Maricopas, and others. Documentaries project the feeling that reservations should be eliminated because the conditions are so bad. There is no effort to present the bright side of Indian life.

With the rise of ethnic studies programs and courses in minority-group history, the situation has become worse. People who support these programs assume that by communicating the best aspects of a group they have somehow solved the major problems of that group in its relations with the rest of society. By emphasizing that black is beautiful or that Indians have contributed the names of rivers to the road map, many people feel that they have done justice to the group concerned.

One theory of interpretation of Indian history that has arisen in the past several years is that all of the Indian war chiefs were patriots defending their lands. This is the "patriot chief" interpretation of history. Fundamentally it is a good theory in that it places a more equal balance to interpreting certain Indian wars as wars of resistance. It gets away from the tendency, seen earlier in this century, to classify all Indian warriors as renegades. But there is a tendency to overlook the obvious renegades, Indians who were treacherous and would have been renegades had there been no whites to fight. The patriot chiefs interpretation also conveniently overlooks the fact that every significant leader of the previous century was eventually done in by his own people in one way or another. Sitting Bull was killed by Indian police working for the government. Geronimo was captured by an army led by Apache scouts who sided with the United States.

If the weak points of each minority group's history are to be covered over by a sweetness-and-light interpretation based on what we would like to think happened rather than what did happen, we doom ourselves to decades of further racial strife. Most of the study programs today emphasize the goodness that is inherent in the different minority communities, instead of trying to present a balanced story. There are basically two schools of interpretation running through all of these efforts as the demand for black, red, and brown pride dominates the programs.

One theory derives from the "All-American Platoon" concept of a decade ago. Under this theory members of the respective racial minority groups had an important role in the great events of American history. Crispus Attucks, a black, almost single-handedly started the Revolutionary War, while Eli Parker, the Seneca Indian general, won the Civil War and would have concluded it sooner had not there been so many stupid whites abroad in those days. This is the "cameo" theory of history. It takes a basic "manifest destiny" white interpretation of history and lovingly plugs a few feathers, woolly heads, and sombreros into the famous events of American history. No one tries to explain what an Indian is who was helping the whites destroy his own people, since we are now all Americans and have these great events in common.

The absurdity of the cameo school of ethnic pride is self-apparent. Little Mexican children are taught that there were some good Mexicans at the Alamo. They can therefore be happy that Mexicans have been involved in the significant events of Texas history. Little is said about the Mexicans on the other side at the Alamo. The result is a denial of a substantial Mexican heritage by creating the feeling that "we all did it together." If this trend continues I would not be surprised to discover that Columbus had a Cherokee on board when he set sail from Spain in search of the Indies.

The cameo school smothers any differences that existed historically by presenting a history in which all groups have participated through representatives. Regardless of Crispus Attuck's valiant behavior during the Revolution, it is doubtful that he envisioned another century of slavery for blacks as a cause worth defending.

The other basic school of interpretation is a projection backward of the material blessings of the white middle class. It seeks to identify where all the material wealth originated and finds that each minority group *contributed* something. It can therefore be called the contribution school. Under this conception we should all love Indians because they contributed corn, squash, potatoes, tobacco, coffee, rubber, and other agricultural products. In like manner, blacks and Mexicans are credited with Carver's work on the peanut, blood transfusion, and tacos and tamales.

The ludicrous implication of the contribution school visualizes the minority groups clamoring to enter American society, lined up with an abundance of foods and fancies, presenting them to whites in a never-ending stream of generosity. If the different minority groups were given an overriding 2 percent royalty on their contributions, the same way whites have managed to give themselves royalties for their inventions, this school would have a more realistic impact on minority groups.

The danger with both of these types of ethnic studies theories is that they present an unrealistic account of the role of minority groups in American history. Certainly there is more to the story of the American Indian than providing cocoa and popcorn for Columbus' landing party. When the clashes of history are smoothed over in favor of a mushy togetherness feeling, then people begin to wonder what has happened in the recent past that has created the conditions of today. It has been the feeling of younger people that contemporary problems have arisen because community leadership has been consistently betraying them. Older statesmen are called Uncle Toms, and the entire fabric of accumulated wisdom and experience of the older generation of minority groups is destroyed.

Rising against the simplistic cameo and contribution schools is the contemporary desire by church leaders to make Christianity relevant to minority groups by transposing the entire Christian myth and archetypes into Indian, black, and Mexican terms. Thus Father Groppi, noted white-black priest, wants to have black churches show a black Christ. This is absurd, because Christ was, as everyone knows, a Presbyterian, and he was a white man. That is to say, for nearly two thousand years he has been a white man. To suddenly show him as black, Mexican, or Indian takes away the whole meaning of the myth.

The Indian counterpart of the black Christ is the Christmas card portraying the Holy Family living in a hogan in Monument Valley on the Navajo reservation. As the shepherds sing and gather their flocks, little groups of Navajo angels announce the birth of the Christchild. The scene is totally patronizing and unrealistic. If the Christchild was born on the Navajo reservation, his chances of surviving the first two years of life would be less than those of the original Jesus with Herod chasing him. (We have not yet reached the point of showing three officials from the Bureau of Indian Affairs coming up the canyon as the Three Wise Men, but someone with a keen sense of relevancy will try it sooner or later.)

This type of religious paternalism overlooks the fact that the original figures of religious myths were designed to communicate doctrines. It satisfies itself by presenting its basic figures as so universalized that anyone can participate at any time in history. Thus the religion that it is trying to communicate becomes ahistorical as Mickey Mouse and Snow White were ahistorical.

If the attempted renovation of religious imagery is ever combined with the dominant schools of ethnic studies, the result will be the last Supper as the gathering of the "All-American Platoon" highlighted by the contributions of each group represented. Instead of simple bread and wine the table will be overflowing with pizza, tamales, greens, peanuts, popcorn, German sausage, and hamburgers. Everyone will feel that they have had a part in the creation of the great American Christian social order. Godless Communism will be vanquished.

Under present conceptions of ethnic studies there can be no lasting benefit either to minority groups or to society at large. The pride that can be built into children and youth by acknowledgment of the validity of their group certainly cannot be built by simply transferring symbols and interpretations arising in white cultural history into an Indian, black, or Mexican setting. The result will be to make the minority groups bear the white man's burden by using his symbols and stereotypes as if they were their own.

There must be a drive within each minority group to understand its own uniqueness. This can only be done by examining what experiences were relevant to the group, not what experiences of white America the group wishes itself to be represented in. As an example, the discovery of gold in California was a significant event in the experience of white America. The discovery itself was irrelevant to the western Indian tribes, but the migrations caused by the discovery of gold were vitally important. The two histories can dovetail around this topic but ultimately each interpretation must depend upon its orientation to the group involved.

What has been important and continues to be important is the Constitution of the United States and its continual adaptation to contemporary situations. With the Constitution as a framework and reference point, it would appear that a number of conflicting interpretations of the experience of America could be validly given. While they might conflict at every point as each group defines to its own satisfaction what its experience has meant, recognition that within the Constitutional framework we are engaged in a living process of intergroup relationships would mean that no one group could define the meaning of American society to the exclusion of any other.

Self-awareness of each group must define a series of histories about the American experience. Manifest destiny has dominated thinking in the past because it has had an abstract quality that appeared to interpret experiences accurately. Nearly every racial and ethnic group has had to bow down before this conception of history and conform to an understanding of the world that it did not ultimately believe. Martin Luther King, Jr., spoke to his people on the basis of self-awareness the night before he died. He told them that they as a people would reach the promised land. Without the same sense of destiny, minority groups will simply be adopting the outmoded forms of stereotyping by which whites have deluded themselves for centuries.

We can survive as a society if we reject the conquest-oriented interpretation of the Constitution. While some Indian nationalists want the whole country back, a guarantee of adequate protection of existing treaty rights would provide a meaningful compromise. The Constitution should provide a sense of balance between groups as it has between conflicting desires of individuals.

As each group defines the ideas and doctrines necessary to maintain its own sense of dignity and identity, similarities in goals can be drawn that will have relevance beyond immediate group aspirations. Stereotyping will change radically because the ideological basis for portraying the members of any group will depend on that group's values. Plots in books and movies will have to show life as it is seen from within the group. Society will become broader and more cosmopolitan as innovative themes are presented to it. The universal sense of inhumanity will take on an aspect of concreteness. From the variety of cultural behavior patterns we can devise a new understanding of humanity.

The problem of stereotyping is not so much a racial problem as it is a problem of limited knowledge and perspective. Even though minority groups have suffered in the past by ridiculous characterizations of themselves by white society, they must not fall into the same trap by simply reversing the process that has stereotyped them. Minority groups must thrust through the rhetorical blockade by creating within themselves a sense of "peoplehood." This ultimately means the creation of a new history and not mere amendments to the historical interpretations of white America.

Wounded Knee

Dee Brown

There was no hope on earth, and God seemed to have forgotten us. Some said they saw the Son of God; others did not see Him. If He had come, He would do some great things as He had done before. We doubted it because we had seen neither Him nor His works.

The people did not know; they did not care. They snatched at the hope. They screamed like crazy men to Him for mercy. They caught at the promise they heard He had made.

The white men were frightened and called for soldiers. We had begged for life, and the white men thought we wanted theirs. We heard that soldiers were coming. We did not fear. We hoped that we could tell them our troubles, and get help. A white man said the soldiers meant to kill us. We did not believe it, but some were frightened and ran away to the Badlands.

—Red Cloud

Had it not been for the sustaining force of the Ghost Dance religion, the Sioux in their grief and anger over the assassination of Sitting Bull might have risen up against the guns of the soldiers. So prevalent was their belief that the white men would soon disappear and that with the next greening of the grass their dead relatives and friends would return, they made no retaliations. By the hundreds, however, the leaderless Hunkpapas fled from Standing Rock, seeking refuge in one of the Ghost Dance camps or with the last of the great chiefs, Red Cloud, at Pine Ridge. In the Moon When the Deer Shed Their Horns (December 17) about a hundred of these fleeing Hunkpapas reached Big Foot's Minneconjou camp near Cherry Creek. That same day the War Department issued orders for the arrest and imprisonment of Big Foot. He was on the list of "fomenters of disturbances."

As soon as Big Foot learned that Sitting Bull had been killed, he started his people toward Pine Ridge, hoping that Red Cloud could protect them from the soldiers. En route, he fell ill of pneumonia, and when hemorrhaging began, he had to travel in a wagon. On December 28, as they neared Porcupine Creek, the Minneconjous sighted four troops of cavalry approaching. Big Foot immediately ordered a white flag run up over his wagon. About two o'clock in the afternoon he raised up from his blankets to greet Major Samuel Whitside, Seventh U.S. Cavalry. Big Foot's blankets were stained with blood from his lungs, and as he talked in a hoarse whisper with Whitside, red drops fell from his nose and froze in the bitter cold.

Whitside told Big Foot that he had orders to take him to a cavalry camp on Wounded Knee Creek. The Minneconjou chief replied that he was going in that direction; he was taking his people to Pine Ridge for safety.

Turning to his half-breed scout, John Shangreau, Major Whitside ordered him to begin disarming Big Foot's band.

"Look here, Major," Shangreau replied, "if you do that, there is liable to be a fight here; and if there is, you will kill all those women and children and the men will get away from you."

Whitside insisted that his orders were to capture Big Foot's Indians and disarm and dismount them.

"We better take them to camp and then take their horses from them and their guns," Shangreau declared.

"All right," Whitside agreed. "You tell Big Foot to move down to camp at Wounded Knee."

The major glanced at the ailing chief, and then gave an order for his Army ambulance to be brought forward. The ambulance would be warmer and would give Big Foot an easier ride than the jolting springless wagon. After the chief was transferred to the ambulance, Whitside formed a column for the march to Wounded Knee Creek. Two troops of cavalry took the lead, the ambulance and wagons following, the Indians herded into a compact group behind them, with the other two cavalry troops and a battery of two Hotchkiss guns bringing up the rear.

Twilight was falling when the column crawled over the last rise in the land and began descending the slope toward Chankpe Opi Wakpala, the creek called Wounded Knee. The wintry dusk and the tiny crystals of ice dancing in the dying light added a supernatural quality to the somber landscape. Somewhere along this frozen stream the heart of Crazy Horse lay in a secret place, and the Ghost Dancers believed that his disembodied spirit was waiting impatiently for the new earth that would surely come with the first green grass of spring.

At the cavalry tent camp on Wounded Knee Creek, the Indians were halted and children counted. There were 120 men and 230 women and children. Because of the gathering darkness, Major Whitside decided to wait until morning before disarming his prisoners. He assigned them a camping area immediately to the south of the military camp, issued them rations, and as there was a shortage of tepee covers, he furnished them several tents. Whitside ordered a stove placed in Big Foot's tent and sent a regimental surgeon to administer to the sick chief. To make certain that none of his prisoners escaped, the major stationed two troops of cavalry as sentinels around the Sioux tepees, and then posted his two Hotchkiss guns on top of a rise overlooking the camp. The barrels of these rifled guns, which could hurl explosive charges for more than two miles, were positioned to rake the length of the Indian lodges.

Later in the darkness of that December night the remainder of the Seventh Regiment marched in from the east and quietly bivouacked north of Major Whitside's troops. Colonel James W. Forsyth, commanding Custer's former regiment, now took charge of operations. He informed Whitside that he had received orders to take Big Foot's band to the Union Pacific Railroad for shipment to a military prison in Omaha.

After placing two more Hotchkiss guns on the slope beside the others, Forsyth and his officers settled down for the evening with a keg of whiskey to celebrate the capture of Big Foot.

The chief lay in his tent, too ill to sleep, barely able to breathe. Even with their protective Ghost Shirts and their belief in the prophecies of the new Messiah, his people were fearful of the pony soldiers camped all around them. Fourteen years before, on the Little Bighorn, some of these warriors had helped defeat some of these soldier chiefs—Moylan, Varnum, Wallace, Godfrey, Edgerly—and the Indians wondered if revenge could still be in their hearts.

"The following morning there was a bugle call," said Wasumaza, one of Big Foot's warriors who years afterward was to change his name to Dewey Beard. "Then I saw the soldiers mounting their horses and surrounding us. It was announced that all men should come to the center for a talk and that after the talk they were to move on to Pine Ridge agency. Big Foot was brought out of his tepee and sat in front of his tent and the older men were gathered around him and sitting right near him in the center."

After issuing hardtack for breakfast rations, Colonel Forsyth informed the Indians that they were now to be disarmed. "They called for guns and arms," White Lance said, "so all of us gave the guns and they were stacked up in the center." The soldier chiefs were not satisfied with the number of weapons surrendered, and so they sent details of troopers to search the tepees. "They would go right into the tents and come out with bundles and tear them open," Dog Chief said. "They brought our axes, knives, and tent stakes and piled them near the guns."

Still not satisfied, the soldier chiefs ordered the warriors to remove their blankets and submit to searches for weapons. The Indians' faces showed their anger, but only the medicine man, Yellow Bird, made any overt protest. He danced a few Ghost Dance steps, and chanted one of the holy songs, assuring the warriors that the soldiers' bullets could not penetrate their sacred garments. "The bullets will not go toward you," he chanted in Sioux. "The prairie is large and the bullets will not go toward you."

The troopers found only two rifles, one of them a new Winchester belonging to a young Minneconjou named Black Coyote. Black Coyote raised the Winchester above his head, shouting that he paid much money for the rifle and that it belonged to him. Some years afterward Dewey Beard recalled that Black Coyote was deaf. "If they had left him alone he was going to put his gun down where he should. They grabbed him and spinned him in the east direction. He was still unconcerned even then. He hadn't his gun pointed at anyone. His intention was to put that gun down. They came on and grabbed the gun that he was going to put down. Right after they spun him around there was the report of a gun, which was quite loud. I couldn't say that anyone was shot, but following that was a crash."

"It sounded much like the sound of tearing canvas, that was the crash," Rough Feather said. Afraid-of-the-Enemy described it as a "lightning crash."

Turning Hawk said that Black Coyote "was a crazy man, a young man of very bad influence and in fact a nobody." He said that Black Coyote fired his gun and that "immediately the soldiers returned fire and indiscriminate killing followed."

In the first seconds of violence, the firing of carbines was deafening, filling the air with powder smoke. Among the dying who lay sprawled on the frozen ground was Big Foot. Then there was a brief lull in the rattle of arms, with small groups of Indians and soldiers grappling at close quarters, using knives, clubs, and pistols. As few of the Indians had arms, they soon had to flee, and then the big Hotchkiss guns on the hill opened up on them, firing almost a shell a second, raking the Indian camp, shredding the tepees with flying shrapnel, killing men, women, and children.

"We tried to run," Louise Weasel Bear said, "but they shot us like we were a buffalo. I know there are some good white people, but the soldiers must be mean to shoot children and women. Indian soldiers would not do that to white children."

"I was running away from the place and followed those who were running away," said Hakiktawin, another of the young women. "My grandfather and grandmother and brother were killed as we crossed the ravine, and then I was shot on the right hip clear through and on my right wrist where I did not go any further as I was not able to walk, and after the soldier picked me up where a little girl came to me and crawled into the blanket."

When the madness ended, Big Foot and more than half of his people were dead or seriously wounded; 153 were known dead, but many of the wounded crawled away to die afterward. One estimate placed the final total of dead at very nearly three hundred of the original 350 men, women, and children. The soldiers lost twenty-five dead and thirty-nine wounded, most of them struck by their own bullets or shrapnel.

After the wounded cavalrymen were started for the agency at Pine Ridge, a detail of soldiers went over the Wounded Knee battlefield, gathering up Indians who were still alive and loading them into wagons. As it was apparent by the end of the day that a blizzard was approaching, the dead Indians were left lying where they had fallen. (After the blizzard, when a burial party returned to Wounded Knee, they found the bodies, including Big Foot's, frozen into grotesque shapes.)

The wagonloads of wounded Sioux (four men and forty-seven women and children) reached Pine Ridge after dark. Because all available barracks were filled with soldiers, they were left lying in the open wagons in the bitter cold while an inept Army officer searched for shelter. Finally the Episcopal mission was opened, the benches taken out, and hay scattered over the rough flooring.

It was the fourth day after Christmas in the Year of Our Lord 1890. When the first torn and bleeding bodies were carried into the candlelit church, those who were conscious could see Christmas greenery hanging from the open rafters. Across the chancel front above the pulpit was strung a crudely lettered banner: PEACE ON EARTH, GOOD WILL TO MEN.

I did not know then how much was ended. When I look back now from this high hill of my old age, I can still see the butchered women and children lying heaped and scattered all along the crooked gulch as plain as when I saw them with eyes still young. And I can see that something else died there in the bloody mud, and was buried in the blizzard. A people's dream died there. It was a beautiful dream . . . the nation's hoop is broken and scattered. There is no center any longer, and the sacred tree is dead.
—Black Elk

Intergroup Hostility and Social Cohesion
Robert F. Murphy

Georg Simmel (1955:33–4) noted that warfare is frequently the only mode of social interaction between primitive societies. He saw the social relations of such groups to be characterized by diametric opposition between the norms of behavior applicable to members of the ingroup, on one hand, and toward members of outgroups, on the other. This dichotomy was internally self-consistent to Simmel, and he wrote (ibid:34):

For this reason, the same drive to expand and to act, which *within* the group requires unconditional peace for the integration of interests and for unfettered interaction, may appear to the outside world as a tendency toward war.

Intergroup conflict was viewed by Simmel as having positive functions; it provides the basis for group formation and cohesion, and it accentuates and maintains group boundaries. Conflict, then, is not aberrant or dysfunctional. Rather, it structures social relations both within and between societies.

Lewis Coser (1956:95), writing to Simmel's general thesis, points out that social cohesion does not automatically follow from conflict, for "social systems lacking social solidarity are likely to disintegrate in the face of conflict, although some unity may be despotically enforced." The corollary proposition is offered that:

. . . if the basic social structure is stable, if basic values are not questioned, cohesion is usually strengthened by war through challenge to, and revitalization of, values and goals which have been taken for granted (ibid:90).

Coser's view by no means contradicts that of Simmel but is an elaboration of the latter's thesis, as cited above, that intergroup hostility and social cohesion are only analytically different aspects of the same social process. Conflict and social solidarity are mutually re-enforcing; conflict promotes social integration, and solidarity is necessary if the group is to take effective common action against the outer world.

The present paper will analyze the warfare pattern of a Brazilian Indian group, the Mundurucú, in the light of the propositions given by Simmel and elaborated by Coser. We will go beyond the thesis that warfare contributes to the maintenance of the social structure to consider also how this social structure organized the membership for military activity. Further, the thesis will be advanced that this type of social structure actually generated the bellicose activities and attitudes that functioned to preserve it, and that this circular relationship allowed Mundurucú society to continue through a period during which it was subjected to severe internal and external threats. Finally, we will conclude with a general hypothesis upon the relation between social structure, social cohesion, and conflict.

THE MUNDURUCÚ

The Mundurucú, a Tupian speaking people, are presently located in a region of mixed forest and savannah east of the Tapajós River in the state of Pará, Brazil, between the sixth and eighth degrees of south latitude. Highly acculturated and almost assimilated remnants of the tribe are also found on the Secundurí, Abacaxí and Maués Rivers in the adjoining state of Amazonas. The Mundurucú were first reported upon in the latter region in 1768 (Monteiro Noronha, 1862). Their military strength was rapidly impressed upon the colonists of the Amazon Valley, for they commenced a series of strong attacks upon forts along the Amazon River that continued until the colonial government retaliated and in 1795 struck at the Mundurucú homeland on the upper Tapajós River. There is no information on the impact of this attack on the Mundurucú, but they ceased raiding white settlements immediately thereafter and in time became active allies of the colonists and the Portuguese colonial government. So rapidly did the Mundurucú adapt to the whites that by 1817 Ayres de Casal (1817:237) wrote, "Nearly all of the Mundurucú hordes are today our allies, and some already are Christians." But the Mundurucú had by no means become pacific, and raids, often instigated by the whites, were pushed with unabated fury against other Indian tribes.

Shortly after their contact with the white colonists, segments of the Mundurucú were evidently in the process of migrating northward along the Tapajós River and into the country between the Tapajós and Madeira Rivers. The Mundurucú who settled in these more northerly regions soon became assimilated into the neo-Brazilian population. Missions and mission-sponsored reductions were established in their midst at several locales, and their inhabitants intermarried with the Portuguese and mestizo colonists. The population of these Indian reductions declined throughout the century; Coudreau (1897:8) states that the old Mundurucú reduction of Uxituba had 485 Indians in 1833, 343 in 1848, 100 in 1869 and only 50 in 1895. Others, such as Boim and Itaituba, lost their Indian character and became Brazilian towns. By 1885 the process had advanced so far that Charles F. Hartt (1885:117) noted: "The Mundurucú of the Tapajós, below the rapids, are now all civilized and so mixed with the general population that their nationality has in large part been lost."

The balance of the tribe, which remained south, or upstream, of the head of navigation of the Tapajós River, maintained relative autonomy. They conducted trade, at first in manioc flour and later in raw latex, with Brazilian traders who seasonally ascended the river, but no permanent Brazilian settlements were located above the Cachoeira de Maranhão, a series of impassable rapids. At the end of the century, however, the boom in rubber extraction attracted permanent trading posts to the upper Tapajós River, and a Catholic mission was established on the banks of the river.

The rubber boom terminated the isolation of the Mundurucú of the upper Tapajós. The population became involved in rubber production for barter, and, although the new economic pursuit did not seriously hamper their traditional subsistence activities, it placed severe inhibitions upon the extensive sorties formerly customary.

Warfare did not end until about 1912, over a century after the Mundurucú had made peace with the whites. During this time certain internal modifications had occurred in the social structure, but social cohesion had remained intact and the boundaries of the society were still sharply defined and vigorously maintained. Although members were lost to Brazilian society, a hard core of population living near the upper Tapajós River made war upon other Indian groups with energy and success. This was not "aboriginal" warfare; it was frequently waged on behalf of the whites and with firearms supplied by them. But the only information on Mundurucú warfare of any value pertains to the 19th century and was derived from older informants and published sources. This, then, is the proper time dimension of our study, and we turn now to a consideration of the relevant aspects of Mundurucú culture during this period.

The Mundurucú villages were located in the midst of grass-covered savannahs surrounded by dense forest, but their subsistence economy was essentially the same as other groups of the Amazon rain forest. Hunting was important throughout the year, and fishing was primarily a dry season activity. Garden crops included the usual range of Tropical Forest vegetables and fruits, and bitter manioc was the staple product. Manioc flour, known as *farinha* in Brazil, was also traded to the whites by the Mundurucú and constituted their most important commercial commodity in the period prior to the rubber boom.

The division of labor and the organization of work reflected certain basic aspects of Mundurucú social structure. The men hunted and fished and carried out the strenuous task of garden clearing, while the women did the rest of the horticultural work and tended the households. Residence was matrilocal, and the females of each house formed a nucleus of matrilineally related kinswomen; each such household was also a communal work and consumption unit. Each Mundurucú village had about three to five such houses and a men's house; the latter was the locus of male activity, for all the village men slept, ate, worked, and relaxed within its confines.

The membership of the men's house was eclectic in relation to descent. The Mundurucú were divided into more than forty patrilineal clans, linked by loose and unnamed phratric affiliations, and parcelled almost equally between patrilineal, exogamous moieties. But the matrilocal residence rule and the resultant shift of men from their natal households and, commonly, villages, continually blocked the formation of co-resident descent groups.

Despite the diversity of their local and lineal origins, the men of a village, and ultimately of the whole tribe, were expected to maintain harmonious and cooperative relations. Cooperation in economic activities transcended the minimal necessities of their ecological adaptation, and any open show of aggression between men was strictly prohibited. The men's house provided the organizational framework within which this unity was expressed, while male values were supernaturally reinforced by their possession of the sacred trumpets, or *karökö*. Each village maintained a set of three of these instruments, and they were absolutely taboo to the eyes of the women, who were thought to have once owned them.

Political controls were not elaborate. Each village had a chief whose position was bolstered by the fact that his sons were generally exempt from the matrilocal residence rule. Although there were no patterns of continuous supravillage leadership, relations between communities were very close and involved intermarriage and joint participation in ceremonies and warfare. Tribal feeling was highly developed and conflict between villages was totally absent.

THE CONDUCT OF WARFARE

Mundurucú warfare was distinguished by a complete lack of any defensive psychology, and the Mundurucú looked upon themselves as aggressors and victors. They have been described as ". . . one of the most valorous and feared [tribes] of all the hinterland of Amazons" (Almieda Serra 1869:4), while, on the other hand, the French explorer Henri Coudreau (1897:142) wrote in righteous indignation that, "The Mundurucú practice neither justice, nor duel, nor warfare, but only assassination." This harsh judgment seems not to fit the people who extended my wife and me kindness and hospitality, and who were invariably soft-spoken, humorous, and gentle. But these same gentle people spoke at length and with great animation of their former prowess as warriors and of expeditions against other tribes in which the enemy men and women were killed and decapitated and their children stolen. Nothing about their own culture interested the Mundurucú as much as the extinct but still remembered patterns of warfare, and the older men were zealous informants on that subject.

The human world was seen by the Mundurucú to consist of two distinct spheres; there were "people" or Mundurucú, and *pariwat*, a term referring to any non-Mundurucú human. With the exception of the neighboring Apiacá Indians and the white men, all pariwat were enemies. An enemy was not merely a person to be guarded against but was a proper object of attack, and the Mundurucú pursued this end with extraordinary vigor and stamina. Before 1795 they attacked Santarém and ranged near the mouth of the Amazon to strike the fort of Gurupá. Hartt (1885:116) stated that Mundurucú war parties had penetrated into the eastern part of the province of Maranhão, where they were beaten back by "Apinagés."[1] Tocantins (1877:98) claimed that the Mundurucú knew the city of Cuyabá in Mato Grosso, and informants told of raids as far as

[1]This seemingly incredible sortie was still remembered by the Urubú Indians of the upper Gurupí River in the state of Maranhão, according to a personal communication from the Brazilian ethnologist, Dr. Darcy Ribeiro.

the upper waters of the Juruena, São Manoel, and Madeira Rivers. These expeditions apparently carried the warriors over 500 miles from home and must have involved trips of well over 1,000 miles. And the Mundurucú traveled solely by foot; bark canoes were made and used only for the purpose of crossing large streams. These were exceptional journeys, but even short expeditions could well take a party over 100 miles from home; and 100 miles through dense, trackless forest and across major streams is no mean trip.

It is obvious that Mundurucú warfare consisted of much more than sporadic and short forays. The average party campaigned only during the dry season, setting out when the rivers fell in May and returning before they again rose in November. Longer expeditions set out at the end of the rains and remained in the field throughout the rainy season and the following dry period, returning before the next rains.

As among the Indians of the North American Plains, youths sought openly for the excitement of war and looked upon it as a means of self-validation and aggrandizement of prestige. But unlike the Plains Indians, the Mundurucú did not openly assert this prestige once it was won; if anything, the person who achieved status became even more self-effacing and less prone to open competitiveness. The young men, however, did not embark upon raids by themselves. They expressed their desire to the chief of the village in words indicative of the martial disposition of the society: "My grandfather, take us to hunt the pariwat. We wish to die in the forest, not in the village." The chief consulted with the older men in order to decide whether the occasion was auspicious. If there was general approval, he proceeded to organize a war party that would include the eager young but would be under the competent direction of experienced elders, for age in Mundurucú society was an important criterion of status.

Although the initiative for a war originated in one village, men from several villages participated. The determination of a village to form a war party was quickly communicated to other communities, but a formal invitation had to be extended. This was carried by a man of the *Muchacha* society, a group of older warriors who were especially well versed in Mundurucú lore and songs and who had taken enemy heads. As the messenger neared each village he sounded three short blasts on a horn used only by members of the society, and was answered by a like signal from a Muchacha of the village being invited. After entering the village, he delivered the invitation and proceeded on his itinerary, collecting volunteers from a number of communities.

Intervillage cooperation enabled the Mundurucú to place large war parties in the field without stripping any one village of all its manpower. Those who took part generally desired to clear land for gardens first, but even when this was not possible or when the expedition lasted more than a year, the horticultural cycle could be maintained by those remaining behind. The problem of leadership of a group drawn from several communities was resolved by delegating authority to two village chiefs who were also members of the Muchacha society. Actually, the two formal leaders did not have absolute control, and all important decisions were made by the older men of the expedition acting as a body.

The war party was accompanied by the wives of the warriors and a number of unmarried girls. Their tasks were to carry cooking utensils and all of the equipment of the men, except for their arms, thus leaving the males unencumbered for hunting and fighting. They also cooked, fetched water and firewood and performed other female services. Contrary to Spix and von Martius' (1831:1313) assertion that the women helped on the battlefield, informants said that the women were always left at a safe distance from the scene of combat. The men then proceeded to encircle the enemy village under cover of darkness.

No warfare rituals were held prior to the departure of the expedition, but the most powerful shaman available always accompanied the war party and throughout the course of march was able to ascertain events in the enemy village by sending one of his instruments abroad to spy upon the foe. Once the village had been encircled, the shaman blew ant-eater hair or macaw feathers in the direction of the houses in order to put the enemy into a deep sleep. Eagle feathers were similarly directed at the village in the belief that this would cause the defenders to become confused and impotent in the face of attack.

When the occupants of the village were benumbed, the warriors waited for the cry of a species of bird that breaks into song at dawn. When this signal was heard, the chiefs sounded blasts on their horns and cried the order to attack. Incendiary arrows, made by affixing dried corn-cobs to the end of the arrow shaft, were ignited and loosed at the thatch roofs of the houses. The Mundurucú then broke from cover and dashed into the clearing of the enemy village, emitting wild shouts calculated to terrify the people. Adult males and females were killed and decapitated, and prepubescent children of both sexes were captured by the attackers. The Mundurucú then beat a hasty retreat before the enemy could reorganize his forces and summon additional support.

The retiring Mundurucú force drove its captive children ahead hurriedly and stopped at the temporary shelter only long enough to pick up the women and supplies. They then made a day and night forced march until they had reached a safe distance from the enemy. At this point, the expedition turned toward home or, frequently, to new fields of conquest.

A central object of the raid was the taking of enemy heads, and a strict protocol was observed in the preparation of the trophies. After killing an enemy man or woman, the warrior quickly decapitated the corpse. The spine was severed at the foramen magnum, but the skin was cut around the chest, shoulders, and back to leave a substantial flap below the point of severance. The excess skin compensated for the inevitable shrinkage that accompanied desiccation. A piece of wood was then thrust into the mouth of the trophy to prevent its locking closed in rigor mortis. During the return march the head was preserved by removing the brains, boiling it, and then drying it near a bonfire.

The war party broke up after reaching Mundurucú country, and the participants proceeded to their respective villages. Signals were sounded on horns a short distance outside the villages, and two messengers were sent to inform the people of the results of the raid. The boys of the community went to meet the waiting warriors and received the trophy heads from them. They ran ahead to the men's house and displayed the prizes to the older men and told them who had taken each. The warriors and their accompanying women then entered the village, and each delivered his captive children to the care of his wife and went to the men's house, where the trophy heads were returned to their owners.

Although the waiting members of the community showed joy at the return of the war party, especially if it had been successful, mourning was in order for those who had fallen in the fray. Among the Mundurucú, each clan recognizes certain other clans of the opposite moiety as their *iboiwatitit*, or people who have the responsibility of burying the dead of the clan. This function is looked upon as more than a duty; moieties are conceived as ritually hostile bodies, and the iboiwatitit consider it a pleasure to bury the dead of the complementary clan. When the whole body is not available, it is considered necessary to the maintenance of proper relations between moieties that some part of the dead be buried. Since it was not expedient to bring the dead back to Mundurucú territory for interment, it was customary for a member of a slain warrior's iboiwatitit to sever his humerus and return it for the mortuary rites. This practice was said to have been followed also in the cases of men who were too severely wounded to continue the homeward journey; needless to say, they died shortly thereafter. When it was impossible to retrieve the humerus of the dead, a piece of arrow cane was cut to simulate the bone.

The iboiwatitit member who had brought the arm bone of the dead back to the village would place it in a basket in his wife's dwelling and keep it there for about a month. People from other villages were invited to attend the burial, and on this occasion other members of the deceased's iboiwatitit engaged in ritual dispute for the honor of burying the bone. The humerus was always retained by the man who had secured it, and it was buried in the floor of his house.

Thus far we have discussed the roles of war leaders, the Muchacha society, the shaman, and the iboiwatitit of the fallen warrior, but other social statuses connected with warfare became activated after the return of the expedition. A wounded warrior was treated as if dead for one year after the hostilities; he had no sexual relations, his hair was allowed to grow long, and the use of his name was tabooed during that period.

The most important status was that of a taker of a trophy head, who was referred to as *Dajeboiši*. Literally, the title means "mother of the peccary," an allusion to the Mundurucú view of other tribes as being equivalent to game animals. The "mother" part of the term is derived from the trophy head's power to attract game and to cause their numerical increase, and the headhunter was so titled because of his obvious fertility promoting function; paradoxically for such a seemingly masculine status, he symbolically filled a female role.

The trophy head was believed to exert a powerful charm over the spirit protectors of the animal world and thus improved the supply and availability of game. Each time that the men of the village went hunting, the Dajeboiši took his trophy a short distance into the forest, where its magical effect was exercised. But the supernatural power of the head could only be maintained when certain precautions were observed. Both the taker of the head and his wife were prohibited from sexual intercourse and were supposed to avoid looking upon any person who had recently indulged in the act. Accordingly, they lived very restrained and sequestered lives; the Dajeboiši spent most of his time lying in his hammock, and his wife was assigned special assistants to perform her household and garden chores.

The Dajeboiši was also responsible for sponsoring a series of ceremonies that took place during three successive rainy seasons following the return of the expedition. During the first, which took place shortly after the return of the war party, feather pendants were attached to the ears of the trophy head; certain clans had the prerogative of affixing the feathers of particular species of birds. Also, the eye sockets were sealed with beeswax and two paca teeth were placed across each eye. During the second phase of the ceremony, the ornaments and skin were stripped from the skull and it was retired to a corner of the men's house. The third part of the ceremony was devoted to stringing the enemy's teeth on a woven cotton belt. This ornament served as a permanent trophy of the slain enemy, and the skull was left to deteriorate in the men's house.

The final phase of the ceremony involved the greatest degree of intervillage participation, for it served as a ceremonial reunion of the *Darekši* or "mothers of the arrow." The *Darekši* was a society devoted to the celebration of Mundurucú arms, and included all adult males. At this time, a great feast was held, martial songs were sung, and the young boys were given instruction in the songs of the Darekši. At the conclusion of the celebration, the ceremonial cycle terminated and the Dajeboiši and his wife resumed their normal life.[2]

No special honor was accorded the warrior who captured children. They were turned over to his wife to rear as her own. Having been incorporated into the kinship system through adoption, the children were accorded the treatment appropriate to their relationship status. In time, they married members of the opposite moiety and lived through a normal Mundurucú life cycle. Contemporary informants affirm that captives were in no way treated as inferiors, although their origins were certainly remembered. Young men were said to have taken part in Mundurucú war parties, even in attacks against their native group. No cases of defection were reported.

GOALS OF WARFARE

George Fathauer (1954:110) maintains in a recent article that the Mohave "conception of war was largely non-instrumental: it was an end in itself." The Mundurucú looked upon warfare in much the same way; war was considered an essential and unquestioned part of their way of life, and foreign tribes were attacked because they were enemies by definition. This basic orientation emerged clearly from interviews with informants. Unless direct, specific questions were asked, the Mundurucú never assigned specific causes to particular wars. The necessity of ever having to defend their home territory was denied, and provocation by other groups was not remembered as a cause of war in Mundurucú tradition. It might be said that enemy tribes caused the Mundurucú to go to war simply by existing, and the word for enemy meant merely any group that was not Mundurucú.

Despite this seemingly undirected aggressiveness, it was possible to establish through direct questioning and by analysis of field data that certain individual and social goals were realized through warfare. The more important of these goals will be analyzed and their significance as causes of the institution of warfare will be evaluated in the following section.

The Mundurucú were partially motivated to war by the quest for manufactured goods, which, as noted earlier, were obtained from the Brazilians in return for service as mercenary warriors against unpacified tribes. The symbiotic relationship that became established was noted by Chandless (1862:276) who wrote that the Mundurucú were "honest and faithful," and "very friendly toward white people, warring only against unpacified Indians while protecting those friendly with the whites."

[2]A fuller description of the ceremonies held subsequent to a successful raid will be published in a forthcoming monograph (Murphy n.d.).

The scope and importance of Mundurucú mercenary activities is impressive. In the early 19th century, the whites urged them to attack the troublesome Mura Indians of the lower Madeira River, and so great was their success that the Mura were scattered as far as the vicinity of Ega, hundreds of miles up the Amazon River (Bates 1863:168–9). Ayres de Casal (1817:237–8) reported that many of the victims of the Mundurucú, among them the Mura, were forced to seek the protection of the white settlements. The traders who employed the Mundurucú thus obtained a dual advantage; the hostiles were not only quelled but were driven into the arms of the labor-hungry whites.

Later references also attest to the alliance with the Brazilians. The Mundurucú were enlisted by colonial officials during the Revolution of the Cabañas in 1835–36, and one of their leaders in the war was given an honorary commission in the army in recognition of his services (Hartt 1885:132). Bates (1863:162) reports that in about 1853 the Mundurucú were instrumental in helping the Brazilians of the Madeira River to suppress the Arara Indians, and Tocantins (1877:140) states that shortly before his journey to the Mundurucú, the latter struck at a marauding group of Parintintin Indians at the behest of the Brazilians. Coudreau (1897:39–40) relates another case of mercenary service by the Mundurucú, whom he characterizes as a people "known for selling their military valor to whoever wants to pay for it." On this occasion, three traders of the Madeira River had been killed by hostile Indians, and their colleagues went to the Mundurucú of the upper Tapajós River and offered merchandise in return for a retaliatory expedition. The offer was accepted but the sortie was a failure, for most of the 60 men and 40 women who took part in the raid died of illness before contacting the enemy.

Although mercenary service is one of the more interesting aspects of Mundurucú warfare during the 19th century, contemporary informants hardly thought it worthy of mention. They acknowledged their alliance with the whites with some pride, but viewed their efforts as civilizing missions against the "savage Indians," or "Indians of the forest." Their attitude was clearly that they did what had to be done and had always been done; the remuneration was secondary.

It is impossible to determine what proportion of Mundurucú warfare in the last century was instigated by the whites, but it is clear that many, and probably most, raids were conducted against groups having no enmity or even contact with Brazilian society. It is evident that the Mundurucú did not remain warlike solely for reasons of material gain, but mercenary service did serve to encourage the perpetuation of a deeply rooted pattern. Whether or not economic and ecological conditions stimulated warfare in the preceding century is difficult to ascertain. It is known that the area of Mundurucú occupation expanded northward in the late 18th and early 19th centuries into regions formerly inhabited by other groups. While the Mundurucú moved into a vacuum that they had helped to create, it is almost certain that assimilation and depopulation due to disease had decimated the ranks of the previous occupants far more than had Mundurucú arms, and the population of the latter was already on the wane. Additional territory was hardly the goal of the migrant Mundurucú; the lure of manufactured articles available through trade with the white settlements offers a more adequate explanation of their northward drift to the lower Madeira and Tapajós Rivers.

The secondary nature of economic goals in Mundurucú warfare is even more manifest when looting is considered. No objects of significant economic value were taken, and the raiders maintained their mobility by traveling light. Captive children were a far more important class of booty than were material items. Captive-taking was a means of strengthening the group through the addition of new members, but it is not certain whether the increment compensated for the loss of mature warriors and their female followers. If, however, one accepts intense warfare as a given factor, the capture of children was important to its successful continuance. Moreover, the Mundurucú valued and desired children, and the captives were treated as the captor's own.

The Mundurucú warrior was strongly motivated by the desire to achieve prestige through the demonstration of valor, especially as signified by the taking of a trophy head. The Dajeboiši was subjected to very onerous restrictions, but he was rewarded by the lifetime respect of his fellowmen. However, if he was to maintain his position and advance to the high status of a Muchacha, it was expected that he would also become a font of traditional lore and songs. Prestige was not openly asserted among the Mundurucú, and the tone of the society was strongly egalitarian. Decision-making was decentralized and informal and joint activity depended upon the consensus of the participants, but the successful headhunter exerted considerable influence in the attainment of such consensus—albeit through subdued means.

Despite the fact that individual wars were undertaken because of the desire of the participants to gain prestige, it would be most dubious to admit this as a fundamental cause of warfare. It seems almost a truism to say that the individual who demonstrates proficiency in the attainment of a socially desirable goal will himself be valued and that this will motivate him to appropriate action, but this still does not answer the question of why the goal and the accompanying activity is valued. Newcomb (1950:329) has stated the same case with cogency in regard to Plains warfare.

The trophy head was prized as a symbol of Mundurucú prowess and of its owner's status, but it was also sought because it was the center of a number of magico-religious observances. The trophy was thought to be pleasing to the spirit protectors of the game animals because it had inherent power, contingent upon the proper observance of connected ritual acts. The possession of a trophy head thus resulted in greater economic abundance, and in this sense it served the same general purpose as does the Jivaro *tsantsa*. However, this aspect of the trophy quest does not cast much light upon Mundurucú headhunting, for alternate ways of pleasing the spirits were known and practiced. The ceremonial and shamanistic techniques of propitiating the spirit protectors of game animals were complex both in practice and in ideational content. In contrast, the linkage of the trophy head and the spirits was vague and ephemeral; it is probable that headhunting developed subsequent to the rites connected with the animal spirits and had become only loosely integrated with them. It is to be expected that any important social activity will become value and belief cathected in this manner, but it would be erroneous to proceed to explain the activity by its supporting ideology.

Finally, it should be considered that the Mundurucú looked upon fighting as a source of sport and excitement. The enemy was looked upon as game to be hunted, and the Mundurucú still speak of the pariwat in the same terms that they reserve for peccary and tapir. War was a relief from boredom, but it is not surprising that peace would be boring to people who consider themselves warriors. One might ask why they did not relieve boredom in log racing as do some groups, or in drinking bouts as did many of their neighbors. In short, can we not look upon activity and play drives as being inherent within the species and proceed from that vantage to explain the particular way they are manifested in particular cultures?

FUNCTIONS OF MUNDURUCÚ WARFARE

The manifest goals of warfare provide us with an understanding of the incentives that motivated the Mundurucú warrior. The religious and sportive aspects of warfare were found to be considerably more ephemeral than were the economic and prestige goals involved, but even the latter two depended upon the existence of a social organization that allowed and encouraged intensive military activity by its very nature. Moreover, the most important single motivation to hostility was a generalized aggressiveness that recognized no specific aims, and this factor yields the most important single clue to an understanding of Mundurucú warfare. If specific goals do not fully explain the extent and intensity of the pattern, and if the pressure of external circumstances did not force battle, then the main dynamics of warfare must be sought within the structure of the society. We must explain the function of warfare, or the social conditions that caused the Mundurucú to direct enormous hostility against an amorphously inimical outside world.

As a first step toward answering this question, we turn briefly to a reexamination of Mundurucú military organization. Leaving out of consideration for the moment the bellicosity of the Mundurucú, the single factor that contributed most to the success of their arms was the tribal organization of war parties. The recruitment of men from a number of communities aggrandized their expeditions while leaving unimpaired the economic and defensive functions of the villages. Tribalism was also central to the ceremonies that were held at the conclusion of a war. On these occasions the tribal warrior society, or Darekši, gathered to celebrate the prowess of Mundurucú arms, and the widely scattered members of certain clans assembled to exercise their prerogative of attaching particular decorations to the trophy heads.

Intercommunity cooperation in warfare was facilitated by the peculiar juxtaposition of matrilocal residence and patrilineal descent. The male Mundurucú population was thereby linked by cross-cutting ties of residential affinity and affiliation by descent. For example, any Mundurucú man was a member of his own village, in most cases a native of another village, and in several instances a former resident of the village of a divorced wife; he was also linked by ties of patrilineal descent to all the villages in which members of his clan resided. On the other hand, he was not involved in any cohesive and localized lineage unit. The kinship structure imposed no boundaries upon the local group; the male social world was the tribe.

The manner in which bonds were extended throughout the tribe necessitated certain social adjustments. The residence rule destroyed the residential basis of patrilineality and thereby weakened clanship. Correspondingly, the only enduring group of coresident, consanguineal kinsmen was the extended family of women related in the female line. Such aggregates of females posed a threat to the superordinate position of the men which was resolved through several means, one of the most important of which was residence in the men's house. This unit freed the male from the necessity of becoming integrated into the economy and authority structure of his wife's household in villages in which he had no supporting group of kinsmen. Although he owed respect and some service to his father-in-law, the locus of his social and economic life was the men's house; this provided the framework within which a group of men from diverse villages was welded into a highly unitary working and fighting unit. Their position as a militant and self-conscious social entity, demarcated from and superior to the women, was reinforced by the cult of the sacred musical instruments. Thus male solidarity was promoted on a tribal level through the dispersal of patrilineal kinsmen, and on the village level through the men's house.

The organization of 19th-century Mundurucú society made male solidarity on the village and tribal level not only possible but a functional necessity. Conflict had to be rigorously suppressed, for if men became arrayed in overt violence along lines of residential affinity, it would pit patrilineal kin against each other and destroy the very fabric of the kinship structure. And if the combatants aligned themselves according to kinship affiliations, strife could break out within villages and even within households. The Mundurucú situation is opposite that found in some segmentary societies, in which, following Fortes' (1945:240–4) analysis, strife between kinship-territorial units of similar scope is actually productive of social equilibrium.

The necessity for suppressing overt conflict as the only alternative to serious disruptions of social relations was complemented by the necessity for male cohesion and unity in villages whose hereditary inhabitants were the women. As a result, Mundurucú ethical values enjoined absolute harmony and cooperation upon all the males of the tribe. No such feeling was expected in inter-female relations. The female ingroup was limited to the membership of one or two extended families; beyond these limits, open jealousy and fighting could and did occur. This dichotomy in ethical values is understandable when one considers how different were the male and female social contexts.

Interpersonal and intergroup grievances will arise in all human societies as a necessary concomitant of social life, and the Mundurucú are no exception to this rule. Despite the surface tranquility of interpersonal relations among the males, numerous causes of latent antagonism existed. One potentially disruptive factor of especial significance to the problem at hand was that patrilineal succession to the chieftaincy was assured by exempting the chief's sons from the matrilocal rule. The extended family of the chief thus became the largest and most cohesive such unit in the village, for it retained sons while gathering sons-in-law. The presence of his own patrilineal kinsmen reinforced the chief's position, but it also resulted in antagonism and resentment on the part of the other men of the village, over whom he exerted no lineage-based authority. Evidence to support this statement can be found in contemporary Mundurucú society in a number of cases of sorcery accusation and punishment. In one village the chief and his son were both slain as suspected witches. In another, the family of the chief wished to execute an accused sorcerer against the will of the other residents, and in a third village the family of the chief protected one of their number against the intention of the other villagers to execute him. No evidence of such tensions would have been manifest to the casual observer in any of the three villages; the disaffected parties usually maintain cordial and cooperative relations with their antagonists both before and after the climax of the train of events, but they generally move from the village as soon as convenient. These conflicts, then, are instrumental in furthering the fragmentation of villages under the current condition of pacification.

Given the potentially centrifugal nature of leadership, descent, and residence, warfare functioned to preserve, or at least prolong, the cohesiveness of Mundurucú society. The chief was able to maintain his leadership over his lineally eclectic group of followers through his position as war leader and his complementary role as mediator between them and Brazilian society. To the Mundurucú these are the essential functions of chieftainship, and contemporary informants commonly ascribe the decline of nucleated village life to the disappearance of such attributes of leadership.

Of even greater importance to the integration of Mundurucú society, warfare activated and intensified male unity and values, both of which functioned to make matrilocality viable. Finally, the only permissible intrasocietal mechanism for the release of aggression was sorcery and the killing of sorcerers, and the previously cited cases indicate that they created as many tensions as they resolved. Actually, the only way in which hostility could be unleashed without damage to the society was against the outside world. Paradoxically for a people who considered all the world as an enemy, the true cause of enmity came from within their own society.

Much of the preceding argument has hinged upon the matrilocal and patrilineal character of Mundurucú society. In a recent article I showed that Mundurucú social structure in the 19th century could only be understood as a result of post-contact change and that the aboriginal society was organized on patrilocal and patrilineal lines (Murphy 1956). The fact that the Mundurucú were vigorous warriors before their shift to matrilocality suggests that warfare acquired new functions subsequent to that change and consequent upon it. These new functions, as they have been outlined in this paper, provide us with an understanding of how Mundurucú society remained cohesive and maintained its boundaries through more than a century of contact with the whites.

We will now broaden our analysis of the function of warfare within Mundurucú society to the closely related problem of its function within the structure of Mundurucú-Brazilian relationships. The two bases of this symbiosis were trade and war. Matrilocality evolved as a result of trade relations with the whites, but it was workable in a patrilineal society only when intrasocietal hostilities were repressed and latent antagonisms channeled into intense warfare. Warfare and the connected ceremonies also helped to perpetuate the system of clanship in this newly-evolved type of society, for they constituted almost the only occasions upon which corporate functions of the fragmented descent groups were exercised. Conversely, matrilocality and patrilineality provided the structure for warfare on a tribal scale and thus enabled the Mundurucú successfully to pursue hostilities against comparatively undisrupted tribes during a period when their own numbers were being reduced through disease and emigration to Brazilian settlements. And by frequently undertaking raids in the service of the whites, the Mundurucú had solidified their peaceful relationship with the technologically and numerically superior society. The Brazilians were willing to respect the autonomy of the Mundurucú as long as it was useful to them. We may conclude that the system of matrilocality and patrilineality and the institution of warfare were mutually reinforcing and served to maintain Mundurucú society during a period that witnessed the disappearance or dissolution of many of their neighbors.

CONCLUSION

Our analysis of the functions of Mundurucú warfare has concluded that the institution operated to preserve the integration and solidarity of Mundurucú society. These findings accord closely with Simmel's theory of conflict and are also substantiated by Fernandes' (1952:354) conclusion on the functions of Tupinamba warfare. The means by which this social end was accomplished can be viewed as a variable of the Mundurucú type of society. The latter was of a unique order; it was structured so as to ramify kinship bonds throughout the tribe, but it was extremely vulnerable to any open display of aggression within the group. This, and the ambivalent position of the men, resulted in the suppression of hostility and the emphasis upon solidarity that characterized male social relations. Such solidarity could be maintained only through the release of latent aggression in a socially valued manner upon surrogate objects. Mundurucú warfare thus corresponds to Coser's (1956:48) formulation of the "safety valve" mechanism in society:

Social systems provide for specific institutions which serve to drain off hostile and aggressive sentiments. These safety valve institutions help to maintain the system by preventing otherwise probable conflict or by reducing its disruptive effects. They provide substitute objects upon which to displace hostile sentiments, as well as means of abreaction. Through these safety valves, hostility is prevented from turning against its original object.

The achievement of specific ends or the defeat of a particular enemy were secondary considerations in Mundurucú warfare. They fought any group and they fought for the sake of fighting. The ultimate source of their bellicosity was the repressed hostility generated within the society, and the ultimate source of repression was the potential destructiveness of intrasocietal aggression.

Safety valve institutions of one kind or another are probably universal in culture. Coser (ibid:41) distinguishes two means by which aggressiveness may safely be released by the members of a society. These are:

... *Ventilsitten*, which provide a socially sanctioned framework for carrying out conflict without leading to consequences that disrupt relations within a group, and those safety-valve institutions which serve to divert hostility onto substitute objects or which function as channels for cathartic release.

Mundurucú warfare and sorcery fall into the class of "safety-valve institutions"; the structure of the society is such that Ventilsitten would be impossible insofar as the Mundurucú cannot publicly acknowledge the existence of intrasocietal hostilities. The institutionalized public arguments and wrestling matches of the Trumaí Indians (Murphy and Quain 1955:57–59) and the spear throwing bouts between Upper Xingú tribes (Galvão 1950:366) are illustrations of cases in which hostility is allowed to appear in a controlled and sanctioned context and is thereby dissipated. Sides are drawn and the issue is resolved among the Upper Xingú groups; the Mundurucú cannot even afford to take sides openly.

Coser (1956:156–7) has considered the relationship between conflict and the rigidity of the social structure, which he defines as "the degree to which it disallows direct expression of antagonistic claims," and concludes:

Our hypothesis, that the need for safety-valve institutions increases with the rigidity of the social system, may be extended to suggest that unrealistic [i.e. cathartic and not oriented toward the frustrating object] conflict may be expected to occur as a consequence of rigidity present in the social structure.

Mundurucú warfare was clearly "unrealistic" and the social structure was rigid in Coser's sense. It is possible to broaden our example to include a larger category of rigid social structures and to consider their functional concomitants. I would propose as a statistically testable hypothesis that matrilocal societies must repress open aggression in order to insure cohesion and continuity. If we take any matrilocal and matrilineal or bilateral society as our model, the system of residence tends to disperse males at least throughout the local community. Thus, any male will have close ties of kinship and economic interdependence with his housemates, his natal household, the households of his maternal uncles, and the households of his brothers. The same is true of patrilocal societies from the viewpoint of the women, but males are the principal political role-players in all human societies. Any conflict involving men therefore becomes a matter of deep community concern. As among the Mundurucú, if the lines of allegiance in a conflict situation are drawn according to kinship in any matrilocal society, bonds of local contiguity will be sundered; if primary loyalty is given to bonds of residence, the ties of kinship will be broken. In short, when the residence and kin groups of the male do not coincide, he acquires multiple commitments that may come into conflict. Also, the individual male will more readily repress his grievances if he cannot rely upon the full support of a solidary group.

Brief reference to the ethnographic literature suggests that the social solidarity of matrilocal groups is not restricted to my model. Writing of the Apinayé, Nimuendajú (1939:129) says:

I have never heard of a case of rape nor witnessed anything of publicly scandalous adultery, larceny, or slander. Only when intoxicated do these natives inflict damage on property and bodily maltreatment on persons or commit manslaughter. Compared with any Šerente settlement the village of Bacaba, at least, is a model of internal peace and harmony, and this would hold for Gato Preto, too, in the absence of alcohol.

The Šerente and the Apinayé are Gê-speaking groups of eastern Brazil and are culturally quite similar. The principal difference between them is that the fractious Šerente are patrilineal and patrilocal, while the harmonious Apinayé are matrilineal and matrilocal. Turning to North America, we have the classical example of the matrilocal and "Apollonian" Puebloans. Ellis (1951:199) has noted of Pueblo warfare:

Beyond protection, warfare served to provide legitimate outlet for the frustrations and aggressions arising from unpermitted competition or suspicions thereof among peoples of the same general culture.

The repression of open conflict among the Puebloans accounts for the latent hostility that many ethnologists have seen seething below surface relations. Under modern conditions this often results in community fission, and the same process can be noted among the contemporary, nonwarring Mundurucú. Lacking adequate safety-valves for the release of aggression, the Mundurucú now tend to withdraw from the frustrating situation.

Not all matrilocal groups repress aggression to the same extent as do the Mundurucú, nor are they as warlike. The greater emphasis of the Mundurucú upon social cohesion and external aggression stems from the persistence of patrilineal clans in a matrilocal society. This factor, combined with intervillage matrilocality, made hostility even more explosive and internal release systems less workable. It oriented the group toward warfare and provided the organization for its effective pursuit. Some deviation from our model is expectable, for there is no fixed and unvarying reservoir of aggression in society; it has its roots in the social structure, as does its expression Our thesis states only that matrilocal societies must repress the open expression of intrasocietal conflict and that this repressed hostility, variable in intensity, will be released through acceptable and nondisruptive means within the society, or through warfare, or through both. But warfare, it can be concluded, is an especially effective means of promoting social cohesion in that it provides an occasion upon which the members of the society unite and submerge their factional differences in the vigorous pursuit of a common purpose.

REFERENCES

ALMEIDA SERRA, RICARDO, "Navegação do Rio Tapajóz para o Para (1779)." *Revista do Instituto Historico e Geografico Brasileiro* 9:1–16, 1869.

AYRES DE CASAL, MANOEL, *Corografia brazilica.* Rio de Janeiro, 1817.

BATES, HENRY W., *The naturalist on the river Amazons.* London, 1863.

CHANDLESS, W., "Notes on the rivers Arinos, Juruena, and Tapajós." *Journal of the Royal Geographic Society* 36:119–128, 1862.

COSER, LEWIS A., *The functions of social conflict.* (Glencoe: The Free Press, 1956).

COUDREAU, HENRI, *Voyage au Tapajóz, 1896.* Paris, 1897.

ELLIS, FLORENCE HAWLEY, "Patterns of aggression and the war cult in Southwestern Pueblos." *Southwestern Journal of Anthropology* 7:177–201, 1951.

FATHAUER, GEORGE, "The structure and causation of Mohave warfare." *Southwestern Journal of Anthropology* 10:97–118, 1954.

FERNANDES, FLORESTAN, *A função social de la guerra na sociedade Tupinamba.* São Paulo, 1952.

FORTES, MEYER, *The dynamics of clanship among the Tallensi.* (London: Oxford Press, 1945).

GALVAO, EDUARDO, "U uso do propulsor entre as tribos do alto Xingu." *Revista do Museu Paulista* 4:353–68, 1950.

HARTT, CHARLES F., "Contribuiçoes para a etnologia do Valle do Amazonas. *Archivos do Museu Nacional* 6:1–174. Rio de Janeiro, 1885.

MONTEIRO NORONHA, JOSE, *Roteiro da viagem da cidade do Pará até as ultimas colonias dos Dominios Portuguezes em os Rios Amazonas e Negro, 1768.* Pará, 1862.

MURPHY, ROBERT F., "Matrilocality and patrilineality in Mundurucú society." *American Anthropologist* 58:414–34, 1956. N. d. "Mundurucú religion." Ms.

MURPHY, ROBERT F. and BUELL QUAIN, "The Trumaí Indians of Central Brazil." *American Ethnological Society*, Monograph XXIV, 1955.

NEWCOMB, W. W., "A re-examination of the causes of Plains warfare." *American Anthropologist* 52:317–30, 1950.

NIMUENDAJU, CURT, *The Apinayé* (translated by Robert H. Lowie). Catholic University of America, Anthropological Series No. 8, 1939.

SIMMEL, GEORG, *Conflict* (translated by Kurt Wolff). (Glencoe: The Free Press, 1955).

SPIX, JOHANN B. VON and KARL F. P. VON MARTIUS, *Reise in Brasilien*, Vol. 3, München, 1831.

TOCANTINS, ANTONIO M. G., "Estudos sobre a tribu 'Mundurukú.' " *Revista do Instituto Historico e Geografico Brasileiro* 40, No. 2:73–161. Rio de Janeiro, 1877.

Shakespeare in the Bush

Laura Bohannan

Just before I left Oxford for the Tiv in West Africa, conversation turned to the season at Stratford. "You Americans," said a friend, "often have difficulty with Shakespeare. He was, after all, a very English poet, and one can easily misinterpret the universal by misunderstanding the particular."

I protested that human nature is pretty much the same the whole world over; at least the general plot and motivation of the greater tragedies would always be clear—everywhere—although some details of custom might have to be explained and difficulties of translation might produce other slight changes. To end an argument we could not conclude, my friend gave me a copy of *Hamlet* to study in the African bush: it would, he hoped, lift my mind above its primitive surroundings, and possibly I might, by prolonged meditation, achieve the grace of correct interpretation.

It was my second field trip to the African tribe, and I thought myself ready to live in one of its remote sections—an area difficult to cross even on foot. I eventually settled on the hillock of a very knowledgeable old man, the head of a homestead of some hundred and forty people, all of whom were either his close relatives or their wives and children. Like the other elders of the vicinity, the old man spent most of his time performing ceremonies seldom seen these days in the more accessible parts of the tribe. I was delighted. Soon there would be three months of enforced isolation and leisure, between the harvest that takes place just before the rising of the swamps and the clearing of new farms when the water goes down. Then, I thought, they would have even more time to perform ceremonies and explain them to me.

I was quite mistaken. Most of the ceremonies demanded the presence of elders from several homesteads. As the swamps rose, the old men found it too difficult to walk from one homestead to the next, and the ceremonies gradually ceased. As the swamps rose even higher, all activities but one came to an end. The women brewed beer from maize and millet. Men, women, and children sat on their hillocks and drank it.

People began to drink at dawn. By midmorning the whole homestead was singing, dancing, and drumming. When it rained, people had to sit inside their huts: there they drank and sang or they drank and told stories. In any case, by noon or before, I either had to join the party or retire to my own hut and my books. "One does not discuss serious matters when there is beer. Come, drink with us." Since I lacked their capacity for the thick native beer, I spent more and more time with *Hamlet*. Before the end of the second month, grace descended on me. I was quite sure that *Hamlet* had only one possible interpretation, and that one universally obvious.

Early every morning, in the hope of having some serious talk before the beer party, I used to call on the old man at his reception hut—a circle of posts supporting a thatched roof above a low mud wall to keep out wind and rain. One day I crawled through the low doorway and found most of the men of the homestead sitting huddled in their ragged cloths on stools, low plank beds, and reclining chairs, warming themselves against the chill of the rain around a smoky fire. In the center were three pots of beer. The party had started.

The old man greeted me cordially. "Sit down and drink." I accepted a large calabash full of beer, poured some into a small drinking gourd, and tossed it down. Then I poured some more into the same gourd for the man second in seniority to my host before I handed my calabash over to a young man for further distribution. Important people shouldn't ladle beer themselves.

"It is better like this," the old man said, looking at me approvingly and plucking at the thatch that had caught in my hair. "You should sit and drink with us more often. Your servants tell me that when you are not with us, you sit inside your hut looking at a paper."

The old man was acquainted with four kinds of "papers": tax receipts, bride price receipts, court fee receipts, and letters. The messenger who brought him letters from the chief used them mainly as a badge of office, for he always knew what was in them and told the old man. Personal letters for the few who had relatives in the government or mission stations were kept until someone went to a large market where there was a letter writer and reader. Since my arrival, letters were brought to me to be read. A few men also brought me bride price receipts, privately, with requests to change the figures to a higher sum. I found moral arguments were of no avail, since in-laws are fair game, and the technical hazards of forgery difficult to explain to an illiterate people. I did not wish them to think me silly enough to look at any such papers for days on end, and I hastily explained that my "paper" was one of the "things of long ago" of my country.

"Ah," said the old man. "Tell us."

I protested that I was not a storyteller. Storytelling is a skilled art among them; their standards are high, and the audiences critical—and vocal in their criticism. I protested in vain. This morning they wanted to hear a story while they drank. They threatened to tell me no more stories until I told them one of mine. Finally, the old man promised that no one would criticize my style "for we know you are struggling with our language." "But," put in one of the elders, "you must explain what we do not understand, as we do when we tell you our stories." Realizing that here was my chance to prove *Hamlet* universally intelligible, I agreed.

The old man handed me some more beer to help me on with my storytelling. Men filled their long wooden pipes and knocked coals from the fire to place in the pipe bowls; then, puffing contentedly, they sat back to listen. I began in the proper style, "Not yesterday, not yesterday, but long ago, a thing occurred. One night three men were keeping watch outside the homestead of the great chief, when suddenly they saw the former chief approach them."

"Why was he no longer their chief?"

"He was dead," I explained. "That is why they were troubled and afraid when they saw him."

"Impossible," began one of the elders, handing his pipe on to his neighbor, who interrupted, "Of course it wasn't the dead chief. It was an omen sent by a witch. Go on."

Slightly shaken, I continued. "One of these three was a man who knew things"—the closest translation for scholar, but unfortunately it also meant witch. The second elder looked triumphantly at the first. "So he spoke to the dead chief saying, 'Tell us what we must do so you may rest in your grave,' but the dead chief did not answer. He vanished, and they could see him no more. Then the man who knew things—his name was Horatio—said this event was the affair of the dead chief's son, Hamlet."

There was a general shaking of heads round the circle. "Had the dead chief no living brothers? Or was this son the chief?"

"No," I replied. "That is, he had one living brother who became the chief when the elder brother died."

The old man muttered: such omens were matters for chiefs and elders, not for youngsters; no good could come of going behind a chief's back; clearly Horatio was not a man who knew things.

"Yes, he was," I insisted, shooing a chicken away from my beer. "In our country the son is next to the father. The dead chief's younger brother had become the great chief. He had also married his elder brother's widow only about a month after the funeral."

"He did well," the old man beamed and announced to the others, "I told you that if we knew more about Europeans, we would find they really were very like us. In our country also," he added to me, "the younger brother marries the elder brother's widow and becomes the father of his children. Now, if your uncle, who married your widowed mother, is your father's full brother, then he will be a real father to you. Did Hamlet's father and uncle have one mother?"

His question barely penetrated my mind; I was too upset and thrown too far off balance by having one of the most important elements of *Hamlet* knocked straight out of the picture. Rather uncertainly I said that I thought they had the same mother, but I wasn't sure—the story didn't say. The old man told me severely that these genealogical details made all the difference and that when I got home I must ask the elders about it. He shouted out the door to one of his younger wives to bring his goatskin bag.

Determined to save what I could of the mother motif, I took a deep breath and began again. "The son Hamlet was very sad because his mother had married again so quickly. There was no need for her to do so, and it is our custom for a widow not to go to her next husband until she has mourned for two years."

"Two years is too long," objected the wife, who had appeared with the old man's battered goatskin bag. "Who will hoe your farms for you while you have no husband?"

"Hamlet," I retorted without thinking, "was old enough to hoe his mother's farms himself. There was no need for her to remarry." No one looked convinced. I gave up. "His mother and the great chief told Hamlet not to be sad, for the great chief himself would be a father to Hamlet. Furthermore, Hamlet would be the next chief: therefore he must stay to learn the things of a chief. Hamlet agreed to remain, and all the rest went off to drink beer."

While I paused, perplexed at how to render Hamlet's disgusted soliloquy to an audience convinced that Claudius and Gertrude had behaved in the best possible manner, one of the younger men asked me who had married the other wives of the dead chief.

"He had no other wives," I told him.

"But a chief must have many wives! How else can he brew beer and prepare food for all his guests?"

I said firmly that in our country even chiefs had only one wife, that they had servants to do their work, and that they paid them from tax money.

It was better, they returned, for a chief to have many wives and sons who would help him hoe his farms and feed his people; then everyone loved the chief who gave much and took nothing—taxes were a bad thing.

I agreed with the last comment, but for the rest fell back on their favorite way of fobbing off my questions: "That is the way it is done, so that is how we do it."

I decided to skip the soliloquy. Even if Claudius was here thought quite right to marry his brother's widow, there remained the poison motif, and I knew they would disapprove of fratricide. More hopefully I resumed, "That night Hamlet kept watch with the three who had seen his dead father. The dead chief again appeared, and although the others were afraid, Hamlet followed his dead father off to one side. When they were alone, Hamlet's dead father spoke."

"Omens can't talk!" The old man was emphatic.

"Hamlet's dead father wasn't an omen. Seeing him might have been an omen, but he was not." My audience looked as confused as I sounded. "It *was* Hamlet's dead father. It was a thing we call a 'ghost.' " I had to use the English word, for unlike many of the neighboring tribes, these people didn't believe in the survival after death of any individuating part of the personality.

"What is a 'ghost?' An omen?"

"No, a 'ghost' is someone who is dead but who walks around and can talk, and people can hear him and see him but not touch him."

They objected. "One can touch zombis."

"No, no! It was not a dead body the witches had animated to sacrifice and eat. No one else made Hamlet's dead father walk. He did it himself."

"Dead men can't walk," protested my audience as one man.

I was quite willing to compromise. "A 'ghost' is the dead man's shadow."

But again they objected. "Dead men cast no shadows."

"They do in my country," I snapped.

The old man quelled the babble of disbelief that arose immediately and told me with that insincere, but courteous, agreement one extends to the fancies of the young, ignorant, and superstitious, "No doubt in your country the dead can also walk without being zombis." From the depths of his bag he produced a withered fragment of kola nut, bit off one end to show it wasn't poisoned, and handed me the rest as a peace offering.

"Anyhow," I resumed, "Hamlet's dead father said that his own brother, the one who became chief, had poisoned him. He wanted Hamlet to avenge him. Hamlet believed this in his heart, for he did not like his father's brother." I took another swallow of beer. "In the country of the great chief, living in the same homestead, for it was a very large one, was an important elder who was often with the chief to advise and help him. His name was Polonius. Hamlet was courting his daughter, but her father and her brother . . . [I cast hastily about for some tribal analogy] warned her not to let Hamlet visit her when she was alone on her farm, for he would be a great chief and so could not marry her."

"Why not?" asked the wife, who had settled down on the edge of the old man's chair. He frowned at her for asking stupid questions and growled, "They lived in the same homestead."

"That was not the reason," I informed them. "Polonius was a stranger who lived in the homestead because he helped the chief, not because he was a relative."

"Then why couldn't Hamlet marry her?"

"He could have," I explained, "but Polonius didn't think he would. After all, Hamlet was a man of great importance who ought to marry a chief's daughter, for in his country a man could have only one wife. Polonius was afraid that if Hamlet made love to his daughter, then no one else would give a high price for her."

"That might be true," remarked one of the shrewder elders, "but a chief's son would give his mistress's father enough presents and patronage to more than make up the difference. Polonius sounds like a fool to me."

"Many people think he was," I agreed. "Meanwhile Polonius sent his son Laertes off to Paris to learn the things of that country, for it was the homestead of a very great chief indeed. Because he was afraid that Laertes might waste a lot of money on beer and women and gambling, or get into trouble by fighting, he sent one of his servants to Paris secretly, to spy out what Laertes was doing. One day Hamlet came upon Polonius's daughter Ophelia. He behaved so oddly he frightened her. Indeed"—I was fumbling for words to express the dubious quality of Hamlet's madness—"the chief and many others had also noticed that when Hamlet talked one could understand the words but not what they meant. Many people thought that he had become mad." My audience suddenly became much more attentive. "The great chief wanted to know what was wrong with

Hamlet, so he sent for two of Hamlet's age mates [school friends would have taken long explanation] to talk to Hamlet and find out what troubled his heart. Hamlet, seeing that they had been bribed by the chief to betray him, told them nothing. Polonius, however, insisted that Hamlet was mad because he had been forbidden to see Ophelia, whom he loved."

"Why," inquired a bewildered voice, "should anyone bewitch Hamlet on that account?"

"Bewitch him?"

"Yes, only witchcraft can make anyone mad, unless, of course, one sees the beings that lurk in the forest."

I stopped being a storyteller, took out my notebook and demanded to be told more about these two causes of madness. Even while they spoke and I jotted notes, I tried to calculate the effect of this new factor on the plot. Hamlet had not been exposed to the beings that lurk in the forests. Only his relatives in the male line could bewitch him. Barring relatives not mentioned by Shakespeare, it had to be Claudius who was attempting to harm him. And, of course, it was.

For the moment I staved off questions by saying that the great chief also refused to believe that Hamlet was mad for the love of Ophelia and nothing else. "He was sure that something much more important was troubling Hamlet's heart."

"Now Hamlet's age mates," I continued, "had brought with them a famous storyteller. Hamlet decided to have this man tell the chief and all his homestead a story about a man who had poisoned his brother because he desired his brother's wife and wished to be chief himself. Hamlet was sure the great chief could not hear the story without making a sign if he was indeed guilty, and then he would discover whether his dead father had told him the truth."

The old man interrupted, with deep cunning, "Why should a father lie to his son?" he asked.

I hedged: "Hamlet wasn't sure that it really was his dead father." It was impossible to say anything, in that language, about devil-inspired visions.

"You mean," he said, "it actually was an omen, and he knew witches sometimes send false ones. Hamlet was a fool not to go to one skilled in reading omens and divining the truth in the first place. A man-who-sees-the-truth could have told him how his father died, if he really had been poisoned, and if there was witchcraft in it; then Hamlet could have called the elders to settle the matter."

The shrewd elder ventured to disagree. "Because his father's brother was a great chief, one-who-sees-the-truth might therefore have been afraid to tell it. I think it was for that reason that a friend of Hamlet's father—a witch and an elder—sent an omen so his friend's son would know. Was the omen true?"

"Yes," I said, abandoning ghosts and the devil; a witch-sent omen it would have to be. "It was true, for when the storyteller was telling his tale before all the homestead, the great chief rose in fear. Afraid that Hamlet knew his secret he planned to have him killed."

The stage set of the next bit presented some difficulties of translation. I began cautiously. "The great chief told Hamlet's mother to find out from her son what he knew. But because a woman's children are always first in her heart, he had the important elder Polonius hide behind a cloth that hung against the wall of

Hamlet's mother's sleeping hut. Hamlet started to scold his mother for what she had done."

There was a shocked murmur from everyone. A man should never scold his mother.

"She called out in fear, and Polonius moved behind the cloth. Shouting, 'A rat!' Hamlet took his machete and slashed through the cloth." I paused for dramatic effect. "He had killed Polonius!"

The old men looked at each other in supreme disgust. "That Polonius truly was a fool and a man who knew nothing! What child would not know enough to shout, 'It's me!'" With a pang, I remembered that these people are ardent hunters, always armed with bow, arrow, and machete; at the first rustle in the grass an arrow is aimed and ready, and the hunter shouts "Game!" If no human voice answers immediately the arrow speeds on its way. Like a good hunter Hamlet had shouted, "A rat!"

I rushed in to save Polonius's reputation. "Polonius did speak. Hamlet heard him. But he thought it was the chief and wished to kill him to avenge his father. He had meant to kill him earlier that evening. . . ." I broke down, unable to describe to these pagans, who had no belief in individual afterlife, the difference between dying at one's prayers and dying "unhousell'd, disappointed, unaneled."

This time I had shocked my audience seriously. "For a man to raise his hand against his father's brother and the one who has become his father—that is a terrible thing. The elders ought to let such a man be bewitched."

I nibbled at my kola nut in some perplexity, then pointed out that after all the man had killed Hamlet's father.

"No," pronounced the old man, speaking less to me than to the young men sitting behind the elders. "If your father's brother has killed your father, you must appeal to your father's age mates; *they* may avenge him. No man may use violence against his senior relatives." Another thought struck him. "But if his father's brother had indeed been wicked enough to bewitch Hamlet and make him mad that would be a good story indeed, for it would be his fault that Hamlet, being mad, no longer had any sense and thus was ready to kill his father's brother."

There was a murmur of applause. *Hamlet* was again a good story to them, but it no longer seemed quite the same story to me. As I thought over the coming complications of plot and motive, I lost courage and decided to skim over dangerous ground quickly.

"The great chief," I went on, "was not sorry that Hamlet had killed Polonius. It gave him a reason to send Hamlet away, with his two treacherous age mates, with letters to a chief of a far country, saying that Hamlet should be killed. But Hamlet changed the writing on their papers, so that the chief killed his age mates instead." I encountered a reproachful glare from one of the men whom I had told undetectable forgery was not merely immoral but beyond human skill. I looked the other way.

"Before Hamlet could return, Laertes came back for his father's funeral. The great chief told him Hamlet had killed Polonius. Laertes swore to kill Hamlet because of this, and because his sister Ophelia, hearing her father had been killed by the man she loved, went mad and drowned in the river."

"Have you already forgotten what we told you?" The old man was reproachful. "One cannot take vengeance on a madman; Hamlet killed Polonius in his madness. As for the girl, she not only went mad, she was drowned. Only witches can make people drown. Water itself can't hurt anything. It is merely something one drinks and bathes in."

I began to get cross. "If you don't like the story, I'll stop."

The old man made soothing noises and himself poured me some more beer. "You tell the story well, and we are listening. But it is clear that the elders of your country have never told you what the story really means. No, don't interrupt! We believe you when you say your marriage customs are different, or your clothes and weapons. But people are the same everywhere; therefore, there are always witches and it is we, the elders, who know how witches work. We told you it was the great chief who wished to kill Hamlet, and now your own words have proved us right. Who were Ophelia's male relatives?"

"There were only her father and her brother." Hamlet was clearly out of my hands.

"There must have been many more; this also you must ask of your elders when you get back to your country. From what you tell us, since Polonius was dead, it must have been Laertes who killed Ophelia, although I do not see the reason for it."

We had emptied one pot of beer and the old men argued the point with slightly tipsy interest. Finally one of them demanded of me, "What did the servant of Polonius say on his return?"

With difficulty I recollected Reynaldo and his mission. "I don't think he did return before Polonius was killed."

"Listen," said the elder, "and I will tell you how it was and how your story will go, then you may tell me if I am right. Polonius knew his son would get into trouble, and so he did. He had many fines to pay for fighting, and debts from gambling. But he had only two ways of getting money quickly. One was to marry off his sister at once, but it is difficult to find a man who will marry a woman desired by the son of a chief. For if the chief's heir commits adultery with your wife, what can you do? Only a fool calls a case against a man who will someday be his judge. Therefore Laertes had to take the second way: he killed his sister by witchcraft, drowning her so he could secretly sell her body to the witches."

I raised an objection. "They found her body and buried it. Indeed Laertes jumped into the grave to see his sister once more—so, you see, the body was truly there. Hamlet, who had just come back, jumped in after him."

"What did I tell you?" The elder appealed to the others. "Laertes was up to no good with his sister's body. Hamlet prevented him, because the chief's heir, like a chief, does not wish any other man to grow rich and powerful. Laertes would be angry, because he would have killed his sister without benefit to himself. In our country he would try to kill Hamlet for that reason. Is this not what happened?"

"More or less," I admitted. "When the great chief found Hamlet was still alive, he encouraged Laertes to try to kill Hamlet and arranged a fight with machetes between them. In the fight both the young men were wounded to death. Hamlet's mother drank the poisoned beer that the chief meant for Hamlet in case he won the fight. When he saw his mother die of poison, Hamlet, dying, managed to kill his father's brother with his machete."

"You see, I was right!" exclaimed the elder.

"That was a very good story," added the old man, "and you told it with very few mistakes. There was just one more error, at the very end. The poison Hamlet's mother drank was obviously meant for the survivor of the fight, whichever it was. If Laertes had won, the great chief would have poisoned him, for no one would know that he arranged Hamlet's death. Then, too, he need not fear Laertes' witchcraft; it takes a strong heart to kill one's only sister by witchcraft.

"Sometime," concluded the old man, gathering his ragged toga about him, "you must tell us some more stories of your country. We, who are elders, will instruct you in their true meaning, so that when you return to your own land your elders will see that you have not been sitting in the bush, but among those who know things and who have taught you wisdom."

10 / The Anthropologist at Work

Introduction

It is the job of the anthropologist to study cultures other than our own. In earlier days, anthropologists limited themselves almost exclusively to non-Western and preliterate groups. In those days the study of complex Western and other literate societies were in the domain of Sociology. In recent years, however, this distinction has become somewhat blurred and Anthropology has widened its horizons to all cultures and to comparisons among them.

Anthropological fieldwork has always been a highly personal affair. The sheer logistics of living among remote tribal people and of attempting to make sense out of their way of life has consumed most of the anthropologists' energies. Participating in the group activities, learning the language, and recording responses to general interviewing and questioning was and is a widespread practice. In recent years anthropologists have become somewhat more self-conscious about examining their own patterns of work and giving increasing attention to specific methods. Since related fields such as Psychology are somewhat more advanced methodologically, there has been a good deal of borrowing of methods that are applicable to other cultures.

In addition to a consideration of technical methods and tools, anthropological fieldwork also leads to considerations involving personal and professional *ethics*. The anthropologist faces ethical questions from the moment that he begins to think about going to the field until long after he has left it. He knows that his intrusion into a small community is certain to interrupt people's established routines. It may even have serious and unpredictable effects, such as the first introduction of Western epidemic disease into a population. After he has left the field and begins to prepare his data for publication, he must make carefully-considered decisions on such matters as to whether to use the real names of his informants, whether to identify the locality by name, whether to omit data that is politically "hot," and the like. Poor judgment in these and similar matters can lead to hostile or legal actions against the people who confided in him.

Many of the populations studied have already come under considerable Western influence long before an anthropologist arrives on the scene. The activities of generations of Western explorers, traders, colonists, soldiers, administrators, missionaries, tourists, and other such agents of contact have had the net effect of decimating many non-Western populations (as we have already seen in Chapter Seven). By comparison, the anthropologist's intrusion is rather slight; and, in fact, he may actually be helpful to the group in their relations with a Western administration to which they are subject. It is significant that one of the earliest "anthropological" associations bore the title of Aborigines' Protection Society (London, 1837). At the outset, it is sometimes difficult to define one's role to the satisfaction of the people, since their past experience may have convinced them that Westerners play only a limited number of unpopular roles—as tax collectors, labor recruiters, or the like.

The inherent difficulty of understanding a foreign worldview has resulted in the development of an anthropological methodology known as "participant observation." Like other scientists, anthropologists have a wide array of more-or-less standardized techniques and instruments for obtaining precise and thorough information of certain types that have proved to be useful in all cross-cultural studies. Frequently, he starts by simply "walking over the ground," making sketch maps of the community and surrounding terrain. He may also spend a good deal of time, early in his stay, taking a census of some or all of the households, asking about the number of people in the household, their ages, their kinship relations to each other and to members of other households and more of the like. These and similar survey techniques (measuring landholdings, making inventories of crops and trade goods, etc.) require only modest language skills and little initial insight into local values. In addition, such undertakings give the anthropologist a chance to meet people—and give people a chance to meet *him*—in a casual, non-threatening way. Later, this general information about "who's who" and "what's where" becomes increasingly important as he tries to understand and explain his further observations.

As time goes on and as he becomes more involved with the people among whom he is living the anthropologist's daily routine becomes more and more tailored to that of the community. And his methods of getting information— while accompanying hunters, helping to build a house, or sitting around a pot of beer—likewise are shaped by the habits and expectations of his informants. In short, he or she gradually becomes more of a participant and less of an outside observer. In a sense, the goal of the anthropologist is to *learn* the local culture, not just learn *about* it. One major emphasis is upon learning the language of the community—the importance of this being clear from Whorf's article in Chapter Eleven—but there is much else that he can usefully learn by practicing it.

The consensus of fieldworkers is that it takes about six months of trial and (mostly) error before one begins to understand very much of what is being said and done around him (See Chagnon's comment in his article in Chapter Two). From this point on, the anthropologist may begin to take an active role in ceremonies and other activities that he has witnessed passively up to then. Such participation is his best way of testing the accuracy of his observation and understanding, and his inevitable experiences with "using the wrong fork" add to the depth and detail of his evolving insights. For example, in the previous chapter, Bohannan's article, "Shakespeare in the Bush," evokes the air of kindly tolerance with which a gathering of Tiv elders greet her effort to participate in one of their story-telling entertainments.

If he or she is lucky, the anthropologist may find some of his informants meeting them halfway. One of the most-prized methods of anthropological research is to develop intense rapport with one or two thoughtful informants and to talk with them about the general aims and methods of anthropology. Often, such informants—ideally-placed as insiders—pick up sufficient skills in observation and literacy that they can present the anthropologist with ready-made field notes. Later, such an informant may keep the anthropologist supplied with current "newsletters" after he or she has returned from the field. Or, alternatively, the anthropologist may arrange for the informant to come see how things are done in the anthropologist's home society.

A whole anthology devoted to the trials and triumphs of cross-cultural friendships has been published under the title *In the Company of Man: Twenty Portraits of Anthropological Informants* (Casagrande, 1964). Needless to say, such relationships can be intense and extended without necessarily being affectionate. In "The Frightened Witch" (Chapter Seven), Bohannan says of her complex symbiosis with the local headman: "there were awkward moments with Shingir, but we were too useful to each other not to try to forget them as quickly as possible."

The sensitive article by Albert reprinted in this chapter illustrates a number of themes that we have discussed. There is, first of all, the genuine friendship that developed between Albert and Muntu. As she puts it: "despite the strains and difficulties of cross-cultural communication, I discovered how important support and forgiveness are between friends living in an unfriendly environment." And it is clear in the article how vital to her fieldwork this friendship was.

Albert touches also upon the tragic and explosive aspects of the colonial setting of her fieldwork when she describes the resident Westerners as "neither giving nor getting trust and affection, decreasingly certain of the meaningfulness of their 'civilizing mission.' " To make headway in this tense situation, she was obliged to learn a locally-accepted role, chosen—and, apparently, *well*-chosen —for her by Muntu. Learning the role was difficult, and she eventually grew tired of playing it. As with many anthropologists she found that, in addition to the specifics of her field data, she also "learned what it is like to be pressured by society into appropriate behavior for a social role I did not choose." The role of the participant-observer can be very demanding.

And so can the role of informant-observed, according to Deloria. In his "Anthropologists and Other Friends," Deloria turns the full force of his trenchant wit upon the foibles of academic "grantsmen" in general and upon anthropologists in particular. His complaints are exaggerated for the sake of parody; but there is no doubt that anthropologists, as authorities, sometimes lead others—informants, as well as policy-makers—to interpret social problems by use of slogans and stereotypes ill-fitted for the purpose. Faced with critiques of this sort, the members of the American Anthropological Association have formulated a code of ethics intended to avoid the unintended abuses of the past. And many individual anthropologists are now experimenting with research techniques designed to minimize the imposition of the fieldworker's view upon the community.

In a final article that reads like a scientific "whodunit," Oakley and Weiner provide us with a brief example of the laboratory atmosphere and technology characteristic of the investigations pursued by physical anthropologists, as well as archaeologists.

REFERENCES

CASAGRANDE, JOSEPH B., ed., *In the Company of Man: Twenty Portraits of Anthropological Informants* (New York: Harper & Row, 1964).

My "Boy," Muntu

Ethel M. Albert

"Find a boy who bakes good bread, and the rest will be easy." This was the most important advice given me as I left Belgium for Africa in February, 1956. I had reason to remember it more than once in the sixteen months I was in Africa. My destination was Ruanda-Urundi, a Belgian trusteeship sandwiched between Belgian Congo and Tanganyika Territory. . . .

• • •

Within a few days I had learned, among other things, that even in French-speaking Belgian Africa, the English word, "boy," is standard usage for a native male servant of any age. I needed an experienced man who could get along in the bush. When the news of my need spread, a stream of applicants appeared at the guest house. One of the last to arrive was Muntu. Even before the interview was over, I had decided that he would be my "boy." My snap judgment of his worth was well confirmed in his fifteen months as my "boy." We had a lively, intimate relationship that is not easily classified. In a feudal environment, he became my privileged personal servant, I his superior and protector.

Muntu's ability to bake good bread was the first item established in our interview. He assured me that he was a good cook and laundry man, and he volunteered the information that he understood white standards of housekeeping cleanliness. Although he was a native of Ruanda, most of his jobs had been in Urundi, several of them in the bush.[1] To my great relief, Muntu spoke passable French. I would not have to learn Swahili, the local master-servant *lingua franca*. He estimated his age at about 38, and I was glad to have a mature hand. He seemed well above average in intelligence and had a very engaging personality. His enthusiastic letters of reference justified in part his demand for twice the going wages. For twenty-four dollars a month and various extras, I would have at my disposal a whole spectrum of skills needed to assure the success of a lone female anthropologist in the central African hinterland.

Very early, Muntu made certain that I knew he was one of the Batutsi, the upper class of Ruanda and Urundi.[2] Six feet tall, he was just average height among these narrow-headed, slender giants. Hamitic herders, the Batutsi had migrated into the area several centuries ago and become the rulers of Bahutu, the short and broad Bantu farmers who make up more than 85 percent of the popu-

[1] Ruanda and Urundi are administratively unified under the Belgian trusteeship government. Contiguous but independent kingdoms, they are sufficiently alike in social and political organization, ethnic composition, and language to be indistinguishable to the non-specialist. The peoples themselves, however, with some justification, insist upon keeping their separate identities clear.

[2] In Bantu languages, *mu-* is the singular prefix and *ba-* the plural prefix for terms designating human beings; thus, Mututsi and Batutsi, Muhutu and Bahutu, for the principal ethnic groups of Ruanda and Urundi. Sometimes the alternative form, Watutsi, appears in the literature, a reasonable transliteration of the soft "b" sound in the languages of Ruanda and Urundi.

lation. True to the standards of his aristocratic background, Muntu was dignified, his manners elegant, his speech fluent. Like many of his compatriots, he had adopted Western dress. His white shirt, blue trousers, and tan sweater were spotlessly clean though ragged. Only later did I learn that his good clothes would be left at home until after he had received from me the gift of two tailor-made khaki safari suits, at four dollars apiece.

In my second-hand Ford pick-up truck, driven by Musazi, a chauffeur loaned me by I.R.S.A.C., I travelled about Urundi with Muntu to choose a research site. . . .

Muntu knew the roads, the names of the princes and what to do at each stop. When I chose the house at Mutumba, he sent for the local chief—a Mututsi who was about 6 feet 6 inches tall—and instructed him to have ready for my return within a week the repairs needed in the house and three new straw-and-reed houses for my staff. Apparently I had only to tell Muntu what I wanted and leave the rest to him.

With the details of safaris taken care of by Muntu, I was free to look around at the wonderful country and people. Urundi is a land of hills, steeply planted with banana trees, beans, peas, maize, and sorghum. The straw-covered, bee-hive-shaped houses, encircled by fences, dot the hills at irregular intervals. Each family occupies its own hill. Grazing on the hillsides in small herds of five to ten are the prize possessions of the Barundi, their cows. Their magnificent curved horns spread upwards or outwards to a length of a yard or more.

In the large commercial center of Usumbura and in the capital city of Kitega, I had met the king and some of the princes of Urundi, dressed in well-tailored business suits and driving large American cars. Western influence is in evidence even on the back roads. Many men wear shorts and shirts. Those who can afford them have sweaters or coats. For, although Urundi lies between two and three degrees south of the equator, the altitude is high—6500 to 8500 feet and more—and the average daily temperature 68° F. the year round. In town or country, however, the principal manner of dress is an adaptation of the traditional freely-hanging robe, knotted at one shoulder. Dark cotton cloth and blankets serve for everyday attire. But the wealthy and those on holiday wear two or three long robes, one over the other, of bright colored cotton prints. They are secured at one shoulder with a long, raffia tassel and trail the dust behind. Heavy copper bracelets and other traditional jewelry are now seen only rarely. The long spear or staff persists, as necessary to sartorial elegance in Urundi as the walking stick in England.

Muntu had a roving eye. Following it taught me local standards of feminine beauty: a narrow Hamitic nose, good height, narrow waist, and full hips. It taught me also to distinguish the sexes, not always easy for the newcomer. Barundi women are on the average only slightly shorter than the men, some of the Batutsi women cutting fine figures at over 6 feet in height. Bahutu women, however, like Bahutu men, are usually not much above 5 feet tall. Women also wear robes knotted at the shoulder, sometimes with blouse and long, full skirt barely visible underneath. Most of the women shave their heads, and so do most of the men. Often, especially among Bahutu, the women are as muscular as their husbands. Defined as the stronger sex, the women carry the heavy burdens and do the farm work. Masculine tasks are herding, building, and walking long distances—sometimes fifty miles in two days—on errands or as porters for Batutsi and others in positions of authority.

. . .

On the morning after our arrival, Muntu hired a man to carry up water, another to chop wood for his kitchen stove and my fireplace, and a pair of night watchmen, each at the local rate of fifteen to twenty cents a day. In stormy haggling sessions, he supplemented the canned goods with local produce. He turned out soups of dried peas and peanuts, excellent sauces for chicken, omelettes, sweet potatoes, or cooked bananas as vegetables, and fried bananas or pancakes for dessert. He did not use for my table the chief foods of the neighbors—cassava, beans, and sorghum. About a quart of thin, blue milk each morning, obtained under protest from cow-owning Barundi, was boiled to use with breakfast oatmeal. The bright spot in the menu was each week's batch of fine white bread baked in a makeshift outdoor oven.

Muntu was fanatical about cleanliness. He explained to all its urgency in the dirty and disease-ridden back country. The green cement floors were scrubbed by his assistant every day. His mornings and afternoons were filled with washing and ironing, expertly done. Two pails of water steamed on the stove until I could stop work to have my bath. Sunset was at 6:00 p.m.—plus or minus five minutes according to the season—and the evening began as Muntu lighted the kerosene pressure lamps. The table was laid and dinner served. Quiet descended for a little while on the otherwise noisy and busy household. Some evenings there were interviews after dinner, but sometimes Muntu called me out to watch the dancers he had invited. A small fire against the bitter cold, a 20-liter pot of banana beer from my storeroom for a dozen men dancing and singing, were entertainment enough until bedtime. Muntu had more than made good his claims of competence.

The second day at Mutumba, Muntu asked me for sixty francs ($1.20) to purchase a pot of banana beer. The first in an almost endless series, the pot of beer represented the solution to the problem of how to explain to the Barundi my mission in Mutumba. Muntu had it all figured out, or, clever Mututsi, figured it out on the spot. "For these people," he told me, "you are a *mwamikazi*, like the wife of a king or rich Mututsi. You will have to invite them to visit, and you must offer beer and tobacco, the way any *mwamikazi* in Urundi does." Patiently and intelligently, he explained how princes and aristocrats had in the past placed each of their several wives on separate estates. Each *mwamikazi* governed the household, supervised the workers, kept food and drink in readiness for visitors. She listened to the troubles of her husband's serfs and gave charity to the needy. Above all, she received on her own account formal requests for gifts from those who wished to become her personal followers.

Although I was an *umuzungu*—an outsider, a white—I could prove my good will by being generous with beer and cigarettes, blankets and lengths of cotton cloth, and clothing for the otherwise naked children. Wealthy by local standards and belonging to the same "race" as the powerful administrators of Urundi, I entered the field with the attributes of social superiority as it is defined in the country. I had a great deal to learn about my part as *mwamikazi* in this anthropological play, but it was on the whole wonderfully successful. Nobody was taken in by the fiction, yet it was a legitimate way to give me an acceptable place in the community. People came to visit and to talk. They told others about the new household. I was warned not to offend my guests by suggesting that my beer was purchasing their information. Still, there were rarely objections to my taking notes. The Barundi can play a profitable game as well as any.

The neighbors soon formed the habit of visiting the house at Mutumba in the morning or afternoon or evening, as inclination and leisure permitted. They came singly or in pairs or groups as chance arranged it. Muntu was a versatile impresario for a would-be *mwamikazi*. His air of authority and knowledge of traditional amenities won him immediate approval from the few local Batutsi, who soon came to talk to me. For Bahutu, he used the quite different approach he deemed suitable for peasants. He jokingly proposed marriage to the worn-out widows who stopped to sell a basket of peas or indulge their curiosity. He gave bananas or sweets to the children as he chatted with their mothers about his six youngsters back in Astrida. He gave beer and cigarettes to the men and discussed local affairs with them seriously and wisely.

In the regular course of events, I would look around after breakfast to see who was there and tell Muntu whom I wanted to interview. With appropriate ceremony, he ushered the visitors into the livingroom. A camp-bed served as my sofa, and Muntu seated the visitors in the chairs arranged in a circle facing the sofa. To the senior person among them, he gave a gourd of banana beer and a drinking tube, and on the coffee table in front of me he placed my cup of tea or coffee. He called my interpreter and left us to a few hours of conversation. Once the visitors had left, he scrubbed away furiously at the mud or dust their bare feet had tracked in and poured vast quantities of disinfectant around to destroy any chiggers or fleas that might have strayed from the never-washed cotton robes. If a guest became boisterous after too much banana beer, Muntu somehow knew and would come, no matter what the hour, to announce that it was time for me to eat. No Murundi, no matter how drunk, would stay after that, for it is strictly taboo to be present while a superior eats.

Returning visits—and in the process, getting to know something about household affairs in Urundi—presented grave difficulties. It was bad manners to visit anyone at home without advance notice. They would be shamed if there were no beer to offer a distinguished visitor. The yard might not be swept clear of cowdung or banana peels, or it might be cluttered up with mats on which beans or cassava were drying. The mistress of the house would be in work clothes and dirty. Some of the women were rather direct in teaching me my manners. If I arrived uninvited and unannounced, the pounding of cassava in the mortar or the breaking up of firewood would become more vigorous, the noise making conversation impossible. Or, a five-mile hike might end in nothing when a child waiting at the yard entrance offered the socially acceptable lie that nobody was home. Only after several months did I hear the friendly reproach, "You went by our door without stopping to greet us," the signal that I could thereafter drop in unannounced.

By the time my research routine was established, I realized that I much preferred Muntu to Musazi, the chauffeur, or my interpreter, first Charles, then Stanislas. . . .

My preference for Muntu seemed natural enough. He was the first one hired and the only one so competent that I did not have to take time away from field work to supervise him. He was decidedly more intelligent than the others and understood better than they the purpose of my research. We were nearly the same age and early formed the habit of talking about local events, life in general, his youthful experiences or the way things were in my country.

Occasionally, of course, Muntu gave me cause for complaint. His mania for cleanliness did not always reach as far as the kitchen. Worse yet, on his own initiative, he undertook to induct a half-dozen country boys into the arts of housekeeping. As a result, the dishes were not always properly washed, and the fleas of his apprentices sometimes found their way into my bed.

Like virtually every other citizen of Ruanda and Urundi, Muntu drank a great deal. He knew my tolerance for drunkenness was low. Still, he could not prevent himself from coming, in a very dignified stagger, to my living room to describe the wonderful party at which he had got drunk. His one truly puzzling offense was loud quarreling, behavior unbecoming to a Mututsi, usually with Musazi. He was otherwise very decorous in public, even when drunk, no matter whether we were at a wedding near Mutumba or at the great national dance celebrations in Kitega.

There was something about "medicines" in Muntu's quarrels with Musazi. Musazi had smelled out most of the curers and witches in the vicinity. I was glad to know who they were for my own purposes, but surely his interest was of a different order. I interrupted one of the more vociferous quarrels to demand an explanation. Muntu was in a rage and seemed on the point of murdering his kitchen assistant. Stanislas, his head hanging, translated: Musazi had bribed the kitchen boy with a pair of shoes to get him to slip some *inzaratsi* into my soup, and Muntu had caught the lad at it. *Inzaratsi* had been described to me as a potion that would cause the consumer to yearn for the presence of the one who had paid for it. I was certain that Musazi had no amorous designs on me, but what he was up to I could not even imagine.

Brought so close to home, the potions and poisons so constantly discussed by my visitors took on greater importance than material for a file on witchcraft. One day, Musazi himself was found placing a powder of some kind in Muntu's bed. Even without chemical analysis to determine scientifically the properties of the powders and potions, it was obvious that they were active agents in demoralizing my household. I could no longer reasonably assume that I had no right to interfere in the personal affairs of my staff, mature men though they were. I called the three men into my living room for an after-dinner discussion.

• • •

To begin, I announced that the irregularities of behavior of Musazi and Muntu were disrespectful of me, disruptive of my work, and no longer tolerable. Musazi was warned that he would be sent packing back to Astrida the next time he misbehaved. Muntu was warned that no more shouting would be borne. With pained surprise, Stanislas corrected me. There was no sense in a council if the decision were already made. Stanislas could not, as in regular interviews, be merely a translator. He was one of Musazi's peers and owed him support. My place, I was told, was to issue a warning to Musazi in the presence of his friends —not privately as in the past—so that they could try to persuade him to change if he had been doing wrong things. I had also to hear Musazi's complaints against me.

There was always more to be gained from following Barundi rules than from standing on what I viewed as my rights. I restated my complaints against Musazi—his drinking, his quarrels with Muntu, his indiscreet affairs with girls in the vicinity, and so on. I then reasserted my right to fire him, should he disregard a final warning. All three men demurred. I had taken Musazi to work for me, and he was therefore my responsibility. I had to realize that his misbehavior came from the weakness of his character, not from malice. He needed help. Muntu and Stanislas joined together to defend Musazi's rights and their own. Each asked me whether he, too, would be fired if he did something wrong. Mustering my courage, I replied that nobody should expect to be kept on in a job if he did not do it well.

Somehow, the discussion turned to the question of what it was like to be a white, alone in the bush. They wanted to know whether I was afraid. I assured them that I had no reason to be, for I had them to protect me. After a moment of silence, Stanislas, speaking quietly and with eyes lowered, said, "But you know, if we became angry with you, we could do you great harm." Realizing how true this was, I had a bad moment. He continued, "You know, if we were angry, we could all run away." I still do not know whether this was a veiled threat of much worse or Stanislas' idea of real harm to me. I laughed it off, arguing, "That would be very foolish, for then you would have no salary." But from that time forward, my sympathy was somewhat greater for the whites living in Africa, isolated from their own kind, outnumbered, and resented, neither giving nor getting trust and affection, decreasingly certain of the meaningfulness of their "civilizing mission," increasingly certain that they had much to fear.

Musazi at last presented his chief complaint. Every day, I invited people into the house to drink, but never until this night had he been invited. Taken by surprise, I left it to Stanislas and Muntu to explain to Musazi that the beer was not for sociability but for getting information. Nevertheless, to raise morale, I promised to invite him from time to time. The council dispersed, the outcome inconclusive but all of us in good humor.

It was no good. Musazi's brain was soaked in alcohol and his soul in despair. He continued to do the same things, and I sent him back to Astrida in the pick-up truck, telling him I would telegraph when I wanted him to come and get me. About half way there, he wrecked the truck—as he had repeatedly told Stanislas and Muntu he would one day do—killing the two passengers he had picked up on the way.

It was clearly an error—an expensive and dangerous one—to regard my partly Westernized Batutsi staff as my "employees." They were my "children," my dependents. In spite of myself, I was changing in actions and attitudes from democratic, egalitarian liberalism—in which impersonal employer-employee relationships make sense—to the benevolent if burdensome despotism of the *mwamikazi*. What Muntu had told me about the protective role of the head of a household was repeated and elaborated by rich and poor, Mututsi and Muhutu, male and female. The power of the council of elders to decide the fate of inferiors, it was admitted, was relative to the justness of the superior person. Musazi was a bad child, for though I had the duty to be generous, to correct him when he was wrong, to try to make peace between him and my other "children," he owed it to me to be docile and obedient. The wickedness of men like Musazi, it was admitted, was characteristic of Batutsi, who are said never to forgive an injustice and to live only for the opportunity to harm those they hate.

The key to the underlying causes of Musazi's unforgiving hostility came from a detailed discussion of the relationships between superiors and inferiors. In each family household and at each princely court, the superior chooses his *umutoni*, his favorite. To Musazi, to Stanislas, and to my Barundi neighbors, Muntu, technically my "boy," was my *umutoni*, my favorite. People who wanted to visit me or to ask a gift of me had first to offer a gift—a pot of beer or a basket of peas—to Muntu. He, in theory, would then recommend the petitioner to my attention.

Almost nobody sought out Musazi with pots of beer, for he had no influence to open the way for them to obtain a gift from me. Bitter rivalry in the family and at the courts was the common state of affairs. The *umutoni* was hated by the less successful aspirants to the privileged and profitable position. Plotting for his downfall, by calumny or poison, was standard practice. Musazi must have been bitterly resentful of Muntu's advantage, good enough reason for Muntu to be hysterically afraid of him. It cannot have mattered to Musazi, or to Muntu, or to the neighbors, that to me, Muntu's distributing beer and cigarettes was part of his job as my "boy," nor can it have mattered that I had not known I had an *umutoni*.

• • •

Because Muntu spoke French, wore Western clothes, and usually presented a dignified and cheerful face, it was easy to forget how thoroughly he belonged to his culture and how great the conflicts were between the old and new ways. His ambition to fulfill the pattern of the Mututsi aristocrat was intense, perhaps pathological. He was desperately poor and wildly spendthrift when he had money. High social position was expensive. He was a mature man whose judgment was respected in councils, and he was the father of many children in a part of the world where fatherhood defines masculinity. Yet, to earn his living, he did woman's work, a matter about which he occasionally made a bitter joke. Here, then, was Muntu, at dinner time serving a white woman, an hour later drinking on equal and intimate terms with a prince. He must surely have had mixed feelings about himself and about me.

• • •

The one time in the fifteen months of our association Muntu lost his temper with me was over an imagined accusation of theft. The burst of rage came at a point where my own temper was not under good control. Life in Mutumba was wearing, and I needed a rest. We were both shouting. I stopped making my part of the noise when I found my clenched fist within an inch of Muntu's jaw. The shock of the spectacle of myself at the point of physical violence helped me to recover my control. It gave him a chance to get hold of himself. His parting shot, delivered in a quiet way, was, "After all, mademoiselle, you are *umuzungu* [a white]. If you stay in Urundi a long time, you will become like the other whites." In the earlier, rougher days of European occupation, he had suffered many a whipping, unable to fight back, from white men and women as well. He knew me well enough by then to know that the invidious comparison would hurt, the more so since he was so nearly right.

The *mwamikazi* game had begun to pall. I was feeling foolish, a soft touch for my "boy," my interpreter, for any Murundi who came along. Like anyone else, I am a child of my culture. It took a great many talks with Barundi to grasp the idea that what was good about a gift—whether it was a cigarette or a cow—was not only the material benefit as such but also, and perhaps more important, the meaning of the gift. "You give only to those you like, and everyone wants to be liked." Where I come from, I explained in some humility, we think it is either wealth or affection that is sought, not both at once. Before the lesson was quite driven home, I had burst out to Muntu in anger against a woman who had been rude enough to ask for a gift within an hour after meeting me. "Asking is all the Barundi know how to do! Wealth is all they think about!" Muntu inquired respectfully, "Do you not also think always of money?" "Of course not!" I countered. "Then, mademoiselle, it is because, unlike us, you have enough." Touché!

• • •

In our evening talks, Muntu told me a little about his history. His father had not liked him, because he was not brave. He had never claimed his inheritance, though now that his father was old, he was thinking of going to ask for cows and lands. His parents had been divorced, but, like other boys, he was educated by his father. He had to learn how to care for cows, how to speak well, and how to behave toward his betters and his inferiors. His father sometimes sent him with the cows at night to use other men's pastures. This infringement of grazing rights resulted almost inevitably in night fighting with spears, swords, and knives. Muntu lacked spirit for the fights. He showed me the scar on his ankle, a souvenir of the spear his father hurled at him to teach him courage. He ran away to the Catholic mission where he began to learn many things—how to write, to wear Western clothes, to work in the kitchen. One day, he saw one of the fathers slap the face of a boy at the school. "Even at the school, they hit people for nothing." He ran away and found work as a kitchen helper in a private home. There again, he was oppressed by violence and repeatedly ran away from it.

Muntu's father figured in another source of unhappiness, his wife and children. In a country where divorce is frequent, he had been married to Maria for about twenty years. She was terribly jealous, though her own record for fidelity was not very good. She asked me on each return to Astrida whether Muntu had been carrying on with women. I could tell her truthfully that if he had been, I had seen nothing of it.

Muntu had fallen in love with Maria when he was 16 or 17—much below normal marriage age for Batutsi. She had already borne a child to a wandering Arab, but she was beautiful and passionate, and Muntu wanted her. His father objected to the marriage. They had the same clan name, and although there were no direct taboos, the old man was fearful. He consulted a seer, who warned that if Muntu married this woman, she would die, and he would have no children by her. Another woman was suggested, but Muntu refused her. Since his father would not, Muntu himself paid the brideprice for Maria. Several times he repeated the moral of the story: Maria has borne him eight children, of whom six were still alive. The woman his father wanted him to marry had died a few months after her marriage to another man. "That is why I cannot believe in the things that are said by our seers."

It was not a happy marriage. Muntu preferred safari work so that he would not have to be with Maria all the time. She, jealous and always without money, would not leave him but grew thin and unhappy when he was away. Worst of all, she was not bringing up the children properly. Muntu wept when he talked about his oldest daughter. At 15, a stately and beautiful Mututsi girl and fully mature, she was pregnant, but no man had paid for her. He had done so much for her, spending all his money and selling his cows to pay for curing her tuberculosis. He had obtained a scholarship for her to go to school and become educated in European things. Now she had done this. She was in love with a worthless fellow who had begotten children with other women, none of them paid for. He dared not scold her, for she might then run away to Congo or to Uganda and live out her life as a prostitute.

Muntu's oldest son, about 13 years old, was also a keen disappointment. A bright boy, he did not like school and wanted to go to work. It embittered Muntu. "My son is a fool. If I only had had his opportunity, I would not have to be a servant. I could be a clerk or a chief, something worthwhile." He took little comfort from the fact that other fathers the world over faced similar problems with their sons.

Muntu was hardly aware of the three other girls, still children. But the little boy, about 4 years old, really warmed his heart. The child resembled him closely and tagged along with him whenever he was back home in Astrida. Except for this little one, Muntu was a sad old man when he spoke of his children. Yet, usually, he kept a cheerful face and straight posture. As he himself said, one did not always have to think about these things, there were many other things to keep busy with.

• • •

Perhaps the most striking part of Muntu's service to me as an anthropologist resulted from his skill in handling people. He reassured the timid, persuaded the recalcitrant, chased away the merely greedy or curious. He was able to procure for me nearly any variety of informant and any kind of object for the museum of Urundi at Kitega. If I wanted to interview an old man who remembered about military organization in the old days, if I wanted to talk to several women about child-rearing, even if I wanted information from a curer or the neighborhood witch, Muntu knew how to get them for me.

• • •

In Urundi, as a stranger, I learned what it is like to be pressured by society into appropriate behavior for a social role I did not choose. From Muntu, I learned what an old-fashioned, feudal personal relationship is like. Despite the strains and difficulties of cross-cultural communication, I discovered how important support and forgiveness are between friends living in an unfriendly environment. For a while at least, Muntu had come close to making a *mwamikazi* of me.

The initial sympathy between Muntu and me, lost for a while, returned before my research tour ended. With such different backgrounds and personalities, it is astonishing that we understood each other as well as we did. Muntu's understanding of me was keen. He had surely never read Freud, but he was an uncanny analyst of my actions and accidents, my considered opinions and slips of the tongue. We could not, however, agree about everything. I could not persuade him that my kitchen spices and the flowers in my garden were amenities and not the secret magic by which I, alone among all the whites he had ever known, had avoided becoming ill in the bush. He continued to believe that my curry powder and marigolds had protected me against malaria and dysentery. I could offer no better explanation than his good care and my good luck.

One other matter on which Muntu and I did not agree was the question of my weight. He, following the standards of his country, liked women to be plump. I, typical American, was most unhappy over the ten pounds I had gained on my starchy diet. He was genuinely upset when I spoke of putting off weight. People would think he had not taken good care of me, his wife would reproach him for ingratitude toward me, my brothers back home would be angry. I decided to wait until my departure from Urundi in July, 1957, before going on a diet. It was the least I could do before saying good-by to Muntu.

Anthropologists and Other Friends

Vine Deloria, Jr.

Into each life, it is said, some rain must fall. Some people have bad horoscopes, others take tips on the stock market. McNamara created the TFX and the Edsel. Churches possess the real world. But Indians have been cursed above all other people in history. Indians have anthropologists.

Every summer when school is out a veritable stream of immigrants heads into Indian country. Indeed the Oregon Trail was never so heavily populated as are Route 66 and Highway 18 in the summer time. From every rock and cranny in the East *they* emerge, as if responding to some primeval fertility rite, and flock to the reservations.

"They" are the anthropologists. Social anthropologists, historical anthropologists, political anthropologists, economic anthropologists, all brands of the species, embark on the great summer adventure. For purposes of this discussion we shall refer only to the generic name, anthropologists. They are the most prominent members of the scholarly community that infests the land of the free, and in the summer time, the homes of the braves.

The origin of the anthropologist is a mystery hidden in the historical mists. Indians are certain that all societies of the Near East had anthropologists at one time because all those societies are now defunct.

Indians are equally certain that Columbus brought anthropologists on his ships when he came to the New World. How else could he have made so many wrong deductions about where he was?

While their historical precedent is uncertain, anthropologists can readily be identified on the reservations. Go into any crowd of people. Pick out a tall gaunt white man wearing Bermuda shorts, a World War II Army Air Force flying jacket, an Australian bush hat, tennis shoes, and packing a large knapsack incorrectly strapped on his back. He will invariably have a thin sexy wife with stringy hair, an IQ of 191, and a vocabulary in which even the prepositions have eleven syllables.

He usually has a camera, tape recorder, telescope, hoola hoop, and life jacket all hanging from his elongated frame. He rarely has a pen, pencil, chisel, stylus, stick, paint brush, or instrument to record his observations.

This creature is an anthropologist.

An anthropologist comes out to Indian reservations to make OBSERVATIONS. During the winter these observations will become books by which future anthropologists will be trained, so that they can come out to reservations years from now and verify the observations they have studied.

After the books are written, summaries of the books appear in the scholarly journals in the guise of articles. These articles "tell it like it is" and serve as a catalyst to inspire other anthropologists to make the great pilgrimage next summer

The summaries are then condensed for two purposes. Some condensations are sent to government agencies as reports justifying the previous summer's research. Others are sent to foundations in an effort to finance the next summer's expedition west.

The reports are spread all around the government agencies and foundations all winter. The only problem is that no one has time to read them. So five-thousand-dollar-a-year secretaries are assigned to decode them. Since the secretaries cannot read complex theories, they reduce the reports to the best slogan possible and forget the reports.

The slogans become conference themes in the early spring, when the anthropologist expeditions are being planned. The slogans turn into battle cries of opposing groups of anthropologists who chance to meet on the reservations the following summer.

Each summer there is a new battle cry, which inspires new insights into the nature of the "Indian problem." One summer Indians will be greeted with the joyful cry of "Indians are bilingual!" The following summer this great truth will be expanded to "Indians are not only bilingual, THEY ARE BICULTURAL!"

Biculturality creates great problems for the opposing anthropological camp. For two summers they have been bested in sloganeering and their funds are running low. So the opposing school of thought breaks into the clear faster than Gale Sayers playing against the little leaguers. "Indians," the losing "anthros" cry, "are a FOLK people!" The tide of battle turns and a balance, so dearly sought by Mother Nature, is finally achieved.

Thus go the anthropological wars, testing whether this school or that school can endure longest. And the battlefields, unfortunately, are the lives of Indian people.

You may be curious as to why the anthropologist never carries a writing instrument. He never makes a mark because he ALREADY KNOWS what he is going to find. He need not record anything except his daily expenses for the audit, for the anthro found his answer in the books he read the winter before. No, the anthropologist is only out on the reservations to VERIFY what he has suspected all along—Indians are a very quaint people who bear watching.

The anthro is usually devoted to PURE RESEARCH. Pure research is a body of knowledge absolutely devoid of useful application and incapable of meaningful digestion. Pure research is an abstraction of scholarly suspicions concerning some obscure theory originally expounded in pre-Revolutionary days and systematically checked each summer since then. A 1969 thesis restating a proposition of 1773 complete with footnotes to all material published between 1773 and 1969 is pure research.

There are, however, anthropologists who are not as clever at collecting footnotes. They depend upon their field observations and write long adventurous narratives in which their personal observations are used to verify their suspicions. Their reports, books, and articles are called APPLIED RESEARCH. The difference, then, between Pure and Applied research is primarily one of footnotes. Pure has many footnotes, Applied has few footnotes. Relevancy to subject matter is not discussed in polite company.

Anthropologists came to Indian country only after the tribes had agreed to live on reservations and had given up their warlike ways. Had the tribes been given a choice of fighting the cavalry or the anthropologists, there is little doubt as to who they would have chosen. In a crisis situation men always attack the biggest threat to their existence. A warrior killed in battle could always go to the Happy Hunting Grounds. But where does an Indian laid low by an anthro go? To the library?

Behind each successful man stands a woman and behind each policy and program with which Indians are plagued, if traced completely back to its origin, stands the anthropologist.

The fundamental thesis of the anthropologist is that people are objects for observation, people are then considered objects for experimentation, for manipulation, and for eventual extinction. The anthropologist thus furnishes the justification for treating Indian people like so many chessmen available for anyone to play with.

The massive volume of useless knowledge produced by anthropologists attempting to capture real Indians in a network of theories has contributed substantially to the invisibility of Indian people today. After all, who can conceive of a food-gathering, berry-picking, semi-nomadic, fire-worshiping, high-plains-and-mountain-dwelling, horse-riding, canoe-toting, bead-using, pottery-making, ribbon-coveting, wickiup-sheltered people who began *flourishing* when Alfred Frump mentioned them in 1803 in his great work on Indians entitled *Our Feathered Friends* as real?

Not even Indians can relate themselves to this type of creature who, to anthropologists, is the "real" Indian. Indian people begin to feel that they are merely shadows of a mythical super-Indian. Many anthros spare no expense to reinforce this sense of inadequacy in order to further support their influence over Indian people.

In Washington, bureaucrats and Congressmen are outraged to discover that this "berry-picking food gatherer" has not entered the mainstream of American society. Programs begin to shift their ideological orientation to cover the missing aspect which allowed the berry picker to "flourish." Programs and the people they serve thus often have a hidden area of misunderstanding which neither administrators nor recipients realize.

Over the years anthropologists have succeeded in burying Indian communities so completely beneath the mass of irrelevant information that the total impact of the scholarly community on Indian people has become one of simple authority. Many Indians have come to parrot the ideas of anthropologists because it appears that the anthropologists know everything about Indian communities. Thus many ideas that pass for Indian thinking are in reality theories originally advanced by anthropologists and echoed by Indian people in an attempt to communicate the real situation.

Since 1955 there have been a number of workshops conducted in Indian country as a device for training "young Indian leaders." Churches, white Indian-interest groups, colleges, and finally, poverty programs have each gone the workshop route as the most feasible means for introducing new ideas into younger Indians so as to create "leaders."

The tragic nature of the workshops is apparent when one examines their history. One core group of anthropologists, helpful in 1955 and succeeding years, has institutionalized the workshop and the courses taught in it. Trudging valiantly from workshop to workshop, from state to state, college to college, tribe to tribe, area to area, these noble spirits have served as the catalyst for the creation of workshops which are identical in purpose and content and often in the student body itself.

The anthropological message to young Indians has not varied a jot or tittle in ten years. It is the same message these anthros learned as fuzzy-cheeked graduate students in the post-war years—Indians are a folk people, whites are an urban people, and never the twain shall meet.

Derived from this basic premise have been such sterling insights as Indians are between two cultures, Indians are bicultural, Indians have lost their identity, and Indians are warriors. These insights, propounded every year with deadening regularity and an overtone of Sinaitic authority, have come to occupy a key block in the development of young Indian people. For these slogans have come to be excuses for Indian failures. They are crutches by which young Indians have avoided the arduous task of thinking out the implications of the status of Indian people in the modern world.

Indian Affairs today suffers from an intellectual stagnation that is astounding. Creative thought is sparse. Where the younger black students were the trigger to the Civil Rights movements with sit-ins in the South, young Indians have become unwitting missionaries spreading ancient anthropological doctrines which hardly relate to either anthropology or to Indians. The young blacks invented Black Power and pushed the whole society to consider the implications of discrimination which in turn created racial nationalism. Young Indians have barely been able to parody some black slogans and have created none of their own.

If there is one single cause which has importance today for Indian people, it is tribalism. But creation of modern tribalism has been stifled by the ready acceptance of the "Indians-are-a-folk-people" premise of the anthropologists. Creative thought in Indian Affairs has not, therefore, come from younger Indians. Rather it has come from the generation of Indians supposedly brainwashed by government schools and derided as "puppets" of the Bureau of Indian Affairs.

Because other groups have been spurred on by their younger generation, Indians have come to believe that through education a new generation of leaders will arise to solve the pressing contemporary problems. Tribal leaders have been taught to accept this thesis by the scholarly community in its annual invasion of the reservations. Bureau of Indian Affairs educators harp continually on this theme. Wherever authority raises its head in Indian country, this thesis is its message.

The facts prove the opposite, however. Relatively untouched by anthropologists, educators, and scholars are the Apache tribes of the Southwest. The Mescalero, San Carlos, White Mountain, and Jicarilla Apaches have very few young people in college compared with other tribes. They have even fewer people in the annual workshop orgy during the summers. If ever there was a distinction between folk and urban, this group of Indians characterizes the revered anthropological gulf.

Concern among the Apaches is, however, tribal. There is little sense of a "lost identity." Apaches could not care less about the anthropological dilemmas that worry other tribes. Instead they continue to work on the massive plans for development which they themselves have created. Tribal identity is assumed, not defined, by the reservation people. Freedom to choose from a wide variety of paths of progress is a characteristic of the Apaches; they don't worry about what type of Indianism is "real." Above all, they cannot be ego-fed by abstract theories and hence unwittingly manipulated.

With many young people from other tribes the situation is quite different. Some young Indians attend workshops over and over again. Folk theories pronounced by authoritative anthropologists become opportunities to escape responsibility. If, by definition, the Indian is hopelessly caught between two cultures, why struggle? Why not blame all one's lack of success on this tremendous gulf between two opposing cultures? Workshops have become, therefore, summer retreats for non-thought rather than strategy sessions for leadership enhancement.

Herein lies the Indian sin against the anthropologist. Only those anthropologists who appear to boost Indian ego and expound theories dear to the hearts of workshop Indians are invited to teach at workshops. They become human recordings of social confusion which are played and replayed each summer to the delight of people who refuse to move on into the real world.

The workshop anthro is thus a unique creature, partially self-created and partially supported by the refusal of Indian young people to consider their problems in their own context. The normal process of maturing has been confused with cultural difference. So maturation is cast aside in favor of cult recitation of great truths which appear to explain the immaturity of young people.

While the anthro is, in a very real sense, the victim of the Indians, he should nevertheless recognize the role he has been asked to play and refuse to play it. Instead, the temptation to appear relevant to a generation of young Indians has clouded his sense of proportion. Workshop anthros often ask Indians of tender age to give their authoritative answers to problems which an entire generation of Indians is just now beginning to solve. Thus, where the answer to reservation health problems may be adequate housing in areas where there has *never* been adequate housing, young Indians are shaped in their thinking processes to consider vague doctrines on the nature of man and his society.

It is very unsettling for a teen-age Indian to become an instant authority equal in status with the Ph.D. interrogating him. Yet the very human desire is to play that game every summer, for the status acquired in the game is heady. And as according to current rules of the game, answers can only be given in vocabulary created by the Ph.D., the entire leadership-training process internalizes itself and has no outlet beyond the immediate group. Real problems, superimposed upon the ordinary problems of maturing, thus become insoluble burdens that crush people of great leadership potential.

Let us take some specific examples. One workshop discussed the thesis that Indians were in a terrible crisis. They were, in the words of friendly anthro guides, BETWEEN TWO WORLDS. People between two worlds, the students were told, DRANK. For the anthropologists, it was a valid explanation of drinking on the reservation. For the young Indians, it was an authoritative definition of their role as Indians. Real Indians, they began to think, drank and their task was to become real Indians for only in that way could they re-create the glories of the past.

So they DRANK.

I lost some good friends who DRANK too much.

Abstract theories create abstract action. Lumping together the variety of tribal problems and seeking the demonic principle at work which is destroying Indian people may be intellectually satisfying. But it does not change the real situation. By concentrating on great abstractions, anthropologists have unintentionally removed many young Indians from the world in which problems are solved to the lands of makebelieve.

Regardless of theory, the Pyramid Lake Paiutes and the Gila River Pima Maricopas are poor because they have been systematically cheated out of their water rights, and on desert reservations water is the most important single factor in life. No matter how many worlds Indians straddle, the Plains Indians have an inadequate land base that continues to shrink because of land sales. Straddling worlds is irrelevant to straddling small pieces of land and trying to earn a living.

Along the Missouri River the Sioux used to live in comparative peace and harmony. Although the allotments were small, families were able to achieve a fair standard of living through a combination of gardening and livestock raising and supplemental work. Little cash income was required because the basic necessities of food, shelter, and community life were provided.

After World War II anthropologists came to call. They were horrified that the Indians didn't carry on their old customs such as dancing, feasts, and giveaways. In fact, the people did keep up a substantial number of customs. But these customs had been transposed into church gatherings, participation in the county fair, and tribal celebrations, particularly fairs and rodeos.

The people did Indian dances. BUT THEY DIDN'T DO THEM ALL THE TIME.

Suddenly the Sioux were presented with an authority figure who bemoaned the fact that whenever he visited the reservations the Sioux were not out dancing in the manner of their ancestors. In a real sense, they were not real.

Today the summers are taken up with one great orgy of dancing and celebrating as each small community of Indians sponsors a weekend pow-wow for the people in the surrounding communities. Gone are the little gardens which used to provide fresh vegetables in the summer and canned goods in the winter. Gone are the chickens which provided eggs and Sunday dinner. In the winter the situation becomes critical for families who spent the summer dancing. While the poverty programs have done much to counteract the situation, few Indians recognize that the condition was artificial from start to finish. The people were innocently led astray and even the anthropologists did not realize what had happened.

Another beautiful example of nonsensical scholarly dribble that has had a great effect on Indians' lives was an event that happened in the summer of 1968. A proposal was written to solve the desperate credit needs of reservation communities. Without a sufficient amount of capital to begin small businesses, no area can achieve economic stability. Tribes had sought a credit bill in Congress for ten years without any noticeable movement in the two Interior committees.

So a scheme was devised in a place far from Indian country to make use of existing funds in the community to generate credit within the reservation for use by the people. The basic document stated that like all undeveloped areas, Indian reservations have a great deal of HOARDED wealth. The trick, according to this group of experts, was to gain the Indians' confidence, get them to bring their hoarded wealth from hiding, and make them invest that wealth in reservation banks, mutual funds, and small businesses.

I could not believe the proposition myself. I had visited a great many reservations and seen the abject poverty, most of its cause directly attributed to the refusal by Congress to provide credit or to bureaucratic ineptness. I had served on the Board of Inquiry into Hunger and Malnutrition in the United States and had been shaken at what we had found, not only in Indian reservations, but in rural America generally. If there was hoarded wealth on those reservations, it was very well hidden!

Yet people I talked with concerning the idea were pretty much convinced that the authors of the document had hit the nail on the head. Some yearned to get the program going to see what could be done on specific reservations. One reservation suggested had had employment only once before in this century. That was during the Depression, when CCC camps were put up on the reservation and conservation was used to provide employment for the people. That era lasted about three or four years and then World War II forced cancellation of the camps.

I could not be convinced that wages earned in the CCC camps had been carefully preserved through the great blizzard of 1949, through the Korean War, through the prosperous days of the 1950's, through the Vietnam struggle, and were now gathering mildew in their hiding places beneath the dirt floors of the log cabins on the reservation. The proposal was designed for the days of Silas Marner in merry old England, when the industrial revolution was just beginning to reach into the countryside.

Hopefully the project has been dropped. To be kindly, it was unrealistic from the very inception. But in my mind's eye I can still visualize what the scene would be as one of its proponents described it to me.

From every nook and cranny, from every butte and mesa, Indians came swarming into Pine Ridge, South Dakota. In wagons and old cars they came, afoot and astride their ponies. Into the agency they moved, a relentless stream of investors. At a table sat two accountants and a distinguished economist, recording each family's investment in a massive bank deposit book. Gradually the little leather pouches were piled higher and higher as thousands of dollars of coin of the realm once again greeted the sun.

Rare coin collectors stood off to the side, looking for large greenbacks, Spanish doubloons, and Greek drachmas, hidden since pre-Colonial times. Occasionally a Viking coin, evidence of Leif Ericson's tourist activities, came to the table, greeted by opposing scholars as authentic and counterfeit as ideology dictated. With pleased looks the economists, anthropologists, and other scholars stood observing the scene. At last, they chortled, Indians were in the mainstream of American life.

I do not place much faith in well-footnoted proposals.

One of the wildest theories, to my way of thinking, has been advocated by some very dear friends of mine. Since we cuss and discuss the theory with monotonous regularity, I feel free to outline my side of the controversy. Their side has had the benefit of publication in scholarly journals for years.

The Oglala Sioux are perhaps the most famous of the Sioux bands. Among their past leaders were Red Cloud, the only Indian who ever defeated the United States in war, and Crazy Horse, most revered of the Sioux war chiefs. The Oglala were, and perhaps still are, the meanest group of Indians ever assembled. They would take after a cavalry troop just to see if their bow strings were taut enough.

After they had settled on the reservation, the Oglalas made a fairly smooth transition to the new life. They had good herds of cattle, they settled along the numerous creeks that cross the reservation, and they created a very strong community spirit. The Episcopalians and the Roman Catholics had the missionary franchise on the reservation and the tribe was pretty evenly split between the two. In the Episcopal church, at least, the congregations were fairly self-governing and stable.

During the years since the reservation was created, members of other tribes came to visit and ended up as residents. Dull Knife's Cheyennes hid at Pine Ridge for a while and a group of them came to be permanent residents. Osages, Kaws, and other Oklahoma tribes also had scattered families living on the reservation.

Over the years the Oglala Sioux have had a number of problems. Their population has grown faster than their means of support. The government allowed white farmers to come into the eastern part of the reservation and create a county, with the best farm lands owned or operated by whites. The reservation was allotted and when ownership became too complicated, control of the land passed out of Indian hands. The government displaced a number of families during the last world war by taking a part of the reservation for use as a bombing range to train crews for combat. Only in 1968 was the land returned to tribal and individual use.

The tribe became a favorite subject for study quite early because of its romantic past. Gradually theories arose attempting to explain the apparent lack of progress of the Oglala Sioux. The real issue, white control of the reservation, was overlooked completely. Instead, every conceivable intangible cultural distinction was used to explain lack of economic, social, and educational progress of a people who were, to all intents and purposes, absentee landlords because of the government policy of leasing their lands to whites.

One study advanced the startling proposition that Indians with many cattle were, on the average, better off than Indians without cattle. Cattle Indians, apparently, had more capital and income than did non-cattle Indians. The study had innumerable charts and graphs which demonstrated this great truth beyond doubt of a reasonably prudent man.

Studies of this type were common but unexciting. They lacked that certain flair of insight so beloved by anthropologists. Then one day a famous anthropologist advanced the thesis, probably valid at the time and in the manner in which he advanced it, that the Oglala were WARRIORS WITHOUT WEAPONS.

The chase was on.

From every library stack in the nation anthropologists converged on the innocent Oglala Sioux to test this new thesis before the ink dried on the scholarly journals. Outfitting the anthropological expeditions to Pine Ridge became the number-one industry of the small off-reservation Nebraska towns south of Pine Ridge. Surely supplying the Third Crusade to the Holy Land was a minor feat compared with the task of keeping the anthropologists at Pine Ridge.

Every conceivable difference between the Oglala Sioux and the folks at Hyannisport was attributed to the quaint warrior tradition of the Oglala Sioux. From lack of roads to unshined shoes Sioux problems were generated, so the anthros discovered, by the refusal of the white man to recognize the great desire of the Oglalas to go to war. Why expect an Oglala to become a small businessman when he was only waiting for that wagon train to come around the bend?

The very real and human problems of the reservation were considered to be merely by-products of the failure of a warrior people to become domesticated. The fairly respectable thesis of past exploits in war, perhaps romanticized for morale purposes, became a demonic spiritual force all its own. Some Indians, in a tongue-in-cheek manner for which Indians are justly famous, suggested that a subsidized wagon train be run through the reservation each morning at 9 a.m. and the reservation people paid a minimum wage for attacking it.

By outlining this problem I am not deriding the Sioux. I lived eighteen years on that reservation and know many of the problems it suffers. How, I ask, can the Oglala Sioux make any headway in education when their lack of education is ascribed to a desire to go to war? Would not perhaps an incredibly low per capita income, virtually non-existent housing, extremely inadequate roads, and domination by white farmers and ranchers make some difference? If the little Sioux boy or girl had no breakfast, had to walk miles to a small school, and had no decent clothes and place to study in a one-room log cabin, should the level of education be comparable to New Trier High School?

What use would roads, houses, schools, businesses, income, be to a people that everyone expected would soon depart on the hunt or warpath? I would submit that a great deal of the lack of progress at Pine Ridge is occasioned by people who believe they are helping the Oglalas when they insist on seeing, in the life of the people of that reservation, only those things which they want to see. Real problems and real people become invisible before the great romantic notion that the Sioux yearn for the days of Crazy Horse and Red Cloud and will do nothing until those days return.

The logical conclusion of this rampage of "warriorism" was the creation of a type of education which claimed to make "modern Indians" out of these warriors. I will not argue right or wrong about the process, since too few Indian people on the Sioux reservations have become acquainted with it, and many of those who have, accept it as the latest revelation from on high.

The question of the Oglala Sioux is a question that plagues every Indian tribe in the nation, if it will closely examine itself. Tribes have been defined as one thing, the definition has been completely explored, test scores have been advanced promoting and deriding the thesis, and finally the conclusion has been reached—Indians must be redefined in terms that white men will accept, even if that means re-Indianizing them according to a white man's idea of what they were like in the past and should logically become in the future.

What, I ask, would a school board in Moline, Illinois, or Skokie, even, do if the scholarly community tried to reorient their educational system to conform with outmoded ideas of Sweden in the glory days of Gustavus Adolphus? Would they be expected to sing *"Ein Feste Burg"* and charge out of the mists at the Roman Catholics to save the Reformation every morning as school began?

Or the Irish? Would they submit to a group of Indians coming to Boston and telling them what a modern Irishman was like? Expecting them to dress in green and hunt leprechauns so as to live on the leprechaun's hidden gold would hardly provide a meaningful path for the future.

Again let us consider the implications of theories put forward to solve the problems of poverty among the blacks. Several years ago the word went forth across the land that black poverty was due to the disintegration of the black family, that the black father no longer had a prominent place in the home.

How incredibly short-sighted that thesis was. How typically Anglo-Saxon! How in the world could there have been a black family if people were sold like cattle for two hundred years, if there were large plantations that served merely as farms to breed more slaves, if white owners systematically ravaged black women? When did the black family unit ever become integrated? During the years of the grandfather clause, when post-Civil War Negroes were denied the vote because their grandfathers hadn't been eligible to vote? Thanks to the programs of the Ku Klux Klan?

Academia, and its by-products, continues to become more irrelevant to the needs of people. The rest of America had better beware of having little quaint mores that will attract anthropologists or it will soon become victim of the conceptual prison into which Indians have been thrown.

What difference does it make?

Several years ago an anthropologist stated that over a period of some twenty years he had spent, from all sources, close to ten million dollars studying a tribe of less than a thousand people! Imagine what that amount of money would have meant to that group of people had it been invested in buildings and businesses. There would have been no problems to study!

Therein lies the trap into which American society has fallen and into which we all unknowingly fall. There is an undefined expectation in American society that once a problem is defined, no matter how, and understood by a significant number of people who have some relation to the problem, there is no problem any more.

Poverty programs are the best contemporary example of this thesis. The poor, according to Harrington, are characterized by their invisibility. Once that thesis was accepted, discussions of poverty made the poor so visible that eventually solutions to poverty replaced the visible poor and the poor faded once again into obscurity. And everyone was outraged to discover that three years of discussion and underfunded programs had not solved the problem of poverty.

In defense of the anthropologist it must be recognized that those who do not publish, perish. That those who do not bring in a substantial sum of research money soon slide down the scale of university approval. What university is not equally balanced between the actual education of its students and a multitude of small bureaus, projects, institutes, and programs which are designed to harvest grants for the university?

The implications of the anthropologist, if not for all America, should be clear for the Indian. Compilation of useless knowledge "for knowledge's sake" should be utterly rejected by the Indian people. We should not be objects of observation for those who do nothing to help us. During the crucial days of 1954, when the Senate was pushing for termination of all Indian rights, not one single scholar, anthropologist, sociologist, historian, or economist came forward to support the tribes against the detrimental policy.

How much had scholars learned about Indians from 1492 to 1954 that would have placed termination in a more rational light? Why didn't the academic community march to the side of the tribes? Certainly the past few years have shown how much influence academia can exert when it feels impelled to enlist in a cause? Is Vietnam any more crucial to the moral stance of America than the great debt owed to the Indian tribes?

Perhaps we should suspect the real motives of the academic community. They have the Indian field well defined and under control. Their concern is not the ultimate policy that will affect the Indian people, but merely the creation of new slogans and doctrines by which they can climb the university totem pole. Reduction of people to ciphers for purposes of observation appears to be inconsequential to the anthropologist when compared with immediate benefits he can derive, the production of further prestige, and the chance to appear as the high priest of American society, orienting and manipulating to his heart's desire.

A couple of years ago Roger Jourdain, chairman of the Red Lake Chippewa tribe of Minnesota, casually had the anthropologists escorted from his reservation. This was the tip of the iceberg breaking through into visibility. If only more Indians had the insight of Jourdain. Why should we continue to be the private zoos for anthropologists? Why should tribes have to compete with scholars for funds when the scholarly productions are so useless and irrelevant to real life?

I would advocate a policy to be adopted by Indian tribes which would soon clarify the respective roles of anthropologists and tribes. Each anthro desiring to study a tribe should be made to apply to the tribal council for permission to do his study. He would be given such permission only if he raised as a contribution to the tribal budget an amount of money equal to the amount he proposed to spend in his study. Anthropologists would thus become productive members of Indian society instead of ideological vultures.

This proposal was discussed at one time in Indian circles. It curled no small number of anthropological hairdos. Irrational shrieks of "academic freedom" rose like rockets from launching pads. The very idea of putting a tax on useless information was intolerable to the anthros we talked with.

But the question is very simple. Are the anthros concerned about "freedom" or "license"? Academic freedom certainly does not imply that one group of people have to become chessmen for another group of people. Why should Indian communities be subjected to prying non-Indians any more than other communities? Should any group have a franchise to stick its nose into someone else's business? No.

Realistically, Indian people will continue to allow their communities to be turned inside out until they come to realize the damage that is being done them. Then they will seal up the reservations until no further knowledge, useless or otherwise, is created. Thus the pendulum will swing radically from one extreme to another, whereas with understanding between the two groups it would not have to swing at all.

Recently, the world of the anthropologist has produced a book the influence of which will be very great. And very detrimental to Indian people. Perhaps when the implications of this book reach the tribes in the form of government programs, they will finally awaken and push the parasitic scholars off the reservations and set up realistic guidelines by which they can control what is written and said about them.

The book is called *Man's Rise to Civilization as Shown by the Indians of North America from Primeval Times to the Coming of the Industrial State*. It exemplifies all the sacred innuendos by which Indians have been hidden from view over the years. The unexamined premises under which the book was written are many and the book will merely serve to reinforce existing stereotypes concerning Indians which have been so detrimental for years.

The explanation of the book, as found on the jacket, indicates sufficiently the assumptions under which the book was written. In the foreword, by Elman R. Service, Professor of Anthropology at Michigan, it is noted that "beginning with the most pitiful and primitive Indians found by explorers, the Digger Indians of Nevada and Utah, Mr. Farb shows that even they are much above the highest non-human primate." Thank you, Mr. Farb, we were pretty worried about that.

The back of the jacket describes Mr. Farb as having been acclaimed by Stewart Udall, former Secretary of the Interior, as "one of the finest conservation spokesmen of our period." This statement will raise the question in Indians' minds of who *read* the book to Stewart Udall.

Being acclaimed as a conservationist by Udall is not exactly gathering laurels either. Udall has allowed Pyramid Lake in Nevada to languish some eight years with a mere pittance of water although it is the finest natural water resource in the state. And although he has repeatedly promised the Pyramid Lake Paiute tribe water for the lake. In many people's minds the best way to eradicate a species is to authorize Udall to conserve it. In his own inimitable style he will accomplish the task posthaste.

Farb's basic assumption is that somehow Indians have risen to civilized heights by being the victims of four centuries of systematic genocide. Under these assumptions the European Jews should be the most civilized people on earth from their graduate course in gas ovens given by Eichmann.

The implications of Farb's book are even more frightening. Indians, people will feel, weren't really as good as we thought, *therefore* we must hurry them on their way to civilization. Indians weren't really conservationists, therefore all this business about them having an attachment to their lands is bunk. Why not, therefore, go ahead with the plan for wholesale mortgage of Indian lands, they aren't using them anyway.

One has only to read Stewart Udall's review of Farb's book to understand the implication of it for future Indian policy. It is a justification for all the irrational policy decisions which Udall had wished he had been able to make but which Indian people brought to a halt. Many Indians still remember Udall's frantic ramblings at Santa Fe in 1966 when he questioned and answered himself on why Indians had not made progress like his friends in Arizona. His answer: because they didn't have the management tools that IBM, General Motors, and Bell Telephone had.

The eventual solution, as proposed by the Department of the Interior, was the creation of a bill under which land could be mortgaged for development, with bureaucrats "giving" technical advice and sharing none of the responsibility for failure, should it occur. The Udall Omnibus Bill was basically to continue "man's rise to civilization" by systematic confiscation of existing capital owned by those-to-be-civilized, through the device of ill-advised mortgages.

Farb continues to use phrases such as "test tubes" and "living laboratories" in describing the development, or rather unfolding, of Indian cultural change. In essence, then, Indian communities exist primarily for people to experiment with. Bureaucratically this means "pilot projects." Anthropologically, as we have seen, it means the continued treatment of Indian people as objects for observation.

One classic statement—"Modern American society has little place for institutionalized rites of rebellion, because it is a democratic society; it is characteristic of a democratic society always to question and challenge, never to be certain of itself"—blithely dismisses social reality.

American society has, in fact, institutionalized rebellion by making it popular. Once popularized, rebellions become fads and are so universalized that *not* to be rebellious is to be square, out of it, irrelevant. Television ads make a big noise about the great rebellions going on in the auto industry. Deodorants and soaps are always new, a radical departure from the old. Cigarette smokers are cautioned to break away from the crowd. Unless a man is rebelling, he is not really a man. And to achieve relevance in American society a person must always be the pioneer, the innovator, against the establishment.

The import of institutionalizing rebellion is that when real rebellion occurs society climbs the walls in its fright. I keenly remember our confrontation with Department of the Interior officials at Santa Fe, when several advised us to go home or we would be "terminated." A democratic society is always up tight about real rebellions because its very operating premise is that rebellions are nice. When rebellions turn out to be not so nice, panic prevails.

Democratic society is always absolutely sure of itself. It could not be otherwise, for to be unsure would call into question the very basis of the political institutions which gave it existence. Even more horrifying would be an examination of the economic realities underlying the society.

With institutionalized rebellion a way of life, one of the major differences between white and Indians emerges—ingratitude. Whites always expect Indians to be grateful according to the whites' ideas of gratitude. Or else they expect ingratitude to be expressed in institutionalized behavior, as other members of society have been taught to do. When Indians do not respond in accustomed ways, because the way is irrelevant to Indian modes of expression, Indian response is attributed to the innate savagery of the Indian.

Sometimes Farb's anthropological references to the Plains Indians are irrelevant and ridden with historical mythologies in several respects. The Mandans, for example, are found to be extinct—which they will be happy to know about. Plains Indians in general are declared to be as make-believe as a movie set— which will make them welcome Farb warmly when he next appears in the plains.

Most unforgivable is the statement that Sitting Bull was accidentally killed. For if Sitting Bull was accidentally killed, then President Kennedy's death was merely the result of Oswald carelessly cleaning his rifle. The two deaths had the same motivation—political assassination.

Man's Rise to Civilization may have redeeming anthropological features; it certainly has sufficient footnotes to make it PURE rather than APPLIED research. The question for Indian people, and the ultimate question for Americans, is: What effect will it have over the lives of people?

There should be little doubt that this book tends to reinforce the anti-Indian school of thought and to sidestep the entire issue of Indian society, culture, or what have you. Unless there is a frank understanding between the two people, red and white, so that the relationship between them is honest, sincere, and equal, talk about culture will not really matter. The white man will continue to take Indian land because he will feel that he is HELPING to bring civilization to the poor savages.

Thus has it ever been with anthropologists. In believing they could find the key to man's behavior, they have, like the churches, become forerunners of destruction. Like the missionaries, anthropologists have become intolerably certain that they represent ultimate truth.

The rest of America had better wake up before their entire lives are secretly manipulated by the musings of this breed. For the time is coming when middle class America will become credit-card-carrying, turnpike-commuting, condominium-dwelling, fraternity-joining, churchgoing, sports-watching, time-purchase-buying, television-watching, magazine-subscribing, politically inert transmigrated urbanites who, through the phenomenon of the second car and the shopping center have become golf-playing, wife-swapping, etc., etc., etc., suburbanites. Or has that day dawned? If so, you will understand what has been happening to Indian communities for a long, long time.

I would expect an instantaneous rebuttal by the "knowledgeable" anthros that these sentiments do not "represent" all the Indians. They don't TODAY. They will TOMORROW. In the meantime it would be wise for anthropologists to get down from their thrones of authority and PURE research and begin helping Indian tribes instead of preying on them. For the wheel of Karma grinds slowly but it does grind finely. And it makes a complete circle.

Piltdown Man

Kenneth P. Oakley and J. S. Weiner

The remarkable story of Piltdown Man began 43 years ago when Charles Dawson, country solicitor and amateur archaeologist and geologist brought to the Natural History Museum in London and handed to Smith Woodward, Keeper of Geology, a number of specimens. These included fragments of thick human skull bones, chocolate brown in colour, some fossilized hippopotamus and early elephant teeth and some crude flint tools. They had been found, he said, as a result of workmen digging gravel for paths at Barkham Manor, Piltdown, not far from Uckfield in Sussex. The gravel was an ancient river deposit, reputed to be 80 feet above the present river level, where in fact remains dating from near the beginning of the Ice Age were to be expected according to local geological opinion at that time. Woodward agreed to join Dawson in carrying out excavations at the site at the end of May and during June 1912. As a result more specimens were found including a fragment of ape-like jawbone with two teeth, still more bits of skull, several fossil animal teeth and bones, several flint tools—and later on a remarkable bone implement. Scrappy though the remains were they presented a remarkably complete picture of a fossil man, his tools, contemporary animals, in gravel dating possibly from early in the Ice Age or even just before.

But there were difficulties. Trouble arose at the first scientific meeting at which Dawson's discovery was described—a meeting of the Geological Society of London in December 1912. The dispute was about Woodward's conclusion that the cranial bones and jaw both belonged to a single individual—whom he called *Eoanthropus, The Dawn Man*—a strange mixture of man and ape. Woodward gave many good reasons why he thought that the jaw must belong to the brain-case even though, as he pointed out, it was very like an ape's, while the brain-case was certainly very human. Despite this extraordinary combination we must agree about the logic of his conclusion based on the evidence available to him. His belief that a new fossil ancestor of man had indeed been found was bold and courageous and at the time scientifically justifiable.

Woodward's argument ran as follows. All the remains in the gravel were found very close together—within a yard or so of each other. The lower jaw and the brain-case were very similar in appearance. They were both of a similar brown color, and also apparently in the same state of fossilization. The jaw, even though ape-like, did have some important human features—particularly in the teeth. The molar teeth had apparently been worn to a flatness never seen in apes, and only to be expected if the jaw had belonged to a type of human being. The roots of the teeth (as seen in the X-ray pictures of the time) were also much more like those of human teeth. And finally, the appearances of this apelike man at the beginning of the Ice Age was just what many authorities had expected to find.

In July 1913 a new specimen was found, a canine tooth, ape-like, but worn in a way never found in modern apes. This was strong support for Woodward's interpretation.

For all that, controversy continued to rage as to whether it was really correct to link the jaw and the brain-case. Woodward's opponents—first Professor David Waterston of King's College, London, and next Dr. Gerrit Miller in America and Prof. Boule in France—were not convinced. They could not see how anatomically the jaw could have worked as part of a human skull when it was constructed in so very different a way. But the opposition case was a good deal weaker than Woodward's. They could not explain the extraordinary wear of the teeth. The opponents also had to explain the amazing coincidence of finding, in one place close together, a brain-case without a jaw, and a jaw without a brain-case, all apparently in the same state of preservation. But they decided it was a coincidence, astonishing though it seemed. They maintained that there were two different fossils there, a fossil man, and a fossil ape, both of an extreme antiquity.

But this view was dealt a severe blow when the remains of a second Piltdown Man were reported in 1915 as coming from a place about two miles away from the first site. Here again there were pieces of thick brain-case like those found at the original site, and with them a molar tooth, again similar to those in the jaw of the first Piltdown Man. From now on Woodward's ideas held the field and most scientists agreed with him. In those days the climate of scientific opinion was extremely favorable to the view that the human ancestor would show such a combination of features of ape and man. It seemed quite feasible, therefore, that a human ancestor should have pronounced chimpanzee characters such as large projecting eye-teeth. Darwin had even sketched such a type hypothetically. And what made it all the more acceptable was that there was nothing to contradict it in the few other human fossils known at the time. Piltdown Man fitted in rather well as a more primitive being than either Java Man or Heidelberg Man.

But he began to fit in less and less well as a lot more human fossils were found in Java and China and South Africa. They all differed from Piltdown Man in their skull characters. Their brain-cases were far more ape-like than his, and their jaws decidedly less so. They formed a fairly consistent line of evolution if Piltdown Man was left out. Still, as long as the apparent extreme age of Piltdown Man remained unquestioned this situation could be accepted. Why should there not be two lines of human evolution one arising from Piltdown and the other from a different ancestral type.

We can sum up this stage of the prolonged controversy, by saying that if the Piltdown remains were old enough they could be accepted—odd and isolated though Piltdown Man seemed to be. But that situation was not to remain undisturbed for much longer. In 1949 the application of a chemical method of dating fossils threw the whole thing into the melting pot again. By this time we had developed the fluorine dating method. This is based on the fact that buried bones adsorb fluorine from the soil and the amount increases with time. When a number of bones are found at the same site their fluorine content can be used to tell us which is the older.

When we applied this test to the Piltdown remains we found to our great surprise neither the jaw bone nor the brain-case contained more than small traces of fluorine, while the early fossils from the gravel such as the extinct elephant's teeth contained a great deal. This meant that Piltdown Man did not date from before the Ice Age. Both jaw and skull appeared to be comparatively recent as fossils, not older than the latter part of the Ice Age.

Our drastic reduction in the age of the Piltdown skull from 500,000 years old to possibly *not more than* 50,000, made it an evolutionary absurdity. It meant in other words that here in late times was a creature for whom there were no known ancestors and no known descendants. Being so recent he could no longer be claimed as an ancestor of *Homo sapiens* who was already in existence in the latter part of the Ice Age. Piltdown Man was therefore a grotesque and quite irrelevant dead end.

Those who believed that the remains were made up of two separate fossils, an ape and a man, did not gain much either from this change of dating. The idea of a fossil ape in England in the second half of the Ice Age seemed highly unlikely considering the entire absence of such remains from the whole of Europe over the last million years; and in any case Woodward's arguments for linking jaw and brain-case still held.

As things stood till July 1953 it all made nonsense. The idea of a Piltdown Man at the end of the Ice Age was extremely difficult to understand, but the idea of a fossil ape of that age in England was equally impossible to accept. Yet these appeared to be the only possible natural explanations.

When we came to reconsider the matter, purely from the anatomical point of view, we were struck by the fact that after all was said and done, the only really strong evidence to link the jaw and brain-case was the peculiar wear of the molars and eye-tooth.

If the wear could not be accounted for by any *natural* explanation, how else? And if the close association of jaw and brain-case could not be accounted for naturally how else could it be? One possibility that could explain nearly all the contradictions was to suppose that a broken bit of modern ape jaw had been deliberately placed with the more ancient brain-case, and that to disguise its modern character and link it with the human brain-case, the bone had been suitably stained, and the teeth deliberately ground down. If this were so we would have a fairly complete explanation of all the circumstances of the find, the suggestion would fit in with the new evidence that it was not of great antiquity, and it would also explain the impossibility of making evolutionary sense out of Piltdown Man.

This idea could clearly be tested by looking again at the anatomy of the original specimens, and also by improving and extending the chemical methods of dating. This was done.

We started from the fact that if the jaw-bone were modern it should have contained less fluorine than the brain-case. The first analysis in 1949 failed to show any significant difference. The amounts we were dealing with were too small to be measured except approximately. But the analysis was accurate enough to prove that neither the brain-case nor the jaw-bone was of the great antiquity previously claimed, though it was not sufficiently accurate to distinguish between a very late fossil and a recent specimen. So, in the autumn of 1953 we drilled into the bones more boldly. And the new and larger samples were analysed in the Government Chemist's Department using a more refined technique. The fluorine in the brain-case turned out to be just high enough to suggest that it was ancient, but the jawbones and teeth were found to contain no more fluorine than modern bones and teeth.

That being so, their organic or protein content should have been high. We obtained a direct indication of this in the course of re-drilling the jawbone. There was a distinct smell of burning as the rapidly rotating burr penetrated deeply. Moreover, the ejected drillings consisted of minute shavings, indicating that the mineral matter in the jawbone was held together by an organic matrix. When we drilled the cranial bones in the same way, there was no smell, and the ejected material consisted of powder, showing that the organic matrix had largely gone.

By chemical analysis we confirmed that the jawbone and teeth contained the same amount of nitrogen and organic carbon as modern specimens. The brain-case on the other hand contained much less. Used as a cross-check to the fluorine test this evidence was conclusive. But we did not let the matter rest there. We confirmed that the jawbone and teeth are really modern by several other methods. We had to make quite sure that the organic matter was not gelatine or glue with which the specimen had been impregnated as a means of hardening it.

The electron-microscope revealed perfectly preserved fibres of organic tissue in a decalcified sample of the jawbone. In contrast to this in the brain-case all trace of such fibres has disappeared. So the jawbone is without doubt modern. And we have also been able to show that it had been colored artificially with iron to match the brain-case bones.

Thus studies of its composition left no doubt that the Piltdown jaw was a bogus fossil, and this conclusion was supported by independent investigation of the anatomical aspects. This side of the work was largely carried out by Professor (now Sir Wilfrid) Le Gros Clark.

What we call the Piltdown *jaw* is only a broken fragment. It consists of the greater part of the right side of a jaw, with two of the grinding teeth in position. The front part is broken off, and also the joint surface by which it hinges with the rest of the skull.

Nearly all anatomists have been agreed for some time that there were really only two features that distinguished it from the jaw of a modern large ape— such as an orang or chimpanzee. These two features are the curious flat wear of the teeth and the apparent shortness of the roots as seen in the X-ray of the jaw taken in 1913. In apes, the roots of the molar teeth are much longer.

We have had new and better X-ray pictures taken and they show that the roots are really much longer than was thought. In fact they are just like the roots of modern apes' teeth.

The other feature, the flatness of the wear, was very puzzling, because, while in human jaws the molar teeth commonly wear down to a flat surface quite early, this is never the case with apes' molars at a corresponding stage of wear.

That is what suggested that the flatness in the Piltdown molars might have been produced artificially, in order, presumably, to imitate the human type of wear.

It immediately led us to carry out experimental filing of modern apes' teeth and to make a most minute study of the Piltdown teeth. A critical and close examination with the microscope at once showed up a number of very curious features that seem to have escaped attention so far. For one thing, the flatness of the biting surface of the molars is astonishingly even all over—as though they had indeed been flattened down by filing or grinding, and the margins of the flat surface are most unusually sharp, instead of being bevelled as you would expect in naturally worn teeth. When, in the course of natural wear, the enamel of a tooth first becomes worn off, the dentine (being less hard) is more rapidly worn away and produces hollows, below the level of the surrounding enamel. But in the Piltdown molars the exposed dentine is actually quite flat and flush the surrounding enamel.

The Piltdown molars show another curious feature. Normally in the lower molar teeth the outer side is worn away quicker than the inner side because it is overlapped by the upper teeth and so gets more worn with chewing. But in the Piltdown molars much more of the enamel has been worn away on the *inner side*—that is, the *wrong way round!* Sir Wilfrid Le Gros Clark has said that in the large number of teeth in human and ape jaws, recent and fossil, that he has examined, he has never come across an example in which the inner side of the tooth is so much more worn down than the outer side. But, when an ape's molar is ground down artificially this is just the appearance you do get.

A close examination with the microscope shows a series of criss-cross scratches on the biting surface of the teeth—further evidence of the use of an abrasive of some sort.

The canine or eye-tooth that was found separately from the jaw is modern too, judged by the very small amount of fluorine, and the large amount of nitrogen, it contains. It has a dark coating which has been examined by authorities at the National Gallery. They reported that it is an oil paint—probably Vandyke brown.

There has always been rather a mystery about this eye-tooth. An X-ray picture shows that it is a young tooth—probably one that has only just come through at the time of its owner's death. But it is so severely worn that the whole of the enamel on the inner side of the tooth has been *entirely* worn away. And, more than that, it has been worn away in a peculiar manner never seen in either man or ape.

This contradiction is explained at once if the crown of the tooth has been ground down deliberately. A new X-ray has shown that so much of the top of the tooth has been ground away that at one point there is a small hole into the pulp cavity and this hole has been plugged with some kind of plastic material. This entirely unnatural state of affairs was not shown up in the early X-rays—because unfortunately they were not taken at just the right angle.

This independent anatomical evidence makes it quite certain that the teeth are modern ape's teeth that have been skilfully and deliberately disguised. With Sir Wilfrid Le Gros Clark's assistance we have tried to decide whether the jaw and the teeth are those of a chimpanzee or an orang-utan.

Some anatomists have wondered whether it really is possible to produce all the appearances of the Piltdown molars by filing down the teeth of any modern ape. But we found that you can do it quite easily provided you use the teeth of an orang-utan. The resemblance between our experiments and the Piltdown teeth is really rather startling, because it is possible to produce just the same shape of tooth, and the same appearance of the exposed patches of dentine on the biting surface. And in X-ray photographs also they look almost identical.

We have in fact reproduced the whole jaw, and the eye-tooth, and we are reasonably sure that the Piltdown specimen is actually that of an orang-utan—probably a female not yet fully grown.

It seems clear then that the Dawn Man of Piltdown has been effectively disposed of, and that for forty years a female ape's jaw has masqueraded as one of our ancestors. The remains were originally supposed to date from just before the Ice Age and the skull was accompanied by tools and fossil animals which supported this idea. We have considered the question of their authenticity very thoroughly.

The flint implements are rough flakes that might be of any age. They are of a reddish color, matching that of the gravel, but they have been artificially stained, in one case with chromium as well as iron. We know this from Dr. E. T. Hall's spectrographic analysis in the Clarendon Laboratory, Oxford, as well as through chemical tests carried out in the Mineral Laboratory of the Natural History Museum. When we chipped the implement to get a sample for chemical analysis we found that below the stain there was a white crust—just like the flints you get on the chalk downs—whereas the local gravel flints are brown throughout.

Even more striking as a forgery is the famous bone implement. It is a large slab of fossil elephant thighbone supposed to have been pointed at one end by its prehistoric owner. But if you try to whittle down a piece of bone when it is fresh, even with a good steel knife, you find it is very difficult—with a flint tool it would be impossible. Even in 1914 some were doubtful about this specimen; and the French archaeologist, Abbé Breuil, realizing the impossibility of its having been shaped with a flint knife, later suggested that the bone had been gnawed by a giant beaver.

A more detailed examination of the cuts has made it obvious that they were produced by a modern steel knife. The fluorine test has established that the bone *is* a fossilised bone, and we have shown that you can sharpen a fossilised bone of this kind with a knife, just as you can shape a lump of chalk. Clearly the Piltdown bone implement must have been made in this way.

So much for the tools. The animal remains from Piltdown have been famous because they include the remains of a rare type of elephant, of mastodon and of a rare type of rhinoceros, known to have become extinct in Britain early in the Ice Age. The great interest in them lay in the fact that such fossils have never been found anywhere else in Southern England. And little wonder, because we now believe that all these animal fossils were planted in the Piltdown gravel, in order to suggest that the skull was that of a man living before the Ice Age.

Proof that the elephant teeth are of foreign origin is supplied by a new method of relative dating. Dr. C. F. Davidson and Mr. S. H. U. Bowie of the Geological Survey of Great Britain have been studying uranium in fossils. Uranium, like fluorine, accumulates in buried bones and teeth, but at rates varying from place to place. The uranium content of a fossil can be estimated by measuring its radioactivity. Some of the Piltdown fossils have the same radioactivity as those genuinely found in deposits dating from before the Ice Age in East Anglia, but the three bits of Piltdown elephant teeth are more than ten times as radioactive. Indeed, they are more radioactive than fossils from anywhere of the same period that have been tested, with the only exception of some from Tunisia. So we must infer that these pieces actually came from a collection of foreign fossils. Their red-brown colour suggested to us that they had been artificially stained, and indeed we found traces of chromium on them as well as iron.

The dark brown hippopotamus molar tooth from Piltdown was formerly supposed to be of the same age as the elephant teeth, but unlike them it contains very little fluorine. On the other hand it has lost almost all trace of organic matter which indicates that it is certainly ancient. Cream-white hippopotamus teeth from caves in Mediterranean islands have just this composition. The Piltdown specimen only differs from them in its dark color. On testing it we found that it too contains the tell-tale chromium.

For a long time we believed that the human skull bones had been genuinely found in the Piltdown gravel, but eventually we found evidence that they too were fraudulently introduced into the Piltdown gravel.

Their fluorine content is just enough to show that they are ancient specimens, perhaps even prehistoric—but we now have proof that their dark brown color is entirely artificial. Dr. G. F. Claringbull, Keeper of Minerals in the Natural History Museum, made an X-ray analysis of the mineral structure of the Piltdown bones for us. This revealed that the phosphate mineral in the human brain-case has been partly changed to gypsum (calcium sulphate). But gypsum is not found in the Piltdown gravel. Moreover, experiments by Dr. M. H. Hey in The Mineral Laboratory of the Museum have shown that if you stain a partially fossilised bone with an acid iron sulphate solution the bone is partly changed to gypsum. We have no doubt that the Piltdown skull was stained in this way to match the gravel in which it was to be planted. The unusual thickness of the bones suggests that the skull used as a basis of this hoax was a pathological specimen obtained presumably from an ancient grave (but where, who knows?).

The "second Piltdown skull" was apparently made up by placing an artificially abraded molar tooth of an orang-utan with a piece of exceptionally thick forehead (frontal) bone, evidently part of the first skull that had been held in reserve and a scrap of the back of another skull stained in the same way. This last occipital fragment was not unusually thick, but then it was chosen to duplicate the *thinnest* part of the first skull.

We think that the chromium detected in the jaw-bone, in some of the skull-bones, in many of the fossil animal bones and teeth, and on one of the flints, indicates that a dichromate solution was at first used by the forger in an attempt to assist the oxidation of the iron salts used to stain these specimens.

After we had presented these results to the Geological Society of London in June 1954, Sir Gavin de Beer, Director of the British Museum (Natural History) concluded a broadcast with these words:

"We have laid the ghost of Piltdown Man, who, as it happens, never fitted very happily into any scheme of man's evolution. Indeed we have gained, because half a dozen new experimental methods of studying fossils have now been developed which will not only make any repetition of such a hoax impossible in future but will materially assist the scientific study of fossils."

11 / Patterns of Communication

Introduction

The fundamental basis upon which the distinctive and unique fabric of human culture is built consists of language and patterns of communication. Without the development of communication patterns it would be impossible to develop and transmit to successive generations culture patterns that distinguish human from nonhuman behavior.

Of all of the various fields of Anthropology, Linguistics is generally considered to be the most advanced in terms of methods and findings. Indeed, some would claim that Linguistics, in introducing the concept of the "phoneme," has isolated a basic structural building block analogous in importance and implication to the discovery of the atom as a building block by the physicist. Most linguists in their study of language would agree that the two fundamental concepts that provide the foundation for most frequent studies are the phoneme and the morpheme.

A phoneme is the briefest *significant* sound unit within a given language. The method by which phonemes are abstracted from a language is illustrated by Hockett later in the chapter. The point to be emphasized here is that in every human language studied, it has been possible for linguists to reduce the seemingly-infinite "blooming and buzzing" of speech sounds to a description in terms of a few dozen elemental phonemes, plus a series of orderly, predictable variations on each.

This, in itself, had a great effect on the morale of those who study other aspects of cultural behavior, for it suggested that the bewildering variety of beliefs and behaviors that flood in upon the cross-cultural observer might, likewise, be able to be described in an economical, orderly way rather than impressionistically. (Impressionistic descriptions are notoriously subjective and cannot be compared cross-culturally with any degree of precision.) There is still much to be done, of course, but the consistent adoption of a linguistic perspective and the tailoring of linguistic methods to other kinds of research has already paid off on many occasions.

Of course, linguists also study many aspects of language beyond the sounds of speech and, in these cases too, their findings provide both direct aid and indirect stimulation for non-linguists. Frequently, an anthropologist preparing for fieldwork is able to draw upon the literature of Linguistics to learn the language of the group to be studied. Previous linguistic studies of the area may also have turned up unsuspected historical affinities between the people of the area and people some distance away, thereby pointing the anthropologist to the possible source of traits and institutions that seem anomalous in the setting where he observes them. That is, they may have been "brought" by migrants from the distant group. The variety of studies that linguists pursue and their direct bearing upon the understanding of other cultural behavior is well-illustrated in the articles in this chapter.

In his article on Communication, Sapir introduces the novel idea that every social "thing," including social institutions, should be viewed not as a static entity but, rather as a sum total of communicative acts among the members of that society. The sample analysis which he offers at the outset of the essay shows the full significance of this viewpoint.

Sapir compares communication in a primitive social setting with communication in a modern Western society. His conclusion is one generally accepted among anthropologists: namely, that the primary processes of communication (language, gesture, etc.) are of a comparable order of complexity in all societies: while the difference comes in the elaboration of media for transmitting messages farther and faster. In the body of the article he also touches on special aspects of Linguistics that have come to be known as "Sociolinguistics" and "Paralinguistics"—topics which are represented in the later article by Jaquith.

When Whorf first published his essay on "The Relation of Habitual Thought and Behavior to Language," it created a sensation—and a certain sense of despair—among anthropologists. Many felt that Whorf had proved that the speakers of a particular language were so totally imprisoned by the worldview encapsulated in their language-and-thought that it was futile even to try to "cross over" from one tradition to another; the anthropological enterprise of discovering how the world looked to a member of a non-Western community seemed illusory.

This was largely a misunderstanding of Whorf's hypothesis (also known as the Sapir-Whorf hypothesis). Whorf himself was careful to emphasize, starting with the title of the essay, that he was talking about *habitual* thought and behavior—"thoughtless" thought, so to speak. He did not mean to deny that a person could, by *critical* attention, begin to see the (habitual) main themes and patterns in another tradition, for this is precisely what he claimed to have done in the case of the Hopi.

For a description and illustration of linguistic methods "without tears," it would be difficult to beat Hockett's article, "How to Learn Martian." In this whimsical scenario, Hockett shows how a linguist boils a stream of speech sounds down to a limited number of elemental units, the phonemes. And mid-way through the article, he pauses to summarize what linguists have discovered about the role of phonemes and other such signals in human communication.

In "Tabooed Words in Comic Strips" Jaquith illustrates in a humorous setting the way that language use becomes tailored to specific social situations. When speaking before a large audience we use a vocabulary and style that would be entirely inappropriate for an intimate chat with a lover, and vice versa. The study of this phenomenon constitutes Sociolinguistics.

"Paralinguistic" behavior; that is, patterned behavior which accompanies speech and may either reinforce the verbal message (e.g., raising the eyebrows while saying "What a surprise!") or else belie it is also presented by Sapir, who gives a very sensitive explanation of how a variety of non-verbal factors affect overall communication. For example, the same words associated with different gestures might have quite different meanings. We can all think of examples of parents speaking to their children while winking to another adult to signal that he does not mean what he is saying to the child. Like Sociolinguistics,

Paralinguistics adds a new dimension to the study of the overall meaning of language and provides new examples of how thoroughly-patterned our behavior, is, even in minor, often unconscious ways.

Communication [1]

Edward Sapir

It is obvious that for the building up of society, its units and subdivisions, and the understandings which prevail between its members some processes of communication are needed. While we often speak of society as though it were a static structure defined by tradition, it is, in the more intimate sense, nothing of the kind, but a highly intricate network of partial or complete understandings between the members of organizational units of every degree of size and complexity, ranging from a pair of lovers or a family to a league of nations or that ever increasing portion of humanity which can be reached by the press through all its transnational ramifications. It is only apparently a static sum of social institutions; actually it is being reanimated or creatively reaffirmed from day to day by particular acts of a communicative nature which obtain among individuals participating in it. Thus the Republican party cannot be said to exist as such, but only to the extent that its tradition is being constantly added to and upheld by such simple acts of communication as that John Doe votes the Republican ticket, thereby communicating a certain kind of message, or that a half-dozen individuals meet at a certain time and place, formally or informally, in order to communicate ideas to each other and eventually to decide what points of national interest, real or supposed, are to be allowed to come up many months later for discussion in a gathering of members of the party. The Republican party as a historic entity is merely abstracted from thousands upon thousands of such single acts of communication, which have in common certain persistent features of reference. If we extend this example into every conceivable field in which communication has a place, we soon realize that every cultural pattern and every single act of social behavior involve communication in either an explicit or an implicit sense.

One may conveniently distinguish between certain fundamental techniques, or primary processes, which are communicative in character, and certain secondary techniques which facilitate the process of communication. The distinction is perhaps of no great psychological importance but has a very real historical and sociological significance, inasmuch as the fundamental processes are common to all mankind, while the secondary techniques emerge only at relatively sophisticated levels of civilization. Among the primary communicative processes of society may be mentioned: language; gesture, in its widest sense; the imitation of overt behavior; and a large and ill-defined group of implicit processes which grow out of overt behavior and which may be rather vaguely referred to as "social suggestion."

Language is the most explicit type of communicative behavior that we know of. It need not here be defined beyond pointing out that it consists in every case known to us of an absolutely complete referential apparatus of phonetic symbols which have the property of locating every known social referent, in-

[1] *Encyclopaedia of the Social Sciences*, (New York: Macmillan, 1931), 4:78–81.

cluding all the recognized data of perception which the society that it serves carries in its tradition. Language is the communicative process par excellence in every known society, and it is exceedingly important to observe that whatever may be the shortcomings of a primitive society judged from the vantage point of civilization, its language inevitably forms as sure, complete, and potentially creative an apparatus of referential symbolism as the most sophisticated language that we know of. What this means for a theory of communication is that the mechanics of significant understanding between human beings are as sure and complex and rich in overtones in one society as in another, primitive or sophisticated.

Gesture includes much more than the manipulation of the hands and other visible and movable parts of the organism. Intonations of the voice may register attitudes and feelings quite as significantly as the clenched first, the wave of the hand, the shrugging of the shoulders, or the lifting of the eyebrows. The field of gesture interplays constantly with that of language proper, but there are many facts of a psychological and historical order which show that there are subtle yet firm lines of demarcation between them. Thus, to give but one example, the consistent message delivered by language symbolism in the narrow sense, whether by speech or by writing, may flatly contradict the message communicated by the synchronous system of gestures, consisting of movements of the hands and head, intonations of the voice, and breathing symbolisms. The former system may be entirely conscious, the latter entirely unconscious. Linguistic, as opposed to gesture, communication tends to be the official and socially accredited one; hence one may intuitively interpret the relatively unconscious symbolisms of gesture as psychologically more significant in a given context than the words actually used. In such cases as these we have a conflict between explicit and implicit communications in the growth of the individual's social experience.

The primary condition for the consolidation of society is the imitation of overt behavior. Such imitation, while not communicative in intent, has always the retroactive value of a communication, for in the process of falling in with the ways of society one in effect acquiesces in the meanings that inhere in these ways. When one learns to go to church, for instance, because other members of the community set the pace for this kind of activity, it is as though a communication had been received and acted upon. It is the function of language to articulate and rationalize the full content of these informal communications in the growth of the individual's social experience.

Even less directly communicative in character than overt behavior and its imitation is "social suggestion" as the sum total of new acts and new meanings that are implicitly made possible by these types of social behavior. Thus, the particular method of revolting against the habit of church going in a given society, while contradictory, on the surface, of the conventional meanings of that society, may nevertheless receive all its social significance from hundreds of existing prior communications that belong to the culture of the group as a whole. The importance of the unformulated and unverbalized communications of society is so great that one who is not intuitively familiar with them is likely to be baffled by the significance of certain kinds of behavior, even if he is thoroughly aware of their external forms and of the verbal symbols that accompany them. It is largely the function of the artist to make articulate these more subtle intentions of society.

Communicative processes do not merely apply to society as such; they are indefinitely varied as to form and meaning for the various types of personal relationship into which society resolves itself. Thus a fixed type of conduct or a linguistic symbol has by no means necessarily the same communicative significance within the confines of the family, among the members of an economic group, and in the nation at large. Generally speaking, the smaller the circle and the more complex the understandings already arrived at within it, the more economical can the act of communication afford to become. A single word passed between members of an intimate group, in spite of its apparent vagueness and ambiguity, may constitute a far more precise communication than volumes of carefully prepared correspondence interchanged between two governments.

There seem to be three main classes of techniques which have for their object the facilitation of the primary communicative processes of society. These may be referred to as: language transfers; symbolisms arising from special technical situations; and the creation of physical conditions favorable for the communicative act. Of language transfers the best known example is writing. The Morse telegraph code is another example. These and many other communicative techniques have this in common, that while they are overtly not at all like each other, their organization is based on the primary symbolic organization which has arisen in the domain of speech. Psychologically, therefore, they extend the communicative character of speech to situations in which for one reason or another speech is not possible.

In the more special class of communicative symbolism one cannot make a word-to-word translation, as it were, back to speech but can only paraphrase in speech the intent of the communication. Here belong such symbolic systems as wigwagging, the use of railroad lights, bugle calls in the army, and smoke signals. It is interesting to observe that, while they are late in developing in the history of society, they are very much less complex in structure than language itself. They are of value partly in helping out a situation where neither language nor some form of language transfer can be applied, partly where it is desired to encourage the automatic nature of the desired response. Thus, because language is extraordinarily rich in meaning, it sometimes becomes a little annoying or even dangerous to rely upon it where only a simple this or that, or yes or no, is expected to be the response.

The importance of extending the physical conditions allowing for communication is obvious. The railroad, the telegraph, the telephone, the radio, and the airplane are among the best examples. It is to be noted that such instruments as the railroad and the radio are not communicative in character as such; they become so only because they facilitate the presentation of types of stimuli which act as symbols of communication or which contain implications of communicative significance. Thus, a telephone is of no use unless the party at the other end understands the language of the person calling up. Again, the fact that a railroad runs me to a certain point is of no real communicative importance unless there are fixed bonds of interest which connect me with the inhabitants of the place. The failure to bear in mind these obvious points has tended to make some writers exaggerate the importance of the spread in modern times of such inventions as the railroad and the telephone.

The history of civilization has been marked by a progressive increase in the radius of communication. In a typically primitive society communication is reserved for the members of the tribe and, at best, a small number of surrounding tribes with whom relations are intermittent rather than continuous and who act as a kind of buffer between the significant psychological world—the world of one's own tribal culture—and the great unknown or unreal that lies beyond. Today, in our own civilization, the appearance of a new fashion in Paris is linked by a series of rapid and necessary events with the appearance of the same fashion in such distant places as Berlin, London, New York, San Francisco, and Yokohama. The underlying reason for this remarkable change in the radius and rapidity of communication is the gradual diffusion of cultural traits, in other words, of meaningful cultural reactions. Among the various types of cultural diffusion that of language itself is of paramount importance. Secondary technical devices making for ease of communication are also, of course, of prime importance.

The multiplication of far-reaching techniques of communication has two important results. In the first place, it increases the sheer radius of communication, so that for certain purposes the whole civilized world is made the psychological equivalent of a primitive tribe. In the second place, it lessens the importance of mere geographical contiguity. Owing to the technical nature of these sophisticated communicative devices, parts of the world that are geographically remote may, in terms of behavior, be actually much closer to each other than adjoining regions, which, from the historical standpoint, are supposed to share a larger body of common understandings. This means, of course, a tendency to remap the world both sociologically and psychologically. Even now it is possible to say that the scattered "scientific world" is a social unity which has no clearcut geographical location. Further, the world of urban understanding in America contrasts rather sharply with the rural world. The weakening of the geographical factor in social organization must in the long run profoundly modify our attitude toward the meaning of personal relations and of social classes and even of nationalities.

The increasing ease of communication is purchased at a price, for it is becoming increasingly difficult to keep an intended communication within the desired bounds. A humble example of this new problem is the inadvisability of making certain kinds of statement on the telephone. Another example is the insidious cheapening of literary and artistic values due to the foreseen and economically advantageous "widening of the appeal." All effects which demand a certain intimacy of understanding tend to become difficult and are therefore avoided. It is a question whether the obvious increase of overt communication is not constantly being corrected, as it were, by the creation of new obstacles to communication. The fear of being too easily understood may, in many cases, be more aptly defined as the fear of being understood by too many—so many, indeed, as to endanger the psychological reality of the image of the enlarged self confronting the not-self.

On the whole, however, it is rather the obstacles to communication that are felt as annoying or ominous. The most important of these obstacles in the modern world is undoubtedly the great diversity of languages. The enormous amount of energy put into the task of translation implies a passionate desire to make as light of the language difficulty as possible. In the long run it seems almost unavoidable that the civilized world will adopt some one language of intercommunication, say English or Esperanto, which can be set aside for denotive purposes pure and simple.

The Relation of Habitual
Thought and Behavior to Language
Benjamin L. Whorf

Human beings do not live in the objective world alone, nor alone in the world of social activity as ordinarily understood, but are very much at the mercy of the particular language which has become the medium of expression for their society. It is quite an illusion to imagine that one adjusts to reality essentially without the use of language and that language is merely an incidental means of solving specific problems of communication or reflection. The fact of the matter is that the "real world" is to a large extent unconsciously built up on the language habits of the group. . . . We see and hear and otherwise experience very largely as we do because the language habits of our community predispose certain choices of interpretation.[1]

—*Edward Sapir*

There will probably be general assent to the proposition that an accepted pattern of using words is often prior to certain lines of thinking and forms of behavior, but he who assents often sees in such a statement nothing more than a platitudinous recognition of the hypnotic power of philosophical and learned terminology on the one hand or of catchwords, slogans, and rallying cries on the other. To see only thus far is to miss the point of one of the important interconnections which Sapir saw between language, culture, and psychology, and succinctly expressed in the introductory quotation. It is not so much in these special uses of language as in its constant ways of arranging data and its most ordinary everyday analysis of phenomena that we need to recognize the influence it has on other activities, cultural and personal.

THE NAME OF THE SITUATION AS AFFECTING BEHAVIOR

I came in touch with an aspect of this problem before I had studied under Dr. Sapir, and in a field usually considered remote from linguistics. It was in the

[1]Reprinted from pp. 75–93, *Language, culture, and personality, essays in memory of Edward Sapir*, edited by Leslie Spier (Menasha, Wis.: Sapir Memorial Publication Fund, 1941). The article was written in the summer of 1939.

course of my professional work for a fire insurance company, in which I undertook the task of analyzing many hundreds of reports of circumstances surrounding the start of fires, and in some cases, of explosions. My analysis was directed toward purely physical conditions, such as defective wiring, presence or lack of air spaces between metal flues and woodwork, etc., and the results were presented in these terms. Indeed it was undertaken with no thought that any other significances would or could be revealed. But in due course it became evident that not only a physical situation *qua* physics, but the meaning of that situation to people, was sometimes a factor, through the behavior of the people, in the start of the fire. And this factor of meaning was clearest when it was a *Linguistic Meaning*, residing in the name or the linguistic description commonly applied to the situation. Thus, around a storage of what are called "gasoline drums," behavior will tend to a certain type, that is, great care will be exercised; while around a storage of what are called "empty gasoline drums," it will tend to be different—careless, with little repression of smoking or of tossing cigarette stubs about. Yet the "empty" drums are perhaps the more dangerous, since they contain explosive vapor. Physically the situation is hazardous, but the linguistic analysis according to regular analogy must employ the word 'empty,' which inevitably suggests lack of hazard. The word 'empty' is used in two linguistic patterns: (1) as a virtual synonym for 'null and void, negative, inert," (2) applied in analysis of physical situations without regard to, e.g., vapor, liquid vestiges, or stray rubbish, in the container. The situation is named in one pattern (2) and the name is then "acted out" or "lived up to" in another (1), this being a general formula for the linguistic conditioning of behavior into hazardous forms.

In a wood distillation plant the metal stills were insulated with a composition prepared from limestone and called at the plant "spun limestone." No attempt was made to protect this covering from excessive heat or the contact of flame. After a period of use, the fire below one of the stills spread to the "limestone," which to everyone's great surprise burned vigorously. Exposure to acetic acid fumes from the stills had converted part of the limestone (calcium carbonate) to calcium acetate. This when heated in a fire decomposes, forming inflammable acetone. Behavior that tolerated fire close to the covering was induced by use of the name "limestone," which because it ends in "stone" implies noncombustibility.

· · ·

A drying room for hides was arranged with a blower at one end to make a current of air along the room and thence outdoors through a vent at the other end. Fire started at a hot bearing on the blower, which blew the flames directly into the hides and fanned them along the room, destroying the entire stock. This hazardous setup followed naturally from the term 'blower' with its linguistic equivalence to 'that which blows,' implying that its function necessarily is to 'blow.' Also its function is verbalized as 'blowing air for drying,' overlooking that it can blow other things, e.g., flames and sparks. In reality, a blower simply makes a current of air and can exhaust as well as blow. It should have been installed at the vent end to *draw* the air over the hides, then through the hazard (its own casing and bearings), and thence outdoors.

Beside a coal-fired melting pot for lead reclaiming was dumped a pile of "scrap lead"—a misleading verbalization, for it consisted of the lead sheets of old radio condensers, which still had paraffin paper between them. Soon the paraffin blazed up and fired the roof, half of which was burned off.

Such examples, which could be greatly multiplied, will suffice to show how the cue to a certain line of behavior is often given by the analogies of the linguistic formula in which the situation is spoken of, and by which to some degree it is analyzed, classified, and allotted its place in that world which is "to a large extent unconsciously built up on the language habits of the group." And we always assume that the linguistic analysis made by our group reflects reality better than it does.

GRAMMATICAL PATTERNS AS INTERPRETATIONS OF EXPERIENCE

The linguistic material in the above examples is limited to single words, phrases, and patterns of limited range. One cannot study the behavioral compulsiveness of such material without suspecting a much more far-reaching compulsion from large-scale patterning of grammatical categories, such as plurality, gender and similar classifications (animate, inanimate, etc.), tenses, voices, and other verb forms, classifications of the type of "parts of speech," and the matter of whether a given experience is denoted by a unit morpheme, an inflected word, or a syntactical combination. A category such as number (singular vs. plural) is an attempted interpretation of a whole large order of experience, virtually of the world or of nature; it attempts to say how experience is to be segmented, what experience is to be called "one" and what "several." But the difficulty of appraising such a far-reaching influence is great because of its background character, because of the difficulty of standing aside from our own language, which is a habit and a cultural *non est disputandum*, and scrutinizing it objectively. And if we take a very dissimilar language, this language becomes a part of nature, and we even do to it what we have already done to nature. We tend to think in our own language in order to examine the exotic language. . . .

In my study of the Hopi language, what I now see as an opportunity to work on this problem was first thrust upon me before I was clearly aware of the problem. . . .

The work began to assume the character of a comparison between Hopi and western European languages. It also became evident that even the grammar of Hopi bore a relation to Hopi culture, and the grammar of European tongues to our own "Western" or "European" culture. And it appeared that the interrelation brought in those large subsummations of experience by language, such as our own terms 'time,' 'space,' 'substance,' and 'matter.' Since, with respect to the traits compared, there is little difference between English, French, German, or other European languages with the *possible* (but doubtful) exception of Balto-Slavic and non-Indo-European, I have lumped these languages into one group called SAE, or "Standard Average European."

That portion of the whole investigation here to be reported may be summed up in two questions: (1) Are our own concepts of 'time,' 'space,' and 'matter' given in substantially the same form by experience to all men, or are they in part conditioned by the structure of particular languages? (2) Are there traceable affinities between (a) cultural and behavioral norms and (b) large-scale linguistic patterns? . . .

PLURALITY AND NUMERATION IN SAE AND HOPI

In our language, that is SAE, plurality and cardinal numbers are applied in two ways: to real plurals and imaginary plurals. Or more exactly if less tersely: perceptible spatial aggregates and metaphorical aggregates. We say 'ten men' and also 'ten days.' Ten men either are or could be objectively perceived as ten, ten in one group perception[2]—ten men on a street corner, for instance. But 'ten days' cannot be objectively experienced. We experience only one day, today; the other nine (or even all ten) are something conjured up from memory or imagination. If 'ten days' be regarded as a group it must be as an "imaginary," mentally constructed group. Whence comes this mental pattern? Just as in the case of the fire-causing errors, from the fact that our language confuses the two different situations, has but one pattern for both. When we speak of 'ten steps forward, ten strokes on a bell,' or any similarly described cyclic sequence, "times" of any sort, we are doing the same thing as with 'days.' *Cyclicity* brings the response of imaginary plurals. But a likeness of cyclicity to aggregates is not unmistakably given by experience prior to language, or it would be found in all languages, and it is not.

Our *awareness* of time and cyclicity does contain something immediate and subjective—the basic sense of "becoming later and later." But in the habitual thought of us SAE people, this is covered under something quite different, which though mental should not be called subjective. I call it *objectified*, or imaginary, because it is patterned on the *outer* world. It is this that reflects our linguistic usage. Our tongue makes no distinction between numbers counted on discrete entities and numbers that are simply "counting itself." Habitual thought then assumes that in the latter the numbers are just as much counted on "something" as in the former. This is objectification. Concepts of time lose contact with the subjective experience of "becoming later" and are objectified as counted *quantities*, especially as lengths, made up of units as a length can be visibly marked off into inches. A 'length of time' is envisioned as a row of similar units, like a row of bottles.

In Hopi there is a different linguistic situation. Plurals and cardinals are used only for entities that form or can form an objective group. There are no imaginary plurals, but instead ordinals used with singulars. Such an expression as 'ten days' is not used. The equivalent statement is an operational one that reaches one day by a suitable count. 'They stayed ten days' becomes 'they stayed until the eleventh day' or 'they left after the tenth day.' 'Ten days is greater than nine days' becomes 'the tenth day is later than the ninth.' Our "length of time" is not regarded as a length but as a relation between two events in lateness. Instead of our linguistically promoted objectification of that datum of consciousness we call 'time,' the Hopi language has not laid down any pattern that would cloak the subjective "becoming later" that is the essence of time.

NOUNS OF PHYSICAL QUANTITY IN SAE AND HOPI

We have two kinds of nouns denoting physical things: individual nouns, and mass nouns, e.g., 'water, milk, wood, granite, sand, flour, meat.' Individual

---

[2]As we say, 'ten at the *same time*,' showing that in our language and thought we restate the fact of group perception in terms of a concept 'time,' the large linguistic component of which will appear in the course of this paper.

nouns denote bodies with definite outlines: 'a tree, a stick, a man, a hill.' Mass nouns denote homogeneous continua without implied boundaries. The distinction is marked by linguistic form; e.g., mass nouns lack plurals,[3] in English drop articles, and in French take the partitive article *du, de la, des*. The distinction is more widespread in language than in the observable appearance of things. Rather few natural occurrences present themselves as unbounded extents; 'air' of course, and often 'water, rain, snow, sand, rock, dirt, grass.' We do not encounter 'butter, meat, cloth, iron, glass,' or most "materials" in such kind of manifestation, but in bodies small or large with definite outlines. The distinction is somewhat forced upon our description of events by an unavoidable pattern in language. It is so inconvenient in a great many cases that we need some way of individualizing the mass noun by further linguistic devices. This is partly done by names of body-types· 'stick of wood, piece of cloth, pane of glass, cake of soap'; also, and even more, by introducing names of containers though their contents be the real issue: 'glass of water, cup of coffee, dish of food, bag of flour, bottle of beer.' These very common container formulas, in which 'of' has an obvious, visually perceptible meaning ("contents"), influence our feeling about the less obvious type-body formulas: 'stick of wood, lump of dough,' etc. The formulas are very similar: individual noun plus a similar relator (English 'of'). In the obvious case this relator denotes contents. In the inobvious one it "suggests" contents. Hence the 'lumps, chunks, blocks, pieces,' etc., seem to contain something, a "stuff," "substance," or "matter" that answers to the 'water,' 'coffee,' 'flour' in the container formulas. So with SAE people the philosophic "substance" and "matter" are also the naïve idea; they are instantly acceptable, "common sense." It is so through linguistic habit. Our language patterns often require us to name a physical thing by a binomial that splits the reference into a formless item plus a form.

Hopi is again different. It has a formally distinguished class of nouns. But this class contains no formal subclass of mass nouns. All nouns have an individual sense and both singular and plural forms. Nouns translating most nearly our mass nouns still refer to vague bodies or vaguely bounded extents. They imply indefiniteness, but not lack, of outline and size. In specific statements, 'water' means one certain mass or quantity of water, not what we call "the substance water." Generality of statement is conveyed through the verb or predicator, not the noun. Since nouns are individual already, they are not individualized by either type-bodies or names of containers, if there is no special need to emphasize shape or container. The noun itself implies a suitable type-body or container. One says, not 'a glass of water' but *ka·yi* 'a water,' not 'a pool of water' but *pa·hǝ*,[4] not 'a dish of cornflour' but *ŋǝmni* 'a (quantity of) cornflour,'

---

[3] It is no exception to this rule of lacking a plural that a mass noun may sometimes coincide in lexeme with an individual noun that of course has a plural; e.g., 'stone' (no pl.) with 'a stone' (pl. 'stones'). The plural form denoting varieties, e.g., 'wines' is of course a different sort of thing from the true plural; it is a curious outgrowth from the SAE mass nouns, leading to still another sort of imaginary aggregates, which will have to be omitted from this paper.

[4] Hopi has two words for water quantities; *kǝ·yi* and *pa·ǝh*. The difference is something like that between 'stone' and 'rock' in English, *pa·ǝh* implying greater size and "wildness"; flowing water, whether or not outdoors or in nature, is *pa·ǝh*; so is 'moisture.' But, unlike 'stone' and 'rock,' the difference is essential, not pertaining to a connotative margin, and the two can hardly ever be interchanged.

not 'a piece of meat' but *sikʷi* 'a meat.' The language has neither need for nor analogies on which to build the concept of existence as a duality of formless item and form. It deals with formlessness through other symbols than nouns.

DURATION, INTENSITY, AND TENDENCY IN SAE AND HOPI

To fit discourse to manifold actual situations, all languages need to express durations, intensities, and tendencies. It is characteristic of SAE and perhaps of many other language types to express them metaphorically. The metaphors are those of spatial extension, i.e., of size, number (plurality), position, shape, and motion. We express duration by 'long, short, great, much, quick, slow,' etc.; intensity by 'large, great, much, heavy, light, high, low, sharp, faint,' etc.; tendency by 'more, increase, grow, turn, get, approach, go, come, rise, fall, stop, smooth, even, rapid, slow'; and so on through an almost inexhaustible list of metaphors that we hardly recognize as such, since they are virtually the only linguistic media available. The nonmetaphorical terms in this field, like 'early, late, soon, lasting, intense, very, tending,' are a mere handful, quite inadequate to the needs.

It is clear how this condition "fits in." It is part of our whole scheme of *objectifying*—imaginatively spatializing qualities and potentials that are quite nonspatial (so far as any spatially perceptive senses can tell us). Noun-meaning (with us) proceeds from physical bodies to referents of far other sort. Since physical bodies and their outlines in *perceived space* are denoted by size and shape terms and reckoned by cardinal numbers and plurals, these patterns of denotation and reckoning extend to the symbols of nonspatial meanings, and so suggest an *imaginary space*. Physical shapes 'move, stop, rise, sink, approach,' etc., in perceived space; why not these other referents in their imaginary space? This has gone so far that we can hardly refer to the simplest nonspatial situation without constant resort to physical metaphors. I "grasp" the "thread" of another's arguments, but if its "level" is "over my head" my attention may "wander" and "lose touch" with the "drift" of it, so that when he "comes" to his "point" we differ "widely," our "views" being indeed so "far apart" that the "things" he says "appear" "much" too arbitrary, or even "a lot" of nonsense!

The absence of such metaphor from Hopi speech is striking. Use of space terms when there is no space involved is *not there*—as if on it had been laid the taboo teetotal! The reason is clear when we know that Hopi has abundant conjugational and lexical means of expressing duration, intensity, and tendency directly as such, and that major grammatical patterns do not, as with us, provide analogies for an imaginary space.

HABITUAL BEHAVIOR FEATURES OF HOPI CULTURE

Our behavior, and that of Hopi, can be seen to be coordinated in many ways to the linguistically conditioned microcosm. As in my fire casebook, people act about situations in ways which are like the ways they talk about them. A characteristic of Hopi behavior is the emphasis on preparation. This includes announcing and getting ready for events well beforehand, elaborate precautions to insure persistence of desired conditions, and stress on good will as the preparer of right results. Consider the analogies of the day-counting pattern alone. Time is mainly reckoned "by day" (*talk, -tala*) or "by night" (*tok*), which words are not nouns but tensors, the first formed on a root "light, day," the second on a root "sleep." The count is by *ordinals*. This is not the pattern of counting a number of different men or things, even though they appear successively, for, even then, they *could* gather into an assemblage. It is the pattern of counting successive reappearances of the *same* man or thing, incapable of forming an assemblage. The analogy is not to behave about day-cyclicity as to several men ("several days"), which is what *we* tend to do, but to behave as to the successive visits of the *same man*. One does not alter several men by working upon just one, but one can prepare and so alter the later visits of the same man by working to affect the visit he is making now. This is the way the Hopi deal with the future —by working within a present situation which is expected to carry impresses, both obvious and occult, forward into the future event of interest. One might say that Hopi society understands our proverb 'Well begun is half done,' but not our 'Tomorrow is another day.' This may explain much in Hopi character.

This Hopi preparing behavior may be roughly divided into announcing, outer preparing, inner preparing, covert participation, and persistence. Announcing, or preparative publicity, is an important function in the hands of a special official, the Crier Chief. Outer preparing is preparation involving much visible activity, not all necessarily directly useful within our understanding. It includes ordinary practicing, rehearsing, getting ready, introductory formalities, preparing of special food, etc. (all of these to a degree that may seem overelaborate to us), intensive sustained muscular activity like running, racing, dancing, which is thought to increase the intensity of development of events (such as growth of crops), mimetic and other magic, preparations based on esoteric theory involving perhaps occult instruments like prayer sticks, prayer feathers, and prayer meal, and finally the great cyclic ceremonies and dances, which have the significance of preparing rain and crops. From one of the verbs meaning "prepare" is derived the noun for "harvest" or "crop": *na'twani* 'the prepared' or the 'in preparation.'[5]

Inner preparing is use of prayer and meditation, and at lesser intensity good wishes and good will, to further desired results. Hopi attitudes stress the power of desire and thought. With their "microcosm" it is utterly natural that they should. Desire and thought are the earliest, and therefore the most important, most critical and crucial, stage of preparing. Moreover, to the Hopi, one's desires and thoughts influence not only his own actions, but all nature as well. This too is wholly natural. Consciousness itself is aware of work, of the feel of effort and energy, in desire and thinking. Experience more basic than language tells us that, if energy is expended, effects are produced. *We* tend to believe that our bodies can stop up this energy, prevent it from affecting other things until we will our *bodies* to overt action. But this may be so only because we have our own linguistic basis for a theory that formless items like "matter" are things in themselves, malleable only by similar things, by more matter, and hence insulated from the powers of life and thought. It is no more unnatural to think that thought contacts everything and pervades the universe than to think, as we all do, that light kindled outdoors does this. And it is not unnatural to suppose

---

[5]The Hopi verbs of preparing naturally do not correspond neatly to our "prepare"; so that *na'twani* could also be rendered 'the practiced-upon, the tried-for,' and otherwise.

that thought, like any other force, leaves everywhere traces of effect. Now, when *we* think of a certain actual rosebush, we do not suppose that our thought goes to that actual bush, and engages with it, like a searchlight turned upon it. What then do we suppose our consciousness is dealing with when we are thinking of that rosebush? Probably we think it is dealing with a "mental image" which is not the rosebush but a mental surrogate of it. But why should it be *natural* to think that our thought deals with a surrogate and not with the real rosebush? Quite possibly because we are dimly aware that we carry about with us a whole imaginary space, full of mental surrogates. To us, mental surrogates are old familiar fare. Along with the images of imaginary space, which we perhaps secretly know to be only imaginary, we tuck the thought-of actually existing rosebush, which may be quite another story, perhaps just because we have that very convenient "place" for it. The Hopi thought-world has no imaginary space. The corollary to this is that it may not locate thought dealing with real space anywhere but in real space, nor insulate real space from the effects of thought. A Hopi would naturally suppose that his thought (or he himself) traffics with the actual rosebush—or more likely, corn plant—that he is thinking about. The thought then should leave some trace of itself with the plant in the field. If it is a good thought, one about health and growth, it is good for the plant; if a bad thought, the reverse.

The Hopi emphasize the intensity-factor of thought. Thought to be most effective should be vivid in consciousness, definite, steady, sustained, charged with strongly felt good intentions. They render the idea in English as 'concentrating, holding it in your heart, putting your mind on it, earnestly hoping.' Thought power is the force behind ceremonies, prayer sticks, ritual smoking, etc. The prayer pipe is regarded as an aid to "concentrating" (so said my informant). Its name, *na'twanpi*, means 'instrument of preparing.'

Covert participation is mental collaboration from people who do not take part in the actual affair, be it a job of work, hunt, race, or ceremony, but direct their thought and good will toward the affair's success. Announcements often seek to enlist the support of such mental helpers as well as of overt participants, and contain exhortations to the people to aid with their active good will.[6] A similarity to our concepts of a sympathetic audience or the cheering section at a football game should not obscure the fact that it is primarily the power of directed thought, and not merely sympathy or encouragement, that is expected of covert participants. In fact these latter get in their deadliest work before, not during, the game! A corollary to the power of thought is the power of wrong thought for evil; hence one purpose of covert participation is to obtain the mass force of many good wishers to offset the harmful thought of ill wishers. Such attitudes greatly favor cooperation and community spirit. Not that the Hopi community is not full of rivalries and colliding interests. Against the tendency to social disintegration in such a small, isolated group, the theory of "preparing" by the power of thought, logically leading to the great power of the combined, intensified, and harmonized thought of the whole community, must help vastly

[6]See, e.g., Ernest Beaglehole, *Notes on Hopi economic life* (Yale University Publications in Anthropology, no. 15, 1937), especially the reference to the announcement of a rabbit hunt, and on p. 30, description of the activities in connection with the cleaning of Toreva Spring—announcing, various preparing activities, and finally, preparing the continuity of the good results already obtained and the continued flow of the spring.

toward the rather remarkable degree of cooperation that, in spite of much private bickering, the Hopi village displays in all the important cultural activities.

Hopi "preparing" activities again show a result of their linguistic thought background in an emphasis on persistence and constant insistent repetition. A sense of the cumulative value of innumerable small momenta is dulled by an objectified, spatialized view of time like ours, enhanced by a way of thinking close to the subjective awareness of duration, of the ceaseless "latering" of events. To us, for whom time is a motion on a space, unvarying repetition seems to scatter its force along a row of units of that space, and be wasted. To the Hopi, for whom time is not a motion but a "getting later" of everything that has ever been done, unvarying repetition is not wasted but accumulated. It is storing up an invisible change that holds over into later events.[7] As we have seen, it is as if the return of the day were felt as the return of the same person, a little older but with all the impresses of yesterday, not as "another day," i.e., like an entirely different person. This principle joined with that of thought-power and with traits of general Pueblo culture is expressed in the theory of the Hopi ceremonial dance for furthering rain and crops, as well as in its short, piston-like tread, repeated thousands of times, hour after hour.

SOME IMPRESSES OF LINGUISTIC HABIT IN WESTERN CIVILIZATION

It is harder to do justice in few words to the linguistically conditioned features of our own culture than in the case of the Hopi, because of both vast scope and difficulty of objectivity—because of our deeply ingrained familiarity with the attitudes to be analyzed. I wish merely to sketch certain characteristics adjusted to our linguistic binomialism of form plus formless item or "substance," to our metaphoricalness, our imaginary space, and our objectified time. These, as we have seen, are linguistic.

From the form-plus-substance dichotomy the philosophical views most traditionally characteristic of the "Western world" have derived huge support. Here belong materialism, psychophysical parallelism, physics——at least in its traditional Newtonian form—and dualistic views of the universe in general. Indeed here belongs almost everything that is "hard, practical common sense." Monistic, holistic, and relativistic views of reality appeal to philosophers and some scientists, but they are badly handicapped in appealing to the "common sense" of the Western average man—not because nature herself refutes them (if she did, philosophers could have discovered this much), but because they must be talked about in what amounts to a new language. "Common sense," as its name shows, and "practicality" as its name does not show, are largely matters of talking so that one is readily understood. It is sometimes stated that Newtonian space, time,

[7]This notion of storing up power, which seems implied by much Hopi behavior, has an analog in physics: acceleration. It might be said that the linguistic background of Hopi thought equips it to recognize naturally that force manifests not as motion or velocity, but as cumulation or acceleration. Our linguistic background tends to hinder in us this same recognition, for having legitimately conceived force to be that which produces change, we then think of change by our linguistic metaphorical analog, motion, instead of by a pure motionless changingness concept, i.e., accumulation or acceleration. Hence it comes to our naïve feeling as a shock to find from physical experiments that it is not possible to define force by motion, that motion and speed, as also "being at rest," are wholly relative, and that force can be measured only by acceleration.

and matter are sensed by everyone intuitively, whereupon relativity is cited as showing how mathematical analysis can prove intuition wrong. This, besides being unfair to intuition, is an attempt to answer offhand question (1) put at the outset of this paper, to answer which this research was undertaken. Presentation of the findings now nears its end, and I think the answer is clear. The offhand answer, laying the blame upon intuition for our slowness in discovering mysteries of the Cosmos, such as relativity, is the wrong one. The right answer is: Newtonian space, time, and matter are no intuitions. They are recepts from culture and language. That is where Newton got them.

Our objectified view of time is, however, favorable to historicity and to everything connected with the keeping of records, while the Hopi view is unfavorable thereto. The latter is too subtle, complex, and everdeveloping, supplying no ready-made answer to the question of when "one" event ends and "another" begins. When it is implicit that everything that ever happened still is, but is in a necessarily different form from what memory or record reports, there is less incentive to study the past. As for the present, the incentive would be not to record it but to treat it as "preparing." But *our* objectified time puts before imagination something like a ribbon or scroll marked off into equal blank spaces, suggesting that each be filled with an entry. Writing has no doubt helped toward our linguistic treatment of time, even as the linguistic treatment has guided the uses of writing. Through this give-and-take between language and the whole culture we get, for instance:

1. Records, diaries, bookkeeping, accounting, mathematics stimulated by accounting.
2. Interest in exact sequence, dating, calendars, chronology, clocks, time wages, time graphs, time as used in physics.
3. Annals, histories, the historical attitude, interest in the past, archaeology, attitudes of introjection toward past periods, e.g., classicism, romanticism.

Just as we conceive our objectified time as extending in the future in the same way that it extends in the past, so we set down our estimates of the future in the same shape as our records of the past, producing programs, schedules, budgets. The formal equality of the spacelike units by which we measure and conceive time leads us to consider the "formless item" or "substance" of time to be homogeneous and in ratio to the number of units. Hence our prorata allocation of value to time, lending itself to the building up of a commercial structure based on time-prorata values: time wages (time work constantly supersedes piece work), rent, credit, interest, depreciation charges, and insurance premiums. No doubt this vast system, once built, would continue to run under any sort of linguistic treatment of time; but that it should have been built at all, reaching the magnitude and particular form it has in the Western world, is a fact decidedly in consonance with the patterns of the SAE languages. Whether such a civilization as ours would be possible with widely different linguistic handling of time is a large question—in our civilization, our linguistic patterns and the fitting of our behavior to the temporal order are what they are, and they are in accord. We are of course stimulated to use calendars, clocks, and watches, and to try to measure time ever more precisely; this aids science, and science in turn, following these well-worn cultural grooves, gives back to culture an ever-growing store of applications, habits, and values, with which culture again directs science. But what lies outside this spiral? Science is beginning to find that there is something in the Cosmos that is not in accord with the concepts we have formed in mounting the spiral. It is trying to frame a *new language* by which to adjust itself to a wider universe.

It is clear how the emphasis on "saving time" which goes with all the above and is very obvious objectification of time, leads to a high valuation of "speed," which shows itself a great deal in our behavior.

Still another behavioral effect is that the character of monotony and regularity possessed by our image of time as an evenly scaled limitless tape measure persuades us to behave as if that monotony were more true of events than it really is. That is, it helps to routinize us. We tend to select and favor whatever bears out this view, to "play up to" the routine aspects of existence. One phase of this is behavior evincing a false sense of security or an assumption that all will always go smoothly, and a lack in foreseeing and protecting ourselves against hazards. Our technique of harnessing energy does well in routine performance, and it is along routine lines that we chiefly strive to improve it—we are, for example, relatively uninterested in stopping the energy from causing accidents, fires, and explosions, which it is doing constantly and on a wide scale. Such indifference to the unexpectedness of life would be disastrous to a society as small, isolated, and precariously poised as the Hopi society is, or rather once was.

Thus our linguistically determined thought world not only collaborates with our cultural idols and ideals, but engages even our unconscious personal reactions in its patterns and gives them certain typical characters. One such character, as we have seen, is *carelessness*, as in reckless driving or throwing cigarette stubs into waste paper. Another of different sort is *gesturing* when we talk. Very many of the gestures made by English-speaking people at least, and probably by all SAE speakers, serve to illustrate, by a movement in space, not a real spatial reference but one of the nonspatial references that our language handles by metaphors of imaginary space. That is, we are more apt to make a grasping gesture when we speak of grasping an elusive idea than when we speak of grasping a doorknob. The gesture seeks to make a metaphorical and hence somewhat unclear reference more clear. But, if a language refers to nonspatials without implying a spatial analogy, the reference is not made any clearer by gesture. The Hopi gesture very little, perhaps not at all in the sense we understand as gesture.

It would seem as if kinesthesia, or the sensing of muscular movement, though arising before language, should be made more highly conscious by linguistic use of imaginary space and metaphorical images of motion. Kinesthesia is marked in two facets of European culture: art and sport. European sculpture, an art in which Europe excels, is strongly kinesthetic, conveying great sense of the body's motions; European painting likewise. The dance in our culture expresses delight in motion rather than symbolism or ceremonial, and our music is greatly influenced by our dance forms. Our sports are strongly imbued with this element of the "poetry of motion." Hopi races and games seem to emphasize rather the virtues of endurance and sustained intensity. Hopi dancing is highly symbolic and is performed with great intensity and earnestness, but has not much movement or swing.

Synesthesia, or suggestion by certain sense receptions of characters belonging to another sense, as of light and color by sounds and vice versa, should be made more conscious by a linguistic metaphorical system that refers to non-spatial experiences by terms for spatial ones, though undoubtedly it arises from a deeper source. Probably in the first instance metaphor arises from synesthesia and not the reverse; yet metaphor need not become firmly rooted in linguistic pattern, as Hopi shows. Nonspatial experience has one well-organized sense, *hearing*—for smell and taste are but little organized. Nonspatial consciousness is a realm chiefly of thought, feeling, and *sound*. Spatial consciousness is a realm of light, color, sight, and touch, and presents shapes and dimensions. Our metaphorical system, by naming nonspatial experiences after spatial ones, imputes to sounds, smells, tastes, emotions, and thoughts qualities like the colors, luminosities, shapes, angles, textures, and motions of spatial experience. And to some extent the reverse transference occurs; for, after much talking about tones as high, low, sharp, dull, heavy, brilliant, slow, the talker finds it easy to think of some factors in spatial experience as like factors of tone. Thus we speak of "tones" of color, a gray "monotone," a "loud" necktie, a "taste" in dress: all spatial metaphor in reverse. Now European art is distinctive in the way it seeks deliberately to play with synesthesia. Music tries to suggest scenes, color, movement, geometric design; painting and sculpture are often consciously guided by the analogies of music's rhythm; colors are conjoined with feeling for the analogy to concords and discords. The European theater and opera seek a synthesis of many arts. It may be that in this way our metaphorical language that is in some sense a confusion of thought is producing, through art, a result of far-reaching value—a deeper esthetic sense leading toward a more direct apprehension of underlying unity behind the phenomena so variously reported by our sense channels.

HISTORICAL IMPLICATIONS

How does such a network of language, culture, and behavior come about historically? Which was first: the language patterns or the cultural norms? In main they have grown up together, constantly influencing each other. But in this partnership the nature of the language is the factor that limits free plasticity and rigidifies channels of development in the more autocratic way. This is so because a language is a system, not just an assemblage of norms. Large systematic outlines can change to something really new only very slowly, while many other cultural innovations are made with comparative quickness. Language thus represents the mass mind; it is affected by inventions and innovations, but affected little and slowly, whereas *to* inventors and innovators it legislates with the decree immediate.

The growth of the SAE language-culture complex dates from ancient times. Much of its metaphorical reference to the nonspatial by the spatial was already fixed in the ancient tongues, and more especially in Latin. It is indeed a marked trait of Latin. If we compare, say Hebrew, we find that, while Hebrew has some allusion to not-space as space, Latin has more. Latin terms for nonspatials, like *educo, religio, principia, comprehendo,* are usually metaphorized physical references: lead out, tying back, etc. This is not true of all languages—it is quite untrue of Hopi. The fact that in Latin the direction of development happened to be from spatial to nonspatial (partly because of secondary stimulation to abstract thinking when the intellectually crude Romans encountered Greek culture) and that later tongues were strongly stimulated to mimic Latin, seems a likely reason for a belief, which still lingers on among linguists, that this is the natural direction of semantic change in all languages, and for the persistent notion in Western learned circles (in strong contrast to Eastern ones) that objective experience is prior to subjective. Philosophies make out a weighty case for the reverse, and certainly the direction of development is sometimes the reverse. Thus the Hopi word for "heart" can be shown to be a late formation within Hopi from a root meaning think or remember. Or consider what has happened to the word "radio" in such a sentence as "he bought a new radio," as compared to its prior meaning "science of wireless telephony."

In the Middle Ages the patterns already formed in Latin began to interweave with the increased mechanical invention, industry, trade, and scholastic and scientific thought. The need for measurement in industry and trade, the stores and bulks of "stuffs" in various containers, the typebodies in which various goods were handled, standardizing of measure and weight units, invention of clocks and measurement of "time," keeping of records, accounts, chronicles, histories, growth of mathematics and the partnership of mathematics and science, all cooperated to bring our thought and language world into its present form.

In Hopi history, could we read it, we should find a different type of language and a different set of cultural and environmental influences working together. A peaceful agricultural society isolated by geographic features and nomad enemies in a land of scanty rainfall, arid agriculture that could be made successful only by the utmost perseverance (hence the value of persistence and repetition), necessity for collaboration (hence emphasis on the psychology of teamwork and on mental factors in general), corn and rain as primary criteria of value, need of extensive *preparations* and precautions to assure crops in the poor soil and precarious climate, keen realization of dependence upon nature favoring prayer and a religious attitude toward the forces of nature, especially prayer and religion directed toward the ever-needed blessing, rain—these things interacted with Hopi linguistic patterns to mold them, to be molded again by them, and so little by little to shape the Hopi world-outlook.

To sum up the matter, our first question asked in the beginning is answered thus: Concepts of "time" and "matter" are not given in substantially the same form by experience to all men but depend upon the nature of the language or languages through the use of which they have been developed. They do not depend so much upon *any one system* (e.g., tense, or nouns) within the grammar as upon the ways of analyzing and reporting experience which have become fixed in the language as integrated "fashions of speaking" and which cut across the typical grammatical classifications, so that such a "fashion" may include lexical, morphological, syntactic, and otherwise systemically diverse means coordinated in a certain frame of consistency. Our own "time" differs markedly from Hopi "duration." It is conceived as like a space of strictly limited dimensions, or sometimes as like a motion upon such a space, and employed as an intellectual tool accordingly. Hopi "duration" seems to be inconceivable in terms of space or motion, being the mode in which life differs from form, and consciousness *in toto* from the spatial elements of consciousness. Certain ideas born of our own time-concept, such as that of absolute simultaneity, would be either very difficult to express or impossible and devoid of meaning under the

Hopi conception, and would be replaced by operational concepts. Our "matter" is the physical subtype of "substance" or "stuff," which is conceived as the formless extensional item that must be joined with form before there can be real existence. In Hopi there seems to be nothing corresponding to it; there are no formless extensional items; existence may or may not have form, but what it also has, with or without form, is intensity and duration, these being nonextensional and at bottom the same.

But what about our concept of "space," which was also included in our first question? There is no such striking difference between Hopi and SAE about space as about time, and probably the apprehension of space is given in substantially the same form by experience irrespective of language. The experiments of the Gestalt psychologists with visual perception appear to establish this as a fact. But the *concept of space* will vary somewhat with language, because, as an intellectual tool,[8] it is so closely linked with the concomitant employment of other intellectual tools, of the order of "time" and "matter," which are linguistically conditioned. We see things with our eyes in the same space forms as the Hopi, but our idea of space has also the property of acting as a surrogate of nonspatial relationships like time, intensity, tendency, and as a void to be filled with imagined formless items, one of which may even be called 'space.' Space as sensed by the Hopi would not be connected mentally with such surrogates, but would be comparatively "pure," unmixed with extraneous notions.

As for our second question: There are connections but not correlations or diagnostic correspondences between cultural norms and linguistic patterns. Although it would be impossible to infer the existence of Crier Chiefs from the lack of tenses in Hopi, or vice versa, there is a relation between a language and the rest of the culture of the society which uses it. There are cases where the "fashions of speaking" are closely integrated with the whole general culture, whether or not this be universally true, and there are connections within this integration, between the kind of linguistic analyses employed and various behavioral reactions and also the shapes taken by various cultural developments. Thus the importance of Crier Chiefs does have a connection, not with tenselessness itself, but with a system of thought in which categories different from our tenses are natural. These connections are to be found not so much by focusing attention on the typical rubrics of linguistic, ethnographic, or sociological description as by examining the culture and the language (always and only when the two have been together historically for a considerable time) as a whole in which concatenations that run across these departmental lines may be expected to exist, and, if they do exist, eventually to be discoverable by study.

[8]Here belong "Newtonian" and "Euclidean" space, etc.

How to Learn Martian

Charles F. Hockett

Once upon a time, people thought that a vocabulary and the grammar rules were the whole story on learning a language. But modern linguistics finds it's both more complicated, and also somewhat simpler than that . . .

An agent of the Galactic Federation, sent to Earth to case the joint secretly for either friendly or inimical purposes, could do a good deal worse than to make a survey of the scientific terms that appear, quite casually, in contemporary science fiction. True enough, there would be some discrepancy between the state of scientific development suggested by such a survey and the actual state of development in laboratory and industry—atomic energy was spoken of quite freely in our type of fiction for decades before technology caught up with imagination, and, in reverse, real recent developments in some fields are only now beginning to find their way into science fiction. If the agent's sole aim were to measure our technological potential, science fiction would be of no great help. But if he also wanted to determine the degree of general *technological readiness* of the whole population—at least in so-called "civilized" parts of the world— then the suggested survey would be of considerable value.

One score on which, as a measure of real technological development, our agent's study of science fiction might badly mislead him, is in the matter of communication, particularly the basic form of human communication, *language.* An occasional term of modern linguistics turns up from time to time in science fiction: "phoneme," in particular, is a word to conjure with just as much as is "transistor" or "cybernetics." The effect sought by the use of such a word is spoiled if the story-writer pauses to explain: the use must be casual, implying that the reader knows all about such things. And, because many of our magazines regularly run factual articles or departments, and we addicts regularly read them, this assumption of the story-writer is very often true.

If we can pride ourselves on the number of modern developments which were anticipated by the lively imaginations of an earlier generation of authors, I think perhaps we should temper this pride with a bit of shame that we have been such Johnny-come-latelies about phonemes, morphemes, intonations, constructions, immediate constituents, the impact of language on culture, and the like. Do you know when the fundamental principle of phonemics was first expounded?

It was explained rather clearly—though of course without the word "phoneme" —by a twelfth-century Icelander who was annoyed by the inaccuracy with which his compatriots put down written marks to represent Icelandic speech. We can probably forgive ourselves for not having known about this particular early episode, especially since modern linguists had forgotten all about it and had to rediscover the principle for themselves. But even in modern times the phonemic principle was stated, in one way or another, as early as about 1910:

the earliest mention I have been able to track down in science fiction postdates World War II.

Maybe we should catch up. If our authors would like to follow their usual custom of being ahead of the times instead of lagging behind, they must at least know what the times have to offer. If we readers insist that they should do this, they will.

We are going along on the first voyage to Mars, and very conveniently we shall find intelligent oxygen-breathing beings with respiratory and digestive tracts shaped very much like our own. (Later on we can point out why this last assumption is so convenient.) Our ship lands; we make the first hesitant contact with the Martians; and before long our xenologist, Ferdinand Edward Leonard, B.A., M.A., Ph.D., M.D., X.D.—who is about as chock full of modern anthropological, linguistic, communicative, engineering, psychiatric, and biological training as one skin can be stuffed with—sits down with a Martian to try to find out something about the latter's language.[1] (Hidden assumption: Martians can sit down.) For short, we shall call these two "Ferdie" and "Marty"—the latter because even Ferdie won't be able to learn, or to pronounce, Marty's real name for quite a while. (Query: Do Martians have personal names?)

Ferdie points to the Martian's foot and says, of course in English, "What do you call that in your language?" Marty certainly does not understand, but at this moment he makes a bit of vocal sound, something like GAH-djik. Ferdie puts this down in his little notebook, and writes the English word "foot" by it. What Ferdie puts down to represent the Martian "word"—if it really is a word, and not just Marty clearing his throat in the typical Martian manner—doesn't look quite like what we have written above, because Ferdie has a special set of written marks which he can use more efficiently and accurately for the purpose (a "phonetic alphabet"); but we needn't bother with this, because it is merely a convenience, not an essential. Now Ferdie is not being a fool and jumping to conclusions when he makes his notebook entry. He knows perfectly well that the sound Marty has made may not only not mean "foot," but may not even be a word at all. Ferdie makes his entry only as a memory aid: it will be easy enough to scratch it out when and if necessary.

Ferdie also says GAHdjik himself—or tries to—and observes Marty's reaction. Just for fun, we shall pretend that Marty does not react, so that this time Ferdie has gained nothing.

Next Ferdie points to something else, gets another reaction from Marty which may be a "word," writes it down, and tries to imitate it. Then he points to a third thing. After a while, having elicited a number of such bits of what may be speech, Ferdie returns to Marty's foot. This time what Marty says doesn't sound like GAHdjik, but more like KAHchuk.

Right at this point, Ferdie comes face to face with the most ticklish and crucial problem which can be encountered by a xenologist or by an Earth lin-

---

[1] Roger Williams, of Rhode Island and Providence Plantations fame, wrote a little book called *Key Into the Language of America*—a grammar of a language spoken by a few hundred Indians in his vicinity, which was but one of *several hundred* distinct languages spoken in aboriginal North America. Some of our exploring science-fiction heroes fall into this same error. If there are millions of intelligent beings on Mars, there may be thousands of Martian languages.

guist. (We except, of course, the task of working with the dragonlike inhabitants of Antares II, whose languages make use not of sound but of heat-waves.) Has friend Marty given two different "words" for two different meanings? Has he given two distinct "words" for a single meaning? Or has he simply said the same "word" twice, with slight differences in pronunciation which are clear to Ferdie but which would be entirely overlooked by Marty's fellows?

Since this problem lies at the very heart of phonemics, we had better return to Earth momentarily and look at some more homely examples of what is involved.

Suppose that your name is Paul Revere and that you want to arrange for me, over in Boston, to send you some sort of a signal across the Charles River so that you can know whether the British are coming by land or by sea. This is all you want to know—it is already clear that they are going to be coming one way or the other, but you need to know which way. What we have to do is to establish a code containing just two signals. One of the signals will mean "they're coming by land," and the other will mean "they're coming by sea." The physical circumstances have something to do with what kinds of signals we can choose. They must both be something that you, over on the Cambridge side of the river, can easily detect, so that a shout or halloo wouldn't do very well. Since it will be night, some sort of arrangement of lights—up in a high place—would be a good idea.

Another consideration is that there must be no possible danger of my sending one signal and you receiving what is apparently the other. That is, we want to keep the two signals physically distinct, so that there will be no danger of mis-understanding. Shall we use a red lantern for "by sea" and a green one for "by land"? No—green might not show up too well, and what's more, we haven't got a green lantern. But I know there are two lanterns over in the basement of the Old North Church: suppose I put just one of them up in the tower for one of the signals, but both of them, at opposite sides, for the other. "One, if by land, and two, if by sea?" Agreed! Good luck on your ride! Hope a fog doesn't come up.

People can make signals out of anything they can *control* and can *observe*, and they can make the signals mean anything they wish. We constantly establish little short-term signaling systems, use them, and then discard them. A wave of the hand, a drop of a handkerchief, a wink of the eye, the raising of a window blind, the toot of an auto horn—such events are assigned special meaning over and over again. Some signaling systems are a little more elaborate and a bit more enduring—for example, the pattern of lights, stable or winking, shown at night by a plane for takeoff, for landing, or during flight. The really elaborate systems are hardly "invented," but merely passed down from generation to generation, with gradual changes; among these, of course, belongs language it-self. Now, however varied these different systems may be, they all conform to certain fundamental principles. One of these—the one in which we are con-cerned here—is that the users of the signals must be able to tell them apart. This sounds simple and obvious enough, but it has some pretty complicated results.

Paul Revere and his side-kick had no trouble on this score, because they needed only two signals—all Paul had to have was one item of information of the either-this-or-that sort. But suppose you had to work out a signaling-system which will include hundreds or thousands of distinct signals. Keeping them physically apart and easily distinguished is in this case much more difficult.

One technique that anyone confronted with such a design-problem is bound to hit on is to set up some fairly small repertory of basic elements, each of them quite different physically from any of the others, and then arrange for the actual signals to consist of some sort of arrangement or combination of the fundamental elements. Suppose Paul and his henchman had needed a couple of hundred different signals. They could have arranged, for example, for a row of five lights to be put up in the old North Church tower, each light either red or green or amber: this yields two hundred and forty-three distinct combinations, yet calls for only fifteen lanterns to be available—one of each color for each of the five positions.

It is pretty obvious that this set of two hundred and forty-three signals would be much easier for Paul to read from across the river than, say, the same number of signals consisting each of a lantern of a different shade. The human eye, true enough, can distinguish several thousand shades of color, but finer distinctions are not easy to detect, and for rapid and efficient use ought not to be involved. Even as it is, if Paul's assistant is only able to find four really red lamps and has to fill in with one which is rather orange, there will be the possibility that the orange lamp, intended as functionally "red," will be interpreted by Paul as "amber." This danger can be avoided if Paul knows in advance that the "red" lamps will in actual transmission vary somewhat in precise shade, without making any significant difference in the signal.

This sort of thing has actually happened in every known case of a really complicated signaling system, including language. When a linguist goes to work on a language he has never heard before, he can count on certain things along this line. The colored lanterns in this case are different motions of lips, tongue, throat, and lungs, which produce kinds of sound which can be heard, and told apart, by human ears.

The investigator knows that the people who speak the language will make *distinctive* use only of certain differences of articulatory motion—that is, maybe they will use relatively red, relatively green, and relatively amber lanterns, but not also orange or blue. He knows that if an articulatory motion of an ambiguous sort occurs, it will count as a "mistake" and will be allowed for by the speakers of the language—since orange is not functional, the actual appearance of an orange lantern must be a mistake for red or for amber. But he does not know in advance just what differences of articulatory motion will be thus used.

After all, a lantern-code could make use of any number of different ranges of spectral colors, providing that no two of the significantly different shades were so close together as to give rise to serious danger of confusion. In just the same way, there are any number of ways in which a selection can be made, from the "spectrum" of all possible speech-sound, of "shades" to be used distinctively. The only way to find out what selection is actually made by the speakers of a given language is—but let's watch Ferdie and Marty again and see if we can find out.

We left Ferdie confronting the problem of *GAHdjik* and *KAHchuk*. Assuming that each of these is really speech, not just Martian throat-clearing, then there are three possibilities:

(1) They are two different words with two different meanings. If we were in the position of Marty, the first time a xenologist pointed to our ear we might say *ear*, and at a subsequent time we might think he was asking what the organ is used for, and so say *hear*. *Ear* and *hear* are pretty similar: a Frenchman or Italian who knew no English might easily wonder whether they were two words or just one.

(2) They are two different words, but for essentially one and the same meaning. When we pronounce *room* with the vowel sound of *cooed* we are using one word; when we pronounce it with the vowel sound of *could* we are really using a different word. But it would be hard to find any difference in the meaning of the two.

(3) Marty has simply said the same word twice: the apparent variation in pronunciation would not be noticed by his fellow Martians. A speaker of Hindustani, hearing us say *pie* or *tie* or *cow* several times, might be convinced that we were pronouncing the initial *p-* (or *t-* or *k-*) now in one way, now in another, since Hindustani breaks up the "spectrum" of possible speech sound a little more finely in this particular region.

There are several things Ferdie can do to try to solve this problem. First, he points to Marty's foot again and says *KAHchuk*, to observe the response; a little while later, he makes the same gesture and says *GAHdjik*. For good measure, he also tries *GAHdjik*, and *KAHchik*, and even *gahDJIK* and *kahCHIK*, making the second syllable louder than the first. The hope is that he can manage to get something out of Marty's reactions which will indicate acceptance or rejection of the various pronunciations. If Marty accepts all the pronunciations except the last two, then Ferdie has fairly good indication that the answer is the second or third of the possibilities, rather than the first. Of course he can't yet be absolutely certain; perhaps Martians are too polite to criticize, or perhaps we simply haven't yet learned to read their gestures of acceptance and rejection.

Another procedure is available. Ferdie looks through his notebook and notices an entry *GOOpit*, apparently meaning "small tuft of green hair sprouting from the back of a Martian's neck," and an entry *KOOsahng*, which seems to refer to a low-growing yellowish shrub that is plentiful in the vicinity. This is what Ferdie does and how Marty reacts:

> *Ferdie* (pointing to the tuft of hair): "*GOOpit.*"
> *Marty* (closing his middle eye—apparently the gesture of assent). "*FUM.*"
> *Ferdie* (pointing to the bush): "*KOOsahng.*"
> *Marty:* "*FUM.*"
> *Ferdie* (the tuft of hair): "*KOOpit.*"
> *Marty:* "*FUM. NAHboo GOOpit.*"
> *Ferdie* (the bush): "*GOOsahng.*"
> *Marty:* "*FUM. NAHboo KOOsahng.*"
> *Ferdie* (pointing to the spaceship in which we arrived): "*GOOpit.*"
> *Marty* (popping all three eyes out on their stalks): "*HLA – HLA – HLA – HLA! EEkup SAHCH bahKEENdut!*"

This last response, whatever it actually means, is certainly different enough from the others to be indicative. Ferdie concludes that he can probably work on the theory that the last response was rejection, the others all acceptance. But what does this tell him? It tells him the following:

(1) *GOOpit* (or *KOOpit*) does *not* mean "spaceship."

(2) The pronunciations *GOOpit* and *KOOpit* may sound different to us English-speaking Earthlings, but to Marty they are all the same.

(3) The pronunciations *KOOsahng* and *GOOsahng* are also all the same for Marty.

(4) The pronunciations *GAHdjik, GAHdjuk, KAHchik, KAHchuk* sound quite varied to us, with our English-speaking habits, but the differences are irrelevant for Marty's language.

Or, in short, for the last three points, the difference between an initial *k*-sound and an initial *g*-sound, which is distinctive for us, is not functional in Marty's language. Ferdie has reached one conclusion about the phonemic system of Marty's language: in the region of the spectrum where English distinguishes between two phonemes, *k* and *g*, Marty's language has only one.

It is entertaining to follow the hard step-by-step field-work of a xenologist or a linguist this far, but after this it quickly becomes boring, at least for everyone but the investigator himself—and, often enough, for him, too. Because what he has to do is simply more of the same—over and over and over again, eliciting, recording, checking, correcting, reaching an occasional tentative conclusion, finding out he was wrong and revising. It is a routine sort of task, before long, but unfortunately it is not one which can be assigned to any sort of machine. (At least, a machine that could perform the task would have to have all the logic *and illogic*, all the strengths *and weaknesses*, of human beings.)

Ferdie's aim can be stated rather easily. He wants to reach the point where he can supply an accurate description of all the *differences in pronunciation* which are *distinctive* in the linguistic signaling of Marty and his fellows. He wants to be able to state what shades of lanterns are used, in what sequences the different colors are allowed to occur, and just what range of spectral shades counts as an instance of each color. All of this constitutes the *phonemic system* of Marty's language.

Maybe you think it need not take Ferdie very long to achieve this aim. Well, if Earth languages are any guide, there is a good chance that our ship hasn't brought along enough food to supply Ferdie while he finishes the job; unless he can get along on Martian lizard-weed, the native staple, he is out of luck. In a day or so, a well-trained Earth linguist, working with a completely new language, can get the cultural wax out of his ears and begin to hear something that sounds like it might really be a language. Before that, everything is a mumbling buzz. In another ten or so days of hard work, the linguist can get perhaps ninety percent of what counts in the sound-making and sound-recognizing habits of the language, though his own hearing may not yet be too well trained for the new system. In another hundred days he can get perhaps ninety percent *of the remainder*. Sometimes it is years before he gets it all.

However, this rather long program shouldn't discourage us, since Ferdie can be making effective practical use of the local Martian dialect long before the full cycle is up. Ninety percent is actually pretty good, though so long as, in his own attempts at speaking Martian, Ferdie uses only ninety per cent, he will impress Marty as having a pretty unMartian accent. Let us see what "ninety per cent" means and why it is effective.

The phonemic system of Marty's language—or of any other—is a set of distinctive *differences* between pronunciations. The units which we call "phonemes" are in themselves of no importance: it is the differences between them that count. A given phoneme, in terms of its use in communication, is nothing except something which is different from all the other phonemes in the system. In Morse code, a "dot" is a "dot" and a "dash" is a "dash" whether the former is a short voltage pulse and the latter a long one, or the former is a wave of a flag in one direction and the latter a wave in the other direction. This is why we will irritate Ferdie no end if we ask him, after his first day's work, "Well, do they have a phoneme K?" or "Well, is K a phoneme in Martian?" If you want to compare languages with each other, the sort of question which must be asked—the sort that will be meaningful to Ferdie even if he can't yet answer it—is "Does Marty have a phonemic contrast between K and G?"

The difference between K and G is distinctive in English, so that we have two phonemes rather than just one in this general region of the spectrum, because a great many pairs of words are kept apart by the difference and by nothing else: *good : could, gap : cap, glue : clue, bag : back, bigger : bicker,* and so on. In Marty's language there are no pairs of words kept apart in just this way. On the other hand, the difference between EE and AH is distinctive in Marty's language—as in ours—because *KEEtah* means "eyestalk" while *KAHtah* means "setting of Deimos."

The sole function of phonemes, then, is to be different from each other, and, in being so, to keep words and utterances—whole signals—apart. But some differences between phonemes do a lot more of this work than do others. The difference between K and G in English carries, relatively speaking, a fairly large share of the total load, as you can easily see by looking for more pairs of words like those which we gave above—it is easy to list hundreds. The difference between the *sh*-sound of *she* or *hush* and the *zh*-sound in the middle of *pleasure* is also functional, but this distinction doesn't carry very much of the total load. If you look hard, you may be able to find three or four pairs of words in which this difference is the only one—one example is *measure* and *mesher*—but there are very few.

Actually, a technique deriving from information theory makes it theoretically possible to express the "functional load" of different phonemic contrasts in a language in quantitative terms, to any desired degree of accuracy. But the amount of counting and computing which is involved is enormous, and would hardly be undertaken without a properly designed computing machine—and then it costs lots of money instead of lots of time, which for linguists is even worse. But we don't need such figures here; the general principle is, we hope, clear enough.

It is because of this that Ferdie can begin making effective use of Martian long before he has ferreted out and pinned down every last vestige of distinctive difference in articulation of which the language makes some use. It is obvious on the face of it that the differences which he discovers first are bound to be, by and large, the differences of greatest functional importance. Working just with these in his own attempts to speak Martian, he will sometimes be misunderstood—but we misunderstand each other from time to time even under the best of circumstances. If you want further empirical evidence, you need only think of the German or the Frenchman who makes you understand him with imperfect English—or of you, yourself, managing to communicate in imperfect French or German.

If there *are* Martians, and they *are* intelligent and have a language, and if they *do* have upper respiratory and alimentary tracts shaped much like our own, and ears much like ours, and, finally, if they *do* make use of these organs in speech communication—given all these ifs, then the procedures of Ferdinand Edward Leonard will work, and he will be able to "break" the phonemic system of the language.

But suppose that the Martians fail on just one of the above ifs. Suppose that they have two tongues and no nose. How, then, is Ferdinand Edward Leonard to imitate and to learn to recognize their speech sounds?

Suppose something even more drastic. Suppose that the Martians communicate with a system just as complex as human language and with much the same essential structure, but that instead of modulating sound they modulate a carrier at frequencies above the reach of human ears—or radio waves, or a light beam, or odors, or electrical flows, or some kind of energy transmitted through the "sub-ether." What kind of equipment and training shall we give our xenologists to handle situations of this sort? There are still certain fundamental design-features which any such language-like communications system is bound to include, but the problem of observation and analysis is tremendously harder.

Tabooed Words in Comic Strips:

A Transparent Mask

James R. Jaquith

Consistently, though with low frequency, comic strip readers are confronted with varying combinations of such graphs as #, ⊚ , !!!, ✳ , * and ⌄⌃⌄. These graphs appear as utterance partials in speech balloons. The remainders of the utterances are presented as conventional letter-based words. This paper considers the structure and functions of such usage. The data comprise 148 linguistic frames, each consisting wholly or partly of nonletter graphs (hereinafter referred to as NLG's) such as the above. They are the yield from a three-year systematic scan of two large urban newspapers, the comic strip contents of which were nonoverlapping during the gathering period. About 10% of the sample comes from magazine advertising and humor texts unaccompanied by cartoons. One frame comes from a humorous report in a usually sober national news magazine. That only 148 frames came to the writer's attention during three years of close observation constitutes some measure of the frequency of this usage.

It does not seem reasonable to contend, prior to analysis, that the use of NLG's does or does not constitute writing. In a loose popular sense the contention that comic strip NLG's are indeed writing appears to be defensible from three points of view. First, NLG's are graphic. Second, the number of mutually discriminable types of NLG's is limited. In fact, only 14 of the NLG types comprise more than 1% each of the total sample. Together, these 14 types amount to 93%. Nine of them (!, *, #, %, $, &, ¢, @, ?) are common typewriter NLG's. Most of the remaining 27 types are linked uniquely to one or another artist. The most specialized (ш ,ф ,ю , Я) are identifiable as Russian and Russian-like letter graphs, employed to communicate either that a Russian comic strip actor's uttering of English tabooed forms was in his native accent or that he was using Russian tabooed forms. Third, combinations of NLG's such as the above (they never occur singly in comic strip context) communicate culturally relevant information.

Evidence bearing on the general cultural parameters of what is being communicated is available to the writer from three sources.

1. Letters from editors of comic strip syndicates which discuss the issues explicitly. That is, NLG's are used to mask forms which are regarded as offensive to a significant number of readers.

2. Three cartoons which juxtapose use of NLG's with explicit recognition of their domain referent. One shows two children writing the comic strip kind of NLG's. One child comments, "Look! I'm typin' all the words Mommy won't let us say!" Another shows a photograph of a myna bird with a balloon containing nothing but NLG's. The final paragraph of the short article accompanying the picture is as follows: "At this point, the ladies complained to an interested newsman, their ears were distinctly assailed by an unspeakable imprecation uttered by one of the mynas—they couldn't say which one. This bird, they insisted, had uttered—directly and unmistakably at them—a two-word Anglo-Saxonism ending in 'you'." The third illustrative cartoon is really a spoof on this issue. It shows a man and a woman. The latter inquires, "%$?" The man, puzzled, asks in turn, "What kind of profanity is that, Liz?" The woman responds, "That's no profanity, Dick! I just wanted to know what percentage of the gross we're getting for this picture!"

3. Several hundred responses to a short questionnaire administered to undergraduate students at a Midwestern university. With but a single exception consensus was complete: the domain suggested by comic strip NLG's is that variously referred to as 'cursing,' 'swearing,' 'profanity' and 'dirty words.' Even the exception might be explained on grounds other than ignorance, e.g., inhibitions of the modesty sort.

For a graphic technique to qualify as writing, technically, readers must be able to establish fixed and predictable relationships between the graphs they are reading and one or more orders of units in the language being written.

Typically, these units are (1) morphemes, as in the well known case of Chinese (or Arabic numbers and a few other graphs in European writing), (2) syllables, as in the system devised by Sequoya for Cherokee or Japanese katakana and hiragana, (3) phonemes, in the case of any alphabetic system, and (4) in the case of comic strip NLG's letter graphs of the English alphabet could in principle constitute referents just as they do in ciphers such as the Morse code.

Putting comic strip NLG's to such tests is not a simple matter, because the investigator can never really be sure which English forms are thus masked. The problem is not a hopeless one, however, a useful approach being in fact available. For one thing, the inventory of tabooed English forms is quite limited. And it is the case that forms tabooed in one context are not necessarily tabooed in all or even in many contexts. Indeed, in some contexts it is the absence of a form that is tabooed. This fact, presumably, leads comic strip artists to suggest that in a given story situation dirty words are appropriate and/or that their absence is inappropriate. At the same time, however, publishers have decided—ultimately on economic grounds—not to present dirty words in conventional letter graphs to children and other comic strip readers whose sensibilities might thus be assaulted. Hence NLG's, a device explicitly and self-consciously adopted to mask forms deemed offensive to readers and, ipso facto, threatening to circulation.

Analysis of the syntactic frames in which NLG's appear in the sample shows each to be classifiable into one of four classes, each defined by the part(s) of speech demanded by the frame. These are, in descending order of frequency:

1. Adjective frame (40% of all occurrences), e.g., "None of your - - - - - - business!" Highest frequency filters (from the questionnaire mentioned above damn(ed), goddamn(ed), fuckin(g), motherfuckin(g).

2. Expletive frame (30% of all occurrences): "- - - - - !" Highest frequency fillers: damn! Jesus Christ! shit! sonofabitch!

3. Noun frame (18% of all occurrences), e.g., "I think those two - - - - - are trying to doublecross us!" Highest frequency fillers: bastards, motherfuckers, sonsobitches.

4. Imperative frame (9% of all occurrences), e.g., "- - - - - this digit dialing!" Highest frequency fillers: damn, fuck, screw.

There is in addition a very small category (3% of all occurrences) to which the label 'idiom frame' might be attached. By contrast with types 1–4 above, precise lexical selection is significantly easier since in such cases the NLG slot is coextensive with the tabooed component of an established idiom. As such, ambiguity of referent is reduced nearly to zero, a fact which makes testing NLG groups as writing much simpler. Two illustrations from the sample are "You can all go to - - - - - !" and "At this point Hoffa gave one of the reporters a good-natured kick in the - - - -."

It should be made clear that the inventory of forms tabooed by producers of comic strips is minimal in the sense that it includes only relatively hard core dirty words. Fringe-area forms, some of which are clearly euphemistic reinterpretations of hard core originals, occur frequently in conventional letter graphs, i.e., as English written words. Examples are gosh, golly, dadburned, gee, darn, heck.

It is apparent, then, that NLG slots cannot be filled at random from the total inventories of English adjectives, nouns, etc. There are two factors which, together, severely restrict the number of possible fillers for a given slot and, in so doing, make analysis possible. The first, applicable to all or most English frames, is that a particular part of speech is called for. The second is that the filler for a comic strip NLG slot must be selected from a very restricted sublexicon, i.e., dirty word adjectives, dirty word nouns, etc.

• • •

Comic strip reading, then, can be thought of as a kind of multiple-choice, fill-in game, and a certain case can be made for regarding it as an effective pedagogical device in the enculturation of a domain which one segment of its perpetuators profess to censor out. That is, the comic strip world seems to have fashioned for itself a kind of best-of-both-worlds, have-your-cake-and-eat-it-too compromise between profit and social reality: the NLG.